Government and Politics of the United States

Second Edition

Nigel Bowles

First edition 1993
Reprinted twice
Second edition 1998

Published by
PALGRAVE
Houndmills, Basingstoke, Hampshire RG21 6XS and
175 Fifth Avenue, New York, N. Y. 10010
Companies and representatives throughout the world

PALGRAVE is the new global academic imprint of
St. Martin's Press LLC Scholarly and Reference Division and
Palgrave Publishers Ltd (formerly Macmillan Press Ltd).

ISBN-13: 978-0-333-69478-7   hardback
ISBN-10: 0-333-694478-3   hardback
ISBN-13: 978-0-333-69486-2   paperback
ISBN-10: 0-333-69486-4   paperback

This book is printed on paper suitable for recycling and made from fully managed and sustained forest sources.

A catalogue record for this book is available from the British Library.

Transferred to digital printing 2002

Copy-edited and typeset by Povey-Edmondson
Tavistock and Rochdale, England

Printed and bound in Great Britain by
Antony Rowe Ltd, Eastbourne

Government and Politics of the United States

COMPARATIVE GOVERNMENT AND POLITICS
Founding Series Editor: The late **Vincent Wright**

Published

Rudy Andeweg and Galen A. Irwin
Governance and Politics of the Netherlands (2nd edition)

Tim Bale
European Politics: A Comparative Introduction

Nigel Bowles
Government and Politics of the United States (2nd edition)

Paul Brooker
Non-Democratic Regimes: Theory, Government and Politics

Robert Elgie
Political Leadership in Liberal Democracies

Rod Hague and Martin Harrop
*Comparative Government and Politics: An Introduction (6th edition)

Paul Heywood
The Government and Politics of Spain

B. Guy Peters
Comparative Politics: Theories and Methods
[Rights: World excluding North America]

Tony Saich
Governance and Politics of China (2nd edition)

Anne Stevens
Government and Politics of France (3rd edition)

Ramesh Thakur
The Government and Politics of India

Forthcoming

Judy Batt
Government and Politics in Eastern Europe

Robert Leonardi
Government and Politics in Italy

* Published in North America as **Political Science: A Comparative Introduction (4th edition)**

Comparative Government and Politics
Series Standing Order
ISBN 0–333–71693–0 hardcover
ISBN 0–333–69335–3 paperback
(outside North America only)

You can receive future titles in this series as they are published by placing a standing order. Please contact your bookseller or, in the case of difficulty, write to us at the address below with your name and address, the title of the series and the ISBN quoted above.

Customer Services Department, Macmillan Distribution Ltd
Houndmills, Basingstoke, Hampshire RG21 6XS, England

Dedicated to the memory of
Colin Moss
1954–1996
friend and scholar

Contents

List of Tables, Figures, Exhibits and Maps

Tables

Figure

Exhibits

Map

Preface to the Second Edition

My need for help has not diminished in the four years since publication of the first edition; nor, fortunately, has the propensity of my friends to supply it. Those whose generous support and advice I acknowledged in the "Preface to the First Edition", I warmly thank once more. In particular, I thank Desmond King both for his wise counsel regarding the new chapter entitled "The Politics of Cities and Suburbs", and for his generous support.

I am especially indebted to Katharine Ellis, my wife, whose love and intellectual support are essential and, happily, complete. Katharine tolerates the intrusion of American politics into her different intellectual world of nineteenth-century French cultural history with grace and understanding.

Several colleagues and students have kindly identified errors of omission, commission, or interpretation: I thank them all. I thank, too, the Principal and Fellows of St Anne's College, Oxford, and colleagues in the Politics Sub-faculty at Oxford, for a happy and stimulating environment in which to work. I am much indebted to my colleagues in the PPE School (Terry O'Shaughnessy, Alison Denham, Roger Crisp, Marc Stears, Lisa Finneran, Rob McMahon, and Paul Martin) for their generous support, as I am also to those many students at St Anne's College and other colleges in Oxford who have made me think harder about numerous questions in this book's large subject. For that, and for their intellectual curiosity and enthusiasm, I am most grateful. Vincent Wright, whose observations about the probable reception of the book's first edition proved characteristically astute, has again been a perceptive critic and supportive friend; so too has David Goldey, whose unwavering encouragement and constructive criticisms are invaluable. I am also grateful to my publisher Steven Kennedy for his professionalism.

Since the publication of the First Edition, Colin Moss, a close friend of integrity and warmth with whom I often talked about American history and politics, has died. This edition is affectionately dedicated to his memory, and a proportion of royalties earned from its sale will be donated to the Cancer Research Campaign.

Responsibility for errors of fact or interpretation remains with me alone.

Charlbury   Nigel Bowles

Note: With regard to the question of the use of pronouns, I have tried to ensure that the male pronoun is used only on those occasions when the reference is to a man or to an office which has been held solely by men. Where the reference is to a woman, I use the female pronoun, and where it is made to an office which has been held both by men and women, the phase "he or she" or "she or he" is used.

Preface to the First Edition and Acknowledgements

Shortly before the publication of his own textbook, my former supervisor directed me in colourful terms never to agree to write one of my own. Textbooks, he insisted, were regarded by colleagues who had written one of their own as unwelcome competition; by those who had not, as intrinsically unscholarly; and by students, degradingly and dispiritingly, as cribs. Many years later, a senior colleague asked me to write a textbook on United States government. Recalling the warning which I had received some years before from my supervisor, I demurred, but the pugnacious reply suggested that it would be unwise to decline. I warmly acknowledge my great debt to Vincent Wright, editor of the series in which this book appears, former supervisor, unembarrassed purveyor of conflicting advice, friend, and colleague. Without his early warning about the pitfalls of writing a textbook, I should have enjoyed his invitation to write it less than I did. Without his steady guidance and patience over the four years that the book has taken to complete, it would not have appeared. Without his unstinting intellectual support, it would be more deeply flawed than it is.

I am also greatly indebted to Katharine Ellis, David Goldey and Desmond King for their intellectual support, friendship, and many kindnesses. All three read the entire text, and the final draft was immeasurably improved by their critical but constructive observations. Desmond generously read several chapters in more than one draft, for which I am particularly grateful. Alan Ware read the full second draft, and made many helpful suggestions; I thank him most warmly, as I do Malcolm Anderson, Roger Crisp, Ruth Deech, and Michael Hart, each of whom read individual chapters. I also thank Herb Alexander for his assistance with campaign finance data. I am also grateful to other colleagues in the Sub-faculty of Politics at Oxford, especially Tim Hames, Gillian Peele, and Byron Shafer, for the intellectual stimulation of their company and conversation. I also thank Mark Habeeb and Richard Hodder-Williams, from whose writings and conversation on American politics over many years I have gained greatly. Warm thanks are also due to Steven Kennedy at the publishers for his professionalism and patience.

Undergraduate and postgraduate students with whom I have worked at Edinburgh and Oxford, especially Mark Brough, Gareth Davies, Chris Howard, and Robert Singh, have helped considerably in clarifying for me some of the questions addressed in this book. I am very grateful to them.

Most of the work for the book was undertaken at Oxford in the libraries of Rhodes House, St Anne's College, and the Law Faculty Library; my thanks are due to the staff of all three libraries, especially to Alan Bell and David Smith, for their kindness and professionalism. I am grateful to the Principal and Fellows of St Anne's College, Oxford, for creating a supportive and stimulating environment in which to read, think and write. In particular, I express my warm thanks to my colleagues in the PPE School, Gabriele Taylor and Terry O'Shaughnessy, for their support. Terry drew my attention to Keynes's note of a conversation with President Roosevelt in 1941; I thank him for it.

Thanks are due to many others but there is space to mention just two. Both, sadly, have departed: Tony Allt, who first introduced me to American political history, and Philip Williams, whose knowledge and understanding of this vast subject were profound, and whose enthusiasm for it was inspirational.

Responsibility for errors of fact or interpretation is mine alone.

Charlbury   NIGEL BOWLES

"The other main criticism . . . relates to the organs of government. To the outsider it looks almost incredibly inefficient. One wonders how decisions are ever reached at all. There is no clear hierarchy of authority. The different departments of the Government criticise one another in public and produce rival programmes. There is perpetual internecine warfare between prominent personalities. Individuals rise and fall in general esteem with bewildering rapidity. New groupings of administrative power and influence spring up every day. Members of the so-called Cabinet make public speeches containing urgent proposals which are not agreed as Government policy . . . Nothing is ever settled in principle. There is just endless debate and endless sitting around . . . Suddenly some drastic, clear-cut decision is reached, by what process one cannot understand, and all the talk seems to have gone for nothing, being a fifth wheel to the coach, the ultimate decision appearing to be largely independent of the immense *parlez-vous*, responsible and irresponsible that had preceded it. Nothing is secret, nothing confidential. The President laughed when I said his method of deceiving the enemy was apparently to publish so much vital information that they would not have the time to read it."

(John Maynard Keynes, XXIII, 105-k, July 1941).

The United States: state boundaries

and major cities

1

Introduction

This book is an introduction to the government and politics of the United States of America. Its main subjects are the structure and organization of the Federal government, and the politics of Federal policy-making. Its secondary subjects are the politics of States, cities, and regions, especially in so far as their governments and politics shape the formation and implementation of Federal policy. Central to the book and its subject is the Constitution of the United States, a document written in 1787, ratified by the then thirteen states in 1789, first formally amended in 1791 with the addition of the ten articles of the Bill of Rights, and on seventeen occasions since (see Appendixes 1 and 2).

Political Values and Society

The United States was born in a revolutionary war against colonial Britain, and the country's revolutionary values have never been fully shed. The flight to Canada of 80,000 loyalists during and after the War of Independence (which lasted from 1775 to 1783) accounts partly for the different pattern and culture of politics in Canada and the United States. Unlike Canada, the United States is a republic, has never had either a Tory or a significant socialist party, and despite its periods of progressive social reform, has lacked both a comprehensive social democratic tradition and discourse. As American socialism has been a marginal political force, so American conservatism has taken neither the welfarist Christian Democratic forms familiar in Italy and Germany, nor the paternalist Tory form it adopted in Britain and retained even after the granting of universal suffrage. Only the Thatcherite faction within the British Conservative Party has had much in common with the dynamic, free- market, ideologies that unite rather than divide the two major American parties. Even that slender tie is more apparent than real: no politician in the United States would join with British counterparts in celebrating the virtues of a strong central state as Margaret Thatcher did in all matters save that of business regulation. Antipathy to government in general, and to centralized government in particular, unites most Americans, as does the corollary of a vigorous defence of political and civil rights.

1

A democratic ethos underpins public debate in the United States. American politics proceed with the presumption, if not always the fact, of disclosure and openness, of free debate and publication, in pursuit of negotiated agreements about public policy between individuals who are equal before the law. Links between America's political values and its institutions of government were apparent from well before the first stirrings of revolt against Britain in 1773, and have been declared publicly in key documents. From the Declaration of Independence in 1776, through President Lincoln's Gettysburg Address in 1863, to President Johnson's speech in 1965 before the Joint Session of Congress, American political rhetoric springs from a tradition in which politicians invoke ideas of progress towards an ideal democratic society within the constitutional framework of republican government. This has been applied not only at home but also, as the Presidencies of Woodrow Wilson, Harry Truman, and John Kennedy show, abroad. As a military superpower since 1945, the United States has wrestled with the tensions arising from turbulent impulses of an evangelistic, democratic creed and the demands of *realpolitik* presented by the need to establish and maintain international order in the interests of American national security. Both abroad and at home, the United States continues to wrestle with the tension between individual liberty and the combined result of great socioeconomic inequality.

Such a distinctive political mix is often held to spring from individual acquisitive freedom, usually regarded as the supreme American political value. Celebrated though this conception of individual freedom is, it collides with equality, another core value, also pronounced in American political thought and practice. Individual freedom has most commonly been understood in the United States as the freedom of individual citizens to become unequal: democracy in America was, as Richard Hofstadter (1948) observed, born in cupidity rather than fraternity. The pursuit of material abundance has blunted the edge of redistributive politics.

Class differences are everywhere apparent in America, but their political implications are dulled because of the greater salience of other social cleavages. In particular, they have been sufficiently cross-cut by ties of race and ethnicity (which successive waves of immigration from different regions and countries have reinforced) for their political significance to be further stifled. Embryonic class loyalties have often expressed themselves in impassioned and violent industrial disputes, but have rarely broken out into wider social conflicts. The overlaying of class division by race, and the pervasive belief in the fact and prospect of upward social mobility, have together drawn the sting of class politics. Save in 1932, 1936, and 1964 (see Chapter 3), it has proved difficult to build Presidential majorities on its foundations. Accordingly, democratic socialism has failed to take root.

Marked more than any other society by mass immigration of those seeking economic betterment or relief from political oppression, the United States is also host to a very large population of African-Americans whose ancestors, uniquely in a diverse society, were involuntary immigrants. Where others fled to America from oppression, blacks were forced there in chains. Slavery shattered black social structures, made marketable property of human beings, and underpinned the South's feudal agricultural regime in the nineteenth century. At fearful human and financial cost, the Civil War (1861–5) ended slavery but led indirectly to the extended subjugation of black Americans through segregation, sharecropping, and the conferment of merely nominal citizenship rights. Not until the years 1954–65 was the lawfulness of southern and border states' enforcement of segregation ended (see Chapter 2). Only then were black civil rights confirmed, and black voting rights guaranteed. That post–war transformation in black civil and political rights has changed American party politics, altered voting patterns, and assisted in the belated modernizing of the south, much of it still relatively backward economically. Yet the bitter aftermath of slavery and segregation still distinguishes black Americans from their fellow citizens, not just from whites but also from Hispanics and the several million immigrants from Asia. A substantial black professional middle class has developed since the 1960s, but blacks remain more heavily represented among the victims and perpetrators of violent crime, the poorest, least well-educated, unhealthy, and worst-housed groups in American society.

Persistent black under-achievement undermines the plausibility of the doctrine of equality, even equality of opportunity, that characterises American society: systematic social disadvantage significantly reduces inner-city black children's prospects of upward social mobility. Despite being an expression of individual freedom, the more general unequal distribution of income, wealth, and property threatens the coherence of American political values: material inequality diminishes the worth both of formal equality before the law, and of individual freedom. Equality of citizenship in law clashes with the fact of practical inequality of political and economic power and, less grandly, of access to the necessities of life. Individual freedom is partly expressed in the pricing of exchanges in markets. Yet, for example market failure, coupled with Federal incapacity and reluctance to act, leave 41 million Americans (most of them white, but including a disproportionate number of blacks) without health care. A collective solution to the problem would impair the myth of individual freedom's supreme claims of morality and efficiency, which explains partly why it has for so long been unaddressed.

The myth of individual freedom nevertheless exerts a powerful hold on American culture. The successful struggle of self-reliant and armed individuals against a violent and hostile frontier, racial segregation, ignorance, injustice, and poverty, has provided the texts, subtexts, and contexts of much American film and literature. Whilst supplying fuel for the nation's physical expansion in the nineteenth century, and its rise to industrial supremacy in both the nineteenth and the twentieth, competitive individual freedom in the pursuit of positional goods has had inequality as both its motive and its result. If the protection of Lockean private property rights was not, as is sometimes claimed, the preoccupation of Federalist proponents (and of some anti-Federalist opponents) of the Constitution in 1789, it was none the less a significant anxiety.

The acquisition and defence of property and wealth has been facilitated in fact, and symbolized in literature and film, by individuals' access to weapons: violence has been less a departure from accepted social practices in America than it has often been their expression. Rooted in its revolutionary birth, in the Constitution's defence of the right to bear arms, and in the exposed and dangerous extension of the frontier, individual possession of arms and their use is a more prominent characteristic of the United States than of any other advanced society except South Africa. The United States is, in many inner-city areas, an exceptionally fragile and violent society. In 1993, there were 630 murders in Canada, but 24,526 in the United States (the population of which is ten times larger). In more than two-thirds of those murders, the assailant's weapon of choice was a gun. More people are killed by guns in the US in a week than in the whole of western Europe in a year. (Bellesiles, 1996). The rate of murder in the United States in 1990 was approximately eight times higher than in Germany, ten times higher than in Japan, and thirteen times higher than in England and Wales. An outgrowth of the heady mixing of individualism and cupidity, armed violence on this scale has made death by gunfire the single largest cause of premature death among black males under the age of twenty-five, and rendered large parts of American cities places of extreme danger.

Violence by individuals finds its counterpart in violence by government: most States' criminal justice systems retain capital punishment. Some permit the execution of the mentally retarded (to which, since the Supreme Court's decision in *Penry* v. *Lynaugh*, 492 U.S. 302 (1989), there is no Federal constitutional bar). In violation of international conventions, some states permit the execution of juveniles: in *Thompson* v. *Oklahoma*, 487 U.S. 815 (1988), the Supreme Court judged that the imposition of a death penalty on a person aged fifteen at the time of an offence's commissioning was unconstitutional, but that imposing the death penalty on a person aged above fifteen was a matter for individual state legislatures to determine.

Group and Individual Interests

Even when unarmed, the individualistic acquisitive exercise of freedom implies a further difficulty for the coherence of American political values. Pluralist descriptions and prescriptions of the formation of public policy as comprising competitive struggles by individuals and groups leave no room for a separate, and separately-defined, public interest. There is a potential and, as the United States' budget deficit has shown, an actual tension between the freedom enjoyed by individuals and groups to pursue their own interests as they perceive them, and the public interest. The product of bargains, negotiations, and struggles between businesspeople and politicians is not self-evidently the 'public interest', even if it may be claimed to be coincident with it. American political theorists have always had difficulty in admitting the existence of a separately-defined public interest. The weakness of the central State, the Federal government, because of its internal fragmentation and its penetration by interest groups, emphasizes the problem: who is to define the public interest, other than freely-competing individuals? This collective action problem lies close to the heart of American government, resisting solution, with grievous consequences for fiscal management and the common good.

Relations between government and people in America are, the Constitution declares, grounded in the affirmation and protection of individual rights. Citizens' rights to be free in their persons and property from government interference is guaranteed, and government is held accountable to citizens by mandatory elections. Freedom of speech, assembly and publication may not be abridged. These rights are enforceable (and enforced) through the courts, providing the edifice of a rights-based liberal political system and society where the concept of citizenship has substance, the notion of subject none, and the possibility of majority tyranny is reduced.

Notions of obligation are nevertheless not absent in America; nor is liberalism's abrogation. Liberalism has itself often assumed highly conformist modes by becoming a doctrine requiring adherence, demanding allegiance to symbols, creeds, and policies which do not themselves comprise part of core American political values. Much illiberal agitation has been perpetrated in liberalism's name: anti-Communist scares after the First and Second world wars; J. Edgar Hoover's equation of dissent with subversion throughout his career as Director of the Federal Bureau of Investigation (FBI) from 1924 to 1972; the emergence of Louis Farrakhan in the late 1980s; and the advance in the 1990s of militia and other right-wing political groups, are but four instances of a paranoid intolerance (Hofstadter, 1966). Such intolerance is often close to the surface of American politics, and sometimes expresses itself in apocalyptic apprehensions. Like many others, J. Edgar Hoover regarded questioning of certain American values and ideals as intolerable and disloyal; he directed the FBI accordingly, at no little cost to the integrity of American public and civil life. Some Members of Congress have at times themselves participated in disparaging attacks upon minority groups and individuals unable effectively to defend themselves.

For example, the US House of Representatives had for much of the twentieth century an "UnAmerican Activities Committee" whose members were bent upon identifying and destroying individuals holding beliefs or engaging in practices deemed "unAmerican", a project powerfully assisted by the perception of an international Communist conspiratorial threat to American freedom. The perceived (insubstantial) internal threat was politically much the more plausible for being liked to a (substantial) external Soviet one. Senator Joseph McCarthy used a Senate Subcommittee to exploit American anxieties about Communism to his own advantage: heedless of the cost to those innocent persons whose reputations he besmirched and some of whose lives he ruined, McCarthy sought to pin the blame for Soviet expansion in Eastern Europe, the Chinese Communist Revolution, and America's disullusioning experience in Korea, upon "traitors" within the Federal government. Since there were so few real Communists within the United States, he took the expedient and irresponsible option of staining others by claiming that America was in the course of betrayal by a conspiratorial elite. In June 1951, McCarthy asked Senate colleagues a characteristically misleading rhetorical question to which he supplied (equally characteristically) a baseless reply:

> How can we account for our present situation unless we believe that men high in this government are concerting to deliver us to disaster? This must be the product of a great conspiracy, a conspiracy on a scale so immense as to dwarf any previous such venture in the history of man. A conspiracy of infamy so black that, when it is finally exposed, its principals shall be forever deserving of the maledictions of all honest men.
>
> (Hofstadter, 1996, p. 8)

McCarthy's success in exploiting domestic fear through identifying a threatening conspiracy against ordinary Americans was not novel. As Richard Hofstadter later argued, America's wealth and the usual absence of sharp class conflict in its history have released an unusually great concentration of political energy upon non-economic divisions of culture, ethnicity, and religion (Hofstadter, 1996, p. 92). Setting aside scholarly arguments about the fact or otherwise of American exceptionalism, many Americans perceive themselves, and the evangelizing democratic project of which they are part, to be exceptional (Shafer, 1991). Yet in no other mature democracy have politicians found it so advantageous to exploit fears of such a way of life's supposed vulnerability.

Anti-immigrant or "nativist" movements arose in the Republic's earliest years, and gained strength after the mid-nineteenth century as immigrants from countries outside northern and western Europe began to arrive in large numbers. Fears that such immigrants threatened America's broadly Protestant cultural heritage, its economic system of free enterprise (because of the influx of socialist ideals which some immigrants, especially Jewish ones, supposedly brought with them), and the jobs of American nationals, became politically salient in the late nineteenth and twentieth centuries. Partly as a reaction to fears of political contagion from the Russian Revolution, the United States pursued a highly discriminatory immigration policy between

1924 and 1965 by which quotas favouring immigrants from northern and western Europe were written in law. (This development is considered further in Chapter 9.)

Radical and cultural differences remain sources of profound social cleavage ripe for exploitation by those politicians and others whose politics are built upon the exploitation of fear and the revelatory discovery of all enveloping conspiracies against American patriots, whether those involving particular ethnic or racial groups, or those with beliefs, views, or lifestyles deemed "unAmerican". Chief among the six characteristics of paranoid politicians which Hofstadter noted are their proclamation of broad conspiracy, their denial of opponents' legitimacy, their rejection of a notion of politics as comprising the susceptibility of interests to bargaining and accommodation, coupled with the assertion that it is instead a struggle over fundamental values (Hofstadter, 1966, pp. 3–39).

The 1990s have seen the shocking and consequential growth of militia groups; most such groups vividly display the characteristics which Hofstadter identified in 1966. In his book *Warrior Dreams* (1994), James Gibson has argued that militia groups' growth in the post Cold War period owed much to a subcultural change reflecting an intense distrust of government arising out of America's defeat in Vietnam. The lagged effects of that disastrous engagement are argued to have deepened a sense of abiding grievance among some of the radical right who charge the Federal government with complicity in America's supposed decline. However, part of the contextual development is partisan: the recasting of the Republican Party in the guise of a socially reactionary right-wing party, a change which began with its electoral success in southern states following passage of the 1964 Civil Rights Act and the 1965 Voting Rights Act, provided a militant setting for right-wing politics. Within the subculture depicted by Gibson, legitimacy was in turn lent to those such as Rush Limbaugh, Oliver North and Gordon Liddy who used radio talk shows as platforms for the dissemination of political extremism. Robert Singh argues that those broadcasters' "marked enthusiasm for the Republican Party . . . and its electoral support by a majority of white southerners for the first time in the region's history, suggested that a politics of extremism that had traditionally been confined to the outer fringes of national American political life was increasingly entering the corridors of the Congress itself" (Singh, *The Farrakhan Phenomenon*, p. 150).

The roots of right-wing extremism in America remain grounded in the twin beliefs (by no means confined to a small number of right-wing extremists) that America is, and should remain, a white, Christian, country but that there exists an extensive conspiracy involving (by some accounts) Jews, Federal bureaucrats, and the United Nations to extinguish American freedoms, especially that of gun-ownership. As *The New York Times* noted in December 1995, three key events in the early 1990s served to confirm extreme right-wing perceptions of the government's treachery:

- a Federal raid on a white supremacist's cabin in Idaho (22 August 1992).
- the bungled Federal pursuit of David Koresh on arms violations. After a fifty-one day siege of his Camp Davidian sect in Waco, Texas (19 April 1993), Federal agents raided the buildings in which Koresh and his followers were living. More than 80 people died in a fire which resulted.
- the passage of the Omnibus Crime Bill in November 1993, which prohibited the ownership of 19 types of semi-automatic assault weapons and stipulated a five-day waiting period for the purchase of guns (see Chapter 7).

Research undertaken by the Southern Poverty Law Center in Montgomery, Alabama, has classified more than 800 groups, including 441 self-identified militia units, forming part of a so-called "patriot movement", of nominally independent organizations but united in their fervent opposition to the Federal Government. Timothy McVeigh, who bombed a Federal building in Oklahoma in 1995 and killed 168 people, belonged to such a group. Yet despite the declared hostility of extremist militia and other right-wing groups towards the Federal government, in the days following the bombing many television news editors prominently broadcast claims that Islamic terrorist groups were responsible for the murders. Such prejudice parading as neutral reporting was supplemented by bigoted observations in certain radio "talk shows". The host of one such programme (broadcast not in a remote, largely white, mid-western state, but in civilized, multi-ethnic, New York) came to the attention of a journalist on *The New York Times:*

> The morning after the Oklahoma City bombing, Bob Grant, the host of a WABC radio talk show in New York, railed at a caller who cautioned against a rush to blame Muslims: "What I would like to do is put you up against the wall with the rest of them, and mow you down along with them – execute you with them," Mr. Grant told the caller. (*The New York Times*, 28 August, 1995)

Physical attacks against Muslims and Muslim property increased in the 1990s. In the twelve months to August 1995, five of the 1,500 mosques in the United States were either destroyed or seriously damaged in arson attacks; in the three days after the Oklahoma City bombing in April 1995, one anti-racist group recorded 222 attacks against Muslims as having taken place (*The New York Times*, 28 August 1995). Among the causes of the increase in such "hate crimes" are, firstly, the increase in the number of Muslims (who now outnumber Episcopalians – Anglicans – by more than two to one); secondly, the acquisition by some Islamic middle-eastern states of radical governments (in Iran's case, a radical-clerical government) opposed to American interests; and, thirdly, in many minds the linking of Muslims with domestic terrorism since the bombing of the World Trade Center in 1993. Other extremist paranoid politicians have prejudices of their own which, in turn, have led them into racist alliances, some of them improbable. Louis Farrakhan, the black leader of the Nation of Islam, is a notorious example: whilst he has some black allies, his identification of Jews, white Americans and the Federal government as black Americans' dedicated, conspiratorial, opponents has caused links to be forged between his own organization, neo-Nazi groups, and the Aryan Nation, an extreme right-wing racist group (Singh, 1997).

As Hofstadter himself acknowledged, political paranoia has scarcely been confined to the United States: the histories of France, Germany, and Italy are replete with examples. Yet the susceptibility of the United States to paranoid politics through appeals to the "fear of catastrophe", and the consequent arousal of social conflicts founded upon "ultimate schemes of values", bringing "fundamental fears and hatreds" to the surface of public life is distinctively American. (Hofstadter, 1966, p. 39) In removing the United States's sole superpower enemy, the Soviet Union's collapse left room for paranoid individuals and radical groups within America to focus upon other objects of discontent, of which Muslims, Jews, black Americans and the Federal government itself are only four examples. Nor have those who conceive of politics in such ultimate terms been confined to the ranks of opposition: most governments of Southern states have for most of the south's history conceived of and practised politics around the stimulation of precisely such fears and hatreds. Catholics (save in Louisiana), Jews, the Federal government and, above all others, black persons were the objects of southern whites' detestation. In his book *Race and Democracy*, a brilliant historical analysis of racial politics in Louisiana, Fairclough has noted with respect to the south that ". . . the term 'racist' has become devalued through overuse: it fails to prepare one for the depths of disgust, contempt, and condescension with which whites, to varying degrees, still regarded their black fellow citizens in the 1950s" (p. 167).

It was upon such sentiments that southern society and southern governments were built before the south's defeat in the Civil War, and after Reconstruction's collapse between 1875 and 1890. Nowhere was consent to prevailing norms elicited and social order maintained with greater ferocity than in the segregated south between that collapse and the passage of the 1964 Civil Rights Act (see Chapter 2). During that period, State contributions reflected the real distribution of local power rather than the normative liberal claims of the Federal Constitution's authors. Most were written to preserve the influence of cotton planters, to keep State government weak in those respects where it suited planters' interests, but to be strong where they required it – not only to disenfranchise black people, but systematically to deprive them of the effective rights of US citizenship and, where necessary, to burn them alive by lynching in order to terrorize other black Americans into submission. Such were the practices of white southern governments and white southern citizens determined to resist democracy and its demands.

The Articles of Confederation

Powers of the Confederal Congress

Between 1781 and 1789, the United States was governed under the *Articles of Confederation*, a Constitution providing for a central government of exceptional weakness, dependent upon the goodwill of the individual States for its functioning. In practice, the thirteen States were unwilling to grant to the Congress of the Confederation the powers which they had denied the British Crown. Each State exercised virtually sovereign powers, even asserting its right to formulate independent foreign policies, and to raise armies and navies. Ministers in London and Paris acted simultaneously on behalf of individual States rather than the United States as a whole. Reacting against unaccountable British power, the Articles established neither an executive nor a judicial branch, but rather a unicameral legislature. Organized along the lines of the Continental Congress which it replaced, it was comparably weak and had power neither to regulate commerce between the States nor to levy taxes. Under this charter of impotence, each State had one vote – a reflection of the sovereignty and nominal equality of each, and an illustration of John Adams's characterization of the Congress as "not a legislative assembly, nor a representative assembly but only a diplomatic assembly". Relationships between the states and the centre of government paralleled those between the legislatures of the thirteen states and their Governors. Lacking independent political bases, the latter were the agents of the former.

The Confederal Congress did have the power to create Executive Departments, but those it established were hampered by the States' assertions of sovereignty and their denial to the centre of adequate funds for the support of Departments' roles. Imposts (requests for import duty) required the States' unanimous consent (which was not forthcoming). Save when external threats were palpable and immediate, the centre was feebly inadequate: the standing army was once reduced to eighty men. Between sessions of Congress, a *Committee of the States* sat, comprising a single delegate from each State. With power to act only in respect of those matters not requiring the assent of nine of the thirteen States, it was a prescription for a government with neither authority nor power. Although intended, the costs of such weakness were high: in the south and the west, the States faced significant threats from Spain which gave cause for general concern, but questions of separate taxation by States and of growing indebtedness were the particular and proximate causes of the undermining of the Articles of Confederation. Taxes on commerce between the States were freely imposed, causing such resentment that war between the States seemed possible: New York actually imposed a tax on all ships trading through her waters to the neighbouring States of New Jersey and Connecticut. It became plain that the States had individual interests in the collectivity's being strengthened and becoming more than merely the sum of its parts.

The Confederation's Collapse

Under the Articles of Confederation, legislative supremacy in the thirteen States had given way to abuses of power, especially unconstitutional incursions into State Judiciaries, and interference with property rights and contracts. In many States, pressure for the repudiation of debts (both to American and foreign merchants and bankers) grew. External debt rose considerably between the end of the War of Independence in 1783 and the collapse of the Confederation. Gradually, creditors (especially British ones) became the target of state legislative action: in flagrant defiance of the 1783 Paris Peace Treaty, the Virginia legislature passed a law to prevent British creditors suing to collect their pre-war debts. In 1786 alone, seven States issued paper money, thereby alarming all creditors, British and American, loyalist and revolutionary. In Massachusetts, impoverished rural debtors in the west of the State rebelled under Daniel Shays in an attempt to prevent county courts from delivering judgment against them. Violent clashes that followed were suppressed by the State militia (financed by exactions on merchants) and not by United States forces (because the United States had insufficient resources to raise them).

General Washington inferred from the rebellion that the Articles of Confederation were inadequate, and feared that European governments (which already accorded the Confederation's ministers little respect) would draw similar conclusions. Washington's anxieties were sufficiently widely shared among senior American politicians to intensify pressures for the drafting of new constitutional arrangements in which the centre would be stronger, popular electoral pressures through legislatures reduced, and the political problems caused by indebtedness resolved. Following an initial meeting in 1786 at Annapolis, the Maryland State capital, attended by delegates from five States to consider difficulties in the commercial relations between them, it was proposed that a further meeting take place at Philadelphia in May 1787 to discuss the amendment of the Articles of Confederation. Congress supported the call for a meeting of delegates:

> for the sole and express purpose of revising the Articles of confederation and reporting to Congress and the several legislatures such alterations and provisions.

The Constitutional Convention and Ratification

At its outset, the Convention's outcome was uncertain, not least because the centre's weakness had attracted some interests as it lost its appeal for others. Smaller States were especially reluctant to cede the sovereignty that they enjoyed under the Articles of Confederation, because the requirement for unanimity on taxation from the centre, and the rule that each State voted as a unit in the Confederal Congress irrespective of resources and size, under-pinned their security. To abandon the rule risked domination by the financially powerful and populous states of Virginia and New York.

Fifty-five delegates met in convention at Independence Hall in Philadel-phia. Ambassadorial duties in Paris and London respectively prevented Thomas Jefferson and John Adams (both of whom were later elected to the Presidency) from attending. Otherwise, the Convention was a galaxy of former rebels against British colonial power: George Washington, Alexander Hamilton, Benjamin Franklin, James Wilson, James Madison, and Gouver-neur Morris were all present. Having participated in the revolution against Britain in 1776, they now found themselves with the task of creating a new political order only six years after the adoption of the existing Confederal one. The proceedings were held in secret and, in order that minds might be changed without difficulty or embarrassment, the votes of individual dele-gates went unrecorded. Instead, States voted as delegations at Philadelphia as they had done in the Confederal Congress. However, Madison took detailed notes of the discussions, and as a result we know a good deal about who said what.

The Constitution that emerged from the negotiations and debates at Philadelphia was, necessarily, a compromise between politicians with differ-ent priorities, interests, and objectives. A short document, the Constitution is, in Supreme Court Justice Sandra O'Connor's words,"animated by an array of intentions"; it not only admits, but implicitly encourages, competing interpretations. Compromise was essential not only to build a coalition in the Constitution's support, but also to avoid equally unpalatable and unwork-able polar options. The Constitution marked an attempt to avoid both the concentration of governing power and its dilution, the national and con-federal alternatives. Its authors had vivid memories of unchecked Executive power exercised from London, experience of the vacuum of Executive power under the Articles of Confederation, and apprehensions about future usur-pation of governing power by a popular legislature. Through the Constitu-tion adopted in 1789, together with the Bill of Rights proposed in December of the same year and ratified in 1791, they addressed all three anxieties. Suspicion of executive power was tempered by the requirements of political order. Crucially, the new Constitution had two features which its predecessor had lacked: an Executive, and the power to act directly upon individuals. The central (Federal) government comprised an institutionally separated Execu-tive, Legislature, and Judiciary, in a Federal system. The States delegated specified powers to the central government but retained substantial and inviolable powers over their own affairs. Some States regarded their member-ship of the new political order as revocable; not until the victory of Union forces in the Civil War was that view refuted.

Key Articles of the Constitution

The Constitution's Article I established a bicameral Legislature, Congress, and describes its powers (see Appendix 1). Members of the House of Representatives (termed Congressmen, Representatives, or Members of Congress) were to be popularly elected by white males (subject in most States until the 1830s to some property qualifications). Members of the Senate (Senators) were to be selected by each state's legislature, but have since the Seventeenth Amendment to the Constitution in 1920 been popularly elected (see Appendix 2). Every State has two Senators, irrespective of population, elected for six-year terms. Apportionment of Congressmen between States varies between one and fifty-two, depending upon population; House terms are two years. At biennial Congressional elections, therefore, all House seats and approximately one-third of Senate seats are contested. The Constitution in many respects makes Congress a remarkably powerful legislature: its single greatest power is the unfettered right to raise taxes and to spend money (through "appropriations") and so to share fully and equally in policy-making. Yet its powers (unlike those of the British House of Commons) are also defined and strictly limited.

Article II established the new executive power in the institution of a single President, separately elected by an Electoral College rather than by popular vote, and Article III an unelected Supreme Court. The powers of all three branches were limited and (albeit imprecisely) specified. The remaining Articles III–VII comprised rules governing processes of policy: relations between the States, procedures for the Constitution's amendment, and for dealing with State debts incurred before the Constitution's ratification. The supremacy of the US Constitution was affirmed, and the means of ratification of the Constitution described.

Article VII required that for the Constitution to be ratified, nine of the thirteen States would have to approve it in Conventions called for the purpose. It was none the less clear that without the support of New York and Virginia, the new Constitution would probably collapse. New Hampshire was the ninth State to ratify the Constitution, but in Virginia and New York opponents were powerful and persuasive. Ratification in both States was achieved only with difficulty, after immense political efforts by both proponents and opponents, and no little good fortune. In New York, Hamilton, Madison, and Jay energetically wrote and published *The Federalist Papers*, contributing not only to the campaign for the ratification of the Constitution by the New York Legislature, but also to later scholarly and judicial understanding of the nature of the Constitution itself. Their literary efforts apart, the narrow victory for ratification in New York owed much to Hamilton and Jay's manoeuvring in the State Legislature where they threatened that if the Constitution were not ratified, they would promote the secession of New York City from New York State and join the Union separately; relations between the city and the State have rarely been entirely comfortable since. Twelve of the thirteen States ratified by the end of 1788; Rhode Island followed in 1790.

Separated Institutions and Shared Government

The United States Constitution is where America's political values and political institutions meet. The link which the Constitution supplies enables the United States to cohere, binding a multicultural, polychromatic, multilingual, ethnically complex, society into one. Constitutionalism is essential to the process whereby the US political system has periodically reconstituted itself, creating a Party system in the early nineteenth century, establishing the permanence of the Union and abolishing slavery in the Civil War, projecting itself into the international system in the twentieth century, and establishing a large, bureaucratic, Federal government to support vast programmes of economic regulation and welfare provision. The Federal Constitution's ambiguities, uncertainties, and intrinsically disputatious provisions have lent it a flexibility that has enabled it to survive, by ensuring its legitimacy in a heterogeneous society subject to repeated demographic shocks of migration and immigration. It has, however, also ensured that agreement on the meaning of its provisions for relations between branches of Federal government, between Federal and State authorities, and for conflicts between competing rights of individuals resist definitive settlement.

Conflicts apparent between American values find structural analogues in competition between and within institutions of government, both separated and Federal. Had clarity, order, and expeditiousness been their priorities, the framers would neither have separated the Executive from the Legislature, nor established a potentially powerful Judiciary, nor divided power between a national government and State governments in a Federal, and hence doubly separated, structure. Both Federalism and the separation of powers were necessary features of a Constitution sufficiently flexible to accommodate political strain and change, but sufficiently resilient to endure. America's vastness and heterogeneity made it necessary to limit the Federal government as well as establishing it.

Federalism, separation of powers, and judicial review are the distinctive structural features of US government and the Constitution's decisive achievement. The structure provides politicians with the opportunity to make government effective whilst preventing them from making it oppressive. Rights of States and individuals against government are guaranteed, and enforced by Federal Courts empowered to determine the constitutionality of Congressional statute and executive action. The Federal government itself is constitutionally empowered to act directly, as its predecessor was not.

The possibility that any one of the three branches might unbalance the tripartite structure is lessened by granting each a different source of power and legitimacy, vesting them with different prerogatives and characteristics, and inducing the Executive and Legislature both to compete and co-operate for influence over policy.

Vertical and Horizontal Separation of Powers

Both the vertical and horizontal separation of powers appear to be nearly complete:

- In the vertical separation, the Constitution grants powers over foreign affairs, defence, monetary policy, and the regulation of commerce between the States to the Federal authorities. The remainder is in theory (though it has not become in practice) the business of the States themselves, or of lower levels of government such as cities, counties and special governing units such as school districts, and commissions which derive their authority from the States. Since 1937 in particular, the Supreme Court's resistance to incursions by Congress into what had hitherto been regarded as traditional State responsibilities has weakened. The boundaries between Federal and State jurisdictions have shifted, and Congress now faces few impediments in constitutional law to extending its regulatory activities. Yet States survive, the fact of their separate existence is constitutionally protected, and the Federal government no longer enjoys the enormous fiscal advantages over the States that it did between the 1930s and the mid-to late 1970s. Although under fiscal pressure themselves, State governments are creative and autonomous actors. They are not independent, but interdependent and interactive with Federal agencies, bound in complex fiscal and administrative patterns of policy-making. That which the Constitution appears completely to separate, policy-making joins.
- In the horizontal separation, the Constitution forbids members of one branch to belong at the same time to another. Neither the President nor any of his Cabinet Secretaries may be members of the Senate or the House of Representatives, or be a Federal Judge or Supreme Court Justice. Congress is entirely separate and politically independent from the Presidency, the President's staff, and the political leaders (Cabinet Secretaries and their senior colleagues) of government departments and agencies. As with Federalism, however, the completeness of separation is more apparent in the structures prescribed by constitutional text than in the processes of policy-making. For government to be effective, unrestrained competition will not suffice; *co-operation* must constantly be sought and achieved. The most important lesson to be learned from relations between the Presidency and Congress since Franklin Roosevelt

took office for the first time in 1933 is that without co-operation, the effectiveness of Federal government deteriorates. However great the strain of eliciting co-operation through negotiation and bargaining, the Constitution's health cannot long withstand either the President or Members of Congress behaving as if the other branch lacked legitimacy. Each has separate sources of legitimacy and strength. Although the American system is Presidential, the Constitution provides neither formal links between the President and the Congress (other than those which the presentation, passage, and vetoing of legislation require), nor sanctions by which the President can coerce legislators or Federal Judges.

The President therefore lacks direct power over legislators. Except in the unimportant and unusual circumstances of disagreement between the two chambers as to the time of adjournment, he cannot dissolve either House of Congress. Since Franklin Roosevelt expanded the size and role of American government so dramatically in the 1930s and 1940s (see Chapter 4), Presidents have, however, been expected to present to Congress legislative proposals they favour: the President is, for example, required in law to propose annually a Budget for the entire Federal government. Nevertheless, the President lacks both the constitutional power and the political means to require or compel them to respond (whether favourably or otherwise) on his proposals. Neither in law nor in practice is Congress the President's creature.

Although the president's political effectiveness in part therefore depends upon Congressional co-operation, he does not hold office subject to Congress's approval, as does the British Prime Minister, subject to the approval of the House of Commons. Indeed, he may face a Congress in which his party colleagues are in the *minority*. Every Republican President since 1954 has had to work with a Congress in which at least one of the two chambers was in the control of Democrats. Richard Nixon's and Gerald Ford's Presidential terms occurred with large Democratic majorities in both houses; Bill Clinton's second term opened with Republican majorities in both. The glue that joins British government so strongly – its party system – is consequently a weaker and often ineffective constitutional adhesive in America. Party leaderships, whether in the White House, Congress, or National Committee, have few sanctions over elected members of the party at any level. Party is usually unable to combine reliably the governing powers the Constitution has so effectively separated. Only under unusual circumstances does it do so, when the normal constitutional constraints weaken, and Presidents have greater freedom of political manoeuvre and initiative. Obstacles to Presidential leadership then shrink, permitting a resourceful Chief Executive the opportunity to chart a course, whether of recovery from economic disaster, or of salvation from foreign threat, and to stick to it.

Diffusion and fragmentation, rather than concentration and coherence, characterise American government, and extraordinary vigour its society. In introducing the subject of the government and politics of the United States, this book attempts to explain the relationships of conflict, competition, and co-operation between the different parts of the democratic and fragmented system that the Constitution encourages and which makes the United States difficult to govern but compelling to study.

2

Political Parties: The Politics of Aggregation and Disaggregation

Party and the Culture of American Politics

Parties are as important to American government and politics as they are to government and politics in other systems. However, party in America differs radically from that elsewhere: the distinctive structure, rules, and culture of American politics produces a party system unlike any other. In Europe, party is everywhere regarded (more or less accurately) as an organizational device binding together members of broadly similar ideological disposition with the purpose of translating it into policy. In the United States, circumstances differ: parties in America have no mass membership, and the combination of the separation of powers and Federalism hinders any attempt at the control of party by leaders.

US parties and the party system are unusual in eight key respects.

Two-party System

The American party system is, except for that in Malta, the purest two-party system in the world. Although other parties exist, only the Republican and Democratic Parties have any prospect of nominating a candidate with a chance of winning the supreme electoral prize of the Presidency. In many States at different times, and in the South for a hundred years after the Civil War, there has been just one party exercising power, ranging from the hegemonic to the merely dominant. Most States are now two-party competitive; none has three major parties. Consequently, both the Republicans and the Democrats (but especially the Democrats, for reasons that will be explained later) are parties of exceptional ideological breadth compared to European parties.

Electoral Bases and Political Purposes of the Parties

Although the names "Republican" and "Democrat" have remained unaltered since the Civil War, neither the Party system they dominate nor the electoral coalitions that support them have been static. Their electoral bases and political purposes have often altered suddenly: the introduction of a major new issue or crisis has caused new cleavages to emerge in the electorate, thereby precipitating partisan realignments. New issues have often been advanced not by the Democrats or the Republicans but by third-party or independent candidates. Eventually, one or both of the two major parties has absorbed the issue, causing the demise of the third party. At other times, partisan change has been slower and more complicated (as since the early 1960s).

The Southern States

The southern States have for most of the Republic's life had a distinctive party system, and in certain respects continue to do so. The Jeffersonian tradition of "States' rights" was exploited by southern States to preserve slavery until 1865. Thereafter, it was used to buttress sharecropping (payment in kind from crops grown on land rented from whites) and segregation from Reconstruction until the passage of five Civil Rights Acts between 1957 and 1968 (see Chapter 3). The South's political development is of cardinal importance for an understanding of the American party system, both outside Congress and within it (where the chairmanships of major committees between 1910 and 1975 were dominated by autonomous, powerful, southern conservatives). The South stands as the great exception to many general rules about American society and politics, but also as Hamlet's ghost. As will be explained later, in no respect has the South had more powerful significance than in the contribution which its social order has made to the maintenance of the Democratic majority in Presidential elections until 1964, and its absence at most Presidential elections since.

Institutional Expression at State Level

The doctrine and practice of Federalism result in parties finding their chief institutional expression at the *State, not at the Federal, level.* Until the early 1970s, this political and statutory focus upon the State rendered national party organizations weak. Since then, national party organizations have acquired new powers over State parties, limiting their autonomy, especially with respect to rules controlling the nomination of candidates for the Presidency. None the less, Federalism continues to fragment American parties.

Quasi-public Institutions

Parties in the United States are quasi-public institutions, not private organizations as they are in most of Western Europe: they are subject to (but often determine) State law passed by State Legislatures.

Open Organizations without Mass Membership

Parties are open organizations and, unlike most West European parties, have no mass membership. Where local political clubs and caucuses survive, their membership is determined by local and not by national considerations. Primaries (see p. 38) give to voters a power over the party unique in Western political systems. The organization of parties in local government jurisdictions such as the counties is, partly in consequence, invariably weak and often non-existent.

Lack of Ideological Coherence

American parties are not strongly programmatic, and have usually lacked most of the ideological coherence typical of many European parties. Historically, parties in America have depended upon their Presidential candidates for the articulation of policy objectives. (The reforms to Presidential nominating politics prior to the 1972 Primary season have, however, sometimes saddled Presidential candidates with commitments from factions in the party which later prove politically damaging.) Candidates for all offices now run under their own programme, not one determined (or even heavily shaped by) a central, State, or local, party organization. Candidates seek less to control government (not least because the structure of American politics makes that very hard to achieve) than to win elections, a characteristic which does not build national or ideologically coherent parties. A centrally-determined ideological programme would have no purpose, could not be imposed upon candidates, and could not be assured of implementation in a system of fragmented government at both Federal and State level. In contrast to the experience of many European states, there have never in the United States been any electorally significant parties dedicated to the overthrow of the political or economic system, or even systematically critical of either. Both major parties support the political and economic orders, and since the end of the Civil War have always done so, save at times of crisis such as that of the Populist challenges in the 1890s. Party competition, though vigorous, occurs within a comparatively narrow ideological range; there exists widespread agreement on fundamental values.

Bridge Across the Political Divide between Institutions

Parties in the United States, although rendered weak by the combination of the separation of powers and Federalism, are vital for efficient government: the unique structure of government in America requires party for the bridging of the political divide between institutions. As Chapter 5 on Congress and Chapter 4 on the Presidency show, while party leaders lack the sanctions available to which party leaders in many west European states are accustomed, and work in a system where compliance has to be elicited rather than demanded, party ties exert a powerful pull on individual politicians in Congress. In the United States, party may indeed be weak, but party also matters: it remains one of the best indicators of why members of Congress vote and behave as they do.

The Development of the American Two-Party System

Dangers of Partisan Allegiance

Party has rarely won the approbation of American voters. It enjoyed neither the favour of the founders nor of the first President of the United States, who perceived in partisan allegiance the seeds of social and political strife (see Exhibit 2.1 for a list of US Presidents 1789–1993, to which it might be helpful in this chapter occasionally to make reference). George Washington himself had no need of party: his reputation ensured that he would face no serious competition to become or remain President, and that his prestige would prove an unshakeable political foundation for his Presidency. The Constitution's exclusion of members of Congress from membership of the Presidential Electoral College was a feeble barrier to party's emergence. Displeased by the factional strife between Jefferson and Hamilton in his own Cabinet, by the fiercely-contested struggle to succeed him in 1796, and fearful of its implications for the future unity of the country, President Washington issued in his Farewell Address of 1796 a forthright warning of the dangers that party, together with sectional interest groups, presented. He and his contemporaries had no experience of party government, but both he and some of them had a lively anxiety about its destructive possibilities, and the rousing of inarticulate and uneducated masses. Nevertheless, as the overwhelming issue of opposition to the colonial power lost its importance after 1776, factional groupings sprang up in several states.

Party before 1800

Most of the delegates to the Philadelphia Convention of 1787, who drafted the Constitution (in the American term, the "Framers"), intended that the role played by the mass of voters should be marginal: a proposal for the President's direct election was rejected because of their aversion to the possible consequences of mass participation. Hamilton, Madison, and Jay (1987) wrote *The Federalist Papers* to advance not a democracy, but a republic buttressed and sustained by its rules and spirit against an effusion of democracy, parties and mass participation. In *Federalist No. 10*, Madison argued that the structure of government would prevent the capture by faction of all branches of government. The notion of government coming under frequent attack from members of an opposition none the less loyal to the constitutional order (and sensitive to the need to preserve the Union) was entirely anathema to Madison and his colleagues.

As with any complicated document whose drafting is the product of compromise and disagreement, the meanings and silences of the US

EXHIBIT 2.1

Presidents and Vice-Presidents of the United States

Year		President	Year	Vice President
1789		George Washington		John Adams
1797		John Adams		Thomas Jefferson
1801		Thomas Jefferson		Aaron Burr
			1805	George Clinton
1809		James Madison		George Clinton
			1813	Elbridge Gerry
1817		James Monroe		DD Tompkins
1825		John Quincy Adams		John Calhoun
1829		Andrew Jackson		John Calhoun
			1833	Martin van Buren
1837		Martin Van Buren		
1841		William Harrison		John Tyler
	1841[1]	John Tyler		
1845		James Polk		George Dallas
1849		Zachary Taylor		Millard Fillmore
	1850[2]	Millard Fillmore		
1853		*Franklin Pierce		William King
1857		*James Buchanan		John Breckinridge
1861		•Abraham Lincoln		Hannibal Hamlin
			1865	Andrew Johnson
1865		*Andrew Johnson		
1869		•Ulysses Grant		Schuyler Colfax
			1873	Henry Wilson
1877		•Rutherford Hayes		William Wheeler
1881		•James Garfield		Chester Arthur
	1881[3]	•Chester Arthur		
1885		*Grover Cleveland		Thomas Hendricks
1889		•Benjamin Harrison		Levi Morton
1893		*Grover Cleveland		Adlai Stevenson

Constitution became the subject of intense dispute after its ratification. Hamilton and his Federalist colleagues understood the Constitution to be a means to the establishment of a powerful national state; Jefferson and his allies were distrustful of a powerful central government and instead saw liberty's best defence in limited government at the centre. As Secretary of State from March 1790, Jefferson strove to weaken the policies of Alexander Hamilton, Secretary of the Treasury and, in particular, opposed Hamilton's plans, published in December 1790, for a national bank. Jefferson's ground for opposition was that the Constitution did not grant to Congress powers to enable the bank to be established. Jefferson's opposition to creating a unitary state through a Federal Constitution was unqualified.

Year	President		Vice President
1897	● William McKinley		Garret Hobart
		1901	Theodore Roosevelt
1901[4]	● Theodore Roosevelt		
1905			Charles Fairbanks
1909	● William Taft		James Sherman
1913	* Woodrow Wilson		Thomas Marshall
1921	● Warren Harding		Calvin Coolidge
1923	● Calvin Coolidge		
		1925	Charles Dawes
1929	● Herbert Hoover		Charles Curtis
1933	* Franklin Roosevelt		John Nance Garner
		1941	Henry Wallace
		1945	Harry Truman
1945	* Harry Truman		
		1949	Alben Barkley
1953	● Dwight Eisenhower		Richard Nixon
1961	* John Kennedy		Lyndon Johnson
1963[5]	* Lyndon Johnson		
1965			Hubert Humphrey
1969	● Richard Nixon		Spiro Agnew
		1973	Gerald Ford
1974	● Gerald Ford		Nelson Rockefeller
1977	* James Carter		Walter Mondale
1981	● Ronald Reagan		George Bush
1989	● George Bush		Danforth Quayle
1993	* William Clinton		Al Gore

● Republican
* Democrat

[1] President Harrison died on 4 April 1841.
[2] President Taylor died on 9 July 1850.
[3] President Garfield was shot on 2 July 1881 and died from his wounds on 19 September.
[4] President McKinley was assassinated in 1901, dying on 6 September.
[5] President Kennedy was assassinated on 22 November 1963.

This broad division between commercial (mainly northern and coastal) and rural (mainly southern and western) interests in the early years of the Republic fuelled emerging partisan divisions in the single-term presidency of John Adams (who succeeded Washington), and in the years of Jeffersonian and Madisonian domination that followed. In 1791, Jefferson succeeded in establishing a compact which united anti-Hamiltonian Republican interests in the South and New York. Partisan divisions over Hamilton's financial policies were soon broadened by fervent disagreement over the course of the French Revolution, the question of war with England or France, ratification of the Jay Treaty (which opened the frontier to the west), and the Federalist President Adams's Naturalization, Alien, and Sedition Acts of 1798 which (among other illiberal measures) criminalised Republican opposition to Federalist politicians. Many of the sources of division between the earliest parties in the Republic continued to divide voters and politicians in the United States long after the nascent party system of the late eighteenth century had disappeared. Indeed, the tensions between the values dividing the Federalists from the Republicans still appear between and within parties in contemporary America.

Washington's Farewell Address (which Hamilton helped to draft) was as much a reaction to developments already apparent as a warning of what might follow. Partisan divisions quickly focused on the office of the Presidency, national party alignments preceded state party alignments – a clear indication of the special significance of the Presidency and the contest for it. The election to the Presidency gave rise to national alignments that have passed through five systems:

- The Virginia dynasty (1800–24)
- Jacksonian democracy (1824–56)
- Civil war, sectionalism, and reconstruction (1856–96)
- Populist discontent, progressive reform, and Republican majorities (1896–1932)
- The New Deal Democratic Coalition (1932–)

The First Party System: The Virginia Dynasty

The constitutional crisis of 1800 followed divisions within President Washington's Cabinet over financial policy, and the struggle to succeed him. Together, they marked the stirrings of party. Reflecting the degree to which party was beginning to determine voting for President in the Electoral College, Thomas Jefferson and Aaron Burr, running together on the Republican ticket against the incumbent Federalist President, John Adams, tied for first place with 73 votes each. The election was therefore thrown into the House of Representatives, which was dominated by Federalists, many of whom had been defeated in the preceding November elections but who retained their seats until the following March. (The Twelfth Amendment, passed in 1804, ended the possibility of another tie between two candidates running on the same ticket; see Appendix 2.) After thirty-five ballots, the House, voting by States, elected Jefferson. Jefferson's Republican Party had swept both the House and Senate elections, and the Federalists were firmly in the minority in Washington, the nation's new capital. Jefferson's own transition from opposition, to party, to presiding over the first party system in American history is gently ironic, but telling. In 1789 he had written scathingly of party spirit: "Such an addiction is the last degradation of a free and moral agent. If I could not go to heaven but with a party, I would not go there at all".

In fact, Jefferson's heavenly passage was on his own party ticket. Before his death, he enjoyed two terms in the White House. His friend and ally Madison took the next two terms, and his "disciple" Monroe the following two. The Federalist Party, greatly diminished by Hamilton's death in 1803, disappeared after the Treaty of Ghent in 1814 ended the second war with Great Britain. The Virginia dynasty, which these three Presidents represented, ended in 1824; the Congressional Party Caucus could not cope with the demands of finding a successor. The election resulted in a stalemate, with none of the four candidates receiving a majority. Accordingly, the election of 1824 was thrown into the House, where John Quincy Adams defeated General Andrew Jackson, the intemperate frontier hero of the Battle of New Orleans.

The Second Party System: Jacksonian Democracy

The 1824 Presidential election was a watershed in the early development of the party system: in the succeeding sixteen years, politicians seeking the Presidency looked beyond Congressional Caucuses to potential supporters in State and local parties. The old cleavage between Federalists and Republicans collapsed under the pressures of the emergence of mass politics, which shifted the selection of the President from Congress to ordinary voters. Between 1830 and 1850, all States removed considerations of property and religion as qualifications for white males to vote. By the time that Martin van Buren (the first President to have been born a citizen of the United States) entered the White House in succession to Jackson in 1836, parties had become firmly entrenched in American polities. They were the means by which elections were organized, by which a structurally divided Federal government was (occasionally) given some coherence, and by which supporters of elected politicians were rewarded with patronage.

At the centre of this transformation from dynastic to mass politics, structured by parties, lay the procedures by which candidates for the Presidency were selected. Either the party had too few elected officials to whom to submit the decision to nominate, or the outcome of a Legislative Caucus was unacceptable to those early party activists in the States and the counties who would campaign for the nominee (Shafer, 1988, pp. 6–14). The new party system was distinctive not only in its organization and relationship between the elected and the electors, but (like the Virginia dynasty) in its bridging of the north–south divide over slavery. It was, unusually in the history of American political parties, a genuinely national two-party system.

Under the leadership of Jackson and a succession of Democratic Presidents after him, the Democratic Party had both northern and southern bases. So, too, did the disparate coalition comprising the (generally unsuccessful) Whig Party, whose name was supposed to link in the public mind the English Whigs' opposition to George III with the American Whigs' opposition to "King" Andrew Jackson (whose enemies described his Presidency as a "reign"). Yet the new Whigs had little more in common than opposition to

Jackson's policies and to his methodical fortifying of party through the spoils which he had introduced, and by which he ensured the allegiance of those Postmasters and Customs Officers who owed their posts to him. The systematic rooting of party in Federal patronage began with Jackson's Presidency; despite later civil service reform, patronage appointments remain an important feature of American executive politics, both in Federal and State governments.

Whig strength was greatest among those who benefited from the transformation of the economy to industrial capitalism, and among socially mobile Protestants in white-collar occupations. Whigs favoured a tariff to protect the infant American industries and labour from foreign competition, a modern, centralized banking system, and the creation of an advanced infrastructure of roads, railways, and canals. Whig support was drawn primarily from "insiders", but Democratic Party support (especially in the north) came, in McPherson's view (1988, p. 30), from:

> workers who resented the de-skilling of artisan occupations and the dependency of wage labour; Catholic immigrants at the bottom of the status and occupational ladder who took umbrage at Yankee Protestant efforts to reform their drinking habits to force their children into public schools; heirs of the Jefferson–Jackson distrust of banks, corporations, or other concentrations of wealth that threatened republican liberty; yeoman farmers in the upcountry or backcountry who disliked city slickers, merchants, banks, Yankees, or anybody else who might interfere with their freedom to live as they pleased.

The possibility that interests might divide cumulatively by region and economic interest along new partisan lines between the slave States of the south and the non-slave States of the north had always been a source of anxiety to those who ascribed the preservation of the Union the highest political priority. The implied threat to the Union was apparent in the Philadelphia Convention, which produced the three-fifths rule compromise in Article I (see Appendix 1) to accommodate the South's adherence to slavery. Washington had been conscious of the dangers: his Farewell Address, cited already for its warning of the "baneful effects of faction" also contained strictures against the emergence of regional parties. In 1796, the question of the preservation of the Union was prominent in the mind of every senior politician, but the longer-term threat posed by the entrenched retention of the peculiar social order, culture, economics and hence politics of the South was clearer to Washington than to some of his contemporaries.

The Third Party System: Civil War and Sectionalism

Intensified abolitionist opinion in the north, and (most especially) pro-slavery opinion in the south, eventually burst through the bounds of the two established parties in a spectacular increase in support for the Liberty Party in the northern states, especially in New Hampshire. In New York, the Democratic Party (already dividing on other, unrelated, issues) split on the question of whether slavery should be permitted in any territory acquired from Mexico in the Mexican War. In Massachusetts, slavery split not the Democrats but the Whigs; throughout the north, abolitionists nominated Van Buren for the Presidency in the 1848 elections under the Free Soil party label. As third-party candidates do at times of incipient or putative realignment, Van Buren ran well but lost (he came second in Massachusetts, New York, and Vermont). As third parties usually do after such promising performances, the Free Soil Party then declined. However, the issue threatening to destabilise the party alignment did not recede.

On the contrary, slavery continued to pose problems which the existing party alignment based on policy differences over banking and the tariff could not solve. Nor, as support for abolition grew, could the issue be avoided. Northern Whigs faced a stark choice: if they were to survive as a national party, they were bound to seek compromise at the price of anti-slavery opinion finding expression in another party. If they were to survive as a northern party, they would have to reject compromise with the grievous consequence of casting off from their southern wing, and so losing the prospect of winning the Presidency. Northern Whigs chose the first option, and sought allies of like mind, most of them in the north.

The problem was exacerbated because of manoeuvring over the greatest political problem of the mid-nineteenth century: the extension of slavery into territories as a result of westward expansion, and the conditions under which new States were to be admitted to the Union. California was admitted as a free State in 1850, but at the price of a more stringent law concerning fugitive slaves. The single most important event that caused the Union to split along new party lines was the passage of the Kansas–Nebraska Act in 1854, which triggered the formation of a new anti-slavery party bringing together many northern Democrats, Free Soilers, and Whigs. The Republican Party, the last major party to be created in American history, was born. Its parents were the former party alignment and the issue of slavery which the old alignment could no longer contain. The new issue cut across existing affiliations, endangering the future of the Union by aligning party with region.

The Court precipitated change. For only the second time in the history of the United States, it declared an Act of Congress (the Missouri Compromise) unconstitutional in the fugitive slave case of *Dred Scott* v. *Sandford* in 1857. Former Vice-President John Calhoun of South Carolina, brilliant exponent of States' rights doctrine and of the claim that slavery was a national condition but freedom sectional, found vindication in a confused and disastrous argument written by Chief Justice Taney, who set out definitively to resolve the legal status of slavery. The Democratic Party, meeting at its singularly ill-chosen convention home of Charleston, South Carolina, split, with many members of southern delegations leaving the hall. The Convention reassembled at Baltimore, where Stephen A. Douglas was nominated for President by the northern faction of the Party, and John Breckinridge of Kentucky for President by the secessionists. The Republicans nominated Lincoln on a platform of opposition to the extension of slavery in the territories, but of no interference with slavery in the southern States.

The election of 1860 confirmed the Republican Party, dedicated to the Union's preservation, as the majority in both Congress and the White House, exposed the north–south rupture of the Democrats, and left Southern Whigs as a dying rump. The South preferred fissure to accommodation, so that its political order might be maintained, and by this preference disposed of the second-party system, with calamitous consequences: America was now thrust into a war more destructive for it than any other in which it has been involved. Throughout the Civil War, two-party politics continued in the north; in the south, there was no opposition to the Confederate government. The cause of good government in the South did not benefit from being denied a vigorous party politics during the War, or after it. Some Democrats in the northern states supported the Union and fought for it – Lincoln's successor as President, Andrew Johnson, was himself a "War Democrat". Other northern Democrats were to varying degrees unsympathetic to the President's war aims. Pressure within the north against the expected emancipation proclamation (issued by Lincoln on 1 January 1863) brought the Democrats substantial gains in the 1862 elections. Lincoln was almost as hard-pressed by radical Republicans as from "Copperheads", the intense northern opponents of the war and of emancipation.

The Civil War has been the only social revolution in American history. At stake was not only the hold on political power but also the unity of the polity, its fundamental character and its social base. After the war, the United States progressed rapidly towards a full capitalist democracy, in which government had an increasingly important hand. In the regulation of banking (and later of interstate commerce); in the making of land grants in the west under the 1862 Homestead Act; in trade and tariff policy; and in the ending of slavery itself, the Republican Party acted as the engine of social, economic, and political change. In this period, the loyalties of many groups of voters to party were established and consolidated; many remained 130 years later.

The Fourth Party System: The Realigning Election of 1896

The period between 1874 and 1892 was one of party deadlock. Except for Grover Cleveland's two conservative Democratic Administrations, Republican candidates won the Presidency (though by small majorities), and the Democratic Party formed the majority in Congress. The forces behind Reconstruction of the South weakened, especially after the 1876 election. Black Americans in the South were excluded from party politics altogether, increasingly ignored by the Republican leadership, and eliminated from electoral politics by the Democratic Party order of enforced segregation in the South. The value of capitalist enterprise came to hold sway over the leaderships of both the Republican and the Democratic parties, although the former was more fully identified with the protection of the interests of industrial and financial capital, as its espousal of the tariff to protect the interests of northern owners of businesses and of workers in them showed.

This system was broken by the general election of 1896, and left the Republicans, in very different political circumstances from those of thirty-five years earlier, once again in control of the White House and Congress. The fourth party system brought Republican domination of contests for the Presidency, Democratic hegemony in the South, and Republican dominance of State-wide and US House elections in the North. The realignment followed a collapse in agricultural prices, and a deep economic depression in 1893, when the two elected branches of the Federal government were under Democratic control. This twin catastrophe occasioned deep resentment among small farmers and debtors (most of them in the southern and western states), and the inequality of income and wealth between west and east, and between debtors and creditors, grew.

For a time there existed the possibility of a new coalition of interests between distressed farmers dependent upon cash-crops, and the growing (though in comparison to Britain and Germany, fragmented) urban working class. It did not materialize. William Jennings Bryan's capture of the Democratic Party for the Populist cause was undertaken on behalf of a rural debtor class whose interests lay in the adoption of inflationary policies. The key issue that marginalized the Democrats was monetary policy, the inflation represented by the Populists' demand for the free coinage of silver (but implying the silver standard) versus the price stability represented by gold. Indebted western farmers favoured a silver standard; their eastern urban creditors, gold. William McKinley, the conservative Republican Governor of Ohio, stood solidly for high tariff barriers against foreign goods and a non-inflationary monetary policy secured by linking the dollar to gold.

In fact, the Civil War alignment by which the Democratic Party's base in the South was strengthened was too secure to be greatly altered. McKinley defeated Bryan by a majority of 95 regionally-concentrated electoral votes. The industrialized north and east turned firmly against the Democrats, aligning ever more staunchly with the Republican Party. The southern States were as solidly Democratic after the convulsions of the 1890s as before, but the Republican Party's significant gains in northern cities sprang from the appeal of the tariff and sound money both to workers and bankers. Bryan's appeal remained rural. His performance in the 1896 election left him and his Democratic successors with little backing in the increasingly important and populous cities of the north and east.

The link between the Republican Party and the interests of finance and business, established so firmly in 1896, has not been broken since. Among workers of the north and east, too, the Republican Party drew on massive support until shortly before the Depression of the 1930s. Except for Woodrow Wilson's victory in 1912 (which Theodore Roosevelt's Progressive candidacy made possible by splitting the Republican vote) and his subsequent re-election, the period from 1896 to 1932 was one of overwhelming Republican dominance. Not until Al Smith's campaign in 1928 attracted the votes of the huge Catholic immigrant populations of the cities did a Democratic candidate for President win a majority of the vote in America's twelve largest cities – although immigrant voters' indifference to the Civil War and incorporation into the Democratic Party through city machines dispensing services (especially patronage) in return for political support caused the Republican plurality to fall in the Presidential elections of 1920 and 1924.

However, even in northern States where Democratic Presidential candidates always lost and Congressional ones usually did, the Republican Party was between 1896 and 1932 dominant rather than hegemonic. The South was by contrast, unwavering in its support for Democrats between Reconstruction and the collapse of segregation in the 1960s. No matter how conservative a view southerners might take of the place of gold in guaranteeing price stability, how hostile they were to organized labour, how suspicious of Catholics, their support for the Democrats as the party of white supremacy in the South overrode those and all other considerations. For so long as the Republican Party represented the alien and hostile forces of Union and desegregation, it found scarcely any support in the South.

The Fifth Party System: The New Deal Coalition

The fifth party system which, in modified form, still operates in the United States, formed as a consequence of the shattering blow delivered to American politics and society by the Great Depression. The onset of its collapse was marked by the beginning of the Wall Street Crash on Thursday 24 October 1929. Within a month of that day's record fall in prices, a vast quantity of wealth was destroyed: the value of equities traded on the New York Stock Exchange fell by 40 per cent. Gross national product (GNP) fell by half in the following three years. Coupled with the entry of a huge wave of immigrants into the electorate, many of whom were of the Catholic, Orthodox, or Jewish faiths from southern and eastern Europe, and who moved predominantly to the large cities of the north-east, the years 1928–36 witnessed a convulsive upheaval of the American party system. Republican domination since 1896 was overturned, control of the Democratic Party by rural interests replaced by a new coalition of the southern and northern underprivileged and "outsiders", and old alignments replaced within many states by a system which (temporarily) owed more to class loyalties across State boundaries.

In the Presidential election of 1932, votes split (as they did throughout Roosevelt's four terms) on economic interest and ideology, between those who stood to gain from an enhanced role in economic management and welfare for the Federal authorities, and those who feared that they would lose by it. Within the Republican Party Herbert Hoover was a moderate, but the Democratic landslide of 1932 swept him from the White House and Franklin Roosevelt into it. Though altered and weakened, parts of the pattern of politics to which the Great Depression gave rise in the United States persist, as Chapter 3 on elections shows. Adherence to lightly-fettered private ownership defended against foreign competition by high tariff walls, characteristic of the Republican Party since Reconstruction, weakened sharply in the course of Roosevelt's four terms. Repeated defeat induced adjustment in all but the most reactionary, the most stubborn, and the most electorally secure.

The Democratic Party offered an interventionist remedy for the crisis, but neither quickly nor without dissent: party polities are seldom so simple in a fragmented system in which ideology and issues are often squeezed by the supreme objective of building a majority for the President. Even Roosevelt did not enter the 1932 campaign as an interventionist. His appeal in that contest sprang from a Progressivism exemplified in the Democratic Party by Woodrow Wilson, and by a readiness (apparent during his governorship of New York) to undertake practical and pragmatic action to alleviate the sharpest distress among the unemployed and poverty-stricken. As President, Franklin Roosevelt personified realignment of opinion around party, building a new and expanded coalition in the northern states on behalf of the propositions that limited redistribution by the Federal government, and government intervention where markets had failed, were consonant with the American political tradition. In the South, he was able to rely upon solid support in the election (provided that southerners could be confident that segregation would not be disturbed) although differences on economic and labour market policy between him and most southerners were numerous. The gospel of the New Deal gave Roosevelt huge new support, and at the 1936 election transformed the Democratic Party into the majority at all levels of government in most states.

The New Deal did not nationalize voting patterns, but the two-party system none the less progressively supplanted sectionalism throughout most non-southern States. The Republican Party was for the next forty years merely a minority Presidential party: Republican candidates won only twice (Dwight Eisenhower defeated the Democratic Governor of Illinois, Adlai Stevenson, in both 1952 and 1956) between the onset of the Great Depression in 1929 and the combination of Great Society and civil rights legislation in Lyndon Johnson's Administration from 1963 onwards. Johnson's Presidency marks the end of the Democratic New Deal majority at Presidential elections. It did not mark its end in Congressional elections, where the Democratic Party continued in the majority as before. Since the passage of the Voting Rights Act in 1965 and the very rapid rise in the enfranchisement of southern blacks which it caused, the only Democratic candidates to have won the Presidency have been Jimmy Carter and Bill Clinton. From 1896 to 1930 the Republican Party was in the majority; from 1932 to 1964, it was supplanted by the Democratic Party. Thereafter, Republican Party candidates dominated the single national race for the White House, while Democratic party candidates enjoyed natural majorities in the House and the Senate until Republicans formed the majority among southern delegations to the House from 1994 onwards. The Fifth party system has metamorphosed: its death, like that of Mark Twain, has been exaggerated. No sixth party system had emerged by the time of Bill Clinton's re-election in 1996; the electoral complexities of the modified and split fifth party system are explored and explained in Chapter 3.

Party Politics in the South

After the Civil War and the Reconstruction that followed, the Democratic Party retained a virtual hegemony throughout the south in non-Presidential elections for ninety years, until the end of Eisenhower's Presidency. In Presidential elections, its dominance was overwhelming. In most parts of the south, and throughout the "black belt" counties (those counties where blacks formed the majority of the adult population but not, of course, of voters) in the Deep South, race mattered above all else. Blacks were systematically excluded from political participation while simultaneously being the social hinge on which southern politics turned. Race was much the most significant cleavage, but not the only one: the interests of poor white farmers often diverged from those of large plantation owners, while the interests of the small urban working class invariably diverged from those of industrialists (as, for example, they did in Birmingham, Alabama). None the less, the regional memories of military defeat at the hands of the north, the common trading interests of a predominantly agrarian region, and the shared interests of all whites, sharecroppers and planters, poverty-stricken and rich, voting and non-voting, in racial matters, overrode all other potential divisions. The intensity and durability of this cleavage enabled Democratic Parties in the southern States to exercise unfettered sway for nearly a century.

They did so on the basis of State Constitutions which, redrafted after Reconstruction and supported by "Jim Crow" laws (enforcing segregation), systematically subjugated blacks and excluded them, directly or indirectly, from electoral politics. Militarily defeated in 1865, the political supremacy of southern white elites was substantially restored by 1880. Segregation won the

Supreme Court's approbation in *Plessy* v. *Ferguson*, 163 US 537, in 1896; southern politicians exercised an effective veto over Democratic presidential nominees; and US Senators from southern states exploited Senate rules to block measures they found repugnant. A remarkable illustration for three-quarters of a century of the power of a cohesive and entrenched minority in a political system which disperses power, the South's resistance survived Lincoln and the Republican Party's enforcement of Reconstruction, and its propagation of civil rights.

The issue of race was not evenly prominent throughout the South. It was at its most salient in the black belt counties, where the economies depended upon the cultivation of cotton, rice, and tobacco. Elsewhere, the lesser significance of race gave a different cast to politics, although only in North Carolina, Virginia, and Tennessee did Republicans have more than a token presence. Republicans in these States voted as they did because they were unionists. They were so either because they were black (a few southern blacks were able to vote between the end of Reconstruction and the Voting Rights Act of 1965, even in Mississippi) or because they were whites with no economic or political stake in cotton, rice, tobacco and the system of sharecropping that accompanied them. They were concentrated in the mountain counties, where there were no plantation crops (and hence no rich planters) and slaves had been few.

Republican Presidential candidates could attract support elsewhere in the South only when the Democratic candidate was repugnant to them: in 1928, Herbert Hoover won Florida, North Carolina, Virginia, Tennessee, and Texas. A "dry" Protestant (he supported the prohibition of alcohol), Hoover won majorities in these five States over the "wet" northern Catholic Democratic candidate, Al Smith. More precisely, he won majorities in those counties of these five States with a small black population, and (in a portent of what was to come in the 1970s and 1980s) in the few growing metropolitan areas of the South. Elsewhere, in counties with a large black population, Smith won despite being a Northern Catholic opposed to prohibition. Otherwise, Republican Presidential candidates were unable to dent the loyalty to the Democratic Party which provided an unyielding institutional barrier in Congress to unwelcome northern intrusion and reform.

Even after the New Deal realignment of 1932, the place of the solid South in the Democratic Party was assured because of the other, less attractive, deal struck by the northern and southern groups within it. Southerners were willing to support Roosevelt's northern candidacy for the Presidency provided he did not challenge segregation. Just as Republican presidential candidates in the last three decades of the twentieth century have been able to rely upon the support of the Rocky Mountain and most mid-western plains states, so between Reconstruction and 1944, Democratic candidates were able to rely upon the South. Hence the region's value to Democratic candidates and Presidents, and their reluctance to upset the mutually satisfactory arrangement. Democratic candidates (all of whom were from outside the South) and Southern politicians and elites gained. Until 1936, the South's leverage over the Democratic convention was reinforced by the "two-thirds rule", which provided that a Presidential candidate had to receive two-thirds of the votes at the convention in order to win. While the primacy of race prevented the replication of national alignments in the South, the creation of a national Democratic majority for the New Deal benefited considerably from solid southern support. Its weakening threatened the capacity of the Democratic Party to build a winning coalition for the Presidency. Once it was disturbed in 1948, with the inclusion in the Democratic platform of a strong civil rights plank urging Congressional action to enfranchise southern blacks and prevent discrimination in employment, the basis of the bargain between south and north was imperilled. The immediate consequence was that half the Alabama delegates and all the delegates from Mississippi rejected the Convention's choice and nominated Strom Thurmond, Democratic Governor of South Carolina. Thurmond, running on the States Rights (or "Dixiecrat") ticket with Governor Fielding Wright of Mississippi, won thirty-nine electoral college votes, all from the Deep South.

The Supreme Court decided in *Smith* v. *Allwright*, 321 US 649 (1944), that the restriction of primary voters to whites violated the Fifteenth Amendment's guarantees of voting rights to black Americans (see Appendix 2). Its unanimous decision in *Brown* v. *Board of Education* in 1954 declared segregated schools inherently unequal and hence a violation of the provisions of the Fourteenth Amendment. These two decisions began to prise apart the Democratic Party: segregationists continued to run and win on the Democratic ticket in the South for election to State Legislatures and Governorships, and to the US Congress, but at national level, Adlai Stevenson, a northern, moderately liberal Governor, lost the Democratic Presidential ticket much southern white support in 1952 and 1956. In the South, Stevenson gained majorities in those two elections only from lower-income white voters. Among middle- and upper-income whites, Eisenhower's advantage was approximately two to one. Southern blacks could not vote in substantial numbers until after the 1965 Voting Rights Act, but northern black voters moved increasingly to support the Democratic ticket in Presidential elections.

Since 1948, most white southern voters have been repelled by the national Democratic Party's support for the extension and defence of civil rights. Southern sensitivities to a civil rights plank in Truman's 1948 platform were reinforced by the passage of the Civil Rights Acts of 1957, 1960, 1964, and 1968, and the Voting Rights Act of 1965. Lyndon Johnson lobbied the first two through the Senate as Majority Leader (leader of the majority Democratic Party), and the final three through Congress as President. Since then, a majority of white voters in most Deep South states have voted at presidential elections for the candidate they have deemed most conservative on civil rights. In the 1960 Presidential election, Richard Nixon and John Kennedy (the Republican and Democratic candidates respectively) expressed similarly cautious views on civil rights. Although neither evinced enthusiasm for the cause, Kennedy's politically adept response to Martin Luther King's imprisonment contrasted favourably with Richard Nixon's unimaginative reaction, and contributed to the further move of black voters from the Republican to the Democratic column. Since 1964, however, there has always been a clear conservative option available to southern voters in Presidential elections. Especially in Presidential and State-wide politics, Republican Party candidates have exploited to their electoral advantage the opportunity presented by the demise of the solidly Democratic South and the persisting salience of racial politics. In addition to the conversion of many southern white Democrats to the Republicans, the inward migration of white (disproportionately Republican) voters and the outward migration of black (mostly Democratic) voters to northern cities have made for a much more competitive southern party politics.

None the less, the speed of Republican advance below the level of the Presidency has been less marked, and is non-linear. Immediately prior to the ending of segregation under the Civil Rights Act of 1964, and the guarantee of black voting rights under the Voting Rights Act of 1965, the Democratic Party's domination of Congressional delegations from most southern States remained virtually complete, as Table 2.1 shows. Its hegemony ended by the 1980s. By the mid-term elections of 1994, even its majority had gone.

In southern State elections, the Democratic advantage is more marked: some southern State Legislatures continue to be dominated by Democrats, with the result that most significant political divisions occur among factions within the Democratic Party rather than between the Democratic and Republican Parties.

American Political Parties as Quasi-Public Institutions

American political parties are not (as parties in most other democratic countries are) private organizations but quasi-public institutions, subject to regulation in public law passed by State Legislatures. State governments may (and do) regulate their organization, their rules, and the conditions by which individual citizens may register as Democrats or Republicans. They may further require primary elections to be held to determine who the candidates for the two major parties shall be at State and Congressional general elections, the dates on which primary elections for different offices take place, the rules governing their administration, and the extent to which parties may lend their support to favoured candidates in Primaries. Political parties in America therefore lack what political parties in almost all other democratic countries take for granted: unfettered control over their own

TABLE 2.1

Party and delegation to Congress, January 1963 and January 1997

State	January 1963 88th Congress, 1st session			
	US House delegation		US Senate delegation	
	Democratic	Republican	Democratic	Republican
Alabama	8	0	2	0
Arkansas	4	0	2	0
Florida	10	2	2	0
Georgia	10	0	2	0
Louisiana	8	0	2	0
Mississippi	8	0	2	0
N. Carolina	9	2	2	0
S. Carolina	6	0	2	0
Tennessee	6	3	2	0
Texas	21	2	1	1
Virginia	8	2	2	0

State	January 1997 105th Congress, 1st session			
	US House delegation		US Senate delegation	
	Democratic	Republican	Democratic	Republican
Alabama	2	5	0	2
Arkansas	2	2	1	1
Florida	8	15	1	1
Georgia	3	8	1	1
Louisiana	2	5	2	0
Mississippi	2	3	0	2
N. Carolina	6	6	0	2
S. Carolina	2	4	1	1
Tennessee	4	5	0	2
Texas	16	14	0	2
Virginia	6	5	1	1

rules and structure. The Federal government has regulated party only indirectly through campaign finance legislation; regulation of political parties themselves has been left entirely to State governments.

All States in the Union regulate political parties operating within their borders, to different extents, in different ways, and with different consequences for the organizational vigour of State parties, and for parties' influence over politics and policy. Power over the Democratic and Republican Parties in the fifty States is therefore shared between the parties and the State governments, but the balance of influence between State governments and parties varies by State. Ingrained suspicion of faction, originating in the earliest days of the Republic (see p. 21 above), provided the cultural foundation for State regulation, but its proximate cause was the rampant corruption in many eastern cities, where party machines developed between the end of the Civil War and the turn of the century, when the power of party over public affairs peaked.

In many port cities in the states of the mid-west and east – especially in Indiana, Missouri, New Jersey, New York, Ohio, and Pennsylvania – politics were constructed by highly-organized machines founded upon exchange and material interest rather than policy. The idea of "machine" suggests a unifying organization which was self-sufficient, inclusive, and directed towards its sustenance and the delivery of votes. The relationship between party and voter was contractual: material assistance and helpful intervention of all kinds were afforded in return for energetic political support. Help of whatever kind needed could be supplied: patronage jobs, whether for the straitened or ambitious), financial or housing assistance to the newly-arrived immigrant family from Europe, a hamper for the widowed at Thanksgiving.

For the city machines, the object was to win elections, and then to control the distribution of the fruits of government. Even in cities where the machine did not dominate, the pattern of polities as mercantilism could be found. Machines reached a high level of development and traded on systematic corruption. In Manhattan, Tammany Hall (named after a mythical native American) was the first classic example of an urban party machine. Its original function was the orthodox one of a bridge between the newly-arrived immigrant and citizenship. For that vital service, it was the monopoly supplier in Manhattan; and on that monopoly its political power was built:

> Whether or not the corner cop would let your youngster play under the water hydrant on a hot day depended on Tammany. It could do anything for a man from granting a bus franchise to a suspension of sentence for a serious crime; whether or not you could build a skyscraper – and how cheaply or expensively. (Gunther, 1947, p. 565)

Corporate and political power occasionally found expression in party organizations fuelled by corporate and personal finance: State politics in Michigan and Wisconsin were dominated in the 1880s, and to a lesser extent in the 1890s, by businessmen-politicians who later came under attack from Progressives seeking an end to corruption.

Having arrived at similar diagnoses for the abuse of political as for corporate power, Progressives prescribed similar remedies for them: regulation of economic monopolies was sought at both Federal and State levels by the creation of commissions whose remit was to secure the public interest by controlling private interests. The exercise of corrupt political power was similarly controlled by regulations designed to weaken the influence of party officials in enhancing the power of citizens through the initiative and referendum (by which voters themselves chose by ballot between policy options); by decreasing the autonomy of elected persons by providing for their recall (ejection from office following a popular vote); by prohibiting party labels altogether in elections for many local offices; and by, in some cases, replacing elected mayors with appointed (and supposedly disinterested and expert) city managers; and, most important by removing the power of recruitment from party notables and vesting it in primary electorates (see Chapter 10). Candidates whose nominations were won through an appeal beyond party bosses were less likely to submit to party discipline thereafter in government.

Much the most important aspect of public regulation of parties has been the control by States of entry to the ballot for State and US Congressional elections through Primaries. Selection of candidates proceeds according to rules set both by the party and by State Legislatures. The intended consequence of the introduction of Primaries by States for State Assembly and US Congressional elections was that parties' capacity to determine who stood in their name at general elections was weakened. This power did not disappear completely in all states. Many local and State parties retained influence over the outcome of Primary elections by ensuring that the candidate favoured by party elites won; some parties even prevented Primaries taking place. In New York, for example, State laws did little to diminish party strength in most counties. Nevertheless, from the time that State governments first regulated them, parties have been unable to determine who participated in Primary elections and who did not. Primaries threw open internal party recruitment decisions to a self-selecting electorate. In Europe, rules governing the selection of candidates confine the decision to party members or a subset of the total party membership; in the United States, selection of candidates is opened to those who "register" themselves as Democrats or Republicans.

States' registration rules vary from severe to lax, but no State confines registration to "members". Indeed, there are no members to whom it might be confined, because American political parties are not mass-membership organizations; opportunities for participation are, therefore, greater. Denied control of who ran for office under the party label, parties in America were (southern courthouse party organizations, and some northern city machines excepted) weakened. Easy entry to the party through the Primary election lessens the attraction of running on a third-party ticket, as explained below. Since parties have no membership, there is no possibility of dissenters or insurgents being expelled. Where organizational centres exist at all, they have few sanctions to hand. Whatever the nature and extent of Primary voters' loyalty to the party, it is unenforceable.

Major city machines (which by the end of Truman's Presidency were all Democratic) formed one of the two major organizational pillars (labour unions were the other) upon which Franklin Roosevelt's Democratic Party was built in government (just as it had been constructed against them when seeking the nomination in 1932). Democratic machines did not make for efficient (still less for good) government, but proved bastions of electoral support for Democratic Presidential candidates, as reliable as the "Solid South", where many rural State and local parties had their own tightly-run organizations centred on courthouses. From Franklin Roosevelt to Lyndon Johnson, every Democratic President was indebted to the Chicago machine, which was established in the mid-1930s, reached a peak of influence in the early 1960s, and lingered until the late 1980s. Over that long period, every Democratic candidate for the Presidency needed its support. John Kennedy's narrow defeat of Richard Nixon in 1960 owed much to his victory in Illinois, made possible by Mayor Daley's corrupt electoral practices. Control of patronage, partly through lax interpretation and imaginative circumvention of Illinois's civil service laws, was complete in Chicago as late as the 1970s, and its extent huge: Daley's machine controlled approximately 30,000 patronage posts in the early part of the decade, in return for the assured and predictable supply of votes by precinct captains (paid local party organizers) and members of his party's local ward committees.

Elsewhere, too, party organizational power reached its apogee only after the introduction of the Direct Primary. The Democratic machine in Manhattan, Tammany Hall, thrived until the mid-1920s and was defeated only with the successful anti-corruption drive by Fiorello La Guardia, the distinguished Mayor of the City of New York, in his three successful mayoral races in 1933, 1937, and 1941. Much later, John Lindsay employed during his tenure as Mayor of the City during the 1970s, no fewer than 13,000 people in "temporary" appointments, and a further 75,000 in other non-competitive, non civil service posts. Although the provision of welfare services is often regarded as the main explanation for the political success of unreformed city machines, patronage was by far the most important currency in which they traded (as it had been of all party organizations, whether machines or not). Had social services been the most important, the New Deal's establishment of social security rights and a primitive system of social welfare would have weakened city machines to a greater extent (or at least more quickly) than it did. In fact, the New Deal often had the consequence of increasing the number of patronage posts at the disposal of city mayors.

Party Organization Today

Machines have largely disappeared, but party organizations of various kinds persist. Parties remain decentralized, but the patterns of organization and the strengths of organizational units vary greatly from State to State, and even from county to county within a State. In organization as in rules, tradition, and political culture, it is more accurate to regard the United States as having a hundred parties rather than two. Viewed nationally, the American party system is a loose confederation of parties drawn into a nominal two-party system.

Nowhere in the United States are party organizations any longer hierarchical command structures, as city machines once were, and as many political parties in Europe remain. The organizational form is not that of a branch, but a caucus–cadre party, in the sense that Maurice Duverger (1954) used the categories in his classic work *Political Parties*. The Democratic and Republican Parties are still of this kind, conforming to Duverger's characterization of them as "decentralized and weakly-knit". They remain primarily "electoral machines" at precinct, ward, city, county, State, and national levels. The two major American parties recruit activists, not members (although parties have often sponsored the establishment and operation of clubs associated with the parties); they reach peaks of activity in periods leading up to elections. American parties accordingly lack the financial support which most European parties enjoy through membership fees. Party organizations at national level do not dominate those in States, nor do the latter dominate those at county level. Since the Chicago machine's end in the early 1980s, city organizations do not usually control wards, nor wards precincts. Each level possesses substantial autonomy from the others, and party activists in each typically respect the independence of other levels.

Using a geological metaphor, Samuel Eldersveld (1982) has characterized this form of non-authoritative relationship as a "stratarchy". Not all State and local parties correspond strictly with this form, but it captures the essence of most party organizations more accurately than do notions of hierarchy and command. State parties work in collaboration with the city and county party organizations below them, and with the national organizations above. Save in the (usually Democratic) machines of some eastern and mid-western cities and in (Republican) State party organizations in New York, Ohio, and Pennsylvania, authority has rarely typified relations between levels of party organization. It certainly does not do so now that party influence over Primary election outcomes is typically slight.

American parties at local, and generally at State, level rely upon small numbers of staff. As Primary elections open the party nomination to almost anyone willing to run for it, so American parties are open to any who have ambitions to participate (though in the great majority of local parties, few do). The Federal nature of American politics was a powerful inhibition to the emergence of centralized parties with branches throughout the country, and developments after 1824 confirmed this trend: Jackson was the first outsider to be elected to the Presidency, having failed to win it as an insider in 1824. The strategy of nomination by Convention that Jackson adopted for his successful campaign in 1828 gave the Presidency (for the first time) a base of power independent of Congress.

There are many forms of local organization, but almost all local parties are loose, flexible, and informal. Factional disputes rarely concern ideological difference, but often have a racial or ethnic dimension; the ordered development of public policy is inhibited by the common condition of rampant factionalism. In the absence of mass involvement, local party organizations are usually run by a stable group of activists virtually autonomously from other local party organizations in the county or city. In the city machines of the eastern and northern past, local party precinct or ward organizations formed part of a much more hierarchical party structure suited to maintaining a full register of party sympathizers, meeting their many needs, and delivering blocks of votes on election day. But this hierarchical form of party based on powerful control of material incentives was never typical of American local or city party organization and except, in attenuated forms, has now disappeared.

If the city machine lay at one pole, so the other was marked by a virtual absence of organization and party activists; it is the latter that has continued. Such leadership as there is in such weak and fluid conditions depends on powers of persuasion rather than authority deriving from party rules. The leadership's resources are few: the material incentives upon which precinct captains in Chicago and Kansas City thrived during the heyday of the Democratic machines in those two cities are now virtually absent. The spread of civil service conditions and the increased density of union membership among State and local government workers have reduced local political patronage. The Courts have further eroded the use of patronage for traditional local and State party organizations. As a result, it is now virtually impossible to draw into local and city parties the volunteer labour which engaged in the detailed canvassing essential to the reliable production of blocks of votes at elections. This loss of patronage over local and State governments has dramatically reduced the political power of local and State party organizations. The Supreme Court's reapportionment decisions, by increasing the number of single-member districts for state assembly and US House elections, have made states less amenable to party control. Finally, the key role of mediator between government and voters, which used to be monopolized at elections by parties, has been replaced almost everywhere by electoral organizations based on individual candidates and constructed by political consultants who communicate with voters by television advertisements produced by media consultants (see Exhibit 3.1 p. 81). Party labels are still necessary, but local and State party organizations are now usually marginal to the tasks of campaigning and winning elections.

Some factors mitigate organizational weakness: most State party organizations now have permanent staff and a head office in which they work to raise money, conduct opinion polls, and supply party candidates running for office at all levels of government within the State with data and analyses of issues. Functions of this kind enhance the capacity of State party officials to defuse factional conflict within the party, and to infuse a spirit of common purpose, but the State party central committee rarely concerns itself with developing policy as a result. Since State party organizations are usually wholly separate from party organizations in the State Legislature (as each party's national committee is separate from the two Congressional parties) there would be little point in their attempting to do so.

It is commonly observed that American parties find their primary organizational expression at the local rather than the State or national level. By contrast, the national organizations have always been weak: Schattschneider (1942) wrote that the national organizations possess "only the transparent filaments of the ghost of a party". The national organization of the President's party has since the 1960s enjoyed little autonomy from the White House: President Johnson regarded the Chairman of the Democratic National Committee (DNC) as the chairman of *his* party; and President Nixon took much the same view of the Chairman of the Republican National Committee (RNC). Nixon's campaign for the 1972 Presidential election was run wholly independently of the RNC; George McGovern's Democratic campaign in the same year was also largely independent of the DNC. It is therefore especially ironic that Nixon's personal campaign staff, the Committee to Re-elect the President (CREEP) should have revealed their ignorance of the marginal political importance of the DNC by attempting in 1972 to find campaign intelligence in the Committee's headquarters (where there would have been none of value) as well as their incompetence by bungling the burglary of the DNC's offices in the Watergate Building.

In the 1980s, the financial and organizational renaissance of the Republican Party was built by its chairman, Bill Brock, on sophisticated direct mailing techniques to targeted potential supporters. President Reagan had the good political sense not to impose a chairman of his own upon the National Committee when he won the Republican nomination in 1980, but to retain Brock, who continued his work. The greatly enhanced organizational power and financial resources of the RNC contributed to the marked revival in Republican electoral fortunes in the Senate in the early and mid-1980s, and to the success of the Republican Party in altering economic and defence policy during Reagan's Presidency. The Democrats' national party organization also improved in quality and increased in influence, although not to the same extent as the Republicans. The national Democratic Party's new arrangements for delegate selection to the Presidential nominating convention following the McGovern–Fraser Commission's reforms after 1968 helped to centralize the distribution of power within it.

National party organizations are now much more important for fund-raising. Not only has the RNC used modern technologies to identify potential supporters and to raise money from them, but its role in disbursing funds to Congressional candidates has also grown. The national organizations of both major parties now play major roles in distributing funds to State and local parties in order to maximize the vote in Presidential elections (where the candidates are notionally funded entirely from public sources, as Chapter 3 explains). Although much less significant than Political Action Committees (PACs) in financing campaigns for both Federal and State office, parties remain more important than they were prior to the enactment of the Federal Election Campaign Act of 1971 (FECA; see Chapter 3) and its major amendments in 1974, 1976, and 1979. The national party organizations' standing in law was also strengthened by Supreme Court decisions that have favoured them over state and local parties. In *Cousins* v. *Wigoda*, 419 US 477 (1975), the Court determined that a State's certification of delegates elected under the law of that State cannot override national party rules governing the selection of delegates.

The Bipolar American Party System

State laws regulating political parties discriminate in favour of the two major parties and against third-party and independent candidates, which, since the legislators who write the laws are either Republicans or Democrats, is unsurprising. Prime among these laws is the device of making access to the election ballot by third parties contingent upon a prior demonstration of support. Before the last decade of the nineteenth century, third parties could not be marginalized in this way, since ballots were then supplied by parties at the polling station – a procedure which made voting virtually a public activity, because party workers noted carefully which voters asked for which ballot. Since 1890, so-called "Australian" ballots have been provided by the State governments on which parties were listed, and between which voters made their choice in secret. Parties were accordingly given the legal status they had previously lacked; equally, it was a standing which States could and did deny to minor parties by drafting rules with which (as was intended) they were often unable to comply.

For the Presidential election, the task of securing access to the ballot by third-party and independent candidates is made more difficult by the variations in rules between the fifty States and the District of Columbia. Demonstrating support sufficient to meet the different demands made by the States is an onerous burden for a candidate's lawyers and campaign managers, especially since the petitions have to be signed and presented within specified periods. Some States require few signatures on a petition for access to the ballot (just twenty-five in Tennessee) while others require a percentage of the registered electorate (California required more than 100,000 for John Anderson in his independent candidacy for the Presidency in 1980). New York law requires that a petitioner obtain a certain number of signatures in every one of the State's counties.

For the Presidency, for Congressional races, and for State contests, the patchwork of State laws inhibits third-party challenges and increases the incentive for candidates to seek access to the ballot by running for a major-party nomination in the Primary. Most states hold Primaries only for those parties that secured a substantial proportion of the popular vote in the preceding election. Federal Courts have in recent years upheld the right of

States to prevent the electoral process from slipping into disrepute, but have indicated their unwillingness to uphold the constitutionality of laws designed to protect the two major parties from competition by third parties.

Despite the height of barriers to third parties, elections for offices at all levels attract many more candidates than the nominees of the Democratic and Republican parties alone. Third-party (and fourth- and fifth-party) candidates frequently appear on ballot papers, especially those for the Presidency and for Governorships in the states. The Libertarian Party, the Communist Party, and the Socialist Party, invariably nominate candidates for the Presidency. In the 1980 Presidential election there were, in addition to the candidates of the Democratic and Republican Parties – President Carter and Governor Reagan respectively – eleven minor party candidates. The best-known of them, John B. Anderson, ran as an Independent (despite having been the Republican whip in the US House of Representatives) and took 6.1 per cent of the vote. In 1948, Strom Thurmond's segregationist candidacy (see p. 34 above) brought him 2.40 per cent of the vote and thirty-nine Electoral College votes. Some third-party candidates have performed more strongly: Governor Wallace of Alabama won 13.53 per cent of the popular vote, and forty-six Electoral College votes, in the bitter election of 1968, while Ross Perot took 19.0 per cent of the popular vote (but no Electoral College votes) in his independent 1992 campaign. Most powerful of all was Theodore Roosevelt's candidacy for the Progressive Party in 1912, when he won 27.39 per cent of the popular vote and eighty-eight Electoral College votes.

Third parties have displayed political strength in some states at certain times because of new issues or crises of unusual, if parochial, intensity. For example, the Progressive Party was a powerful force in Wisconsin state politics in the 1934 and 1936 elections, having sprung from factional divisions in the Republican Party between the Progressives (dominated by the La Follette family) and the Stalwarts (the conservative wing of the party). In New York, Conservative, Liberal, and Right to Life parties are still active in the State's politics: James Buckley was elected to the US Senate from New York on the Conservative ticket in 1970. However, New York's party politics are unusually complicated, not least because the State's election law permits nomination by more than one party, and multiple ballot placement. Some candidates secure the backing not only of one or two minor parties, but of both the Democratic and Republican Parties.

Measured by the number of parties whose names appear on the ballot paper, the party system in the United States is multiple; measured by the distribution of the vote, it is two-party; measured by election result, the system is the purest two-party system in the world. Every member of the US Senate and every member of the US House (bar the socialist Bernard Sanders of Vermont) in the 105th Congress elected in 1996 was either a Democrat or a Republican. Since 1856, every President has been the nominee of one of the two main parties and so, since 1945, has been every Governor of every State. The party labels that apply at the national level have also tended to apply at State and local levels; this has been so since the second party system of Whigs and Democrats in the first half of the nineteenth century (see p. 25). Forty-nine of the State Legislatures have scarcely any independent, and usually no third-party, representation.

No socialist or social democratic party has ever established itself in the United States. This is another distinguishing feature of American party politics: all other industrial democracies have (or have had) socialist or social democratic parties of significant size. Class conflict has often broken out in the United States' commercial and industrial development; it has taken intense forms in the coal industry throughout the twentieth century, and has been apparent at various times in vehicle manufacturing, the docks, road and rail transport. Yet class has played little part in party politics: only in 1932 and 1936 has the national political alignment been largely founded upon it. Several factors account for this distinctive characteristic: universal male suffrage preceded industrialization in America rather than, as in most of Europe, following it, while ethnic and racial cleavages in American society, far from being cumulative with that of class, have cut across it. Socialist and social democratic parties have also been hindered by factors of a more general kind that have militated against the emergence of third parties. Discriminatory rules written by state legislatures against third parties, a single-member district voting system, quadrennial elections by a winner-take-all system in the Electoral College for a single-person Executive, together discriminate fiercely against all third-party candidates. At State level, too, the executive is single, not multiple. The consequences for states are similar to those for the Federal government in the case of the Presidency.

The requirement to unite in the campaign of a single national victor exercises a powerful centripetal force on State party organizations. It is in the election to the Presidency that powerful regional interests and divisions are overcome. There are no rewards for coming second, and no prospect of displacing the winner before the end of the four-year cycle. Even the questionable luxury of parliamentary opposition as compensation for defeat is denied the loser. The party without the Presidency lacks even a leader. The singularity of the Presidency and of the competition for it therefore has powerful implications for the nature of the American party system. Like third parties in another polity with single-member districts, the United Kingdom, third and fourth parties with evenly-spread minority support fare badly at the polls. Unlike the United Kingdom, however, regional parties enjoying spatially- concentrated support and some electoral reward have never emerged in the United States.

President Washington's first concern was, as noted on p. 26 above, the nascent fissure between south and north on the question of race and which, were it to become aligned with party, would raise the gravest doubts about the capacity of the nation to survive. The Civil War raised such doubts. Since 1865, however, even at times when it seemed to some politicians most propitious to form a regional or ethnic party, the two-party system has not been seriously threatened. With the exceptions of 1948 and 1968, neither the South between Reconstruction and the struggle for civil rights ninety years later, nor blacks at any time in their history, have formed sectional parties. His independent candidacy in 1968 apart, George Wallace remained in the Democratic Party; other southern Democrats changed their registration to Republican. No ambitious southern politician entertained hopes that a third party based on segregationist principles might compete with the Democrats or Republicans over the long-term: a two-party system with primary selection offered sufficient scope for ambition's realization.

Weakness of American Political Parties

The constitutional rules establishing and maintaining the separation of powers have not changed fundamentally since 1789. Those concerning Federalism have been modified – by war, constitutional amendment, and Court decisions. None the less, the states retain importance as the basic organizational units around which party is constructed in the United States and between which quadrennial association takes place through the processes for the nomination and election of the President. Much of the scholarly literature on American political parties published since the mid-1970s is concerned with their decline. The two basic constitutional rules of a separation of powers and Presidential system at the national level, with a Federal structure, merely tend to weakness while ensuring distinctiveness. The Presidential system splits parties at the national level by dividing the Executive from Legislative power, by establishing two Elective Branches of Federal government, and two distinct fields of party competition. One is led by the Chief Executive, and the other by the majority party in Congress. The division of the structures of government results in the division, and weakening, of the party system. The full constitutional independence from the Executive enjoyed by Members of Congress invites dissension between them and the President. The prospect of government, so powerful an inducement to political loyalty in many European parliamentary systems (notably the British) is absent from Congress because the Constitution forbids it. The implication is that, while Members of Congress and the President may share party membership, the separation of powers renders unity of purpose between them weaker than in parliamentary systems. Party is the only bridge across the gulf between President and Congress, but it is alarmingly rickety.

At State and local levels, party has undoubtedly lost much of the power it once enjoyed. The McGovern–Fraser Commission reforms of the Democratic Party's nominating processes following the disastrous Presidential nominating Convention at Chicago in 1968 (when the party's divisions were damagingly exposed) removed from State party notables the power to choose a candidate. Choices in the Presidential nominating process are now made by Primary electorates, who had to varying extents in different States and cities enjoyed similar power over sub-Presidential elections. Combined with the emergence of new issues on to the public agenda in the 1960s and 1970s, which split the Democratic Party in particular (civil rights and affirmative action; environmentalism; women's rights; gay rights), the loss of Presidential nominating powers weakened State parties while centralizing party authority in the national Convention. These developments strengthened candidates at all levels of government. In the 1970s and 1980s they found themselves able to take advantage of television, video, and mass- mailing techniques to make direct appeals to Primary voters over the heads of party notables. In their different ways, Governors Jimmy Carter and Jerry Brown, and Representative John Anderson illustrate the extent to which politicians outside the ranks of the party elite have been able to launch and sustain campaigns for the Presidency (and in Carter's case, spectacularly to succeed). All have depended upon exploiting the weakness of party to advance their candidacies.

If party is in these senses weaker, it is also in certain settings more coherent. The correspondence between ideology and party affiliation was for both voters and elected politicians long indeterminate. It is still far from complete: American parties are not held together by ideological glue. While the Republican Party has become more coherently conservative since the collapse of the one-party South in the 1960s, and the Democratic Party has lost the majority of its deeply conservative wing (mainly, but not exclusively, from the south), there is often little ideological coherence within each of the major parties in cities and States. Free entry to the two parties through the Primary system, coupled with the extraordinary cultural and ethnic heterogeneity of America, results in party labels proving a poor guide to similarities and dissimilarities in both ideology and policy between State parties. The striking ideological consistency of some third parties in America remains an unaffordable luxury for the two major ones. Excellent examples of "catch-all" parties, their flexible capacity to absorb new movements, to adapt to new issues and pressures, does much to explain their longevity and their resistance to easy ideological categorization.

None the less, the creation of two-party systems in the southern States caused by the ending of segregation has resulted in southern Democratic Parties losing almost all politicians having the most conservative views on civil rights: whereas the Democratic Party nationally contained as recently as 1970 the most conservative and the most liberal voices on civil rights policy, it no longer does so. US Senators and Congressmen from southern states are in most cases now either conservative Republicans, or Democrats who are fully part of the national Democratic Party alignment. The Republican Party's most moderate voices in Congress are to be found in the Senate, where mobilization by candidates independent of party is easiest; the liberal, progressive wing of the party that was politically significant before the mid-1970s has now virtually disappeared.

The Democratic Party remains a broader coalition than the Republican Party on issues of defence, fiscal policy, welfare, education, and on the new issues of environmentalism, gay rights, and women's rights. Almost all liberal politicians, and most liberal voters, are now Democrats: Presidents Reagan and Bush had little difficulty in marginalizing their Democratic opponents between 1980 and 1988 by stigmatizing them as liberals. The party system from 1932 to the early 1960s, with the Republican Party having large moderate and liberal factions, and the Democratic Party a large conservative wing, has therefore been replaced by one in which ideology no longer cross-cuts party allegiance at wide angles. This development has powerfully affected public policy. President Reagan's radical programme of tax reductions and defence spending increases in 1981 was passed by Congress because of the virtually unanimous support from the (then majority) Senate Republicans and the (large minority) House Republicans (see Chapter 10). In the House, the President needed to win the support of Democratic conservatives in matters of taxation and defence in order to secure majorities. However, Republican successes at the preceding November elections, coupled with the shrinking of the Democrats' conservative wing, meant that he had to rely upon his own party colleagues in the House for most of his support. Greater ideological coherence of parties does not, of course, ensure ease of government; nor did the older cross-cutting patterns of ideological and partisan majorities in Congress thwart all legislative progress. For President Reagan, ideological harmony was insufficient to bridge the gap between the White House and Congress, not least because the Presidency, Senate, and House at no point in his administration lay in the same partisan hands. For Presidents Roosevelt, Truman, Kennedy, and Johnson, when neither party was neatly coincident with ideological division, it was necessary to craft legislative majorities from shifting bases of partisan and ideological sources of support.

Conclusion

Party in America has always been distinctive, and continues to be so. Increased ideological coherence in recent years has modified the character of American parties but not fundamentally altered their nature. Parties have "weakened" in fewer respects than is sometimes supposed: machines have vanished, but they were never typical of party organization in most of the country, where they remain loosely organized (at the local and state levels, looser than ever). They have come to be dominated at all levels by candidates whose campaigns for office are increasingly independent of the party whose label they seek, though often not independent of interest groups from whom many receive heavy financial support via Political Action Committees (PACs).

Despite the decline in the identification of voters with party and the candidate-centred nature of the electoral process, the American two-party system remains substantially intact. Buttressed by single-member plurality election rules, the single national electoral prize of the United States' Presidency, and the fifty single State prizes of the Governorships, the two-party system has, since the early 1970s, extended into the formerly solidly Democratic southern States. It has thereby virtually ended the abnormality of party politics in the South by introducing a party system not dissimilar to that elsewhere. The old one-party system in the South had immense consequences for American politics and government; the transition from a single- to a two-party system has had comparable significance for election processes and results. Neither of the two parties has become a mass membership organization. Both parties continue to find their major organizational expression at State rather than national level; and both are still heavily regulated by State legislatures which share responsibility with the national Party Conventions, and with State and local parties, for determining party rules.

The increase in the proportion of voters who identify themselves as independents has resulted neither in the growth of third parties nor in a growth of independent candidacies. The label of one of the parties remains a prerequisite for election to public office (save, of course, for those offices that State Legislatures classify as non-partisan). Party remains the major means by which governments are organized, and by which electoral outcomes at all levels of American government are structured. Difficult as government is in America, it would be formidably demanding without party.

3

Elections and the Politics of Participation

Four related problems are examined in this chapter:

1. Who has been *able to vote* and why?
2. Who *votes* and who *abstains* and why?
3. *How* do Americans run for election and vote?
4. *For whom* do Americans vote?

Who Has Been Able to Vote

The question "Who may vote in the United States?" is now easily answered. Every American citizen may vote, irrespective of wealth, gender, race, or ethnicity, provided that she or he is not serving a sentence for a crime or (in many States), has never been convicted of a crime.

Limitations on the Franchise

It was not always so. Not until the ratification of the Nineteenth Amendment in 1920 were the rights of women to vote assured in Federal constitutional law (see Appendix 2); not until 1924 were native Americans granted full US citizenship; and only with the passage of the Voting Rights Act in 1965 were the rights of black Americans to vote guaranteed by the Federal government.

Property qualifications for voting, though rarely severe, enjoyed widespread support at the time of the Philadelphia Convention in 1787 (see Chapter 2); those for office-holding were usually larger, and often prohibitive. Except for Vermont, every State set property qualifications of some sort. Even Benjamin Franklin, one of the most democratic of all the founders, regarded the prospect of the enfranchisement of the landless as "an impropriety". Most States also barred Catholics and former loyalists from voting.

Property qualifications were dispensed with quickly in the early years of the Republic, and had disappeared by 1830; religious tests followed within the following two decades. Admission of new States in the west and south

(Indiana in 1816; Illinois in 1818, and Alabama in 1819) prompted the partial democratization of politics in the other States. Whereas in 1800 only two States chose members of the Electoral College for the election of the President by popular ballot, by 1832 voters in every State except South Carolina did so. Together with the stimulus provided by the creation of a mass politics organized and mediated by party (see Chapter 2), this change caused the size of the electorate to double between 1820 and 1830. Party power was both symbolized and expressed by nominating Conventions, machines, and (except in the rigidly patriarchal South, where political power was the preserve of the landed gentry) compromise and bargaining in the face of popular pressures.

The Struggle for Women's and Black Suffrage

Although the extension of democracy was much more advanced in the United States than in other countries, blacks and women were excluded from it. The struggle for women's suffrage was shorter than that for blacks, and (in public, at least) mainly pacific. American suffragettes encountered considerable opposition to their cause, by no means all of it from men. Most southern black women were in practice deprived of their Fifteenth and Nineteenth Amendment voting rights until 1965, but other women had secured the vote with the Nineteenth Amendment's ratification in 1920. Unlike in Britain, where the vote was at first granted only to women aged over thirty, no such distinction was made in the United States; all women (except southern blacks) aged over twenty-one were able to vote in the 1920 Presidential election. As with black voting rights, so with women's: many states guaranteed them before the Federal government did so. In the same decade in which southern states began to disenfranchise blacks following the end of Reconstruction, Colorado became the first state to extend the franchise to women, in 1893 (the same year in which New Zealand became the first country to establish women's voting rights). Wyoming had acted in 1869, but was at that time still only a territory. Twelve other states, many of them in the west, where women had partly freed themselves from the traditional roles ascribed to them in the east, granted women's suffrage before 1919.

The struggle for black suffrage divided the United States much more deeply and bitterly than that for women's suffrage, because the whole of southern politics turned upon the exclusion of blacks from southern society. Yet the problems posed by racial division were not confined to the South: prior to the Civil War's outbreak, there was substantial resistance in northern states to voting rights for blacks. Attempts by Republicans in New York to enfranchise all black males (where they had been subject to a $250 property qualification long after it had been abolished for whites) foundered on united Democratic opposition and the fears of many Republicans, who voted against an equal suffrage amendment even as they supported Lincoln's candidacy. Even at the war's end, black men could vote in only six northern states. After Lincoln's assassination in 1865, attempts by Radical Republicans in Congress to enfranchise blacks failed at the first attempt with President Andrew Johnson's veto, and passed at the second attempt only over it.

In the wake of the Civil War, the Fourteenth Amendment was passed by Congress in 1866 and ratified by the States two years later, marking a decisively important development of the Federal constitution. It reversed the relationship between the States and the Federal government that had been applied previously by extending Federal guarantees to all persons against the deprivation of life, liberty, or property without due process of law. The equal protection of the law was similarly guaranteed. Yet the Civil War had not caused northern Unionists to become integrationists: segregation and racism were rife in northern as well as southern States, and public opinion was generally hostile to ideas of political and social equality for blacks. Moreover, many Republicans were alarmed by the prospect that southern representation would increase with slavery's abolition and the superseding of the notorious Article 1, Section 3 of the Constitution, which had bribed slave States into the Union at the 1787 Convention (see Appendix 1). According to that provision, each slave was denied citizenship but counted as three-fifths of a person for the purpose of calculating the seats to which slave-holding States were entitled in the US House of Representatives. The abolition of slavery by the Thirteenth Amendment in December 1865, coupled with the end of the Civil War, meant that southern representation in Congress would increase (since blacks were now free and counted not as two-thirds of a person but as full citizens for apportionment purposes). Were southern States to prevent blacks from voting, the South would not only have a majority in the Electoral College and Congress, but also one composed of southern white rebels. Section 2 of the Fourteenth Amendment therefore reduced representation proportionately, as voting rights were abridged by State governments, although in practice this provision was later ignored.

Ten of the former Confederate States refused to ratify the Fourteenth Amendment, and radical Republicans in Congress responded with punitive ferocity: the First Reconstruction Act of 1867 provided for brutal military rule in every southern State except Tennessee. Re-establishment of civilian rule was made contingent upon ratification of the Fourteenth Amendment and the establishment of black suffrage. After the governments of the south were reconstructed according to the north's requirements, their constitutions rewritten, suffrage extended, and legislatures reapportioned, the states were readmitted. The Fourteenth Amendment (and the Fifteenth which, following it, declared that the right of United States' citizens to vote shall not be abridged by Federal or state governments "on account of race, color, or previous condition of servitude") were duly ratified in 1868 and 1870, respectively. Unlike the Fourteenth, the Fifteenth Amendment leaves no doubt about Congressional intent.

Congress, acting at the customary invitation of the drafters of the Fifteenth Amendment "to enforce this article by appropriate legislation", passed the Enforcement Acts in 1870–1. The Acts were implemented by the despatch of Federal troops and marshals to execute court decrees. The US Justice Department prosecuted State employees who sought to apply election laws in racially-biased ways. Between 1870 and 1877, the Department prosecuted an average of 700 cases every year, but the proportion of successful prosecutions fell from 74 per cent in 1870 to just 10 per cent by 1877, aided in part by two narrow interpretations of the Enforcement Acts by the Supreme Court in *United States* v. *Cruickshank*, 92 US 542, and *United States* v. *Reese*, 92 US 214, in 1876. Strengthened by the Court's judgment that to convict under the Enforcement Acts it would be necessary for the prosecution to show that the accused had intended to interfere with an individual's voting because he was a black who intended to vote, white resistance to black suffrage grew quickly. "States' Rights" became a code phrase for those who sought to extinguish the citizenship rights of black Americans; it was used until the 1960s and 1970s by those southern politicians who sought to resist their extension and protection. The re-establishment of white supremacy in the South and the consequent disenfranchisement of blacks also owed much to the corrupt 1876 Presidential election: the victory of the Republican Rutherford B. Hayes was bought at the price of Republican acquiescence in the re-establishment of the old white southern order. In the ninety years that followed, the citizenship of southern blacks was largely fictitious.

Black voting (and even black representation) continued until the 1890s in parts of the South, but between 1890 and 1910 all southern State constitutions were rewritten with the intention of disenfranchising black voters. Between the end of Reconstruction in the 1880s and the passage of the Voting Rights Act in 1965, blacks who attempted to vote had to endure the multiple jeopardy of discriminatory literacy tests (in the application of which, white officials were given substantial discretion in order that illiterate white voters need not be excluded from the rolls), long residence requirements, the poll tax, and the threat of white violence. States with few black voters took more limited measures, usually relying upon the poll tax. The disenfranchising of approximately half the white electorate, and almost all poor white males (because of the poll tax), were more often the unintended consequences. The difficulty of avoiding catching poor white voters in the trap that ensnared all blacks was considerable, and often the subject of bitter divisions among whites.

Primary elections nominate for office; general elections elect to office. Introduced elsewhere during the Progressive period in order to combat the

motives vs. outcomes

power of corrupt party bosses, the introduction of the Direct Primary in the South early in the twentieth century had a sinister motive and consequence. It helped in the re-establishment and maintenance of white supremacy and the exclusion of blacks from the electoral process. As a party rather than a State matter, the Primary was held to lie outside the purview of the Federal Courts – a view helpfully and technically sustained by the Supreme Court until 1944. This was an attractive defence for white politicians, because the South was between the Civil War and the 1960s a one-party region. The only significant electoral contest therefore took place in the Democratic Primary, exclusion from which rendered blacks electorally powerless. The Democratic Party was for a hundred years the chosen and manipulated vehicle of white political power in the southern states.

The Federal Courts hesitated to strike down the white Primary at the centre of this edifice. The Texas State Legislature, dominated by the Ku Klux Klan, declared in 1923 that no black voter would henceforth be allowed to participate in a Democratic Primary within the State. After the head of the El Paso chapter of the National Association for the Advancement of Colored People (NAACP), Dr L. A. Nixon, was denied a ballot paper in the 1924 Primary election, he filed a suit in the Federal District Court against the election officer concerned. The question before the District Court was whether the Primary was an "election" within the meaning of the Fifteenth Amendment. The defence held that the election was a private matter, notwithstanding its having been organized under the State's auspices.

The case eventually came to the Supreme Court in 1927. Justice Oliver Wendell Holmes, writing an opinion for a unanimous Court in *Nixon* v. *Herndon*, 273 US 536, struck down the Texas statute on the grounds that it violated the Fourteenth Amendment. The State legislature responded by delegating to the Texas Democratic Party's Executive Committee the determination of qualifications for participation in the party's Primary, an action which, by the narrowest of margins, the Supreme Court in 1932 found unconstitutional after the redoubtable Dr Nixon had again pursued the case through Federal courts: Justice Cardozo, writing for the majority in *Nixon* v. *Condon*, 286 US 73, observed that whatever power a State party had to determine its membership lay with its Convention. The Texas party needed no clearer invitation: the Party's Executive Committee rescinded the restriction that Cardozo and his colleagues had rejected, and the State party convention proceeded to restrict membership of the party to whites.

Basing its judgment on Cardozo's ruling, the Court in *Grovey* v. *Townsend*, 295 US 45 (1935), distinguished between the "privilege" of membership in a political party and the right to vote in a general election. The claim that the first of these, as measured by participation in the Primary, was indissolubly linked to the second (especially in the South) did not find favour with the Court. The Court's judgment in *Smith* v. *Allwright*, 321 US 649 (1944), overruled *Grovey* on Fifteenth Amendment grounds. The case was significant in two respects: first, in disposing of the fiction peddled by southern white politicians that Democratic parties in the south were, by placing restrictions upon participation in Primaries, acting entirely independently of State Legislatures; and second, in establishing afresh the constitutionality of Federal interference in the election process to secure individual voting rights of American citizens where they had been violated.

Alabama responded quickly to the Court's judgment by adopting a constitutional amendment requiring that a person seeking to register to vote would have to be able to read and write, "to understand and explain any article of the United States Constitution", to have "worked or been regularly engaged in some lawful employment, business, or occupation, trade, or calling for the greater part of the twelve months" preceding the application for registration. The amendment also provided that registration be contingent upon the applicant being a person "of good character and who understands the duties and obligations of good citizenship under a republican form of government". The purpose was to enable local registration officers to find reason to deny registration to black applicants by granting them a discretion which legislators could be confident would be used systematically to prevent blacks from voting. The language of the amendment mattered little, and afforded no defence whatever to blacks: local, white officials would determine who voted and who did not. If black respondents were to demonstrate knowledge of constitutional matters, they could be excluded by unanswerable questions: "How many bubbles are there in a bar of soap?" was the paradigmatic case.

Little progress towards enforcing civil and voting rights was made during Franklin Roosevelt's Presidency. Politics explain the silence. Roosevelt well understood that the maintenance of his electoral and Congressional coalitions depended upon northern Democrats conniving at the perpetuation of racist policies and politics which constituted the central nervous system of Democratic Parties in the southern states. Repugnant though many northern Democrats found southern practices, their priority was to secure the New Deal, which was in turn dependent upon maximizing party votes in Congress, the price for which was that such advances as there were by Federal authorities in the extension of black civil and voting rights came only from the Supreme Court.

The first movement of Executive and Legislature towards enforcement of the Fifteenth Amendment in the post-Reconstruction period came in 1957, eighty-seven years after the Amendment's ratification. President Eisenhower faced a Congress with Democratic majorities. While he privately supported both the guarantee of the suffrage to southern blacks and the end of segregation, his need for southern Democratic support modified his calculation. It was left to Attorney General Herbert Brownell to press for passage of civil rights legislation, and to Speaker Rayburn and (especially) Senate Majority Leader Lyndon Johnson to create the conditions within Congress for its enactment. The 1957 Act created a Civil Rights Commission, a Civil Rights Division within the Justice Department, and empowered the Attorney General to seek an injunction when a citizen was deprived of her or his vote. The Act was nevertheless hedged around with restrictions, and weakened by provisions for only light penalties. Its importance lay in its being the first Civil Rights Act since Reconstruction; its more perceptive supporters regarded it as a harbinger of further progress.

The 1964 Civil Rights Act and the 1965 Voting Rights Act

The most important Civil Rights Act of the twentieth century was that of 1964, passed in unamended form during Lyndon Johnson's first year as President. The most significant titles (sections) of the Act were Sections II and III, providing for the desegregation of public facilities, and for injunctive relief against discrimination in such places. Title I, however, amended and tightened earlier Acts primarily by weakening the obstacle presented by literacy tests in the South. In Court, people having received education to the sixth grade (reached at approximately the age of eleven) would henceforth be presumed literate in cases coming before the Court.

Title I of the 1964 Act is of less significance than the Voting Rights Act of 1965. Its passage followed savage violence by white state troopers under the authority of Governor George Wallace against participants in Dr Martin Luther King's campaign of voter registration in Alabama, and in particular against peaceful marchers near Selma, Alabama, in March 1965. Clubs, bullwhips, tear gas, and electric cattle prods were used by the police. Bullets were used (with fatal consequences) by the Ku Klux Klan. It is doubtful whether, in the absence of official white brutality, televised to great political effect across America, and organized by Wallace with a mixture of cynicism and supine incompetence, President Johnson could have galvanised Congress to act.

The President signed the Bill into law on 6 August 1965. The Act suspended literacy tests for a period of five years from the last case of voting discrimination, and abandoned individual litigation on behalf of individual citizens denied the vote. Buttressed with the Federal guarantee sealed by a Presidential commitment, the Act placed under Federal control the registration of voters in areas where blacks had been disenfranchised. Within three months of passing into law, Federal officials were registering voters in thirty-two counties in Alabama, Louisiana, Mississippi, and South Carolina. Georgia, Virginia, and parts of North Carolina were also caught in the net. The constitutionality of the Act was sustained by a unanimous judgement of the Court in *South Carolina* v. *Katzenbach, Attorney General*, 383 US 301 (1966). In *Harper* v. *Virginia State Board of Elections*, 383 US 663 (1966), the Court determined that the payment of poll taxes as a condition for voting was unconstitutional.

In the five years following the passage of the 1965 Act, 1.5 million blacks registered to vote in the southern States. Over the longer period of 1960–80, black registration nearly doubled. The Act was reauthorized again in 1975, and once more (after President Reagan had attempted unsuccessfully to weaken it) in 1982. The 1965 Act suspended the use of state literacy tests, prohibited state residency requirements beyond thirty days as a bar on voting in Presidential elections, and established uniform national rules for absentee registration and voting in presidential elections. Eletion law had fallen almost completely under Federal control. Additions made to the legislation in its several reauthorizations require the provision of bilingual ballots, extend the scope of the Act to cover all or part of ten additional states, and guarantee the voting rights of other specified racial groups including Asian Americans, Hispanic Americans, native Alaskans, and native Americans. In twenty-six States, changes in State election laws are now required to have the prior approval of the US Justice Department before taking effect.

Apportionment of Electoral Districts

Denial of the suffrage was long compounded by malapportionment of electoral districts, a subject the Supreme Court had long avoided, no President could solve, and southern Congressional chairmen had every interest in deflecting. It was neither solely an injustice afflicting southern States nor simply one infringing upon black rights. In 1946, Justice Frankfurter declared in *Colegrove* v. *Green*, 328 US 549, that the Federal Courts should decline to enter the "political thicket" of apportionment questions, and leave their resolution to elected politicians. This position did not last long. In *Gomillion* v. *Lightfoot* 364 US 399 (1960), the Court considered a case arising from the attempts of the city government of Muskegee, Alabama, to maintain white rule through gerrymandering, the manipulation of electoral boundaries for political effect. In a brazen attempt to exclude every black from the city's electoral roll, Muskegee's boundaries had been transformed from a square to a complex 28-sided shape. The litigant claimed that his right to vote in municipal elections had thereby been denied. Justice Frankfurter claimed that the case was quite different from *Colegrove*, that the Court had never sanctioned gerrymandering for the purposes of "an unequivocal withdrawal of the vote solely from colored citizens", and that as such *Gomillion* was not subject to the self-denying ordinance the Court had imposed with regard to "political" questions. Giving judgment in favour of the litigant, Frankfurter concluded that he and other black citizens of Muskegee had been deprived of voting rights protected under the Fifteenth Amendment:

> the inescapable human effect of this essay in geometry and geography is to despoil colored citizens and only colored citizens, of their theretofore enjoyed voting rights. That was not [the intended effect of] *Colegrove* v. *Green*.

Until the 1960s, disparities between the size of State legislative districts occurred throughout the United States, resulting in the over-representation of rural areas and the under- representation of urban ones. In the South, malapportionment, the failure to change constituency boundaries to reflect population changes and movements (redistricting), and gerrymandering had the additional object and consequence of minimising black voting strength. In its most extreme form, where it was supplemented by the county-unit rule which treated counties as legislative districts with equal representation in the state House, the ratio between sparsely-populated rural counties and Fulton County (most of Atlanta) was as great as 99 to 1. *Baker* v. *Carr*, 369 US 186, which the Supreme Court decided in 1962, addressed just such a problem from Tennessee, where the legislature had not reapportioned the state since 1901. Justice Brennan, writing an opinion for the Court's majority of seven, devoted most of his judgment to the prior questions of jurisdiction and justiciability. Having disposed of them, he found the failure to reapportion a denial of Fourteenth Amendment rights.

Having established the Federal Courts' right to deal with apportionment questions, *Baker* v. *Carr* precipitated a flood of cases which continued through to the 1980s. Among these was litigation to end the Georgia county-unit system which, in the 1963 case *Gray* v. *Sanders*, 372 US 368, was ruled unconstitutional on the grounds that the Fifteenth, Seventeenth, and Nineteenth Amendments required equality of voting power within a given electoral unit (as, for example, with the election of a Governor in a State). In 1964, the Court ruled in *Wesberry* v. *Sanders,* 376 US 1, that the malapportionment of US Congressional Districts in Georgia could no more be justified under the requirement of Article 1, Section 2, of the US Constitution than the malapportionment of State Legislative Districts could be under the Fourteenth Amendment. The Court ruled that although "mathematical precision" might not be capable of achievement, the "principle of equal representation for equal numbers of people [was] the fundamental goal for the House of Representatives". In the same year, the Court struck down in *Reynolds* v. *Sims*, 377 US 533, the county-unit rule in Alabama, by which one senator was elected from each of the State's thirty-five counties, irrespective of population. The population of Alabama's counties varied between 15,000 in the least-populated rural counties to more than 600,000 in Jefferson County (the city of Birmingham); such differential weighting of votes within the State could not be justified by the Court, and was duly declared a violation of the Fourteenth Amendment. Alabama's object (the over-representation of white-dominated rural interests and the marginalization of the working-class and heavily black city) was unconstitutional.

In practice, mathematical precision and exactly equal population of representative districts for every legislative body in the United States excepting the United States Senate alone is just what the Warren Court and the succeeding Burger Court have required. No diminution of the value of the vote of one citizen or votes of groups of citizens is now tolerated by the Federal Courts through variation in the size of state assembly or US Congressional Districts. Whereas the variation in the size of parliamentary constituencies in Britain is (at its most extreme) considerable, the State with the greatest variation in size in the 1980s was Alabama where the deviation was a trivial 2.45 per cent. In the early 1960s when *Baker, Wesberry*, and *Reynolds* were decided, no State in the Union applied Warren's principle. Every State now does so. The Court has, however, declined to declare gerrymandering for partisan (as opposed to racial) advantage unconstitutional. Gubernatorial and State legislative elections occurring at the end of each decade prior to the new census therefore have special significance: a party controlling both a State Legislature and the State governorship is well placed to redistrict to its own advantage.

After the reauthorization of the Voting Rights Act in 1982, Congress, the Courts, and the Civil Rights Division of the Justice Department came to interpret the Act's prohibition of racial minority voting strength as requiring that, where a minority district can be created, it must be. The ruling resulted in some convoluted electoral geography: in order to capture a black voting majority in North Carolina's twelfth Congressional District, the state legislature concocted a long, snaking, distrist across the centre of the state; at one point it was little wider than one of the two Interstate highways around which the District was drawn. Five disaffected white voters filed suit in Federal Court, holding that the creation of "majority–minority" Districts violated their Fourteenth Amendment rights to equal protection of the laws. In *Shaw* v. *Reno*, 113 S.Ct. 2816 (1993), the Court judged (by a vote of 5–4) that the creation of such bizarrely-shaped districts was constitutionally doubtful. Much litigation followed, especially in southern States: the tangled problems of equality presented by minority representation is greater there because black populations are more dispersed in the South (still characterized for the most part by small towns) than in the north (where black populations are concentrated in central cities). There is no final settlement of the question, partly because there is no single principle of representational equality which finds universal assent. Majority–minority districts continue to be drawn, and black Americans in particular continue to be elected from them.

Despite hostile Supreme Court judgments, more blacks and Hispanics have been elected in the 1990s (especially in the South) because of the creation of districts favourable to them. Blacks themselves have favoured the creation of districts with black majorities. Such a preference none the less threatens the interests of many white Democratic incumbents whose district boundaries would be disadvantageously altered. It is therefore opposed by many elected white Democrats and supported by those Republicans who think that they and their party would gain: an ironic result of majority–

minority districts' creation (especially in southern States) has been that white Democratic candidates have had fewer black voters to rely upon and have therefore had to appeal (with declining success) to white voters.

Who Exercises the Right to Vote and Who Abstains?

In the most distinguished book ever written on the American electorate, *The American Voter* (1960), Angus Campbell, Philip Converse, Warren Miller and Donald Stokes argued that most Americans in the 1950s knew little about politics, had little interest in the subject, failed to organize their thinking about politics in structured or sophisticated modes, and did not categorize their attitudes to politics in coherent ideological terms. Other scholars later argued that much changed in the 1960s as a result of the upsurge of political protest against the involvement of the United States in Vietnam, civil rights marches, and urban violence, with the result that the electorate grew to be better informed, casting more intelligent votes, and came to think about politics in more sophisticated ways. More recent research by Eric Smith in *The Unchanging American Voter* (1989) has demonstrated convincingly that Campbell *et al.*'s thirty-year-old character-isation of the American voter remains broadly accurate.

Although the elective principle cuts deeper into public life in the United States than in any other democracy, the rate of participation in elections is lower than in every democracy except Switzerland; the gap has widened even as the legal and institutional barriers to participation have been lowered. This phenomenon has excited a good deal of scholarly and journalistic attention, not least because of the implications that low turnout may have for political legitimacy. Part of the explanation for this extraordinary apathy had been thought to lie in cumbersome registration procedures. Registration regulations in some states (such as North Dakota, which required no registration, and Maine, Minnesota, and Wisconsin, which permitted voters to register on the day of the election) made entry to the voting roll straightforward. Procedures in many states were much less accommodating, requiring citizens to take positive steps to ensure that their names appear on the electoral roll. An outcome was that, while approximately 80 per cent of those registered to vote turn out on election day, high non-registration rates in many states kept participation low. A *New York Times*/CBS poll taken after the 1988 election showed that 37 per cent of those non-voters questioned cited their failure to register as their reason for not voting.

Nationally, the highest turnout of voters in a Presidential election since Franklin Roosevelt's victory in 1932 was just 62.6 per cent, when John Kennedy defeated Richard Nixon in 1960. Although turnout increased dramatically in the southern States following the passage of the Voting Rights Act in 1965, it declined after 1960 in the country as a whole, falling to 50.1 per cent in 1988, and to less than 50 per cent in 1996. Turnout in

Congressional off-year elections is even lower than in Presidential elections. From its highest points of 45.4 per cent, in both 1962 and 1964, it declined to 33.4 per cent in 1986. Many more fail to vote than support either of the two major candidates in Presidential elections.

Difficulties of voter registration are greater because of Americans' geographic mobility: a third of all US adults change their address every two years. Although the Federal Courts no longer permit States to require more than fifty days' residence before citizens may register to vote, frequency of moving coupled with the disincentive provided by registration requirements reduces registration rates. The blaze of publicity given to the poll leaves few citizens ignorant of the date of the election, but the final date for registration is often little known.

Two further provisions in many State laws reduce voting participation: first, many states "purge" voters from the electoral roll if they do not vote in two consecutive elections; second, and for no good reason, most States deny the vote not only to convicts serving sentences, but also to former convicts. Since the United States jails a large proportion of its population (and a higher proportion than any other major democratic country except for South Africa), the disenfranchisement effect is marked (and greater than elsewhere).

There have been many attempts to remedy the problem of low registration, some taking the form of persuasion, others of legislation. Whenever they deem it to be to their advantage, politicians running for office urge voters to register. Jesse Jackson did so in 1984 and 1988, concentrating his efforts among black voters (though this increased the incentive for opponents to persuade other groups, especially poor, white, rural voters to register). The most coherent of recent reform measures in Congress, the National Voter Registration Act of 1993 (the so-called "motor-voter" bill), requires state governments to ensure that when citizens apply for a driver's licence they are enabled to register to vote. All attempts in Congress to make registration easier have met with the opposition of those who fear that their political interests would be threatened by the registration of minority groups, the ill-educated and the poor, smaller proportions of whom are at present registered, and those who claim either that easier registration would encourage voter fraud, or that the Federal government ought not to involve itself in matters that are properly the province of the States. Between its passage and early 1996, six States challenged in Federal court the constitutionality of the motor-voter law (a Federal mandate for which States have had to pay) but without success.

The Republican vote is more easily mobilized than the Democratic: differential rates of turnout therefore have partisan consequences. Some of the statistics are, none the less, misleading. In particular, it appears at first sight that the election participation rate of blacks is lower than that of whites, and that of Hispanics even lower than that of blacks. In fact, the racial difference is entirely explained by the higher concentrations of blacks and Hispanics among the working class, the occasionally employed, and the unemployed. Some research has even shown that, holding social class constant, blacks participate at a higher level than whites. P. R. Abramson and J. H. Aldrich (1982) have argued that approximately 70 per cent of the decline in presidential elections arises from the combined effect of two trends: the weakening of party loyalties among the American electorate; and a decline in the beliefs about the responsiveness of government.

How Americans Run for Election and Vote

There have been few amendments to the United States Constitution. Since the Bill of Rights of 1791, only seventeen Amendments have been ratified, of which the Twenty-first (which ended prohibition) cancelled the Eighteenth (which imposed it). An indication of the importance of elections to American politics is that, of the remaining fourteen, seven are concerned with election rules, as Table 3.1 shows (see also Appendix 2).

Central as these Amendments suggest the rules and conduct of elections are to American constitutional law, elections in many States confer limited or contingent power. Elections' legitimating power in American politics is weakened (and the ingrained distrust of politicians exemplified) by the widespread use of the referendum, the initiative, and the recall – although these devices are not employed at the Federal level. Study of these tools of direct democracy falls outside the scope of this chapter, but it is important to take brief note of them.

- The *referendum*, presented as a proposition on the ballot paper on election day, is a vote on a policy proposal, a bond issue, or an amendment to the state constitution.
- The *initiative* is a means whereby voters gather signatures on a petition for the holding of a referendum, or require the State legislature to debate a policy proposal.
- The *recall* provides for the removal from office of certain State officials.

As the Progressives dramatically weakened party in the early years of the twentieth century by their introduction of the direct Primary, so they increased popular control over policy- making by these three devices. All three have found powerful expression in California, where Governor Hiram Johnson in 1911 introduced the Initiative in a challenge to the corrupting influence of the monopoly railroad company, the Southern Pacific. In recent years, Propositions have been addressed to a variety of policy questions in California, but most notably to property tax reduction in Proposition 13 in 1978. In 1988, voters in California were faced with twenty-nine initiatives on the State ballot paper, five of which concerned the insurance industry; groups

TABLE 3.1

Amendments to the Constitution Concerned with Electoral Rules

Amendment	Content
Twelfth	Requires that electors vote separately for President and Vice-President (in an attempt to avoid a repeat of the constitutional crisis which developed in the Presidential election of 1800)
Fifteenth	Forbids the denial of the right to vote on grounds of race
Seventeenth	Requires that Senators be popularly elected, having previously been selected by state legislatures
Nineteenth	Forbids denial of the right to vote on grounds of gender
Twenty-Second	Limits all Presidents after Truman to a maximum of two four-year terms of office
Twenty-Fourth	Prohibits the denial of the right to vote by reason of the failure to pay any poll tax or other tax
Twenty-Sixth	Reduces the voting age to eighteen

lobbying for and against them spent some $75 million. Additional initiatives were also put to voters in many of the State's counties. Their proliferation in California has done much to discredit such direct democratic devices: they add to the incoherence of the policy-making process, and may promote a politics of casual irresponsibility (fuelled by intensive special-interest lobbying and campaigns; see Chapter 7) rather than one of deliberation and the careful weighing of alternatives by legislators. For politicians, however, they have the attraction of enabling them to avoid taking decisions on contentious matters from which they can gain no advantage.

Election Campaigns and Finance

Those with ambitions for office must first raise money. Only then can they market themselves. Few candidates do either directly; most hire consultants to do both. Winning elections is costly, and becoming more so, whether the contest be for the Presidency, the House of Representatives or the Senate, a State Governorship, a State Assembly, or the Mayoralty of a city. Congressional elections have become particularly expensive: Federal Election Commission (FEC) data show that candidates in the 1996 House and Senate elections spent more than $766.4 million on their races. Poorly-financed candidates usually lose (especially if they are challengers): in most of the 435 House races, the victorious candidate outspent the loser by a ratio of 10:1. The services of campaign and media consultants, access to prime-time television advertising, opinion polls, advertising hoardings, computer time, and mass mailings demand considerable resources, especially for Senate races in large States, where commercials have to be purchased in several media markets. Candidates for the US House running in densely-populated cities such as Chicago, Los Angeles, or New York have a problem which, though different in kind, is also expensive: the television time they buy tends to be inefficiently spent because the media market is larger than the Congressional District they are contesting.

Driven by the need to raise large sums of money to deter challengers, or to defend oneself against them, and to raise yet larger ones to make credible challenges against incumbents or build a race for an open seat, the means by which candidates raise money has come under close scrutiny. This has been so both in the States (among which regulation of campaign financing has taken widely differing forms) and in campaigns for Federal office, both for the White House and for Capitol Hill. The mixing of politics with money, and the implied potential the resulting cocktail has for corruption at worst, and the improper exercise of influence at least, is a subject as old as American politics. It gained new currency in the 1996 Presidential and Congressional elections, both because of the continuing rapid growth in expenditure (exclusive of "soft" money, discussed below, candidates for Federal office in 1996 spent $2.28 billion in the two-year election cycle), and because of the manner in which much of it was raised. President Clinton's victorious re-election was marred by Vice-President Gore's admission that he had solicited campaign contributions from his office (a violation of the Federal law, which prohibits solicitation or receipt of campaign funds in Federal buildings); by the apparent receipt of funds from foreign sources (a violation of Federal law); by the crass holding of "coffee mornings" at which Clinton and Gore raised large hundreds of thousands of dollars; and by the President's inviting prominent Democratic donors to sleep in the Lincoln Bedroom of the White House.

The financing of Federal elections for both the Presidency and Congress is regulated, but to differing extents, in differing ways, and with different consequences. Since 1976, only one candidate for the Presidential nomination of a major party has elected not to receive public financial support in return for adhering to the complicated legal disclosure requirements. (In 1992, however, the independent candidate, Ross Perot, also elected not to receive public support.) The two parties' nominees have since 1976 run their subsequent general election campaigns from public funds, although, as explained below, so-called "soft" money has increased greatly in amount and importance since 1976; its impact has come to undermine the spirit, though not the letter, of the Federal Election Campaign Finance (FECA) laws of the 1970s. Members of Congress and Senators have not seen fit to apply to their own campaigns even the limitations they set for Presidential candidates, and the funding of Congressional campaigns is consequently relatively unrestricted: Congressional candidates are permitted to raise as much as they can, and to spend as much as they raise.

The general statutory framework within which political relations between the Presidency and the Congress has developed was deeply affected by the traumatic (and linked) national experiences of the Vietnam War and the abuse of executive power by President Nixon. These changes were important in several respects, including the financing of Presidential election campaigns. The Watergate scandal sprang in part from the corrupt mixing of money and politics – specifically, from the illegal activities of Richard Nixon's re-election campaign organization, the Committee to Reelect the President (CREEP), and the subsequent cover-up of those activities by the President and his most senior staff in the White House.

Among Nixon's numerous violations of the constitutional rights of United States citizens was his use of illegally acquired secret campaign funds to finance illegal domestic activity by the CIA. The establishment and operation of an investigative unit in the basement of the White House (the so-called "plumbers" unit on account of its role in plugging leaks from within government) was in itself an illegal act, but was in addition financed in part by an illegal and secret contribution of $2 million which the Milk Producers' Association gave to CREEP in return for President Nixon's backing for increases in milk price supports.

The House Judiciary Committee made reference to the campaign-financing practices of the President in the second Article of Impeachment against the President, which it prepared and approved in 1974. Watergate became synonymous with political corruption; Senator Sam Ervin's investigative Select Committee discovered "rivers of cash" running through Mr Nixon's campaign in 1972: the total amounted to more than $60 million, including sums ranging from $125,000 to $4.47 million from business corporations, many of which maintained secret funds. Over $1.7 million was raised for the campaign from people who were subsequently given ambassadorships. In the 48 hours before the 1971 Federal Election Campaign Act became law, the President's re-election Committees spent almost $5 million, much of it in respect of activities directed against Democratic candidates for the Presidency.

Watergate's exposure prompted thorough reform of Presidential campaign financing, recovering it from the murky reaches of secret contributions in return for Presidential favours to the light of public scrutiny through public financing and public disclosure. Amendments to the 1971 Federal Election Campaign Act (FECA) passed in 1974, 1976 and 1979 provide for the following:

1. Presidential candidates may opt to have their primary campaigns financed partly from the public purse established by a $3 voluntary checkoff on individual income tax returns (exercised by a mere 13 per cent of taxpayers), and their general election campaigns financed entirely from it. Primary candidates qualify for Federal "matching" funds, dollar for dollar, up to $250 per donor, if they can raise $100,000 in individual donations with at least $5,000 in each of twenty States. Most major candidates raise greater sums than the law permits to be matched: by

early January 1996, for example, Clinton had raised more than $20 million despite facing no significant primary opposition. In return for receiving public financial support in the general election (subject to a limit in 1996 of $61.8 million each for Clinton and Dole), the two major party candidates are not permitted to receive private donations. Each of the major parties is, however, permitted to expend limited co-ordinated sums on its nominee's behalf; for 1996, the FEC set the limit at $12.3 million.

2.   In the 1976 case *Buckley* v. *Valeo*, 424 US 1, the Supreme Court decided that the 1971 FECA's limitation on individuals spending their own money on their campaigns even where they were not in receipt of matching funds from the public purse was unconstitutional, since it was held to place "substantial and direct restrictions on the ability of candidates, citizens, and associations to engage in protected political expression, restrictions that the First Amendment cannot tolerate". Accordingly, the amount that candidates or their families may contribute to their own campaigns is the only unlimited source of campaign finance available. *Buckley* v. *Valeo* also struck down the limits on independent expenditures, the overall spending limits on Congressional campaigns, as well as the laws of thirty-one States which placed limitations of varying kinds on candidates' financing their own campaigns for state office.

A Presidential candidate who chooses to receive Federal matching funds may contribute only $50,000 of his personal resources. Having won 19 per cent of the popular vote as an independent candidate in the 1992 Presidential contest (while rejecting public funding and so being exempt from limitations upon his personal contribution to his campaign), Ross Perot elected in 1996 (as the nominee of the Reform Party) to accept public funding. Calculating his public funding entitlement on the basis of his performance in 1992, the FEC allocated him more than $29 million for his 1996 race. By accepting public funding, Perot was thereby subject not only to the limit on his personal contribution but also to the requirement that any further private receipts would have to come from individuals in donations of $1,000 or less.

3.   Contributions from individuals and committees in respect of all campaigns for Federal office are limited: no individual may make contributions of more than $1,000 to any one candidate in any one election (counting Primary, runoff, and general elections separately) nor of more than $20,000 in any one year to a political party. There is a further aggregate limit of $25,000 that any person may lawfully contribute to all Federal elections in any single year. PACs (the formation of which by corporations having business with the government was made illegal in 1940, but legalized in 1976) may not make contributions of more than $5,000 to any one candidate in a single

election; the law places no limit on the total aggregate amount that a PAC may donate. Direct contributions by labour, business, or any other corporate body, are prohibited.

4. Each party receives public financial support for its Presidential nominating Convention.

Parties, Issue Advocacy, and "Soft" Money

Parties' direct contributions to candidates' campaigns for election to the US House and Senate are limited by law: $5,000 per candidate in each election cycle for the House, and $17,500 per candidate in each cycle for the Senate. In addition to such direct support, each party's national and State committee has a specified amount of so-called "hard" money which it may spend on behalf of each US House and Senate candidate. A State party committee may either itself spend the same amount as the national committee, or transfer it to the national committee. Candidates' campaigns do not receive such "co-ordinated expenditures" direct: party committees may decide in conjunction with the candidates how the money is to be spent, but the law stipulates that the responsibility for such contributions lies with the parties. It is the parties that must disclose to the FEC how they are made.

The role of political parties has to this extent been enhanced by the 1979 amendments to the FECA which permit State and local party committees to spend unlimited sums on so-called "grass-roots" political support both for Congressional and Presidential candidates. Parties may also spend unlimited amounts on registration and voter-drive activities for Presidential candidates, and may similarly spend freely on party-building and mobilization work, provided that doing so does not involve them in advocating directly the election of particular candidates for Federal elections. In 1995 and 1996, the Democratic and Republican National Committees spent large sums promoting, respectively, the re-election of Mr Clinton and (once his nomination had been assured by the Spring of 1996) the election of Mr Dole. The parties carefully avoided breaching the law: while promoting the two candidates' electoral interests, advertisements did not explicitly urge viewers to "elect", "support", "vote for", or "defeat" one or the other candidate. Instead, advertisements offered support for, or opposition to, particular views of the two candidates. The Supreme Court blessed such issue advocacy advertising by its key decision in 1996, *Colorado Republican Party* v. *Federal Election Commission* (424 U.S. 261). The Court judged that political parties have the right to spend unlimited amounts in congressional elections provided that such funds are spent "independently", so raising the question of where the boundaries of that elastic notion might lie. The Court held that the First Amendment prevented the government from imposing any limits on what parties may spend of their own funds when such expenditures are not in fact discussed with a candidate or with his or her agents. The judgment was nearly more radical: four Justices made clear in minority opinions that they regarded any expenditure limits upon parties as being unconstitutional.

Most of the money raised to pay for such issue advocacy advertisements was "soft", much of it transferred to State parties that were subject to looser FEC rules than national committees: A. Corrado has shown that, in 1996, the Democratic National Committee transferred 56 per cent of its 'soft' money to State and local party committees, and the Republican National Committee 43 per cent (Corrado, 1997). The 1996 campaign showed that the loopholes in campaign finance law which permit the raising of "soft" money and its expenditure in this way are enormous: President Johnson's characterization of campaign finance laws in 1967 as "more loophole than law [which] invite evasion and circumvention" applies with similar force to the corrupting cancer of "soft" money in the late 1990s. The weakness of current federal election law on *contributions* is that, while direct contributions to candidates in federal elections from businesses, unions, and other interest groups are prohibited, direct donations to political parties are unrestricted. The Center for Responsive Politics calculates that the parties raised $263.5 million for the 1996 poll, triple the amount collected in 1992. The weakness of current federal election law on *expenditure* is that while certain types of spending might reasonably be regarded in law as being "independent", they are intended to have particular electoral effects in particular campaigns, and often do so. Both parties are skilled at putting "soft" money to highly creative use while remaining technically independent of individual candidates' campaigns.

In 1996, the President and Vice-President were drawn heavily into the raising of funds for the DNC from corporations and individuals. (It later emerged that among the large corporations and interest groups which responded to such solicitation of funds were foreign companies – a breach of Federal law.) Following access to the President, participation in White House meetings, invitations to White House coffee mornings, and even overnight stays in the Lincoln Bedroom of the White House, significant sums of money were collected. Federal law prohibits any exchange of "consideration, favor, or reward for any political activity or for the support of . . . any candidate or any political party in connection with any election". In the light of that bar, the coincidence of timing in the holding of White House coffee mornings and the subsequent receipt of donations to the DNC from some of those who attended is striking, as *The Washington Post* of 22 March 1997 reported:

> businesswoman Pauline Kanchanalak, an American resident who has interests in China, met with the president for coffee on June 18 last year. She brought along five associates for what press reports described as a meeting about "US policy toward China" Three Democratic National Committee officials also came along – then DNC chairman Donald

Fowler, DNC finance chair Marvin Rosen and John Huang, the DNC's assiduous fund-raiser. That same day, Kanchanalak contributed $85,000 to the DNC.

White House records show that donations arising from coffee mornings were planned to realise $400,000 each. Harold Ickes, a senior White House staff member, told the President and Vice-President in January 1996 that "We estimate that approximately $180 million will have to be raised during calendar 1996 during the ten-month period January through October". In the following month, he emphasized the implications of that revenue requirement: "The fundraising needs for the DNC will require a very substantial commitment of time from the President, the Vice President, the First Lady and Mrs Gore". While the need to raise funds therefore shaped the President's and Vice-President's timetables, the project succeeded: three coffee mornings in January 1996 raised $1.2 million, tidily meeting the planned yield. One DNC internal paper records the President as having undertaken seventeen fund-raising engagements in September alone.

The 1996 campaign for the Presidency was marked by the raising of money which, if not actually illegal, gave rise to questions of impropriety. Section 607 of the Federal criminal code makes it an offence for "any person to solicit or receive any contribution in any room or building occupied in the discharge of official duties" (such as the White House or Congress). Vice-President Gore has nevertheless acknowledged making telephone calls from his office (albeit using a DNC credit card), so raising the question of whether he violated Section 607 (for which there is a penalty of up to three years in prison). Together with other allegations about the means which the DNC and RNC used to raise funds in 1996, and many disreputable congressional fund-raising methods amounting to overt shakedown, the White House's involvement became the subject of Congressional investigations in 1997.

With large quantities of "soft" money fuelling the two parties' National Committees' issue advocacy, Presidential candidates in 1996 were free to spend much of the public funds given to them on direct campaigning costs: Clinton in particular was able to spend public funds with exceptional freedom on television advertising in the campaign's final month. Of the $232 million which Clinton and Dole spent on the primary and general elections, nearly half was spent on advertising. Without a primary opponent, Clinton enjoyed a considerable financial advantage over his challenger: he needed to spend much less on fund-raising, and so was able to devote more to advertising.

Political Action Committees

Political Action Committees (PACs) exist because the FECA permits them to be used by corporations to make donations to candidates for Federal office, something which corporations and labour unions are prohibited from doing direct. Corporations, labour unions, and other corporate bodies accordingly establish PACs, for which they solicit financial support. In 1974, 608 PACs were registered with the Federal Election Commission. The number almost doubled by 1976, and reached more than 4,000 by December 1995. Corporate PACs remain the largest category, with 1,674 committees, followed by non-connected (1,020); trade/membership/health (815); and labour (334).

The key provision in FECA was that permitting large unions and business corporations having contracts with the US government to form political funds. These funds, "connected" PACs, raise money from people employed by the corporation or from members of the labour union; they rarely solicit donations from the general public, although they are in law free to do so. "Unconnected", or "independent" PACs were entirely legal before the FECA amendments but have benefited from technological advances of the kind which enable sophisticated mass-mailings to be undertaken with the object of raising money from selected people and groups among the public. The Supreme Court's decision in *FEC* v. *NICPAC*, 466 US 935 (1985) established that no limits may be placed on spending by PACs on a candidate's behalf provided that the expenditure incurred was not made in collaboration with the candidate – provided, in other words, that the PAC's legal independence was maintained in the expenditure. Such "independent" funding usually takes the form of hostile and negative campaign advertising, of which the most notorious example was the $8.5 million spent by the National Security PAC to produce the "Willie Horton" television advertisements attacking Michael Dukakis in 1988. However, independent PAC expenditure is also prominent in Congressional races: in 1990, the National Association of Realtors' independent expenditure committee spent slightly more than $1 million on behalf of nine candidates. Although the Supreme Court has held that independent spending cannot be limited constitutionally, contributions to PACs can: they may not receive contributions of more than $5,000 from any one individual.

Although Presidential election campaigns receive public support under FECA's provisions, PACs contribute to the parties' support for the election expenditure of the candidates. Federal law limits to $15,000 the amount that any one PAC may lawfully contribute to a national party, but the amount that PACs may lawfully contribute to State and local parties is subject to restrictions in some States, but not in others. Exploratory, pre-Primary campaigns are generally financed from PACs formed by a candidate or by Foundations (which have the tax advantage that they may lawfully receive direct and tax-deductible donations). Such candidate and officeholder PACs are used to finance an undeclared candidate's political travel and related expenses.

Most PAC funding of Congressional candidates is directed towards two categories of politician in the two Houses: incumbents; and Committee chairpersons and party leaders. The alteration in financial flows from PACs following the change in party control of the House and Senate in the 1994 mid-term elections illustrates the point. FEC data show that for the Congressional elections of 1988, 1990, 1992, and 1994, incumbent Democratic Senators enjoyed an advantage in PAC funding over their Republican challengers of nearly five to one. In 1996, incumbent Republican Senators' advantage over Democratic challengers was more than five to one. Although a few Members of Congress make a point of accepting no PAC money, others are heavily dependent upon it: nine House members (eight of whom were Democrats) drew four-fifths or more of their total campaign receipts from PACs in the 1989–90 election cycle. PAC money therefore increases the non-competitive character of House, and to a lesser extent, Senate, elections; the rule that permits candidates to retain PAC and other contributions which candidates receive and find surplus to their requirements for future election expenditure accentuates it further. The result is that well before the beginning of the next election year, many incumbent Congressmen and Senators have large financial resources with which to deter possible Primary or general election rivals. *Congressional Quarterly* reported in February 1997 that the thirty Senators elected in 1992 and standing for re-election in 1998 had already raised an average of $1.4 million (Congressional Quarterly Weekly Report, 22 February 1997). A Senator anticipating re-election costs of $5 million (much less than some Senators in fact raise and spend) therefore has to raise more than $2,000 every day of his or her six-year term. Senators' need for cash accordingly structures their political calculations. The effect is much the same for Congressmen who, running for office biennially, are also constantly engaged in a search for cash sums. While running for the House costs less than running for the Senate, many incumbents raise and spend more than $1 million.

The consequences of PAC funding are difficult to determine. Some newspapers, of which *The Washington Post* is the leading example, have campaigned for years in favour of a radical reform of the financing of elections, and against what they take to be the corrupting influence of special interest money. It might be thought implausible to claim that the expenditure of large sums of money in support of election campaigns by PAC fund directors does not affect the votes of those financed. Yet there is no compelling evidence either that PAC money determines the outcomes of election campaigns, or that the receipt of PAC money shapes the voting behaviour of Members of Congress. The limitations placed upon PAC donations to individual candidates themselves restrict the extent to which candidates may feel themselves under an obligation. Yet Barney Frank, a US Congressman from Massachusetts, once observed that "Elected officials are the only human beings in the world who are supposed to take large sums of money on a regular basis from absolute strangers without it having any effect on their behavior". As anthropologists have long understood, no gifts are pure.

The problems presented by the attempts of interest groups to influence election outcomes are not new (see Chapter 7). Under current law and FEC regulations, PACs' involvement is at least publicly disclosed and discussed. That marks a welcome improvement on the hidden slush funds of earlier years: the Federal Election Commission keeps and scrutinises full records of the financing of Congressional and Presidential elections, and the records are freely available for public and media inspection. Yet anxieties remain. The activities of PACs and the rising cost of campaigning prompt troubling questions about the hidden influence that concentrated private interests exercise over legislators. They also expand the already swollen advantages of incumbency. Interest groups' legal circumvention of the limits on individual contributions to PACs by collecting them and distributing them to candidates in so-called "bundling" operations with the intention of increasing their impact intensifies alarm about PACs' influence, and reduces the worth of limits on PAC donations to individual candidates.

In Presidential elections, "soft" money has weakened the defences against corruption established by the FECA and its amendments during the 1970s. Their public declarations of support for reform notwithstanding, there is little will among President Clinton, Congressmen, or Senators to reform a system which sustains most of them in public office so reliably. The most coherent and responsible reform measure yet proposed, the McCain–Feingold–Thompson Bill, fell six votes short of the 60 needed in 1996. Its three key provisions provide the core around which reform efforts can honourably continue, but with little prospect of short-term success:

1. Voluntary expenditure limits for primary and general elections with the ceiling a function of the size of a state's voting age population. In return for accepting these limits, candidates would have received half an hour of free television time, discounted rates from broadcasters for additional advertising time and reduced postage costs.
2. Direct contributions from PACs would have been prohibited.
3. Political parties' freedom to use "soft" money would have been restricted substantially.

Primary Election Campaigns

Since the early part of the twentieth century, the selection of party candidates for many elective public offices in the United States has lain with voters, and not with party bosses. As Chapter 2 demonstrated, there were exceptions to this rule–notably in many large cities, where the bosses of political machines determined who ran under the party label, and later distributed the fruits of victory through patronage. It is none the less now a nearly universal principle that the selection of candidates to run under a party label lies with those voters who identify with a party rather than with those within a party's (usually weak) organization.

States differ in the severity of the requirements they make of voters intending to participate in Primary elections. Approximately 80 per cent of the States demand some form of public statement of affiliation before permitting a voter to participate in a party's Primary; in most of these States, the declaration has to be made between two weeks and a year in advance of the election. Primaries can therefore be more or less "open" to all who wish to participate, or effectively "closed" to all except those who identify with the party over a substantial period of time.

State laws also differ in their rules regarding State parties' endorsement of candidates in primaries. California prohibits such endorsement; Connecticut and Massachusetts permit it. Whatever the variations among the States, the Primary device tends to weaken a party by denying it control over candidates' nomination. Moreover, by effectively permitting anyone identifying with a political party to seek its nomination for public office, Primaries and caucuses double the vulnerability of politicians to defeat, and hence their sensitivity to the politics of faction within a party.

In its most extreme form, it has in recent years resulted in parasitism – unwelcome attachment to the party by foreign and bizarre factions. The most striking example is that of Lyndon Larouche, who ran for the Democratic nomination for President in 1988 on a remarkable platform which included compulsory quarantining for AIDS victims and the identification of Queen Elizabeth II as the head of an international drug smuggling conspiracy. Two of Larouche's followers in fact won the Democratic nominations for Secretary of State and Lieutenant Governor in Illinois in March 1986.

Odd cases apart, the Primary system none the less provides a means whereby factions within a party struggle for the nomination by appealing to different groups of voters. Primary voters may be (and often are) radically different from general election voters. Winning a party's nomination through appealing to activists whom a candidate's campaign workers mobilize with energy and skill may constitute a considerable achievement. However, if the factional base on which victory within the party is built is narrow, it may prove difficult to unite the party around a candidacy in the general election, and impossible to expand the coalition to include independent voters and those who normally identify with the opposing party. Under the old order prevailing before the McGovern–Fraser report (see p. 76), Democratic Party elites could (and did) take these factors into account for Presidential elections: the object in selecting a nominee was to select one who maximised the party's prospects of victory in the general election. Primaries at all levels have in general removed (or at the very least, greatly weakened) the capacity of party leaders to exercise this degree of influence. The extension of Primaries, which bind delegates to a candidate to the Presidential contest, has increased the clement of randomness in the candidate selection process.

Both American political parties have as their supreme purpose the quadrennial selection of a candidate who will win the Presidency, though the Democratic Party conspicuously failed in this regard for twenty years following the reforms of the late 1960s. The increase in randomness through the delegation of the nomination to Primary and caucus electorates had graver consequences for the Democrats than for the Republicans, because the greater width of their coalitional base makes it more liable to fragment following the selection of a divisive candidate. Primaries were adopted by most States for the Presidential nominating process because it was calculated (correctly) that to do so would enable them to conform safely with the requirements of the national party, which gradually assumed jurisdiction over State party selection rules. These now fall into four types:

- Much the commonest (especially in the Democratic Party) is the *proportional representation preference Primary*, in which delegates are distributed between the candidates according to the vote received.
- The *advisory presidential preference Primary*, in which votes are recorded for both Presidential candidates and delegates to the Convention, who may be denoted as supporting a particular candidate or none.
- The binding *"winner takes all" Primary*, in which two types of delegate are elected: those from the State's congressional districts, and those from the State as a whole. Delegates are obliged to vote for the winners of the races in each Congressional district and that in the State as a whole.
- The *delegate selection Primary*, in which only the names of the delegates appear on the ballot, with or without the name of the Presidential candidates whom they prefer.

Promoted as an exercise in broadening participation in the selection of the Democratic Party's candidate for the Presidency, Primaries and caucuses are a minority sport. Rates of participation in Democratic and Republican Primaries are much smaller even than in the general election: only 14.1 million voters took part in the 1996 Republican Primaries. Even in southern states where Republican allegiance has grown so greatly since the 1960s, participation in the 1996 Republican primary elections was low: 280,000 voters turned out in South Carolina, and 550,000 in Georgia. In New England, where Republican strength has weakened during the same period, only 275,000 voters participated in the party's Connecticut Primary.

The first Primary of the Presidential election season always takes place in New Hampshire, a small state almost as unrepresentative of the country as it is of the Democratic Party. Low participation exaggerates its unrepresentative character, especially for Democratic candidates: of the 4,282 delegates present at the Democratic Convention in New York City in 1992, 286 were elected from New York, and 382 from California, but only 18 from New Hampshire.

Caucuses are even less representative than Primaries, and are ideally suited to candidates with unrepresentative but ardent followings, as the etymology of "caucus" might be thought to indicate: it derives from an Indian word meaning "to gather together and make a great noise". In 1988, Jesse Jackson (the most politically liberal of the Democratic candidates) ran most strongly in those States such as Iowa (which select all of their delegates through caucuses) and those such as Texas (which select some of them in this way). Pat Robertson (much the most culturally conservative of the Republican candidates) also did markedly better in caucuses than in Primaries. By contrast, George Bush, from the centre of the Republican Party, lost seven of the ten caucuses but only one of the forty-one Primaries in which he was a candidate.

For candidates in both parties, the object in each Primary or caucus is to win as many delegates as possible, so that victory is inevitable at the respective Party Conventions. Unlike the Electoral College in the general election, where the winner of a state takes all of that State's Electoral College votes, a proportional rule applies in most Primaries: delegates to the Democratic Convention in 1992 from each state were divided in rough proportion between the candidates for the nomination, a rule that has often had important consequences. Thus, once Clinton was ahead in the 1992 Democratic Primary races, he could (and did) keep adding to his delegate total whether or not he was the plurality winner in individual Primary races or not.

The Democratic Party's nomination rules in 1996 continued to provide for the representation of senior party officials in addition to the delegates selected by Primary and caucus voters. (In the wake of the implementation of the McGovern–Fraser Commission reforms in 1972, the number of such delegates had fallen to just fifty in 1980.) In 1984, the number of super-delegates was sharply increased to give senior party officials a louder voice: in 1996, 768 superdelegates (US Senators; US Congressmen; Chairs of State parties; and State Governors) attended the Chicago Convention, some 20 per cent of the total number of delegates.

In 1996, the absence of serious opposition to Clinton's renomination had given him walkover victories in Primaries and caucuses, and an effective monopoly of delegates at the Convention. In years when the nomination is contested, however, superdelegates may have a role to play. In the 1988 campaign, for example, Governor Michael Dukakis had to secure 50 per cent + 1 of the 4,160 Democratic delegates attending the party's Convention in Atlanta. In the Democratic nomination process, Dukakis won too few delegates in Primaries and caucuses to gain the nomination, but had a sufficiently large plurality to ensure that superdelegates switched their support to him. The system was intended to benefit the candidate likely to be closest to the median voter in the general election. So, in this case, it did, by working to the advantage of Dukakis and against that of his main challenger, Jesse Jackson. Unfortunately for Governor Dukakis, he was in the general election only second-closest to the median voter: Vice-President Bush defeated him.

The displacement of party elites by Primary electorates has greatly enhanced the importance of television to the outcome of the elections. Early Primaries and caucuses receive the heaviest coverage; later ones receive less, irrespective of the number of delegates at stake, or of the representativeness of the State. Early momentum is essential for later success, and may be acquired with the assistance of journalists' interpretations of Primary election results. These are invariably influential because of the prominence accorded them, and contentious because they often rest on erroneous expectations of how the candidates would run against each other. For example, it was alleged that Jimmy Carter's elevation by weekly magazines and television alike as front-runner for the Democratic nomination after the 1976 Iowa caucuses owed much to Johnny Apple's interpretation of the result in the *New York Times* – despite his having secured only 29 per cent of the vote, and delegates uncommitted to any candidate having won 39 per cent.

Party Conventions

Prior to the McGovern–Fraser reforms, accepted by the Democratic National Committee in 1971, and introduced for the 1972 Presidential elections, the nominees of the two major parties for the office of President were chosen at the nominating Conventions. The highly divisive Democratic Convention of 1968 saw Hubert Humphrey nominated without his having run in a single Primary, a point which factional opponents exploited to secure Humphrey's agreement to the formation of the McGovern–Fraser Commission, whose recommendations have had the effect of virtually nationalizing Democratic Party nominating rules, ceding the task of nomination to Primary and caucus electorates, and rendering the Convention a political shell. Having lost their central function, the two parties' Conventions now ratify decisions taken previously, although, in the unlikely event that no candidate secured the majority required, the nomination would revert to the Convention. There is no prospect of the Convention regaining its former institutional role.

Enticed by drama, television and press journalists nevertheless continue to cover Conventions in depth, often contriving substance from theatrical froth. Convention halls now provide little space for delegates (who have no remaining substantive function save that of being seen to enthuse) but much for television, whose demands dominate. While the occasion (funded by Federal taxpayers and corporate sponsors) is more memorable for pageantry than political substance, the Convention retains three purposes:

- That of *unifying the party* and of *presenting the nominee as a potential President*. Prior to the Convention, the focus has been upon the struggle within the parties; at the Convention, the new theme is upon the party as a united force. A divided party Convention risks damaging the candidate, as the Democratic Convention damaged Hubert Humphrey in 1968, and the Republican Convention harmed George Bush in 1992.
- That of *balancing the ticket* by the selection of a *running-mate as Vice-President*. The balance generally takes geographical and ideological forms. Thus, in choosing Hubert Humphrey in 1964, Lyndon Johnson selected a northern liberal to balance his own image (though not his moderately liberal record) as a centrist southerner; in choosing Governor Spiro Agnew of Maryland four years later in 1968, Richard Nixon selected a conservative from the east coast to counterbalance his own moderate Californian Republicanism. Walter Mondale sought gender balance by his selection of Geraldine Ferraro in 1984. Racial balance has not yet been achieved, but Bob Dole tried hard to persuade General Colin Powell to join the ticket in 1996. Only exceptionally has a modern candidate sought to reinforce the ticket he leads by selecting a candidate in his own ideological image and from his own part of the country, as Governor Clinton did by selecting Senator Gore in 1992.
- That of presenting the *party's platform*. This is usually carefully constructed in order to placate influential dissidents. In 1988, for example, Jesse Jackson succeeded in extracting some platform concessions from Governor Dukakis; the exercise is none the less usually for purposes of presentation only. Unlike a party manifesto in Britain, where the only significant internal political constraint upon the implementation of its provisions lies in the bureaucracy, and where the executive can usually corral majorities for its policies in the legislature without difficulty, American Presidents have no reliable institutional means of converting party aspiration into policy. Party platforms, whilst given extensive coverage in the major newspapers, are more important for the healing of internal party injuries than they are as statements of policy intent.

General Elections

Conventions concluded, running-mates nominated by the candidate, visions of unity extended beyond the party faithful to the undecided electorate, the campaign for the Presidency and other Federal offices slips into a short summer remission until Labor Day on the first Monday in September. That is traditionally the last day of the lull and heralds the onset of the frenetic two months until election day, which is always held on the first Tuesday after the first Monday in November.

In election years, the Presidential election dominates national news, but State and local media markets reflect the importance of State and local electoral politics too. Even at the level of the Presidency, the general election is really fifty-one separate elections rather than a national election. The object is to win a clear majority in the Electoral College; the means to achieving this end is to win a plurality in enough states to secure it, as is explained in greater detail below in the discussion of the Electoral College.

In California, and in most other States, votes are counted by machine. The Californian practice is for voters to indicate their preference by punching a card, the votes later being counted by machine. The design of the machine can either facilitate "party-line" voting, where voters, by pulling a lever, may vote "down-the-line" for all of a party's candidates for all offices, or make it easier to "split the ticket" (which, before the introduction of the Australian ballot, meant that party tickets were literally torn by voters) and vote separately for each office. Provision is also made for "write-in" votes, by which candidates whose names do not appear on the official ballot paper may none the less receive support.

The US Constitution did not make the Presidency subject to popular election. Article 2, Section I, modified by the Twelfth Amendment, provides for each State to choose (by whatever means each State determines) a number of electors equivalent in number to its total Congressional delegation (see Appendixes 1 and 2). It is the electors' task to elect the President. Since each State has two Senators irrespective of size or population, and has a number of Representatives ranging from one to fifty-two (in California), the variation in voting strength in the Electoral College is between three and fifty-four. (Since the ratification of the Twenty-Third Amendment in 1961, the District of Columbia has for the purposes of Presidential elections only been treated as if it were a State, and so has as many electors as it would have if it were a State.) The electors meet in the month after the popular vote, effectively ratifying it; and the person elected takes office on 20 January of the following year, taking the oath of office at the prompting of the Chief Justice and in the presence of the outgoing President, senior members of the old and new Administrations, and members of both Houses of Congress.

Each State votes in the Electoral College as a unit, and the plurality winner (who, because of the usual absence of third-party candidates is normally also the majority winner) takes all the State's Electoral College Votes. Unlike in Presidential Primaries, the Presidential election itself does not operate according to proportional or near-proportional voting rules. The winner of the popular vote for the Presidency in a State takes all of that State's votes (except in Maine, where the state legislature has provided that two of the state's four Electoral College votes should be determined by Congressional district). States with tiny populations are accordingly over-represented in the Electoral College, although this does not induce candidates to spend much time campaigning in them. Most campaigning is undertaken in the eight largest States (California, Florida, Illinois, Michigan, Ohio, Pennsylvania, New York, and Texas) which together account for 218 Electoral College votes from predominantly urban and suburban States. This in turn comprises the bulk of the total required to win: since the total number of votes in the College is 538 (435 votes equivalent to the total number of Representatives; 100 Senators, and the three votes of the District of Columbia) a candidate requires 50 per cent + 1 of 538 to win the Presidency – 270 Electoral College votes.

It is the Electoral College vote, not the popular vote, that matters. The latter is technically merely a vote to choose electors, all other means of selecting them having been dispensed with in the nineteenth century. In fact, the popular vote has importance because it has become structured by party – a development not anticipated at Philadelphia in 1787. The distribution of the popular vote determines the composition of the Electoral College.

Electors now have autonomy but do not (dare not) exercise it; instead, they act not as independent representatives but merely as agents of the voters' will. The possibility that a candidate might win the popular vote and lose in the Electoral College none the less remains. It is easy to see how it might arise. For example, let us suppose that the Republican Party's candidate for the Presidency were to accumulate large pluralities in several states, so that when the popular vote was aggregated across the country her or his vote total was greater than her or his opponent's. Let us further suppose that the Democratic Party's nominee for the Presidency accumulated a majority of Electoral College votes despite recording only slim majorities (or, where there was a third-party candidate, pluralities) in the states where she or he was victorious. The application of the unit rule rather than proportional representation would under these circumstances have had the effect of turning small State-wide majorities into a majority in the Electoral College.

The risk of such an occurrence has kindled anxiety on the grounds of its perceived unfairness and its damaging consequences for the legitimacy of the person securing a majority in the Electoral College having been denied one in the popular vote. In 1876 and in 1888, the winner of the popular vote lost in the College (although voter fraud on the first of these occasions was, in any case, extensive). Such an outcome has nearly resulted in the more recent past: in 1976, a shift of a mere 9,000 votes in the states of Ohio and Hawaii would have given President Ford an Electoral College victory, though he secured more than 1.5 million fewer votes than Jimmy Carter in the popular vote. Similar marginal shifts in the 1960 race would have brought Richard Nixon to the White House eight years before he finally managed it in 1968. Even then, Nixon came close to failing to secure a majority in the Electoral College because George Wallace's third-party appeal was heavily concentrated in the south, giving him forty-six votes and nearly causing the election to be decided in the House of Representatives.

No election has been thrown into the House under this rule in the twentieth century (largely because the stability of the two-party system has come under serious attack only twice – in 1912 with Theodore Roosevelt's defection as a Progressive, and again in 1968). If it were to happen, the voting strength of the large States would be dramatically reduced and that of the small States enhanced: each State has one vote, which it may cast for any one of the first three candidates in the Electoral College's ballot. An absolute majority is required for election. Such a procedure might produce a bizarre result, so undermining the winner's legitimacy and thereby intensifying pressure for modifying the Electoral College's rules or even abolishing the College altogether. Widespread though dissatisfaction has been with the potential for difficulty, embarrassment, and chaos, no alterations have been made to the rules since the passage of the Twelfth Amendment in 1804.

The Media

Television and the press dominate the setting of American elections (see Exhibit 3.1). The building of coalitions among influential politicians remains the key to Presidential leadership in government, but in campaigning has largely been replaced by the creation of powerful images. This process has been assisted materially by the controlling importance of television in election campaigns at all levels, but especially for the Presidency. Successful campaign consultants establish positive images of their client, and negative ones of their opponent. In this comparatively fluid, entrepreneurial, environment for the selection of each party's candidate for President, editors and journalists select the items, questions, and issues they believe worthy of viewers' attention. Newspapers continue to compete in the setting of the campaign agenda, but the stories which they initiate gain national prominence only through their subsequently being replayed on television. Television's interpretations of Primary election results, or of candidates' behaviour on the campaign trail, can enhance or undermine candidates' prospects in the next Primary election.

Intimately aware of television's centrality to electoral politics, candidates calculate their every word and action in the light of it. The scheduling of campaigns is determined in large part by the judgments which a candidate's campaign managers make of the utility of particular engagements for presentation on television. The writing of candidates' speeches by the campaign's speechwriters is shaped by the search for 30-second "sound bites" – snippets containing a pithy phrase likely to be identified and used in television news programmes which are now national programmes. If a candidate's stand on an issue cannot be condensed into a suitably compelling phrase, it is unlikely to be reported. Editors, as well as candidates and their managers, know that discussions of welfare reform or of the relationship between the fiscal and external deficits make bad television. Photo oppor-

---

EXHIBIT 3.1

Television and US Elections: the Medium and the Message

Television has exaggerated features of American electioneering that were already apparent: the presentation of politics as a horse race in which the result is all that matters, and the associated concentration upon personality. The triumph of symbol over substance is exaggerated by television, but was not invented by it. There is none the less a technological imperative at work: the medium accommodates complexity and nuance only with difficulty. Thirty- or sixty-minute analytical programmes offer programme-makers the opportunity to explore the complexities and contingencies which 30-second news coverage inescapably prevents, but they are of importance only to a small section of the viewing public. The mass of television viewers base their understanding of electoral politics in America on the three network channels and Cable News Network (CNN). All offer brief snippets of coverage on their thirty-minute news programmes, and thereby confirm rather than mitigate the logic of the technology, which is to concentrate upon questions of personality rather than policy, upon symbol rather than substance, and upon images created rather than essence revealed.

Washington types [handwritten marginalia]

tunities are sought by editors and provided by campaign managers. The focus of television news is firstly upon image, secondly upon phrase, and only incidentally upon substance. Television news coverage trivialises politics at all times, but does so especially during election campaigns.

All recent Presidential elections are replete with examples of these techniques and their dispiriting implications, but they have increasingly been adopted by campaign managers for other public offices. Indeed, below the level of the Presidency, "attack" and "comparative" advertisements (which draw deliberately misleading comparisons between the candidates) are common. In the 1988 Gubernatorial race in North Carolina, the Democratic candidate, Robert B. Jordan, ran an attack commercial disparaging Governor Martin's formulating of the 1988 state budget by using a team of chimpanzees writing on flip charts, and playing with calculators. As the announcer accused the Governor of "monkeying with the budget", a chimpanzee somersaulted on a desk while another performed on roller skates in front of the cameras. In the 1990 Democratic Gubernatorial Primary election in Texas, Mark White (a former Governor) paraded before enlarged photographs of convicted murderers whose death sentences he had refused to commute, comparing his enthusiasm for electrocution with what he characterised as his opponents' lack of zeal.

The popularity of negative advertising springs from the evidence that positive advertising has less effect upon voters, that negative advertisements arouse and maintain the interest of voters more easily than positive ones, and that negative attacks place opponents disadvantageously on the defensive.

Get book on media [handwritten marginalia]

Bush's negative advertising campaign against Dukakis in 1988 serves as a successful illustration of all three. As in the campaigns of 1968, 1972, 1980, and 1984, the symbolically important themes of law and order, and patriotism, were successfully exploited by Mr Bush in 1988 in advertisements charging that the Democratic candidate had departed from mainstream American public opinion.

For Whom Do Americans Vote?

Party and Voting

Part of the argument of Chapter 2 was that, although party in America is distinctive, and in certain respects weak, party matters. It certainly matters in voting, where it simplifies decision-making for the electorate.

Tickets are, as discussed below, now frequently split by voters between candidates of different parties; party none the less continues to act as a Primary voting cue. The party label enables voters to choose without having extensive or detailed comparative information on the candidates whose names appear on the long ballot. Most voters choose how to vote according to their party allegiances, and their voting patterns tend (in the absence of a convulsive realignment of social groups and parties caused by the appearance of a new issue disrupting established alignments and breaking stable coalitions) to be stable over the short-to-medium term. Many of the scholarly debates about electoral behaviour have as their focus the changing relationship between parties and the electorate. The structuring of electoral choice by party remains enormously important in American politics despite the shift towards an entrepreneurial polities in which candidates depend upon themselves and their campaign consultants rather than upon the party for finance and the building of bases of support. The importance of the attachments of voters to parties is plain. These attachments have regional, class, ethnic, educational, gender, age, and racial bases, as Table 3.2 shows.

Economic depression fathered the large New Deal coalition. In the early form it took in the 1932 and 1936 Presidential elections, the coalition comprised an alliance between voters in the north and the south, workers in industry, and those in agriculture. With the exception of the South, it also comprised the unusual alignment for the United States of party with class: the Democrats represented those without capital or resources, those with only their labour to sell, and those millions of unemployed having no one to whom they might sell it. In more detail, the coalition consisted of the industrial working class, the poor, liberal intellectuals, most Catholics, Irish-Americans, Italian-Americans, and later, southern and eastern European immigrants (all of whom Democratic Parties in industrial cities accommodated and absorbed), Jews, northern blacks, voters in the (mostly rural) South, the industrial east and mid-west, and the Pacific west. The coalition was united around the common interest its constituent groups shared in extensive Federal macroeconomic intervention in the economy, the creation of social welfare programmes, the regulation of labour markets, and the direct creation of work, to counter the spectacular failures and social injustices of the free enterprise system which President Hoover and the Republican Party represented and defended.

At the Presidential level, the New Deal coalition remained intact until 1948. It was weakened as a result of the civil rights challenge that threatened to split its northern and southern wings, fell under the weight of Dwight Eisenhower's wide personal appeal, which in turn derived from the confidence he inspired in the electorate, and was (with the exception of much of the south and west) reassembled by John Kennedy and spectacularly (though briefly) expanded by Lyndon Johnson in 1964. It collapsed as the Democratic Party was torn asunder by Vietnam, the crisis of the cities, law and order, civil rights, and women's rights in 1968 and 1972. With the qualified exception of 1976, it was not re-assembled in Presidential elections until 1992, and then in a form much less dependent on white southern support.

Individual candidates have made, and continue to make, a difference to their party's fortunes: Eisenhower would have defeated any candidate whichever party's nomination he decided to seek (or take) in 1952. Ronald Reagan's personal electoral appeal in 1984 would have overwhelmed any Democratic candidate; George McGovern's perceived extremism would have made the task of almost any Republican opponent simple (which makes the decision to burgle the Democratic National Committee Headquarters all the more foolish). None the less, it is not accidental that Democratic candidates should have won seven of the nine Presidential elections between 1932 and 1964, or that Republican nominees should have won five of the seven since that date. Party allegiances shape outcomes. Beginning in the 1960s, the outcomes began to alter. Party allegiances have altered, too.

The first and decisively important conceptualisation of "realignment" was provided by Key (1955) who argued in a major article that some Presidential elections (those he dubbed "critical") resulted in a change in the composition of the coalitions supporting the two parties, and a transfer in governmental power between them. Critical elections were not the only means by which coalition composition and governmental change might be brought about; change often came about more slowly through a "secular realignment".

Key's successors have used the concept of realignment extensively. Among these scholars, none has exploited and developed it to better effect than Burnham (1970), who identified six factors which set critical realignments apart from temporary realignments arising from "deviating" elections (such as Eisenhower's second victory over Governor Adlai Stevenson in 1956). In

TABLE 3.2

Presidential Vote by Social Groups, percentages

Percentage of total			1992			1996		
			Clinton	Bush	Perot	Clinton	Dole	Perot
1992 All	*1996 All*							
100	100		43	38	19	49	41	9
		Party						
35	39	Republicans	11	72	18	13	80	6
38	35	Democrats	77	10	13	84	10	5
27	26	Independent	38	32	30	43	36	18
		Ideology						
21	20	Liberals	68	14	18	78	11	7
49	47	Moderates	47	31	21	57	33	9
30	33	Conservatives	18	64	18	20	71	8
		Gender						
47	48	Men	41	38	21	43	44	10
53	52	Women	45	37	17	54	38	7
		Age						
21	17	18–29	43	34	22	53	34	10
36	33	30–44	41	38	21	48	41	9
23	26	45–59	41	40	19	48	41	9
20	24	60+	50	38	12	48	44	7
		Education						
6	7	Non-high school graduate	54	28	18	59	28	11
25	24	High school graduate	43	36	21	51	35	13
29	27	Some college education	41	37	21	48	40	10
23	26	College graduate	39	41	29	44	46	8
16	17	Postgraduate	50	36	14	52	40	5
		Family income						
14	11	< $15,000	58	23	19	59	28	11
24	23	$15,000–29,999	45	35	20	53	36	9
30	27	$30,000–49,999	41	38	21	48	40	10
20	21	$50,000–74,999	40	41	18	47	45	7
12	18	> $75,000	36	48	16	41	51	7
		Race						
87	83	White	39	40	20	43	46	9
8	10	Black	83	10	7	84	12	4
2	5	Hispanic	61	25	14	72	21	6

Table 3.2 continued opposite

Table 3.2 continued

| Percentage of total | | | 1992 | | | 1996 | | |
			Clinton	Bush	Perot	Clinton	Dole	Perot
1992 All	*1996 All*	**Religion**						
56	52	Protestant and other Christian	37	43	20	42	44	9
27	29	Catholic	44	35	20	53	37	9
4	3	Jewish	80	11	9	78	16	3
		Family financial situation compared with 4 years previously						
24	33	Better	24	61	15	66	26	6
34	20	Worse	61	14	25	27	57	13
41	45	About the same	41	42	17	46	45	8
		Unionization						
19	23	Union households	55	24	21	59	30	9
81	77	Non-union households	41	40	19	46	45	8
1992 votes		Clinton (44)	85	9	4			
		Bush (34)	13	82	4			
		Perot (12)	22	44	32			

Burnham's formulation, critical realignments are marked by the following features:

- A short-lived but intense *disruption* of traditional patterns of voting behaviour.
- Abnormally high *political intensity*, which manifests itself in the nominating process and disputes over the drafting of the party platform.
- A considerable increase in *ideological polarisation*, at first within one or more of the major parties and then between them, occasioned by external stresses in the socioeconomic system.
- Higher than normal *voter participation*.
- The recurrence of *realigning elections* at intervals of approximately thirty-six years.
- Realigning elections often being preceded by *third-party revolts*.

The University of Michigan's Survey Research Center's time-series data show that voters' attitudes towards both parties have shifted. Between 1968 and the mid-1990s, the proportion of voters expressing strong identification with the Republican Party grew from 10 per cent to 16 per cent, and the

EXHIBIT 3.2

The changing political geography of the United States: how the states voted in Presidential elections, 1932–96

Presidential Election 1932

	Popular vote	Electoral College vote
☐ Governor Franklin Roosevelt (Democrat)	22,825,016	472
▦ President Herbert Hoover (Republican)	15,758,397	59

Presidential Election 1968

	Popular vote	Electoral College vote
☐ Vice-President Hubert Humphrey (Democrat)	31,270,533	191
▨ Richard Nixon (Republican)	31,770,237	301
▓ Governor George Wallace (Independent)	9,906,1441	15

Presidential Election 1980

	Popular vote	Electoral College vote
☐ President Jimmy Carter (Democrat)	35,483,820	49
▓ Governor Ronald Reagan	43,901,812	489
John Anderson (Independent)	5,719,722	0

Presidential Election 1996

	Popular vote	Electoral College vote
☐ President Bill Clinton (Democrat)	47,401,054	379
▓ President George Bush (Republican)	39,197,100	159
Ross Perot (Independent)	8,088,100	0

proportion of Republican-leaning independents from 9 per cent to 12 per cent. Strong and weak Democratic identifiers have fallen from 20 per cent to 15 per cent and 25 per cent to 19 per cent respectively. Other data show that in the mid-1990s, more voters held neutral views of both parties than held either positive or negative views, representing a significant shift over two decades. The data suggest that the link between candidates for the Presidency and the party label on which they run, firm in the 1950s, has weakened.

Parties none the less still shape the voting behaviour of most individuals, and the attachment of individuals to a party remains strikingly stable over the short term. Most changes in identification are between some form of independent allegiance (whether leaning to the Democratic Party, leaning to the Republican Party, or neutral between the two) and a weak identification with one or the other of the two parties. Only a third of those who identify themselves as "independents" lean to neither party and express no preference between them. The concept of "independent" has therefore to be applied with care. Pure independents (only 10 per cent of the total electorate in 1994) have a lower rate of voting than those with weak or strong partisan attachments. Presidential elections therefore tend to be decided not by those with a stable and unambiguous party identification, since they change their partisan allegiances only at times of massive and sudden realignment, such as 1896 and 1932. They are decided by those with weak partisan attachments and those independents who lean towards one of the two parties, and who are persuaded to alter their weak attachments or to confirm their leaning according to their view of the policy preferences of the two candidates, or the retrospective judgements they make about the preceding four years. There is none the less evidence to suggest that the core groups at the heart of the Democratic coalition are less loyal to Democratic Presidential candidates than core Republican identifiers are to Republican Presidential candidates.

Of all groups, only blacks remain firmly wedded to the Democratic Party: 86 per cent of those blacks who voted in 1988 supported Dukakis, and (in a three-way race) 84 per cent supported Clinton in 1996. Republican candidates at Presidential or Congressional elections attract few black votes, continuing a pattern begun with Roosevelt's New Deal coalition and confirmed in the early to mid-1960s. John Kennedy, the Democratic President in 1961–63, having associated himself cautiously in the 1960 Presidential election with the civil rights cause, later as President sponsored Executive Orders advancing the cause materially. His successor, Lyndon Johnson, sent four major Civil Rights Bills to Congress, and successfully lobbied to ensure the passage of three of them (see Chapter 2). Johnson thereby completed the attachment of blacks to the Democratic Party, at the price of losing the white South. Economically successful blacks are scarcely more inclined to vote Republican than are poor ones.

Hispanics vote less solidly for the Democratic Party than do blacks. Not only do their circumstances and history differ from those of blacks, but there are many cleavages among them: many Cubans in Florida and Puerto Ricans in New York are immigrants, but many Hispanics in Texas and California are not. (In the south and south-west, many are illegal immigrants, and hence ineligible to vote.) The Republican Party has made considerable efforts to attract Hispanics, and has had some success in doing so, especially in Florida. There, with folk memories of President Kennedy's failed expedition against Castro at the Bay of Pigs in 1961 regularly stirred by Republican candidates, Cuban-Americans (most of them anti-Castro immigrants, or their descendants, from Cuba) remain distrustful of Democratic Presidential candidates' intentions towards Castro's regime. President Clinton, ever watchful for electoral threats, has been careful to blunt the force of such distrust by maintaining a consistently hostile stance towards Castro. Since their rates of birth and of immigration are high, Hispanic Americans are increasingly important to the outcomes of elections in California, Texas, Florida, and New York, and are therefore pursued assiduously by both parties.

As the case of Hispanic voters shows, while Catholics lean to the Democratic cause, they no longer vote as a group. Nor are they decisively swayed by the views of their priests (whose views on social matters are, in any case, by no means uniformly conservative). The new importance in politics and policy since the 1960s of social issues such as the role and rights of women with respect to matters such as abortion and contraception, and the changing size and character of family life in contemporary American society, has not met with a unified Catholic response. It has never done so among lay Catholics, and no longer does so among the priesthood or even the episcopacy. Such expectations as there once were that the conservatism of the Republican Party under the ascendancy of the New Right in general, and Ronald Reagan in particular, would result in Catholics voting *en bloc* for Presidential, if not Congressional, candidates of the more socially conservative party, have been disappointed. Catholics vote as instrumentally as many other groups have come to do; those who continue to agree with their Church's views on social issues do not for the most part let it affect their voting decisions.

Jews, women, blue-collar workers, and union members voted more heavily for Dukakis than for Bush in 1988, and much more heavily for Clinton in 1992 and 1996. Protestants (especially "born-again" fundamentalists) supported Bush heavily, although not as overwhelmingly as they did Reagan, Bush's non-churchgoing, divorced predecessor. In addition to losing some fundamentalist support in 1988 and rather more in 1992, Bush lost many of the Democrats who had defected to Reagan in 1980 and 1984, and other elements of the New Deal coalition who had done the same: those who had come of political age in the 1930s and 1940s, the uneducated, and the poor. George Bush's coalition of support was much closer to the traditional Republican middle and upper-middle class base of white, Protestant Americans than Reagan's broad base in 1984 had been, and shrank further towards that core in 1992. As Table 3.2 showed, Dole was unable in 1996 to improve upon Bush's performance.

Regional loyalties have altered greatly in the post-war era. The disappearance of the solid South is the single most important such change, but other regions' attachments have also changed. New England, once a Republican stronghold, is now (with the qualified exception of New Hampshire) two-party. New Jersey, New York, and Pennsylvania in the east, once Yankee Republican strongholds, have since the early 1970s had Congressional delegations dominated by Democrats but voted for candidates of both parties for the White House.

The question remains of whether a fundamental realignment of the relationship between party and electorate, established in 1932 and 1936 in the form of the New Deal coalition, is occurring in the United States. Of the eight Presidential elections since 1968, five have been won by Republicans and only three by Democrats. Only one of the Republican victories was narrow (1968, in a three-cornered contest between Nixon, Humphrey, and Wallace); and two, in 1972 (between Nixon and McGovern) and 1984 (between Reagan and Mondale), were won by landslides. Of the three Democratic victories, that of Jimmy Carter over Gerald Ford in 1976 was exceptionally close, but in neither of his victories did Bill Clinton secure a majority of the popular vote. While change has occurred, for there to have been a realignment in the terms employed by Key and Burnham it would have been necessary for there to have been a shift in aggregate voting patterns for House elections. That change has not occurred; nor have voters and parties dealigned.

Rather, voting patterns in the United States in Presidential elections have diverged from those in Congressional, Gubernatorial, and State legislative elections. "Ticket-splitting" (voting for one party's candidate for the Presidency and for the other party's candidates for most or all other offices) became common for much of the post-war period. Democrats controlled the House of Representatives between 1955 and 1995. In the Senate, they formed the majority between 1955 and 1981, and between 1987 and 1995. Those periods included all of Richard Nixon's, Gerald Ford's, and George Bush's Presidencies. Below the Federal level, Democrats also controlled most State Legislatures in the period, and most Governorships. This skewed picture suggests why mandates are so difficult for Presidents to claim or exploit: they are usually qualified. Most post-war Presidents have been Republican. All have faced at least one, and generally two, chambers of Congress controlled by the Democrats. Thus the key support of common party links to bridge the gap between the White House and the Congress has since Nixon's Presidency usually been absent. George Bush rightly inferred from this fact that co-operation with his partisan opponents would be essential if he were to have any prospect of achieving his objectives.

The link between Capitol Hill and the White House has weakened in another respect: Presidential coat-tails have shortened since Roosevelt's Presidency. Whereas Roosevelt brought huge numbers of Democrats into Congress on his coat-tails in 1932 and 1936, and Lyndon Johnson did much the same in 1964, recent Presidents have had much less effect on the fortunes of their nominal party colleagues' Congressional electoral fortunes. Richard Nixon's victory did not lead to Republican Congressional successes in 1968: he was the first President in the twentieth century to enter office facing opposition majorities in both Houses. Nor have Nixon's successors done very much better.

A comparison of net seat gains and losses for the Democrats and Republicans in the last major realigning era (the 1930s) with that in the hypothesized realigning period (the late 1970s to the mid-1990s) shows that no classic realignment has occurred. In the three House elections between 1930 and 1934, there was a net shift of 159 seats from the Republicans to the Democrats; and in the three House elections between 1978 and 1982, the net shift from the Democrats to the Republicans was a mere 23. Following the 1936 election, in which Franklin Roosevelt defeated Alf Landon by the largest plurality in history, the party balances favoured the Democrats by 334 to 89 in the House, and 75 to 17 in the Senate. So great was the Democratic dominance that their party's sides of the two chambers could not accommodate them all; this was a condition under which even American Presidents have a prospect of governing. Without unified control at both ends of Pennsylvania Avenue, Presidents have no hope of sustaining enduring policy change. Republican Presidents enjoyed such unified control in the decades after the 1896 realignment; Franklin Roosevelt did so after 1932. Neither Reagan nor Bush did so between 1980 and 1992; nor did Clinton after his victories in 1992 and 1996.

Although split partisan control persisted in Clinton's second term, the cause lay less with the continued vigour of ticket-splitting than with a further concentration in the distribution of Congressional party strength by region. The 1992 and 1996 election results leave open the question of whether the GOP's strength in Presidential polls has been halted or merely interrupted, but results of Congressional races between 1992 and 1996 nevertheless leave less room for doubt about the steady continuing change in the pattern of regional allegiances.

The Republican Party's penetration of the South, which began in the 1960s, moved a decisive stage further in the 1994 mid-term elections with its capture of a majority of House seats in the region. The South, once solidly and durably Democratic, where not only Republican Congressmen but also competitive Republican candidates scarcely existed before 1960, is now the Republicans' heartland. The speed of the Republicans' takeover of southern States and Congressional Districts, steady but slow between 1960 and 1990, has since been rapid. In January 1993, Republicans were still outnumbered in southern State delegations to the US House by 85–52; the 1994 mid-term Republican surge brought the Republicans a majority in the South of 73–64. Clinton's re-election victory notwithstanding, Republican candidates made further advances in the South by winning eighty-two seats to the Democrats' fifty-five, a result founded upon striking successes in open seats. Aggregated House votes for southern Congressional Districts in the 1996 election show that 14.2 million votes went to Republican candidates, compared with 11.4 million for Democrats. In the Senate, too, Republican strength in the South increased from eleven in January 1993 to eighteen in January 1997. (Significantly, the two victorious Democratic Senate candidates from southern states in November 1996 won by only tiny margins.)

Republican gains have not been confined to the South. Democratic candidates in the Rocky Mountain states of Alaska, Arizona, New Mexico, Colorado, Idaho, Montana, Nevada, and Utah have done poorly since 1990, having lost all but four of the eleven seats they held in January 1993. In the sparsely populated mid-western plains states, too, Democrats have been almost eliminated during the 1990s: by January 1997, only one remained.

In the north-east, industrial mid-west, and Pacific west, however, the pattern is one of persisting Democratic strength. Of the twenty House contests in 1996 that resulted in partisan change in these three regions, eighteen were from Republicans to Democrats. Aggregated votes for Congressional Districts in the 1996 election in the north-east, industrial mid-west, and Pacific west, show that Democratic pluralities over Republicans were 2.4, 0.72, and 0.75 million votes, respectively.

The resulting pattern is of Republican majorities in an "L"-shaped area stretching north to south across the Rocky Mountains and great plains states, and along the old confederate south. Within that huge area, Republicans are the majority not only in delegations to both Houses of Congress but, albeit incompletely in the 1992 and 1996 elections, also in the Presidency. Outside that "L"-shaped area, Democratic strength has grown during the 1990s, and is now pronounced: it is from here that the great bulk of Democratic Representatives and Senators come, and from here too that Clinton derived his electoral strength in the 1990s.

Bases of Incumbent Representatives' Power

The most striking result of Congressional elections in the post-war period is that incumbents win. The outcomes of most elections to the House of Representatives are, therefore, highly predictable; those to the Senate are rather less so. Although incumbent re-election rates have long been high, they have risen in recent years to the point where they now approach 100 per cent. Since 1948, the number of Representatives seeking re-election has varied between a low of 369 in 1992, and a high of 411 in 1966. The proportion of those seeking re-election who have won has varied between a low point of 79.3 per cent in 1948 and a high of 98.5 per cent in 1988. The proportion has fallen below 85 per cent only once since 1948, has been above 95 per cent between 1984 and 1990, and above 90 per cent in every election year since 1976, with the sole exception of the Republican landslide of 1994 when it fell to 89.9 per cent.

If Congressmen are to be politically successful (whether through a long-term career in the House itself, by chairing an important committee or winning a position in the party leadership, or by using their House member-ship as a springboard for more illustrious office in the Senate, their State's Governor's mansion, or even the White House) they must first secure their own re-election. The frequency of elections to the House obliges Members of Congress to calculate carefully and constantly the effects upon their re-election prospects of their decisions, speeches, and voting behaviour. Sam Rayburn, the most capable holder of the Office of Speaker in the twentieth century, on more than one occasion advised Democratic colleagues to "vote your District". The Speaker's advice was more guileful than it might appear: as his party's leader in the House, it was Rayburn's task to maximise Democratic voting strength by helping Democrats win re-election. As Rayburn thereby implicitly acknowledged, Members of Congress cannot rely upon party label or organization to shield them from constituents' displeasure if they should be so unwise as to place the interests of another Congressional District, or those of their President, above their District's own. The double jeopardy of Primary and general elections offers opponents from within and without the Representative's own party two opportunities to capitalize. In practice, few Members of Congress thus imperil their careers.

Like their colleagues in the Senate, Congressmen provide themselves with massive resources drawn from public funds to defend themselves from defeat and advance their interests: personal and committee staff; offices in the home District and State; expert advice from Congressional support agencies; free mailings; free trips home, and appearances in television studios. Personal staff have a powerful electoral utility for Members of Congress. By attending efficiently and creatively to District and constituent politics and problems, they underpin incumbents' electoral security. The permanent allocation of many staff dealing with constituent mail to District or State offices symbo-lises and strengthens the link between Representative or Senator and electors. Postal franking privileges are a significant expense to the taxpayer, but wonderfully useful to incumbents for enabling them to keep voters at home fully apprised of their political qualities. A study by the Congressional Research Service has shown that the volume of House mail through the Capitol Hill Post Office is twice as large in election years as it is in off-years. Television studio facilities are also valuable to Members for recording tapes to be broadcast on local television stations.

The systematic exploitation of Congressional perquisites, provided at public expense, buttresses incumbents' electoral security. Irrespective of whether the incumbent won in the most recent election with a tiny majority or by a landslide, the tending of electoral roots is a preoccupation: incumbents' first object is to deter plausible opponents from taking up the challenge of running against them, and their second is to defend their seats against those who are not so deterred. The acquisition and constant replenishment of campaign treasuries greatly enhances such a deterrent effect: in 1990, House incumbents raised on average six times as much finance as their opponents. Under these circumstances, it is to be expected that the quality of many challengers to incumbent Representatives should be poor and their political experience slight: in 1988, only 10 per cent of incumbents seeking re-election faced opponents who had ever been elected to public office, however lowly.

In the 1980s, incumbency was so powerful that it underpinned the Democratic Party's majority in the House, defending it against the growing popularity of conservative Republicanism. In the long run, incumbency offers no defence since the average length of service of Members of Congress is less than twelve years while the duration of the Democratic Congressional majority is three times as long. Only when incumbents decline to run again or die in office (thereby precipitating an "open" race) is a change in the partisan label of the District's Representative more than a remote possibility. In 1992, the unpopularity of Congress, fuelled by public discontent with a paralysis of policy-making and with an apparently widespread abuse by Congressmen of the perquisites of office, many incumbents retired prematurely in order to stave off anticipated defeat. Others were defeated in primaries, many of them taking place for newly-drawn Congressional Districts following the decennial reapportionment and redistricting exercises. Nevertheless, of those who stood for election in November under their party's label, 93.1 per cent were re-elected to office. Even in the 1994 mid-term elections, when Republicans made a net gain of fifty-three House seats to recover the majority status they had lost forty years previously, the incumbency re-election rate remained at 90 per cent. Most Republican gains in 1994 were in open seats (in which they won twenty-two of those previously held by Democrats) and in seats defended by Democratic incumbents in their first term (when incumbents are most vulnerable to defeat). Consistent with the discussion on p. 92 about the regional patterning of partisan strength, nineteen Republican gains in 1994 came in the South, sixteen in the Pacific west, and fifteen in the central plains.

Electoral Bases of Presidential Power

The Democratic coalition's ideological breadth was for long as great an advantage to the Democratic Party in Congressional elections as it was a handicap to its nominee in Presidential elections. In the latter, the Democratic candidate's natural coalitional strength proved vulnerable to Republican poaching through cross-cutting appeals to some of its components. White working-class and lower-middle-class voters have been attracted by campaigns arousing fears of violent crime, as Nixon demonstrated in 1968 and 1972, as Reagan did in 1980 and 1984, and as Bush notoriously did in 1988. Many older Democrats, who remained firm "New Dealers", were persuaded to support Reagan in 1980 and 1984 because of his appeals to patriotism and family values, and his vigorous anti-Communism.

The sources and development of political opportunity for conservative Republicanism in the Presidency are several and complex. Briefly, four strands can be identified:

- The politics of *race*: the national Democratic party's first tentative campaigning embrace of civil rights in 1948 began the process by which (with the exception of 1976) the South has become mainly or completely lost to the Democratic Party at Presidential elections, and the much longer and less certain process by which the Republican Party has become a very serious competitor in southern Senate races, and only a slightly less serious one in many House contests. Civil rights, and the associated policy questions of school bussing, affirmative action, and law and order, have all featured prominently in Presidential elections since 1964. Since 1968 they have done so always to the advantage of the Republican Party, whose candidates have consistently held the more conservative positions. Clinton drew the sting of such attacks in 1992 primarily by his having carefully acquired a conservative record on criminal justice when Governor of Arkansas.
- Levels of *taxation*: in the period from 1961 (and especially from 1963), American politics entered upon fourteen years of rapid change in economic policy generally, and in fiscal policy in particular. As the budget became a manipulable tool of macroeconomic policy rather than an object of policy, so the GNP growth rate rose from the level prevailing under the fiscally prudent Eisenhower Administration. Rising expenditure on the Vietnam War brought about fiscal chaos in 1967 and 1968, which in turn weakened Johnson. Mishandling of macroeconomic policy by Carter between 1977 and 1981 further discredited the Democrats' claims to mastery of macroeconomic policy management. Except for 1976, when President Ford's economic policies were in inflationary disarray following the quadrupling of the price of oil in 1973–4, the economic high ground between 1968 and 1988 belonged to Republican Presidential candidates. It did not belong to them in 1992, when Bush was falsely perceived to be presiding over an economy in recession, or in 1996, when Clinton had benefited from a long and steady economic recovery.
- The *redistributive purpose* of fiscal policy and welfare: Democrats at both ends of Pennsylvania Avenue between 1961 and 1969, and persisting Democratic Congressional majorities thereafter, did not so much extend

the range of New Deal social programmes as take wholly new initiatives in urban, social, transportation, and educational policy which their successors have been obliged to defend politically and fiscally. President Johnson in the late 1960s, and President Carter ten years later, found themselves politically vulnerable to the charge that domestic largesse was responsible for unsustainably large budgetary deficits. President Clinton's signing in 1996 of the Republican Congress's welfare reform bill (which abandoned the main Federal welfare programme, Aid to Families with Dependent Children) innoculated him against the charges that Republican candidates for the Presidency had made against Democratic candidates since the Great Society's implementation in the 1960s.

- *Defence and foreign policy*: both the late 1960s and the late 1970s were periods of convulsive international change, and of domestic trauma, induced in the first instance by American involvement in South-East Asia, and in the second by an emerging crisis in superpower relations complicated by the catastrophic and humiliating failure of American policy towards Iran. The ramifications of all three cases shaped the foreign policy debates in the 1980 campaign for the Presidency. With the collapse of the Soviet Union by the end of the decade, the effects of the first two instances were greatly muted: President Bush was, accordingly but ironically, unable to extract significant advantage from his having led the United States through Communism's collapse. By the same token, President Clinton in 1996 was immune from the attacks that had damaged his Democratic predecessors since 1972 because the issue of Communism was no longer of significance.

Conclusion

As Chapter 2 argued, party in America is distinctive. Party has in the several senses identified in that chapter also weakened in recent years. The prime consequence for elections in the United States is that most candidates for office are dependent upon Primary electorates rather than party officials for nomination. The Presidency, which was until 1972 exempt from this rule, is also now subject to it. The politics of entrepreneurship suffuses elections in America; they are in turn mediated primarily by television rather than by party. Candidates purchase election services and television time; for the most part, party neither buys nor supplies them.

Although neither race nor gender are any longer bars to voting, and the Courts act rigorously to ensure the equal value of votes, comparatively few Americans vote. Elections play a conspicuously large part in American politics but do not in themselves make citizens active participants. Electoral alignments, and alterations to them, are made by the 50 per cent of America's adult population who participate in Presidential elections, and the 35 per cent who take part in Congressional ones. The dominant alignment since 1968 has been of divided electoral power within Washington, by which the electorate has tended to send Republicans to the White House and Democrats to Congress. Divided control has persisted for all but two years in the 1990s, but in two modes: since 1994, a Democratic President has governed with a Republican Congress. Republican Congressional gains in the "L"-shaped swath of states in the Rocky Mountains, plains, and the South may well be stable in the medium-term: southern Democrats certainly appear likely to be in secular decline. Their extinction, however, is not pre-ordained. At the level of the Presidency, however, circumstances are more fluid: Clinton won two successive victories over Republican candidates, who won exceptionally low percentages of the popular vote. While a durable winning Democratic Presidential coalition could emerge on the foundations of Clinton's distinctive mix of regional, class, gender, and racial support, it might founder. There has been no realignment of the classic kind seen in 1896 and 1932, and there is no majority party.

4

The Presidency and the Politics of Leadership

Presidential Leadership

The Executive Branch of the government of the United States has but two elected members: the President and the Vice-President. Only the former matters for what he is; the latter merely for what he might become. Election every four years to the Presidency shapes the electoral and party systems; the outcome of each Presidential election shapes the pattern of government in the succeeding four years. Upon taking the oath of office, a President becomes Commander-in-Chief of the armed forces of the most heavily-armed nation-state on earth, and acquires full command over its strategic and theatre nuclear forces. New roles thrust upon the Presidency in the twentieth century have enhanced its symbolic and substantive significance (see Exhibit 4.1). The elected part of the Executive Branch is singular, not collective, and the President is, in consequence, a prominent national figure: his constituency is the nation, and he therefore enjoys a singular electoral legitimacy. Both the United States Congress and the Supreme Court are institutions with multiple memberships. The Presidency is a club of one.

Yet those elected to this supreme national office do not govern alone. The Presidency of the United States is not the government of the United States. Governing America requires politicians in separated institutions to co-operate because unfettered competition between them obstructs rather than facilitates policy-making. While seeking co-operation, a President must also attempt to lead because the holder of no other office is institutionally equipped to do so. A President must, however, also accept that other politicians in other institutions have their own separate bases of legitimacy and power, their own perspectives upon policy and politics, and their own priorities. A President cannot lead unless he appreciates the perspectives of other elected politicians, and accepts their legitimacy.

98

A President has no party colleagues whose primary task it is to sustain a government in office or to enable him to prosper against an opposition; such a bulwark of party government in Britain is absent in America. Presidents are obliged to exercise political leadership in a system of government whose structure has survived essentially unaltered through two centuries. Alluring as the potential power of the office appears to Presidential candidates, the task of realizing governing power in a Federal system of separated institutions has frustrated all post-war Presidents, and defeated most. Both Presidents and scholars of the Presidency have sometimes concluded that the institution's power is illusory; the more discriminating have always understood its constitutional grant of powers to be confined in scope and contingent in application. Presidents are obliged to bargain with other politicians, having independent bases of power over whom they have no authority but merely the possibility of influence.

Presidential leadership consists of two elements:

1. The strategic capacity to set the nation's *political agenda* by exploiting such prerogatives as the Constitution grants him, and choosing between policy options and priorities.
2. The tactical capacity to *negotiate* and *bargain* with other politicians in order that his declared policies might win the approval of Congress and of public opinion, leading to their implementation by the Federal bureaucracy and lower-level governments according to his expressed preferences.

This chapter first explores the nature and implications of the dilemma which these two aspects of leadership present for Presidents. The formal grant of powers to the Presidency by the Constitution, and those powers which, though not specified in it, are either implied by it or held to be inherent in the role of Chief Executive, are then examined; other powers granted to the President by statute and custom are examined here and in later chapters. The part which the mass media, and particularly television, have played in the portrayal of the Presidency to the electorate, is considered, together with an account of the nature of Presidential power, and the circumstances under which Presidents may make it effective. Presidential power is considered in the context of an examination of the scale and nature of changes in the Presidential role in the twentieth century (especially since the beginning of Franklin Roosevelt's Administration in March 1933) and in relation to other institutions of government. Analysis follows of the expansion of the Presidential staff system in response to the growth of the executive departments and agencies, and then of the key relationship between the Presidency and Congress. The problem of the President's relations to the Federal Courts is considered separately in Chapter 6, while the place of the Presidency in economic and foreign policy is examined in Chapters 11 and 12.

Prerogative Powers of the Presidency

Article II of the Constitution (see Appendix 1) reveals why the office of the Presidency should be the supremely attractive elective office in the United States, the office around which the party system is structured, and the focus of national political attention (see Exhibit 4.1).

It is on the constitutional foundations of Article II, upon its explicit grants and limitations of power, and upon statutory delegation of powers by Congress, that the contemporary Presidency is built. Some of the constitutional powers are exclusive: those of the pardon and the Presidential veto, for example, are his alone. Others, such as the formulation and consideration of legislation, are in practice shared between the executive and legislative branches. In any event, the present nature, sweep, and grandeur of the Presidency cannot be inferred from the explicit grants of power alone. The modern Presidency is the complex product of a Constitution that has itself been amended (though, as far as the Presidency is concerned, with respect to

---

EXHIBIT 4.1

The Office of the Presidency: Article II of the Constitution

- The *Executive power of the Federal government* is vested in the President.
- The President has the power to appoint *ambassadors, members of the Cabinet, Justices of the Supreme Court* and *Judges of lower Federal Courts*, with the advice and consent of the Senate.
- The President may recommend to the Congress such *legislative measures* as he deems appropriate and, subject to two-thirds of both Houses of Congress overriding his decision, *veto* bills emerging from Congress.
- The President has the power to make *treaties* with foreign nations, with the advice and consent of two-thirds of the Senate.
- The President is *Commander-in-Chief* of the armed forces of the United States.
- The President may require the *opinion in writing* of the principal officer of each of the Executive Departments.
- The President has the power to grant *reprieves* and *pardons*, save in the cases of impeachment. The President is, like all other officers of the United States, subject to *removal* from office by *articles of impeachment* voted by the House, and to subsequent trial by the Senate, for "Treason, Bribery, or other High Crimes and Misdemeanours".

the method of election only, and not to its formal executive powers) and reinterpreted by society and the Supreme Court acting in a continuing, if often disputatious, constitutional debate.

Inherent Powers of the Presidency

The extent and character of Presidential power has in particular, come to be shaped by part of that debate concerning those powers that many Presidents have claimed to be inherent in the office, or implied by the Constitutional document itself. Many ends to which government is necessarily and properly devoted (and to which the Constitution's framers plainly expected American government to be) were not specifically provided for in the Constitution of 1789; nor could they have been. This was Chief Justice Marshall's view, as it had earlier been Madison's, when he wrote the forty-fourth of *The Federalist Papers:*

> Had the convention attempted a positive enumeration of the powers necessary and proper for carrying their other powers into effect, the attempt would have involved a complete digest of laws on every subject to which the Constitution relates; accommodated too not only to the existing state of things, but to all the possible changes which futurity may produce . . . No axiom is more clearly established in law, or in reason, than that whenever the end is required, the means are authorized; whenever a general power to do a thing is given, every particular power for doing it is included.

The power of the Presidency cannot properly be confined to the particular powers specified in the Constitution. Presidents have claimed for themselves certain powers which they deem to be inherent in the Constitutional grant of authority in Article II, in a statutory delegation of power by Congress to the Presidency, or implied by either of these. In the Republic's 200 years, no such claim was more sweeping than President Lincoln's suspension of *habeas corpus* during the Civil War under a claim of emergency powers. By his action, Lincoln authorized his military commanders to declare martial law, and to try civilian offenders in military courts. The principled objections of Chief Justice Taney to Lincoln's deliberate setting aside of his oath to defend the Constitution did not move the President. Lincoln took the view that the Constitution could not survive if the Union failed.

The claims of more recent Presidents to be acting under inherent powers have met less frequently with assent from Court or public. Acting, like Lincoln, in a time of war, President Truman attempted in the spring of 1952 to resolve a dispute over new wage contracts in the steel industry by ordering that the works be seized. Truman resorted to a defence similar to Lincoln's: it was for the President to determine the national interest, and to act accordingly. Having pushed his case dangerously far, he retreated a little, but the Justice Department rashly returned to the fray in the Federal District Court by claiming that the Courts had no power to restrain a President. Only the ballot box, and the ultimate sanction of impeachment, were available to check the Chief Executive. The court declared this unattractive doctrine to be unconstitutional. By a majority, of 6:3, the Supreme Court found in *Youngstown Sheet and Tube Co.* v. *Sawyer*, 343 US 579 (1952), that the President's directive:

> cannot properly be sustained as an exercise of the President's military power as Commander in Chief of the Armed Forces . . . we cannot with faithfulness to our constitutional system hold that the Commander in Chief of the Armed Forces has the ultimate power as such to take possession of private property in order to keep labour disputes from stopping production. This is a job for the Nation's lawmakers, not for its military authorities.

None the less, as the presence of three dissenting voices indicates, the problem of the inherent powers of the Presidency is contentious and not easily resolved. There is (by definition) no unambiguous constitutional text that resolves the difficulty, since it is to the unwritten constitutional provisions of inherent powers that Presidents in such circumstances appeal. Reliance upon constitutional commentators is necessary for Courts to adjudicate, together with judgements about the gravity of the circumstances in which the inherent power is claimed, and the sweep of the inherent power in question. Many incline to the view that claims of inherent powers are empty. Yet the Constitution's brevity and generality require gaps to be filled if government is to work. It would be a ludicrous requirement (and make a nonsense of the Constitution both as a document and as a framework for working and workable government) were powers to be exercised only where they were expressly and explicitly granted. The process of filling constitutional gaps has been untidy, intellectually inconsistent and highly contentious, but necessary. Not confined to the judicial branch, it has involved all three branches, interested groups, and mass public opinion.

The principle of the Presidency's inherent powers is now generally conceded, even though its extent remains a matter of dispute. The President's special prerogatives in foreign affairs have long been acknowledged by Congressional and judicial politicians alike, especially since the Supreme Court's decision in *United States* v. *Curtiss-Wright Export Corporation,* 299 US 304 (1936). There, the Court held that Federal power over external policy was distinct from, and distinctly greater than, Federal power over domestic policy, and that the realm of external policy was one in which the President's power was special and pronounced. In foreign affairs, the latitude granted to Presidents by Courts, Congress, and public alike, is large, but Presidents do not have free rein. However, with respect to general claims of inherent power, Presidents have fared less well than they have in foreign affairs.

President Nixon spent much of his Presidency attempting to expand executive prerogatives across the entire range of government. The judgment in the summer of 1974 that triggered his resignation was made in the case of *United States* v. *Nixon*, 418 US 683, where the President declined to release sixty-four tape-recordings of White House conversations. His defence had two elements: first, that the Special Prosecutor who had secured a *subpoena* directing Nixon to produce them was a member of the Executive Branch under Nixon's authority as President; and second, that the tapes could be withheld from the Prosecutor and anyone else who sought them because they were privileged material. (The real reason for his not wishing to release the material was that one of the *subpoenaed* tapes was of a conversation between Nixon and Haldeman, his Chief of Staff, in which the use of the CIA to obstruct the FBI's investigation of the Watergate break-in was discussed.) Nixon's claim was not founded on the claim that the contents of particular tapes or parts of tapes were privileged, but that all Presidential communications were so. The *subpoena*, by contrast, referred to specified, dated, recordings. The Special Prosecutor had not embarked upon an unlimited or undefined enquiry. Nixon contended that executive privilege was absolute; the Court judged that it was not.

Claims by Presidents that they have certain inherent powers have been advanced with greater insistence in the twentieth century because of the growth in the size and importance of both the government and the Presidency. Throughout the century, but particularly since 1933, the Federal government has acquired two huge and continuing responsibilities which, as they have fundamentally expanded its capacity and reach, have effected a proportionately greater aggrandizement of the executive. Within an enlarged system of government, Congress has vested the President with responsibility both for the management of national economic policy and also for the direction of foreign and defence policies. These two developments have had four related results:

- The *budget* and *programmes* of the Federal government have increased in size and number (see Chapter 8).
- The relation of the Federal to the State governments has changed and become infinitely more *complex* fiscally, organizationally, and politically (see Chapter 10).
- The nature of the Presidency has altered, its prominence has increased, and its *centrality* in the political life of the nation has become established and permanent.
- The relationships of the Presidency with Congress and the Executive Branch have become the most significant in American government. Presidents' *political direction* of their relations with Congress is among

their most important tasks, and that of relations with the rest of the Executive Branch scarcely less so because the maintenance of co-operative and productive relations with both is essential if Presidents are to make and sustain their priorities at all stages of the policy process.

The expansion of government has caused a greater growth of the Presidency. The modern American Presidency could not have assumed the large, bureaucratized form it has in the absence of more general political pressures upon government to expand. In consequence, the Presidency is now far more prominent within the structure of Federal government than those who drafted the Constitution envisaged that it either could or should be.

The Presidency and the Mass Media

While the Presidency's constitutional authority is limited, its prominence is great – largely because of the advent of radio from Roosevelt's presidency onwards, and to television from Eisenhower's. The electronic media have played major parts in changing the nature of the Presidency, in enhancing its significance as the source of strategic leadership in an otherwise fragmented political system, and in establishing it permanently at the centre of the country's government (see also Exhibit 2.1 on pp. 22–3). Theodore Roosevelt and Woodrow Wilson showed that a mass Presidential politics could be created without a mass media, but it would probably be impossible to sustain in its absence.

The trappings of Presidential office are intimately familiar: Flag, Oval Office, Marine helicopter on the south lawn of the White House. The rhetoric, actions (whether contrived or important), resignation, successes, failures, and deaths of Presidents have their place in national and individual memories. Whether of President Kennedy's lonely burden during the Cuban Missile Crisis in October 1962, of his violent death and Lyndon Johnson's taking of the oath of office aboard Air Force One thirteen months later, of Johnson's transformation both of the legal and political status of black Americans and the place and politics of the southern states by his sponsorship of civil and voting rights legislation, or of President Bush's leadership of the Allies in the Gulf War, the Presidency has come to represent, though not always to comprise, the very centre of government. It remains the only possible source of consistent national political leadership.

That the office and its occupants dominate public perceptions and understanding of government in the United States (though to a greater extent abroad than at home) is explained in large part by television's focus upon them. The technology of television tends to fasten upon the graphic images of events and to eschew the complexities of process (see Exhibit 3.1 on p. 81); the training of television journalists confirms the tendency. If most students studying the American system for the first time bring with them one assumption, it is that the system is fully Presidential. This assumption has been reinforced by the need of television itself and those who work with it to simplify rather than to clarify, and to infer from Presidential visual prominence, Presidential government. For Presidents themselves, television has a corresponding utility in reaching over the heads of Congressional politicians and, less easily, over the heads of media producers, editors, and journalists, directly to voters. Appreciation of the subtly contingent nature of Presidential power has none the less been inhibited rather than advanced by television's ubiquity and cultural pervasiveness.

Most voters in the United States acquire most of their information about, and understanding of, politics and government from television. The consequences of the way in which television portrays politics for voters' understanding of politics have prompted much academic disagreement. Television is not a neutral technology: its operation has implications (albeit of imprecise and contingent kinds) for American politics. Television fastens more easily on the actions (whether trivial or important) of an individual Chief Executive than it does, for example, upon the deliberations of a Congressional Subcommittee taking evidence from expert witnesses on technical but substantively important questions of corporate tax law; the latter are rarely covered by television. Without a single figure, television would be hard-pressed to make sense of American politics. Whereas in the nineteenth century newspaper coverage of Congress exceeded that of the President, the focus is now on the White House, and Presidents receive far more television coverage than do Congress or the Supreme Court.

The Presidency and the media have a symbiotic and mutually parasitic relationship. Staff in the White House press office strive to control the President's dealings with the electronic and printed media to his (and sometimes their) advantage. This effort is constantly made (and has been made since Theodore Roosevelt first invited journalists into the White House under strict procedural rules), but is most obvious in time of war, where the incentive and opportunities for control are high and coincident. Yet the press in general, and television in particular, also threaten Presidents. Potentially, they may expose corruption and mischief, and enforce accountability. The relationship is rarely smooth, and usually deteriorates as a Presidency ages and political problems grow. The development of the relationship between Presidents and journalists has not been simple: Presidents have not learned to exploit the medium more systematically to their advantage with the passing years, even though the quality of advice from specialist White House staff available to them has become infinitely more sophisticated. Reagan's ease before cameras and his deceptively relaxed exploitation of the medium during his first term in office inclined some observers rashly to conclude that television would henceforth be the ally of Presidents and not, as had been the case under Johnson, Ford, Nixon, and Carter, their foe.

The Vice-Presidency

The growth of government in the twentieth century, and the simultaneous focus of the printed and electronic media upon the Presidency has left the Vice-Presidency little changed. Those who hold it still have no constitutional role other than to wait for the President's death, or to seek the succession when the Twenty-Second Amendment prevents an incumbent President from running for office for a third term (see Appendix 2). With two exceptions in the post-war period, all Vice-Presidents have led institutional lives of political frustration and (usually) obscurity. Neither the Constitution nor custom grants the Vice-President any responsibilities beyond that of presiding over the Senate. That duty is trivial: Vice-Presidents usually prefer to leave the task to the President *pro tempore* (for the time being) and appear in the chamber only to break a tie vote or at the Majority Leadership's request to assist in procedural manoeuvres.

Save in the case of Vice-President Mondale between 1977 and 1981, no post-war Vice-President has been able to make much of the office during his tenure, whether in his guise as the President's deputy in the Executive Branch, or as the Senate's President. In an attempt to clothe the institutionally naked, recent Presidents have occasionally given Vice-Presidents either substantive tasks or party political ones. President Kennedy appointed Vice-President Johnson to the position of Chairman of the Space Council; President Nixon gave Vice-President Agnew the responsibility of maintaining political support for the administration among groups of conservative voters; President Bush named Vice-President Quayle the Chairman of the Competitiveness Council, in which role he strove to weaken the force of regulations issued by executive agencies under the authority of Congressional statutes governing environmental protection and civil rights.

Selection of the Vice-President

Although Vice-Presidents have little to do, their selection as a Presidential candidate's running-mate typically proceeds on the assumption that a ticket must have a "balance" of geography and ideology, if not of gender and ethnicity. Hence Adlai Stevenson, the quintessential northern liberal intellectual, balanced his candidacy in 1952 with that of the conservative southerner, Senator John Sparkman of Alabama. John Kennedy balanced the ticket in 1960 by selecting Lyndon Johnson (thereby ensuring that he would win at least both Massachusetts and Texas). By selecting Walter Mondale, Jimmy Carter chose a Vice-Presidential candidate who was northern, liberal, and a distinguished Democratic US Senator. Carter had none of these assets, weaknesses which were as apparent in government as on the campaign trail.

To his credit, Carter discerned Mondale's compensating qualities, and used them to the administration's advantage. In contrast to most of his predecessors in the White House, Carter regarded his Vice-President as a colleague rather than as a subordinate. Their staff organizations were effectively integrated, while Mondale had an office adjacent to the President's own in the West Wing of the White House and not in the East Wing, the remote part of the White House to which Vice-Presidents are usually assigned. Carter worked closely with his Vice- President, drawing on his experience and advice in all major policy matters; he ordered that Mondale be party (without exception) to all of the President's national security briefings, and that he be fully conversant with nuclear decision-making procedures. Such openness was wholly unprecedented: Franklin Roosevelt, for example, had kept Vice-President Truman ignorant of the very existence of the United States' nuclear weapons programme.

Succession to the Presidency

Characteristically, Truman thought the Vice-Presidency to be as useful as a "fifth teat on a cow". One of his predecessors, John Nance Garner, Franklin Roosevelt's Vice-President between 1933 and 1941, once declared that the office was "not worth a bucket of warm spit". However, while Vice-Presidents are nothing, they may become everything. This is so most dramatically following a President's death: a mere fourteen weeks after being told of the existence of America's atomic weapons programme, Truman ordered the use of atom bombs against Hiroshima and Nagasaki. Less dramatically, it is the case with election to the highest office after having held the second highest. Since 1945, Vice-Presidents Harry Truman, Richard Nixon, Lyndon Johnson, Gerald Ford, and George Bush have succeeded directly to the Presidency: Truman and Johnson by the natural death and assassination respectively of Roosevelt and Kennedy; Nixon after a gap of eight years following the end of his Vice-Presidency under Eisenhower; Ford because of Nixon's enforced resignation; and Bush by election after Reagan's second term. The Vice-Presidency has in the post-war years become the office most likely to assist Presidential ambitions.

Prior to the ratification of the Twenty-Fifth Amendment to the constitution in 1967, a vacancy in the Vice-Presidency would not be filled until the following Presidential election. Thus, until January 1965 (when he began the term to which he was elected in November 1964) Lyndon Johnson had no Vice-President. Had Johnson himself died in the period between his accession to the Presidency upon Kennedy's assassination and his taking of the oath of office in January 1965, the Presidency would have fallen to the holder of the office next in succession: the Speaker of the House of Representatives, as provided by statute under the authority of Article 2, Section 6 of the Constitution (see Appendix 1). The Twenty-Fifth Amendment stipulates that in the event of a vacancy occurring in the Vice-Presidency following the death of the incumbent or of his succession to the Presidency itself, the new President shall nominate a new Vice-President who takes office upon majority votes of both Houses of Congress. This procedure was followed when Vice-President Agnew resigned his office in 1973. Gerald Ford was nominated to succeed him, and later himself became President following Mr Nixon's resignation in August 1974; Ford's elevation itself caused a vacancy in the Vice-Presidency which was filled by the nomination and confirmation of Nelson Rockefeller, a former Governor of New York. Between the time of Rockefeller's confirmation and the Democratic succession under Carter in January 1977, both the Presidency and the Vice-Presidency were therefore held by people who had been elected to neither office.

Franklin Roosevelt, Harry Truman, and the Modern Presidency

A clear break in the nature, possibilities and purposes of the Office of the Presidency came in March 1933, with Franklin Roosevelt's statement of purpose in his inaugural address. Prior to this, the Presidency usually lay at the heart of American government only in three exceptional circumstances: responses to foreign threats such as those presented by the British incursions in 1812 and by the European war in 1917–18; imperialist policies adopted towards Mexico in the mid- nineteenth century and, later, towards Spanish possessions in the Caribbean and Pacific; and the response to the threat of secession presented to the Federal government by the rebellion of the southern states in the Civil War of 1861–5. In each instance, the Constitution's grant of power to the President under the "Commander-in-Chief" clause accorded Presidents Madison, Polk, McKinley, Theodore Roosevelt, Wilson and Lincoln a uniquely powerful position within government.

Setting a National Agenda

Emergency is still a sufficient condition for Presidential domination, but is no longer necessary. Narrow interpretations of executive power as defined by Article II of the Constitution are redundant. Economic collapse between 1929 and 1933 caused the attention of the nation's new mass electorate to focus on the institution of the Presidency in its search for escape from misery. Only from the Presidency was there a possibility that a new national agenda might be set, and a plausible hope of the sluggish and disordered responses of a fragmented Congress being overcome by sustained and coherent executive leadership. The constitutional foundation of Presidential powers did not alter under the pressure of events. Yet upon an unchanged base, the processes of Presidential politics, and especially of Presidential–Congressional relations, changed radically between the period from 1929–33 and that from 1933–7, between Herbert Hoover's single term and the first term of his successor, Franklin Roosevelt.

Herbert Hoover's failure to offer strategic leadership lay not in an intrinsic weakness of the office he held, but in his own hostility to expanding government in general, and the Presidency in particular, in the cause of correcting the failure of markets to meet the gravest emergency. The economic collapse over which he presided brought about his defeat in the 1932 Presidential election, propelling his Democratic opponent Franklin Roosevelt to the White House four months later. Roosevelt chose to attack through direct Federal intervention the financial collapse and huge loss of output. In the short term, he proposed a package of emergency measures to Congress (most of which were enacted) to arrest financial collapse, and later during his first two terms proposed measures that increased the direct role of government in the economy, acknowledged limited Federal responsibilities for the welfare of Americans, regulated industry and finance, and provided for a new framework of labour law.

Roosevelt's three complete terms in office marked radical departures not only in the output of policy, but also in the organization of the Executive Branch, in the place of the Presidency in the political life of the nation, in the Presidency's relation to the other two branches, its relationship to the electorate and the parties, to the Federal bureaucracy, and in the relations between the Federal and State governments. The Federal government, which previously spent less than either State or local governments, had spent almost twice as much by the end of Roosevelt's second term.

Roosevelt's economic policies contributed to the salvation of American capitalism, and his foreign policies established the United States as a military and economic superpower – but his reformulation of the role of the office he held was imperative for the achievement of both. The change has been sustained and confirmed by all his successors, irrespective of their views on the proper size and role of government. Conservative or liberal, Republican or Democrat, Presidents elected since Franklin Roosevelt have presided over a heavily-staffed Presidency at the nominal head of a substantial Federal bureaucracy. Harry Truman, Roosevelt's successor in the White House, willingly embraced an extension of the role of the Federal government in the domestic economy and in welfare and education policy. For Truman, too, the role of Commander-in-Chief was one that carried with it inescapable burdens and responsibilities which most of his predecessors had known either in exceptional circumstances or not at all.

The United States as a World Power

The United States' emergence from the second World War in the unique condition among Western allies of economic strength, coupled to a novel (albeit short-lived) monopoly of nuclear weapons, and overwhelming conventional military advantage, had immense significance for the Presidency's conduct of foreign affairs. When America's engagement with the world was occasional, and its maintenance of large standing military forces the exceptional condition of wartime rather than the constant experience of peace, the importance and prominence of the Presidency fluctuated, too. America's spectacular escape from the depression of the 1930s, occasioned by the vast growth in the country's capacity during the war and the absorption of its production through domestic mass consumption after it, together with the interests attaching to its new status as the pre-eminent world power after 1945, made Presidential activism obligatory in the sustenance of the first, and the discharge of the second.

Franklin Roosevelt and Harry Truman thus altered permanently the place of the Presidency in the American political system. Passivity would never again be an option for holders of the office. Roosevelt's successors could not plausibly claim that the management of the economy was not their responsibility; nor was it in their electoral interests to do so. Despite the still comparatively scant provision of income support and welfare in America, and the widespread antipathy to welfare dependence, they also found it politically impossible to claim that the welfare of American citizens unable to provide for themselves and their dependents in a market economy was none of their concern. Much as Ronald Reagan railed against "big government" on the hustings, neither a reduction in the size of the Presidency nor the complete removal of the welfare safety net was on his agenda.

The Obligation to Bargain

The fundamental structural peculiarities of the Federal government – separation of powers and Federalism – render effective Presidential leadership rare. Policy change is difficult to effect in America, even for powerful Presidents in propitious circumstances. With the loss of American hegemony in the international system since the mid-1960s, the task has become harder still. The United States' mass of Treaty obligations, and military, trading, and financial ties with other nations in a global order which it no longer dominates makes Presidents' satisfaction of voters' expectations effectively impossible to realise, not least because such expectations often conflict. Presidents are more often tethered than they are free.

Political skill is indubitably a factor in the success that Presidents have in asserting leadership – whether of a kind susceptible to quantification (as in the proportion of bills that have been passed by Congress proposed by Presidents) or not (as in the revival of national morale or purpose). Lyndon Johnson's persuasive political skills provide a remarkable instance of the first kind; Dwight Eisenhower's and Ronald Reagan's strategic skills of the second; and Franklin Roosevelt's of both. Since Presidents can exercise neither strategic nor persuasive leadership by relying upon their limited resources of authority, much depends upon the skill with which a President is able to bring political influence and persuasion to bear.

The governing problem for Presidents is therefore the following: the Presidency is an office whose occupants are expected to deliver successful economic, foreign, defence, environmental and educational policy, and to provide the country with a vision and purpose. "Political leadership" in its strategic sense in the variegated country that in the US can come from no one but the President, since he and he alone has a national constituency, the sole national electoral legitimacy that flows from it, and both the incentive and the opportunity to act. Other politicians exercise great power within their cities, States, rural counties, or Congressional Committees, but their jurisdictions are in every case limited. The President's jurisdiction is, by contrast, exclusively national.

Yet the design of Federal institutions acts as a forbiddingly high barrier to the president exercising that leadership. The fit between public expectation and constitutional provision is poor – a condition which, though potentially harmful to the office and the system of which it is the central part, is none the less difficult to rectify, short of radical alteration to the structure and rules of government. Such a change, as both constitutional barriers and the evidence of many failed past attempts suggest, is improbable.

Faced with this problem, Presidents are obliged to attempt to make the system work for them. Modern incumbents have employed various institutional devices to make Presidential government more than the fleeting outcome of confluential political advantages, the norm rather than the exception. Half a century after Roosevelt recognised the need for Congress to create a more extensive, institutionalized Presidency in order to address continuing economic and political problems, the dilemma has not been solved: within the framework of the separation of powers and the weak fabric of political parties in America, it cannot be. It has none the less been mitigated to the extent that able Presidents may maximize their influence so as to exploit passing opportunities to their own advantage, and yet do so without infringing constitutional provision.

A President's greatest political asset is that the executive power in the United States is not collective but singular. All Presidents attempt to exploit this compelling singularity in their bargaining with allies and opponents among elected politicians in Congress, unelected ones in the departments and agencies of the Executive Branch, and in their contact with members of interest groups and the general public. A Member of Congress is one of a body of 435, a Senator of a hundred, a Governor of fifty, a President of one. A national constituency is theirs alone, and the solitariness of the Oval Office an unmatched opportunity. The President has competitors everywhere but no peer – hence his nagging governing problem, and tantalizing political opportunity.

The Presidency and the Executive Branch

The growth of government to meet burgeoning domestic needs and responsibilities during the 1930s, together with foreign and defence responsibilities during the 1940s, required the development of a Federal bureaucracy, which in turn has presented Presidents with political competition from unelected officials on the one hand, and unelected Cabinet Secretaries (the heads of the executive departments) on the other.

Presidents' political skills of persuasion and negotiation are as severely tested in their management of relations with the Executive Branch as they are with Congress. All Presidents face the predicament of how to prevail against bureaucrats whose priorities may differ from their own and who (rationally) have political loyalties to members of Congress, to Congressional staff, to clients and interest groups, and legal obligations in respect of the programmes they administer. Bureaucrats have several loyalties, for reasons of law and politics: the Executive Branch is not a Weberian hierarchy led by the President. Such constitutional complexity has not diminished the demands of Chief Executives for speedier and simpler responses from the departments of government nominally beneath them, but has made the straightforward assuaging of their demands improbable.

Cabinet Secretaries, the political heads of executive departments, are nominally the President's subordinates rather than colleagues. Unlike in Britain, members of the President's Cabinet have no prospect of supplanting the chairman of the Cabinet by political manoeuvre or *coup d'etat* between elections; their only means of doing so is through the public quadrennial processes of nomination and election. None the less, Cabinet Secretaries have conflicting priorities: advancing the President's cause may have political appeal in the period immediately following confirmation in office, but is usually overcome in the longer term by each Secretary's need to attend to the priorities and preferences of the department and its clients.

The President's Cabinet is not an executive body: it has no power to decide government policy. Nor are its members independently elected: of all the politicians who sit around the table in the White House Cabinet Room, only the President has an electoral base. The Constitution in Article II refers to "the principal Officer in each of the executive Departments", but only in the context of the President's power to "require the Opinion, in writing" of such officers (see Appendix 1). There is no mention in the Constitution of a Cabinet. Cabinet Secretaries therefore not only pose no threat to the President's position between Presidential elections, but also lack the legitimacy which flows from electoral support. Presidents serve not for so long as they can command the confidence of party colleagues but (short of death, resignation, or impeachment) for the four years specified by the Constitution.

The Constitution prohibits dual membership of executive and legislature with the (intended) result that American Cabinet Secretaries have no roots in the legislature. Not only does the Constitution deny them the opportunity to manoeuvre for the Presidency, but most lack the motive and will to seek it. To the extent that most do not pursue the Chief Executive's job, they do not constantly remind the President of his political mortality. Many American

Cabinet Secretaries come from law firms, corporations, banks, research institutes, and universities, to which they return upon leaving the Department or Agency they run temporarily: moving in and out of government is the norm rather than the exception in American government. Others join the Cabinet from Congress, from which they must resign before taking office, and to which most do not later attempt to return.

Whether by virtue of their own stature or because of the importance of the particular offices they hold, individual Cabinet members in the United States are none the less frequently significant political figures (see Exhibit 4.2). The Departments of State and the Treasury are so important that almost all who have led them were prominent in public life before they arrived. Most have confirmed, and some have enhanced, their standing while in the post. Since the war, Secretaries of State George Marshall, John Foster Dulles, Henry Kissinger, George Schultz, and James Baker ranked second to the Presidents in whose Cabinets they served, not just in protocol but also in the influence they enjoyed over the administration's foreign policies. All had known Washington's byways, Congressional structures and processes, and the foreign policy-making community well before they took the post, and were consequently advantaged in it. Several Secretaries of the Treasury have been no less influential in their own sphere of finance and macroeconomic policy. As Secretary of Defense, Robert McNamara did as much as the two Presidents under whom he served to set and sustain United States policy in Vietnam; in the same office, Caspar Weinberger was the architect of American rearmament between 1981 and 1987.

By apportioning Cabinet posts carefully (see Exhibit 4.2), Presidents can accomplish five ends:

- *Reward important supporters*, as all Presidents frequently do, and as Bush did with his appointment of James Baker as Secretary of State.
- Build support among the *uncommitted* or *former opponents*, as Nixon tried to do with his offer of the post of Secretary of Defense to the Democratic Senator, Henry Jackson, and as Clinton succeeded in doing by appointing William Cohen as Secretary of Defense.
- Build *links with Congress*, as Clinton tried to do by appointing Les Aspin to be Secretary of Defense in 1993, and Daniel Glickman to be Secretary of Agriculture in 1997.
- Strengthen links with *key racial groups,* and with *women,* as all modern Presidents do by appointing at least one black, and one woman. Bush appointed the distinguished black physician Louis Sullivan to be Secretary of Health and Human Services, and Elizabeth Dole to be successively Secretary of Transportation, and Secretary of Labor. President Clinton appointed an Hispanic (Henry Cisneros, the former Mayor of San Antonio) to be Secretary of Housing and Urban Development, two African-Americans (Jesse Brown and Ron Brown)

EXHIBIT 4.2

President Clinton's Cabinet, March 1997 (prior occupation in parentheses)

Secretary of Agriculture	Daniel Glickman (US Representative)
Attorney General	Janet Reno (State Prosecutor)
Secretary of Commerce	William Daley (Lawyer)
Secretary of Defense	William Cohen (US Senator; Member, Senate Armed Services Committee)
Secretary of Education	Richard Riley (Governor of South Carolina)
Secretary of Energy	Federico Pena (Secretary of Housing and Urban Development)
Secretary of Health and Human Services	Donna Shalala (University President)
Secretary of Housing and Urban Development	Andrew Cuomo (Assistant Secretary of Housing and Urban Development)
Secretary of the Interior	Bruce Babbit (Governor of Arizona)
Secretary of Labor	Alexis Herman (White House aide)
Secretary of State	Madeleine Albright (Ambassador to the United Nations)
Secretary of Transportation	Rodney Slater (Federal Highway Administrator)
Secretary of Treasury	Robert Rubin (Investment Banker)
Ambassador to the United Nations	Bill Richardson (Democratic Congressman)
Secretary of Veterans' Affairs	Jesse Brown (Veterans' Interest Group lobbyist)
Director of the Office of Management and Budget	Franklin Raines (Deputy Director, OMB)
Director of Central Intelligence	George Tenet (Deputy Director of Central Intelligence)
National Security Adviser	Samuel Berger (Deputy National Security Adviser)
US Special Trade Representative	Charlene Barshefsky (Acting US Trade Representative)
Administrator of the Environmental Protection Agency	Carol Browner (Florida state government official)
Chairman of the National Economic Council	Gene Sperling (Deputy Director of the NEC)

to be Secretaries of Veterans Affairs and of the Department of Commerce, respectively, and five women (Hazel O'Leary, Donna Shalala, Madeleine Albright, Carol Browner, and Janet Reno) to be Secretaries of Energy, Health and Human Services, Ambassador to the United Nations, EPA Director, and Attorney General, respectively) in his first term. In his second term, Clinton confirmed his commitment to promoting women by naming Madeleine Albright as Secretary of State; she was the first woman appointed to the post.

- Draw into the inner counsels of the Executive Branch those whom a President *trusts*, as Kennedy did with the appointment of his brother, Robert, to the post of Attorney General in 1961, and as Nixon did by his appointment of John Connally to be Secretary of the Treasury in 1971.

Although the Cabinet has political utility for Presidents in its composition, it has much less in governing. Some Presidents (such as Kennedy) have virtually ignored it; others (such as Eisenhower) have found it useful; some (such as Johnson) have used it merely as a device to act out a prepared ritual of purported consultation; one (Reagan) had so tenuous a command of his job that it was alleged that he forgot the name of his Secretary of Housing and Urban Development.

The organization of the Executive Branch, and the political difficulties which its size, complexity and power present for Presidents, are among the political consequences of Roosevelt's radical expansion of the role of the Federal government. To play the expanded role required of the Chief Executive following the collapse of the United States's economy under President Hoover's administration, Roosevelt required the resources of an expanded Executive Branch. New programmes spawned new departments and new agencies (authorized by Congress) to run particular programmes (authorized and appropriated by Congress) within them. By his second term, he appreciated the need for the services of an expanded staff organization responsible exclusively to him.

The Executive Office of the President

Presidents have had the support of staff since 1789. However, until the middle of the nineteenth century, Chief Executives were expected to pay for staff out of their own overall allowance. Congress first specifically appropriated funds for staff (a private secretary, a steward, and a messenger) only during Buchanan's Presidency in 1857. Throughout the nineteenth century, Congress provided increasing support for staff assistants to the President although, as late as 1900, the total number of clerical and administrative staff in the White House was just thirteen. President Hoover benefited from Congressional legislation which increased the complement of secretaries to the President from one to three, permitting the President for the first time to allocate particular tasks to his senior staff. The Executive Office of the President (EOP) was formally established by the Reorganization Act passed by Congress in 1939. The Act sprang indirectly from the work of the President's Committee on Administrative Management, established in March 1936, and chaired by Louis Brownlow, a distinguished scholar of public administration. Brownlow and his collegues argued, in a phrase that has been taken to characterise their approach: "The President needs help". In support of this claim, the Committee recommended the establishment of the EOP as an overarching organization of Presidential staff to support the Presidency as an institution, and the virtually autonomous creation within the EOP of a White House Office for the President's closest personal staff.

As its recommendation that such a White House Office be staffed by a mere six Executive Assistants showed, the intention was not to create a parallel bureaucracy (although that has been the consequence). Each member of the staff should, they argued, in phrases which amused both Roosevelt and the White House press corps to which he revealed them, "be possessed of high competence, great physical vigor, and a passion for anonymity". Roosevelt was especially concerned with the place of the new White House Office within the EOP. At the press conference to publicise the Committee's Report, he justified its radical proposals by emphasising the responsibility carried by the President for the Executive Branch's general management, and the growth of that responsibility since 1933. (It entered a further phase of expansion following Japan's attack on Pearl Harbor on 7 December 1941, and Germany's declaration of war upon the United States four days later.) Rejected by Congress in 1937, the President's proposals, modified slightly to take account of opposition from within the Executive Branch and from Congress, were sent again to Capitol Hill in 1939, where they were this time quickly passed into law.

In addition to the Reorganization Act's substantive importance for the Presidency in making available to the holder of the office resources appropriate for him to make effective his nominal leadership of the Executive Branch, the Act provided for a legislative veto. The legislative veto is a contingent delegation of rule or decision-making authority to the Presidency or an executive agency by which rules may be issued and decisions made subject to Congress retaining the right to veto them and thereby prevent their being applied. The legislative veto was, and remains, a procedure by which the huge task of issuing detailed administrative regulations might be delegated to Executive Branch officials subject to Congress retaining the right to prevent their being issued should it so decide. The Reorganization Act specifically empowered the President to submit reorganization plans to Congress which, unless both houses of Congress vetoed them, would then become law. President Roosevelt submitted such a proposal ("Plan 1") for the establishment of the EOP by incorporating within it the White House Office and the Bureau of the Budget.

At the time of writing, the Executive Office is much more complex, having had staff agencies added to it under the reorganization authority delegated to the President by Congress, and other units established by separate Acts of Congress. The present size, shape, and composition of the EOP are therefore the product of reorganization plans submitted to successive Congresses by successive Presidents, and of Acts of Congress establishing staff agencies such as the Council of Economic Advisers (CEA), and the National Security Council (NSC) within it. However, the genesis of the contemporary White House Office, as of the EOP as a whole, lies in the Reorganization Act of 1939.

The Presidency expanded, therefore, because of the general growth of the Executive Branch between 1933 and 1955; and it has continued to grow in later years despite the much slower growth in Federal civilian personnel. As programmes within the Executive Branch proliferated, so the agencies that ran them developed powerful political links with Congress (which authorized and reauthorized their existence and the programmes they implemented, and regularly appropriated funds for their continuation) and with the Congressional committees that oversaw their operation. Shrewd Presidents appreciate that their political direction and control of the Executive Branch are necessarily limited; they are therefore bound to rely heavily upon the additional, personal, governing resources which the EOP affords them. In practice, this has implied substantial staff assistance within the Executive Office (see Exhibit 4.3). The provision of specialized staff working on the President's behalf offered the possibility that nominal Presidential authority over subordinate but influential bureaucrats might be made more effective by being devolved to his personal senior staff. Executive Office staff are,

---

EXHIBIT 4.3

Expansion of the Executive Office of the President

Between its establishment in 1939 and the end of Eisenhower's Presidency in 1960, the Executive Office of the President (EOP) grew rapidly. A rough measurement of the extent of the increase in staff employed in the Presidential branch can be made by noting its physical expansion into buildings in and around the White House. The old Navy Building into which the Bureau of the Budget (BOB) moved in 1939 was by Eisenhower's Presidency in the 1950s insufficiently large to house all the staff members of the EOP, and is now one of three buildings within which EOP staff work. During the First World War it had housed the three Executive Departments of State, War, and the Navy. Approximately 1,500 people were officially listed as working in the EOP at the end of Mr Bush's Presidency; the real total is higher because of temporary secondments from elsewhere of staff whose salaries are paid by other agencies.

therefore, a means by which a President indirectly extends his persuasive leadership capacity through intervention in policy implementation, particularly by ensuring that his priorities are reflected to the fullest degree possible in decisions, rules, and regulations issued by executive agencies.

Roosevelt's object in the late 1930s was, therefore, similar to that of each of his successors: how to make Presidential leadership over the Executive Branch effective, how to be Chief Executive in fact as well as in the theory of constitutional law. Roosevelt required then, as all Presidents have required since, direct assistance from people dependent on him personally rather than on superiors in departments or clients outside them. For Roosevelt, the problem was novel; for his successors, it has been a familiar feature of the difficulties of Presidential governance. A President neither can nor should scrutinize personally the work of departments on all major matters of government policy. Nor can he alone ensure that Cabinet Secretaries resist the temptation, in John Ehrlichman's words, to "marry the natives" by straying from his policy and advancing their own. An array of senior staff might be able to assist him.

The modern Executive Branch is therefore divided: there is a departmental component (and, within the departments, specialist agencies and regulatory organizations), and a Presidential component consisting of the EOP, which is in turn subdivided, as illustrated in Figure 4.1. These twelve units form the institutional Presidency: the White House Office (WHO), Office of Management and Budget (OMB), National Security Council (NSC), Council of Economic Advisers (CEA), Office of the United States Trade Representative (USTR), Council on Environmental Quality (CEQ), Office of Science and Technology Policy (OSTP), Office of National Drug Control Policy (NDCP), National Economic Council (NEC), Office of Policy Development (OPD), Office of Administration (OA), and the Office of the Vice- President (V-P).

All EOP staff agencies have their importance for government, although to differing extents and in differing ways. The significance of the Council of Economic Advisers, created by the (Keynesian) 1946 Employment Act, and charged with the task of providing economic advice to the President, is considered in Chapter 11, together with the National Economic Council, established by Executive Order at the beginning of Mr Clinton's administration. The place in foreign policy-making of the National Security Council, created by the National Security Act of 1947 and which functions as the highest source of advice to the President on domestic and foreign questions affecting the nation's security, is examined in Chapter 12. Two other key EOP staff agencies are examined here: the White House Office, comprising the personal staff organization immediately around the President himself, and the Office of Management and Budget, the Executive Branch's organization with primary responsibility for the formulation of the President's budget policy.

FIGURE 4.1

The Executive Office of the President Representative

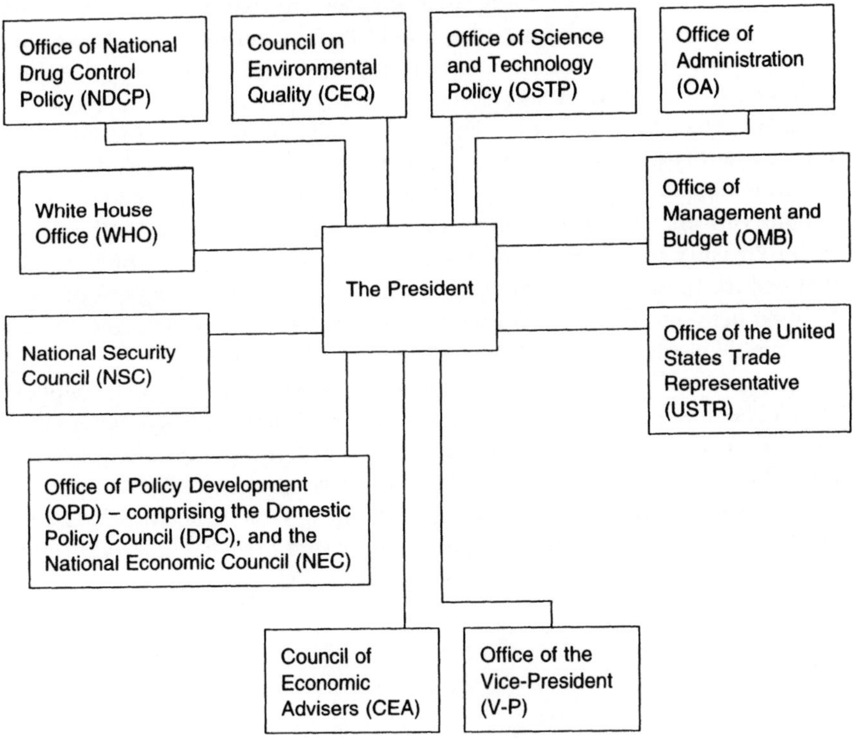

The White House Office

Although formally a part of it, the White House Office is effectively separate from the rest of the EOP. Unlike the three members of the Council of Economic Advisers, or the Director of the Office of Management and Budget, the responsibilities of White House staff, numbering approximately 400, are defined by the President rather than specified in law; they are not subject to confirmation by Congress. They are the President's most intimate advisers, to hire and fire as he sees fit, to organize as he wishes, to undertake the tasks he sets, and responsible to the President alone.

Louis Brownlow had hoped that the White House staff would act with restraint, confining themselves to strictly administrative tasks, and refraining from interposing themselves between the President and his Cabinet. However, the division between administration and politics does not, in practice, exist. All administrations since the implementation of Executive Order 8248 in 1939 have been co-ordinated under the President's direction by a clutch of senior staff whose competitive struggles and activities hold a fascination for the Eastern press and Washington's political classes. Except under President Nixon, their role has not been to assume executive roles by displacing heads of departments and agencies but to build unity by enforcing the President's perspective over semi-autonomous departments and agencies and a fully autonomous Congress. White House staff have the task of advising the President when he requests it, but more usually of assessing the advice of others, whether in Congress or in the departments (see Exhibit 4.4). In their covering papers to the President, staff review the recommendations of Cabinet officers. Preferred courses of action by, for example, the Secretary of the Treasury regarding tax policy are assessed by staff (including, but not confined to, those in the CEA) prior to the President reviewing options and deciding between them. This flow of activity is heavy, constant, and runs in both directions between the White House and the agencies.

The organization of the White House Office has varied over time, between Presidents, and within Presidencies, as Presidents become discontented with existing arrangements. Some, such as Eisenhower, have employed a broadly hierarchical form with a Chief of Staff in charge to whom all papers routed to the President are directed in the first instance. Others, such as Roosevelt and Kennedy, have preferred a more fluid system, in which several senior

---

EXHIBIT 4.4

The Power of White House staff

Harry McPherson, one of the most distinguished of all senior White House staff in the post-war period, was Special Counsel to Lyndon Johnson (a title that gave him some specific tasks, but a more important, general remit). In his book, much the best and perceptive of all Presidential staff memoirs, he has emphasised the entirely conditional nature of the power of senior White House staff, and contrasted its nature with the place of the Vice-President:

> In every case, the special counsel or assistant carried with him the contingent authority of the President. He needed that authority to accomplish anything at all, as the law gave him none of his own. And it was necessarily contingent; the President had to be free to repudiate his assistants' views and apparent commitments. The counsel-assistant's position was almost exactly opposite that of the Vice-President. The Vice-President was powerless, but he was only a moment away from holding enormous power; the special assistant had power, which might be withdrawn just as suddenly. Working for Lyndon Johnson, an assistant did not easily forget that he carried his authority on sufferance.

Source: McPherson (1972), pp. 284–5.

staff have direct access to the President by paper and in person. President Reagan operated in his first term with a triumvirate of senior staff but, following the Iran-*Contra* scandal, with just a Chief of Staff of unusual distinction and standing in Howard Baker, Majority Leader of the Senate between 1981 and 1984.

President Kennedy used the metaphor of "a wheel and a series of spokes" in characterizing the organization of his White House Office, with himself at the hub. However, the White House is not a smoothly-ordered operation whose processes can be captured in one of several geometric forms; only under Eisenhower's Presidency and Sherman Adams's tenure as Chief of Staff did it approach such clarity. Attempts by staff to establish the organization of the White House formally usually fail. Many Presidents, especially self-confident ones, find that fluid staff arrangements best suit their needs, but Lyndon Johnson was notorious for asking senior staff to perform menial tasks, and junior staff to take on major ones (see Exhibit 4.4).

Truman's Counsel, Clark Clifford; Eisenhower's Chief of Staff, Sherman Adams; Kennedy's Counsel, Ted Sorensen; Johnson's two *de facto* Chiefs of Staff, Bill Moyers and Joe Califano, and, most notoriously of all, Richard Nixon's Bob Haldeman and John Ehrlichman all did as much to shape the content, style and perceptions of the modern Presidency as the most senior members of post-war Cabinets have done to shape policy: to have worked in the service of the President of the United States does no harm to one's *curiculum vitae*. Upon leaving the White House, many have proceeded to lucrative careers in lobbying and the law (often indistinguishable activities in Washington), business, or journalism. Many have written of their experiences in Presidential service. Some, especially in the Nixon and Reagan administrations, have after leaving the White House spent time in Federal Courtrooms and jails, and later writing exculpatory memoirs.

Loyalty to the President is a prerequisite; without it, staff have no value to him. Loyalty is invariably demonstrated by staff having worked for the President in his election campaigns or in earlier institutional incarnations. Hence journalists' reference to President Kennedy's staff as "the Irish Mafia", and to President Carter's as "the Georgia Mafia". Most of Kennedy's staff had served him in his campaigns for the House, Senate, or Presidency, and many of President Carter's staff had worked for him when he was Governor of Georgia. Of President Reagan's three senior staff in his first term, two (Meese and Deaver) had served him during his tenure as Governor of California. The third was a remarkable exception to the general rule, in that James Baker had run the Presidential primary election campaigns of Reagan's Republican Party opponents in both 1976 and 1980: Gerald Ford and George Bush. President Bush followed the usual pattern for similar reasons. His senior White House advisers were those whose political judgement and loyalty to him he had cause to trust by reason of their having demonstrated both qualities during his long career in Federal government, and those whose advice and organizational abilities had been apparent during the Primary and general election campaigns of 1988.

Trust between President and staff is essential to the creation of a successful Presidency. However, it can hide neither incompetence and inexperience (as President Carter learned to his cost) nor for criminality (as President Nixon learned to his). Loyalty is a quality most reliably demonstrated in the fire of an election campaign, but experience of the latter is not the ideal apprenticeship for assisting a President in the formidably demanding task of leading America's government. President Carter's staff proved themselves adept at exploiting the new rules of the Democratic Primaries and the new technologies of campaigning in 1976. They had less success in assisting their President to circumvent bureaucratic and Congressional barriers in Washington. To no individual did this apply with greater force than to Hamilton Jordan who, at the tender age of 34 and with no experience in government before 1977, was appointed as White House Chief of Staff by President Carter following the (predictably disastrous) dismissal of four senior Cabinet secretaries and the centralization of power in the White House in 1979.

As loyalty and trust are the first requirement for staff, physical stamina, astute political judgement, and high intellect are the others. Stamina is necessary to survive the punishingly long hours which the difficulty and volume of their work require of senior staff. No senior staff member can expect respite or relaxation during her or his period in the White House. They are never off duty. As McPherson (1972, p. 123), thinking of Johnson, has observed: "Every leader bent on great enterprises consumes his staff as fuel". Staff who lack political judgement are a liability to the President (as Hamilton Jordan was to Carter through his insensitivity to Congressional prerogatives). Powerful intellect is necessary in order to master fast streams of politically complicated policy problems. The finest White House staff combine all four characteristics, serving their Presidents with candour and loyalty, over eighteen-hour days for six (and often seven) days a week, clarifying policy and political options for the President in briefing papers where they distil conflicting opinions from numerous agencies across governments within and outside Washington.

The total number of people working in the White House is difficult to determine, not least because some are in fact paid by other agencies or departments and so do not appear formally on the White House personnel budget. Wayne (1978, pp. 20–1), using figures supplied to him by President Ford's staff secretary, has calculated the number of staff in the White House in 1939 as being very much larger than it is usually portrayed: a grand total of 157. The total grew steadily, reaching 283 at the end of Truman's Presidency, 388 at the end of Eisenhower's, 429 at the end of Kennedy's, and 546 at the end of Johnson's. Approximately half of these were secretarial staff and half professional. Notwithstanding the popular view in Washington during the Watergate crisis that the size of the White House staff had grown rapidly under President Nixon's administration (and that the increase in size had itself contributed materially to the Watergate crisis) the total has altered little since.

Although several Presidents have begun their administrations as Jimmy Carter did, by declaring their intention to rely upon their Cabinets for the making of policy, none have found it a satisfactory instrument for Presidential decision-making. All recent Presidents, Carter included, have found irresistible the political attractions of using staff in the EOP to centralize policy-making in the White House (see Exhibit 4.5). Some, such as Bush, have deliberately created in the EOP new units such as the Office of Drug Control Policy to administer new programmes and so to increase Presidential control over them, lessening the chance of their being undermined by established departments. Both Kennedy and Johnson relied heavily on the Council of Economic Advisers, appreciating it as a counterweight to the established (and invariably more conservative) advice of the Treasury, just across the street from the East Wing of the White House. Others, such as Nixon, have used the National Security Adviser not merely as their primary source of foreign policy advice but also as an executive and personal ambassador, thereby diminishing significantly the influence and standing of the Secretary of State.

The Assistants, Deputy Assistants, and Special Assistants all had particular responsibilities which included, but were not confined to: Communications; Media Affairs and Operations; Public Liaison; Speechwriting; Press

---

EXHIBIT 4.5

The White House Bureaucracy under President Clinton

The official description of President Clinton's White House staff in the last months of his first term was of a large and much more highly structured organization, many of whose members had specific responsibilities rather than the general remit granted to their senior advisers by Presidents Roosevelt and Truman. The 1996/7 edition of the *United States Government Organization Manual* is suggestive more of a bureaucracy than of a small staff unit. Leon Panetta, formerly a Californian Congressman and more recently Clinton's first Director of OMB, was at the head of the list as Chief of Staff, followed by two Deputy Chiefs of Staff, and twenty Assistants to the President. Of the latter group, one was the President's National Security Adviser; one his Press Secretary; one the Counsel to the President; and two were Assistants for Domestic Policy. There were in addition twenty-three Deputy Assistants; a Deputy Counsel; eight Associate Counsels (George Bush, having fewer legal difficulties than his successor, had made do with just five); one Special Counsel; three Special Associate Counsels; and no fewer than fifty Special Assistants.

Advance; Intergovernmental Affairs; Legislative Affairs; Agricultural Trade and Food Assistance; Political Affairs; Scheduling and Appointments; White House Operations; Women's Initiatives and Outreach; National Security Affairs; International Programs; and Presidential Personnel. Below the most senior levels of the staff, many specialists have advanced academic and technical qualifications, matching those of economists in the Council for Economic Affairs (CEA) and on the agency's staff, foreign policy specialists on the National Security Council (NSC), and the bureaucrats throughout the Federal Executive whose work the White House staff shadow and attempt to shape to the President's purposes.

President Nixon believed, not without justification, that there was intense opposition to his domestic and foreign policies within the Federal bureaucracy as well as from partisan opposition in both Houses of Congress. He accordingly sought to centralize power within the White House, and did so to a greater extent than any of those who preceded or have followed him in the Oval Office. The frustration for Presidents in dealing (as they must) with the Federal bureaucracy is that their control over Federal bureaucrats is limited. Civil servants always have, and the President's political appointees in the agencies quickly acquire, political loyalties to clients in the private sector, to lobbyists, to interest groups, and (crucially) to the members and staff of Congressional Committees and Subcommittees that qualify their loyalty to the President of the day. Under these circumstances, Presidents are liable to discover that their policies (and even their instructions) are modified, delayed, or simply ignored by bureaucrats who have both the political incentive (protecting their jobs and their clients' interests by defending the programmes they administer) and the means (by allying themselves with powerful coalitions of Congressional and private interests) to resist the President.

The danger for Presidents in employing a large White House staff to address the problems of bureaucratic resistance and of balkanized administration is that they thereby run the risk of isolating and misleading him. Whereas agency bureaucrats invariably obstruct, White House staff help. Where bureaucrats may delay, White House staff comply. This may delude Presidents into supposing that their instructions are being carried out. In fact (since they have no administrative machine below them to implement decisions) staff can merely relay such instructions, and impress upon bureaucrats the importance of compliance, and attempt to ensure that the President's wishes have been carried out to the extent that Congressional statute and politics grant him such autonomy.

Yet the essential problem remains that the President does not in practice control the Executive Branch. Nor does the degree of Presidential control grow with an increase in the number of staff. At the end of Carter's Presidency, Zbigniew Brzezinski, the National Security Adviser, had more personal staff than the Secretary of Defense, while the Special Assistant for international trade negotiations had a larger personal staff than the Secretary of Commerce, and the Special Assistant for wage and price stability a larger staff than the Secretary of the Treasury (Lowi, 1985, p. 142). Indeed, Carter's Presidency was marked as much as any modern administration by tensions between White House staff and departmental heads.

Those whom the President does control – his immediate staff – are not, and cannot be, executives. This rule does not apply to the institutionalized part of the Executive Office – to the Special Trade Negotiator, or to the National Security Council – to the same extent. Yet attempts by the National Security Adviser and his staff to seize executive authority in circumvention of the Departments of State and Defense have often had damaging consequences for the coherence of policy and for the President's political standing. In the most extreme circumstances, members of the President's National Security staff have attempted to execute policy in defiance of explicit Congressional prohibitions, as the examples of Admiral Poindexter and Colonel Oliver North between 1986 and 1988 show.

White House staff are necessary, but insufficient, for making effective Presidential leadership. Like the President for whom they work, they are in practice obliged to work with an Executive Branch in which power is scattered and divided, where loyalties run to the many agencies in the Executive Departments, to Congress, and to private sector clients, as well as to the President (and often before they run to him). It is, moreover, a system in which bureaucrats are party to other political alliances which grant them substantial autonomy from the Executive Branch's one elected member. Citing Presidential wishes enhances the staff's prospects of success, but provides no guarantee of it.

The Bureau of the Budget/Office of Management and Budget

When originally established by Congress in 1921, the Bureau of the Budget (BOB) was placed not within the Presidency but in the Treasury, because Congress did not wish the President to have direct control over the budget's formation. The Brownlow Committee in 1937 recommended its removal to the EOP, where Presidents would have a greater chance of ensuring that budgets reflected Presidential priorities. "Plan 1" provided for the transfer, and within a few months of the passage of the Reorganization Act of 1939, its staff decamped from the Treasury to the Executive Office Building adjacent to the White House. There, the Bureau of the Budget became a political tool of the Presidency, as Roosevelt had intended (see Exhibit 4.6). Just as the expansion of the White House Office had an expressly political purpose in enabling Roosevelt to make more effective his strategic direction of government, so the BOB's transfer from the independently powerful Treasury Department to the Presidency provided him with an additional resource.

No Chief Executive has any prospect of political leadership without specialist staff to ensure that his fiscal priorities are adhered to throughout the Federal government, and that the financial implications of new legislative proposals are thoroughly examined to ensure that they fit his overall spending policies and do not subvert them.

The significance of political relations between the Presidency and Cabinet Secretaries arises once again here because of their fiscal implications: the practical political independence of Cabinet Secretaries made absolutely necessary the establishment and retention by Presidents of a degree of fiscal control. Roosevelt's exercise of strategic leadership depended upon his being able to impose fiscal policy choices. Had he permitted Departments and Agencies within the Executive Branch to make their own annual budget requests to Congress, he would have lost all influence over government spending, and hence over policy priorities. All budgets reveal political preferences: accordingly, budget requests by Executive Departments to Congress reveal the preferences and priorities of the United States' government. It is therefore essential that the President himself should intervene before budget requests are made in order to ensure that they are fiscally coherent, and that they reflect accurately the priorities he wishes to set for the Executive Branch. The president and his staff will constantly have to intervene after submission of the budget to ensure that his priorities and choices are sustained during their consideration by Congress. Such persuasive leadership through negotiation is essential to the achievement of strategic success. But the huge budget request that is sent to Capitol Hill in January of every year must be the President's aggregated and distinctive choice, not the sum of Departmental aspirations. In this way, BOB expanded Presidential influence over the Executive Branch and provided a coherent

---

EXHIBIT 4.6

Establishment of the Bureau of the Budget (1939)

The President's Executive Order 8248 of 1939 establishing the BOB in the EOP provided the Bureau with authority to perform certain tasks, the four most important of which were:

- *To assist the President with the preparation of the Budget* and the *formulation* of the *government's fiscal policy.*
- To supervise the Budget's *administration.*
- To promote *efficient administration* throughout government.
- To *clear* and *co-ordinate legislative proposals* made by departments and agencies and to advise the President of their significance for his overall budgetary policies.

baseline from which Congress's Appropriations Committees could work in making their judgements of the funds to be spent upon programmes within each executive department and agency.

However unrepresentative their States or Districts of the nation as a whole, Congressional politicians enjoy an electoral legitimacy which every Departmental Secretary lacks. In this setting, Roosevelt intended that the Bureau of the Budget should provide him with dispassionate advice, enabling him to make informed decisions about the fiscal calibration of departmental interests and his own. The alternative course of leaving spending priorities to Cabinet Secretaries and their separate departments in self-interested alliances with other beneficiaries of public spending – members of Congressional Committees and interest groups – would have amounted to abdication of fiscal responsibility. No modern President bent upon strategic leadership could countenance such an outcome (although it should be stressed that the Federal Budget was written in this way until the mid-point of Roosevelt's Presidency).

The Bureau's detachment and expertise provided the foundation for its dominance of fiscal and legislative clearance, and the co-ordination, refinement, and improvement of the Executive Branch's administration. If the disparate elements of the Executive Branch were to be drawn together in the causes of professionalism and efficiency, and the asset of institutional memory (as rare in Washington as it is common in London) to be retained, politicization had to be eschewed. Composed mainly of politically intelligent but non-partisan career civil servants with no programmes or clients to defend, the Bureau had been ideally placed to serve the Presidency. Until Richard Nixon's administration, it did so. In 1970, Nixon reorganized the Bureau, renamed it the Office of Management and Budget (OMB), and altered its role from an institution serving the Presidency to an agency of policy advocacy serving a President. Political control was increased by the traditional expedient in Washington of partisan appointments at senior levels. The Bureau was thereby transformed from the agency of "neutral competence" that Nixon's predecessors had valued to a personal staff unit; and its credibility outside the White House (and especially within Congress) was accordingly diminished. Congress responded by making the OMB Director subject to Senate confirmation. Significantly, having itself been content to rely heavily upon BOB analysis and estimates, Congress created in 1974 the Congressional Budget Office to ensure dispassionate fiscal analysis because it could no longer trust the OMB's own.

The process having been started, Nixon's successors extended it, unheeding of the damage which such politicization did to the OMB's capacity for disinterested budgetary analysis, and hence to the public interest. Under Reagan, the Director of the Budget became a national figure by acting as the chief protagonist for the President's budget. In realizing the administration's object of pressing its budgetary reforms through Congress in a matter of months, dissenting interpretations by the OMB's professional economists were excluded in the cause of generating the fanciful economic assumptions supporting Mr Reagan's budget forecasts which, in consequence, were politically expedient aspirations rather than intellectually robust expectations.

The Presidency and Congress

The Presidency's single most important political relationship is that with Congress. Here is the central link in American government. It is not a sufficient condition of Presidential achievement that Presidents exercise strategic and tactical leadership of Congress by winning votes for their authorizations and appropriations legislation and for confirmation of their nominees to the Executive and Judicial Branches, but it is necessary. Those Presidents (such as Jimmy Carter) who do not reliably achieve legislative leadership are generally regarded as having failed. In the post-war period, John Kennedy has been the only exception to this rule: he achieved little legislative movement on Capitol Hill, and saw most of his proposals languish in Committees where conservative chairmen suffocated them. Kennedy's historical standing is nevertheless high.

Even Kennedy was bound to take the legislative initiative, although he lacked the political opportunity and creativity to sustain it. Since there is no path of retreat either for Presidential aspirants from promising much, or for Presidents themselves from the expanded Presidency, no incumbent can withdraw from political engagement with Congress. For Lyndon Johnson in the mid-1960s, intense lobbying of Congressional chairmen and party leaders was necessary to pass Great Society welfare and education reforms, and three major Civil Rights bills into law. Even Richard Nixon, who conducted Congressional relations with belligerence, was constitutionally bound to seek Senate ratification of the Strategic Arms Limitation (SALT I) and Anti-Ballistic Missile (ABM) Treaties. Fundamentally, his executive agencies' requirement of regular reauthorization and appropriations for their programmes ensured the interaction of Executive and Congress, and compelled Nixon to seek Congressional support. Although his behaviour towards the legislature suggested that he wished it were otherwise, Nixon could not govern independently. His need for finance limited him, just as the Founding Fathers intended, while his own political agenda required authorizing and reauthorizing legislation, as Congress helpfully reminded him. Where, as in his attempts to wage war privately in Cambodia and his refusal to spend lawfully- appropriated funds, Nixon violated explicit Constitutional provision, Congress belatedly restrained him by the War Powers Resolution of 1973, and the Budget and Impoundment Control Act of 1974. In such a setting, Arthur Schlesinger's lengthy indictment of what he took to be an "Imperial" Presidency under its incumbents in the 1960s and early 1970s (he served two of them as a Special Assistant on the White House staff) had some force. Yet American Presidents act "imperially" only when Congresses resile from their constitutional obligations. Though prosecuted by Presidents, the Vietnam War was sustained by annual Congressional appropriations, and often by supplemental appropriations when the expansion of the war exhausted funding.

As with the changing role of the Presidency in general, so with its legislative function, Franklin Roosevelt's administration provides the historical key. Within the constitutional framework, Roosevelt quickly altered popular and Congressional understandings of the Presidency's legislative role. Eisenhower was the last President not to embrace enthusiastically the role of Chief Legislator; his resistance was token, and lasted for only one year. Between the beginning of Eisenhower's Presidency in 1953 and Reagan's in 1981, most major authorizing legislation that Congress considered originated with Presidential proposals. Appropriations bills come to Congress as part of the annual budget message. The Constitution grants Presidents power first, with regard to the vetoing of bills passed by Congress, and second respecting the submission of legislative proposals. Hence the Presidency plays key roles both at the beginning and at the conclusion of the legislative process:

- The first is granted by Article I, Section 7, of the Constitution, providing the President with a qualified veto of legislation presented to him (as all legislation must be) for signature (see Appendix 1). The success of Presidents in using the veto has varied between individuals and the circumstances of their disagreements with Congress. The most successful modern exponent was Gerald Ford, Richard Nixon's appointed successor, whose legislative leadership consisted in his vetoing all measures of which he disapproved and then in lobbying intensively to have the vetoes sustained by Congress. Impossible though it made the development of strategic Presidential leadership, it was the most attractive option for dealing with a hostile Democratic Congress, since it required his opponents to find two-thirds, and not simple, majorities to prevail. President Clinton did not use his veto powers at all during his first two years in office (the first occasion on which a President had not used the veto in an entire Congress since Millard Fillmore withheld his veto-pen between 1851 and 1853), when Democrats formed the majorities in both Houses of Congress. As President Ford had done twenty years before, however, Clinton found the authority to say "no" to legislation passed by hostile party majorities in Congress useful in his third and fourth years in office: in 1995, he vetoed a $16 billion rescission bill. Later, he vetoed the Republican 1996 fiscal year budget containing provisions for reductions in Medicaid, Medicare, welfare, education, and federal environmental programmes.

- The second key role is found in Article II, Section 3, of the Constitution, which deals with the powers and duties of the President, and provides that:

> He shall from time to time give to the Congress Information of the State of the Union, and recommend to their Consideration such Measures as he shall judge necessary and expedient.

This power to recommend is the foundation for Presidential leadership of Congress in both the strategic and tactical senses: it enables the President to choose between options and to decide upon the order of priorities, and the implied power (from which Presidential lobbying of Congress derives its constitutional foundation) to advocate publicly and privately the adoption of his recommended measures places no obligation upon Congress to respond affirmatively. In resourceful hands, the President's power to recommend Congress's agenda is great. Yet the legislative branch has complete constitutional freedom to ignore, reject, or re-order the agenda sent to it from the White House (although it is usually politically more constrained than this formal power suggests). It is none the less upon the power of recommendation, agenda-setting, and lobbying, that all modern Presidents have organized their relations with Congress. To that end, all Presidents since Eisenhower have assigned a number of their White House staff to organize their relations advantageously. Such staff have four main tasks, irrespective of the politics and policies of the President for whom they work:

1. To assume and retain responsibility within the White House for all questions of *legislative strategy* and *tactics.* The timing of legislative initiatives to Congress, the submission to the Senate of Treaties for ratification, and of nominations for confirmation, are matters on which the staff is expected to advise the President and his/her senior policy and political staff. Congressional relations staff maintain active and detailed supervision of the progress made by the President's bills, Treaties, and nominations, identify obstacles and difficulties, and seek to eliminate or circumvent them.
2. To attend to the political needs of Congressional *allies,* to cultivate the *uncommitted,* to *marginalize opponents.*
3. To co-ordinate the *lobbying work* of the entire administration by ensuring that Congressional relations staff in every agency advance the President's priorities, rather than departmental and agency ones. The fragmentation of American government makes this both difficult (because the Executive Branch is large and its individual components have powerful countervailing incentives to pursue separate interests) and important (because the President's causes may easily be harmed by semi-autonomous agencies).

4. To ensure that due regard be paid to the views of *known* and *potential supporters* in both Congressional parties on legislation, Treaties, and nominees, in order that political difficulties are identified before submission rather than discovered afterwards. The President's Congressional relations staff are therefore ambassadors in both directions along Pennsylvania Avenue: representatives of the President's views and purposes to Representatives and Senators, and of theirs to him.

Presidential leadership in the sense of the President's persuasive capacity to negotiate and bargain is exemplified in his relations with Congress. Persuasion is necessary because the separation of powers grants Congress autonomy, thereby denying Presidents authority over them. Neither the President nor his staff, neither his Cabinet colleagues nor his political appointees within the Federal bureaucracy, are members of the legislature. There is no requirement that the legislature should respond affirmatively to his requests nor, indeed, an obligation upon them to make any response at all. Presidents cannot count upon Congressional acquiescence. Declaration of agenda items and the setting of priorities are but the first strategic steps in making leadership effective. Presidents must exercise to the full their tactical powers of persuasion through political pressure where they can exert it, and bargaining and negotiation where they cannot, in order to win support.

Legislating in America is an imprecise and uncertain process. The rise of the Presidency to permanent prominence in the twentieth century, and the resulting popular expectations of it, have confirmed the role of President as Chief Legislator, but have not equipped the President to perform it with the reliability that British Prime Ministers typically enjoy.

Essentially, the explanation lies in the continuing separation of executive and legislature: the President cannot command a legislature from which s/he is separated because that separation disables party and denies him/her stable support. Even the presence in Congress of majorities for the same party in control of the White House provides no guarantee that a President will secure approval for those legislative proposals, Treaties, or nominations s/he submits to Congress. Nearly unbroken Democratic party advantage between 1933 and 1994 did not ensure the adoption of a stream of legislation proposed by Democratic Presidents. Nor has it placed insuperable obstacles in the governing paths of Republican Presidents. Since the White House has lain in Republican hands for most of the post-war period, while one or both Houses of Congress have usually been in the control of the Democrats, this has been the commonest condition of partisan relations between the White House and Capitol Hill.

Republican Presidents have therefore had to accustom themselves to the politics of divided party control, and have been obliged to adjust their tactics accordingly. Were parties to command the undiluted support of their Congressional members, Presidents Nixon and Ford would have had no success whatever in their relations with Congress, since they faced Demo-cratic opposition in both chambers throughout their terms. If party were all, President Eisenhower would have had little success for the last six years of his two terms, but have achieved much for the first two when he was buoyed by Republican majorities (albeit small ones) in both the House and Senate. President Reagan's record, too, would have been less impressive in 1981 than it appeared to be, since control of Congress was divided for the first six years of his two terms. Examination of the legislative records of successive Presidents and Congresses working under different partisan and external political circumstances shows that Republican Presidents are much more successful than they would be if the divisions between Congressional parties were pure, and the results of party-line votes predictable.

Equally, the history of relations between Democratic Presidents and the Democratic Congresses with which they have worked in the post-war period is one of recurrent friction and frustration. John Kennedy's term of office was marked more by legislative frustration, as the then baronial chairmen of the House Judiciary and Rules Committees refused to allow his legislative proposals for new civil rights legislation to come to the Floor of the House for debate and a vote. Other Committee chairmen emulated their refusal to co-operate. One such was Wilbur Mills of the House Ways and Means Committee, who showed himself to be an effective opponent of Keynesian demand management (not least because its effective implementation would have weakened the political power of his Committee). More recently, Jimmy Carter's term of office was conspicuous for heavy legislative failure. His proposals for the containment of health care costs expired in Congress. The energy bill which finally emerged from Congress bore little resemblance to the legislation the President had proposed. The SALT II Treaty which he had negotiated with Leonid Brezhnev was withdrawn from further consideration by the Senate when the Soviet Union's invasion of Afghanistan made political defeat certain. President Clinton, too, failed to secure passage of his major health care reform in 1993/4, despite large numerical majorities in both chambers. Ironically, he enjoyed much greater *political* success in the 104th Congress (1995/6) when he faced Republican majorities in both chambers than he had in the 103rd: the President adapted to mixed government with extraordinary political agility.

The clarity of the Presidential imprint upon Congress's legislative process depends, therefore, upon much more than the bare numerical indicators of party balance in each chamber. As Chapter 5 on Congress will show, ideological divisions in both House and Senate cut across party cleavages because of the peculiar historical pattern of the American party system, and in particular because of the one-party politics of the South between Recon-struction and the passage into law of the Civil Rights Act of 1964 and the Voting Rights Act of 1965 (see Chapter 2). Since these two Acts transformed the politics of the South into a two-party competitive system, the nature of the cross-cutting cleavage has altered.

However, even major changes in the political agenda such as this have not resulted in the fusing of ideology with party in the classic European mould. While the Democratic Party in Congress claims the loyalties of most Congressional liberals, many moderates and conservatives are also Democrats. Similarly, the Republican Party in Congress is an ideological coalition of many conservatives and moderates of different stripes, and a (very) few liberals. Congressional parties reflect, therefore, the diversity of parties across the country. The heterogeneity of American society and the fragmented character of its political structures, sanctified by Constitutional prescription, is constitutive at most of a politics of inducement, not of compulsion. Congressional parties do not easily cohere because other forces – regional, economic, ethnic – often exert greater gravitational pull than does loyalty to a party which has little or no influence over its members' political fates.

Prime among these cross-cutting influences is ideology, the single most significant cleavage between conservatives on the one hand, and a liberal–moderate grouping on the other. The dominant questions of public policy have changed so greatly since the period prior to the passage of the Civil Rights legislation of the mid-1960s, that the political significance of the Conservative Coalition, drawn from the bulk of the Republican Party and a minority of the Democratic Party, has declined: the old southern Democratic boll-weevils are now few in number, while liberal Republicans are an endangered species. Its importance for the Presidency lay with the consequences it had for the legislative role of the Chief Executive. The coalition dogged four post-war Democratic Presidents (Harry Truman, John Kennedy, Lyndon Johnson, and Jimmy Carter), often nullifying their nominal party advantage in Congress. By the same token, it aided immeasurably the lots of four Republicans (Dwight Eisenhower, Richard Nixon, Gerald Ford, and Ronald Reagan).

Conclusion

Presidential policy-making failure is commoner than Presidential success. The Federal and fragmented American political system is characterized by the scattering of institutional power; the society that sustains it is a mosaic. Such a setting is hostile to Presidential government. Yet, limited though the strategic power of the President to set the political agenda is, and constrained as he is in his exercise of leadership through persuasion and negotiation, he is bound constantly to attempt both. The reason is plain: if strategic leadership does not come from the President, it can come from no one else. Elective politicians on Capitol Hill, unelected Judges in the Federal Courts, State Governors, legislators, and Judges in the State Courts, city mayors and local politicians, and unelected bureaucrats throughout the 85,000 governments within the United States often have both the capacity and the incentive to delay, weaken, amend, or nullify initiatives and proposals from the President. The President, alone among the very large class of elected office-holders across America, has both the strategic opportunity and obligation to set both an agenda for the United States and the tactical means for its achievement.

5

Congress and the Politics of Legislative Competition

Procedural and Structural Dimensions

Congress is the first branch of government. A bicameral institution, it is organized by membership of party, Committees, Subcommittees, and bipartisan caucuses. Unlike the British Parliament, the United States Congress is not constitutionally supreme: it may not invade certain specified (and other implied and inferred) rights of American citizens. These limitations are significant constraints on Congress's capacity to act, and hence upon majoritarianism; the United States remains a polity founded on the defence of individual rights from encroachment by government. Permeated by its members' political calculations, and cross-cut by ideological, regional, racial, and ethnic interests, its powers are limited by the principles of separation of powers and Federalism in the Constitution, by other constitutional rights (particularly by the Bill of Rights and the Fourteenth Amendment; see Appendix 2) and by the Constitution's guardians, the Federal Courts.

Congress has six dimensions, the first five of which are structural, and the sixth procedural:

- The *bicameral dimension*, as a divided legislature of two contrasting, autonomous, and competitive chambers.
- The *institutional dimension*, as the Federal legislature separated from the other two branches of government.
- The *individual dimension*, of 535 legislators with their own agendas and the capacities to pursue them.
- The *specialised and fissiparous dimension* of committees, characterised by a division of labour in respect of the "marking up" (drafting) of legislation and the oversight of the executive and judicial branches.
- The *aggregative and collective dimension* of party, whereby the fissiparous tendencies of Congress are partly overcome.
- The *procedural dimension* of legislation, and scrutiny of the executive (the accepted American term is "oversight"), in which the first five dimensions are all, to varying extents, apparent.

135

Subject to biennial primary elections typically lying beyond parties' organizational influence, Members of Congress are highly sensitive to their districts' politics. Such sensitivity is apparent in their voting on bills and amendments to them, in their speeches, in their relations with their constituents, in their interventions in Committee and Subcommittee hearings, and in the choices they make about the Committees and Subcommittees to which they wish to belong. None the less, this fragmented grounding of Congressional behaviour in the politics of 435 Districts does not preclude Representatives from taking broader views of government's purposes. Still less does it so preclude Senators, the demographic and political heterogeneity of whose States affords most of them political latitude denied to members of the House. Both chambers have developed means whereby the fragmentary character of the institution as a whole is contained and productively channelled into legislation which is more than the sum of its many parts.

The Bicameral Dimension

The Federal legislature is not an undifferentiated whole. The bicameral order is reflected in the physical division between the two chambers and the large supporting complexes of offices, Committee rooms, restaurants, and gymnasia. Bicameral roots support a legislature divided by culture, constituency, prerogatives, rules, size, tenure, and organization. In the organization of parties within Congress, in their procedural and organizational rules, the two chambers are separate and self-governing bodies. Neither chamber dominates the other: whilst the types of power granted to each chamber by the Constitution are not identical, their extent is comparable. Each forms a key part in the constitutional order and in the processes of government; each has interests of its own as well as those which it shares with the other. Neither is a "dignified" part of the United States Constitution, as the House of Lords usually is of the British (although discussion of the role of the Senate at the Constitutional Convention alluded to the possibility that the Senate might, like the Lords, act to "cool the passions" of the popularly-elected House of Representatives). Both chambers are much more central to policy processes in the United States than is the House of Commons to them in Britain, primarily because both have autonomy from the executive.

Bicameralism complicates the legislative process. In their constituency bases, members' terms of service, size of chamber, rules, organization, and nature of party organization, the Senate and the House differ. Not only do individual members of each chamber differ from their colleagues within the same chamber and from those in the other, so the two chambers often have different interests as collectivities. With 435 Representatives directed much more towards the production of legislation than are the 100 Senators, the House remains the more formally and hierarchically organized of the two; the division of labour is also more pronounced. Members of the House spend much of their working time examining in detail legislation before the standing Committee or Committees of which they are members.

Bicameralism reflects the framers' determination to weaken the legislature, and so reduce the probability of its dominating the Federal executive. It also reflects the compromise between the political interests of populous and less-populated States during the Constitutional Convention in 1787 (when several States already had bicameral legislatures of their own). By the "Connecticut Compromise", delegates to the Convention eventually agreed that membership of the House should be distributed between States by population, and that of the Senate divided equally among the States irrespective of area or population. The number of Representatives is now fixed at 435; the least populous States have just one Representative each, and the most populous (California) has fifty-two. The number of Senators rises by two with the admission of a new State to the Union: following the admission of Alaska in January 1959, and of Hawaii in August of the same year, the size of the upper chamber therefore increased from 96 to 98, and then to 100.

The Constitution makes no distinction in the general extent of powers granted to the two chambers, and competition between them is often sharp. The Constitution does, however, grant the Chambers powers of slightly different kinds: the House considers tax legislation first, while the Senate has the responsibility for advising and consenting on nominations to the executive and judiciary, and for the ratification of international treaties. The implication is that the House (and particularly its Ways and Means Committee) has primacy in national fiscal policy, and that the Senate (particularly its Foreign Relations Committee) has primacy in foreign policy (although qualified by the overall leadership of the President in foreign affairs). Responsibility for confirmation and ratification enhances the Senate's role in oversight of the executive and the judiciary.

Formal equality of the two chambers notwithstanding, membership of the Senate carries greater prestige than membership of the House. Members of both chambers subscribe to this view, as is indicated by the many Representatives who leave the House to run for the Senate. By contrast, Senators never voluntarily leave the Senate to run for a seat in the House. Having a much smaller chamber with longer terms, membership of the Senate is regarded by most politicians as the more desirable for its being rarer and less frequently exposed to electoral contests. Except for the Presidency, the Speakership of the House of Representatives and one or two senior party colleagues and committee chairmen, and the Governorships of California, Florida, Illinois, New York, and Texas, only Senators have the potential to establish themselves as national figures.

Senators are collectively jealous of the powers granted to their Chamber by the Constitution, and individually aware that as the House has for many of them formed their stepping-stone to the Senate, so the Senate may be a launch-pad for the Vice-Presidency and Presidency. Presidents Truman,

Kennedy, Nixon, and Johnson were all previously Senators (three had also been Vice-President). At any one time, as many as a dozen Senators may be considered (if only by themselves) as candidates for the Presidency or Vice-Presidency, whether at the next or at some future presidential election. Senators' ambitions for the Presidency help shape their thinking and voting on the Floor and in Committee and Subcommittee, and in their speech-making. Many Senators now see themselves, not as most of their predecessors in the 1950s and 1960s did, as spokespersons for their States, but for the nation. The Senate, which in the 1950s was generally viewed by most Senators as the summit of their political ambitions, is now increasingly viewed as a base for the fulfilment of ambition elsewhere. To this end, Senators use the Senate as a forum in which they can offer a lead on matters of national importance with a view to seeking the nation's highest office.

Circumstances, culture, and condition differ greatly between the two chambers, but each presents difficulties to a President seeking to lead. It is not merely that Congress is separated from the Executive but that this institutional separation of a divided Congress from the Executive presents different incentives for Presidents, Congressmen, and Senators. They have various (but apparently compelling) reasons for having their own perspectives on public policy. The combination of the three electoral bases of the three institutions, the contrasting internal organization of the two chambers, together with the weakness of party which in part flows from separation, makes the aggregation of interest within Congress politically difficult, since Congress is both a legislative and representative body. The care and attention that Members of Congress devote to representing constituents makes legislating difficult in a cause greater than the sum of Congress's individual parts. On many issues, Members of Congress and Senators often have little interest in seeking rational solutions to national problems. The first concern of Congressional politicians in particular lies with serving their own political needs: those of their party, House, President, and their country are of less moment.

Bicameralism results in two separately-constituted, separately-elected, legislative bodies, responding in different ways to different constituencies, circumstances, and political pressures. Opportunities for delay and obfuscation in such a body are many. Tenacity, invention, and bargaining are therefore necessary qualities for successful legislators in the United States Congress, and for Presidents who attempt to give legislative leadership by identifying a national agenda and pressing Congress to adopt it as their own.

The Institutional Dimension

Congress is also a single institution: as the Federal legislature, it has collective institutional interests of its own, binding House and Senate together against the Executive. This expression can and does bridge partisan division: Congress expressed a collective will against the Executive with respect to the control both of fiscal and of foreign policy during President Nixon's second term. The Watergate affair's importance lay in the Executive's abuse of power and the unconstitutional infringement by the Executive of powers held by Congress, rather than in party political struggle. The Constitution's provision for the impeachment of Executive officers and members of the Federal judiciary illustrates both the separation and the unification of Congress. The articles of impeachment against President Nixon were voted by the House Judiciary Committee; had the President not resigned, he would have been tried by the Senate.

Congress and the Executive

Chapter 4 illustrated the importance of staff within the Executive in serving the administrative, electoral, and governing needs of Presidents. The Executive's single greatest asset in its relations with Congress until the Nixon Presidency was its virtual monopoly of expertise, the experience and understanding possessed by some senior Committee Chairmen of policy questions notwithstanding. Of all the legacies to the 1950s and 1960s of the expansion of the Presidency under Franklin Roosevelt and Harry Truman, this was one of the most significant. When Members of Congress sought technical information or guidance on a particular topic, they approached executive agencies. The relationship was partly one of reliance borne of an underlying trust, but it also illustrated asymmetries of information and expertise intrinsic to the relationship between Congress and the Executive, which became less acceptable to many legislators as both the scope of Federal regulation at home and the peacetime interests of the United States abroad grew. It had special political significance in foreign affairs and defence policy, where the Executive's monopoly of information was supplemented by Congress's disinclination to probe too deeply for fear of encroaching on Presidential prerogatives. Yet at hearings held by the Joint Committee on the Organization of Congress which drafted the Legislative Reorganization Act of 1946, many witnesses testified to the deplorable inadequacy of Congressional staff resources, and of Congress's consequent dependence upon hastily-gathered information from the Executive Branch, journalists, and lobbyists. For Congress, one of three co-equal branches of government, to be collectively and individually dependent upon external sources of data risks both its independence and its standing. The 1946 Act accordingly provided for increases in the number of staff provided to members and to Committees as a counter to the Executive's resources, themselves so massively enhanced by adaptation to the demands of the New Deal and the Second World War.

Vietnam and Watergate, together with the politicization of the Budget Bureau, induced Congress to attempt afresh to end its dependence upon the

Executive for policy information and analysis. Congressional trust in the Executive was undermined by President Johnson's conduct of the Vietnam War, and by pervasive corruption under Nixon. The "neutral competence" of the Bureau of the Budget, which derived from its being heavily staffed by civil servants was rapidly weakening by the late 1960s as the Bureau became more thoroughly politicized. Congress was accordingly less inclined to trust its budgetary proposals. Unable to rely upon the expertise of Executive Branch agencies, Congress recruited its own numerous professional staff to work for individual members, committees, and for the Legislature as a whole (see Chapter 4).

Increased provision for staff since the Johnson and Nixon Presidencies has strengthened Congress as a single institution. The United States Congress is now a competing source of expertise in the formation, legislation, and evaluation of public policy. The participation of the United States Congress in legislation and oversight is powerfully shaped by professional staff. They supply data, expertise, analysis, advice, and speeches, draft questions to Executive officials and others giving testimony before Committees, and provide answers to constituents and journalists. Without them, Congress could not have experienced the institutional "resurgence" that James Sundquist (1981) identified and which has so greatly complicated and altered the politics of Presidential–Congressional relations (and hence the making of public policy) since the mid-1970s. Asymmetries between the two branches remain, none the less. Congress delegates powers to the Executive to implement particular public policies precisely because of the Executive branch's huge bureaucratic assets: the familiar principal–agent problem is intrinsic to any legislature so empowering an Executive. Where, as in the case of the Federal government, that executive is also formally separated from the legislature, iterated conflict between them about the extent of Executive autonomy is certain. Under Speaker Gingrich's leadership, the radical 104th Congress cut staff budgets and numbers, thereby increasing the Executive's informational advantages over Congress. Gingrich's reform may appear perverse in its effects, but he intended his policy to increase his own control over his party colleagues. In the short run, it did so; by the end of the 104th Congress, many of his colleagues had asserted their autonomy from him and his agenda.

Congress as a Bureaucracy

Congress is therefore not a simple legislature composed of 535 elected members sitting in two chambers. It is also a large bureaucracy sited in more than twenty buildings. In addition to elected Representatives and Senators, there are more than 26,000 unelected staff. The 1997 budget for the entire legislative branch amounted to some $2.2 billion.

The professional staff comprise four broad categories:

- *Congressional research* and *support agency* staff.
- *Committee* and *Subcommittee* staff.
- *Leadership* staff.
- *Personal* staff.

The roles of Committee, Subcommittee and Leadership staff are discussed in the sections dealing with Committees and parties. The subject of Congressional research/support agency staffing is illustrated in Exhibit 5.1 in its institutional dimension supporting Congress as a whole: the Library of Congress with its specialist subdivision, the Congressional Research Service; the General Accounting Office; and the Congressional Budget Office. (The Office of Technology Assessment, a research agency, was abolished in September 1995 as part of the new Republican majority's campaign against what was presented as wasted public resources.) These three major Congressional agencies are the collective expression of Congress's determination to defend its place in the constitutional order against the Executive. All serve both the House and the Senate, and all assist Congress in its oversight of the Executive as well as in legislation and representation. The first two existed long before the eruption of Executive–Legislative conflict in the latter phase of the Johnson administration and throughout Nixon's, but grew in size and importance because of it. The third and fourth were created in response to that conflict.

The Individual Dimension

The points of cohesion within Congress are few, those of incohesion many; pressures within Congress are more centrifugal than centripetal. The passage of legislation that serves the public interest rather than the interests of individuals or groups is, accordingly, difficult. There are in Congress, as in European legislatures, complex relationships between the structures of government and the processes of politics and policy formation: the constitutional order provides incentives to certain types of political behaviour and disincentives to others, as the authors of the Constitution appreciated. *The Federalist Papers* provide a clear statement of the political behaviour expected of Representatives, subjected to popular biennial elections, drawing their political strength from constituencies that were in most cases small and reasonably homogeneous. (Although still relatively homogeneous, they are now very large by European standards.) The authors contend that these circumstances would cause members of the House of Representatives to be highly sensitive to popular opinion. Madison, when arguing in *Federalist*

EXHIBIT 5.1

Congressional Research/Support Agency Staffing

(1) **The Congressional Research Service** (CRS) of the Library of Congress. Its much smaller predecessor, the Legislative Reference Service, was founded in 1914. The CRS provides a policy analysis and information service for Congressional Committees and for individual Congressmen and Senators. Located within the Library of Congress (which has a larger public role) the CRS has a wide remit, preparing briefs and more detailed analyses across the entire range of American public policy. Its professional staff in 1993 numbered 814.

(2) **The General Accounting Office** (GAO) was established in 1921 by the Budget and Accounting Act which provided for sweeping reforms of the Federal Budget. Its 5,000 staff, comprising accountants, auditors, economists and (inevitably) lawyers, assess the efficiency and value of programmes administered by Federal government departments and funded by Congress.

(3) **The Congressional Budget Office** (CBO) was established by the 1974 Budget and Impoundment Control Act. The CBO, comprising more than 200 professional staff, is Congress's main source of expertise on public finance and hence, because of the centrality of the Budget to Congressional politics, the Congressional agency most in the public eye. Its place in the Congressional budget process is considered more fully in Chapter 11.

No. 62 for the necessity of a second chamber, the Senate, insisted that the House of Representatives would be liable to:

> yield to the impulse of sudden and violent passions, and to be seduced by factious leaders into intemperate and pernicious resolutions.

This view had force in the early years of the Republic, but (notwithstanding the febrile atmosphere of the first few weeks of the 104th Congress in 1995), has little in the late 1990s. Far from being prey to factious leaders, its members typically prove difficult to galvanize, their 535 individual interests resistant to aggregation. Innovative departures from incremental additions to policies, whether in economics, welfare, or defence, are difficult for Congressional leaders to secure (as the experience of the 104th Congress indicates). Sensitivity to public opinion, however, is palpable: Members of Congress spend much time, money, and effort in attending to constituents' complaints about their treatment by Federal agencies. Such complaints are usually prosaic, personal, and non-political, but Members' staff ensure that (where expedient) their successful handling receives favourable publicity in Members' Districts, as reports on local television stations across the country illustrate.

Local pressures weigh massively with politicians seeking re-election. Whereas, in the early nineteenth century, Congress was characterized by high membership turnover, it has not been since 1945. Unlike in Britain, where Members of Parliament are elected or defeated almost entirely because of their party affiliation, Congresswomen and men are heavily dependent for their re-election upon their advertised capacity to represent their constituents' interests. For the most part, they are (or become) skilled at doing so, as Chapter 3 showed. The proportion of incumbent members of the House seeking re-election actually re-elected has long been high. Until the 1992 election, the proportion of incumbents winning by substantial margins was not only high but rising to levels of more than 85 per cent; the 1992 elections, however, saw the measure slip back to approximately two-thirds.

As Madison expected, Members of the House of Representatives are highly responsive to their constituents' expressed needs and wishes. However, for Presidents seeking to make their role as legislative leaders effective, the House is a body whose structure and rules appear to foster recalcitrant behaviour. Since Presidents, unlike House Members, attempt to govern under a constitutional prohibition from serving more than eight years in office, the virtual absence of electoral threat to the incumbency of House members is frustrating. Circumstances in the Senate are different, and the incentives to which electoral politics give rise are less clear-cut. Senators run for election every six years, not every two. Many are therefore less sensitive to the electoral consequences of their political behaviour between polls. Senate elections usually attract more able, and better-financed, challengers to incumbents than do elections in the House. Whereas House Congressional District boundaries are redrawn (and often gerrymandered) every decade, State boundaries cannot be adjusted. Most elections are, accordingly, more competitive, with the result that the proportion of Senate incumbents winning re-election is above 90 per cent almost as rarely as that of House incumbents is below it.

Membership Resources

Since the Second World War, the personal staffs of Representatives and Senators have grown by between five and six times. Such staff buttress incumbents against challenges; accordingly, Congressional politicians fiercely defend the arrangement. Even zealous Congressional Republican followers of Speaker Gingrich early in 1995, while agreeing to reductions in committee staff, resisted cuts in their own. In 1995, some 7,500 staff worked for individual Representatives, and a further 4,200 for individual Senators. Each Representative's staff hiring allowance is nearly $600,000; this amount is supplemented by a consolidated allowance of between $152,000 and $350,000 each, the precise amount varying with transport costs to the Home District and the cost of local office rents.

Senators' personal staff allowances are larger than those for Representatives. Staff hiring budgets vary (but not proportionately) with State population between $1.8 million and more than $2.5 million. There are further substantial allowances for office equipment and furniture expenses, and for the renting of between 4,800 and 8,000 square feet of office space in the home State. Senators from the largest States who also chair a major Committee have as many as 70 staff.

There are two organizational points of special importance here:

- Whereas committee staff are concerned with the legislative and oversight work of the committee, personal staff attend solely to the fortunes of the single politician for whom they work.
- Personal staff are not confined to Washington. Particularly in large Senate offices, many staff are employed not in one of the large Congressional office buildings on Capitol Hill but at home in offices spread throughout the State or District. It is there, and not in Washington, that much constituency service work is done.

Constituency service work in fact requires several offices across States and Districts. Some Senators in large and populous States maintain five or more separate offices; and many Congressmen keep three or more District offices in addition to their main office in Washington. In State and District offices, most work is concerned with social security, Medicare, veterans' benefits, and tax problems. An indication of the importance attached to such activity is that in 1995, nearly half of Representatives' personal staff were based in offices within the Congressional District. The comparable proportion of Senate personal staff was a third. David Price (1989, pp. 437–8) characterizes the work of Congressional offices in general as operating an appeals process for bureaucratic decisions functionally similar to that of ombudsmen in Britain, Sweden, and Norway. It also resembles that of members of the French National Assembly.

Most staff based in Washington deal with legislative and political matters of concern to their Representative or Senator. Organization of staff within Congressional offices varies with different politicians' differing needs, but all have a senior political adviser, and an Administrative Assistant charged with the smooth and effective operation of the office. The resulting undertaking is considerable: the concentration of highly motivated, ambitious, young people (most are under the age of thirty-five) in an entrepreneurial politician's office makes for a competitive and often fraught environment. Struggles for space, status, advancement, and influence result. Many staff have political ambitions of their own and quickly discover that there are few political rewards for the self-effacing.

Committee and Subcommittee chairs, and ranking members of Committees and Subcommittees, enjoy the support of specialist Committee staff. (Since rules changes instigated by Gingrich and his Republican leadership colleagues in January 1995, the employment of staff has, however, formally become the exclusive responsibility of *full* committee chairmen.) Other members of committees are not provided with committee staff and must rely upon one or more of their personal staff to support their committee work. All Senators and Representatives employ Legislative Assistants in this role, writing speeches, preparing and giving briefings on committee business. Other personal staff liaise with the media, seeking to feed stories to the press and television, often by means of sending videotapes, professionally-produced in studios on Capitol Hill, of their principal's views on the subjects of the week, arranging for media coverage of events organized during the member's visits to the District or State, and organizing press conferences. For all but the dozen or so Congressional politicians of national standing, this work is primarily with the newspapers and television stations in the home District or State. Most Congressional politicians, lacking any prospect of gaining regular national media attention, therefore focus not on Washington, but upon viewers and readers back home.

The Specialized and Fissiparous Dimension

Committee/Subcommittee Structure

Both the House and the Senate organize their legislative and oversight activity around a complicated structure of Committees and Subcommittees. Committees are of four kinds:

- *Conference Committees*, as the procedural aspect of bicameralism, are convened *ad hoc* enabling the Senators and Representatives selected to serve on them to agree a common version of a Bill previously passed by the two chambers in different forms.
- *Standing Committees and Subcommittees* lie at Congress's heart. Their members consider and examine legislative proposals, whether from the White House or from within Congress. Members of both House and Senate Committees also oversee the work of Executive agencies, examining the extent to which departments and agencies (all of which are authorized and funded by Congress, and none of which can exist without Congressional approval) execute the law in the manner Congress intended.
- *Select or Special Committees* are established for special oversight purposes or to examine particular problems. Some are permanent; others have a limited life. Examples include the Senate's Select Committees on Aging; Ethics; Intelligence; Indian Affairs; and the House's Select Committee on Intelligence. The best-known (and that with the greatest political impact) was the Senate Select Committee on the Watergate affair, chaired by Senator Sam Ervin.

- *Joint Committees of Congress*, of which there are four. Two, the Joint Economic Committee and the Joint Committee on Taxation, deal with matters of economic policy in general and fiscal policy in particular. The other two, the Joint Committee on the Library and the Joint Committee on Printing, are politically unimportant.

Importance of Committees

Committees are central not just to Congress as an institution, but also to the processes of American government. They are organizational centres of legislation, of oversight, and of representation. Different committees engage in these three activities in different proportions at different times. Standing committees engage in all three types of work: they are centres of power and expertise, strengthened by the functional division of labour between them. Members of committees and their substantial staffs are therefore specialists, especially in the House, where the principle of the division of labour is more pronounced.

Congress does most of its work in committees and subcommittees. It is here that hearings on Authorizing and Appropriations Bills take place, with testimony given by witnesses from the Executive Branch, members of groups with an interest in the proposed legislation, and disinterested experts. It is here, too, that Representatives and Senators produce a draft of the legislation during the "mark-up" (drafting) sessions of the committee before reporting the Bill to the Floor of the chamber.

To an even greater extent than with legislation, Standing and Select Committees and Subcommittees are the primary foci for scrutinising the implementation of policy by executive departments, agencies, bureaux, and regulatory commissions. Oversight is necessarily specialized, and one in which Subcommittees, with their smaller jurisdictions, are better placed to work than the full Chambers: as Chapter 8 shows, cyclic re-authorization and appropriations legislation provide scheduled opportunities for such scrutiny and influence. Even in legislation and oversight, however, members of Committees never lose sight of the importance of representing their constituents' interests.

This use of committees shows that Congress does not provide for a simple translation of majority preferences into policy. Building coalitions in Congress for political change is difficult unless its benefits are widely distributed among those voting on the measure – unless, in other words, there is something in it for those whose support is sought. Distributive politics has long been an attractive game to play in Congress: a Federal initiative to tighten pollution controls is more likely to win support if it results in the widespread distribution of grants. As the Committee structure facilitates distributive politics so it may inhibit political reform: Congress's multiple institutional points of access may serve as points of veto.

Senate and House Committees: Similarities

Senate Committees now differ from House Committees in some respects, but are similar in others. They share the following features:

- Chairs are always in the hands of the *majority party.*
- The most senior member of the *minority party* on each committee has the title "ranking member".
- Political power in both chambers is *unevenly distributed* among committees and subcommittees.

The heavy fiscal deficits incurred in the 1980s, and the associated effective abandonment of the progressive liberal purpose that informed the Roosevelt, Truman, and Johnson Presidencies, weakened all authorizing committees except Senate Armed Services (which itself manages shrinking rather than expanding budgets), and elevated the importance of Appropriations, Finance (Ways and Means in the House), and Budget. Committees with an explicitly regulatory purpose, such as the House Commerce Committee, which has jurisdiction over electricity, nuclear, telecommunications, and finance, also became foci of special political attention and governing importance.

Senate and House Committees: Differences

They differ in the following respects:

- The *remit* of Standing Committees in the Senate is broader than that in the House. For example, the Senate Committee on Commerce, Science, and Transportation, covers the following policy areas: aviation; consumer affairs; international trade; tourism; manufacturing and competitiveness; telecommunications; merchant shipping; road and rail transport; commercial fishing; science; technology; and space. The House assigns this large cluster of loosely-related fields to four committees.
- There are *fewer subcommittees* in the Senate than in the House.
- Since the Senate is less than a quarter the size of the House, Senators belong to *more committees* than their House counterparts and so are able to serve *more objectives* by their Committee assignments than are Representatives.
- Most Senators are *generalists,* whereas almost all majority of Representatives apart from the party leaders are *specialists.*
- Each Senate Committee and Subcommittee has *fewer members* than do panels in the House. The largest Senate Committee, Appropriations, has only twenty-eight members; the largest House Committee in the 105th Congress, Transportation and Infrastructure, has seventy-three members (many of them attracted by prospect of channelling capital project funds to their own Districts).

- Senate Committees are in most cases significantly *less important to the careers* of Senators than House Committees are to the careers of Members of Congress.
- The *ratio of majority* to *minority parties* on Senate Committees is determined differently in the Senate from the House. Whereas House majorities are expanded in party ratios on committees in order to increase party control, Senate ratios are set more leniently.

Standing Committees in the House and the Senate

There are nineteen Standing Committees (excluding the Select Committee on Intelligence) in the House, and seventeen (excluding the Select Committees on Intelligence, and on Ethics, and the Special Committee on Ageing) in the Senate. Most are further divided into subcommittees. In both chambers, Standing Committees are one of two kinds: authorizing, or appropriating. The former create new programmes and modify existing ones, while the latter provide finance for them. Committee jurisdictions cover the entire range of public policy, and there is substantial overlap between the jurisdictions of different committees. The correspondence between the committee structures of the House and the Senate is none the less incomplete, since each chamber is responsible for the organization of its committees, as it is for its rules. The House of Representatives' rules require that every standing committee with twenty or more members must have at least four subcommittees. This rule was adopted in 1975, partly in order to ensure that the power and influence of Committee chairmen was kept under tighter control than in the sixty years following the ending in 1910 of Speaker Cannon's domination of the House. The importance of subcommittees in the House also reflects the growth of Federal regulation and programmes, and the consequent need that Congress has to oversee them. Powerful individual incentives also apply: the preoccupation of Representatives with re-election, and their ambitions for power within the House or for higher office elsewhere mean that Subcommittees provide a convenient stage for political entrepreneurship, for demonstrating their political sagacity to existing or potential constituents. The change towards "subcommittee government" after the 1970s reforms advanced furthest in the House: there, most Bills receive at least their first mark-up in subcommittee (in contrast to circumstances in the Senate, where most marking-up of Bills and hearings on them occurs in full committee).

The distinction between *authorizing* and *appropriating* Committees is fundamental (see Exhibit 5.2). Authorizing Committees consider proposals for new agencies or programmes, or for the reauthorization of existing ones. If committees approve them, they attach limits to the public money that may be spent on them. Appropriations Committees (one in each chamber, each with functionally-divided subcommittees) finance government programmes by appropriating public money to them. Except for those programmes where entitlements to benefits are included in the Bill authorizing the programme, an Act of Congress enjoys no funding, and hence is null and void, without appropriations being voted by the Appropriations Subcommittees and Committees of both chambers. Appropriations Committees derive their considerable power from controlling government finance. With the addition of the Budget Committees in both chambers under the Budget and Impoundment Control Act of 1974, which have the remit of setting overall budget targets and obliging other Committees to meet them (explained in detail in Chapter 11), this categorization is inadequate. In addition to considering all Standing Committees as being either authorizing or appropriating, we may identify a third category of committee (though these are not separately recognized in Congressional rules or procedures): Control Committees. These control money, legislation, and the ethical behaviour of Members of Congress; all are forms of Standing Committee.

Authorizing and Control Committees differ between the House and Senate, and within each Chamber. Some are important, some less so. Some are prestigious, others are not. The importance of some has increased over time, while that of others has diminished. Some Committees therefore offer attractions to all members within each Chamber because of their importance and prestige, while others are important to members with certain constituency or policy interests, and irrelevant to those without them. Some are long-lived; others are recent creations formed to address new problems. Some committees have retained old jurisdictions; others have seen their jurisdiction altered. Few generalizations can be made about Congressional Committees: House Committees of all kinds, but especially Subcommittees, are usually more important than Committees and Subcommittees in the Senate. They are more important in the procedures of the House, for the policy questions with which it deals, and for the careers of its members.

Within the Control category, four Committees have particular significance: Senate Finance and House Ways and Means (which write tax legislation); and the Budget Committees in each chamber. Tax and spending policy is the heart of Congress's work; those committees concerned with the politics of revenue-raising and spending have always exploited their functional importance to their political advantage. A programme initiated by the Executive Branch to build and deploy a new class of strategic nuclear weapons such as the MX Missile, or the B2 bomber, requires the passage through Congress of authorizing legislation to permit the programme to go ahead, and appropriating legislation to finance it. Before dealing with it on the Floor of the House or Senate, the House National Security Committee and the Senate Armed Services Committee must consider whether to authorize the programme. If the Authorizing Committees in both chambers do so, they will each determine not only its size and character, but also a financial ceiling: a specified number of B2 bombers with a ceiling on the total price. If the Committee's version of the legislation is granted a Rule

EXHIBIT 5.2

House and Senate Standing Committees

HOUSE

Authorizing

Agriculture	Government Reform	Science
Banking and Financial	and Oversight	Select Intelligence
Services	International Relations	Small Business
Commerce	Judiciary	Transportation and
Education and the	National Security	Infrastructure
Workforce	Resources	Veterans' Affairs
		Ways and Means

Appropriations
Appropriations

Control

Appropriations	House Oversight	Standards of Official
Budget	Rules	Conduct
		Ways and Means

SENATE

Authorizing

Agriculture, Nutrition	Energy and Natural	Indian Affairs
and Forestry	Resources	Judiciary
Armed Services	Environment and Public	Labor and Human
Banking, Housing and	Works	Resources
Urban Affairs	Finance	Rules and
Commerce, Science and	Foreign Relations	Administration
Transportation	Governmental Affairs	Small Business
		Veterans' Affairs

Appropriations
Appropriations

Control
Budget
Finance
Rules and Administration

(specifying the conditions for its consideration in on the House Floor) by the eponymous House Committee, is subsequently passed by the House and Senate, and then passed again, this time in identical form by both House and Senate after differences between the two Chambers have been eliminated in a Conference Committee of the two Chambers, it may be sent to the President for signature or veto. But even if it is signed, the programme will still need to be financed by the wholly separate (and similarly complicated) action of Appropriations Committees in both chambers.

Both Appropriations Committees (which because of their financial control function may also be regarded as Control Committees) are powerful because they allocate approximately a third of Federal expenditure. Each is similarly organized around groups of semi-autonomous Subcommittees responsible for groups of Executive departments, agencies, bureaux, and regulatory commissions. The full Committees, invariably deferring to the Subcommittees, may appropriate funds for programmes to the ceilings determined by the Authorizing Committees and approved by both Chambers, but not beyond them. They are not obliged to appropriate funds at the authorized ceilings, at the levels requested by the President in his budget message. Indeed, they are not obliged to make any appropriations available at all. A decision by the House Armed Services Committee to authorize the construction and deployment of x number of missiles at a total cost of $y may be modified by a subsequent decision of the House Appropriations Committee's Subcommittee on the Armed Services (subject to confirmation by the full House Appropriations Committee) to provide funding of $0.8y – or even (which is unusual but not unknown) by its refusal to appropriate any funds for the project.

In practice, the spectrum of politically plausible choices is smaller than that which is theoretically possible. Nevertheless, the width of the theoretical choices shows how great are Congress's powers, especially in comparison with the limp financial control exerted by most West European legislatures. The power of the Appropriations Committees to cut spending has frequently been a source of tension with the committees that authorize defence spending – the Senate Armed Services Committee and the House National Security Committee. Congress as a whole acts entirely autonomously in determining public spending, subject only to the threat or fact of a Presidential veto. Authorizing Committees determined to set spending levels for a programme above the President's request face no constitutional obstacle – only the political one of judging whether such determination can be sustained on the Floor, in the Conference Committee, and in the Oval Office.

Tax-writing committees enjoy jurisdiction over spending programmes for all the major entitlement programmes: Medicare (assistance for the elderly with their hospital costs), unemployment compensation; social security, welfare; and, in Finance's case, for Medicaid (a joint Federal–State programme to assist the poor with their medical costs). All lie beyond the control of Appropriations Committees, since payments are made under them as of right according to criteria specified in the authorizing legislation. Both also have the responsibility of considering legislation to raise the debt limit, which must pass if the Federal government is to continue to function. (It became politically more significant during the 1980s as total government debt grew rapidly.) These responsibilities are in addition to their primary shared function of writing tax law. The general decline in Committee Chairmen's power since Congressional reform in the early 1970s notwithstanding, the Chairmen between 1987 and 1992, Congressman Dan Rosten-kowski, and Senator Lloyd Bentsen, were among the most powerful figures in Federal budgetary politics.

All three categories of committees and their associated subcommittees may hold hearings on subjects within their jurisdictions in order to oversee the implementation of policy by departments and agencies for which they have responsibility. All may also consider legislative proposals referred to them. Hence the House National Security Committee and Senate Armed Services Committee may hold hearings on requests by the Administration for changes in the force structure of the US Army, for a new class of aircraft carriers for the US Navy, or on topical questions of its members' choosing related to the performance of particular weapons systems, on the wisdom of the President's naval policy, on the quality of advice made by the Joint Chiefs of Staff to the President, or on the lessons to be learned from a military engagement such as the deployment of the US Marines to Lebanon, or the invasion of Grenada.

House Committees

Congressmen are assigned to Committees by their parties' Steering Commit-tees. For Representatives, whose policy interests, unlike those of Senators, are usually dominated by those which fall within their committees' jurisdic-tions, these decisions shape their careers. Changes to House Rules passed at the beginning of the 104th Congress provide that members may serve on no more than two full committees and four subcommittees; chairmen and ranking members (the most senior minority party member on a committee) may, however, serve on all subcommittees *ex officio*. A further change for the 104th Congress caused three full committees to be abolished – the first occasion since the Democrats had retaken control of the House forty years earlier that the number of House Committees had been cut.

Richard Fenno (1973) has argued that Members of Congress have three main political purposes: re-election; the achievement of power and influence within the House; and the making of good public policy. Committee membership is a means to these ends: a seat on the House Agriculture Committee will serve excellently both re-election and policy interests of a Representative from a rural Congressional District in southern Illinois; it would not only not assist a Representative from Chicago (in the northern part of the same state) but would probably damage her or him politically. Assignments matter also to Congressional Party Leaders and to the Con-gressional Parties more generally: committees' ideological balances, the quality of their membership, and their importance, can be and are modified by recruiting certain colleagues to particular committees, and excluding others. Democrats construct the membership of the Steering Committee to reflect the regional, economic, ideological and ethnic interests within the

Party. When the Democrats have had the majority, the Democratic Speaker has chaired it; now that they do not, the Minority Leader does so. Composition of the Republicans' Committee on Committees reflects the party's heavy southern weighting: of the twenty-six members in July 1997, eleven are from the Deep South. Decisions by these assignment Committees of both parties are formally subject to the approval of the full caucus meeting at the beginning of every Congress and then to the approval of the full House; informally, such decisions were, at the beginning of the 104th Congress, heavily influenced by Gingrich at the height of his political power. The single most important reform adopted by Republicans following the 1994 elections was to give Gingrich effective control of a quarter of the votes on the Committee on Committees: it was a power which he used to extraordinary effect.

Before 1975, Committee chairs were allocated purely by seniority, regardless of capacity, energy, or ideology. This rule encouraged Congressmen to serve what amounted to apprenticeships, because they had no prospect of acquiring power without having done so. Sam Rayburn served in every Congress from 1913 to 1961 and waited eighteen years before becoming chairman of the Interstate and Commerce Committee (an especially important Committee during the 1930s, when much of Roosevelt's New Deal legislation was sent to it); later he served as Speaker of the House on three separate occasions, from 1940–47, 1949–53, and 1955–61. He had pithy advice for new members of the House with high hopes of gaining power: "If you want to get along, go along". Power in committees came to those who obeyed House norms, and survived. Distribution of power within the House was by age; the chamber accordingly became a gerontocracy and, because southern State Legislatures avoided redistricting in order to maintain the over-representation of rural bases of political power, a gerontocracy dominated by southern rural conservatives. The seniority rule applied to both Democrats and Republicans; party leaders had to take it into account. John McCormack, Speaker of the House during the 1960s, advised freshmen: "Whenever you pass a committee chairman in the House, you bow from the waist. I do".

Those who sought to reform Congress in the 1970s were in general antipathetic to the seniority rule, but they had other interests: liberals sought the weakening of the institutional power bases of conservatives; freshmen of all stripes sought power more quickly than the old rules permitted; and Republicans of conservative and moderate persuasions were keen to weaken Democratic power bases irrespective of the ideologies of chairmen. For all three groups, the motives were entirely political, and opportunities were seized in the turbulent circumstances following Richard Nixon's enforced resignation and the last agonizing months of the Vietnam War. The reforms of 1973 and 1975 had four main consequences for committees and their chairpersons:

1. The abolition of the convention that Committee chairs (most of them conservatives) should be assigned automatically on the basis of *seniority* (a convention that had been but rarely broken before) and its replacement by the rule that it be made subject to the vote of the *caucus* (which conservatives did not dominate).

2. The devolution of a substantial portion of legislative and oversight work to *subcommittees* from committees. In order to diffuse authority and influence, House rules stipulated that every Standing Committee with twenty or more members must have at least four Subcommittees. (Later changes to House rules in 1995 restricted all committees except Appropriations, Government Reform and Oversight, and Transportation and Infrastructure, to a maximum of five subcommittees, and concentrated staff recruitment and deployment powers in the hands of full committee chairpersons.)

3. The overturning of the rule permitting Members to chair more than one Subcommittee, thereby weakening the power of chairmen further and dispersing power through the middle ranks of the House Democratic Caucus.

4. The expansion of the *Speaker*'s power, especially by greatly increasing his formal and practical powers over the Rules Committee, and of the Democratic Party Caucus.

Implementation of the 1970s reforms led to the House coming more closely to resemble the Senate in so far as the old hierarchical order with committee chairs at its apex was replaced by a flatter distribution of authority. The concentration of power in the Speakership in the early months of 1995 slowed, rather than halted, this long-run development: the broad thrust of House rule changes from 1973 to 1997 has been to decentralize power from committee Chairpersons to committee members.

All institutional rules are politically informed. Though many are unanticipated, all have political consequences, too. By making committee chairpersons subject to confirmation by the party caucus at the beginning of every new Congress, the House majority obliged chairpersons to pay careful attention to their colleagues' views. Furthermore, since the votes of every member of the Democratic caucus count equally, the views of impatient freshmen members of the caucus carry as much weight in the confirmation process as those of the halt, the lame, and the venerable. Speaker Gingrich's reforms of January 1995 were not all of a piece: they weakened the autonomy of Subcommittees and increased the authority of full committee chairpersons. Yet the limit of three terms imposed upon chairpersons limited their medium-term leverage over colleagues. Moreover, as the gathering rebellion against Gingrich in 1996 and 1997 from within his own party showed, the power of individual Republican Congressmen was as marked in those years as that of individual Democrats had been at the beginning of the decade.

The practice whereby the most senior member of a committee *normally* chairs it remains (see Exhibit 5.3). House Committees were in the 1950s, 1960s, and the first half of the 1970s chaired by old white men, most of whom were southerners. After the reforms, little on the surface might appear to have changed: immediately prior to the 1988 elections, seven House committees were chaired by men over the age of 70. As late as 1992, old white men, a smaller proportion of whom are southerners (largely because the South is no longer a one-party region and its Democratic members are now proportionately less important within the Democratic Party), still predominated. The seniority principle enjoys general support because it provides assurance of promotion in parties that are divided internally. Its application sometimes results in members supporting those with whom they have little in common in order that the established mode of succession may be maintained, and their own prospects of a committee chairmanship be enhanced.

Beneath the veil of the seniority principle's continuity, the politics of relations between chairpersons and committees, and of recruitment to the chairs of committees have in any case changed completely since the reforms. The "Subcommittee Bill of Rights" in the 1970s enabled astute Congressmen to influence particular areas of policy while still in their first few terms. To that extent, chairpersons of full committees prudently took careful account of the views, objectives, and capabilities of party leaders and committee colleagues. Where chairpersons failed to take such account and persistently departed from party policy, they imperilled their chairmanships – as the veteran Mississippi conservative Sonny Montgomery discovered when the Democratic caucus came within four votes of depriving him of his chair following the 1992 elections.

Following the Republicans' remarkable triumph in the 1994 mid-term Congressional elections, Gingrich appointed some chairpersons to committees in open defiance of the seniority rule in order to place ideologically congenial colleagues in positions of influence: he promoted two fiscal conservatives, John Kasich and Bob Livingston, to the Chairmanships of the key Budget and Appropriations Committees, respectively. Nevertheless, the seniority rule continues to be more often observed than violated, and few chairpersons are either young or newcomers to the House: immediately after Gingrich and his trusted conservative allies had effected their changes, the average chairman was male, white, 60 years old, and with nine terms of service in the House. It remains to be seen whether another of Gingrich's alterations to House rules, the provision that no member may chair a committee for more than six years, will survive the ambitions of those who would gain from its being amended.

Notwithstanding the six-year limits upon their chairmanships since the 1995 changes to the House's rules, all chairmen retain some powers which resourceful politicians exploit to influence their committees' business and policy jurisdictions. All possess the formal authority to summon meetings of

---

EXHIBIT 5.3

House Committee Chairmen and Ranking Members, January 1997

Committee	Chairman	Ranking Member
Agriculture	Bob Smith (R-OR)	Charles Stenholm (D-TX)
Appropriations	Robert Livingston (R-LA)	David Obey (D-WS)
Banking and Financial Services	Jim Leach (R-IO)	Henry Gonzalez (D-TX)
Budget	John Kasich (R-OH)	John Spratt (D-SC)
Commerce	Thomas Bliley (R-VA)	John Dingell (D-MI)
Education and the Workforce	Bill Goodling (R-PA)	William Clay (D-MO)
Government Reform and Oversight	Dan Burton (R-IN)	Henry Waxman (D-CA)
House Oversight	Bill Thomas (R-CA)	Sam Gejdenson (D-CO)
International Relations	Ben Gilman (R-NY)	Lee Hamilton (D-IN)
Judiciary	Henry Hyde (R-IL)	John Conyers (D-NY)
National Security	Floyd Spence (R-SC)	Ron Dellums (D-CA)
Resources	Don Young (R-AK)	George Miller (D-CA)
Rules	Gerald Solomon (R-NY)	Joe Moakley (D-MA)
Science	James Sensenbrenner (R-WS)	George Brown (D-CA)
Select Intelligence	Porter Goss (R-FL)	Norman Dicks (D-WA)
Small Business	James Talent (R-MO)	John LaFalce (D-NY)
Standards of Official Conduct	James Hansen (R-UT)	Howard Berman (D-CA)
Transportation and Infrastructure	Bud Shuster (R-PA)	James Oberstar (D-MN)
Veterans' Affairs	Bob Stump (R-AZ)	Lane Evans (D-IL)
Ways and Means	Bill Archer (R-TX)	Charles Rangel (D-NY)

---

their committees; to determine its business; to hasten, retard, or halt the progress of the legislation before it; to recruit and dismiss committee (and, since January 1995, subcommittee) staff; to ensure the orderly management of the committee; and to allocate resources among its members. Some politicians are better at exploiting these formal powers than others, but none have the unfettered powers enjoyed by their predecessors in the period between 1910 and 1975.

Senate Committees

Although the Senate is the House's full constitutional equal, it labours under the disadvantage of having to organize its work of legislation and oversight (particularly to scrutinize nominations made by the President to the Federal

Judiciary, and the Executive Branch) with a much smaller membership than in the House. Senators' allocation of their time and the choices which they make about the committees to which they wish to belong reflect their political purposes and calculations. As for Congressmen in the House, the choices which Senators make about Committee membership are not free: if they were, most would choose Appropriations, Finance, and Foreign Relations. Nevertheless, with only a hundred Senators to authorize, appropriate, and oversee government, each Senator sits on more committees than does a Member of the House.

In the 103rd Congress, which met in 1993–4, there were 2,043 meetings of Senate committees and subcommittees, only about half as many as in the mid-1970s, when a Democratic Senate spent much time overseeing Republican Presidents, but about as many as took place in the 1950s. Committees and subcommittees continue to be important as arenas for the Senate at work, and politically significant for Senators themselves. However, the Senate Floor has in recent years acquired greater importance as a centre of decision-making. In the 1950s, committee decisions were invariably ratified by the full Senate; now, committees cannot be certain that their versions of bills will find straightforward confirmation. Senators who are not members of a particular committee have, therefore, the chance of participating in the decision-making on a Bill once it reaches the Floor where access to the debate is more open. (Their counterparts in the House are less fortunate since debate on the House Floor is more tightly controlled under the Rule granted by the Rules Committee.)

Unlike the House, the Senate permits committees to determine how many subcommittees they are to have. Some full committees establish many subcommittees (Commerce, Science, and Transportation has seven, while Appropriations has thirteen); others have few. Seven (Budget; Indian Affairs; Rules and Administration; Select Intelligence; Small Business; and Veterans' Affairs) have none at all. Similarly, the variation among Senators' subcommittee burdens is great – although the average is inevitably higher than in the House. In the 104th Congress (1995–6), the average number of panels per Senator was 10.8; among Representatives, the figure was 4.8. Senators change their committee membership more frequently than do Representatives; the number and jurisdiction of Senate subcommittees often change with them, particularly following a change in party control or chairmanship, either of which may transform the way in which a committee conducts its business. For example, when the Chairmanship of the Judiciary Committee passed from the southern conservative James Eastland to Edward Kennedy in 1979, the new Chairman abolished six subcommittees, and added three new ones in order to facilitate his establishment of a new liberal agenda for the Committee.

Following the House's review and modification of its committee structure and operation in the 1970s, the Senate made changes of its own, albeit with less sweeping consequences. Attempting to make the Senate's committee system more efficient and less burdensome for Senators, the Stevenson Committee recommended a reduction in the number of committees and subcommittees, and that committees be prevented from establishing new subcommittees without the permission of the full Chamber. Other recommendations were that Senators be allowed to serve on no more than two major committees (all Standing Committees except Rules and Administration, and Veterans Affairs), and that no Senator could chair more than three committees, of which only one could be a full committee. Unlike the House, the Senate is not heavily bound by rules: having accepted most of the Stevenson Committee's proposed new rules, the Senate gradually diluted them in the course of the following decade. In practice, most Senators retain wide-ranging committee responsibilities. Discharging them poses difficulties of judgement and organization, not least because of the risk that a Primary or general election opponent might exploit absence or inattention. Yet compression of the Senate's effective working week to three days causes Committee meetings to clash. Senators must therefore choose how to allocate the average of less than two and a half hours in their typical eleven-hour day which one Senate study in 1976 showed they spent in committees. Multiple committee memberships still make raising quora difficult: the few Senators present at most committee meetings usually carry some colleagues' proxy votes, and reliance upon staff is heavy. Chairmanship of full committees takes precedence. The unequal importance of Senate subcommittees mitigates the problem: some scarcely ever meet, and are marginal to legislation, representation, and oversight.

Attempts to alleviate the problem have failed. From 1977, every Senator was permitted to join no more than eleven committees and subcommittees, but by 1984, fifty had been exempted from the rule. It is uncertain whether further rules changes introduced in 1997 limiting the number of subcommittees upon which Senators could sit will endure. To seasoned observers of the United States Senate, the change's extent is startling. In 1997, for example, a Senator of just two years' standing, Fred Thompson (R-TN), took up the chairmanship of a full Committee (Governmental Affairs); such a development would have been unthinkable in earlier years of the twentieth century. In order both to assist his party and to further his own ambitions, Thompson then exploited his bracing institutional advantage position by holding extended hearings into the unedifying means by which President Clinton raised campaign funds in 1996.

An underlying problem is that the breadth of committee responsibilities presents attractive political opportunities to individual Senators, but problems for the Senate's efficient operation. Coupled with "sunshine" laws which require Senate committees to hold most hearings in public, with the result that policy-making is more transparent to lobbyists and the press, the tasks of co-ordinating Senate business, building coalitions, and aggregating interests within and between committees is harder. The Senate is probably a weaker institution in the late 1990s than it was in the 1970s and 1980s, but its members are individually more assertive and more powerful. The Senate is therefore characterized by a marked and continuing dispersion of authority and power, as Trent Lott (R-MS) discovered in his first, and deeply frustrating, year as Majority Leader following Senator Dole's resignation.

An implication of such power dispersal and multiple responsibilities is that Senators depend heavily upon staff to assist them in every aspect of their work. Clashing committee and other obligations may oblige Senators to rely on staff to attend those meetings they themselves cannot: staff invariably outnumber Senators at committee hearings and mark-ups. Many hearings attract only one or two Senators besides the chairperson; in some, the chairperson may be alone with the majority committee staff, the minority committee staff, and the personal staff representatives of Senators detained elsewhere. Nor are staff required merely to attend and report: if they are to manage their time, Senators are bound to trust their staff to exercise vicarious political judgement.

In hearings on the question of competing demands on Senators' time, Senator Dan Quayle reported to his colleagues on the Senate Select Committee to Study the Senate Committee System that on one morning in the summer of 1984, forty-nine Senators had more than one committee or subcommittee meeting they were due to attend, and that eleven had three or more. Ironically, Quayle's hearings also suffered from some Senators' inability to attend because of other committee engagements: of the twelve members on that Committee, nine had scheduling conflicts.

The Aggregative and Collective Dimension

Party in Congress offers the possibility that interests in each chamber might be aggregated, and individual preferences and parochial concerns overcome in pursuit of collective ends. Committees and subcommittees are Congress in its specialist mode and its fissiparous dimension; party is Congress in its aggregative mode and collective dimension. Party provides the core of coalitions around which legislative majorities are built. Less frequently, party provides a means for the expression of opposition to the policies of the President, and the President's party in Congress. The hold of Congressional parties over their members is in most respects weak, yet the political forces binding them together are more powerful than those that would unfasten them. Their continued existence shows how, even in the American system of government, centripetal forces can overcome centrifugal ones if the calculus of political incentive is appropriately configured.

Such a calculus is the product of an interest that all members of each party share, regardless of their ideology, or regional, economic, ethnic, or constituency interest. They need one another's support to attain their individual objectives. A Senator who, after years of service on a committee finds himself about to succeed the current chairperson following her or his retirement, has an overriding interest in his party retaining a Senate majority. His political ambitions will be frustrated if he becomes the minority party's most senior member on the committee: opposition is not a happy condition for serious politicians, since it leaves them deciding what to say rather than what to do. Senators of each party therefore share the objective at each Congressional election of ensuring that their party enjoys majority control. A conservative Republican Senator from Mississippi may have little in common except party label with a moderate Republican colleague from Vermont. Crucially, however, shared partisanship gives each a common interest in the other securing re-election, in so far as that may be required for either of them to gain the chair of a committee which they have spent their careers seeking. Such mutual interest, realised through the mechanism of party, holds together what would otherwise be a rickety agglomeration of interests. The House is more amenable to party leadership: as events in 1995 showed, it can on rare occasions even be characterized by firm party control. For so long a barrier to conservative Republican hopes, the House briefly became, under Speaker Gingrich's leadership in 1995, a vehicle for them: the "Contract with America", the electoral vehicle for Gingrich's assault upon the Democratic majority in November 1994, took legislative form in ten major Floor votes within one hundred days of the 104th Congress convening.

If expressed at all, the public or national interest on behalf of which party leaders in Congress build coalitions of support from among their party colleagues, is that voiced by the President. Partisan links between a President and colleagues on Capitol Hill are usually weak. Unlike a British Prime Minister's power over party colleagues in the House of Commons, links between President and nominal party colleagues in Congress are not strengthened by the powerful inducement of patronage. Partisanship is none the less one of the few instruments of persuasion at his disposal, and one which party leaders in Congress attempt to exploit at his behest. When President Johnson sent numerous legislative proposals on welfare, education and civil rights to Capitol Hill in the mid-1960s, much of the assembly of supporting coalitions for them was undertaken by the Congressional leadership, together with designated Floor leaders, who co-ordinated supporters and potential supporters on the Floor of each chamber, in close liaison with the President and the White House staff. President Reagan acted similarly with Republican colleagues in the House and Senate in respect of his fiscal package in 1981.

Since neither the President nor his Cabinet colleagues may be members of Congress, they must rely upon political allies in Congress for assistance with their legislation. For example, in the case of the 1964 Civil Rights Act, President Johnson directed an intensive lobbying operation, with the assistance of his senior staff, who themselves communicated with the Majority

TABLE 5.1

Party Balances in Congress, 1929–97[1]

Year	Congress	Senate D	R		House D	R	
1929–31	71st	39	56	(1)	167	267	(1)
1931–33	72nd	47	48	(1)	220	214	(1)
1933–35	73rd	60	35	(1)	310	117	(5)
1935–37	74th	69	25	(2)	319	103	(10)
1937–39	75th	76	16	(4)	331	89	(13)
1939–41	76th	69	23	(4)	261	164	(4)
1941–43	77th	66	28	(2)	268	162	(4)
1943–45	78th	58	37	(1)	218	208	(4)
1945–47	79th	56	38	(1)	240	190	(1)
1947–49	80th	45	51		188	245	(1)
1949–51	81st	54	42		263	171	(1)
1951–53	82nd	49	47		234	199	(1)
1953–55	83rd	47	48	(1)	211	221	(1)
1955–57	84th	48	47	(1)	232	203	
1957–59	85th	49	47		233	200	
1959–61	86th	64	34		283	153	
1961–63	87th	64	36		262	175	
1963–65	88th	67	33		258	176	(1)
1965–67	89th	68	32		295	140	
1967–69	90th	64	36		248	187	
1969–71	91st	58	42		243	192	
1971–73	92nd	54	44	(2)	255	180	
1973–75	93rd	56	42	(2)	242	192	
1975–77	94th	61	37	(2)	291	144	
1977–79	95th	61	38	(1)	292	143	
1979–81	96th	58	41	(1)	277	158	
1981–83	97th	46	53	(1)	243	192	
1983–85	98th	46	54		268	167	
1985–87	99th	47	53		253	182	
1987–89	100th	55	45		258	177	
1989–91	101st	55	45		260	175	
1991–93	102nd	56	44		267	167	(1)
1993–95	103rd	57	43		258	175	(1)
1995–97	104th	47	53		203	231	(1)
1997–99	105th	45	55		207	227	(1)

[1] Vacancies excluded; other parties and independents numbered in parentheses.

Leader of the Senate, Mike Mansfield; the Speaker of the House, John McCormack; and Hubert Humphrey, the Floor Leader for the Bill in the Senate. Close collaboration between Presidents and their allies in Congress is a necessary but not a sufficient condition of legislative success for Presidents who give legislative leadership. The further condition to be satisfied is that Congressional leaders are themselves able to elicit support from their colleagues: as Presidents cannot rely upon members of the legislature following their lead, so Congressional leaders cannot rely upon *their* colleagues following *theirs*.

Party leaders have as their first concern the party's collective interests, the clarity of which priority those whom they would lead rarely share. Party leaders in Congress must attempt to maintain coherence and order within their own party, so that when the White House is occupied by a President of their own party he may be supported, and when it is not he may be opposed (see Table 5.1). Congressional party leaders' effectiveness derives from influence, not authority. Leading entails deciding. Most decisions by party leaders on policy matters threaten the interests of at least some colleagues and may provoke open dissent, thereby undermining party harmony. Party leaders therefore have to strike finely-judged balances between defensive caution (which invites frustration) and aggressive entrepreneurship (which risks dissension). Like Presidents, prudent party leaders pay their colleagues courteous and close attention, and assess carefully whose views and intentions they should take into account. Since party leaders will always need the assistance of Congressional colleagues, they are bound to attend to their political needs and ambitions. Party leaders can assist colleagues during campaigns (both by speaking for them and by financial support through their personal PACs), invite them to social gatherings, and ensure that they receive more than their fair share of the credit at times of political success (such as after the passage of a Bill).

Party Organization in the House

The Speakership

House party leadership structure has developed from the Constitution's provision for a Speaker. The Constitution does not, however, specify the manner of the Speaker's election, which is for the House to determine (see Appendix 1). The vote on the Speakership takes place with every Congress. It usually does so on pure party lines: every Democratic Representative votes for the Democratic candidate, and every Republican Representative for the Republican. As in other respects, however, Gingrich's Speakership has seen well-established practices broken: following his admission that he did not seek legal advice on the use of foundations classed by the Internal Revenue Service as tax-exempt, and that he had given inaccurate information to the

House Ethics Committee charged with investigating the case against him, Gingrich faced opposition from within his own party to his election as Speaker in January 1997. The vote took place after Gingrich's allies had exerted intense pressure upon wavering Republicans to toe the party line in an attempt to fend off Democratic attacks. (There was a splendid irony in the House Chaplain's prayer for the day expressing the hope that the House might be steeped in "righteousness like an ever-flowing stream", especially since Gingrich owed his own rise to prominence in 1989 to his devastating attacks upon the ethical standards of then Speaker, Jim Wright.)

Six of Gingrich's colleagues voted "Present" (effectively, a means of abstention); two voted for Jim Leach, Chairman of the Banking Committee; and two (one of whom was Leach) for former members of the House. Apart from the latter two votes serving to remind scholars of the quaint rule that theoretically allows a person other than a Member of Congress to be elected to the Speakership, the extraordinary vote served as a public indication of the grave disquiet to which Gingrich's ethically unattractive behaviour had given rise, even among many of his own colleagues. Those voting "Present" do not count, Gingrich did not vote, and others were either ill or detained; since every Democrat voted for Richard Gephardt, Gingrich therefore achieved the required majority of 216 votes with a margin of only three to spare.

The Speakership developed from the role of presiding officer in the 1st Congress to that of party leader under Henry Clay in the first decade of the nineteenth century. (Clay was elected Speaker while a freshman, an unthinkable event in today's House.) Until 1910, the Speaker sat at the head of the House's power structure. In the Speakership were vested powers of recognition of those who wished to speak on the Floor, the assignment of members to committees, the choosing of committee chairpersons, and the personal chairing of the Rules Committee, whose power it was to determine which items of legislation from committees should proceed to the Floor. The combination of powers resulted in party control of legislative business in the House throughout the nineteenth century, reflecting in part the power exercised by party bosses in urban machines over the selection of candidates for Congress. The last three prerogatives were finally stripped from Speaker Joe Cannon between 1909 and 1911 as a reaction against the excesses of party control (which is to say, *his* control) exemplified during his tenure in office.

The Speaker is the *de facto* leader and spokesman of the majority party in the House; he is a partisan politician, not a neutral chairperson overseeing debate. Because the Democrats have had majorities in the House since 1955 (and for all but four of the twenty-two years before that), the advantage of electing the Speaker irrespective of the party affiliation of the President or of the party balance in the Senate (see Exhibit 5.4) has usually been theirs. Thus even when, as in President Reagan's first six years, both the White House and the Senate have lain in Republican hands, the Democrats' national political fortunes have been bolstered by their supplying the Speaker. When a party lacks a President, the Speaker is the closest it may come to having a national leader: for six of Ronald Reagan's eight years in the White House, Tip O'Neill served as Speaker – in effect, as an unofficial leader of the Democratic opposition. Gingrich played a similar role with great effect for the first year of the 104th Congress.

Until the revolt of newly-elected Representatives in the 94th Congress of 1975–6, legislative power in the House lay with virtually autonomous Committee Chairmen. As part of the spate of Congressional reform in the 1970s, the revitalized party caucus returned to the Speaker effective control of the Rules Committee. The Speaker does not chair it, but chooses the Chairman and nominates other members. While this does not give him a free hand, placing the Committee under his effective control (especially in the short run) has given the Speaker the power to determine which legislation moves from committees to the Floor. As the former Speaker, Jim Wright, has observed, the Rules Committee is the leadership's agent. Setting the agenda is almost as great a political power as the ability to dispose of the items upon it. Combining the Leadership's own abundant scheduling powers with the institutional resource of the Rules Committee is a potent source of political power. As the rapid movement of the legislative components of the "Contract with America" to Floor votes in 1995 showed, the change has strengthened the Speaker's power to manage legislation in the post-reform Congress. That, in turn, has assisted the majority party, and protected committee versions of Bills from amendment in the Committee of the Whole. The Speaker's preferences are rarely opposed by party colleagues, and even less often successfully so; that Gingrich was so often opposed in 1996 and 1997 is a measure of the political damage which he suffered through the Ethics Committee's investigations and findings.

EXHIBIT 5.4

Democratic and Republican House Leadership in the 105th Congress

REPUBLICAN

Speaker	Newt Gingrich (Georgia)
Majority Leader	Dick Armey (Texas)
Majority Whip	Tom DeLay (Texas)
Conference Chairman	John A. Boehner (Ohio)

DEMOCRATIC

Majority Leader	Richard A. Gephardt (Missouri)
Majority Whip	David E. Bonior (Michigan)
Caucus Chairman	Vic Fazio (California)

Making the Speakership's formal powers effective is contingent upon the abilities and purposes of the individual Speaker, the political environment, and the support of the party caucus. Limited scope for expensive domestic policy initiatives since 1981 has restricted subcommittees' freedom to subvert the purposes of the congressional party leaderships, but the Speaker remains dependent upon the support of colleagues for the maintenance of his office's effectiveness. The revolts against the Speaker before the First World War and in 1996/7, and those against Committee barons in the mid-1970s, show that majority sentiment in Congressional parties cannot for long be resisted, especially now that Representatives have the technological means and staff resources to defend their political interests so vigorously.

The Majority Leader and Majority Whip

In support of the Speaker, and immediately below him in seniority within the majority party is the Majority Leader, whose primary task is that of assisting the Speaker in legislative scheduling, bargaining, exhortation, and coalition formation. As Dick Armey showed in the 104th Congress, this is a highly political matter, and not merely a technical or administrative one. Legislation can be scheduled to suit the interests of the House majority, to facilitate liaison with the Senate or to frustrate it, to accommodate or resist a President's wishes, to enhance a Bill's prospects of success, or to weaken them.

The complex and diverse coalitions that comprise the two Congressional Parties in the House require elaborate Whip structures for communication within the party. In addition to the Majority Whip himself, there is a leadership organization comprising a Chief Deputy Whip (who has his own staff), sixteen Deputy Whips, and forty-eight Assistant Whips, covering nearly every State. In all, therefore, more than a quarter of Republicans in the House are Whips, reflecting not only the Party's diversity, but also the paramount need for communication among its disparate elements to the leadership to be extensive and active if intra-party coalitions are to be built and repaired constantly. Former Speaker Jim Wright once observed that the two tasks of House Whips are:

> gathering intelligence, knowing where the votes are . . . Their second function is persuasion, producing the votes.

The first of these tasks is relatively straightforward; the second is problematic. Since Members of Congress are entrepreneurial, individually seeking both re-election and political power, the task of aggregation is exceptionally difficult (as the crumbling of Republican Party cohesion in 1982–6, and 1996–7 showed). In neither Congressional party is there a norm or an expectation of fierce party discipline: leaders have few usable and durable sanctions with which to enforce it, and none to compare with those powerful deterrents to dissension which operate in the fused systems of government in Germany and the United Kingdom.

The Minority Leader and Minority Whip

There is no Minority Speaker: the Democratic Party's leader in the House is the Minority Leader. He has no capacity to engage in scheduling, but like the majority leadership, has as his first task the cultivation of party loyalty and effectiveness in an institution whose structures, procedures, and culture are hostile to the concentration of authority. He therefore acts as the party's principal spokesman in the House (a task which, as Richard Gephardt discovered from 1996 onwards, is not necessarily congruent with larger ambitions for a party's Presidential nomination). The Minority Leader is assisted by his Deputy, the Minority Whip, and twelve Regional Whips. Since the House is a more partisan body than the Senate, the minority party there usually counts for little.

Party Organization in the Senate

Majority Leadership

The Senate has no Speaker, nor an office with comparable powers and prerogatives. The Vice-President of the United States is the President of the Senate, but has no power other than to make a casting vote in the event of a tie on the Floor. He rarely presides over the Senate; in his place there is the President *pro tempore*, who has no more power over the Chamber's proceedings than has the Vice-President. Nevertheless, both parties have Leaders, and a Whip elected by the Senate Conference (the party caucus) when it convenes after each Congressional election. For all that it lacks the powers of the House Speakership, the office of the leader of the largest party, the Majority Leadership, has often been important. Since 1955, it has been held by just four Democrats (Lyndon Johnson, 1955–61; Mike Mansfield, 1961–77; Robert Byrd, 1977–81 and 1987–89; and by George Mitchell from 1989–1995) and three Republicans (Howard Baker, 1981–85; Robert Dole, 1985–87, and 1995–96; and, since the summer of 1996, by Trent Lott).

There are fewer and weaker mechanisms in the Senate for enforcing majorities than there are in the House. Senate rules have the consequence of elevating individual members of the chamber rather than creating majorities, and Senate leaders are obliged to exercise their duties primarily through custom rather than by rules. Emphasizing that party leaders have little authority, that the leadership is informally at least collective, bound in practice to depend upon and defer to other senior members, and heavily reliant for day-to-day functions upon staff, Davidson (1989, p. 285) defines Senate Party Leaders' responsibilities as follows:

1: managing the affairs of their senatorial parties;
2: scheduling Senate floor business in accord with workload needs and individual senators' desires;
3: monitoring floor deliberations, which includes seeking unanimous consent agreements governing debates and votes;
4: serving as a conduit between the Senate, the White House, and the House;
5: speaking for the Senate through the media.

No Majority Leader enjoys the formal powers over the scheduling of legislation and the assignment of members to Committees which the rules of the House of Representatives grants the Speaker, or which Robert Taft and Lyndon Johnson enjoyed between 1953 and 1958 (when a large class of liberal Democratic Senators determined to forge a new agenda for the national party was elected). Having been elected Minority Leader in 1953 after only four years' membership of the Senate, Johnson assumed the Majority Leadership in 1955 when the Democrats regained their majority following the 1954 mid-term elections.

Influential though Robert Taft had been in enhancing the prominence of the office, Lyndon Johnson was the politician who effectively defined the office of Senate Majority Leader. Positioning himself broadly in the ideological mainstream of his diverse party, he led from the front, exploiting every opportunity to strengthen the office he held, his own prospects of Presidential office, and the fortunes of Senate Democrats. He did so by attending constantly to long-established political friendships, establishing the foundations of new ones, and investing political capital in those whom he might persuade to support him on particular issues. He sought legislative compromise where (as was usually the case) he could not achieve complete victory, while supporting President Eisenhower on matters of national importance, and where the President's own position enjoyed such popular support as to make opposition to it unwise.

None of Lyndon Johnson's successors has approached the office as he did. None has had the same objectives or opportunities, or worked under constraints similar in kind or extent. Part of the explanation lies in the changes that Johnson himself wrought. As he paid due regard within the Senate to the norms of collegiality and deferred to the Chairmen of committees, his centralization of power weakened the baronial power-bases of these chairpersons. Nelson Polsby (1969) attributes the significant weakening of the "Inner Club" of senior Senators partly to Johnson's transformation of the office of Majority Leader between 1955 and 1960.

Recent Majority Leaders have worked in an institution that obliges them to cultivate goodwill if collective objectives are to be achieved. Abraham Ribicoff, a member of the Senate in the final phase of its pre-reform period in the 1960s, but who continued to serve in it after the convulsive internal and external changes of the 1960s and 1970s, characterized the difference by pointing to Majority Leader Byrd's anxious willingness to serve his fellow Democratic Senators: were he ever to have taken a pencil out of his pocket in the presence of the Majority Leader, he remarked, it was certain that Senator Byrd would offer to sharpen it for him. Byrd's was a willingness born of necessity. The clashing ambitions of entrepreneurial colleagues have obliged all of Johnson's successors to mediate between the President and Senators, persuading, cajoling, and cautiously crafting agreement. Robert Dole has himself characterized the post he twice held as "majority pleader", something which no Speaker of the House of recent years could claim about the Speakership.

Recruitment to the top party leadership positions in the Senate is uncertain; there is only a weak custom (and certainly no right) of accession to the Majority Leadership from the Whip's office. In early 1984, for example, it was impossible to predict with any confidence who would succeed Howard Baker as Senate Majority Leader. Whereas no Member of the modern House can expect to be elected as Speaker without having long served the party in more junior positions, the Senate Majority Leadership can be sought and won by those with little seniority in the body. George Mitchell became Majority Leader in 1990 just ten years after his appointment to the US Senate from Maine following Senator Muskie's appointment as President Carter's Secretary of State.

Minority Leadership

Although the Democrats controlled the House even during the height of President Reagan's power, party control in the Senate switched between the two parties during his Presidency as it has done during President Clinton's in the 1990s. To that extent, the post of Minority Leader in the Senate has acquired an importance which that of Minority Leader in the House usually lacks since majorities there have been less durable. Weaker traditions of party control coupled with laxer and fewer rules make the task of leading the majority party in the Senate even harder. The Majority and Minority Leaders are bound to work with each other as colleagues in the task of managing Senate business, as well as against each other in their roles as partisan and competitive politicians.

Whip System

By contrast with the House, the Whip system in the Senate is undeveloped. There are Majority and Minority Whips, with Chief Deputy Whips and Deputy Whips below them. None the less, they work in a political setting quite different from that in the House: the Senate is an institution designed to enable its members to gain regional and national attention, not to produce legislation with despatch. Party control is, accordingly, difficult for party leaders to secure.

Party and Voting

Where constituency interests are affected, Members of Congress and Senators tread carefully. If, for example, they calculate that to support the President would prompt heavy criticism from constituents, thereby increasing their vulnerability to Primary or general election defeat, they will not hesitate to oppose him. Similarly, however assiduous the party Whips, they will not persuade colleagues to risk their careers for the sake of supporting the party. Where constituency interests are unaffected or marginal, Presidential leadership and party membership are two important variables involved in explaining why Members of Congress vote as they do. Presidential success in this regard is none the less mainly a function of the existence, size, and ideological composition of the majority held by the President's party in each Chamber. President Roosevelt's extraordinary legislative accomplishments between 1933 and 1938 owed much to his personal political qualities, but ideologically favourable large partisan majorities in the House and the Senate were a prerequisite of success. In the United States Congress, pure party-line voting occurs only upon unusual occasions and in unusual circumstances: Republican unity on taxation and budget measures in 1981 and in 1995 are two such cases. The exception discussed above of Mr Gingrich in January 1997 notwithstanding, votes on the organization of each chamber (the House's election of the Speaker; and the setting and modification of party ratios on Committees), normally produce a predictable and pure division between the two parties.

Has Party Voting Declined?

If that much about party voting is straightforward, little else is. It is unclear whether party voting (defined as those votes when a majority of one party votes opposes a majority of the other party) has declined in the twentieth century. Most studies which use as their data set aggregate roll call voting statistics suggest that decline has occurred. During the high tide of party strength within Congress from 1890 to 1915, more than half of all votes in some years resulted in more than 90 per cent of one party's members voting against more than 90 per cent of the other party's. Since the end of the Second World War, aggregate measures of this kind reveal that such partisan division has never exceeded 10 per cent. None the less, other studies using more confined data comprising votes on the few major bills in each session of Congress reveal no such long-run decline. A further measure of party voting is the percentage of party unity votes where members of each party vote with their party colleagues. From 1968 to 1994, House Democrats voted at their low point 70 per cent, Senate Democrats 71 per cent, House Republicans 71 per cent, and Senate Republicans 66 per cent. At their high point, House Democrats voted 88 per cent (in the 100th Congress in 1987 and 1988, and in the 103rd Congress in 1993–4), Senate Democrats 87 per cent, House Republicans 87 per cent, Senate Republicans 86 per cent. Democrats in both the House and the Senate displayed a secular increase in their party unity scores throughout the period from 1968 to 1994.

Cleavage Factors in Party Voting

The extent of party unity varies between policy areas and within policy areas over time. Differential fracturing of this sort was revealed between the 1930s and the early 1980s by both the appearance and the success of the conservative coalition of Republicans and southern Democrats, prompted by shared political imperatives uniting conservatives in the two parties. The major factional cleavage within the Democratic Party has been between its northern and southern wings, occasioned most sharply by civil rights, but also by fiscal policy, and social questions including school prayer, abortion, and wider cultural values. Defined as a majority of southern Democrats voting with a majority of Republicans, the Conservative Coalition has appeared in Congressional votes more frequently than it has won them. Both its appearance and its success rate have declined markedly since the first year of Reagan's Presidency, when it enjoyed striking success, especially in the House. Among the reasons for the decline of the Conservative Coalition is the South's transformation: enfranchisement of southern blacks has produced two-party competitive Congressional elections in much of the region, and a dependence of many remaining Southern Democrats upon black support. Since the passage of the 1965 Voting Rights Act (see Chapter 3), Southern Democrats in Congress have increasingly voted like their colleagues in the North – especially on issues important to blacks, such as education, welfare, employment, and civil rights. The ideological interests of Democrats and Republicans from the South therefore coincide less frequently than they once did. Given, too, the pronounced unity within the Republican Party on budgetary questions, and the Party's possession of majorities in both chambers, the Conservative Coalition's political significance is much diminished.

The Democratic Party has been the most susceptible to cross-party ideological appeals, but the Republican Party has not been exempt. Although its liberal wing has withered since the 1960s, the Congressional party retains many moderate elements whose members continue to support certain Federal welfare programmes. The Republican Party (founded as an almost exclusively northern party of union) in Congress contained for much of the post-war period many (such as Governor Nelson Rockefeller and Senator Jacob Javits) who were ardent champions of progress in civil rights, others (such as Vice-President Nixon and President Bush) who with varying degrees of reluctance have accepted most civil rights legislation, as well as those conservative others (such as Senator Goldwater, President Nixon, President Reagan, and Pat Buchanan) who have found it expedient to oppose most of it. The latter group has become very much stronger as the party's southern component has grown from virtually nothing in 1960 to a majority in the region by the mid-1990s.

Caucuses

Party membership is the best predictor of how an individual Member of Congress or Senator will vote, but is on most issues still a less than excellent one. The social, geographic, ethnic, racial, and economic heterogeneity of America makes the containing by two parties of social cleavages impossible. In addition to their party membership, most Congressional politicians belong to cross-party caucuses or to intra-party caucuses (factions) (see Exhibit 5.5). They may be confined to the House (as most are), to the Senate or, in some cases, be drawn from both Chambers. Within the cross-party (and most numerous) category, different types of caucus cater to distinct kinds of interest: geographic; social; economic; and policy. Intra-party caucuses consist of factional groups within each party which seek to enlarge their influence. Most caucuses have a small staff; all elect officers.

EXHIBIT 5.5

Typical Cross-Party Caucuses

Geographic	Congressional Sunbelt Caucus
	Long Island Congressional Caucus
	Tennessee Valley Authority Caucus
Social	Congressional Black Caucus
	Women's Policy, Inc.
	Congressional Hispanic Caucus
Economic	Congressional Competitiveness Caucus
	Congressional Soybean Caucus
	Flat Tax Caucus
	Congressional Steel Caucus
	Senate Textile Committee
Policy	Concerned Senators for the Arts
	House Education Task Force
	Narcotics Abuse and Control Caucus
	Nuclear Waste Caucus
	Factional
	Conservative Democratic Forum
	Democratic Study Group (liberal group)
	Republican Class of the 100th Congress

The purposes of bipartisan caucuses vary, but the following three features are shared:

- *Provision* and *exchange* of *information* between members.
- Offering of *amendments* on *pending legislation.*
- Building of *wider support* for *Caucus policy* on particular issues of concern to its members.

For individual members, the costs of joining a caucus are low, but the rewards may be high; while some Members will seek the Chairmanship of a caucus, most are content to draw upon the benefits of membership. Caucuses frequently work closely with interest groups outside Congress to draft legislation, assisting individual legislators in promoting their policies and careers and, at best, mitigating the worst effects of the relative structural and partisan rigidities of Congress.

The Procedural Dimension

The procedural dimension has two aspects: the first is of the legislative process; and the second that of oversight. Only the first of these is considered here; the second is examined in Chapter 8. Two chambers share the legislative function, and every Bill that becomes law has to be passed in identical form by both. This rarely happens at the first time of asking because Bills suffer different fates in the two places, being subject to various amendments as they are considered by committees, subcommittees, and finally by all Members of Congress and Senators on the Floor of each chamber. Conference Committees, composed of members from each chamber, are therefore constituted for each Bill after it has passed all of the stages in each Chamber. Most legislation is minor, uncontentious, and passed quickly. Provided that the two parties' Calendar Watchers (usually staff members of the Policy Committees) raise no objection, such legislation before the Senate is listed by the Majority Leader one day prior to the formal seeking of approval on the Floor. Similar procedures apply in the House with respect to uncontroversial legislation.

Fewer major Bills originate in the Executive Branch than did so before the Reagan Presidency, but most still do. The clearest example is that of the annual Budget: all departments' and agencies' annual requests for appropriations are supervised by the Office of Management and Budget before being sent to Congress in the President's Budget message. Bills re-authorizing agencies and programmes are also prepared in the Executive Branch. Bills are physically despatched from the White House to Congress where they are introduced, under prior arrangement, by sympathetic Senators and Congressmen whose names appear on the Bill as sponsors. In the House, all Bills, including those sent up by the President and the myriad of trivial ones introduced by Congressmen (motivated more by the prospect of winning favourable publicity with interest groups or constituents than by serious legislative intent) are introduced into the House by being dropped into a mahogany box known as the "hopper" near the Speaker's podium in the front of the chamber. In the Senate, Bills are introduced either directly from the floor by the sponsoring Senator, or by being sent to Senate clerks for publication in the *Congressional Record*. Most Bills thus introduced into Congress every session die. In order to become law, a Bill must pass all of the many institutional obstacles to passage within the two-year time limit of each Congress. For example, in the 103rd Congress, which ran from 1993 to 1994, 6,647 bills were introduced in the House and 3,177 into the Senate. Of these – nearly 10,000 pieces of legislation – a mere 465 became public laws.

Following their introduction, Bills are referred to a Standing Committee of the House by the Speaker, and to a Standing Committee of the Senate by that Chamber's presiding officer. A bill re-authorizing support for Amtrak, the inter-city passenger railway system, will in the House be referred to the Transportation and Infrastructure Committee, and in the Senate to the Commerce, Science and Transportation Committee, both of which would in the first instance refer it to the Surface Transportation subcommittees. It is in these subcommittees that Congress does most of its work on the legislation, hearing expert testimony from disinterested and interested witnesses alike, from politicians in senior positions within government departments and agencies, and civil servants lower down, and from lobbyists and experts outside government or operating at the permeable boundaries of government in Washington, where the public world meshes with the private. All witnesses are questioned during the hearings.

The sponsor of a Bill in each chamber, together with such of his or her co-sponsoring colleagues whose names the sponsor finds it advantageous to have associated with the Bill, always seek to divert a Bill from a committee that may be hostile to it. Presidents and Congressional party leaders behave similarly in respect of their own legislation. Where committee jurisdictions overlap, providing no single path for a Bill, obstacles presented by particular committees to a Bill's passage can be circumvented. Formal powers granted to the Speaker by the House make this easier in the larger, rule-bound House, than in the Senate. For example, President Carter found that the prospect of the House passing his contentious Energy Bill in 1977 improved with the Speaker's establishment of one *ad hoc* committee to consider it as a whole rather than risk its being addressed in parts by several Committees. The Bill duly fared better in the House than in the Senate, where three Committees held separate hearings and produced their own drafts, none of which closely resembled the President's own proposal.

At the start of the 104th Congress, the Republican majority abolished joint referrals, and amended House rules to enable the Speaker to "designate a committee of primary jurisdiction". With the vigorous support of the seventy-three conservative GOP freshmen, the Speaker and his colleagues drafted the alteration to enhance his discretion in determining the most effective political means for steering the Republican agenda through Congress by granting to him, for example, the power to send different parts of a bill to different committees. Gingrich quickly added to his powers by creating task forces where he thought it advantageous to circumvent established committees. The formal change in rules and practices did not make Gingrich all-powerful: the Speaker overreached himself, prompting some of his colleagues to rebel against his presumption.

Committee hurdles cannot, in any case, always be so easily jumped. Many Bills are often submitted to more than one committee, either sequentially or simultaneously. Overlapping jurisdictions, deliberately arranged in order to maximize participation and opportunities for the claiming of credit, fuel multiple referrals. Some authorizing committees, of which the House Commerce Committee is a striking example, have jurisdictions sufficiently broad to enable their chairmen to conduct oversight of a wide range of public policy, and to claim major legislative roles. Attempts by committees to invade the territory of one another are resented, but reflect the competitive political struggle within Congress and are, accordingly, ineradicable.

When a subcommittee has completed its hearings, and marking-up, it votes on whether to report the Bill to the full committee. If the subcommittee chairman wishes to proceed and has judged his colleagues' views soundly, the Bill will progress to the full committee. For major legislation, the full committee will hold hearings, consider amendments, and eventually produce a (probably somewhat different) draft of its own. Consideration is then given to reporting the Bill to the Floor. The Floors of both Chambers are now very much more important to the content of legislation than they were before the reforms of the 1970s, and further revisions may take place there.

Legislation in the House

Their varying tenures, constituencies, Constitutional responsibilities, and the exclusive powers that each Chamber has over its rules, causes the formal bicameralism of Congress to issue in distinctive legislative cultures. The House's is tightly rule-bound: legislation proceeds through dense institutional structures under detailed rules. The Senate gives freer rein to its members' individual characters, needs, and ambitions. Davidson and Oleszek (1981) characterize this contrast between the ordered procedures of the House and the relative looseness of the Senate as reflecting the former's pursuit of "majority rule" within the 435 member chamber, and the Senate's underpinning of its 100 members' "individual rights". The difference is incompletely realized. Nevertheless, procedures for considering legislation on the House floor remain formal and detailed; those in the Senate are, by comparison, informal and general. In the House, a bill reported to the Floor from Committee is listed in order on one of four calendars, according to its type:

- *The Union Calendar* is that which encompasses all *taxation* and *appropriations* Bills.
- The *House Calendar* encompasses all other *major public legislation.*
- The *Private Calendar*, upon which bills dealing with *special private subjects* including special grants of citizenship are placed.
- The *Corrections Calendar*, upon which the Speaker may place bills intended to repeal obsolete or needlessly burdensome laws. A three-fifths vote is needed for passage, and most amendments are prohibited.

House rules assign the Corrections Calendar to the second and fourth Tuesdays in each month, subject to the Speaker's discretion. Other days are set aside for business arising under special provisions including, for example, that falling under the scope of the *Discharge Calendar* – used for those bills which, having been before a Standing Committee for thirty working days, are released from that committee's consideration directly to the Floor via a discharge petition signed by a majority of House Members.

On every Monday and Tuesday, members may move the consideration of legislation under *Suspension of the Rules*, enabling debate of uncontroversial matters to be expedited. Since this procedure is under the Speaker's control, the temptation to employ it on behalf of important legislation (especially late in the session when pressures on the timetable are intense) may be irresistible. It has in recent years become the object of considerable criticism, especially where it prevents full legislative scrutiny.

House rules grant to five Committees the right of direct access to the Floor for certain bills. Appropriations; Budget; House Oversight; Rules; and Standards of Official Conduct may all bring such measures directly to the Floor provided that other business is not pending there. For most purposes, these provisions grant a privileged status to appropriations bills, to budget resolutions, and to the leadership's rules for the ordering and scheduling of business on the Floor. All three are best understood as instances of the House leadership's power. Accordingly, they may be brought to the Floor for debate at any time of the Majority Leadership's choosing. Otherwise, except in the rare event of its being subject to a Discharge Petition, no Bill may come to the Floor without first having its terms of debate set by the Rules Committee, in the form of a "Rule" being granted to it. Unlike other Standing Committees, Rules conducts no hearings on legislation. It is the sole gatekeeper to the Floor, establishing rules for the consideration of authorizing legislation on the Floor of the House. The Committee may grant four types of Rule. All specify the time available for general debate, exclusive of the time necessary to debate amendments:

- An *Open Rule*, permitting the proposal and debate of amendments germane to the subject of the Bill.
- A *Closed Rule*. If pure, no amendments may be offered to the Bill; otherwise, only those amendments from, for example, the primary committee reporting the legislation may be permitted.
- A *Modified Closed Rule*, according to which some parts of a Bill may be subject to amendment and some not.
- *Waiver Rules* may be granted by the Committee, and are frequently included within one of the above Rules. They may permit the waiving of points of order raised against parts of the Bill, or dispense with customary rules of procedure.

The House is not bound to accept a Rule granted by the Rules Committee, and votes on every Rule prior to debating the Bill itself. On the rare occasions that Rules are defeated, the consequences may be considerable.

Whoever controls the Rules Committee therefore acts as gatekeeper of legislation to the House Floor, and is able to influence legislation by the selective opening, bolting, and temporary closing of the gate. When, as in the 1950s and 1960s, the Committee was dominated by southern conservative Democrats, it checked the liberal and moderate majority. The Committee could not act in the absence of the conservative Democratic Chairman, Howard Smith, who accordingly used the pretext of attending to urgent business on his Virginia farm when he needed to prevent a Bill proceeding to the Floor. Alliance with like-minded conservative colleagues on the Committee (most Republicans and southern Democrats) presented a fixed obstacle to liberal legislation, especially on civil rights. Seeking a Discharge Petition (whereby business before the Committee could be released from it by a vote of the House against the Chairman's wishes) was not politically prudent because all Members of the House were reluctant to irritate a powerful Chairman whose support they might themselves require for other legislation in the future.

A Rule having been granted by the Rules Committee, and approved by the House, general debate proceeds on the Floor under the special procedures applying to the Committee of the Whole House, into which form the House now technically resolves itself. The Speaker does not preside at this stage, but vacates the chair in favour of a colleague; the quorum for debate is just 100 members (rather than the 50 per cent + 1, or 218, which is normally required) and the debate proceeds under the guidance of the Majority and Minority Floor Managers (normally the Chair and Ranking Members of the Standing Committee which reported the legislation to the Floor). They are typically charged, respectively, with assisting the Bill's passage, and with bringing about its demise. Debate is usually confined to the reading of set-piece speeches, equally divided between each side. The main political activity in the Committee of the Whole occurs not in the general debate, but in the consideration of amendments. This stage, under which amendments can be made and substitute clauses offered, also proceeds under strict rules: each amendment may be the subject of no more than one five-minute speech in support or opposition.

Once all amendments have been voted upon, the Committee of the Whole "rises", and resumes its former existence as the full House under the Speaker's Chairmanship. The House reviews the Committee's actions by voting on the amendments. The penultimate stage, for a motion to be offered to recommit the Bill to the Standing Committee which reported it, is invariably rejected. A vote is then taken on Final Passage by each member wishing to vote using a plastic identity card in one of forty machines on the Floor and pressing a button to indicate whether she or he wishes to vote "yea", "nay", or "present" (abstain). If the Bill is passed, and the Senate has not already considered it, it is then sent there.

Legislation in the Senate

The Senate has no functional equivalent of the House Rules Committee; its Rules Committee, is not an analogue of the House Rules Committee, but deals with internal procedural matters only. There is just one Senate Calendar for legislation: the Calendar of General Orders. Treaties and nominations for which the Constitution gives the Senate special responsibility for considering are placed on the Executive Calendar. Most legislation reaches the Senate Floor by an agreement of Unanimous Consent which, dispensing with the rules nominally controlling Floor procedure, set terms and conditions under which debate is actually to be conducted.

The Senate retains only filaments of the club-like culture for which it was celebrated in the 1950s. Less raucously partisan than the House, it attaches greater importance to Floor deliberation but less to detailed legislative work in Committees than its much larger neighbour. Protection of the individual rights and standing of each Senator are reinforced by the Senate's procedures, and makes the scheduling of legislation by the Senate leadership a strenuous task. With the aid of his colleagues in the leadership and staff, the Senate Majority Leader is condemned to initiate legislation, guide its passage through the Senate, speak on its behalf, while lacking any significant control over it. The variable which Majority Leaders would doubtless most like to control (but which there is least prospect of their controlling) is that of the schedules of their party colleagues. As Senators spend more time in their States, aping the behaviour of House colleagues, so the planning of legislative schedules becomes ever harder. In response to Senators' pleas to spend more time, and to spend it more predictably, away from Washington attending to their individual political needs, the Senate now works only three weeks in four.

One Senate rule illustrates how the Senate continues to set a higher priority on the protection of the rights of individual members to object to proposed legislation before the Senate: unlike the House, the Senate preserves the practice of permitting unlimited debate through the filibuster by which individual Senators may deliberately prolong debate by continuing to speak. Prolix members of the House were controlled by party leaders as early as 1841. By the end of the nineteenth century, the small Republican majority in the House prompted Speakers Reed and Cannon to limit strictly the Democrats' frustration of their opponents' legislative intent by declining to respond to a quorum call. Speaker Cannon justified new limits upon obstructive tactics by emphasizing the Constitutional obligation placed upon the House to facilitate the emergence of the majority will:

> I say that a majority under the Constitution is allowed to legislate, and that if a contrary practice has grown up, such practice is unrepublican, undemocratic, against sound policy and contrary to the Constitution.

Such majoritarian sentiment finds only faint echoes in the Senate. The filibuster's roots are so deep in the Senate's institutional culture that even when it has been employed (as it often has) since 1945 by conservative southerners against northern liberals to defeat civil rights legislation, proposals to abolish it have been few. Filibustering requires physical stamina and organizational skill: Senator Strom Thurmond of South Carolina, then a Democrat, now a Republican, but always a conservative, spoke for more than 24 hours continuously in 1957 against the Civil Rights Bill. Such a herculean performance would not be possible in the House of Representatives, where speeches of five to ten minutes are the norm.

Although the Senate had as early as 1917 weakened the force of the filibuster by providing in Rule XXII that a filibuster might be stopped under certain circumstances, the hurdles to invoking it were high. The 1964 Civil Rights Act passed only after a bitter battle to vote "cloture" – that is, to close the debate. Thus it was upon the cloture vote that the political struggle concentrated rather than upon the Bill itself. To that extent, the battle was especially difficult because a cloture vote requires (under current Senate rules) the approval of three-fifths of the Senate, after which each Senator is permitted to speak for a further hour. Until the modification of Rule XXII in 1975 made the granting of cloture easier, few cloture votes had succeeded. Since 1975, many have. However, although more filibusters have been halted by cloture votes in the last quarter of the twentieth century, filibustering itself has become more, not less, common in the same period: only twenty-three filibusters occurred in the nineteenth century, but 191 occurred between 1970 and 1994 alone (Binder and Smith, 1997, p. 11). The Senate is an institution in which the majority has increasing difficulty in exercising its will.

Conference Committees

After Final Passage by both House and Senate, a Bill invariably exists in two different forms. Appropriations Bills rarely emerge from the two chambers in precisely the same condition; Authorization Bills often fail to do so, especially where their subject is important and the subject of fierce debate and disagreement. However, the Constitution requires that each Chamber pass identical versions, so that an agreed Bill may be sent to the President for his signature or veto. Congress therefore provides for a Conference Committee to eliminate the differences.

Conference Committees are not Standing Committees. Their membership is not fixed, but set freshly in respect of each Bill with a membership drawn from both Chambers. Each Chamber has the right to name as many of its members as it wishes to serve on the Committee. In practice, conferees are nominated from the Standing Committees which held hearings on the Bill and reported it to the Floors of the House and Senate. Formally, the power to name members is vested in the Speaker and Presiding Officer of the Senate; in practice, the power is delegated to the Chairman and Ranking Member of the committees from which the members are drawn. The party balance within each chamber's share of the Conference roughly matches that within the chamber as a whole (and the ratio that is usually applied to determine the distribution of party positions on each Standing Committee).

Conference Committees' importance and size vary considerably. Some Conferences modify Bills significantly, while others merely eliminate inconsequential differences. A Conference comprising between nine and fifteen Representatives and six and thirteen Senators is typical, but the variation is wide. Some major pieces of legislation (especially "Omnibus" bills embracing large areas of policy) are discussed in conferences composed of more than 200 members: the Omnibus Budget reconciliation conference of 1986, and the Omnibus Trade legislation of 1988 are two examples. Conferences of this size are always divided into subconferences; the 1988 Trade Bill had no fewer than thirteen.

Conference Committees act as forcing mechanisms. They either amend both versions so as to arrive at a new draft, or simply agree to the version passed in one of the two Chambers. The common draft is then returned to the Floors of the House and Senate; in the House, no further amendments are permitted. Only if both Houses then approve it in the form agreed to by the Conference Committee may it be sent to the President for his signature and formal passage into law. It then becomes an Act of Congress.

Conclusion

The United States Congress was not designed so that policy-making might be made simple. Yet Congress has developed institutional techniques for the control and channelling of problems embedded in the Constitutional order. The outcome invariably appears disordered, and often is. Of Congress's two functions, as a representative and as a policy-making institution, the former is discharged with conspicuously greater enthusiasm, effectiveness, and efficiency than the latter. Here lies the primary interest in analysing Congress: the tensions between its five dimensions, and their resolution in the sixth: the centrifugal political and financial forces on the one hand (especially those arising from Congressional districts, home States, and constituents within them), and the countervailing centripetal forces of party and President which provide incentives to Representatives and Senators to participate in the aggregation of interests and the formation, legislation, implementation, and evaluation of public policy.

None the less, by comparison with the powers of legislatures elsewhere, Congress's autonomy from the executive grants it powers over public policy and a role in national politics much greater than those of legislatures in all other advanced liberal democracies. In the formation of national budgets, of many aspects of defence policy, in the regulation of industrial pollution, safety at work, banks, financial markets, labour markets, telecommunications, and elections, Congress's power to regulate under the provisions of the Constitution's interstate commerce clause is unfettered and intensively employed. The separation of powers ensures that Congress is not subject to the will of the executive; Presidents who suppose otherwise are always disabused.

If its autonomy is complete, its capacity to set and sustain the national political agenda is slight. The bicameral Congress is ill-fitted to give coherent leadership or to act speedily. These possibilities it cedes to the Presidency. Congress has no prospect of competing durably with the President in national leadership. In so far as it is an untidy institution with a deficient capacity to aggregate interests, it reflects the diverse and contradictory aspirations and preferences of American voters, interest groups, and of its own membership.

6

The Supreme Court and the Politics of Adjudication

The Supreme Court is thickly immersed in the formulation, implementation, and evaluation of public policy in the United States. Whether or not the authors of the Constitution intended it, many of the Court's judgments have political consequences. The Court's role differs from those of the other branches because its members are politically appointed, not elected. They are, however, bound to maintain the legitimacy of the institution of which they are members. Accordingly, its appointive character does not diminish the extent to which the Court is political, but modulates its expression.

The Federal Courts in general, and the Supreme Court in particular, are apparent anomalies in a political system characterized more than any in Europe by the principle of electoral accountability. Federal Judges are formally neither accountable to electors nor answerable to a body of elective politicians. Yet what appears at first to be constitutionally anomalous flows from the characteristically American cultural distrust of the unfettered exercise of power by politicians. Majority and minority groups across the United States and throughout American history have good cause to distrust the rule of politicians unchecked between elections (and sometimes in spite of them). Nevertheless, the Court is not a final arbiter in matters of public policy (although many suppose it to be so). Its lack of enforcement powers has occasionally resulted in its decisions being vigorously (and sometimes successfully) resisted by communities or regions, or overturned by Congressional action or constitutional amendment.

The Organization and Role of the Judicary

The Structure of State Courts

Article III, Section 1 of the US Constitution establishes a Supreme Court, and permits Congress to form lower Federal Courts (see Appendix 1). The Constitution assumes throughout, and at points explicitly discusses, the existence of Courts falling under the jurisdiction of the then thirteen States.

181

There is no doubting the superiority of the United States Constitution in the event of a clash between it and the Constitutions or laws of the several States. The Constitution of the United States, and the laws and Treaties made under it by the Federal authorities shall, declares Article VI:

> be the supreme Law of the Land; and the Judges in every State shall be bound thereby, any Thing in the Constitution or Laws of any State to the Contrary notwithstanding.

Equally, the States are sovereign. Legal entities in their own right, they have full authority under the US Constitution to establish their own Courts. Thus there are in the United States fifty-two distinct legal systems: one for the United States as a whole, but administered by a three-tier system of Federal courts; fifty for the individual States; and one for the District of Columbia. Most law in the United States is State law; some law is entirely a matter for States. Federal law is interstitiary. Most Courts are State and municipal Courts. Most Judges are State and municipal Judges: of the 29,500 Judges in the United States, only 1,500 are members of the Federal bench. While all State law must accord with the provisions of the United States Constitution and Federal law, this requirement permits wide latitude in the content of law between the States and in its interpretation by State Judges.

Recruitment of Judges to State Courts varies between States. In fourteen States, Judges are popularly elected on a partisan ticket; and non-partisan elections are used in a further eighteen; in three, the Legislature elects; in nine (mainly in the east) the Governor appoints (in some States with confirmation by the State Senate, and in others by a council). In fifteen, the "Missouri Plan" is applied: the Governor appoints from a list of three candidates nominated by a special commission generally comprising lawyers selected by Judges, and non-lawyers selected by the Governor. Judges chosen by this last method are subject to periodic re-election by citizens of the State. The salience of law and order as a political issue notwithstanding, judicial elections rarely arouse much interest among voters. Incumbency offers some advantage in most States, especially since most voters know little of those standing for election. In few judicial elections are policy issues addressed.

The structure of the Courts in the States varies in detail; among municipalities, it varies rather more. Some of the differences consist in the idiosyncrasies of local nomenclature and procedural embellishment; others are substantive.

At the lowest level, Justices of the Peace preside over minor civil and criminal cases. The first Courts of significance within the States are Municipal Courts, which have jurisdiction over civil cases involving small claims, and misdemeanours in criminal cases. Within each State, there are Courts for each County (County Courts) divided in some States between Courts dealing with civil and criminal matters, and in others along more complicated functional lines. Above County Courts lie, in most States and in all large ones, the Intermediate Courts of Appeal. Appearing under a variety of names such as the Appellate Division, or Intermediate Court of Appeal, the functions of such Courts are almost always entirely appellate, as their several titles suggest. As with County Courts, the structure of the Intermediate Courts of Appeal varies from State to State. In some, such as New York, it is of extraordinary complexity and hence invites resourceful lawyers to prolong appeals. The Court of last resort within each State is the highest Court to which a case may be taken, unless it involves a substantial Federal question. In this event, it may in theory be taken on appeal to the US Supreme Court. In practice, the US Supreme Court denies most appeals to it from State Supreme Courts. (State Supreme Courts have different names in different states: "State Judicial Court" in Massachusetts and Maine, and – doubly confusingly – the "Court of Appeals" in New York, where "Supreme Court" is reserved for trial Courts – the equivalent elsewhere of Municipal Courts.)

The Structure of Federal Courts

The Federal Courts are divided into legislative and constitutional courts. The former special courts include the US Tax Court; the US Court of Appeals for the Armed Services, and the United States Court of Veterans Appeals. Their specialist character precludes their further discussion here.

There are three layers to the Federal Court system: the US Supreme Court; the US (Circuit) Courts of Appeals, and the US District Courts. Of these three, the Constitution established only the first by name, but enabled Congress to create a supporting Federal Judicial system by creating "such inferior Courts as the Congress may from time to time ordain and establish". Circuit Courts were created by the Judiciary Act of 1789, one of the first Congress's first Acts, and District Courts by the Judiciary Act of 1891.

Federal District Courts

There are currently 90 US District Courts and 649 US District Judges (including seven in Puerto Rico). Twenty-six States consist of just one District; the rest have two or more, and the three most populous states (California, New York, and Texas) each has four. Some districts have only one or two Judges, while major cities have many (the southern District of New York has twenty-seven). With the minor exception since 1979 of the appeal of civil cases to the US District Court first heard before a US magistrate, the District Courts have no appellate jurisdiction, but an original jurisdiction only: all crimes against the United States, all financially substantial (above $10,000) civil cases under Federal law or the Federal Constitution, the review and enforcement of orders and actions of certain Federal agencies, and in other cases determined by the US Congress.

District Courts bear the brunt of the judicial burden in the Federal system. That burden is only occasionally relieved by the creation of additional Courts at the District level and the appointment of further Judges. In 1977, 117 new Judgeships were created, and a further 53 in 1984. Unlike the Supreme Court, District Court Judges enjoy the support of a secretariat, from law clerks to secretaries and probation officers. District Courts handle a wide range of cases, including criminal prosecutions, petitions from prisoners, civil rights, labour law, social security law, torts, and contracts. The formal process of recruitment of Judges to the District Courts is the same as for the other two levels in the Federal system: the President nominates candidates whose names are then placed before the Senate for confirmation or rejection.

The US (Circuit) Courts of Appeals

The thirteen Appeals Courts and the 179 Judges within them are often named "Circuit Courts" because each Justice of the US Supreme Court, in being assigned to head one of the Circuit Courts by way of overseeing its work, was until the Judiciary Act of 1869 required to "ride circuit" across the States comprising each division, or Circuit, of this Appellate division of the Federal Judicial system. Each Judge has three clerks (only one fewer than most Associate Justices of the Supreme Court).

Eleven of the Circuit Courts cover defined geographical areas of whole states; the twelfth covers the District of Columbia, the seat of Federal government. For example, the Second Circuit comprises the states of New York, Connecticut, and Vermont. In establishing the Federal Courts by the 1789 Judiciary Act, Congress provided for the number of Circuit Courts to be equivalent to the number of Supreme Court Justices. Increased workloads in the late nineteenth century caused Congress in 1891 belatedly to recognize the need to establish full-time Courts of Appeal between the overburdened District and Supreme Courts. Eighty-five per cent of Federal cases reaching the Circuit Courts proceed no further.

Only one geographical circuit has been added since the Second World War: the old Fifth Circuit was divided in 1980 to create a new, Eleventh Circuit in the south-eastern states. The division reflected the growth of cases from the states of Florida and Georgia in the south-eastern part of the old Fifth Circuit, and from Texas in the south-western part, and won Congressional approval only after both conservatives and liberals were satisfied that the amended structure would not harm their interests. In the summer of 1997, however, the House passed a Bill providing for a commission to consider the distribution of Federal Judgeships, with a special brief to consider whether the huge 9th Circuit (California, eight other western states, and two Pacific territories) should be divided.

The US Court of Appeals for the Thirteenth Circuit, which has no defined geographical area, was formed in 1982 following the consolidation of the Court of Customs and Patent Appeals with the jurisdictional aspects of the Court of Claims.

The United States Supreme Court

From 1789 until the Civil War, the relationship between the Federal and State governments dominated all other questions before the Court. In McCloskey's words (1960, p. 29), the survival of the Union "inhered in almost every constitutional case the Supreme Court faced". Neither the Constitutional Convention nor the States' ratification of the Constitution had settled the nature of the new polity. Nor did resolution of that question await revelation by close examination of the Constitution's text, of the Constitutional debates, or *The Federalist Papers*. Constitutional arguments proceeded in Courts, in Congress, and in State Legislatures throughout the period, but not until the end of the Civil War was the question of the polity's indissolubility finally answered. Related questions of the extent of the States' sovereignty and the meaning of the Tenth Amendment still exercise the Federal Courts, as the discussion in Chapter 9 shows. Nor will the boundaries of Federal and state action ever be definitively settled: neither the Constitution nor the judgments of the Court provide for agreement either on underlying principle or on the application of constitutional principle to new controversies and cases.

Between 1865 and 1941, the Court's prime concern was the constitutional basis of the Federal government's intervention in the economy. The period opens in the aftermath of the final establishment of the indissolubility of the Union, of the end to the frontier, in the founding for the first time of a *nation*, in the completion of transcontinental railroad links, through the formation of independent regulatory commissions from 1883 onwards, and the growing regulation of the national economy in the last decade of the nineteenth century and in the period leading up to the First World War. Following the quiescence of the decade that followed the war came the assertion by President Roosevelt in the New Deal of the Federal government's power to shape macroeconomic policy, and to regulate agriculture, finance, and industry. Roosevelt's policies met with short-lived but vigorous resistance from an activist and conservative Court majority. Following wholesale changes in the Court's composition, attention gradually turned to questions of racial equality, privacy, and freedom of speech.

The importance of racial politics throughout American history has been fully reflected in their appearance before the Supreme Court, culminating in *Plessy* v. *Ferguson*, 163 US 537 (1896), and *Brown* v. *Board of Education, Topeka*, 347 US 483 (1954). *Plessy* sanctioned the practice in southern states of maintaining separate but notionally equal schools segregated by race; *Brown* overturned it. In both cases, the Court's decision shaped the way in which race was subsequently addressed by the States, the Congress, and the Presidency. While no decision of the Court in the twentieth century has had greater repercussions than *Brown*, individual rights have occupied almost as much of the Court's attention since 1944, as Exhibit 6.1 shows.

The Judicial branch has no political role of the kind the executive and legislative branches do. But in establishing a Federal Judiciary whose members are appointed by the head of the Executive Branch subject to the confirmation of one part of the Legislative Branch, the framers did not hide their inclusion of the Supreme and inferior Federal courts within the political realm. Since the legitimacy of American policy-makers rests so heavily upon election, an unelected Court armed with the power of judicial review limits majoritarianism, thereby posing problems of legitimacy which Justices of the Court cannot escape. The legitimacy of Federal Judges and Justices derives

---

EXHIBIT 6.1

The Supreme Court and Individual Rights

- *Smith* v. *Allwright*, 321 US 649 (1944), struck down the all-white Primary, long-employed as a means of excluding southern blacks from political participation.
- *Baker* v. Carr, 369 US 186 (1962), *Reynolds* v. *Sims*, 377 US 533 (1964), and *Wesberry* v. *Sanders*, 376 US 1 (1964), ended the practice of gerrymandering by rural white elites in order to exclude blacks and other disfavoured groups from electoral politics.
- *Gideon* v. *Wainwright*, 372 US 335 (1963), guaranteed legal representation to indigent persons charged with serious crimes, and *Miranda* v. *Arizona*, 384 US 436 (1966), set rigorous procedural standards for the admission of evidence through confession in criminal trials, thereby guaranteeing compliance with the Fifth Amendment's protection against self incrimination (although the ruling has since been eroded).
- *Griswold* v. *Connecticut*, 381 US 479 (1966), overturned state laws that forbade the use of contraception. *Roe* v. *Wade*, 410 US 113 (1973), overturned State laws restricting abortion in the first three months of pregnancy. *Webster* v. *Reproductive Health Services* (1989) limited Roe's scope by upholding the constitutionality of five provisions of a Missouri statute regulating the circumstances under which late abortions should be performed, and banning the use of public employees and facilities to perform abortions not necessary to save the mother's life. By extension, the Court granted greater scope to the State Legislatures to determine abortion policy. *Casey* v. *Planned Parenthood of Pennsylvania*, 112 S.Ct. 2791 (1992) marked a division between those conservatives on the bench who held that *Roe* should be overturned, and others who argued that it should be upheld as precedent.

from three sources: first, from the symbolic and substantive importance of their roles as guardians of constitutionally-guaranteed freedoms and rights; second, from the review of their fitness for the task by the President and his staff prior to their nomination, and the Senate's examination of them prior to their confirmation; third, from the Court's application of judicial restraint to avoid finding acts or actions unconstitutional unless they very plainly are.

The Supreme Court's Jurisdiction

The Supreme Court is the only judicial body named by the Constitution, whose functions are explicitly discussed in it, and upon which duties are laid. Article III, Section 2, lists them:

> The judicial Power shall extend to all Cases, in Law and Equity, arising under this Constitution, the Laws of the United States, and Treaties made, or which shall be made, under their Authority; – to all Cases affecting Ambassadors, other public Ministers and Consuls; – to all Cases of admiralty and maritime Jurisdiction; – to Controversies to which the United States shall be a Party.

Appellate and Original Jurisdiction

For all practical purposes, the Supreme Court has an "appellate jurisdiction" only. Its small "original jurisdiction" (that class of cases for which the Supreme Court is the court of first instance) derives not from an Act of Congress (as does that of the Federal District Courts) but from the Constitution itself (and is limited further by the Eleventh Amendment). Chief Justice Marshall built his judgment in *Marbury* v. *Madison*, 1 Cranch 137 (1803), on precisely this point – that the grant of original jurisdiction could not be modified by Act of Congress as (so he claimed) had happened with respect to the Judiciary Act of 1789's grant to the Court of the power to issue a writ of *mandamus* – an instruction. The remaining categories of original jurisdiction are:

- Cases involving *two or more States*.
- Cases between the *United States* and an *individual State*.
- Cases affecting *foreign ambassadors* and *foreign "Ministers and Consuls"*.
- Cases initiated by a *State* against a *citizen of another state* or *"foreign States, Citizens, or Subjects"*.

These categories are unimportant and, except in cases between the United States and another State, the Supreme Court's jurisdiction is not exclusive. With the Court's approval, Congress has extended concurrent original jurisdiction to Federal District courts in the other three categories listed above. Consequently, most cases of original jurisdiction heard by the Court are between two States of the Union: most are boundary disputes, especially acrimonious where resources are involved. Examples include minerals beneath Lake Erie in a dispute between Michigan and Ohio; water in a long-running controversy between Arizona and California; and, more exotically, oyster beds between Maryland and Virginia. Cases between the United States and an individual State have also usually concerned resource exploitation rights. Since the Court is poorly equipped to ascertain the facts of a case as trial courts are accustomed to do, it refers most original jurisdiction cases to a "special master", usually a retired Federal Judge, who examines the case, and recommends a disposition to the Supreme Court (which it is not bound to accept).

Though of much greater importance, the Court's appellate jurisdiction may be limited by Congress, as Article III, Section 2 notes:

> In all the other Cases . . . the supreme Court shall have appellate jurisdiction, both as to Law and Fact, with such Exceptions, and under such Regulations, as the Congress shall make.

In *Wiscart* v. *Dauchy* 3 Dallas 321 (1796), the Court accepted that in the absence of a statute passed in an Act of Congress, the Court could not assume jurisdiction. In principle, this leaves the way open for Congress to eliminate the Court's appellate functions – a possibility that has often appealed to Members of Congress opposed to particular judgments of the Court. In practice, Congress has not legislated exceptions to the Court's "core" functions, but the Court has always accepted Congress's power to determine what lies within its appellate jurisdiction. Congress's determination to defend the triangular separation of power between itself, the Executive, and the Court has increased its reluctance to reduce the Court's appellate jurisdiction. Members of Congress and others in public life have often displayed (or affected) outrage with judgments of the Court's majority. Yet most have also been mindful of the defence which the Court may provide to Congress against the Executive, and so have been reluctant to consent to the Court being constrained. Others have recalled that since most Americans are members of at least one minority group, the collective interest is best served by the Court defending Constitutional rights as it judges for itself. Congress has consequently shown little enthusiasm for restricting appellate powers of the Court.

The Constitution's language on this point is, none the less, plain. In *Ex parte McCardle*, 7 Wallace 506 (1869), the Court addressed the petition of a Mississippi newspaper editor that a writ of *habeas corpus* be issued. Mr McCardle, the editor in question, was held in custody for trial by a military commission for his publication of articles in his newspaper that were allegedly "incendiary and libellous". Fearing that the Court would move to declare the Reconstruction Acts unconstitutional, Congress, by an Act of March 1868, removed the Court's jurisdiction in respect of appeals from the Circuit Courts regarding writs of *habeas corpus* arising under the Reconstruction Act of 1867. Quoting the terms in which Article III, Section 2 qualified the grant of appellate jurisdiction to the Court, Chief Justice Chase declared that the Court could not judge the case:

> Without jurisdiction the court cannot proceed at all in any cause. Jurisdiction is power to declare the law, and when it ceases to exist, the only function remaining to the court is that of announcing the fact and dismissing the case . . . this court cannot proceed to pronounce judgment in this case, for it has no longer jurisdiction of the appeal; and judicial duty is not less fitly performed by declining ungranted jurisdiction than in exercising firmly that which the constitution and the laws confer.

Congress's reluctance in practice to exercise its right under Article III, Section 2, is illustrated by two issues that prompted impassioned debate: anti-Communism in the 1950s; and school prayer in the 1980s. In the 1950s, the force of anti-Communist sentiment was so great and the anxieties it produced so intense that in 1958, Senate Majority Leader Lyndon Johnson secured by just one vote the tabling of the Jenner–Butler Bill to deprive the Court of jurisdiction in most security cases. In the 1980s, the US Senate defeated an attempt to exclude all school prayer cases from the jurisdiction of the Federal courts by a vote of 62 to 36. Other attempts to restrict the Courts' appellate jurisdiction over elements of the social agenda promoted by President Reagan and some of his supporters also failed in the 1980s.

"Standing" of the Parties and Judicial Restraint

In all cases arising under the Court's appellate jurisdiction, the party or parties bringing suit must have "standing": they must have a direct and personal interest in the outcome of the case. The rule ensures that great though the wider significance of an individual case may be, it derives from the Court's judgment in a particular case concerning parties who themselves contest the constitutionality of an Act or an action in specific, and not general, terms. In the absence of such a case or controversy, where one of the parties claims that her or his Constitutional rights (which must be a specific right or rights) have been infringed, the Court cannot act. The Court cannot offer advisory opinions on major questions of public concern, or on hypothetical questions, simply because a majority of Justices think a constitutional question involved. This restriction is a key element in 'judicial restraint" – a doctrine by no means confined to some conservatives alone. Judicial restraint matters. If the Court were to abandon or weaken it, the foundations of its legitimacy and effectiveness would be weakened.

Procedure

Appeal and certiorari

Most cases that come to the Court for review do so either on appeal as a matter of right, or through the granting of *certiorari* where there exists no right but merely the privilege of petitioning the Court for the granting of a writ that the case may be "made more certain". Even in cases of appeal by right, the Court may dismiss the appeal (as it does in approximately nine-tenths of appeals brought to it) if the Justices determine either that no substantial Federal question is involved or if they discover that the Federal question was not raised at an early stage in proceedings in the State Court. There have been various moves to abolish the right of appeal and confine all cases of review to *certiorari* but, at the time of writing, cases of appeal may be brought to the Supreme Court by right:

- On appeal from the highest relevant State Court that has held a Federal statute to be unconstitutional.
- On appeal from the highest relevant State Court that has upheld a statute of the State or a provision in the State's constitution over a challenge that it conflicts with the United States Constitution, a Federal statute, or a Treaty.
- On appeal from a Federal District or Circuit Court where the United States is a party in a suit following the judgment of the Federal Court that part or all of a Federal statute or Treaty is unconstitutional.
- On appeal from a US Circuit Court of Appeals following a judgment by it that a State law conflicts with the United States Constitution, a Federal statute, or a Treaty.
- On appeal from a special District Court comprising three Judges, which has issued or denied an injunction in cases specified by Congress in statute (especially regarding voting and civil rights, and reapportionment cases) or from any other Federal court.

There is no right of appeal to the US Supreme Court in other cases. A writ of *certiorari* may be granted, according to Rule 19 of the Court, only "when there are special and important reasons therefor", but these now account for nine-tenths of all the cases which the Supreme Court accepts for review, including the following instances:

- When two Federal District Courts or US Circuit Courts of Appeals have delivered conflicting decisions (as happened when the Public Accommodations Title III of the 1964 Civil Rights Act was upheld and struck down by different District Courts).
- When a State Court or a US Circuit Court of Appeals has given judgment on an important Federal question which the Supreme Court has not considered.

- When a State Court or US Circuit Court of Appeals has made a judgment conflicting with a Supreme Court precedent.
- When a Federal District Court or US Circuit Court of Appeals has made procedural errors of such significance as to require the Supreme Court to exercise its authority.

Petitions for *certiorari* are considered at the Conference which meets on most Fridays during the Court's term; under the 1925 Judiciary Act, the Court has unfettered discretion over whether to grant them. Only one justice has to support a petition's inclusion in the "discuss" list for it to be considered. Records of such cases, the briefs from the plaintiff and the respondent, in addition to any briefs filed by other parties (*amicus curiae,* see p. 192) are then issued to each justice for consideration prior to the Conference.

Although only one vote is necessary for the case to be considered at Friday Conferences, for *certiorari* to be granted, four votes are required. Occasionally, Justices may change their minds after listening to colleagues at the Conference, as happened in a case of brutality by prison authorities in Florida: in *Brooks* v. *Florida,* 389 US 413 (1967), Chief Justice Warren dissented, scathingly but alone, from his eight colleagues' refusal to grant *certiorari.* His dissent not only persuaded his colleagues to grant it, but also thereafter to issue a unanimous *per curiam* opinion reversing the lower Court's decision. Such drama is untypical: 85 per cent or more of the petitions discussed at the Friday Conference are not accepted for review. They may be (i) summarily reversed; (ii) summarily affirmed; (iii) "vacated and the case remanded" back to the lower Court to be decided in the light of a particular decision of the Supreme Court; or (iv) dismissed because the petition is held by six or more of the Justices not to involve a substantial Federal question, or because they think that the Supreme Court has no jurisdiction in the case. The Conference is therefore a sifting mechanism, both to ensure that the Court's role adheres to Article III of the Constitution, and to control the burden of work.

The Conference is the only regular meeting of the nine Justices. In his book *The Politics of the US Supreme Court*, Richard Hodder-Williams (1980, p. 81) cites Justice Lewis Powell's observation that prior to becoming a member of the Court he had supposed that it would act as a collegial body whose dominant procedural characteristics would be "consultation and deliberation". In fact, as Powell discovered, the Court is "a bastion of jealously preserved individualism". Justices depend very largely upon themselves and their law clerks, who usually serve for a year. In 1989, each of the Justices had four law clerks, except for Chief Justices Rehnquist and Stevens, who chose to have three and two respectively. In addition, the Associate Justices have two secretaries and the Chief Justice three. Although the Federal Executive and Legislature enjoy large staff resources, the Court does not.

Oral Argument

The public phase of the Court's activity takes place in the chamber of the Court itself. Oral argument there takes place during two weeks each month (normally from Monday to Wednesday, but sometimes from Monday to Thursday), in two sessions: from 10 am–12 noon, and from 1 pm–3 pm. The public may attend: there are 188 seats in the public gallery, and a further 112 for members of the bar, Justices' families, and the press. Time for oral argument is limited – usually to thirty minutes for each side. Occasionally, this allowance is doubled, and even more rarely increased still further: reflecting the case's importance, argument in *Brown* v. *Board of Education II* (1955) (see pp. 213–15) was allotted fourteen hours. Justices' views about the importance of oral argument for the clarification of opinions vary. Justice Douglas thought it often decisive; Chief Justice Warren did not. It is in any event the only occasion on which the Court performs its functions publicly. Lawyers admitted to practise before the Court (not itself a difficult hurdle, but a privilege which the Supreme Court may remove in the event of his or her disbarment by the state bar of which she or he is a member – as former President Richard Nixon and two of his Attorneys-General, John Mitchell and Richard Kleindienst, were) must accustom themselves to interruption from the bench. Some Justices (Antonin Scalia is a good, though to some of his colleagues, an irritating, example) make a practice of interrupting frequently.

Filing of Written Briefs

By the time that oral argument takes place on one of the six or seven days allotted for it each month, the Justices have, with their clerks' assistance, and after much reading and assessment, already considered the case before them. Justices' dependence on written briefs submitted not just by the plaintiffs and respondents in the case, but also by groups with an interest in the case who may file briefs as "a friend of the Court" (*amicus curiae*), is high. *Amicus curiae* briefs enable interested organisations (especially groups such as the NAACP in the 1950s and 1960s (see Chapter 3), the American Civil Liberties Union, the AFL-CIO, or the National Organisation of Women, and the United States government) to make known their views and add to the case of the plaintiff or the respondent. The number of such briefs filed has increased in recent years, and some cases attract many of them. Cases having a major commercial significance instantly draw the attention of corporate lawyers. The gender-discrimination case *Liberty Mutual* v. *Wetzel*, 421 US 1010 (1975) attracted the National Association of Manufacturers, the US Chamber of Commerce, AT&T, General Motors, and Westinghouse Electric. Twenty-one major airlines (who employed more than 100,000 women) joined the fray, to the pleasure and profit of their lawyers (Hodder-Williams, 1980, pp. 89–90). *Amicus curiae* briefs are often an attractive option for groups denied access or remedy elsewhere, whether in the States, or in the Federal Executive or Legislature. The NAACP employed the tactic in segregation and voting rights' cases in the 1950s and early 1960s. The Federal government also employs it: for the Reagan Administration it was one means by which the President (vainly) attempted to implement his policies on school prayer and abortion.

Oral argument having been concluded, the public phase of the Court's work ends. Justices then meet (without clerical assistance) in Conference, privately. This is the same Friday (and, since 1974, on Wednesday afternoons, too) meeting of Conference at which petitions for *certiorari* are heard. Cases heard by the Justices in oral argument that week, and those recently discussed in conferences without having proceeded to oral argument, are discussed here.

Both at this stage and later, when the opinion or opinions of the Court on the case in question are written, the Chief Justice has the opportunity to exercise special influence. He speaks first in Conference, chairs the meeting, and votes last (Associate Justices vote in ascending order of seniority). He may, if he thinks it appropriate, decide in the light of his colleagues' votes and arguments to vote differently from the way he had intended. Extensive and frequently vigorous discussion may take place, unlimited by time, following which a preliminary vote is taken (which commits no one). The second, and final, vote takes place later, following drafting of opinions when such general implications as the Court's majority may decide to make are determined. This initial vote is simply on whether the lower court's judgment should be upheld or rejected (in the language of the Court, "affirmed" or "reversed").

If, whether by conviction or calculation, the Chief Justice finds himself in the majority, he then has the responsibility (which he discharges within a fortnight of the Conference ending) of assigning the writing of the "opinion", or draft judgment. He may either request a colleague to write it, or write it himself. The opportunity to choose is considerable, enabling a resourceful Chief to frame the opinion in order that it should win the assent of his colleagues, or have wide or narrow implications as he thinks best. This can usually best be done if he writes it himself, but since his colleagues' views will invariably be well known, to him, he may think it advantageous for political, personal, or collegial reasons to give the job to a colleague. If the Court's heavy workload is to be shared fairly, it is important that assignments be widely distributed. In practice, Chief Justices assign most opinions to their colleagues, with the result that each Justice typically writes between fourteen and eighteen opinions in each term. Both Warren and Burger assigned only about one in ten cases to themselves. If the Chief Justice finds himself in the minority (as Chief Justice Rehnquist has often done) the senior Associate Justice assigns the writing of the majority opinion.

The Chief Justice may think it wise or necessary to write the opinion himself, in order (for example) that the Court's judgment be seen to carry the fullest weight with lower courts, and with Congressional and public opinion. *Brown* v. *Board of Education* in 1954 is the paradigmatic example: it was essential that such a momentous case should be written by the Chief Justice, and that the final draft should command the unanimous backing of the Court. The same was true of the Court's unanimous decision in *United States* v. *Richard M. Nixon*, 418 US 683 (1974), where the President's own appointee to the Chief Justiceship, Warren Burger, wrote the opinion that precipitated the end of Nixon's career.

While the immediate objective of an opinion's author is to secure the assent of at least four colleagues, the value of the opinion as settled law is diminished if, in the rush to achieve consensus, intellectual coherence, clarity, and force are lost. Drafting and redrafting of an opinion often fails to persuade those who were initially unpersuaded at Conference. They may then join with other colleagues in the minority and by means of a single dissenting judgment oppose the majority judgment. Alternatively, they may write a separate opinion of their own, dissenting from the majority but on different grounds. Past dissents are often cited by members of the Court's majority when overturning judgments made by their predecessors. In writing dissenting opinions, Justices occasionally invite future members of the Court to consider their arguments (another indication that the Court's decisions are contributions to constitutional evolution rather than final and decisive judgments.) The clearest instance of a dissent coming to represent the majority view is the lone argument of John Harlan (a former slave-owner) in *Plessy* v. *Ferguson*, 163 US 537, in 1896:

> Our Constitution is color-blind, and neither knows nor tolerates classes among citizens. In respect of civil rights, all citizens are equal before the law. The humblest is the peer of the most powerful.

The increasing complexity of the issues involved in the cases before the Court has increased the incidence not only of dissents but of plurality decisions, where Justices give different reasons for their decision. A majority may therefore contain several separate opinions. *New York Times Company* v. *United States*, 403 US 713 (1971), the so-called *Pentagon Papers* case, drew nine opinions from the bench, as *Dred Scott* v. *Sandford* 19 Howard 393 (1857) had done. Such revealed divisions usually muddy the reasoning undergirding the Court's judgment.

Drafting of the opinion makes heavy jurisprudential and diplomatic demands upon the author. In his work on draft opinions printed and circulated within the Supreme Court, Bernard Schwartz (1985, p. 19) claims that the decision process is "essentially . . . political". Justices are, as he shows, often open to persuasion by the arguments which their colleagues deploy. For example, in the years following *Brown*, the Court granted *certiorari* in cases involving sit-in protests by blacks against restaurants that served food to whites only. Decided shortly before discrimination in public places and public accommodations became illegal, *Bell* v. *Maryland* 378 US 226 (1964), concerned the arrest and conviction of blacks for violating state trespass laws for having refused to leave a whites-only restaurant in Baltimore until they were served a meal. Declining to reverse the convictions on narrow, technical, grounds (as President Kennedy's Solicitor-General urged in an *amicus curiae* brief) the Court opted to address the central question, and voted five to four in conference to affirm the convictions. The Chief Justice found himself in the minority (adamantly so) and Justice Black, the then senior Associate Justice, in the majority.

It was therefore Black's task to assign the opinion, and he did so to himself. He initially drafted an opinion in which he claimed that the State could not itself be held to be acting prejudicially (against the requirements of the Fourteenth Amendment) if it were merely enforcing trespass laws at the request of the owner of the restaurant. The Fourteenth Amendment was designed to prohibit discriminatory action by a State, and not by a private person or company. Such an interpretation had been upheld by the Court as recently as 1948 in *Shelley* v. *Kraemer*, 344 US 1.

Circulation of draft opinions occurred at the same time as the Senate filibuster on Title II of the Civil Rights Act, and Justice Brennan was alarmed at the prospect that Black's opinion as drafted would unwisely call the constitutionality of Title II into question. He proposed instead that the convictions should be reversed under laws prohibiting discrimination in public facilities in Baltimore passed since the convictions took place. Three of Brennan's colleagues, including the Chief Justice, agreed to support his draft. Brennan's opinion became the majority opinion of the Court when Justice Stewart supported it in order to prevent a majority forming behind an alternative opinion circulated by Justice Clark, reversing the convictions on the grounds that they violated the Fourteenth Amendment because of the State's close involvement in enforcing private discrimination. Clark preferred Brennan's politically subtle judgment (that in the difficult circumstances of 1964 the case would be better decided on narrow grounds) to be supported, and joined him accordingly. The constitutional question involved was therefore avoided by the Court, partly because it was expected that it would be addressed by the Congress and Executive shortly afterwards through the 1964 Civil Rights Act.

A Justice may (as *Bell* v. *Maryland* showed) alter her or his mind up to and including Opinion Day, when the final written opinions of the Court are published. A collective view cannot, therefore, be imposed by Justices in the drafting of a judgment. It may, by careful crafting and modification, be elicited.

Judical Review

Judicial review occurs frequently in Federal systems, where the boundaries between the Federal and provincial authorities are often unclear, and in separated systems of government, where boundaries between the branches are imprecisely drawn, contested, or both. For both reasons, judicial review in the United States is especially important because of the Court's capacity to determine the constitutionality of laws passed by a democratically-elected Congress, and the constitutionality of the actions of the single elected Executive and of unelected officials. The Court's power of judicial review was implied by the Constitution without being expressly granted. It was certainly regarded by several of the founders as being logically required in order to defend the Constitution they had written. It was not, however, unambiguously affirmed as a power of the Court until Chief Justice Marshall's seminal judgment in *Marbury* v. *Madison* in 1803.

Such apparently sweeping power in a democracy to overrule the actions and decisions of elected people is contentious. The Court was not designed to be a representative institution, but its power, coupled with its appointive character, alarms those who see liberty's best defence in democratic accountability. Judicial review is both anti-majoritarian and undemocratic, yet the United States Constitution was constructed neither as a simply majoritarian nor as a wholly democratic system.

Functions of Judicial Review

The Supreme Court has two tasks. The first it shares with Supreme Courts in other countries: the interpretation of legislation, and judging the lawfulness of the actions of public officials. Unlike Courts in the United Kingdom, however, the US Supreme Court is a branch of government in a Constitution which divides powers between the branches, between the Federal and State governments, and guarantees to citizens of the United States a panoply of rights against government. Unlike the *Conseil Constitutionnel* under the French Fifth Republic, its importance derives (as discussed on p. 187 above) from its appellate rather than its original jurisdiction. The Court's decisively important task is its second: determining the fit between Constitutional and Statute Law, pronouncing upon the constitutionality of an Act of Congress, of a Title, clause, or clauses within the Act, or the constitutionality of an act of a State Legislature, or an action of an elected politician or unelected official.

With respect to the first task, the Court's construction of a statute can be overturned by an Act of Congress, although pressure on Congress's time usually makes this harder to achieve than those Members of Congress and Senators most opposed to the Court's judgment wish. The greater power of the Court lies in judicial review where Congress may not overturn the Court's construction of the Constitution except by initiating a Constitutional amendment (an altogether more difficult task than amending a statute). Congress may also, as explained earlier, forestall judicial review by explicitly making exceptions to the Court's appellate powers.

Since government in America at both Federal and State level is held accountable not only by the frequency of elections, but also by Constitutional guarantees, the arrangement requires an arbiter. Hamilton, in *Federalist* No. 78, reminded his readers of what the Constitution itself declares: the Constitution is supreme. It is by implication the task of the Supreme Court (and that of those inferior Federal Courts created by Congress) to determine whether or not individual statutes or actions by public officials accord with it. If they do not, they are unconstitutional, null and void, and must be amended as appropriate or rescinded:

> A constitution is, in fact, and must be regarded by the Judges as, a fundamental law. It therefore belongs to them to ascertain its meaning as well as the meaning of any particular act proceeding from the legislative body. If there should happen to be an irreconcilable variance between the two, that which has the superior obligation and validity ought, of course, to be preferred: or, in other words, the Constitution ought to be preferred to the statute, the intention of the people to the intention of their agents.

This is an instructive commentary on what came to be accepted as the Court's decisive power. Although Hamilton acknowledges that the Constitution does not explicitly grant it, he insists that central to the jurisdiction of the proposed Supreme Court is the power of judicial review. In so far as any constitution limited upon a Legislature's freedom of action, the doctrine of judicial review was logically entailed. The experience of most of the States themselves showed this clearly enough in different settings: judicial review was a common State practice, both prior to the adoption of the Constitution in 1789, and afterwards. At least eight States in their conventions held to ratify the new US Constitution explicitly accepted that the Supreme Court would possess the power to declare Acts of Congress null and void (Abraham, 1986, p. 322). The lacunae, ambiguities, and uncertainties of the Constitution were from the time of its defence by the authors of *The Federalist* pregnant with future political dispute. Hamilton was not alone in holding that judgment of cases arising from them was the proper province of the Court. If its members did not defend the new constitutional order's integrity, who might properly and plausibly do so? Where else could the Constitution be impartially interpreted free from the pressures generated in a popularly-elected Legislature? Both the doctrine and practice of judicial review are not merely consistent with the separation of powers and the doctrine of limited government, but are implied by them.

Marbury v. Madison (1803)

Although Hamilton's discussion of the Supreme Court's role was predicated on the Court's power to declare "all acts contrary to the manifest tenor of the Constitution void", and despite a number of State Supreme Courts themselves having practised judicial review, the Court explicitly assumed the power only in 1803, sixteen years after the Republic's founding. It did so in one of the most important cases ever to come before it: *Marbury* v. *Madison*, 1 Cranch 137 (1803). The case was extraordinary for taking the process by which the Court had in its first fourteen years begun to establish its province a decisive stage further: the power of judicial review of Federal statutes was here explicitly claimed, and the basis for the further power of judicial review over State Statutes and actions laid. It was also shocking by modern standards for the Chief Justice, John Marshall, having, in his previous incarnation as President Adams's Secretary of State, been intimately involved in the political circumstances which gave rise to the case.

Those circumstances were as follows: after Thomas Jefferson's victory in the Presidential election of 1800 over John Adams, the incumbent President, Adams strove desperately to pack the Judicial branch with his Federalist supporters before he left office in March 1801. The attempt was largely successful because the Senate, in which the Federalist Party had a majority, was as anxious to confirm the Federalist nominees in their posts before Jefferson took the oath of office as Adams was to nominate them. Among the nominees was Marshall himself; he stayed on in government (long after his mentor had left it) by moving from the State Department to the Chief Justiceship of the Supreme Court. As Adams's Secretary of State, it had been Marshall's official responsibility to deliver letters of commission to the new appointees following their confirmation by the Senate and the signing of their commissions by the President. He did so in all the important cases, but failed in respect of seventeen Justices of the Peace (posts created under the District of Columbia Organic Law Act in early 1801, during the transition between Adams and Jefferson).

Upon taking office in March 1801, President Jefferson declined to order that the remaining seventeen letters of commission be delivered by James Madison, the new Secretary of State. Four of the disappointed office-seekers challenged the President in the Supreme Court, petitioning it to issue a writ of *mandamus*, commanding Madison to serve the letters of commission, under the powers granted the Court by Section 13 of the Judiciary Act of 1789. The circumstances were thus highly charged. A Federalist appointee confirmed in office by a Federalist Senate led a Court in judgment of an intensely political case over a question of patronage. Marshall rose to the occasion. In his opinion, he disposed of any doubt either that William Marbury, one of the four, was entitled to his commission, or that the laws of the United States afforded him a remedy. He was, and they did. The third question was the difficult one, the hinge on which Marshall's judgment turned: did the Supreme Court have the power to issue such a writ?

He established by argument that Section 13 of the Judiciary Act of 1789, which granted to the Supreme Court the power to issue writs of *mandamus*, was unconstitutional. Marshall asserted that by doing so, Congress had expanded the original jurisdiction granted the Court by the Constitution. This was a contentious claim. It could more reasonably have been argued that Congress was merely granting the Court procedural power to issue such a writ when this would be appropriate in respect of cases properly brought before the Court on either its original or its appellate docket. However, Marshall held that Section 13 represented a substantive addition to the powers of the Court; he did so because to have interpreted it as merely a procedural power would have denied him the opportunity he wished to exploit. Article III of the Constitution permitted no such expansion. He reasoned that the writ therefore could not be issued. This judgment circumvented political opposition. Marshall well understood the implications of any miscalculation: Madison would probably refuse to obey a writ of *mandamus* were one to be issued. A constitutional crisis would certainly result. Justices of the Supreme Court have no powers of enforcement save the authority which they command by virtue of their standing in defence of the constitutional order. Marbury therefore lost his case; he and his three colleagues did not secure the jobs they sought. But this outcome amounted to no inglorious retreat on Marshall's part. His decisive achievement in *Marbury* was still to come.

Marshall drew on Hamilton's case, forcefully presented in *The Federalist Papers*, dealing with the relationship between the judicial branch and the other two. Constitutional prohibitions of certain actions, such as those against a Bill of Attainder (the extinction of a person's civil rights in consequence of a death sentence, or outlawry following a conviction) or *ex post facto* law could, he argued, have no force unless their prohibition were to be enforced by the Court. Marshall added that, just as Congress's scope of action is restricted by the provisions of the Constitution, so is the Court's. He reminded the readers of his judgment that he and his colleagues had taken an oath of office to discharge their duties "according to the constitution and laws of the United States". "Why", he then asked:

> does a Judge swear to discharge his duties agreeably to the constitution of the United States, if that constitution forms no rule for his government? . . . If such be the real state of things, this is worse than solemn mockery. Thus, the particular phraseology of the constitution of the United States confirms and strengthens the principle, supposed to be essential to all written constitutions, that a law repugnant to the constitution is void; and that courts, as well as other departments, are bound by that instrument.

Marshall thus wrote Hamilton's argument and the Constitution's logic into constitutional law by denying the Court he led a power granted it by an Act of Congress which he declared unconstitutional. By finding that the Court lacked a trivial and particular power, he imparted to it an infinitely greater one. The threat of conflict between the judiciary and the executive was adroitly avoided, and the place of the Court in the constitutional order strengthened.

It was the first and last occasion on which Marshall declared an Act of Congress unconstitutional, an indication neither of his nor of the Court's weakness, but of his circumspection in establishing its legitimacy and power, and of Congress's disinclination to challenge this subtle affirmation of the Court's independence. There was none the less a further step to the Court's full assertion of judicial review: its capacity to declare acts of State Legislatures or actions of State officials unconstitutional. Steps towards this had been taken in *Chisholm* v. *Georgia*, 2 Dallas 419 (1793) and in *Marbury* v. *Madison*, but only with Marshall's unanimous opinion for the Court in *Fletcher* v. *Peck*, 6 Cranch 87 (1810) did the Court establish its right (much as that right was contested) to declare an Act of a State Legislature unconstitutional. In prohibiting the state of Georgia from rescinding a corrupt sale of land because to do so would impair the obligation of a contract, it also established that State governments are bound by contracts to which they are a party.

The Supreme Court and the Elected Branches

In the first year of the Republic, Congress established, through the 1789 Judiciary Act, that the Court should comprise a Chief Justice and five Associate Justices. The number of Judges was increased by an Act of 1869 to nine, at which figure it has since remained (except in the periods between a Justice's resignation or death and the confirmation of her or his successor).

By its powers to create additional District and Circuit Courts, to alter the number of Justices on the Supreme Court, to set judicial salaries, to restrict appellate powers, and through the important role of the Senate in considering the President's nominees to the Courts, Congress involves itself in the politics of the Federal Courts in general and the US Supreme Court in particular. Recruitment to the Federal Courts involves both the Senate and the President. Following confirmation, Federal Judges and Justices enjoy substantial autonomy; during the Senate confirmation process, many endure close scrutiny from elected politicians.

The intermeshing of the Federal Courts in general and of the US Supreme Court in particular with the elected branches is none the less of greatest significance in the appointments process. The Court comprises six white men, two white women, and one black man. Like their colleagues in the District and Circuit Courts, Supreme Court Justices are appointed, subject to the confirmation of the Senate (see Exhibit 6.2). Once confirmed by the Senate, they are formally unaccountable. Their appointments are for life (which usually means that they serve until death, or close to it). In recent years, Hugo Black retired after thirty-four years on the Court, and died shortly afterwards. Except when Justices move to other posts (as Abraham Goldberg did upon his appointment as Ambassador to the United Nations in 1965) they rarely retire when still active and in good health; some continue in post when neither. Article III, Section 1 of the Constitution places just one qualification upon life tenure – that Justices of the Supreme Court and Judges of the inferior Federal Courts "shall hold their offices during good Behavior".

Article III, Section 1 of the Constitution prescribes that members of the Federal bench were to receive at "stated times . . . a Compensation which shall not be diminished during their Continuance in Office". In *Federalist* No.79, Hamilton held that tenure and a regular salary "affords a better prospect of their independence than is discoverable in the constitutions of any of the States in regard to their own Judges". None the less, the Constitution made no allowance for inflation, and hence no provision for judicial salaries to be protected from its effects. Both in 1964 and 1973, when inflation had eroded judicial salaries, in pointed displays of one branch's displeasure with the decisions of another, Congress raised the pay of District and Circuit Court Judges by more than it did the salaries of Supreme Court Justices.

Most of those appointed to the Court are well into middle age; few have been appointed when younger than fifty. Of those nominated to the Court and confirmed since the beginning of Franklin Roosevelt's administration, William O. Douglas was the youngest (aged forty) at the time of his confirmation, and Clarence Thomas almost as young at forty-three in 1991. Most have been in their late fifties or early sixties. The average age of the Court therefore tends to be high; in the 1980s, it became exceptionally so. In late 1987, as President Reagan (the oldest President in American history) struggled to find a successor to Justice Powell, who had resigned earlier in the year at the age of 79, Justice Brennan was 80 years old, his colleagues Marshall and White were 79, and Justice Blackmun 78. Brennan resigned only in 1990, Marshall in 1991, White in 1993, and Blackmun in 1994. The intellectual demands made by the job of Supreme Court justice are considerable, and the stamina required to meet those demands by no means insignificant. Justices of advanced years labour under burdens that very few of their peers contemplate, still less endure. Venting his frustration at his large workload in his old age, Justice Blackmun observed in 1984 that being a Justice was "a rotten way to earn a living".

None the less, guarding the Court's independence from interference by Congress or the Presidency is so important that there have been no serious attempts to require the retirement of Justices at a certain age. However,

EXHIBIT 6.2

Justices of the United States Supreme Court

(Chief Justices in **bold** type)

Justice	State	Term	Years in office
John Jay	NY	**1789–1795**	**6**
John Rutledge	SC	1789–1791	2
William Cushing	MA	1789–1810	21
James Wilson	PA	1789–1798	9
John Blair	VA	1790–1796	7
James Iredell	NC	1790–1799	9
Thomas Johnson	MD	1792–1793	1
William Paterson	NJ	1793–1806	13
John Rutledge	SC	**1795–1795**	–
Samuel Chase	MD	1796–1811	15
Oliver Ellsworth	CT	**1796–1799**	**4**
Bushrod Washington	VA	1799–1829	31
Alfred Moore	NC	1800–1804	3
John Marshall	VA	**1801–1835**	**34**
William Johnson	SC	1804–1834	30
Brock Livingston	NY	1807–1823	16
Thomas Todd	KY	1807–1826	18
Joseph Story	MA	1812–1845	33
Gabriel Duval	MD	1811–1835	23
Smith Thompson	NY	1823–1843	20
Robert Trimble	KY	1826–1828	2
John McLean	OH	1830–1861	32
Henry Baldwin	PA	1830–1844	14
James Wayne	GA	1835–1867	32
Roger Taney	MD	**1836–1864**	**28**
Philip Barbour	VA	1836–1841	5
John Catron	TN	1837–1865	28
John McKinley	AL	1838–1852	14
Peter Daniel	VA	1842–1860	18
Samuel Nelson	NY	1845–1872	27
Levi Woodbury	NH	1845–1851	6
Robert Grier	PA	1846–1870	23
Benjamin Curtis	MA	1851–1857	6
John Campbell	AL	1853–1861	8
Nathan Clifford	ME	1858–1881	23
Noah Swayne	OH	1862–1881	18
Samuel Miller	IO	1862–1890	28
David Davis	IL	1862–1877	14
Stephen Field	CA	1863–1897	34
Salmon Chase	OH	**1864–1873**	**9**
William Strong	PA	1870–1880	10
Joseph Bradley	NY	1870–1892	21
Ward Hunt	NY	1873–1882	10
Morrison Waite	OH	**1874–1888**	**14**

Justice	State	Term	Years in office
John Harlan	KY	1877–1911	34
William Woods	GA	1881–1887	6
Stanley Matthews	OH	1881–1889	8
Horace Gray	MA	1882–1902	20
Samuel Blatchford	NY	1882–1893	11
Lucius Lamar	MS	1888–1893	5
Melville Fuller	**IL**	**1888–1910**	**21**
David Brewer	KA	1890–1910	20
Henry Brown	MI	1891–1906	15
George Shiras	PA	1892–1903	10
Howell Jackson	TN	1893–1895	2
Edward White	LA	1894–1910	16
Rufus Peckham	NY	1896–1909	13
Joseph McKenna	CA	1898–1925	26
Oliver Holmes	MA	1902–1932	29
William Day	OH	1903–1922	19
William Moody	MA	1906–1910	4
Horace Lurton	TN	1910–1914	4
Charles Hughes	NY	1910–1916	5
Willis van Devanter	WY	1911–1937	26
Edward White	**LA**	**1910–1921**	**10**
Joseph Lamar	GA	1911–1916	6
Mahlon Pitney	NJ	1912–1922	10
James McReynolds	TN	1914–1941	26
Louis Brandeis	MA	1916–1939	22
John Clarke	OH	1916–1922	5
William Taft	**CT**	**1921–1930**	**8**
George Sutherland	UT	1922–1938	15
Pierce Butler	MN	1923–1939	16
Edward Sanford	TN	1923–1930	7
Harlan Stone	NY	1925–1941	16
Charles Hughes	**NY**	**1930–1941**	**11**
Owen Roberts	PA	1930–1945	15
Benjamin Cardozo	NY	1932–1938	6
Hugo Black	AL	1937–1971	34
Stanley Reed	KY	1938–1957	19
Felix Frankfurter	MA	1939–1962	23
William Douglas	CT	1939–1975	36
Frank Murphy	MI	1940–1949	9
Harlan Stone	**NY**	**1941–1946**	**5**
Robert Jackson	NY	1941–1954	13
Wiley Rutledge	IO	1943–1949	6
Harold Burton	OH	1945–1958	13
Fred Vinson	**KY**	**1946–1953**	**7**
Tom Clark	TX	1949–1967	18
Sherman Minton	IN	1949–1956	7
Earl Warren	**CA**	**1953–1969**	**16**
John Harlan	KY	1955–1971	16

Exhibit 6.2 continued overleaf

EXHIBIT 6.2 continued

Justice	State	Term	Years in office
William Brennan	NJ	1956–1990	34
Charles Whittaker	MO	1957–1962	5
Potter Stewart	OH	1958–1981	22
Byron White	CO	1962–1993	31
Arthur Goldberg	IL	1962–1965	2
Abe Fortas	TN	1965–1969	3
Thurgood Marshall	NY	1967–1991	24
Warren Burger	**MN**	**1969–1986**	**17**
Harry Blackmun	MN	1970–1994	24
William Rehnquist	**AZ**	**1972–1986**	**14**
Lewis Powell	VA	1972–1988	16
John Paul Stevens	IL	1975–	
Sandra O'Connor	AZ	1981–	
Antonin Scalia	NJ	1986–	
William Rehnquist	AZ	1986–	
Anthony Kennedy	CA	1988–	
David Souter	NH	1990–	
Clarence Thomas	GA	1991–	
Ruth Bader Ginsburg	DC	1993–	
Stephen Breyer	CA	1994–	

under the compromise eventually passed following the defeat of the core of Roosevelt's "Court-packing" Bill in 1937 (see p. 290), the financial pain of retirement endured by Federal Judges and Justices has been eased by establishing exceptionally generous pension arrangements. This inducement notwithstanding, Supreme Court Justices tend to carry on. Liberal and moderate members of the Court remained on the Court throughout the 1980s partly in order to deny President Reagan (for whose politics they did not care, and whose view of the Court's proper role they did not accept) the opportunity to nominate their successors. Ironically, the opportunity to replace them fell to another conservative President, George Bush.

The composition of the Court is the subject of political dispute almost as intense as its judgments. Processes of selection and confirmation of nominees to the Court involve both the Executive and Legislative Branches. The President proposes a name to the Senate which, after hearings and voting by the Judiciary Committee, confirms, denies, or declines to act upon the nomination. The Senate is under no obligation to confirm a President's nominees to the Court (although Presidents frustrated by the Senate's resistance to their will have often claimed that it is). The Constitution grants to the Senate a full role in considering the worth of nominees to the Federal bench at all levels. Its role is not ancillary. By reason of its importance and prominence in American government, nominations to the Supreme Court naturally attract particularly close attention from the Senate Judiciary Committee and the full Senate.

The manner of their appointment made the Federal Judiciary's role inescapably political from the first. The autonomy which the Constitution guaranteed them after confirmation by the Senate gave them the freedom to judge without fear of retribution. They were obliged only to make judgments on the cases before them, so that limited government within the framework of the Constitution might be ensured. Since the Constitution has been modified more by judgments of the Federal Courts than it has by the cumbersome process of amendment, this task is at once difficult and essential. It is assuredly political, but equally certainly not just political.

Threats, Manipulation, and Impeachment

Franklin Roosevelt's attempt in 1937 to increase the number of Justices on the Bench so that the Court's opposition to his New Deal legislation might be overcome remains the only attempt by a President or Congress to modify the size of the Court for unambiguously partisan ends. Although Roosevelt proposed the expansion of the Court following his own triumphant re-election in 1936, when he benefited additionally from enormous partisan advantage in Congress, the plan made no progress. Instead, it weakened the President and divided the Democratic Party. Roosevelt's offence was constitutional rather than simply political, and widely regarded as such. Buoyed by his enormous victory in the election, he reckoned that he could assert his power over the then conservative, activist, Bench that had assaulted the New Deal. Rashly, he pressed the plan on Congress without prior warning either to the Democratic leadership or his own Cabinet.

In seeking to make the Supreme Court more pliable in the face of a liberal President's legislative designs, Roosevelt's proposal opened the way for a future conservative President to employ the Court for very different political ends. The Constitution's greatest strength is often held to be its flexibility. Yet its resilience is as important, tempered by the jealousy with which institutional balances of power are defended. In August 1937, Roosevelt's Bill died in Congress, to the relief of his Vice-President and other allies, but not before damage had been done to the New Deal coalition in Congress. In the interim, the circumstances that had prompted Roosevelt to strike against the Court had in any case changed. Justice Van Devanter (one of the five conservative members of the bench) retired in May (less than four months after the Court-packing Bill was sent to Congress), and Justice Roberts, who had voted to strike down much New Deal legislation as unconstitutional, now changed his disposition and in a series of pending cases supported the Administration's view as represented by the Solicitor-General.

The formal autonomy of Supreme Court Justices is virtually complete. The sanction of impeachment, which applies to Justices and Federal Judges as it does to Presidents, is so drastic a remedy that in recent times it has not been pursued with great seriousness against any Justice. Justice Douglas was the subject of a feeble impeachment attempt in 1953 by a minor Congressman from Georgia following his vote to grant a stay of execution against Ethel and Julius Rosenberg; and again in 1970, but this time in bungled fashion by the Republican House Minority Leader, Gerald Ford, who claimed that Douglas had in his book *Points of Rebellion* (1970) endorsed revolution, that he had shockingly liberal views on censorship and, drawing on material supplied from FBI files by Attorney-General Mitchell (later convicted of serious crimes arising from the Watergate Affair), that he had links to organised crime. (The first and third claims were ludicrous, and the second politically expedient for Ford.) The attempt was, as Ford later conceded, unwise. At the prompting of the John Birch Society, following the seminal decision prohibiting school segregation in *Brown* v. *Board of Education, Topeka* (1954), some southern politicians sought to impeach most, if not all, of the Warren Court, but it came to nothing.

The impeachment of lower Federal Court Judges is rare, but not unknown. In all, eleven Federal Judges have been impeached by the House; all but one have been convicted by the Senate.

Autonomy, Longevity, and Justices' Behaviour

Judges and Justices themselves determine the time of their retirement (if death does not carry them away first). The arrangement grants Federal Judges and Justices greater autonomy in office than it does power to the Presidents who nominate them. What appears to most Presidents to be a valuable opportunity to shape the direction of politics and policy after (often long after) they themselves have left the White House amounts to less than it often seems. Thus, Justice William Brennan continued to sit on the Court and exercise influence over its more liberal wing thirty years after his nomination by the Republican President Eisenhower who, under the provisions of the Twenty-Second Amendment, was prevented from offering himself as a candidate for re-election in 1960 to a third term. However indirectly, Presidents' influence over policy continues from the graves of both their political and mortal lives.

Such longevity cuts two ways. It can work to the advantage of a President when his nominees to the Supreme Court, and to the Federal District and Circuit Courts, show on the bench the qualities, characteristics, and judicial philosophy that originally caused him to nominate them. Where they do not behave according to expectations, disappointment results.

Grants of power to one branch of Federal government are normally qualified either by their being shared, or by their setting in train processes that take away with the left hand what the constitution gives with the right. Both apply here. Presidents in practice share the appointment function with the Senate. Following confirmation, Presidents lose all control, and most of their influence, over their nominees. Ambitious Judges of the District and Circuit Courts may build a judicial record with half an eye on prospects for future advancement and are, to that extent, constrained. Supreme Court Justices, however, can advance no further. Ambition satisfied, their autonomy is complete; their independence, however, is qualified by prudential attention to the political circumstances within which they make their judgments and their anticipated ramifications.

It is therefore unsurprising that Justices should sometimes take a different course on the Bench from that which the President who nominated them anticipated. Though superficially attractive, classifying Justices simply as "conservative" or "liberal" often propounds a false polarity. In so far as Presidents think in these terms, they are bound to be disappointed. It is unclear, for example, how a "conservative" Chief Justice such as Burger should have judged cases involving enforcement of school desegregation, or variations on the *Miranda* case (see p. 186) involving the exclusion of improperly-obtained evidence. As a conservative, Burger (no doubt with Nixon's support) would feel bound to defend the rule of *stare decisis*, that of letting the precedent stand. Overturning precedent is not the act of a conservative judge, as Justice Souter reminded conservative critics in *Casey*. Yet to sustain precedent in new cases in the 1970s concerning the exclusion of improperly-obtained evidence was to uphold *Miranda*, a "liberal" decision. Complexities of judicial decision-making, and the inapplicability of a linear model covering all cases before the Court with 'conservatives" to the right of the scale, and "liberals" to the left, make Presidential disappointment still more likely. There is no logical inconsistency in a Justice adopting a conservative interpretation of the Constitutional limits on pornography, and a liberal interpretation of the constitutionality of the Federal regulation of the wages and conditions of employees of state and local governments. Indeed, many Federal Judges have done so.

The tangential influence which Presidents exert over judicial policy-making has been a cause of great anguish to Presidents of all persuasions. Theodore Roosevelt was furious that Oliver Wendell Holmes should have had the temerity to judge an important anti-trust case differently from the way he had expected and wished. Much later, President Truman took the view that his nomination of Judge Tom Clark had perhaps been unwise:

> it isn't so much that he's a bad man. It's just that he's such a dumb son of a bitch. He's about the dumbest man I think I've ever run across . . . I never will know what got into me when I made that appointment, and I'm as sorry as I can be for doing it. (Miller, 1974, p. 226)

Truman's conservative Republican successor in the White House, Dwight Eisenhower, had in his first year in office the opportunity to nominate a

Chief Justice, and later regretted his choice. Earl Warren, as Republican Governor of California during the Second World War, had approved of President Roosevelt's Executive Order confining American citizens of Japanese descent to prison camps. The combination of Warren's leadership of the Court between 1953 and 1969, and William Brennan's liberal jurisprudence, underpinned the Court's reforming opinions in those years. Eisenhower, who died in the year Warren retired, was privately displeased by the Warren Court's decision in *Brown* and angered by its judgments in cases involving the rights of accused people in the 1960s. Eisenhower was unmoved by Warren's defence of the application of the rules of due process to all Americans. including members of the Communist Party. On their way to Winston Churchill's funeral in 1965, Eisenhower angrily told Warren that Communists should be "killed".

Expectation of political propinquity is only one reason why a President appoints a particular individual: payment of political debts is another. Warren's nomination by Eisenhower owed much to the support which the then Governor of California gave to Eisenhower at the 1952 Republican Convention. Cultivation by Presidents of political advantage among ethnic, racial, and religious groups, and among women's organisations, also informs their choices. Presidents may also hope to cultivate constituents. For example, while Johnson's nomination of Thurgood Marshall in 1967 had much to do with his expectation that Marshall would continue judicially from the bench what Johnson had started politically from the Oval Office in civil rights and the Great Society, it had rather more to do with Johnson's view that it would be politically advantageous to nominate a black man to the Court. (Marshall had the added symbolic distinction of having argued the case for the litigants in *Brown* v. *Board of Education* thirteen years earlier, see p. 213.) Equally, by nominating Sandra Day O'Connor in 1981, President Reagan sent to the Senate for confirmation a conservative and distinguished lawyer. She won the support of conservatives and liberals in the Senate. Conservatives voted to confirm her nomination because she was on almost every matter except abortion solidly conservative: despite her ideological bent, liberals felt obliged to confirm her because of her intellect and her gender – a testimony to Reagan's shrewdness in nominating her.

Unless there is clear evidence that a nominee is corrupt, has poor financial judgment, low moral standards, or is opposed to the law and established political values on such matters as civil rights, she or he is likely to be confirmed. Robert Bork's experience notwithstanding (see p. 211), nominees are in little danger of rejection by the Senate Judiciary Committee or the full Senate simply because of their judicial philosophy. While a nominee with a distinct conservative or liberal record provides Senators with ideological axes to grind with a public platform for their views, opposition of this kind has not normally been sufficient to persuade a majority of the Senate.

Scrutiny Prior to Nomination

In addition to the formal procedures by which the Senate examines nominees, thorough security investigations are made by the FBI of all nominees to Federal Courts, not just those to the Supreme Court. Only rarely are such reports found wanting: the nomination of Alexander Ginsburg to a Federal District Judgeship in 1986 occasioned an FBI report which failed to disclose that Ginsburg, when a student in the 1960s and an Assistant Professor of Law at Harvard in the 1970s, had smoked marijuana. An independent professional assessment is also made: through its Standing Committee on the Federal Judiciary, the American Bar Association (ABA) considers the professional qualifications of people under consideration for nomination and makes them available to the President and the Attorney General. The Committee ranks those it assesses as "Not Qualified", "Qualified", "Well Qualified", or "Exceptionally Well Qualified". The ABA's Standing Committee has no formal veto over nominees, but its imprimatur is effectively a prerequisite for a nomination to be regarded as plausible. For nominees to the Supreme Court, the ABA Committee uses just three classifications – the first and the third of those above, with "Not Opposed" as the weakest expression of support. Several members of the ABA voiced their anxieties and reservations about Justice Bork's nomination to the Court in 1987. They expressed their "concerns as to his judicial temperament, e.g., his compassion, open-mindedness, his sensitivity to the rights of women and minority persons or groups and comparatively extreme views respecting constitutional principles or their application, particularly within the ambit of the 14th Amendment".

Nominations to Federal District Courts and to the US Circuit Courts of Appeals usually arouse little controversy in the Senate. Nominations are frequently being made by the President and considered by the Senate Judiciary Committee. While the formal procedure for nomination and confirmation of Judges to District and Circuit Courts is identical to that for Justices to the Supreme Court, Senators have in practice a fuller role in respect of appointments to the lower courts. Under the Constitution, Presidents appoint subject to the advice and confirmation of the Senate. In practice, the Senator or Senators in the State from which the nominee comes have the right at least to be consulted by the White House prior to the nomination being made, and often in fact to suggest a name or names to the President of a person or persons deemed acceptable. This tradition of "Senatorial Courtesy" applies in all cases where the President and at least one of the two Senators from the nominee's home State are of the same party. If party is shared, the President will require at the very least the acquiescence of the Senator or Senators concerned for the nomination to proceed unhindered; without it, the nomination is likely to fall.

In the modern era (since Franklin Roosevelt was elected to the White House in 1932) only the nominations of Judges Haynsworth, Carswell, and Bork have been denied by the Senate. In addition, the nominations of Justice Abraham Fortas to the post of Chief Justice, and of Judge Homer Thornberry, were filibustered in 1968 and the nominations withdrawn when it became apparent that no vote could be taken on them, and Reagan's nomination of Judge Ginsburg was also withdrawn after it had become clear that it would fail. Between 1789 and 1997, there were 147 nominations to the Supreme Court; twenty-nine failed to win Senate confirmation. Four of the six failures since 1932 illustrate some of the limits on Presidents' capacity to secure confirmation, and on Congress's capacity to deny it.

Of Nixon's six nominations to the Court, two successive ones were rejected (at the time, a unique achievement in the twentieth century, and the first occasion on which it had occurred since 1894, but one that President Reagan emulated). As President, Nixon took the view that the Senate's role of "advice and consent" meant just that, and no more. Its role was to be restricted to that of approval after less than searching examination, a convenient view for one who sought to alter the composition of the Court but anticipated liberal Democratic opposition to his doing so. Nixon nominated the southern conservative Clement Haynsworth (already a Federal Circuit Court Judge) for the vacancy created by the resignation of Justice Fortas in 1969. He did so following a search by his appointees in the Justice Department led by Attorney General John Mitchell for a southerner who would adopt a "strict constructionist" interpretation of the constitution on the Court. Two "strict constructionist" Republican Senators voted against Haynsworth. The Senate Republican leadership also opposed him because of allegations that he had participated in decisions involving corporations in which he held shares. Haynsworth also proved deeply conservative on civil rights questions, and on labour law. Moderate Democrats might none the less have supported him had the Court not become so highly politicized since the fierce conservative opposition to Thurgood Marshall's nomination in 1967. The Senate rejected Haynsworth's nomination by 55 to 45.

Nixon's belligerent response was to nominate G. Harrold Carswell of Florida, also a Circuit Court Judge, whom Mitchell described as "almost too good to be true", which he was, but not in the sense that Mitchell supposed. Senate investigations revealed that Carswell had in 1948 defended segregation in the southern states (unsurprising behaviour by a southern public figure) and at a later date attempted to secure Federal funding for a segregated private golf club in Florida, a new twist on an old southern practice. Carswell suffered from the further, and fatal, defect of stupidity. One of his most ardent supporters confirmed widespread doubts about his own and the nominee's intellectual competence when he argued that the mediocre generality of the population deserved representation on the Court. Senator Roman Hruska, whom Nixon had unwisely charged with the nomination's management on the Senate Floor, observed:

> Even if he is mediocre there are a lot of mediocre Judges and people and lawyers. They are all entitled to a little representation, aren't they, and a little chance? We can't have all Brandeises, Cardozos, and Frankfurters and stuff [*sic*] like that there.

Others, including Louis Pollak, the Dean of Yale Law School, found Carswell's intellectual bankruptcy a matter of anxiety rather than celebration. In Pollak's judgment, Carswell had "more slender credentials than any nominee for the Supreme Court put forth in this century". The nomination was defeated by 51 to 45. Among those who voted against it were thirteen members of the President's own party.

Nixon wrongly claimed that his nominees were rejected solely because of their judicial conservatism. Bruised liberal pride at conservative attacks upon the Court's decision-making aside, their rejection owed less to judicial philosophy than to well-founded doubts about their competence and integrity. Although Nixon claimed that the defeat of Haynsworth's and Carswell's nominations showed that the Senate would not confirm a strict constructionist southerner, he believed Blackmun to be at least as conservative as either of the rejected southerners on "law and order", and "very slightly to the left only in the field of civil rights". Convinced of this or not, the President was naturally anxious to defend himself against the charge that he had given way to pressure from a liberal majority in the Senate for a more moderate appointment to be made. Nominated within a week of Carswell's defeat, Blackmun was overwhelmingly confirmed by 94 to nil. Blackmun was thereafter inclined to adopt a self-deprecatory tone when referring to his having been Nixon's third choice: he was, he said, merely "Old No. 3". Subsequently, another two Nixon appointees were confirmed by a Democratic Senate: Powell of Virginia, by 89 to 1, and Rehnquist by 68 to 26. As with Blackmun's, so Powell's confirmation underlines the disinclination of the Senate to reject nominees purely on ideological grounds.

The only other President to have failed to secure confirmation of two nominees, Ronald Reagan, attempted in 1987 to appoint Judge Bork of the DC Circuit Court of Appeals. Bork's judicial philosophy was thought by many Senators to be too narrow to be of constructive use in judging cases before the Court. He had opposed the Civil Rights Act of 1964 (although he later changed his mind) and executed President Nixon's instruction to dismiss the Watergate Special Prosecutor after Attorney General Elliott Richardson had refused to do so. Either would have harmed his chances with liberals and many moderates; the combination was very damaging. However, the single most important charge against him was that he denied that the Constitution conferred a right of privacy on American citizens. He had taken this view so far as to oppose the Court's decision in *Griswold* v. *Connecticut*, 381 US 479, the 1965 case by which the Court struck down the State of Connecticut's ban on contraception as an unconstitutional invasion of the First Amendment's "penumbra" right of privacy. (No right of privacy was explicitly conferred by the Bill of Rights, but it has been held to be implied by it.) Bork was the first nominee in the post-war period to be rejected because of his interpretation of the Constitution. Following Bork's rejection by the Senate Judiciary Committee, the full Senate voted against confirmation by 58 to 42. All but two of the supporting votes came from Republicans (the two Democrats were both southerners), and all but six of the opposing votes from Republicans (three of whom were New Englanders, and one from Oregon – both areas of residual liberal and moderate Republican strength).

For his second attempt, President Reagan nominated Judge Douglas Ginsburg whom, he averred, was "a man who believes profoundly in the rule of law", and whom he predicted the Senate would dislike as much as they did Bork; the President was wrong in respect of the first, but right on the second. His pose would under any circumstances have been brazen and foolish, but was especially so following the heaviest vote ever against a Supreme Court nominee, when his own influence was palpably waning, and against the considered advice of equally conservative but politically more sensitive Senate colleagues such as Strom Thurmond of South Carolina, who had energetically supported Bork's nomination. In fact, there was no time for Ginsburg's nomination to be considered seriously because he soon disclosed that he had smoked marijuana. The revelation embarrassed conservative supporters, placed Reagan (who, with Nancy Reagan, had exploited politically his opposition to drug-taking, and also set demanding standards of appointees to jobs in the Justice Department) in an impossible position. Both the haste with which Ginsburg's nomination was made, and the offence that caused Ginsburg to withdraw his name from consideration, reflected the disarray within the Reagan White House as the President entered his last year in office.

All Presidents seek to influence the Court's composition, including those who proclaim the importance of the Court remaining free of political taint. In the short term, however, Presidential manipulation of the Court as a whole is virtually impossible. In the long term, ideological manipulation of the entire Federal Courts poses a more significant threat. Between 1933 and 1969, Justices sympathetic to government regulation of the economy but not to government interference in civil and private rights were nominated deliberately by Democratic Presidents of similar mind, and mistakenly by a Republican President. Between 1969 and 1992, Justices in the main antipathetic to both stances were nominated by Republican Presidents overtly hostile to both. The politics of each period showed the risk of the

Court becoming an unbalanced instrument of elected branches rather than a principled defence against their majoritarian predations.

Chief Justices and Leadership of the Court

Earl Warren

Earl Warren stands next to John Marshall as the greatest Chief Justice in the history of the Court, a garland neither easily won nor lightly worn. Chief Justices can shape a Court's direction; Marshall and Warren did so. The task is great, for their political circumstances are even less promising than those of Presidents. Those around them are close to being their equals and enjoy complete autonomy in law if incompletely in political practice. The Court is both a collectivity with an institutional consciousness, and nine individual Judges with the resources to resist coercion. As Chief Justice Rehnquist observed in a speech in 1984, the Court is:

> far more dominated by centrifugal forces, pushing toward individuality and independence, than it is by centripetal forces pulling for hierarchical ordering and institutional unity.

Leadership in these circumstances is difficult to achieve: Chief Justices have even fewer sanctions than Presidents. *Brown* v. *Board of Education* illustrates how a Chief Justice may lead his colleagues. When the Court granted *certiorari* on the case and it was discussed in conference in December 1952, the Chief Justice was Warren's predecessor, Vinson. He was disinclined to overrule *Plessy* v. *Ferguson* by which segregation was held not to violate the Fourteenth Amendment provided that the facilities were equal. No clear view having emerged, the Court set the case for re-argument in the 1953 term, but Vinson died before it could take place. Justice Frankfurter, who, with Alexander Bickel, his law clerk, had applied himself to preparing the ground for overturning *Plessy* in the face of what he expected would be continued opposition from Vinson (of whom he had a poor opinion), memorably observed upon learning of Vinson's death: "This is the first indication I have ever had that there is a God". The second conference on *Brown* took place a year after the first, under Warren, the new Chief Justice, former Republican Governor of California and Thomas Dewey's running-mate in the 1948 Presidential election. Warren was thought to be a safe choice by most Associate Justices (but not by Frankfurter, although he changed his view later). Eisenhower expected Warren to be reliable, but was to be disabused.

Warren inherited *Brown*. His disposal of it established his reputation, changed the South in particular, and American politics in general. From his first re-examination as Chief Justice of *Plessey*, he took the view that the doctrine of "separate but equal" rested upon "a concept of the inherent inferiority of the colored race" to which he did not subscribe. While none of Warren's colleagues contemplated sustaining *Plessy* on such grounds, Justice Reed was reluctant to overturn it, and two other Justices, Jackson and Clark, had reservations. Warren fully appreciated the case's gravity for black Americans, for the South, and for the notion and practice of equality in the United States.

The case was therefore frequently discussed in Conference; Warren regularly postponed votes in order that he might determine precisely where the point of unanimous agreement lay. Warren's first achievement was to recognise the need for unanimity and to persuade his colleagues accordingly; his second was to achieve it. In Conference, in informal groups, during lunch, the case was thoroughly discussed. The Conference vote resulted in an 8 to 1 majority to overturn *Plessy*, with Justice Reed voting to uphold it. In conditions of even greater secrecy than those in which the Supreme Court normally operates, Warren circulated his draft opinions personally to Justices in their chambers as soon as they were received from the Court's printers. He took a copy to Justice Jackson in hospital and collected an annotated version from him later the same day.

Energy, courtesy, collegiality, and good judgment were Warren's decisive advantages as Chief Justice. He was, and continued to be, a politician, albeit a robed and unelected one, responding to different pressures, demands, and circumstances on the Court than those he had known as Governor of California and as a Vice-Presidential candidate. His political skills served him well in preparing a unanimous decision on *Brown*, and particularly in persuading Justice Reed of the importance of a unanimous judgment. Between Warren's first Conference on *Brown* in December 1953 and May of the following year, Warren lunched with his southern colleague Reed on at least twenty occasions. As the Court's opinion gelled, with Frankfurter and Jackson content to subscribe to Warren's opinion and not submit a concurring one of their own (which itself would have impaired the force of the judgment), Warren put his final case to Reed. All the members of the Court had, as Warren impressed upon Reed, to judge carefully the impact of the decision and the means by which it was to be enforced.

Warren secured Reed's vote and unanimity for a short judgment (it takes just eleven pages in its original printing, and a mere seven pages in the Lawyers' edition of the *Supreme Court Reports*). Lacking much in legal scholarship and elegance, it nevertheless represents an astonishing marriage of Warren's judgment of what his colleagues would accept and what he and his colleagues thought required constitutionally in the country. No decision of the Court in the twentieth century has had a greater impact on public policy and politics. The rapid pace of Presidential legislative leadership under Lyndon Johnson between 1963 and 1968 in civil rights would have been politically impossible without the Court's momentous decision in *Brown*, which itself could not have occurred under the leadership either of Warren's predecessor or of his successor. Vinson was not disposed to overturn *Plessy*. It is doubtful if, had he found himself in Warren's place in 1953–4, Chief Justice Burger would have done so either. Even if he had, Burger's weak leadership of the Court between 1969 and 1986 suggests that he could not have led his colleagues to secure a unanimous opinion.

Warren Burger

Where Warren, throughout his fifteen years as Chief Justice, led the Court with diplomatic skill and imagination, Burger's leadership was invariably hesitant and indecisive. His task was in certain respects even more difficult than Warren's. In *Brown*, moral leadership was possible; there existed the opportunity to declare ringing principle. The difficulties of implementation, of applying principle to reality in the complicated formation of detailed policy, were not his. Among the consequences of *Brown* were the establishment of private schools subsidised by state governments, and policies providing for "freedom of choice" in the selection of schools. Both were means of maintaining segregation *de facto* in the light of its withering *de jure*, and were eventually ruled unconstitutional by the Court in *Griffin* v. *County Board of Prince Edward County*, 377 US 218 (1964) and *Alexander* v. *Holmes County Board of Education*, 396 US 19 (1969).

In *Swann* v. *Charlotte-Mecklenburg Board of Education*, 402 US 1 (1971), Chief Justice Burger wrote the unanimous opinion of the Court, affirming the judgment of the Federal District Court requiring the busing of students in Mecklenburg County, North Carolina, in order to achieve school desegregation. Busing aroused considerable controversy throughout the country. Whereas *de jure* segregation was a distinctively southern problem, *de facto* segregation was common in northern cities, a function of racial division in housing. It aroused intense political passions, was exploited in the Presidential elections of 1968 and 1972 by Richard Nixon and George Wallace, divided the Democratic Party not just between south and north, but also between liberals and blue-collar white voters, and made judicial decision-making exceptionally fraught.

From judging whether the doctrine of "separate but equal" could be maintained, the Court moved in Burger's period as Chief Justice to determining what length of bus ride Federal Courts might require to achieve the constitutional end of desegregation, whether schools which were predominantly white were less acceptable than predominantly black ones, and where schools should be built in order to promote integration. Ought they to be constructed in the inner cities, in the suburbs, or in areas between them whose racial composition was changing – and changing very often because of the threat of busing? Details of policy implementation do not make judicial leadership as straightforward as the pronouncement of simple principle sometimes does; these were unpropitious circumstances for any Chief Justice. Nevertheless, instead of overcoming the difficulties facing the Court, Burger compounded them–notably by acting after *Swann* to weaken the force of his judgment. Having written the opinion, Burger became alarmed at the prospect of its being implemented with what he took to be excessive zeal, and wrote to Federal Judges drawing attention to the restrictive language which it contained. It was an act of weakness that detracted from the force of the judgment and made it more rather than less likely that Federal District Courts would implement the original opinion differently according to local circumstances and sentiment.

Other aspects of Burger's leadership also contrasted poorly with that of Warren's. His political judgment was myopic, he made little effort to establish co-operative relations with colleagues, and showed little imagination in assigning opinions. He not only exercised little influence with those Justices who were antipathetic to his conservatism, but also exercised little sway with his natural allies. Harry Blackmun, who had been Burger's best man and remained a close friend, thought Burger's leadership of the Court poor, and became disheartened at the lack of humour on the Court. He particularly resented the Chief Justice's habit of assigning opinions on tedious tax law cases to colleagues with whom he had had a disagreement.

Enforcement of Desegregation

Brown fell into two parts: the principle at stake was decided in 1954 and the remedy followed in 1955. Implementation was, however, protracted and complicated. As late as 1963, the US Commission on Civil Rights reported that fewer than 0.5 per cent of southern blacks were attending integrated schools. Warren's opinion in *Brown I* provoked longer-term conflicts in northern cities which were intensified by the muddle which followed *Swann*. In the shorter term, the opinion occasioned tenacious and often violent southern resistance. Both reflected the Supreme Court's lack of implementation powers. An opinion having been delivered, it remains for it to be enforced. Remedies for the wrongs the Court rights lie in hands other than its own. The Court is therefore dependent upon other Courts, Legislatures, executives, and police forces. It is also critically dependent upon the willingness of the public to accept its judgments.

It is not the case that decisions of the Court are implemented or not, that they meet with resistance or are accepted. Within this misleading polarity lies a range of responses of affected parties and many possible paths of development. De Tocqueville understood that even in the early stages of the Republic America was a highly litigious society; but its enthusiasm for litigation is vastly greater in the late twentieth century. Federal Court decisions are therefore often tested by cases of a slightly different kind by private citizens, corporations, or other affected individuals or bodies. In

Federalist No. 78, Hamilton discussed the nature of judicial power under the proposed Constitution. The third branch of government was, he averred, the weakest:

> The executive not only dispenses the honors but holds the sword of the community. The Legislature not only commands the purse but prescribes the rules by which the duties and rights of every citizen are to be regulated . . . The judiciary, on the contrary, has no influence over either the sword or the purse; no direction either of the strength or of the wealth of the society, and can take no active resolution whatever. It may truly be said to have neither FORCE nor WILL but merely judgment; and must ultimately depend upon the aid of the executive arm even for the efficacy of its judgments . . . the judiciary is beyond comparison the weakest of the three departments of power.

Apart from for a small police force to guard the Justices and the building, the Supreme Court has no greater means of enforcement in the late 1990s than in 1789. Even within the judicial branch, the Supreme Court depends upon District and Circuit Courts to apply the opinion to relevant cases. The resistance of District Court Judges to Supreme Court decisions has been rare, but occasionally of great importance. This was especially so following the second of the Court's Brown opinions, which set out the remedy that Warren and his colleagues had refrained from providing in *Brown I*. Paying (unusually for the Court, but probably necessarily) careful attention to the difficulties of implementation, the opinion in *Brown II* (1955) required the Federal Courts:

> to take such proceedings and enter such orders and decrees consistent with this opinion as are necessary and proper to admit to public schools on a racially nondiscriminatory basis with all deliberate speed the parties to these cases.

Warren's acceptance of Justice Frankfurter's suggestion of the phrase "with all deliberate speed" was an error, as both men later appreciated. Southern politicians interpreted the phrase as permitting much deliberation and little speed, thereby delaying integration for many years. Most Federal Judges complied with *Brown*, although with varying enthusiasm depending upon their own views and ambitions, local political circumstances, and their courage. President Kennedy sought to prevent the appointment of Judges opposed to civil rights, although he did not overcome the device of "Senatorial Courtesy". Most resistance came from southern politicians, as three examples illustrate.

1. State Courts and State Governors vigorously resisted implementation. At Little Rock, Arkansas, in 1957, Governor Faubus used units of the Arkansas National Guard to prevent the Central High School's

integration following earlier approval by the Federal District Court for the eastern District of Arkansas of the School Board's desegregation plan. Faubus testified before the Arkansas State Chancery Court that desegregation of the Central High School might lead to violence. The State Court issued a restraining order preventing implementation, whereupon the Federal District Court ordered that there should be no further delay. The Governor responded by ordering the Arkansas National Guard to prevent black students entering the School, and then defied both President Eisenhower's personal request that he desist and the District Court, which issued a further injunction against further interference with its ruling. Mindful of the potential harm which such action might do the Republican cause in the South during the 1960 Presidential election, Eisenhower declared that he could not imagine any circumstances in which he would use Federal troops to enforce a Federal Court order. Only with great reluctance did he finally resort to Federal force: on 24 September 1957, Eisenhower called the Arkansas National Guard into Federal service and ordered 1,000 paratroopers from Kentucky into Little Rock to oversee the enforcement of the District Court's integration order.

2. In the following decade, two more southern Governors, Ross Barnett of Mississippi and George Wallace of Alabama, also made local political capital from their defiance of the Federal authorities following Federal court orders. In both cases, the political risks for President Kennedy were considerable. He had won both States in 1960, but could win neither in 1964 if as the Democratic candidate he were to alienate white voters on the perpetuation of racial segregation, the issue that mattered to them above all others.

    James Meredith, a black applicant to the University of Mississippi at Oxford (a publicly-funded institution) sought in 1961 an order from the Federal District Court that his application had been blocked solely on account of his race. Like many of his colleagues in Federal Courts in the south until the 1960s, the District Judge in question was concerned more to uphold the racial mores of his State than to enforce unwelcome rulings of the United States Supreme Court. He twice declined to grant Meredith the order he sought, but the Circuit Court overruled him and found the Governor and the Lieutenant Governor in contempt for obstructing Meredith's admission. One of the eight Judges on the Circuit Court then delayed (on four separate occasions) the remanding of the Circuit Court's order until the Supreme Court Justice responsible for the fifth circuit, Hugo Black, used his powers to make the remand order himself.

    Having overcome the resistance of the two lower levels of the Federal Courts, Meredith then faced armed mobs of outraged white Mississippians, in the face of which the weak Barnett took the easiest course open to him, preventing Meredith (in the protective company of lightly-armed Federal marshals) from entering the University. Following seven telephone conversations with the Governor, President Kennedy made a national television broadcast, having accepted and believed Barnett's assurance that Meredith would be registered without the need for Federal force. The violence of the mob was such that the Federal District Court's order could be enforced only with additional Federal assistance. Thirty-five US Marshals were injured by gunfire during the episode, and two people were killed. Kennedy called the Mississippi National Guard into Federal service, and ordered the despatch of troops from Memphis to the University campus. (To the President's fury, the Army responded slowly and inefficiently, thereby increasing the risk that Meredith might be killed, an event that would cause altogether greater conflict.)

The belated arrival of US troops from Memphis enabled the Federal Court order requiring Meredith's admission to be completed. Meredith was protected by a Federal Marshal throughout his four years as a student.

3. Governor George Wallace's recalcitrance at Birmingham in 1963 was of a more theatrical kind than Barnett's had been a year earlier. The last State university in America to be desegregated, the University of Alabama could not long resist the Court orders obtained by two black applicants, but Wallace extracted political advantage and publicity by appearing on television in the main entrance to the University breathing defiance; University officials had drawn chalk lines on the ground so that Wallace would enjoy the best camera angles. As had happened in Arkansas and Mississippi, the President called the State's National Guard into Federal service. Under Robert Kennedy's astute leadership as Attorney General, the US Justice Department secured an order from the Federal District Court in northern Alabama against the Governor. The Federal Judge who granted it declared that if Wallace were to violate the order, he would send him to jail for at least six months – a threat the Governor's lawyers communicated to Wallace. Such an outcome would have served no good purpose, and stirred memories of Reconstruction. Wallace's resistance in the doorway was brief, and characteristically theatrical. Members of the President's Cabinet had telephoned Alabaman businessmen in the hope of persuading them that to resist the Federal Courts would be to court disaster, and that repetition of disruption on such a scale would damage business interests. They in turn pressed this view upon Wallace, who duly gave way.

Lack of enforcement powers does not disable the Court. *Brown* and its sequel excited intense passions and active political, judicial, and direct resistance. Most judgments do not. Indeed, many that do arouse controversy are none the less speedily implemented. The redistricting cases prompted much litigation from outraged southern politicians, greatly vexed at the prospect of their gerrymandered rural bases of power being undermined. However, problems of implementation as such were relatively few, not least because to have refused to redistrict in accordance with the Court's judgment would create legal challenges to subsequent acts of legislatures, on the ground that legislators had been elected unconstitutionally. In the cases of the 1964 Civil Rights Act and the 1965 Voting Rights Act, violence by white southerners (some of them in official uniform, some unofficial, but many in neither) preceded but did not follow either the passage of the two Acts or the Court's finding that both were constitutional.

Conclusion

Over the ferocious dissent of Justices Stone, Brandeis, and Cardozo, Justice Roberts wrote in the majority opinion in *United States* v. *Butler*, 297 US 1 (1936), which struck down both the taxation and expenditure provisions of the Agricultural Adjustment Act of 1933 as unconstitutional that judicial review was much misunderstood:

> It is sometimes said that the court assumes a power to overrule or control the action of the people's representatives. This is a misconception. The Constitution is the supreme law of the land ordained and established by the people. All legislation must conform to the principles it lays down. When an act of congress is appropriately challenged in the courts as not conforming to the constitutional mandate the judicial branch of the Government has only one duty, – to lay the article of the Constitution which is invoked beside the statute which is challenged and to decide whether the latter squares with the former.

In his dissent, Stone complained of Roberts' "tortured construction" of the Constitution. The language of the Constitution provides few straightforward solutions to problems of American government: truths do not lie in the language awaiting discovery by the discerning. Nor is the view that the only construction that Judges and Justices may properly place upon the Constitution is that which its framers intended of much help to Supreme Court Justices. Few parts of the Constitution met with universal approbation from delegates to the Constitutional Convention in 1787; still fewer did so in the State ratifying Conventions. Even those who voted to ratify the Constitution, and those who later supported the adoption of amendments to it, had different reasons for voting as they did, and different views of its likely operation and meaning. Not only was the language of the Constitution itself the product of disagreement and intense debate from the opening of the convention to Rhode Island's belated ratification, the Constitution itself and the amendments that followed were framed in ways that would allow changing interpretations in a changed future.

What the Constitution has meant, and means; how that meaning might be determined and clarified; how it should be applied by the Federal Courts to the cases coming before them; and how the general significance of the decision that emerges should be shaped into a remedy, are fundamental problems. They lie at the core of debates about America's public policy, American citizens' liberties, the defence of individual rights, and the maintenance of limited but effective government. In so far as they must concern themselves with these questions, the Court cannot eschew a political role. Politics is ineradicable from the Federal Courts. It is present in the selection, nomination, and confirmation of Judges and Justices for Federal Courts as it is in State Courts, and it is present in judgments that the Courts must make about the cases before them. It is not, for example, clear why to adhere to *Miranda* is an instance of politicization while to weaken it (as the Burger and Rehnquist Courts have done) is not. With respect to judicial restraint, President Reagan's position was, in any event, inconsistent: much as he advocated the doctrine as a general prescription, he plainly intended that Judges decline to deliberate upon some matters rather than others. Were it otherwise, his administration would not have litigated in Federal Courts with such enthusiasm on school prayer and abortion. Process and result are less easily separable than some conservatives claim.

In matters of recruitment, too, conservative Presidents such as Reagan and Bush have assiduously appointed to the Federal Courts those whom they expect to share their views. Almost all of Reagan's and Bush's nominees (carefully screened by political appointees at the Justice Department) were judicial conservatives. Politics do not explain all judicial recruitment, still less judicial decision-making: the Constitution is no more warm putty in the hands of a President than it is in the hands of a passing majority of the Supreme Court or of the lower Federal Courts. It is not so because *stare decisis* powerfully constrains current action and decision. Another, however paradoxically, is that the Court inhabits a political world. Justices are constrained (though not confined) by public, congressional, and media opinion, and by their need to ensure the broad acceptability of their judgments, and protect their own legitimacy. Therefore, they do not write on a blank sheet of paper, but contribute to a continuing judicial, jurisprudential, and constitutional deliberation among both politicians, lawyers, Judges and the public.

7

Interest Groups

Accountability and the Allocation of Political Power

The First Amendment to the Constitution affirms the right of the people "to petition the government for a redress of grievances". It thereby legitimizes lobbying – of Legislatures, Executive agencies, and Courts – by private interests. Business corporations, labour unions, public interest groups, professional associations, single-issue groups, and coalitions of some or all of these, lobby governments in America on behalf of sectional interests, which may or may not coincide with a (or the) public interest. That private groups pose problems for the polity as a whole has been acknowledged since Hamilton, *et al.* (1987) defended the proposed Constitution to the electors of New York in *The Federalist Papers*. Penetration of the (structurally weak) American state by many groups also poses the question of to whom elected politicians are in practice accountable, and of how political power is allocated. Not all interests are represented before government; many have no representation at all, while that of others is often poorly-financed or organized.

Theoretical Problems Posed by Interest Groups

This chapter examines American interest groups, their roles in American society, and their interactions with the three branches of United States government. Undergirding this examination is a consideration of three connected theoretical problems which interest groups and their operation pose for understanding the operation of the government of United States, and the processes of public policy in which it and other governments in the States and localities are entwined:

- How and by whom contending claims to the legitimate exercise of *political influence* is to be determined in a political system marked by an extensive and vigorous civil society, and a weak State.
- Identifying where the *public interest* lies in the exceptionally cluttered policy-making environment that results.
- Determining where, in consequence, power over public policy and resources lies.

222

These questions are considered throughout this chapter, which begins by an examination of opportunities open to, and constraints upon, interest groups as a whole. The next section considers lobbying of the Courts, Congress, the Presidency, and the executive bureaucracy, while the third analyses different types of group their purposes, and the means available to them to bring pressure to bear upon decision-makers in government.

The Interest Industry

Washington owes its existence, employment, and prosperity to government, and the parasitic representation of interests. Directly or otherwise, most who work in Washington do so because it is the seat of Federal government; interest representation is the third largest source of employment in the city. Metropolitan Washington's rapid spatial and population growth since the late 1960s is owing in large part to the proliferation of groups, a development that has been supplemented by many corporations moving there from New York.

Of the 40,000 active lobbyists in the capital, 5,000 are registered with Congress. Under the *Federal Regulation of Lobbying Act* (PL 601, 1946) any organization which:

> solicits, collects, or receives money . . . to be used to aid in the passage or defeat of legislation by the United States Congress [or] whose principal function is to aid in the passage or defeat of legislation by the United States Congress

is obliged to register with the Secretary of the Senate and the Clerk of the House of Representatives, and to submit quarterly reports on their contributions, loans, and expenditure. Registration is a gesture toward transparency in policy-making, a necessary condition of democratic plurality. As the total number of groups lobbying the Federal government is large, so also is the range of legislative interests which they represent. In one month in 1989 alone, some 150 corporate and business groups; one (foreign government; twenty "interest group" lobbies; five labour organizations; ten State, local, and other government lobbies; fifty-four trade associations; and nine miscellaneous groups filed preliminary lobby registration reports with the Office of Records and Registration of the House of Representatives. Exhibit 7.1 lists some of the trade associations, and the corporate and labour groups who registered in this way, and the interest they had in pending legislation.

Organization

As the scope of State government activity (both that flowing from the autonomous actions of State Legislatures and from regulations imposed by

EXHIBIT 7.1

Groups Lobbying the Federal Government

Group	Interest
Trade Associations	
American Association of Bioanalysts	Clinical laboratories
American Society of Internal Medicine	Medicare/Medicaid and other related issues
National Coal Association	Acid rain, clean coal technology, global warming, parental and medical leave, coal pipelines and energy policy
Office of Professional Employees of the US Department of Agriculture	Credit in Federal retirement system for certain present and former USDA employees
Corporations and Businesses	
Adidas, USA	Trade legislation affecting imports by employer
Charter Medical Corporation	Legislation affecting Medicare and Medical hospitals and health-care industry
Honeywell Inc.	Health of the US defence technological industrial base
National Wildlife Federation	Conservation, environmental quality, fish and wildlife habitat
South Central Bell	Telecommunications legislation
Yamaha Motor Manufacturing Corp. of America	General trade legislation
Labour Organizations	
American Federation of Government Employees	All bills of interest to Federal government employees and District of Columbia employees, Hatch Act Reform,* pay retirement, contracting out
Association of Professional Flight Attendants	Airline safety and personnel-related legislation including HR 638** applicable to flight attendant scheduling
Seafarers International Union	Maritime transportation, labour and other related legislation
United Association of Steamfitters	Labour-related issues, pensions and minimum wage

*The Hatch Act limits spending by, and contributions to, political parties. In particular it protects Federal employees from risk of political intimidation.
**HR638 is an Act of Congress governing hours and conditions of work of flight attendants.

the US Congress) has grown, groups have also organized vigorously in State capitals. As in Washington, groups attempt to influence State executives and party activists during the formation of policy; State Legislatures and the public (through the electronic and printed media) during its legitimation; the Executive and State Judiciary during its implementation; and all branches of government and public opinion during its evaluation. State and local governments regulate the private sector, just as the Federal government does; groups in the private sector accordingly have interests to defend and advance before State governments.

In large states such as California and Texas, the number and range of groups approach that in Washington, since there is similar diversity of economic activity, ethnic composition, and political purpose. The two State capitals, Sacramento and Austin, attract ranks of lawyer-lobbyists who seek to influence State governments as their counterparts in Washington do the Federal government. The particular weakness of political parties in California has itself been partly responsible for the strength of interest groups in the state. Railroad companies dominated California State politics between 1860 and the Progressive revolt in the State of 1910. Progressive reforms deliberately weakened the Legislature through the referendum, the initiative, and the recall, and so further weakened parties, leaving a gap that interest groups have partly filled. In Texas, circumstances are different: the two-party system is dominated by fiscal conservatives, but weakened by factionalism within the Democratic Party, many of whose members are closer to organized oil, banking, and other commercial interests than they are either to their nominal party colleagues or to their constituents. Penetration of Texas state government by organized interests is, accordingly, pronounced.

Interest Representation, Institutional Openness, and Policy-Making

Implications for Representative Democracy

By promoting competition between branches of a weak central state, fragmentation of Federal government begets weakness of central authority, corresponding penetration of government by groups, and relative openness of policy processes. Although an open society, the United States is not an equal one: formal equality before the law sits alongside a profound social and economic inequality which has grown since the tax changes of 1982 redistributed income from the poor to the rich. Congress is most easily lobbied because it is the most open of the two elective branches. However, many corporations have tight and collusive relationships with executive agencies and Congressional Subcommittees that many other organizations lack.

In the twenty-five years immediately after the Second World War, J. Leiper Freeman (1955), Douglass Cater (1964) and Theodore Lowi (1969) separately considered the implications for representative democracy of such relations between social organizations and government. Moving across the permeable boundary between government and civil society, Cater wrote, in *Power in Washington* (1965), that public policy was effectively determined by "sub-governments" operating in "iron triangles" linking government agencies with Congressional Subcommittees and interest groups. Resulting patterns of policy-making exclude the President, non-specialists, and the public from most policy areas, and confine the exercise of influence to specialists – in the Federal bureaucracy, in functionally-specialized Congressional Committees, and in groups with special interests in particular programmes authorized and appropriated by Congress, and implemented by Executive agencies. This is both an ideal-type model and a starting point for the examination of public policy.

Cater's approach was later modified by Hugh Heclo (1978) who, in a subtle essay, argued that the concept of an iron triangle was "not so much wrong as disastrously incomplete", because it took too little account of the "loose-jointed play of influence" accompanying the growth of government, and the refined specialisation and highly-developed professional expertise that characterises both senior civil servants and those in think-tanks and research institutes with whom they deal. Although he fails to sustain the charge of "disastrous" incompleteness, he usefully modifies Cater's account. Cater's metaphor is too rigid, although Heclo acknowledges that he finds it "difficult" to define an issue network or specify precisely how it differs from Cater's formulation. Heclo none the less rightly lays emphasis upon the extreme complexity and fluidity with which networks of interlaced, overlapping, conflictual groups of individuals in law firms, research institutes, universities, lobby firms, and the mass and specialised media interact to influence the policy process.

Legitimating Public Policy

Such complexity offers opportunities to Presidents and political executives in the bureaucracy in dealing with or struggling against expert and professional members of groups within and outside government. Political executives cannot monitor all that bureaucrats do; however, they may intervene and attempt to lead in those areas that they, or the President, determine to be in their or the President's political interest. Congress, however, is a more complex and formidable participant in the policy process than either the iron triangle or the issue-network metaphors suggest: individual Members of Congress and Senators, party leaders, Chairs of Standing Committees, participants in Conference Committees, other members on the Floors of both Chambers, and members of cross-party caucuses may all shape public policy.

Most public policy in the United States is legitimated and implemented in public, and open to public view and private pressures, thereby exacerbating

the weakness of the State and rendering governance more rather than less
difficult. As Steven Krasner has argued in his justly celebrated book
Defending the National Interest (1978), the state in America is weak but
society strong. Martin Sklar (1988, p. 34) takes a similar view, regarding "the
central principle of the American political tradition" as being:

> the supremacy of society over the state: Government and law were to
> adapt to, and serve, the freely developing society. As shaped by strong
> republican imperatives since the Revolution, this tradition posited the
> society as one characterized by equal liberty for all full citizens and special
> privilege or monopoly power for none.

Within this tradition, modern American government is deeply penetrated by
private groups, its processes of public policy-making the product of particularistic patterns of interaction between groups and public officials. None
the less, there are in the United States no instances of the corporatist policy-
making once familiar in Austria, Sweden, and Germany. This condition is
partly explained by the fragmentation of many major economic interests in
the United States: industry, finance, and agriculture are all represented by
several organizations. Industry is represented by the US Chamber of
Commerce, the National Association of Manufacturers, and the National
Alliance of Business (all of which have usually been louder in their public
pronouncements than effective in shaping public policy). Financial interests
are represented by several different organizations, and agriculture by the
American Farm Bureau Federation, the Grange (another union of farmers),
the National Farmers' Union, and the National Farmers' Organization.
Although not unknown, peak organizations are uncharacteristic of most
policy areas, including those of health, defence, agriculture, and the environment.

Interest Groups and the Courts

Federal Courts are open to interest group pressure through litigation.
Although Courts are not lobbied conventionally, groups litigate on their
own behalf, and submit *amicus curiae* briefs (see Chapter 6) to supplement
arguments presented by the adversaries directly involved. In Courts as much
as before Congress, the executive, or public opinion, groups work not alone
but in concert with others.

The most striking instance of a group pursuing cases through the Courts is
in civil rights. Through its Legal Defense and Education Fund, the National
Association for the Advancement of Colored People (NAACP, founded at
the end of the First World War) sought to enforce civil rights by litigating on
behalf of black people denied their constitutional rights under the Fourteenth Amendment. It did so most spectacularly in *Brown* v. *Board of*

Education through its then Chief Counsel, Thurgood Marshall (later appointed to the Supreme Court; see Chapter 6). It has also litigated in order to preserve its avenue of redress through the Courts: in *National Association for the Advancement of Colored People* v. *Button*, 371 US 415 (1963), the Court reversed the Supreme Court of Virginia's judgment to uphold the constitutionality of a 1956 Virginia Statute extending restrictions on barratry (the vexatious encouragement of litigation) in ways that would have had the consequence (as it had the intention) of significantly weakening the NAACP's attempts to enforce the application of *Brown* v. *Board of Education* through State Courts. The NAACP continues to pursue civil rights cases before the Courts. In 1989, it succeeded with the last desegregation case, securing a favourable Court judgment desegregating the public school system in Natchez, Mississippi. It has, however, since enjoyed less success in defending the judgments of the Warren Court regarding the protection of minority rights in employment law.

The NAACP's decision to argue the case for desegregation through the Courts was *faute de mieux*: neither Congress nor the Executive would act. A similar motivation has informed the busy litigation of pro- and anti-abortion groups in recent years. Both the National Right to Life Committee and the National Abortion Rights Action League have (in league with other groups that lobby on one side or the other of the issue) raised income by appeals to sympathetic populations and then pursued cases through both Federal and State Courts. Both in civil rights and in abortion cases, it is the structural fragmentation of the Federal government that permits groups denied satisfaction in one branch to seek it in another.

Congress

Exploitation of Constituency Interests

Congress is the most open branch of the United States government, especially to interest groups. Group pressures are often cumulative with the constituency interests of Members of Congress: homogeneity of most Congressional Districts typically gives rise to ethnic and economic groups with concentrated membership or support in each district. Such cumulation is augmented by private financing of Congressional elections through Political Action Committees (PACs) and reinforced by House elections being held biennially, so rendering Representatives highly sensitive to local opinion. Members of Congress are local political figures running for office by appealing to local people and local groups on local issues: links between local groups and Members of Congress are thereby forged when they first run for office. Once elected, the requirement is to maintain the support of those groups which they judge to be politically advantageous, and to resist, deflect, or disarm those thought to be potentially harmful. These pressures are often exerted upon Representatives during their frequent (publicly-financed) visits to their home District. Local politics form the backcloth against which policy-making in Congress proceeds.

Where a District is dominated by a major economic interest, a Member of Congress rarely determines his or her view on policy matters autonomously. Thus the Representative from the Seventh District of Michigan is obliged to defend the interests of General Motors' workers by supporting limits upon the importing of Japanese vehicles. High-cost tobacco, peanut, rice, and sugar producers in southern States have not only sought, but also achieved and maintained, significant protection against imports from more efficient foreign competitors. Prior to Speaker Gingrich's major reforms of the Committee and Subcommittee structure in 1995, the success of such producers was facilitated by the power of regionally-concentrated Congressional defenders of trade barriers, quotas and tariffs on two of the House Agriculture Committee's key Subcommittees: Cotton, Rice and Sugar; and Tobacco and Peanuts. The Chairmen of both Subcommittees and most of their colleagues represented Districts where the relevant farmers and processors and their employees were significant economic and voting forces. American consumers have accordingly long paid higher prices for tobacco, peanuts, rice and sugar than they would have done under free agricultural trade.

Hearings of Congressional Committees and Subcommittees provide interest groups with formal opportunities to testify on legislative business before the Committee. There are also private opportunities to lobby Members of Congress and Senators. As hearing rooms of Committees in session are usually lined with lobbyists, so lobbyists are invariably to be found waiting in anterooms of Congressional offices for the opportunity to speak to the politicians whose support they solicit. Interest groups seek and accept opportunities to present their case before Committees. If, as Woodrow Wilson once observed, Congress at work is Congress in Committee, then Congress in Committee is where Congress and Interest Groups meet, epitomising society's penetration of the State.

Committees are the primary institutional focus for groups on Capitol Hill. Hearings take place at the discretion of the Chair of the Committee or Subcommittee, and the list of those groups testifying is agreed by the Chair in consultation with colleagues in both the majority and minority parties. Which groups are heard and when, how they are questioned, by whom, in what order, and upon what subjects, can have a critical effect on the influence that the testimony of particular groups may have upon the panel's deliberations. Witnesses may or may not represent the range and intensity of opinion on the particular Bill but will, to the extent that the Chair thinks it expedient, assist her or him in disposing of the Bill as she or he wishes. Chairs may encourage particular supporters to attend, in order either to bolster the Bill's prospects, or to weaken them. Hearings may be kept short, thereby limiting the time available for groups' formal submissions, to the point where prepared testimony may merely be entered into the Committee's records. Alternatively, they may be deliberately protracted, with the consequence either that groups may win sympathy for their cause, or exhaust it. The capacity of Chairmen to influence Committee decisions by the creative use of discretion during hearings is great.

Committees which were once internally hierarchical, highly susceptible to special producer influences and unsympathetic to consumer interests now have flatter distributions of internal authority and are open to a greater variety of pressures. There are three explanations for this. The first has to do with developments within, and the second and third outside, Congress:

1. In comparison with the decades before the early 1970s, the weakened formal power of Committee Chairs, and enhanced importance of Subcommittees as sites for hearings, have increased both the number and the range of interests represented before Congress. Committees that once were dominated by a few special producer interests on major policy questions are now more susceptible to wider influences. Even where a narrow range of interests continues to be protected within Committees and Subcommittees, the increased importance of the House Floor limits the capacity of specialist committees to protect their legislation from competing pressures in Congress as a whole.

2. The composition of interest groups lobbying Congress has changed radically since the 1960s. New types of groups representing single issues, fundamentalist Christians, consumer interests, universities and research institutes, associations of state and local governments, individual foreign governments and their support groups within the United States, and associations acting on behalf of what they claim to be the public interest, have established themselves and intervened in policy-making (especially during the continuous process of policy evaluation). Pure examples of single-issue groups include pro-and anti-abortion groups and the National Rifle Association. Common Cause, founded in 1970, is the clearest example of a public interest group. The National Governors' Association has since the late 1970s become much the most influential representative of sub-Federal governments. Foreign embassies now court Congress on questions of international trade, government contracts, US foreign aid, and immigration, while the America Israel Public Affairs Committee works busily on behalf of Israel's interests (and does so in close co-ordination with the Israeli Embassy).

3. Since the early 1970s, the merging of computing, television and video, telecommunications, and printing technologies, together with rapid and sustained falls in real prices of both hardware and software have resulted in the augmented capacity of groups to produce and disseminate propaganda. These technological developments have spawned new

industries of public relations and media consulting, enabling politicians and lobbyists to promote causes with greater speed and sophistication than was possible previously. Presentation of material, its targeting towards selected groups, and the generation of income from computerized mailings, have greatly assisted lobbying by groups dependent upon mass memberships. New communications technologies have none the less reduced the real cost of group formation and participation in policy-making.

These three interrelated developments have not ended the power of niche producer interests to protect the domestic US industry in league with agencies of the Department of Agriculture and Congressional Subcommittees. They have, however, been sufficient to weaken them and (for example) the capacity of American vehicle manufacturers and pharmaceuticals companies to resist consumer demands for safer cars and drugs by modifying conceptions of newsworthiness and (partly in consequence) the political agenda with which Congress works.

Openness is a necessary but insufficient condition for politics to be plural in practice as well as in theory. Three other conditions must also be satisfied:

1. No single group or class dominates politics and public policy processes, and all groups with an interest in the policy under discussion must be represented in its consideration.
2. Leaders of groups accurately and fully represent their members' views, and the intensity with which those views are held (notwithstanding the problems that intensity poses for rules and norms of democratic decision-making).
3. Political assets and resources are widely and evenly distributed.

These conditions are not reliably satisfied in the making of public policy in the United States. While Congress has undoubtedly become a more open institution since the Congressional reforms of the early to mid-1970s, both on the two Floors and in Committees, the Executive has always been a less transparent branch. There, many private interests enjoy collusive relations with Executive agencies, whether in iron triangles, networks of influence, or through formal mechanisms of their membership of advisory committees in which they seek to deploy their asymmetrical advantages of information and expertise, and thereby exploit their positional advantages over groups without them. Formal equality of access to legislators and executive officials often obscures other paths trodden by groups which enjoy continuous access and influence. Senate Finance and House Ways and Means Committee meetings are open to the public as well as to special interest groups, but the interests of (mostly unorganized) ordinary taxpayers have usually been less well represented on those two Committees than those of major corporations.

None the less, ample resources avail lobbyists little in the absence of credibility, which is built upon the accuracy of the information which a lobbyist provides to policy-makers. Lobbyists and the lobbied trade in the currencies of information, expertise, and influence. Lobbyists can and do bring to Congressional politicians and their staff information, and interpretations of it which, if accurate, can be of significant benefit. As Hall and Wayman (1990, p. 803) have explained:

> group representatives often serve as "service bureaus" or adjuncts to congressional staff. They provide technical information and policy analysis; they provide political intelligence; they draft legislation and craft amendments; they even write speeches or talking points that their supporters can employ in efforts on their behalf.

Lobbyists, who are acknowledged masters of their subjects as well as politically resourceful, can often compensate for their group's lack of financial resources. Providing misleading or inaccurate information to politicians, their staff, and bureaucrats quickly ruins a lobbyist's standing by undermining the credibility of politicians unfortunate (or foolish) enough to rely upon it. Lobbyists who thus damage themselves and others find their access to policy-makers closes and with it any possibility of exercising influence over the marking-up of a Bill, the agency's drafting of regulations, or the holding of oversight hearings on government programmes. The American Medical Association (AMA), whose annual Convention determines policy and whose professional lobbyists in Washington consequently have little autonomy, is one example. The United States Chamber of Commerce, which to many politicians and bureaucrats often appears doctrinaire and inflexible, is another. On the occasions that it has sought to defend the indefensible, as in its opposition to prohibiting the sale of armour-piercing bullets, the National Rifle Association has also harmed its cause.

Successful lobbying comprises less the application of pressure than the communication of accurate information and analysis: incentives to mislead are weak, since the penalty is the loss of trust and the rupturing of valuable relationships. Some private groups' expertise is such that their advice commands attention. Other groups carry such great political weight that they cannot be ignored. There develop between interest groups, Congressional Committees and Subcommittees, and Executive agencies, relationships rather than occasional encounters. Politicians and staff within government learn whom to trust, those upon whose judgement and honesty they may safely depend, and whose opposition will cause them more difficulties than they might prudently risk. Lobbyists learn the importance of when, with whom, and how it is most advantageous to intervene. Relationships between competent lobbyists, agency bureaucrats, and Congressional politicians are positive-sum games: all participants gain.

Some groups are advantaged by the nature of their membership. Thirty-two million citizens over the age of fifty belong to the American Association of Retired Persons (AARP); all have a current or anticipated direct interest in protecting Social Security and Medicare entitlement programmes. All Members of Congress have significant cohorts of retired people within their Districts, and need no reminding of their voting power. No argument is more persuasive than that which resting upon constituents' votes. In the 1980s, the AARP played a strong hand with skill in defending expensive entitlement programmes from budget reductions during a decade when non-entitlement domestic programmes subject to the appropriations process were heavily cut.

The AARP's large membership was acquired, and is maintained, partly for the reasons identified by Mancur Olson in *The Logic of Collective Action* (1965). Olson showed that individuals do not necessarily form or join groups to promote shared interests, even where it would be rational for them all to do so. He noted that the public goods flowing from the activities of groups are provided to all irrespective of whether or not they join the group. In the case of large groups, the temptation is always to "ride free" on the contributions of others, since the benefits will accrue to those who do not contribute as they will to those who do. Only with small groups might individuals have rational egoistic reasons for joining, since in such cases the benefits deriving from the group's activities may be materially less if an individual abstains from membership. Olson argues that groups must offer other, material, benefits if they are to persuade people to pay for membership. The AARP's ability to defend its members' interests is a function of its success in offering a large range of benefits to them. Charles Morris records the AARP in 1996 as offering to its members an affinity credit card; annuities; mail-order pharmaceuticals; a car breakdown rescue service; hotel and car hire discounts; and life, home, and car insurance (Morris, C R, 1996).

The successful employment of such techniques by other groups does not necessarily result in their enjoying comparable success. The AMA's financial and lobbying resources are abundant (in 1995, it had 297,000 members, an annual budget of $200 million, and fifty staff in its Washington headquarters) but have not enabled it to overcome its internal difficulties. Divisions within the Association have grown as the pressures on Federal finances have increased. The size and diversity of the medical profession is such that maintaining unity is difficult; it accordingly becomes easier to defeat. (Appreciating this point, Congress in 1989 deliberately divided the profession by proposing different changes in Medicare fee payments to different categories of physician in an attempt to restrain the growth of the Medicare budget.) The AMA then spent more than $570,000 in an attempt to defeat two Democrats on the Ways and Means Committee's Subcommittee on Medicare – Congressmen Jacobs of Indiana, and Stark of California. Both won their elections, and neither was reluctant to exact retribution. Since the primary utility of PAC funding is to secure access to key legislators, it is foolish to oppose entrenched incumbent Congressmen with jurisdiction over Federal programmes central to the group's interests. The capacity of interest groups to punish politically adept Members of Congress is slight.

Establishment of PACs, and the Federal Election Commission's (FEC) regulation of them requiring that sources and destinations of PAC funds be publicly recorded (see Chapter 3), have allowed examination of the relationship between the money that politicians receive and their votes on questions of interest to PACs and their parent organizations. However, voting is only one form of political behaviour. Others may have greater political significance: the content, tone, and timing of speeches, the audience to which (and the setting within which) they are delivered, also matter. So, too, do the meetings (formal and informal, public and private), conversations, arguments, hints, inflections, and facial expressions of politicians. The time, energy, intensity, and passion that politicians devote to, or withhold from, a cause also reveal their detailed preferences, their views about issues and the importance that they attach to their resolution.

Votes, by comparison, provide only a crude account. Moreover, votes cannot, by definition, measure the efforts that politicians make, successfully or otherwise, to prevent votes being taken at all. It might appear that the rational purpose of the expenditure of PAC funds should be to affect crucial swing marginal votes – yet research by Richard Hall and Frank Wayman (1990) has shown that this is not how PAC money is spent. Nor is it entirely clear (as is commonly argued) that money enables lobbyists to buy access to politicians. Even if this were so, it should prompt the question of what lobbyists do with such access once they have it. If group influence is mediated by access, the relationship between its exercise and its effect should still be apparent in voting patterns, but (as almost all research has shown) it is not. Hall and Wayman argue that while PACs do not purchase support in measurable form, they do at least partly affect the intensity of politicians' devotion to different causes.

John Wright (1990, p. 433) has taken a different approach. He, too, finds no clear relationship between PAC donations and voting, but some between campaign contributions and groups' lobbying patterns. However, studying the Ways and Means Committee, he finds that Representatives' voting decisions are best explained by the number of contacts they had with lobbyists on each side of the issue in question. Wright's research demonstrates a further, important relationship. Since lobbying tends to reinforce opinions that legislators already have, information and interpretations of it supplied to legislators by lobbyists are partly shaped by campaign finance. Such a pattern is classically apparent in iron triangle systems of policy-making, where private economic activities are subsidised through distributive policy: subsidies to tobacco, peanuts, rice, and sugar farming are examples. Throughout the post-war period, it has also been true of tax policy, where sectional interests have until recently succeeded in protecting the many special exemptions and deductions in the tax code.

The passage of the Tax Reform Act of 1986 (HR3838) reveals some of the resources available to many financially powerful groups whose interests were threatened by the Act's provisions for reducing and eliminating tax concessions and shelters. It also illustrates an important feature of modern lobbying: groups rarely lobby alone, but instead pool their resources and expertise in coalition. The Tax Reform Act was opposed by a wide range of groups, including hospitals, charities, bankers and bond underwriters; many groups in this broad coalition without a PAC of their own formed one to channel campaign contributions to Ways and Means members. In the first six months of 1985, PAC contributions to members of the House Ways and Means Committee nearly tripled, compared with the same period in 1983. By seeking to delete Investment Tax Credit from the Federal Tax Code, the Bill's authors struck at a key provision of tax law for manufacturing companies. In addition to their individual and trade association lobbying, twenty-three large corporations, including Goodyear, Du Pont, and AT&T contributed $800,000 to acquire the services of Charls Walker, one of Washington's most senior and most skilful lobbyists, to press their case before Congress and to purchase full-page advertisements in newspapers arguing that the investment tax credit was in the public interest.

The Bill none the less passed, and investment tax credit was deleted from the US Tax Code. Powerful as the groups lobbying for special exemptions were, the forces arrayed against them were formidable: the President and his White House staff, the Treasury Department, and the Chairmen and key members of the Senate Finance and House Ways and Means Committees collaborated to ensure that winning coalitions of legislators could be assembled to support the President's Bill.

Interest Groups and the Presidency

At all stages of public policy-making processes – initiation, formalization, legitimation, implementation, and evaluation – Presidents draw both competition and support from groups. In many areas of distributive policy dominated by subgovernments or issue networks where Federal programmes proceed incrementally from year to year, Presidents may not attempt (whether by deliberate choice or default) to impose their own preferences. In other areas of greater importance to them, Presidents are frequently obstructed in their attempts to formulate and implement policies that they declare to be in the national interest over those they identify (or stigmatize) as being merely the sectional interests of groups. All politicians attempt to present their own interests as being coincident with (and often in fact identical to) the public interest, but the President is in a better position than most to do so. As the sole national elective politician of significance, his singular legitimacy affords him a distinctive advantage in making the claim, and then in seeking to enforce it. To that end, Presidents and their staff attempt to co-opt groups into their presentation of new policies, their lobbying of legislative proposals through Congress or of Presidential appointments through the Senate, and into the detailed implementation of Acts passed by Congress.

The President has the support of specialist White House staff charged with the task of maintaining "Public Relations" – the cultivation of productive relations with groups supportive of the President, and with other groups whose support the President needs but does not reliably have. The broad appeal of both political parties results in ties with groups being less clear-cut than they have traditionally been in Europe: since 1933, labour unions have usually been closer to Democratic Presidents than to Republican ones, but all Republican Presidents have attempted to woo labour unions (President Nixon did so with considerable success, especially in respect of his foreign policy). Democratic Presidents have been similarly resourceful in seeking support from business corporations.

President Carter won support front key interest groups such as the National Educational Association (NEA) (the main teachers' union) during his campaign for the Presidency in 1976. Once in government, he unwisely paid such groups less attention until the appointment of a specialist staff member, Anne Wexler, in 1978. She achieved some success in integrating consumer, environmental, and labour organizations into the President'[s lobbying of Congress. By contrast, President Reagan's coalition-building was usually as efficient in office as it had been in pursuit of it. Reagan understood that coalitions of support were best assembled in Congress after the laying of their foundations outside among powerful supporting groups. Reagan's approach was evident in passing the Omnibus Reconciliation Act and the Economic Recovery Tax Act of 1981 (see p. 378), when he secured the support of business and taxpayers' groups. Since Reagan had enjoyed their backing in the 1980 election, his collaborative campaign with them in 1981 offered the virtues of continuity and political rationality. When added to wide and deep public support, the political context within which Congress voted was shaped to the President's temporary Congressional advantage and to the fiscal benefit of the groups with which he worked.

As support can be critical to the President's political success, so opposition can cause its failure. Opposition of the United States Catholic Conference (USCC) to any Bill providing for Federal aid to public schools but excluding aid to parochial schools, and the equally impassioned opposition of the NEA to any Bill that aided parochial schools on the same terms as public schools, long prevented passage of an Act by entwining the issue with the sensitive First Amendment question of the State's separation from the Church. Only the NEA's change of mind enabled the Elementary and Secondary Education Act to pass. Although other groups worked with

President Johnson to pass the compromise draft bill, the support of the NEA (which in 1964 had a membership of 900,000) and the USCC (much the largest and most powerful representative of non-public elementary and secondary education in the country) was essential.

More than twenty years later, the opposition of groups including the American Civil Liberties Union (ACLU), the National Association for the Advancement of Colored People (NAACP), and the National Organization of Women (NOW) was instrumental in causing the Senate's rejection of President Reagan's nomination of Judge Bork to the Supreme Court (see Chapter 6). In attempting to advance his social agenda through the Courts late in his second term rather than his fiscal one through Congress early in his first, Reagan overestimated his capacity to build a new political coalition for different and more contentious ends.

Interest Groups and the Executive Bureaucracy

Congress's general intent has to be implemented by agencies through the drafting and enforcement of detailed regulations. Groups are, accordingly, obliged to scrutinize and act upon the rules that agencies issue. Group interests are as dependent upon the detailed application of law as upon its general construction, and are assisted by sharing two qualities with agencies and Congressional oversight Subcommittees: first, expertise deriving from their specialization; and second, a powerful stake in the rules being drafted to maximise the benefits accruing to them and minimise the costs imposed upon them. Details of administrative procedure and practice affect present and future profitability and welfare.

Manufacturers consequently attach great importance to rules drafted and implemented by officials in the Occupational Health and Safety Administration (OSHA). Companies that pollute the air, land, and water are similarly attentive to technical regulations drafted and enforced by the Environmental Protection Agency (EPA). The same is true of broadcasters regarding the Federal Communications Commission (FCC), and of stockbrokers respecting the Securities and Exchange Commission (SEC). By the same token, regulatory authorities have regard not only for relations with Subcommittee parents in Congress but also with private interest groups. Purposes are not necessarily shared, nor are modes of operation necessarily collusive. Yet OSHA, EPA, FCC, and the SEC are parts of policy-making, implementing and evaluation networks. These networks may be politically competitive. Enforcement of rules controlling environmental pollution brings competitive group interests to bear: interests of industries and companies may and do diverge and conflict, as (more commonly) do those between most business interests and environmentalists.

Groups are often so closely incorporated into decision-making procedures established by agencies that the boundaries between government and groups are unclear. Formal penetration of economic interests into the bureaucracy through advisory committees has been common since the New Deal. Thus, the Department of Commerce formally incorporates business interests through such committees; the Department of Labor, unions; the Department of Defense, weapons contractors; the Department of the Treasury, banks; and the Department of Housing and Urban Development, companies and groups with policy or commercial interests in the Department's programmes. Less formally, Departments consult constantly with clients and other interested parties in the private sector. Lobbyists for all organized interest groups appreciate fully that their groups' objectives may depend upon how policies affecting them are implemented. Agencies' drafting of rules may confirm political victories embodied in legislation, or negate them. While organized groups must therefore pay heed to bureaucrats' detailed implementation of policy, the activity is so rarefied that none save the informed and organized appreciate it. Fewer still in fact influence those engaged upon it. As Schattschneider argued in 1960, small organized groups often triumph over large unorganized ones; Olson made a similar claim a core part of his thesis in *The Logic of Collective Action*. Such outcomes are especially likely when the interest in outcomes of rule-drafting embraces a public interest and not merely a set of private, sectional, interests, whether they be conflictual or coincident.

Participants in the Interest Industry

Lawyers and Lobbyists for Hire

Just as many of Washington's political consultants specialize in working for candidates of a particular party or ideological persuasion, so many of the city's lobbyists work primarily for Republicans, Democrats, conservatives, liberals, or another identifiable group, or specialize in certain policy areas. Contract lobbying firms of this kind are often retained by interest groups to conduct a particular campaign or to supplement their own lobbying efforts. Former Senators, Members of Congress, and Administration officials figure prominently among Washington's specialized law and lobbying firms. (The lobbying industry is dominated by lawyers, of whom there are 38,000 in Washington alone.) Washington has since the late 1960s increasingly become a city to which many politicians are attracted and which few leave: in 1989, approximately 200 former Members of Congress and Senators had their main residence in the Washington Metropolitan area. Most remain in Washington in order to exploit their former contacts, to employ their knowledge and understanding of the policy process, and to know how, when, and where to intervene to the greatest effect.

Governments

Governments also lobby. Foreign governments represented in Washington lobby, both on their own account through their embassies and by retaining specialist lobbyists to work for them. State, city and county governments lobby individually but also (and increasingly) in associations of State, county, or city governments: the National Governors' Association (NGA) has been especially influential not only in shaping the course of authorizations and appropriations but also in modifying the agenda of public policy. As Governor of Arkansas, President Clinton used his Chairmanship of the NGA creatively to help set the agenda of national debate about both welfare and education policy. Different parts of the Federal government also lobby Congress and, through the Solicitor-General and the submission of *amicus curiae* briefs, the Federal Courts. The White House lobbies Congress constantly – ideally in co-ordination with the departments and agencies, every one of which has its own Congressional relations staff.

A Public-Interest Lobby: Common Cause

Increased wealth; public awareness of negative externalities; diminished trust in government's probity after the abuse of executive power with respect to Vietnam and Watergate; the growing importance of issues as cleavages in society and the correlative weakening of attachment to party (assisted by the greatly enhanced importance of television) have altered group politics. Since the mid-1960s, public and consumer interest groups have been established to pursue new issues. Broadly within the Progressive tradition, such groups claim to promote not a sectional (often profit-making) interest, but the public (non-profit-making) interest. The establishment and growth of public interest lobbies is implicitly damaging to the classical pluralist account of group formation in the United States. Adherents of such interpretations of American politics thought it axiomatic that there was no identifiable public interest on most issues separate and apart from the sum of group interests: the public interest was the result of private interests freely competing. To the extent that public interest lobbies have won support for their identification of such a separately-defined interest, the plausibility of such a view was weakened.

Coalitions are often formed to fight particular campaigns, but public interest groups also sometimes lobby on different sides: in 1989, Common Cause supported the proposed Congressional pay rise while Congress Watch opposed it. The "public interest" is variously defined by different groups in respect of different issues. Common Cause seeks to establish and enforce standards of good government, and ensure politicians' accountability to the public. Public Citizen's objectives are broader but couched less in terms of process than of substance, and tied more closely to consumer interests. None the less, the establishment of groups dedicated to identify and promote a public interest has altered the context of group politics. It has also provided frankly sectional interests with a distinctive competitor whose claims are more difficult to dismiss because they do not derive from parochial financial or political interest.

Founded in August 1970 by John Gardner, Secretary of Health, Education and Welfare under Lyndon Johnson, Common Cause attracted a fee-paying (mainly upper-middle-class and highly educated) membership of 100,000 within six months. In 1995, its annual budget was $10.5 million, and its membership 250,000; it accepted no contributions of more than $100.00 from corporations or labour unions. sixty-six full-time staff worked for the organization in Washington, supported by a further forty full-time and thirty-five part-time employees in forty-six state offices. Its main lobbying target is Congress. Both in Washington and in the States, Common Cause draws on additional voluntary support. The organization is now chaired by Archibald Cox, the distinguished lawyer whom, as Solicitor-General, Robert Bork dismissed during the Watergate crisis.

Common Cause's first major successful campaign was to advance reform of the hierarchical system of Congressional Committee Chairmanships that had undermined liberals' attempts to investigate President Nixon's policy on Vietnam. The group thereafter turned its attention to ethical questions, sought a new lobby registration Act, and campaigned against both the MX missile system and the Strategic Defense Initiative. Whereas most groups representing interests before government lobby as supplicants, Common Cause usually does so as an irritant. Apart from its support for Congressional pay increases, its causes are rarely comforting to incumbent politicians: its prime target is the corrupting influence of private finance on Congress, and its object the maintenance of high ethical standards in government. To that end, Common Cause depends upon the principle of openness. Without extensive and detailed obligations upon PACs and politicians to report to the FEC about their finances, its task would be impossible.

Yet, as openness is a necessary but insufficient condition for plurality, so access to data is an insufficient condition for Common Cause's efficacy. Its expertise in campaign finance law and its creative energy in using information supplied to the FEC confer two significant advantages in the group's competitive struggle with other groups to promote its purpose. In a society where the speed and accuracy with which data are ordered and disseminated are commercially and politically important, Common Cause's proficiency in both respects makes it highly valued by the electronic and print media. That in turn ensures Common Cause prominence in news reports of those subjects in which it is interested.

A Labour Lobby: United Auto Workers

The American Federation of Labor-Congress of Industrial Organizations (AFL-CIO), a weak federation which in 1996 represented seventy-eight independent national affiliates and 13 million trade union members, is the product of an amalgamation in 1955 between, respectively, a craft union federation founded in 1886, and a mass industrial union organization (dedicated to the cause of mobilizing those whom the AFL had deliberately ignored) established in labour's politically buoyant days of the New Deal. The AFL-CIO represents a smaller proportion of the workforce than do the TUC in Britain, the LO in Scandinavia, or the Federation of German Trade Unions in Germany.

Although the proportion of unionized workers in the public sector is high, that of white-collar workers is low (and markedly lower than in Europe). Including those unions outside the AFL-CIO, just 14.9 per cent of US workers belonged to a union in 1995, the number having fallen from more than 25.5 per cent at its peak in 1965. The fall is partly explained by the decline in employment in industries having previously enjoyed high rates of unionization, such as vehicle manufacture and steel. Unions have also been harmed by Republican domination of the White House for all but four years between 1969 and 1993, and by Republican majorities in Congress since 1995. Although American unions have occasionally been courted by Republican Presidents, their interests have rarely been served by them. President Reagan's breaking of a strike by 11,000 air traffic controllers early in his first term signalled his determination to weaken unions. The President's policy was reinforced by his nominating conservatives who shared his views to the National Labor Relations Board and to the Federal Courts. These developments added to the general disadvantage of highly decentralized wage-bargaining and a fragmented movement of more than 200 trade unions. State laws restricting unions' freedom to organize workers further weakened them.

Since John Sweeney was elected as the AFL-CIO's President in 1995, more attention has been paid to organization. A Center for Strategic Campaigns has been established, to assist with unions' organizing campaigns, first-contract negotiations, general bargaining and to improve research support for labour union affiliates. The first nationally co-ordinated political campaign by the AFL-CIO was seen in 1996 (though with mixed results). A National Labor Political Training Center has been established to create a permanent "grassroots" political organization in each Congressional District, with the object of running political campaigns. Organization remains comparatively ineffective: unions face considerable difficulty in achieving the first step, that of certification as a bargaining agent. In the mid-1990s, unions won slightly less than half of National Labor Relations Board (NLRB) elections held to certify a union. Even where certification is achieved, a first contract is successfully negotiated in less than three-quarters of cases.

Individual unions have, however, known considerable influence. At times of high profitability, steel, docks, road transport and automobile unions have secured favourable wage contracts for their members: steel was the clearest example during the 1950s and 1960s. Even in the more difficult circumstances since the oil-induced recession of 1973–5, car workers were for some years partly cushioned against the worst effects of increased foreign competition and declining domestic profitability by effective union organization. The Union of Auto Workers (UAW) has as a key objective the restriction of the import of foreign cars to the United States. Their stance has won strong minority Congressional support, especially from the usual suspects: Representatives whose Districts contain substantial vehicle and component businesses. Their cause has been strengthened by Congressmen, such as Richard Gephardt, who have sought to exploit public anxiety about America's large trade deficit by campaigning against foreign penetration of domestic markets and foreign investment in American corporations. The UAW also retains the familiar objectives of opposition to deregulation (especially where it threatens job security and wage levels); maintenance of domestic spending programmes (especially Social Security and Medicare, upon which retired union members depend); and support for civil rights.

Business Lobbies

Much has changed since the early 1960s, when Bauer, Pool and Dexter noted in their book *American Business and Public Policy* (1963) that 129 of the 166 large corporations which they studied had had no contact with Congress in at least two years. The authors concluded that this remarkable instance of the dog that did not bark was indicative less of business's political naïveté than of its general satisfaction with government policy, the weakness of unions in most industries, and the lightness of regulation. Moreover, the lack of corporate activity reflected politicians' anticipation of business interests: protection by Congressmen from Texas, Louisiana, and Oklahoma of the oil industry's depletion allowance in tax law is just one example. (The allowance was abolished by a liberal Democratic Congress in 1975, in full cry against conservative Congressional privileges and power.)

Lyndon Johnson's Administration and those of the Republican Presidents Nixon and Ford that followed saw significant growth in Federal business regulation. Congresses dominated by Democrats (and often by liberals) between 1964 and 1977 passed a panoply of environmental, health, safety, labour, product standards and civil rights laws and regulations. Regulations written by the Consumer Product Safety Commission (CPSC), OSHA, and EPA, and most decisions of the Departments of Labor, Commerce, and Health, Education, and Welfare reduced the profitability of many American companies, small and large. In the States, too, regulation burgeoned during the same period, with the result that large corporations operating across the United States pressed for Federal regulation to avoid working under different regulations in different States. Growth of consumer and public interest groups also stimulated the surge in corporate representation: General Motors, for example, had thought it unnecessary to establish a lobbying office in Washington. In response to Ralph Nader's exposé of the Chevrolet Corvair (a GM product) as "unsafe at any speed", the company changed its view.

There has never in the United States been a single overarching organization representing business: partly in consequence, neither the National Association of Manufacturers (NAM) (whose membership is drawn mostly from medium-sized firms) nor the United States Chamber of Commerce (USCC) (whose membership comprises mainly small businesses) has enjoyed much political influence, either in the 1950s, when threats to business interests were slight, or in the 1970s, when they became more significant. In both decades, the two organizations were conservative on all political questions, and weakened by their heterogeneous memberships having conflicting interests. Dissatisfaction with both groups among executives of America's largest corporations led to the formation of the Business Roundtable in the early 1970s, which provides higher-quality analysis and lobbying. That in turn stimulated the NAM and the USCC to improve their own analytical work; both now provide economic analysis and econometric modelling, meeting the needs of their memberships and of politicians with whom their lobbyists are in regular contact. These successes notwithstanding, employers still face the problems of maintaining unity on divisive issues, of developing services that individual corporations cannot themselves supply, and of the awkward fact that employers speak with several voices.

Large corporations meet most of their lobbying needs in house, or from contract lobbyists and lawyers retained for particular projects. However, like other groups, business lobbies form *ad hoc* coalitions with other groups on matters of shared interest. Business has also been favoured by the 1974 amendments to the 1971 Federal Election Campaign Act, which repealed the prohibition upon corporations having business with the Federal government from establishing PACs. The amendment's significance springs from the fact of the Federal government's enormous procurement of goods and services from the private sector.

Approximately half of the largest 500 companies in the United States have PACs, but few that sell their products or services to the Federal government or are affected by Federal regulations do not. Notwithstanding corporate celebration of the virtues of fiscal rectitude and reduced public spending, many major corporations are, directly or indirectly, dependent upon Federal government contracts. Indeed, the business success of no less an opponent of the Federal government than Ross Perot depended heavily upon Federal contracts. Business PACs spend more than twice as much as unions in campaign finance, and very much more than public interest, consumer, and environmental groups. While this fact does not ensure that their views prevail (not least because they often conflict with each other), business is now a vigorous participant in lobbying, and facilitates access to policy-makers (though not control over them). Like other PACs, business PACs usually support incumbents more often and more heavily than they do challengers, even where challengers' politics are closer to their own.

Racial and Ethnic Lobbying: American Israel Public Affairs Committee

American policy towards Israel has been influenced by pressure upon successive administrations and Congresses by groups representing nearly 6 million American Jews. Especially influential in New York and the northeast, and disproportionately represented among the nation's academic, professional, financial, and political elites, Jewish lobbies have assiduously sought to advance Israel's security and prosperity.

The lobby on behalf of Israeli causes is dominated by the umbrella organization, the American Israel Public Affairs Committee (AIPAC). Many AIPAC groups (among them the American Jewish Congress and the Anti-Defamation League of B'nai B'rith) have their own representatives in Washington. AIPAC has close working relations with other Jewish organizations, some of which are represented on its Board. It also advises the numerous Jewish PACs across the United States. Its continuing success can be measured by the National Association for Arab Americans, and the main Greek lobby, the American Hellenic Institute Public Affairs Committee (AHIPAC), the second most powerful ethnic lobbying group on foreign policy, having modelled their tactics on AIPAC's own. Despite its acronym, AIPAC is not a PAC: the largest allied PAC is the National Political Action Committee, but nine other PACs, many of them regional, share similar objectives. In law, Israel is not the client of AIPAC, since it is not funded by the Israeli government. None the less, Israel is the *de facto* client of the several Jewish lobbies: it is with its interests alone that they are concerned. AIPAC and its allies are able to draw on the support of not only American Jews but also of most Americans. Despite the decline in support for Israel since the Camp David accords, most Americans continue to approve of the United States' generous financial assistance to Israel through foreign and military aid.

Following its defeat over the sale of Airborne Warning and Control (AWACS) aircraft to Saudi Arabia in 1981, AIPAC transformed itself in a way that augmented its power. Whereas AIPAC had not previously supported conservative Republican candidates, it changed tactics after 1982, successfully courting some Republicans such as Jesse Helms (who had hitherto not been a prominent supporter of Israeli causes) and supporting others such as Senator Alfonse D'Amato, deterring potential Democrats from opposing him for re-election in 1986. AIPAC also extended its lobbying from traditional bases in northern States with large Jewish populations to include Jewish areas in the south and west. The group highlighted its new bipartisan base of support and the fact that AIPAC was a single-issue group, taking no position in other disputes between conservatives and liberals. AIPAC's resources also increased: its budget and the number of its staff increased from $1.3 million and thirty staff in 1980, to $5.7 million and seventy-five staff five years later.

AIPAC's tactical changes and improved circumstances brought their reward. During a period of increasing fiscal difficulty, US support for Israel grew to more than $3 billion by the late 1980s, sustaining Israel's position as the largest single beneficiary of US foreign aid. By the mid-1980s, President Reagan's attempts to sell arms to Arab states met fiercer and more successful resistance in Congress. More politicians were mobilized in AIPAC's support, in part because of fears among some running for re-election that they might otherwise lose, as others had done in 1984 after being targeted for defeat by AIPAC. Far from being invincible, AIPAC has none the less become a formidably powerful lobby on behalf of Israel's interests. Recognizing the organization's power, Secretary of State Schultz was obliged in 1986 to bargain direct with AIPAC to determine what arms sales to Saudi Arabia the administration could propose to Congress without incurring the Israeli lobby's opposition.

Women's Lobbying: The National Organization for Women

Established in June 1966 on the occasion of the Third National Conference of the Commission on the Status of Women, the National Organization for Women (NOW) was in its first ten years concerned primarily with the passage and ratification of the Equal Rights Amendment to the US Constitution. Its stated purposes now include the elimination of discrimination and harassment; securing women's reproductive rights; ending violence against women; eradicating racism, sexism, and homophobia; and promoting social equality and justice.

Its efforts were insufficient to persuade three-quarters of State Legislatures to ratify the amendment: only thirty-five had done so when the three-year extension granted by Congress to the original 1979 deadline expired. Since the Supreme Court's 1973 judgment in *Roe* v. *Wade*, NOW has also emerged as the foremost proponent of freedom of choice for women in opposition to the large and diverse Right to Life movement, in which cause it has been a tenacious litigant. In 1994, for example, the Supreme Court upheld NOW's use of the illiberal Racketeer Influenced and Corrupt Organizations Act (RICO) against pro-life activists who conducted campaigns of harassment (including deprivation of leases) against abortion clinics (*National Organization of Women, Inc.* v. *Scheidler*, 114 S. Ct. 798 [1994]).

NOW's membership of 250,000 is a source of financial strength, but its diversity one of weakness. NOW mitigates the difficulties that internal divisions present by devolving some policy-making power and 4 per cent of national revenues to state organizations, thereby reinforcing links between the national organization and the membership, so lessening the prospects of the former misrepresenting the latter. The Supreme Court's decision in *Webster* (1988) that State Legislatures should have greater latitude to determine abortion policy illustrates the importance of interest groups organizing themselves in state capitals as well as in Washington.

Pure Single-issue Lobbying: National Rifle Association

Of all the lobbies in America, none is better-known outside of the nation's capital than the National Rifle Association (NRA); few are more influential within it. Like AIPAC, the NRA is a single-issue group with a clearly identifiable group of potential supporters – legal owners of the 200 million guns in American citizens' hands. Its resources are large: nearly 3 million members paid fees, giving the organization an income in 1990 of $86.9 million. The group maintains a full-time staff of 550, including twelve professional lobbyists, and retains the services of contract lobbyists in Washington for particular legislative contests. Members are prompted by direct mail to contact legislators when gun controls are being considered. The organization has a PAC: the NRA Political Victory Fund which, by spending $5,948,803 in 1993–94, was the fifth largest PAC in the United States.

The possession of guns enjoys Constitutional protection under the Second Amendment (see Appendix 2). Some hold that the Amendment precludes any restriction on the type (or quantity) of weapons that may be held, but this is a contentious view. Most who supported the Amendment in 1791 were concerned more with providing for adequate state militia than for individual rights to own a gun; it is accordingly unclear whether the Amendment refers to the collective rights of militia or to the rights of individual citizens. The consequences of an armed citizenry have made the nature of, and limitations upon, this right into a bitterly-contested question. The Second Amendment is unique within the Bill of Rights in setting the right to which it refers in a particular organizational and political context. With that setting (and, by implication, limitation) in mind, both the US Congress and State Legislatures have acted to control the types of weapon sold in interstate commerce and within States. The Firearms Act of 1934 required the registration of automatic weapons and sawn-off shotguns; the Federal Firearms Act of 1938 prohibited licensed gun dealers from selling guns in interstate commerce and (for the first time) made it a Federal offence to sell firearms to felons and fugitives, while in 1990 Congress prohibited the sale of AK-47-type semi-automatic weapons. The fact of gun control has been as much a feature of American public policy as its weakness in comparison with all other democracies.

As is invariably the case in American government, where Congress declines to act, Governors and State Legislatures may do so. Where State

Legislatures decline to act, local governments may be permitted (by the States under whose authority they fall) to do so. The result is the familiar and turbulent mix of different laws regulating different types of weapon in different jurisdictions: there are more than 20,000 State and local gun laws. Variegated as gun-control laws therefore are, the constitutionality of control is not in doubt. At both Federal and State level, the courts have frequently upheld the right of Legislatures to restrict the sale, possession, and carrying of certain types of weapon. Unable to pursue judicial challenges to action by State Legislatures, the NRA has been obliged to supplement private lobbying of legislators with well-financed and energetic public campaigns. Few battles which it has conducted in recent years have been more bitter than that which it led unsuccessfully against Maryland's restrictive gun-control law in 1988. Fearful that, if the law won the approval of the State's voters in a referendum, other States would follow suit, the NRA spent $6 million on an intensive advertising campaign. More than $900,000 was spent on a "single market segment", inner-city black people, whom the NRA told would find their ability to buy cheap handguns restricted under the proposed law. The NRA's position was defeated.

State and local regulation is weakened where laws of adjoining States or cities vary (as they usually do); the NRA's major task has therefore been to limit Federal regulation. Despite increased pressure upon Congress to pass more restrictive legislation following attempts on the lives of three post-war Presidents – John Kennedy, Gerald Ford and Ronald Reagan – all of them NRA members, Federal regulation remains weak. Similar pressure followed the assassinations of Martin Luther King and Robert Kennedy in 1968; the mass killings by a man with an AK-47 semi-automatic rifle of children in a school playground at Stockton, California in 1989; and the increased use of semi-automatic weapons by drug dealers in inner-city areas from 1986 onwards. Yet the profusion of restrictions below the Federal level has not been matched in Washington, a significant achievement for the NRA.

In particular, the NRA has resisted more restrictive gun-control laws; in 1986 the organization marked one of its more significant legislative victories with the passage of the McClure–Volkmer Act. It ended the ban on interstate traffic in rifles and shotguns, and overrode all State laws restricting transportation of firearms across State lines.

The NRA's usual approach to gun control legislation is to oppose all restrictions of any kind. Against the united opposition of police organizations, and Handgun Control, Inc., the NRA spent between $1.5 and $3.0 million defeating an attempt (known as the "Brady Amendment", named after President Reagan's Press Secretary who was grievously injured during the attempt on Reagan's life in April 1981) to impose a national waiting period of seven days before a handgun may be collected, so that police checks might be completed on the purchaser. In the final House floor vote, opposition to the Brady Amendment was heaviest in rural areas across the country, especially in the south, mid-west, and far-west.

Few Members of Congress and Senators feel themselves sufficiently immune from defeat to risk incurring the NRA's wrath, and subsequent support for a Primary or general election opponent, because it possesses a formidable capacity to bring pressure to bear on legislators from its large membership. The political sensitivity of the question of the ownership of guns also causes the White House, the Justice Department, and the Treasury Department's Bureau of Alcohol, Tobacco, and Firearms to tread warily for fear of losing the support of gun-owners. Congress and the Executive Branch have little autonomy against the concentrated lobbying and electoral power of the NRA.

The NRA's stubborn resistance to all restrictions has in recent years none the less left it politically exposed. Its opposition to the proposed ban on the manufacture or sale of plastic but usable guns incapable of detection by airport X-ray security equipment was insufficient to prevent passage of the Bill. The Association's opposition to the prohibition of the manufacture and importing of armour-piercing bullets was insufficient to prevent the House passing the Bill with the support of all the major police organizations, the National Coalition to Ban Handguns, and Handgun Control Inc. The NRA's view exposed the NRA to ridicule even in Idaho, where hunting is popular, gun-ownership is restricted only with regard to the carrying of concealed weapons, and support for the NRA is widespread and vigorous: former Governor Cecil Andrus (whose hobby is hunting) referred to the Association as "the gun nuts of the world" for opposing the ban on armour-piercing bullets by observing that he had yet to see an animal in a bullet-proof vest.

In gun-control, therefore, the major lobby dominates, but does not determine, policy. Great as its financial and organizational resources are, its tactical errors, coupled with the publicity afforded violent crime, have enabled its opponents to organize in support of tighter controls – especially on semi-automatic weapons and handguns. Internal divisions within the organization in 1996 and 1997 have also diminished its effectiveness. One such group, Handgun Control Inc., was founded by Sarah Brady, the wife of Mr Reagan's injured Press Secretary. However, the constitutional and ideological foundations of gun-ownership, and the huge resources which the NRA always brings to bear, makes enactment of controls comparable in their severity to those in Canada and other civilized democracies highly unlikely. It is equally improbable that guns will be decontrolled. The clash of opinions on the issue leaves few Congressional politicians exempt from NRA influence. Members from rural areas have even smaller prospects of resisting the Association than those from cities, where pressures from hunters and farmers are slight and those from the families of victims great.

Conclusion

Interest groups attempt to influence public policy by persuading public officials of the merits of their causes and cases. They do not compete for electoral office. Having established rules, agreed purposes, and memberships, interest groups differ from broader social movements lacking these characteristics. Relations between advanced democratic societies and States are mediated more by groups than by party in the United States where organizationally enfeebled political parties contrast with a rich civil society.

Groups have at different times been denounced as being threatening to the Republic, celebrated for expressing democratic participation, excoriated for representing partial interests over the unrepresented public interest, and regarded by some as transmitting public preferences but by others as misrepresenting them. There is no simple solution to the problem of assessing in the aggregate the nature and extent of interest groups' influence over public policy, because they vary with the tactics, resources, legitimacy, substantive expertise, political skill and support of different groups, and with issue, field of activity, and political circumstances. These groups' influence over government, or parts of it, accordingly ranges from insignificant to determinative; and developing a theoretical account to explain such variation is therefore forbiddingly difficult. Nevertheless, interest groups are rightly regarded as a key characteristic of the American political system, marked more than any other democratic order by the weakness and fragmentation of the central government and by the vitality of its society.

8

Bureaucracy: The Fourth Branch of Government

The United States Constitution provides for three branches of government. This chapter examines an unmentioned fourth: the Executive Branch's bureaucracy.

Separation of powers combined with Federalism renders bureaucracy complicated, dispersed and decentralized (both within Washington and throughout the country) and its accountability to representative politicians problematic. The Federal bureaucracy's key organizational units are usually not Departments but the semi-autonomous agencies or bureaux within them. As islands of separately-authorized functional power, agencies are subject to political pressures from the Presidency, from Congress, and from clients seeking to influence bureaucrats' decision-making, both during the formation and the implementation of policy. Presidents attempt to enforce leadership over bureaucrats by making political appointments to the upper reaches of departments and agencies of people loyal to them (at the risk of losing experience and expertise), as well as by establishing their own political and bureaucratic resources within the Executive Office of the President. Reliance upon civil service neutrality, standard in British government practice, offers no solution to American Presidents, who have to compete for influence in a separated and Federal system without a powerful central State over which to preside. It is in the space between the general intent of Presidency and Congress, and its detailed implementation in the forms of administrative decisions and rule-making, that politicians and lobbyists contend with the expertise, experience and longevity of bureaucrats for influence over the implementation of policy.

There is in the United States Federal government no durably dominant centre of power, and no sense of a "State". The Federal government is permanently divided by constitutional separation and by staggered elections to representative posts of different-sized constituencies and often divided further by split-party control of Congress and the Executive. Elected and unelected officials therefore often have compelling incentives to compete openly against one another. Federal executive departments are not ideal types of hierarchical Weberian rationality but are shells within which multiple, semi-autonomous, agencies are placed, each of them separately created by Congress. Each agency's programmes are authorized and re-authorized, funded and overseen by Congressional Committees and Subcommittees. The internal organization of the Federal bureaucracy is tightly and continuously integrated politically with that of Congress in Committees and Subcommittees. Each agency is shadowed by Congressional Subcommittees which, since they created and sustain them, are sometimes refered to as their Congressional "parents". Two consequences flow from these arrangements: first, little collective authority inheres in the Federal government; and second, public administration is thoroughly politicized.

The variation among bureaucratic forms in the Federal government is wide. The major determinants of agencies' design are the political choices of those who establish, sustain, and modify it; this was apparent from the first years of the Republic, when Congress granted to the President much greater leeway in determining the policies to be followed by the Departments of State and War, than it did in the case of the Treasury, where Congressional prerogatives were greater. As Seidman and Gilmour (1986, p. 149) have observed:

> Choices are influenced by a complex of tangible and intangible factors reflecting divergent views about the proper sphere of government activity, politics, institutional folklore, program importance and status, visibility, political and administrative autonomy, and, most important, who should exercise control.

The Federal Civil Service

The Federal government acquired a civil service after most advanced European countries had done so. Well before their industrialization, Germany and France had established public bureaucracies. In France, Napoleon's taxation reforms in the early years of the nineteenth century required the services of a large bureaucracy for their enforcement, although the Napoleonic State was little more than a development of the Jacobin structure. By contrast, the United States lacked the apparatus of a State just as it lacked the popular conception or sense of one. In continental Europe the modern democratic form was established by the institutions of representation being added to a bureaucratic order. In America, the sequence was reversed.

The first act of Presidents from Andrew Jackson onwards was to dismiss all office-holders in the Executive Branch, replacing them with those of proven loyalty, or those whose cases were advanced by supporters to whom they owed political debts. As Senator William March of New York put it, "To the victors belong the spoils" (from which the phrase "spoils system" derives). By this system, all posts in the Federal bureaucracy were in the gift of Presidents.

The Tenure of Office Act, passed in 1867 over President Andrew Johnson's veto, was the first clear indication that Congressional sentiment was moving against the spoils system. It attacked the power of Presidents by preventing their removing, without the Senate's concurrence, individuals appointed to Federal office with the Senate's consent. An amended version of the Act was repealed in 1881, largely because its constitutionality was in doubt. The Pendleton Act was passed in January 1883 during President Arthur's administration, following (and in part because of) President Garfield's assassination by a disappointed office-seeker. It provided for a classified list of merit appointments by "open, competitive examination"; for an end to the assessment of office-holders for political contributions; and for a Civil Service Commission to administer the rules impartially. The new rules initially affected only about 12 per cent of bureaucrats in Federal service, but the proportion grew rapidly under the reforming stimulus of Theodore Roosevelt and Woodrow Wilson in particular. During the same period, the merit principle was widely applied by State governments to their own administration. Merit posts were reserved for the best-qualified applicant, regardless of party, who would thereafter be immune from removal when a change of administration occurred, not required to contribute to any political fund, and protected from other partisan harassment.

Two Presidents (Harrison and Garfield) had lost their lives to the spoils system; another, Theodore Roosevelt, rose to national prominence in part because of his indefatigable enforcement of the Pendleton Act as Civil Service Commissioner. As the drive against patronage grew, it became politically advantageous for Presidents to expand the list as a proportion of all Federal posts, and they duly did so. In the twenty years following the Civil War, the movement for civil service reform took on the character of a crusade, the object being the depoliticization of the bureaucracy on behalf of a public interest. Entire political careers were devoted to the cause. A merit-based civil service was a prerequisite for a modern bureaucracy capable of administering the policies of a government that was taking on regulatory roles. Civil service reform and the attack upon the abuse of monopoly power by large corporations were linked in the Progressive movement, and contributed to the growth of the Federal government's capacities in the years immediately before the First World War. The Pendleton Act did not eliminate the unedifying scramble for Federal posts at the beginning of a new administration, but did greatly diminish both its extent and tendency to corrupt.

Introduction of a merit-based civil service did not remove patronage from American politics; chief executives across America, from the President to many city mayors, still have many appointments within their gift. Development of civil service conditions in Federal, State, and local governments, has

TABLE 8.1

Executive-Level Civilian Federal Appointments (1996 rates)

	Women	Men
Level 1, paying $148,000	4	9
Level 2, paying $133,600	5	26
Level 3, paying 123,100	17	56
Level 4, paying $115,700	95	161
Level 5, paying $108,200	0	6
Total	127	277

therefore occurred alongside the maintenance of the right of most executives in most governments in the United States to make at least some political appointments. In 1996, there were more than 3,200 political appointees in the Federal government alone, but only executive level posts require Senate confirmation. There are five such levels (see Table 8.1).

Specialized Support and Fragmented Government

Nearly three million civilians work for the Federal government, not many more than when President Eisenhower took office in 1953; in proportion to the population, the civil service has shrunk considerably over the period. The fragmentation of the Federal bureaucracy's organization is reflected in its personnel structure. Sixty years after Franklin Roosevelt initiated the rapid expansion of the Federal bureaucracy, there is still little notion of a government-wide career structure for civil servants. In circumstances of functional specialization and agency autonomy, many agencies have effectively independent career structures, and there is little notion of a common civil service as there was in London prior to the creation of the Executive Agencies, or as there still is in Paris. The United States's government tends, as Robert Wood explained in 1970, to recruit by profession. This practice affords the government specialized support at the cost of accentuating its fragmentation.

The example of the Forest Service illustrates the relationship between the functional specialization of agencies within departments and the distinct professional groups recruited to run it. The Forest Service is an agency within the Department of Agriculture run, for the most part, by qualified foresters. The high percentage of the Service's employees who work full-time in the field (or, perhaps more correctly, in the woods) are graduates of Forestry Schools. They are no more likely to transfer from or to other agencies within the department than they are to other agencies in other departments. Their specialization is of a kind whereby their skills cannot be transferred within government (although they may well be marketable within the private sector). Even where skills are transferable between agencies, as is the case with lawyers and budget analysts, who are to be found in every agency and department, most civil servants remain in the agency to which they were originally recruited.

Concentration of professional expertise underpins agencies' autonomy within departments, creating asymmetries of information and expertise *within* departments. It therefore affords agencies greater autonomy from the few political appointees with responsibility for the entire department, and yet greater autonomy from the President. Since the Twenty-second Amendment to the Constitution ensures that the turnover of Presidents is high (see Appendix 2), the longevity of professional bureaucrats in specialized agencies makes the task of Presidents who seek to give a policy lead exceptionally difficult, particularly since links between specialized agencies on the one hand and specialized parental Congressional Subcommittees on the other are intimate.

Civilian Federal Employees

There are four broad categories of civilian Federal employees:

1. Nearly half work for the Post Office, public power systems operated by the Department of Energy, or government agencies with special professional requirements and recruitment procedures such as the Secret Service and the Federal Bureau of Investigation (FBI).

2. The "General Schedule" (GS), a merit-based career system that accounts for slightly more than half of all civilian employees, including, in eighteen grades, the great majority of civil servants working in the main departments and agencies from the most junior grades to the most senior. Recruitment to the GS was until recently undertaken by a standard, competitive, aptitude test, the Professional Administrative Career Examination (PACE). However, in 1982 a Federal District Court judged PACE to be racially discriminatory, and recruitment is now organized by individual agencies to suit their particular requirements. Recruitment procedures have therefore fragmented and become more complicated, further weakening the civil service as a whole.

3. The Senior Executive Service (SES) was established by the Civil Service Reform Act of 1978, President Carter's single most significant domestic reform. Carter intended it to revitalize the senior ranks of the civil service, providing greater mobility between agencies and departments for ambitious and creative senior managers, who were enticed into the SES by the prospect of performance-related bonus payments and career advancement. The Civil Service Reform Act established the SES as a hybrid service, including not only civil servants drawn from the four most senior grades in the GS but also permitting more political appointees in what would previously have been the exclusive preserve of career civil servants.

Ronald Reagan's politicization of the Civil Service exploited the freedom which the legislation gave him to remove SES civil servants from their posts and replace them with political appointees. Reagan devoted more resources to politicizing the bureaucracy than any President before him: 100 staff members in the White House's Office of Presidential Personnel examined potential appointees for loyalty to the President, ideological enthusiasm, and (less reliably) competence. General Accounting Office figures showed that between 1980 and 1986, the number of career civil servants in the SES fell by 5.3 per cent while the number of political appointees in the SES increased by 13.1 per cent. While, as the history of Mr Reagan's Administration revealed, zealotry is an insufficient condition for changing an agency's course, its application between 1981 and 1988 damaged the quality and morale of the civil service considerably.

4. Schedule "C" appointments are conventional political appointments which comprise most Presidential patronage. A report compiled by former Congresswoman Patricia Schroeder's House Civil Service Subcommittee showed that between 1968 and 1988, the number of political appointments listed in the "Plum Book", the official government list of patronage posts, grew by 23 per cent to a total of more than 4,500.

President Reagan's Civil Service Reforms

Reagan's attack upon the civil service cut with the grain of public prejudice and was to that extent politically helpful to him. Attacking the alleged sloth and inefficiency of the Federal bureaucracy is an old and profitable campaigning tactic, but intellectually dishonest. In fact, government bureaucracies necessarily differ considerably from private-sector bureaucracies: they face distinctive problems, and operate under special constraints. In all democracies, governments operate under constraints of equity, accountability, high standards of stewardship, and fairness, which private companies for the most part do not; in no political system are these constraints more elaborate or more closely supervised than in the United States. The view that public administration is inherently less efficient than private industry and commerce, and that government ought to be run like a business is, nevertheless, widespread; it found its clearest expression in President Reagan's attempts to reform the Federal civil service along private-sector lines.

As part of his drive to increase the efficiency of the Federal bureaucracy, President Reagan launched a programme in 1981 entitled Reform '88 to examine particular aspects of managerial practice in government. It was followed in 1982 by the President's Private Sector Survey on Cost Control (the Grace Commission, after its chairman, J. P. Grace, a businessman) whose approach to the problem, like that of Reform '88, sprang from the assumption that the introduction of what was taken to be the rigour of private-sector management techniques and organization into the civil service would improve its efficiency. Reporting in 1984, Grace concluded that savings of over $400 billion could be made with improved management. The CBO and GAO issued their own joint report on Grace's recommendations, concluding that the true savings would be only $100 billion, of which 60 per cent could be achieved not through management improvements but only by policy changes. Of the remaining 40 per cent, most of the savings could be made only if additional costs were to be incurred (such as hiring more Internal Revenue Service officials to collect taxes) or by the contracting-out of services to private companies.

President Reagan took special steps at an early stage of his administration to attack what he and many in his entourage regarded as the generous pay and perquisites of civil servants. Encouraged by many of those whom he had appointed to senior posts in the Office of Personnel Management, he proposed in 1981 that their pay be cut by 5 per cent. He later modified his view, suggesting that the principle of pay comparability with the private sector (which was, in any case, neither universally nor fully applied) should be abandoned in order to allow for government pensions to be uprated in line with the cost of living. Although neither proposal was accepted, Reagan's hostility towards the conception and practice of public service ensured that the conditions of service for Federal civil servants worsened during the 1980s, not least because Members of Congress lacked the courage to increase their own salaries in line with inflation, and continued to be unwilling to support civil servants' receiving higher salaries than their own.

National Commission on the Public Service

Reagan's undermining of the civil service lowered morale within it, and made for difficulties of recruitment and retention, which became especially severe as private sector salaries grew quickly in the mid-to-late 1980s: the gap between government and private sector salaries increased to an average of 25 per cent by August 1988. Following a symposium on public service sponsored by the Brookings Institution and the American Enterprise Institute in 1986, the National Commission on the Public Service was formed, chaired by Paul Volcker, the distinguished former chairman of the Federal Reserve, to examine the problems plaguing the bureaucracy.

Volcker brought integrity and high public standing to the job, and was able to force on to the political agenda the related anxieties he and his colleagues on the Commission had about the civil service's condition: public perceptions of the service; pay and conditions; recruitment and retention; the relationship between political appointments and civil service career posts; education and training. He met with sympathetic hearings from key Congressional Committees, and found in President Bush one who valued public service and public servants.

Among the many proposals to emerge in the Commission's report *Leadership for America* were recommendations for significant pay increases in order to stem the flow of experienced civil servants from government to the private sector, and to restore morale, that the number of political appointments available to the President be set at the reduced figure of 2,000, that managerial and personnel authority be devolved, and, as part of a renewed emphasis upon the importance of the training of civil servants, that a special programme of scholarships be established to encourage able young people to pursue careers in the civil service. The Commission's signal achievement was to alter the terms of public debate about the value and importance of public service.

By raising the subject of public sector reform, as he did in 1993, President Clinton modified the terms of debate about the federal bureaucracy, and responded to intensifying public discontent with the perceived scale and cost of federal regulation. He announced on 7 September of that year a programme entitled the *National Performance Review* consisting of an attempt to improve the quality of Federal service to the public while cutting costs by $108 billion over five years. The President gave responsibility for the development and implementation of the programme (popularly if misleadingly known as Reinventing Government) to Vice-President Gore, who approached the subject with an evangelist's zeal, attempting to exploit it to his electoral advantage in preparation for a Presidential bid in the year 2000. Among the programme's elements were proposals to introduce normal commercial practices into federal procurement, to revise the organization of Departments, and to make provision for financial inducements to civil servants surplus to requirements to resign. Some of the programme's elements could be implemented by executive order of the President. Crucially, however, others required positive steps from Congress. After the Republicans' seizure of majority control in 1994, the programme's many components became the object of intense partisan dispute as part of a broader attack upon a Democratic President and executive agencies led for the most part by Democrat appointees. While the Republican majority failed to abolish any major Department or Agency, it sought (with only partial success) to claim credit for forcing privatization and commercialization on to Federal Agencies' agenda.

Federal Regulation

Whatever the bureaucracy's institutional form, delegation of power to bureaucrats is inescapable. Legislators cannot provide for every contingency in statute; some discretion must be granted to those who execute laws. Implementation of policy therefore requires bureaucrats also to form policy by making decisions within sets of general parameters about particular events. Implementation of policy by bureaucracies over time is the administrative analogue of the courts' development of case law.

Bureaucratic growth in the United States has three main sources:

1. The establishment of a wide range of Federal social security, urban, welfare, and education policies.
2. The growth in the regulatory role of Federal government.
3. The establishment of the United States as a global military and political power.

The first and second of these are overlapping categories: all Federal programmes have regulatory purposes and consequences, irrespective of whether they are administered by notionally independent regulatory commissions or notionally subordinate departments and agencies of the Executive Branch. The third is dealt with in greater detail in Chapter 12.

Most of the expansion in Federal employment (especially of employment in Washington) to have occurred between 1933 and the late 1990s did so between the beginning of Franklin Roosevelt's Presidency and the end of Harry Truman's. In 1933 there was one civil servant for every 280 Americans; by 1953 there was one for every eighty. During this period, the foundations of social security law were laid, the regulatory activity of the Federal government expanded greatly, and the United States moved from isolationism to world-wide military and diplomatic involvement. Contrary to popular opinion, agitated by the false claims of politicians seeking election, Federal employment growth since the beginning of Eisenhower's Presidency has been slow, and much slower than population growth. While the image of Washington as a bloated and expanding Federal animal wins easy applause in election campaigns by stirring old populist sentiment, it is misplaced.

None the less, whether measured by the number of programmes, expenditure, volume of public law administrative regulation or the number of public employees, the Federal government is large. Metropolitan Washington is overwhelmingly dependent upon government for its prosperity; many communities across America also depend upon the Federal government for the maintenance of prosperity through direct Federal employment.

Large though it is, the Federal government relies on lower-level governments to deliver most of the services generated by the expansion of the Federal educational, welfare, and urban programmes of the New Deal and Great Society programmes of the 1930s and 1960s. During the 1960s, employment in state and local government grew by nearly 40 per cent, fuelled by an increase of more than 230 per cent in Federal aid to lower-level governments. Less than 10 per cent of the Federal budget is spent on domestic programmes administered directly by Federal employees. Most Federal programmes are delivered by lower-level governments and other third parties – by officials working for State or city governments, and by private organizations working under contract to Federal agencies or with the assistance of Federal grants. Symbolic of the Federal government's involvement in all fields of public policy is the profusion of Federal buildings and bureaucrats throughout the country: nearly nine out of every ten Federal employees work outside the Washington metropolitan area.

In the nineteenth century, the United States played minor military and diplomatic roles, while domestic Federal responsibilities were mainly confined to the Post Office (which accounted for almost all of the growth in Federal employment up to the outbreak of the Civil War). The Army and Navy, Treasury, and Post Office apart, neither the Federal nor the State governments had many employees. Until the end of the Federalist period, Congress left the running of the Executive Branch to the administration. Thereafter, until the end of the nineteenth century, it exercised direct controls over domestic departments in the formation and implementation of policy. Except for the Departments of State, War, and Navy, where there was general agreement that the Constitution vested special authority and responsibilities in the President, Congress regarded heads of executive departments as being responsible primarily to the legislature, and accordingly oversaw the few domestic departments with care. Its powers over interstate commerce were exercised directly and not through intermediary regulatory commissions.

From the mid-nineteenth century onwards, Congress began to regulate private business on behalf of a wider public interest by devolving powers to executive agencies, usually to independent commissions. Much of the American economy has since fallen under Federal or State regulation. Federal regulation has proceeded in three main phases: (i) beginning in the 1860s and ending with the United States's entry into the First World War; (ii) running from 1933 to 1938; and (iii) lasting for a decade from the middle of the 1960s.

The beginning of the first phase was marked by the passage of the National Currency Act in 1863, and, the following year, of the National Bank Act, which established a Comptroller of the Currency with the power to charter and supervise national banks. In 1887, the Interstate Commerce Act established the Interstate Commerce Commission (ICC), designed to rationalise disorderly competition between railroad companies. After two years in the Interior Department, Congress revised its legal basis and made it an independent Commission in 1889; three of the other commissions formed subsequently during this first period were also independent of the Executive and Legislative Branches.

The ICC's establishment marked a new willingness by the Federal government to control the worst consequences for public health and consumer well-being of hitherto unrestrained market forces. After much vacillation, the Supreme Court upheld the policy-making role of the Interstate Commerce Commission in *Interstate Commerce Commission* v. *Illinois*

Central Railroad Co., 215 US 452 (1910), and extended it in *Houston, East and West Texas Ry. Co.* v. *United States*, 234 US 342 (1914) (which has since become known as the *Shreveport* case). In the latter judgment, the Court upheld the right of Congress to regulate not just interstate commerce, but also intra-state commerce in so far as it had "a close and substantial relation to interstate commerce". *Shreveport* had powerful implications for the ICC's regulatory authority over intra-state railroad rates, for Congressional supremacy over State law in commercial matters, and hence for Congress's consequent freedom to legislate. Although the Constitution grants Congress no powers to regulate intra-state commerce, the interstate power was by the *Shreveport* case deemed effectively unlimited.

In 1890, Congress passed the Sherman Anti-Trust Act, designed to prevent the emergence of (but also, if necessary, to dissolve) monopolies or price-fixing trusts. The Act forbade "every contract, combination . . . or conspiracy in the restraint of trade or commerce", and provided for criminal penalties and civil action. President Woodrow Wilson's inaugural address in March 1913 included the main elements of his "New Freedom", which heralded his sending to Congress three major measures designed to give the public interest a more powerful voice in commerce. All three were passed into law: the Federal Reserve Act; the Federal Trade Commission Act; and the Clayton Anti-Trust Act.

The Federal Reserve Act, passed in December 1913, radically revised the nation's banking system by establishing a Federal central bank with supervisory powers over member banks, and over the nation's money supply. In September of the following year, Congress passed the Federal Trade Commission Act, which was designed to promote open competition and prevent the emergence of monopolies. The Clayton Anti-Trust Act increased competition in business by strengthening the Sherman Act. It also guaranteed the freedom for workers to associate in unions that were specifically excluded from the general prohibition on the formation of "combinations or conspiracies in restraint of trade" to which business corporations were subject.

Enforcement depended upon appropriate regulatory agencies being established, and upon subsequent Congressional support for their re-authorization and appropriations. Responsibility for enforcing the Sherman Act was vested in the Department of Justice's anti-trust division, which has retained it to the time of writing. Responsibility for enforcing the Clayton Act was placed with the Federal Trade Commission (FTC), established a month earlier in 1914 as a wholly independent regulatory commission. It, too, retains the original remit of prohibiting illegal combinations in restraint of trade, price-fixing, discrimination, and other practices against the interest of consumers.

The second phase of Federal regulation encompassed the period from the beginning of Franklin Roosevelt's Presidency in 1933 to the midpoint of his second term in 1938, during which time eight separate regulatory agencies were established to address problems arising from financial ruin and economic collapse. Among them were the National Labor Relations Board, formed by the Wagner Act of 1935; the Federal Deposit Insurance Corporation (FDIC) charged by the Glass–Steagal Act of 1933 (which separated commercial from investment banking) with the insurance of bank deposits up to $10,000 against the default of the member bank; and the Securities Exchange Commission (SEC) established by the Securities Exchange Act of 1934. All National Banks, and all State banks that were members of the Federal Reserve System, were covered by the Glass–Steagal Act. Its primary instrument (disclosure of all pertinent information), employed to counter misrepresentation and fraudulent dealing on Wall Street, has remained a key weapon in the Federal regulatory armoury ever since. In equity markets, the SEC continues to find plenty of work. The antipathy to Federal regulation among many in the Reagan Administration found expression in the easing of restrictions on another major market: Savings and Loans Associations. The incentives to imprudent and even criminal behaviour which the weakening of Federal regulation provided has had damaging effects upon the home loans market. Partly in consequence, the tight leash of the Federal authorities on other financial markets is now unlikely to be loosened. In contrast, some markets, such as insurance, which at present fall within the ambit of State rather than Federal regulators, may be drawn into the Federal net.

Whereas the first phase sprang from the intention to control the detrimental effects of monopoly capital, and the second from the economic crisis, the third was triggered by the articulation of new concerns, especially social regulation, and control of negative externalities. Among the regulatory agencies created in this latter period were the Equal Employment Opportunities Commission (EEOC); the Occupational Health and Safety Administration (OSHA); and the Consumer Product Safety Commission (CPSC). Reliance on GNP growth as the single most important indicator of national welfare came increasingly to be questioned in the mid-1960s as the problems of large pockets of rural and urban poverty, of environmental damage, and of the high risks to the health and safety of workers and consumers became important issues on the political agenda. President Johnson had hastened the change by questioning the adequacy of affluence as an indicator of the quality of life.

The burgeoning consumer interest movement was stimulated by the publication of Ralph Nader's book *Unsafe at Any Speed* (1965), a critical study of the scant attention then paid by car manufacturers to the safety of their products. Nader's book caused the question of car safety in particular, and consumer interests in general, to rise rapidly up the political agenda. It was the first major success for consumer lobbies in America, and prompted government action. The Consumer Product Safety Act, passed by Congress in 1972 with President Nixon's support, established the Consumer Product

Safety Commission (CSPC) to protect consumers against unreasonable risk of injury from hazardous products. Two years before, by an executive reorganization plan that consolidated fifteen scattered units into one, Nixon established the Environmental Protection Agency (EPA), charged with writing regulations enforcing new anti-pollution legislation – work that brings it into conflict with powerful industrial interests.

Bureaucratic Structure and Organization

Executive Departments

Competition between agencies within departments is endemic and ineradicable. Buttressed by functional specialization, some agencies enjoy almost complete autonomy from other agencies in the same department and have been powerfully resistant to attempts by the Secretaries and Under-Secretaries of Departments to enforce a wider or a Presidential view or policy upon them. Agencies are the primary units of importance and interest. Established separately by Congress, they administer distinct programmes authorized and re-authorized by Congress, and for which Congress separately appropriates public money. Their purposes are defined separately in law, and their work is overseen by different Subcommittees. Relations between agencies and their Congressional parents are often closer politically than relations between agencies within what is nominally a single department. Brief examinations of the Departments of Defense, Judiciary, and the Treasury given in Exhibit 8.1 illustrate this characteristic.

Federal Corporations

Regulation, not nationalization, has been the Federal government's chosen policy instrument to modify the operations of the market, and opportunities for privatization have consequently been fewer. There have been just three major exceptions to this preference:

1. Major failures of commercial or financial undertakings, such as the collapse of passenger railroads leading to the formation of Amtrak; and the failure of the Continental Bank of Illinois and of many Savings & Loans Associations in the late 1980s and early 1990s.
2. The operation of public utilities such as the Tennessee Valley Authority and the western power generation plants.
3. The change in the status of the Post Office from a government department to a public corporation in 1970 so that it might have greater autonomy from Congressional pressure to keep postage fees artificially low, thereby starving the organization of investment. (The move has been conspicuously unsuccessful.)

EXHIBIT 8.1

Agencies and their Congressional Parents

- The *Department of Defense* as a whole has as its ostensibly undivided object the defence of the United States. It is, however, subdivided into three major departments (Army, Air Force, and Navy, with the Marine Corps being a semi-autonomous agency within the Navy Department) whose interests frequently collide. Prior to 1949, the Army and Navy were run as wholly separate Departments. The amalgamation in that year of the Departments of Navy and of War (which had itself combined supervision of the Departments of the Army, and Army Air Force) did not end inter-service rivalry. Bureaucratic competition between the services continues, to the detriment of the formulation and execution of American foreign and defence policy. Participation in the Libyan raid by USAF F111s based in Britain sprang partly from the Air Force's desire to record a military "victory" as the Navy, Marine Corps, and Army had already done during the Reagan Administration.

- The *Department of Justice* also harbours powerful and autonomous fiefdoms. Indeed, the clearest instance of agency autonomy was the Federal Bureau of Investigation (FBI) during its heyday under J. Edgar Hoover, its Director for almost half a century. Even after his death, most Americans regard the FBI as an independent and free-standing organization, not as a division of the Department of Justice, which it nominally is. Hoover did not readily submit to the succession of Attorneys General (his nominal superiors) or to Presidents; as an unelected bureaucrat, he possessed effective independence. Resolute in pursuit of those whom he suspected of Communist sympathies, and unenthusiastic in his enforcement of civil rights laws, Hoover was virtually unaccountable.

- The *Department of the Treasury* illustrates the disparate nature of semi-autonomous agencies within a department, a general pattern throughout the Federal bureaucracy. Two agencies within the department have, in practice, substantial independence from each other: the US Secret Service and the Internal Revenue Service (IRS). Created by Act of Congress in 1860 to suppress the counterfeiting of United States's coin, bills, and securities, the US Secret Service is now known less for this work than for its responsibility for ensuring the safety of the President and his family, former Presidents and First Ladies, other senior government figures, and visiting VIPs. The IRS is one of the largest agencies within the United States government, with offices spread throughout the country, engaged in the business of collecting Federal taxes. In addition to its direct relationship with every American tax-payer, it also has close links to the Tax Committees in both Houses of Congress, and to the Joint Committee on Internal Revenue Taxation. Within the Treasury, the functional specialization of the IRS and Secret Service renders them special cases, but only in extent, not in kind. The relationship that each has to the Department of the Treasury as a whole and to other agencies within the department, such as the Bureau of the Mint, is not different in principle from those of other agencies in other departments.

Independent Regulatory Commissions and Executive Regulatory Agencies

Some regulatory bodies, such as the Food and Drug Administration (FDA), are placed within an Executive Department. Others, such as the Federal Election Commission, are in their operation (though not in the selection of their senior officials) formally independent both of Congress and of the Executive. In 1977, the Permanent Subcommittee on Investigations of the Senate Government Operations Committee in 1977 defined a Federal regulatory office as one which:

> (1) has decision-making authority, (2) establishes standards or guidelines conferring benefits and imposing restrictions on business conduct, (3) operates principally in the sphere of domestic business activity, (4) has its head and/or members appointed by the President and in all but one instance, subject to Senate confirmation (FDA is the exception), and (5) has its legal procedures generally governed by the Administrative Procedure Act.

Condition (4) underpins the Commissions' independence: Federal Departments have at their head Secretaries appointed by the President subject to Senate advice and consent, who together comprise the President's Cabinet but (like all political appointees in the departments) are subject to dismissal by the President. Independent Regulatory Commissions are led by independent commissioners who, though appointed on the same terms as Departmental Secretaries, may not be dismissed by the President. Congress has reinforced the relative freedom which this immunity grants them by setting their (staggered) terms of office at between four and fourteen years, according to the provisions of their founding statutes. In most Commissions, the capacity of Presidents and Congresses to interfere is further limited by statutory provisions limiting the number of Commissioners on any one Commission who may be drawn from either political party. Long terms of office increase the prospect that Commissioners will become expert in their work, while granting them almost complete immunity from partisan interference. The old faith in expertise, distrust of politicians, and in organizational solutions to policy problems which together spurred Progressive reformers at the turn of the century still exercises its sway.

As Federal regulations were addressed to interstate commerce, State regulations and regulatory agencies established by state legislatures dealt with intra-state concerns. State regulations are neither necessarily more lax nor more stringent than Federal ones: thus many States operated and enforced civil rights laws long before the Federal authorities acted in 1964, while the regulation of the sale of firearms by many State Legislatures is stronger than that by Congress. The provision in the Trade Bill of 1988 vetoed by President Reagan providing for 90 days' notice to be given to workers was significantly weaker than that already in place in the statutes of many States.

Until the early 1980s, much of America's commercial life was regulated by regulatory commissions: broadcasting; air travel; and rail and road transport. Exploiting growing public discontent with the harmful consequences for consumer choice and interests within a highly-regulated economy (which invariably operated to the benefit of producers), President Carter initiated the deregulation of airline travel with the abolition of the Civil Aeronautics Board under the Airline Deregulation Act of 1978, and the consequential ending of a Federal role in the setting of airline fares. Railroad rates (fares) were similarly deregulated under the Staggers Rail Act of 1980 with the ending of the ICC's original role. Rates are now determined by the market. The activities of savings institutions (whose members' savings were insured by a Federal Agency) were deregulated (and consequently greatly expanded) by the Garn–St Germain Depository Institution Act of 1982; the setting of rates for cable TV were deregulated in 1984 under the Cable Deregulation Act. Deregulation contributed greatly to the disastrous run of insolvencies and associated criminality that undermined the savings and loan industry from 1989 onwards, with the result that a new Federal Agency took over the bankrupt institutions at great public expense. Less dramatically, the rapid rise in prices that followed cable TV deregulation resulted in new regulation passed in the autumn of 1992 over President Bush's veto.

However, the deregulation of the 1980s was partial, even within the airline and railroad industries. Many aspects of both, from operational safety, and the closure of passenger railroad lines, to the occupational health of airline and railroad employees, remain firmly regulated by, among others, the Federal Aviation Agency (FAA), and the Occupational Health and Safety Administration (OHSA). Other areas of economic activity were regulated either for the first time (for example, the futures trading of commodities) or more tightly (as with a range of air, water, and ground pollution controls) during the same period in which airline and railroad rates were deregulated. As the fracas over the lax enforcement of anti-pollution laws at the Environmental Protection Agency (EPA) in 1983 showed, Congressional and public support for deregulation was greater in some areas than others; where a clear public or consumer interest was at stake, pressure for the maintenance or extension of regulation was greater than where it was not. IRCs are still a major component of the Federal bureaucracy, and regulation a common instrument for the control of parts of the economy and of other areas of public life where Congress holds that the public interest cannot be served by an unfettered free market.

Business is not universally opposed to regulation. Regulation has as often served the interests of the regulated industries as those of consumers: agencies have frequently fallen under the effective control of the notionally regulated industry. Many leaders of industries have themselves sought the Federal regulation of their industry, because of the threat that individual States might set stricter standards than the Federal authorities, or because of the extra costs of dealing with different regulations set by different governments, or in the face of pressure from consumers for deregulation. Marver Bernstein (1955) argued that the "capture" of regulatory commissions by the regulated organization is the final phase of a dynamic relationship between the two. Airline deregulation was, for example, fiercely fought by large American airlines and by the unions within the industry whose different purposes regulation served well, and very much better than it did the purposes of passengers. In setting the prices of airline tickets and licensing airline routes within the United States, the Civil Aeronautics Board protected the interests of high-cost airlines with conservative business practices rather than the interests of airline passengers. Similarly, broadcasters had long had their interests defended by the Federal Communications Commission (FCC). Indeed, the FCC (like its predecessor, the Federal Radio Commission) was established at the urging of radio and television companies so that local markets might be protected and their use of frequencies defended.

Administrative Law

Administrative law comprises regulations, rulings, and judgments made by Executive Branch agencies under authority delegated to them by Congress in authorizing legislation. Regulations published by Executive Branch agencies are binding, and identical in their effects to Statute or common law. Congress may delegate powers to agencies broadly or narrowly, but in doing so, it retains the absolute right to modify the nature and extent of the delegation. Indeed, most statutory delegations of authority to agencies and regulatory authorities to issue regulations are subject to Congress retaining the right to veto them. Through re-authorization legislation, Congress may extend, diminish, or abolish altogether the right of Executive agencies to exercise rule-making authority. The example of deregulation of airline rates and routes in Exhibit 8.2 illustrates aspects of the phenomenon.

The *Federal Register* is a daily Federal government publication with a print run of 35,000. The Federal Register Act of 1935 requires all new regulations and administrative orders issued by Executive Branch agencies to be published in it. The Administrative Procedure Act of 1946 similarly requires all Presidential Executive Orders to be published there, and further requires that the details of proposed regulations be published in the Register to give "interested persons an opportunity to participate in the rule-making", thereby legitimating the place of interest groups in the formation of public policy. Executive Orders made by the President have the effect of law, and give effect to provisions of statute law under discretionary authority granted to the President in the original authorizing legislation, treaties, or the Constitution itself.

EXHIBIT 8.2

FAA Regulations

Deregulation of airline rates and routes since 1980 have occurred simultaneously with the tightening of regulations governing aircraft and airport safety by the responsible authority, the Federal Aviation Administration (FAA), an agency of the Department of Transportation. Regular air passengers on a flight to the United States or within it become familiar with Federal regulations covering the safety of passengers in flight and the procedures for emergency evacuation of the aircraft. Such regulations have the force of law, and passengers who break them risk heavy fines on conviction. FAA regulations address not only those questions of smoking in the gangways, the fastening of seatbelts, and the use of the emergency exits, but also thousands of other operational details familiar only to airlines and their employees.

Every detail of civilian aircraft manufacture and operation is subject to FAA regulation and enforced by FAA inspectors. No civilian aircraft may be flown by any airline within the United States unless the type of aircraft and its engines have airworthiness certificates and the individual aircraft is subject to detailed tests specified, approved, and implemented by the FAA. Notices of rules to be issued by the FAA are published in the *Federal Register*.

The complexity of published rules and the financial interest that corporations and other groups have in them, result in frequent hearings by agencies to adjudicate on appeals against their decisions. In more serious and substantial cases, groups may seek the rescinding or alteration of a rule or judgment by filing suit in a Federal court. By determining the lawfulness of particular administrative rules, Courts are therefore inextricably involved not just in policy adjudication but also in the implementation and evaluation of public policy itself. Courts must judge whether or not disputed rules accord with the delegation of authority made to agencies by Congress, or whether such rules are, in the language of the 1946 Act, "arbitrary and capricious".

The Court most directly concerned with major questions of administrative law is the US Court of Appeals for the District of Columbia (the seat of Federal government). Since the passage of the Administrative Procedures Act in 1946, the District of Columbia Court of Appeals has established criteria by which agencies ought to act in particular cases. In determining whether an agency head acted appropriately in exercising his or her authority, courts often require bureaucrats to inform them of the basis for their decisions. Prudence therefore requires administrators to ensure that they are acting within the bounds of the authority granted them by Congress, and full records are kept of the reasoning behind each rule.

Interest groups scour the *Federal Register* for notices of regulations affecting them or their clients, in light of which they take action. They also take note of agencies' failure to issue detailed regulations which implement Congressional statutes. One example among many of the latter is that of the Sierra Club, an environmental interest group (see Exhibit 8.3).

EXHIBIT 8.3

The Sierra Club and the Environmental Protection Agency

In 1992 the Sierra Club gave notice to the Environmental Protection Agency
(EPA) that unless new anti-pollution regulations required by the Clean Air Act
of 1990 were published within sixty days, the Club would file a civil suit against
the Agency (which it subsequently did). The EPA's delay was partly caused by
its being heavily burdened with work, but mainly by its being embroiled in
disputes with the White House, which sought to lessen the regulatory burden
upon business by delaying regulations and weakening their force. For the
Agency, the cost of bowing to Presidential pressure by delaying the issue of
regulations is, first, that the issue comes to the attention of the public and the
courts; but second, that the publicity invites searching Congressional scrutiny in
oversight hearings conducted on the next Re-authorization or Appropriations
Bill.

Congressional Control of the Bureaucracy

The Senate Governmental Affairs Committee's 1977 report on Federal
regulation listed six main objectives of Congressional oversight:

1. Ensuring compliance of Executive agencies with Congressional intent.
2. Determining the effectiveness of regulatory policies.
3. Preventing waste and dishonesty.
4. Preventing abuse in the administrative process.
5. Representing the public interest.
6. Preventing usurpation by agencies of legislative authority.

Congress has extensive formal powers to ensure that these objectives are met.
There are three main tools at its disposal, which are examined in the
following three sections:

(i) The power of confirmation of presidential nominees to executive posts.
(ii) Appropriations and authorization committee hearings.
(iii) The legislative veto.

Congress also has available to it the commissioning of studies by the General
Accounting Office, one of its institutional arms, into the efficiency with
which the Executive Branch executes public law.

The US Senate's Power of "Advise and Consent"

Senate scrutiny of Presidential nominees to political positions in Executive
Departments and agencies is, in combination with authorizing and appro-

priations hearings, a more potent form of oversight than that available to it in respect of appointments to the Judiciary. As the Senate Judiciary Committee has primary responsibility for examining the qualifications of judicial nominees, so other Senate Committees are responsible for scrutinizing nominations to departments and agencies within their functional jurisdiction. Hence, political appointments by the President to agencies within the Department of Agriculture are considered by the Senate Agriculture Committee, and those to the Department of Defense by the Senate Armed Services Committee.

Few nominees to Executive Departments and agencies are rejected, but the greatest value of the advice and consent power lies in deterrence rather than defence: wise Presidents avoid rather than court disputes that would be damaging to them, and so nominate those whom the Senate is likely to confirm, not those whom it is likely to reject. Defying the Senate by deliberately nominating those whom a majority are likely to find repugnant invites rebuff and consequent embarrassment.

Presidents Nixon and Reagan held that the power to "advise and consent" obliged the Senate to accept their choices. Both were wrong. In the twentieth century, the Senate has rejected few nominees to Cabinet-level positions: President Coolidge's nomination of Charles Warren to Attorney General was rejected in 1925; Eisenhower's nomination of Lewis Strauss as Secretary of Commerce was defeated in 1959; Carter's nomination of Theodore Sorensen (formerly President Kennedy's Special Counsel) as Director of Central Intelligence fell in 1977; and Bush's nomination of former Senator John Tower as Secretary of Defense was rejected in 1989. It is commoner for careful soundings of opinion to be taken among key opinion-formers in the relevant Senate Committee before a nomination is made, so that nominees' acceptability can be tested before the formal process begins. Such a practice enables influential Senators to consider the background, politics, character, and behaviour of those whom the President appoints to key policy-making positions within his administration. Presidents and their staff who take seriously the Senate's constitutional right to advise on the acceptability of possible nominees are more likely to secure its consent to them.

The time which Members of Congress have devoted to oversight in Committee and Subcommittee hearings has grown in recent years, partly because of the increased complexity of government regulation, but largely because of Congress's decreased trust in the Executive since the late 1960s. Johnson's conduct of the Vietnam War, and President Nixon's systematic abuse of presidential prerogatives led to Congressional reform and to the revision of formal Executive–Congressional relations. Congress is, in consequence, a livelier competitor of the Executive than it was prior to the late 1960s. By increasing its staff resources, the number and autonomy of Subcommittees, the legislature broke the Executive's monopoly of expertise, and was able to oversee more effectively the implementation of public laws passed by Congress. Two legislative vehicles have had special importance in Congress's attempts to enforce its prerogatives. In fiscal policy, the reforms of the 1974 Budget and Impoundment Control Act have enhanced Congress's capacity to participate in the formation of Federal Budget policy. The consequences of the 1974 Act are difficult to assess because it has been implemented over a period when much else of importance has changed, as is explained in Chapter 11. In military matters, the War Powers Resolution of 1973 marked an attempt to constrain the President's capacity to wage war without Congressional knowledge or sanction. The Resolution's constitutionality has been contested by every President since its passage over Nixon's veto, has been flouted by them all, but has still not been tested in a Federal Court.

Both initiatives none the less reflected Congress's reassertion of its right to participate fully in policy implementation and evaluation, as well as legislation. Congress's role in government and policy-making does not end when the President signs legislation into law, the Supreme Court's judgment in declaring the legislative veto unconstitutional in *Chadha* notwithstanding (see p. 369). On the contrary, Congress properly participates at all stages of the policy process: initiation, legislation, implementation, and evaluation.

Congress cannot itself implement programmes but must ensure that implementation by executive agencies of programmes which it has authorized and for which it has appropriated public money, accords with its intentions. Presidents and their political appointees to departments and agencies often find such oversight unwelcome, but their dismissal of Congress's right to scrutinize programmes in detail (so-called "micro-management") has little constitutional weight. The Constitution gives no part of the United States' government a free hand, and Congress has the incentive, the right and, since the Congressional reforms of the 1970s, the capacity, to examine implementation of programmes and policy as its Members please. Executive officials rarely tell Congressional committees all that they know, whether from a proper concern to maintain executive privilege or an improper attempt to deceive. In the long run, however, the powers of Congress are too extensive and fundamental for Presidents and their executive subordinates to ignore. Presidents cannot govern without Congress.

Authorizing and Appropriating Committee Hearings

Congress typically authorizes programmes for a specified period, varying from every year to every few years. If they are to continue beyond that period, they require re-authorization. Non-entitlement programmes depend for their funding on annual Appropriations Bills. The committee system of Congress is organized to accommodate the periodicity of re-authorization and appropriation; these regular events supply the bulk of authorizing and appropriating Committees' work. Authorization bills enable the Executive

Branch to suggest, and the Legislative Branch to require, that programmes be added, altered, or deleted. Appropriations Bills permit similar scrutiny of the cost of programmes. Both authorization and appropriations hearings in specialized Congressional Committees therefore appear to provide excellent opportunities for Congress to oversee Executive Branch activities: executive officials may be examined about the programmes which they administer, while experts from outside government and witnesses from interest groups are also summoned and questioned about policy and programmes. Congress writes its authorizing and appropriating legislation partly on the basis of the views that Members and their staff hear at such Committee hearings.

Incentives for Representatives and Senators to use the Subcommittees on which they sit as vehicles for overseeing the agencies' execution of programmes which they authorize and finance are, nevertheless, often weak. Relations between agencies and Subcommittees are more often co-operative than conflictual: bureaucrats know that whatever the short-term attractions, the medium- and long-term costs of antagonising Congressional "parents" are high. Where relations between agencies and parent Committees are collaborative, there is, however, a risk that a central purpose of oversight (ensuring that Congress's legislative will is executed) will be compromised. Irrespective of whether co-operation between agencies and Committees in fact compromises oversight, the incentives to Representatives and Senators to engage in general scrutiny of agencies' activities are weak. When, by contrast, errors or disasters occur, politicians engage eagerly in retrospective oversight.

It is Congress's task to set the parameters within which Agency officials act; it cannot be Congress's proper task to do bureaucrats' jobs for them by drafting highly detailed, technical rules. It is neither desirable nor practicable for administrative discretion to be eliminated; the point and purpose of the delegation of powers by Congress to the Executive is that it should not be. Dispassionate bureaucratic expertise is a valuable resource: airline passengers sensibly prefer regulations governing the detection of metal fatigue in aircraft to be drafted and implemented by aerospace engineers rather than by politicians – not because it guarantees that errors will be avoided, but because it reduces the likelihood of their occurring.

Two difficulties arise: the first is that the volume of consequential rule-making by agencies is so large that Appropriations Subcommittees are unable constantly to check that funds are spent by agencies in accordance with the agencies' stated intentions or Congress's will. The second is that Authorizing Committees and Subcommittees are similarly unable to ensure that all rules and actions of the Agency comply with the letter and the spirit of Congress's requirements in the authorizing legislation. Provided that this has no damaging consequences, politicians may be unconcerned. There are only weak incentives for Members of Congress to cross-examine witnesses from agencies in hearings of their Subcommittees simply in order to check whether Congress's intent is being followed. However, in the event (for example) of an airline disaster, the Chairpersons of the Aviation Subcommittees will certainly call public hearings to interrogate FAA and other witnesses to assess whether the Agency has been negligent in the issuing and enforcing of rules under its delegated authority. Attempts by agencies to depart from Congress's appropriating intent are more easily controlled: the Appropriations Committees of both the House and the Senate typically restrict the freedom of agencies to move resources from one programme to another (the "reprogramming" of funds).

Restricting such administrative freedom may be good administrative practice, but it has few political benefits for the Members of Congress who write appropriations law. By calling hearings to examine failures by agencies, Committee Chairs bathe in the light of publicity, projecting themselves as acting in the public interest but to their own political advantage. Examining officials after the fact is both easier and politically more attractive than examining them before it. To that extent, the threefold objectives of Congressional politicians – re-election; the achievement of power within Congress; and the making of sound public policy – can be advanced simultaneously. Generalizing from this particular example suggests, however, that Congress's task of overseeing executive implementation may be executed less than satisfactorily. The FAA's failure (and by extension the failure of any Agency) to make rules for the detailed implementation of Congress's will was in these cases corrected only after the event, and not before.

Studies of Congress's Oversight Function

Most scholars who have written on the subject argue that Congress performs its function of oversight poorly, waiting for intermittent disasters to force issues on to its agenda rather than seeking to avert policy failures through laborious scrutiny of an Agency's activities. However, others have argued that "police-patrol" oversight (Congress conducting oversight of a sample of agency activities on its own initiative "with the aim of detecting and remedying any violations of legislative goals and, by its surveillance, discouraging such violations") is not extensively undertaken, but that "fire-alarm" oversight (by which they refer to the practice of investigating incidents after they occur) is performed extensively and well (McCubbins and Schwartz, 1984). Preferring the latter over the former is, McCubbins and Schwartz write, "eminently rational". It is also possible for Congress, in authorizing legislation, to oblige agencies to report to Congress that the law's requirements are being met, thereby reducing the chance of "fire-alarm" oversight proving inadequate. Yet that course of action which is rationally in the (short-term) interests of individual members of Congress is not necessarily in the (longer-term) interests of Congress as a whole. Still less is it necessarily in the public interest. Congress is institutionally much better equipped to respond to particular violations of Congressional intent than it is to prevent them.

A more comprehensive study by Aberbach (1990), while not disposing of the dilemma of short-versus long-term interests, emphasises that large and highly competent professional committee staff have made the general monitoring of agencies' work a less forbidding task than most writers have supposed. Interviews with senior Congressional Committee staff have de-monstrated their many (and intensively used) informal links with senior agency bureaucrats. Such informal links are the firmer for the widespread practice whereby individuals move within the policy-making communities in Washington: between staff positions on Capitol Hill, law firms, interest groups, political appointments in the Executive Branch, research institutes, and universities. In this context, oversight is not a series of discrete events, but, in fact, interconnected processes in a community of policy-makers embracing agencies, Subcommittees, and interest groups.

In contrast to the circumstances under which Congress worked in the 1950s and 1960s, the quality and quantity of information available to staff about agencies' work is high. Several members of staff working for the Senate Foreign Relations and House Foreign Affairs Committees, or their associated Subcommittees, for example, were well-informed about (and alarmed by) the nature and extent of military support provided by the Executive to Iraq in the weeks prior to Saddam Hussein's invasion of Kuwait in August 1990, and the mixture of commercial and political motives for it. Secrets are difficult to keep in Washington; they are nearly impossible to keep over more than the short term from the extensive staff networks serving Congressional Committees. Informal patterns of communication of this sort are essential for Congressional oversight to be conducted effectively. The expertise, energy, and time devoted by Congressional committee staff to the maintenance of communications with officials in the Executive Branch acts both as a check on agencies and as a deterrent to their departing from Congress's intent.

The Legislative Veto

The legislative veto appears nowhere in the Constitution but was devised by Congress in 1932 to enable the President to reorganize Executive depart-ments and agencies subject to either House disapproving within sixty days. It has since been incorporated into much public law, typically providing for a period of sixty to ninety days after an Executive action during which Congress might approve or reject it. The legislative veto power was lodged in different institutions by different laws: in the House or the Senate (a "one-house" veto), in both Chambers (a "two-house" veto), in a particular Committee, or even in a Committee's Chair.

A legislative veto on an agency having been effected and the agency's decision either approved or disapproved, the President has no further role: the Constitution's requirement that all legislation be presented to him for signature or veto does not apply to legislative vetoes. Legislative vetoes therefore enable Congress to exercise some control over the Executive without resorting to the passage of a new law. The balance is by no means wholly to the disadvantage of the Executive: Congress has to act to nullify the Executive's action; it may not amend those measures sent to it by the President; the President decides what is sent to it, and when. These are considerable advantages for Presidents, especially when compared to the obstacles which their normal legislative proposals have must surmount if they are to pass into law.

However, the failure to adhere to the presentment clause of Article I, Section 7 of the Constitution prompted the Supreme Court to declare in *Chadha* v. *Immigration and Naturalization Service*, 462 US 919 (1983), that the arrangement was unconstitutional. Arguments supporting it founded on considerations of "efficiency" were, the Court declared, unsatisfactory, since the founders did not accord that notion high priority. Since it was partly to provide for a more efficient government than the Articles of Confederation that the founders convened at Philadelphia, this was an odd claim for the Court to make. The legislative veto does indeed invert the legislative process as specified in the Constitution: under it, the executive proposes rules which Congress has the opportunity to veto. It is not clear that the procedure subverts the Constitution. The legislative veto is better regarded as one of many instances by which procedures are adapted within the framework of the Constitution to cope with new circumstances and demands.

The legislative veto's value for Congress's oversight capacity and for the case with which the Executive conducts its business are in any case so pronounced that the Court's cry of unconstitutionality has had little effect other than to call its own judgment into question. President Reagan initially approved of the Court's judgment in *Chadha*. However, he came to recognise that, being denied the opportunity to review Executive Agency decisions, the Legislative Branch could if it chose restrict its delegations of power to the Executive by number and scope, thereby hampering the Executive. Deprived of the legislative veto or devices with the same practical effect, Congress would simply not delegate authority to the executive on terms which granted agencies any significant discretion.

In practice, however, Congress has both defied and circumvented the Court's decision. Between the judgment in *Chadha* (delivered in the summer of 1983) and 1991, Congress defied the Court by writing more than 200 legislative vetoes into law: the Supreme Court had overreached itself, and Congress had both the incentive and the means with which to respond. With the grudging consent of the White House and agencies, Congress has also circumvented the judgment by arriving at informal understandings with agencies which the Supreme Court is powerless to prevent but which constitute a substantial and effective means by which Congress can continue to share in the implementation of legislation.

Conclusion

The President's influence over Congress, and hence his control over the legislative process, is limited by the separation of the Legislature from the Executive. This constitutes a major limitation on the power of the office, because the President is granted no legislative powers beyond those of being permitted to recommend "from time to time" measures to Congress, and the qualified right of veto. The Constitution does, however, explicitly grant him Executive powers, as under Article II: "The Executive Power shall be vested in a President of the United States of America".

At first sight, nothing could be clearer: the grant of power is his alone, and (except in respect of the Senate's obligation to consider Presidential appointments to senior government posts) unqualified. Even where it is explicit, however, the Constitution does not dispose of political problems. In practice, the apparently unfettered power granted to the President over the Executive Departments by Article II, Section 2, of the Constitution is highly constrained. Large and fragmented Federal departments comprising functionally-differentiated agencies are in many cases as much the creatures of Congress and interest group clients as of the Presidency, and in other cases effectively independent. "Clientelism" (capture by interest groups) is a prominent characteristic of some Federal agencies, and one that Presidents have constantly to confront when deciding how they can best implement the programmes which they have succeeded in persuading Congress to pass into law.

The administrative complexities of modern American government do not fit the eighteenth-century Constitution. The framers could not and did not anticipate that the Federal government could or would assume a large role in managing the national economy; in protecting, however imperfectly, its citizens from penury and sickness in old age, or in placing a rudimentary welfare net beneath the poor. Nor could the Framers have expected the United States to expand to a nation of 270 million people, to assemble the most powerful military forces in the history of the world, or to become the largest (and for a time, the hegemonic) global economy. All these functions require vast expenditure of public money and the services of many millions of bureaucrats in departments and agencies of Federal, State, and local governments. Controlling programmes administered by bureaucrats is therefore of central importance to democrats.

The United States Federal government is divided, decentralized, and fragmented. Executive departments owe their existence to Acts of Congress, and their maintenance to Congressional appropriations. The Federal governing process in the United States therefore comprises in part a struggle for control over the many functional islands of the Federal bureaucracy by the Presidency, Congress, the Courts, the departments within which individual agencies are placed, and the clients whom the agencies serve.

9

Federalism and Intergovernmental Policy-Making

The Tenth Amendment to the Constitution (see Appendix 2) reflects an American antipathy to government in general, to a unitary State in particular, and denotes the need to establish criteria for allocating powers to different levels of government without in fact determining them. Since its ratification, the Federal government has become more powerful, but a unitary state has not emerged.

Yet while States retain elements of their sovereignty, their autonomy from the Federal government is heavily circumscribed. The States' constitutional standing has weakened since 1937, while their fiscal condition, which between 1933 and 1980 was sustained by the growth of Federal financial support, deteriorated seriously in the 1980s. The Federal government's freedom to regulate commerce in its many forms and to initiate policy is contingent upon its possessing both political will and resources. The widespread perceived failure of Federal education, welfare, and urban initiatives of both the Great Society of the 1960s and the successor programmes of the 1970s, weakened Congress's will to act progressively in the 1990s and issued in an especially sharp reaction in 1995 following the Republicans' victory in the 1994 mid-terms. The Federal government's fiscal crisis curtailed its capacity to act (as some conservatives intended). Federal authorities being shorn of both capacity and will, the States became the primary centres of the initiation of most domestic public policy (as they have always been of its implementation) despite the crises of public finance that have afflicted them, and well before the passage of the *Personal Responsibility and Work Opportunity Reconciliation Act of 1996* obliged them to assume an enhanced role.

Federalism: Theory and Structure

Although the word "Federalism" does not appear in the Constitution, the document is animated by the concept. Federalism is fundamental to under-

277

standing the structure and operation of government in the United States: the Constitution of 1789 replaced the Articles of Confederation which had provided for a frail centre and powerful states by a new Federal Republic. Under the new regime, the Federal government was granted an autonomy from the States, which the Articles of Confederation had denied to its predecessor. However, the Constitution also afforded the States and localities powerful influence upon the new Federal government through their representation in Congress.

Social, geographical, ethnic, economic, and political diversity coupled with the vastness of the thirteen States required a Federal Constitution. Without it, there could not have been a "United States": the contested meaning of the term enabled proponents and opponents of the proposed Republic to find different constructions and implications in its use. Anti-federalists attacked the essence of the proposed new political order which the State Conventions were asked by the Philadelphia Convention to ratify. Their perception was that the Founders (who for the sake of rhetorical advantage mischievously described themselves as "Federalists") had, in seven short Articles, created not a Federation but a national government. For reasons that George III had taught Americans thoroughly, such an arrangement was to be resisted. In order to assuage fears of an excessively powerful central government, the new Constitution's proponents agreed to the adoption of a Bill of Rights, including the elastic Tenth Amendment.

After ratification, dispute persisted over what had been created; moreover, the Constitution's brevity and imprecision left the question unresolved. Sovereignty was not unambiguously placed in the people, the States, or the new Federal government. Divisions arose. Alexander Hamilton and John Marshall (Secretary of State under Adams, and later Chief Justice) interpreted the Constitution as a broadly nationalist document by which a national government's few enumerated powers were supplemented by implied powers both broad and deep. Hamilton approvingly detected the possibility of a powerful central government in the elasticity of the powers granted to it in Article I. By contrast, Madison and Jefferson (and much later, in starker form, John C. Calhoun) interpreted it as a compact between States, in each of whom sovereignty resided after 1789 as it had done before. Madison claimed in *Federalist* No. 45 that:

> The powers delegated by the proposed Constitution to the federal government are few and defined. Those which are to remain in the State governments are numerous and indefinite.

The Constitution did more than define a ring in which Federal and State governments might compete. Some powers were exclusively those of the Federal authorities (foreign and defence policy; monetary policy; and the maintenance of a postal service); others were denied to Federal and State governments, including the granting of titles of nobility and the passage of *ex post facto* laws. Others powers were granted to Congress but not denied to the States; in these cases, Congress retains the power to pre-empt state action by reason of the Constitution's provision for the supremacy of Federal over State law where the two collide. Other powers may be exercised by State governments only if Congress permits them to do so (for example, the maintenance of troops in peacetime). Although "dual Federalism" explains more about the division of powers between the Federal government and those of the States in the late eighteenth century than it does now, some powers were concurrent from the first.

The Federalists provided less for a national government than for the possibility of its being created. In practice, the Federal government now has most of the Constitutional powers of a fully national government. Such freedom to act, such sovereignty as the States retain, is theirs only because the United States Congress permits it. Under Article I, Section 8, of the Constitution, Congress has effectively unfettered power over many areas of public policy. Individual rights unambiguously protected by the Bill of Rights, and the Thirteenth, Fourteenth, and Fifteenth Amendments, together with the States' constitutional right to tax and the immutability of their borders are the major exceptions. Otherwise, the constitutional guarantee to the states of sovereignty is now, according to the Supreme Court, in the gift of Congress.

Exhibit 9.1 records the Constitution's guarantees to, and limitations on, the States. This definition leaves unaddressed questions of the Fourteenth Amendment, the Commerce clause, and the "Necessary and Proper" clause. They will be dealt with in the section below on the Constitutional law of federalism.

Units of Government

States and cities evoke loyalties from their citizens which (for example) Congressional districts do not. The famous *New Yorker* cartoon cover portraying New York City as the world's centre speaks to an important truth about the dominance of local cultures and politics in the perceptions of Americans. The Jeffersonian tenet, that "all authority resides in the people", retains a strong force in American political culture which is itself characterised in part by localism's persistence (Wolman, 1996, p. 160). The Federal government is one of no fewer than 85,000 governments in the United States; they fall into eight categories.

1. Federal government
    The Federal government is the national government of the United States, and the prime subject of this book. Divided into three branches, the Federal government was established by the ceding of powers by State governments under the Constitution ratified in 1789.

EXHIBIT 9.1

The Constitution's Allocation of Federal and State Powers

Guarantees to the States – General
(1)   "The Powers not delegated to the United States by the Constitution, nor prohibited by it to the States, are reserved to the States respectively, or to the people". **(Tenth Amendment)**
(2)   No new State to be formed from an existing State or States, nor an existing State to be abolished or to have its boundaries altered, "without the consent of the Legislatures of the States concerned as well as of the Congress". **(Article IV, 3.1)**
(3)   Protection by the Federal government against invasion. **(Article IV, 4)**
(4)   Protection against "domestic violence" on application of the State Legislature or of the Executive. **(Article IV, 4)**
(5)   "The United States shall guarantee to every State in this Union a republican form of government." **(Article IV, 4)**
(6)   "Full faith and credit shall be given in each State to the public acts, records, and judicial proceedings of every other State." **(Article IV, 1)**
(7)   "The citizens of each State shall be entitled to all privileges and immunities of citizens in the several States." **(Article IV, 2)**

Limitations Upon the States – General
(1)   The Constitution of the United States, and the treaties and laws made under it are binding upon the States. **(Article VI, 2)**
(2)   All members of the US Congress, the State Legislatures, all Executive and judicial officers of the United States and of the several States are bound by the provisions of the United States Constitution. **(Article VI, 3)**
(3)   States may neither enter into treaties, alliances, or confederations, nor coin money. **(Article I, 10.1)**
(4)   Slavery is forbidden in all states. **(Amendment 13)**
(5)   States may not arrive at agreements or compacts with other States except with the consent of Congress. **(Article I, 10.3)**

Guarantees to the States – Judiciary
(1)   The Supreme Court has original jurisdiction over all controversies between states of the Union. **(Article III, 2.2)**
(2)   A crime must be tried in the State where it has been committed. **(Article III, 2.3)**
(3)   Accused persons shall be extradited "on demand of the executive authority of the State from which he fled" **(Article IV, 2.2)**

Limitations Upon the States – Judiciary
(1)   "The judicial power of the United States shall not be construed to extend to any suit in law or equity, commenced or prosecuted against one of the United States by Citizens of another State, or by Citizens or subjects of any Foreign State." **(Amendment 11)**
(2)   Bills of attainder are prohibited. **(Article I, 10.1)**
(3)   "No State shall make or enforce any law which shall abridge the privileges or immunities of citizens of the United States; nor shall any State deprive any person of life, liberty, or property, without due process of law; nor deny to any person within its jurisdiction the equal protection of the laws." **(Amendment 14)**

(4)   Judges in every State shall be bound by the Constitution of the United States and all treaties and laws made under it, "anything in the Constitution or laws of any State to the contrary notwithstanding". **(Article VI, 2)**

Guarantees to the States – Political Process

Congress
(1)   Members of the United States House of Representatives to be chosen biennially by the people whose qualifications shall be the same as those requisite for electors to the "most numerous branch of the State Legislature". **(Article I, 2.1)**
(2)   Upon election, Representatives and Senators must be inhabitants of the State from which they are chosen. **(Article I, 2.2, and 3.3)**
(3)   Representatives shall be reapportioned among the States according to a decennial census, but each State shall have at least one Representative. **(Article I, 2.3)**
(4)   The Executive authority of each State "shall issue writs of election" to fill vacancies in the representation from a State when they occur. **(Article I, 2.3)**
(5)   The Senate shall be composed of two Senators from each State, shall be chosen every six years by the people whose qualifications shall be the same as those requisite for electors to the "most numerous branch of the State Legislature". Vacancies shall be filled according to procedures determined by the Legislatures of the States. **(Article I, 3.1; Amendment 17)**

President
(1)   The President is to be selected by the electors of the States, with each State having a number of electors equivalent to the total number of its Representatives and Senators. **(Article II, 2)**
(2)   Each State shall have one vote in the event that the election is thrown into the House of Representatives. **(Amendment 12)**
(3)   Presidential appointees shall be subject to confirmation by a majority vote of the Senate. **(Article II, 2.2)**

Constitution Amendments
Amendments may be proposed by two-thirds of the States; to take effect, amendments must be ratified by the Legislatures of three-quarters of the States. **(Article V)**

Foreign Affairs
To take effect, treaties must be ratified by two-thirds of the Senate. **(Article II, 2.2)**

Limitations Upon the States – Political Process

President
"The Congress may determine the time of choosing the elector, and the day on which they shall give their votes; which day shall be the same throughout the United States." **(Article II, 1.3)**

Exhibit 9.1 continued overleaf

EXHIBIT 9.1 continued

Congress
(1)   A Representative must be at least 25 years old and have been a US citizen for at least seven years at the time of election. (**Article I, 2.1**)
(2)   A Senator must be at least 30 years old and have been a US citizen for at least nine years. (**Article I, 3.3**)
(3)   Although the States have the authority to decide the "times, places, and manner of holding elections for senators and representatives", Congress has the power to make or alter them. (**Article I, 4.1**)
(4)   "Each House shall be the judge of the elections, returns and qualifications of its own members." (**Article I, 5.1**)
(5)   Where a State denies the right to vote to any male citizen over the age of eighteen, that State's representation in the House of Representatives shall be reduced "in the proportion which the number of such male citizens shall bear to the whole number of male citizens twenty-one years of age in such State". (**Amendment 14, 2**)
(6)   Except by a two-thirds vote of each chamber of Congress, no person who having taken an oath to uphold the Constitution of the United States and who subsequently engages in "insurrection or rebellion against the same, or given aid or comfort to the enemies thereof" shall hold any office under the United States. (**Amendment 14, 3**)

Voting
(1)   States may not deny or abridge the right of citizens of the United States to vote "on account of race, color, or previous condition of servitude" (Amendment 15), "on account of sex" (Amendment 19), or "on account of age" in the case of those "who are eighteen years of age or older". (**Amendment 26, 1**)
(2)   States may not deny or abridge the right of citizens of the United States to vote "by reason of failure to pay any poll tax or other tax". (**Amendment 24**)

Foreign Affairs
Treaties are binding upon the states as "the supreme law of the land". (**Article VI, 2**)

Guarantees to the States – Commerce and Taxes
(1)   No Federal duties to be laid upon the exports of any state. (**Article I, 9.5**)
(2)   "No preference shall be given by any regulation of commerce or revenue to the ports of one State over those of another: nor shall vessels bound to or from, one State be obliged to enter, clear, or pay duties in another." (**Article IV, 9.6**)

Limitations Upon the States – Commerce and Taxes
(1)   States may not impose duties upon vessels of another State. (**Article I, 9.6**)
(2)   States may not "make anything but gold and silver coin a tender in payment of debts". (**Article I, 10.1**)
(3)   States may not impair contractual obligations. (**Article 10.1**)
(4)   States may not levy imposts or duties without the consent of Congress, "except for what may be absolutely necessary for executing its inspection laws". (**Article I, 10.2**)
(5)   States may not levy any duty upon the tonnage of ships. (**Article I, 10.3**)

2. State Governments

There are fifty State governments, each of which is guaranteed a Republican form of government, certain rights and (limited) sovereignty by the Constitution of the United States. Each has its own Constitution (the fact of which, according to a survey conducted for the Advisory Commission on Intergovernmental Relations in 1992, 52 per cent of adult Americans are unaware), and government established under it. The District of Columbia, the Commonwealth of Puerto Rico, Guam, the Virgin Islands and American Samoa are not States, but have certain powers of self-government and send non-voting delegates (not representatives) to the US House of Representatives.

In *Atkins* v. *Kansas* (1903), the Chief Justice of the Iowa Supreme Court, Judge John F. Dillon, determined that local governments

> are the creatures, mere political subdivisions, of the state for the purpose of exercising a part of its powers. They may exert only such powers as are expressly granted to them or such as may be necessarily implied from those granted.

This judgment, "Dillon's Rule", holds that sub-State-level governments derive their authority from the State and do not possess it in their own right. Though consistently upheld in constitutional law, its practical application is complicated. Dillon's Rule has prevented neither State governments from granting to their local governments measures of home rule, nor Federal and State governments from vesting in local governments responsibilities for delivering specified services to local citizens. The former is merely a devolution of authority from State capitals to cities. Relationships of local to State government are therefore different from those between State and Federal government: the latter is a Federal relationship; the former, unitary. Different States devolve differing amounts of local autonomy (or "Home Rule") to local governments. Some devolve substantial Home Rule powers to cities with regard to the *structure* of city governments; some devolve such powers to cities with regard the *functions* which they are permitted to undertake; and some devolve such powers to cities with regard to *personnel* policies. States also differ in the amount and type of power which they devolve to counties. The practical force of Dillon's Rule is therefore contingent. (see Hanson, 1996, p. 65).

3. County, borough, and parish governments

The *Census of Governments* conducted by the US Bureau of the Census in 1992 recorded 3,043 county, borough and parish governments. All States designate them 'counties' except Alaska and Louisiana, where they are termed boroughs and parishes respectively. They are local governments and judicial districts organized under each State constitution and generally have a wide range of responsibilities.

4. City governments

   The responsibilities of the 19,000 American cities typically include fire, police, street maintenance and cleaning, water and sewerage services, public works, libraries, inspection and regulation of a wide range of commercial activities, health and welfare. Cities may coincide with county boundaries, or spread across them; larger cities often form part of a "metropolitan area", considered in greater detail in Chapter 10.

5. Township Governments

   There are more than 16,000 townships in twenty States, but they constitute significant governments in only eleven. Concentrated in the old Progressive States of Minnesota and Wisconsin, in New York and the States of New England, the functions of township governments are concentrated in police, highways, parks and recreation, and refuse collection services.

6. School District Governments

   Local control is commonly regarded (not altogether accurately) as the most distinctive institutional characteristic of education policy in the United States; 14,400 elected school district governments are its institutional expression. In most States, these single-purpose governments provide substantial independence in both administration and revenue-raising. The Federal government accounts for only 6 per cent of total expenditure on elementary and secondary education, the remainder being split (to differing degrees in different States) between State and local sources.

7. Special district governments

   The 33,000 special districts (1992 data) are local governments which have a single (or few) purposes established under State law. They include authorities, boards, and commissions; and States have various rules governing their creation. Their functions include the operation of local parks, hospitals, and public housing, and the regulation of specialized aspects of local agriculture or commerce.

8. Regional governments

   Regional governments have frequently been established by two or more State or local governments to administer regional policies and public facilities, especially in public transport.

The Development of the Constitutional Law of Federalism

Since neither the debates at the Philadelphia Convention, the Constitution itself, nor the discussion of the proposed Constitution in *The Federalist Papers* definitively allocated powers between the Federal government and the States, it fell to the Supreme Court to play a key part in doing so. In *Ware* v. *Hylton*, 3 Dallas 199 (1796), the Court invalidated a Virginia statute that erased pre-Revolutionary debts of British creditors. Ironically, John

Marshall argued the case for the debtors, but he failed to persuade the Court, whose judgment rested on Article VI, Section 2, of the Constitution–that Treaties should be supreme over State laws. Since *Ware*, many Supreme Court cases have concerned, either directly or indirectly, Federal powers over the States, and State powers over US citizens, to whom the Fourteenth Amendment guaranteed due process and equality in law. The incorporation of the Bill of Rights within the Fourteenth Amendment has been one of the most important developments in the constitutional law of Federalism in the twentieth century.

Establishment of the Federal Government's Supremacy

In 1810, the Marshall Court acted to prevent States impairing contracts in *Fletcher* v. *Peck*, 6 Cranch 87, and in the case of *Dartmouth College* v. *Woodward*, 4 Wheaton 518 (1819) to prevent States from impairing charters. Their significance lay in the use of Federal judicial power to limit the States' freedom of action against private property – in the first case of individuals, and in the second of corporations. However, much the most important case concerning Federal powers arising under Marshall's Chief Justiceship was *McCulloch* v. *Maryland*, 4 Wheaton 316 (1819). It addressed the question of whether Congress had the power under the Constitution to incorporate a bank (the Bank of the United States) and whether a State government (Maryland) could tax it. The issue had divided politicians from the Republic's first year, when President Washington first sought his colleagues' opinions. Hamilton claimed that the bank's establishment was constitutional; Jefferson initially disagreed. In finding that Congress had the power to create such a bank under its implied and resultant powers, Marshall provoked a controversy that went well beyond the confines of the immediate case: the constitutionality of Federally-sponsored internal canal and road improvements was disputed and its political appeal waned as nationalist sentiment faded after the war of 1812. (President Madison vetoed an internal improvements bill on the ground that such works required a constitutional amendment to permit Congress to authorize them.) Marshall's judgment accordingly gave heart to Hamiltonians favouring stronger central authority and a broad construction of Congress's powers, but alarmed those whose interests were threatened by it and who therefore favoured a narrow interpretation.

A remarkable pseudonymous exchange ensued between the numerous supporters of the latter cause (especially slave-holders and southern governments), and Marshall himself in favour of the former. Advocates of States' rights found their voice in the Richmond *Enquirer*, and Marshall in the Philadelphia *Union* and Alexandria *Gazette*. Marshall's central claim, that *McCulloch* had not created an untrammelled unitary authority but sustained a Federal government, the limits of whose powers the Supreme Court would police, had more plausibility in the early nineteenth century than it has in the late twentieth. As the discussion below shows, the charge made by those who opposed Marshall has been in key respects confirmed by the Court since 1937. However, Marshall was not disingenuous: there is nothing in *McCulloch* that is in principle inconsistent with the narrow construction of Federal power in the case of *Schechter Poultry Corporation* v. *United States*, 295 US 495 (1935), but much is inconsistent with *United States* v. *Carolene Products Company*, 304 US 144 (1938), and almost everything with *American Power and Light* v. *SEC*, 329 US 90, 104 (1946) (all three cases are discussed later in this chapter).

Federal powers to regulate commerce were first addressed by the Court in *Gibbons* v. *Ogden*, 9 Wheaton 1 (1824). The case arose because the Constitution's grant of power to Congress "to regulate commerce with foreign nations, and among the several States, and with the Indian tribes" defined neither "interstate commerce" nor the extent of Congress's power. Marshall's opinion in *Gibbons* was plain: Congress did indeed have the power of commercial regulation between the States and there was no clearer case of it than the regulation of navigation in the Federal Coasting Act of 1793, designed for the licensing of ships engaged in interstate coastal traffic. In such circumstances, the Federal regulatory power overrode that of the States.

Civil Rights Cases and Fourteenth Amendment Rights

Marshall prepared the ground for a definition of the extent of Federal power, but could not dispose of the question. In *Dred Scott* v. *Sandford*, 19 Howard 393 (1857) Marshall's successor, Chief Justice Taney, sought to do so. The general issue was the right of southern States to deny citizenship to black people and to class them in law as property. The particular case was whether a black slave could become a citizen of the United States by residing in a part of the United States where slavery was forbidden by the Missouri Compromise of 1820. The Court found that he could not, and that the compromise (which prohibited slavery north of 36° and 30°) was an unconstitutional deprivation of property and a denial of due process of law. Following the Civil War that *Dred Scott* precipitated, the Taney Court's disastrous judgment was reversed by the Thirteenth and Fourteenth Amendments, and the right of States to deny citizenship rights to persons born or naturalized in the United States ended, although, as the period between Reconstruction's end and the Civil Rights Act of 1964 showed, only formally.

As the War established the indissoluble nature of the Union, the Court confirmed it in *Texas* v. *White*, 7 Wallace 700 (1869). In it, Chief Justice Chase reiterated that Federalism in the United States was dual: the States retained their "separate and independent autonomy". However, the Civil War had destroyed the secessionists' claim that the Constitution of 1789 had established merely a compact of sovereign States:

When, therefore, Texas became one of the United States, she entered into an indissoluble relation . . . The act which consummated her admission into the Union was . . . final. The union between Texas and the other States was as complete, as perpetual, and as indissoluble as the union between the original States. The Constitution, in all its provisions, looks to an indestructible Union, composed of indestructible States.

The Civil War had in part occurred precisely because this view was disputed. Reconstruction, during which a triumphalist Congress dictated the course of politics in the South, temporarily extinguished southern States' autonomy. Later, after the Compromise of 1877, by which "Home Rule" in the South began to be re-established as the price for securing the election of Rutherford B. Hayes to the Presidency, the application of the Fourteenth and Fifteenth Amendments to black Americans whose citizenship rights they were intended to guarantee was increasingly resisted by southern governments. The Union's indissolubility notwithstanding, the Amendments that guaranteed citizenship to black people were for a century from the end of Reconstruction rendered inoperative in the South. Civil and voting rights of all black and many poor white southerners were extinguished by State and private violence until the Federal remedy of the 1964 Civil Rights Act.

The *Slaughter-House Cases*, 16 Wallace 36 (1873), concerned the granting of monopoly rights by the state of Louisiana to a private company. In its judgment, the Court, while holding that the Thirteenth, Fourteenth, and Fifteenth Amendments were intended to ensure former slaves' legal equality, nevertheless rejected the claim that the Fourteenth Amendment incorporated the Bill of Rights. Civil Rights were, in the opinion of the Court's majority, derived from State citizenship and unprotected by the Fourteenth Amendment against action by State governments or officials. This second finding vitiated the Fourteenth Amendment: by its judgment in *United States* v. *Reese*, 92 US 214 (1876), the Court swam with the current of public opinion by finding that the 1870 Enforcement Act was not "appropriate legislation" for the enforcement of the Fifteenth Amendment.

As *Reese* undermined the Fifteenth Amendment, so the *Civil Rights Cases*, 109 US 3, following in 1883, voided the Fourteenth. By it, the Court held that since the Fourteenth Amendment made no explicit reference to the denial of citizenship rights by individuals or corporations but prohibited only "State legislation, and State action of every kind". It was held not to prevent discrimination by private individuals. Not until *Heart of Atlanta Motel Inc.* v. *United States*, 379 US 241 (1964) was this principle rejected. In *Plessy* v. *Ferguson*, 163 US 537 (1896), the Court held that State governments' establishment and enforcement of racially-segregated public facilities did not violate the Thirteenth or Fourteenth Amendments. Re-imposition of Federal standards to enforce the Amendments did not come until *Brown* v. *Board of Education* in 1954.

In practice, the Court put the Fourteenth Amendment to altogether different ends from those intended by its supporters: the prevention of any State from interfering with the liberty of contract. The doctrine was first established in *Allgeyer* v. *Louisiana*, 165 US 578 in 1897, but was more fully developed in 1905, when the Court took the case of *Lochner* v. *New York*, 198 US 45. The case came from New York whose government had legislated to prohibit those in the baking industry from working more than ten hours a day or sixty hours a week. In a 5 to 4 decision, the Court found against New York:

> The general right to make a contract in relation to his business is part of the liberty of the individual protected by the Fourteenth Amendment of the Federal Constitution.

The Fourteenth Amendment's primary object, guaranteeing equal citizenship of the United States to all inhabitants of every State in the Union, became lost for half a century as Federal enthusiasm for it diminished and segregation became established, even within Federal employment. (King, 1995b).

Federal Power, and the Interstate Commerce Clause

The Court later upheld the constitutionality of some Federal regulation, while delineating a reserved domain for State action (or inaction) in accordance with the Tenth Amendment. In *Champion* v. *Ames* [Lottery Case], 188 US 321 (1903), the Court upheld Congress's ban upon interstate traffic in lottery tickets, presaging later judgments that the regulation of interstate traffic in unfit foods through the Pure Food and Drug Act, and the banning of interstate traffic in prostitutes through the so-called White Slave Traffic Act were constitutional. The Court also sustained Congressional regulation of women's working hours, of overtime wages, and of Progressive anti-trust legislation.

However, the interstate commerce clause was not regarded as being infinitely elastic in strictly commercial matters. The establishment of three transcontinental railroads by 1869 had assisted in the creation of a single market in the United States, and so to the undermining of Dual Federalism which, however, retained constitutional vitality, artificially preserved by the Court's majority to defend business from State and Federal regulation. The Court's refusal to sanction Federal regulation of child labour illustrated the vigour of Dual Federalism: in *Hammer* v. *Dagenhart*, 247 US 251 (1918), the Court held (with fragile constitutional support) that Federal regulation of interstate commerce in lottery tickets, unfit foods, and prostitutes was justified by reason of the "harmful" nature of the trade. Since the goods moved between States resulting from child labour were harmless, and Congress's interstate commerce power did not extend to the manufacture of the goods themselves, Congress had no power to regulate child labour. It was for the States, not Congress, to decide whether to act. When Congress later imposed an excise tax upon goods produced by children's labour, the Court struck it down in the 1922 case of *Bailey* v. *Drexel Furniture Company* [Child Labor Tax Case], 259 US 20, on the grounds that it had the character of a penalty.

The Sixteenth Amendment, enabling Congress to lay and collect taxes without apportionment among the States according to their population, overturned the judgment of the Court in *Pollock* v. *Farmers' Loan and Trust Company*, 158 US 601 (1895). That judgment had declared unconstitutional those sections of the Wilson–Gorman tariff of 1894 which, at the behest of the populist William Jennings Bryan, had levied taxes upon income from real and personal property. The amendment thereby established the constitutionality of what had been uncertain since a Federal income tax was first imposed during the Civil War. The potential for the Federal government to raise revenue directly from the population for constitutional purposes was apparent both to the Amendment's proponents and opponents. Income tax freed Federal government from the narrow revenue base that constrained it in peacetime during the nineteenth century, when it derived most of its revenues from customs duties and the sale of western lands. Congress had raised no income tax in 1902, but by 1927 income taxes accounted for 60 per cent of Federal revenues, thereby shifting the tax burden in a progressive direction, as both Populists and Progressives had wished. Expansion of the Federal revenue base was a prerequisite of the vast increase in Federal programmes from Franklin Roosevelt's Presidency onwards.

Notwithstanding the growth of Federal regulation between the Interstate Commerce Commission's establishment in 1887 and the First World War, many Supreme Court Justices found dual sovereignty a persuasive doctrine until the 1930s. The doctrine's application damaged the New Deal, and embroiled President, Congress, and Court in constitutional crisis. Three judgments attacked the heart of the President's programme. The issue at stake in the first two remained Congressional scope under the "interstate commerce" and "necessary and proper" clauses; and that in the third concerned Congress's power to tax.

1. *Schechter Poultry Corporation* v. *United States*, 295 US 495 (1935), concerned the code regulating wage rates and hours of workers in the poultry industry in New York, and the production and sale of poultry. The case itself was trivial, concerning a sale which, under the authority of the National Industrial Recovery Act, was deemed by Federal authorities to violate the code's rules. However, the implications of the Court's unanimous finding for the plaintiffs were, potentially, momentous. In judging that "the authority of the Federal government may not be pushed to such an extreme as to destroy the distinction, which the

commerce clause itself establishes, between commerce 'among the several States' and the internal concerns of a State", the Court found that "the Federal Constitution does not provide for it", and thereby struck down the National Industrial Recovery Act as an unconstitutional extension of the interstate commerce power.

2. *United States* v. *Butler*, 297 US 1 (1936) concerned the constitutionality of the Agricultural Adjustment Act of 1933 which turned on the Federal government's regulatory authority deriving from its general powers of taxation and expenditure. Basing his judgment on a simple premise of dual Federalism (which he thought it "hardly necessary to reiterate", but did), Justice Roberts wrote a confused opinion, claiming that no power was specifically delegated to Congress to regulate agricultural production, and that the Tenth Amendment therefore forbade any such power. The general power to tax and spend could not justify compliance with a regulatory act that the Constitution did not permit. To argue otherwise would, Roberts claimed, be to acquiesce in the obliteration of the independence of the individual states, with:

    the United States converted into a central government exercising uncontrolled police power in every state of the Union, superseding all local control or regulation of the affairs or concerns of the states.

3. *Carter* v. *Carter Coal Company*, 298 US 238 (1936) concerned a challenge to the Bituminous Coal Conservation Act's regulation of prices and wages in the soft coal industry. The regulation was overturned on the grounds that local production of a good or mineral was distinct from its disposal or marketing in interstate commerce. The Court held that where *Schechter* concerned the attempted regulation of a good after it had passed through interstate commerce, *Carter* concerned its production prior to such passage but that the latter was no more a part of interstate commerce than the former.

Thus the Court reached the pinnacle of judicial activism in substituting its judgment about policy for that of Congress in the guise of policing the boundaries between Federal and State action. Justice Stone, dissenting with Brandeis and Cardozo, implicitly rejected Roberts's simplistic model of dual Federalism which economic depression, the Federal Government's immense revenue-raising powers, and the New Deal's consequential revision of intergovernmental fiscal relations had damaged. Stone wrote that the power to tax and spend in promotion of the general welfare belonged, to Congress, and that "the power to tax and spend includes the power to relieve a nationwide economic maladjustment by conditional gifts of money".

It was the Court's conservative and interventionist judgments in these three cases that prompted Roosevelt to make his "Court-packing" proposal in 1937 which, whilst unsuccessful, none the less intimidated the Court to the extent that Justices Roberts and Hughes undertook a tactical retreat. In *West Coast Hotel Company* v. *Parrish*, 300 US 379 (1937), the constitutionality of State minimum wage laws was upheld over the dissents of Justices Sutherland, Devanter, Butler and McReynolds. Two cases decided on the same day in 1937 upheld the constitutionality of different parts of the Social Security Act of 1935, the foundation of old age insurance (and, from 1965 onwards, of Medicare): in *Charles C. Steward Machine Co.* v. *Davis*, 301 US 548, and *Helvering* v. *Davis*, 301 US 619, the Court dealt respectively with a payroll tax and unemployment compensation, and with retirement benefits. Relying upon a broad interpretation of the general welfare clause of Article 1, Section 8, the Court upheld its constitutionality, and also found in the former case that Federal funds used to assist States in the administration of unemployment laws constituted not coercion of the States but merely an inducement to them.

Earlier in the same year, the Court had upheld the constitutionality of the National Labor Relations Act in *National Labor Relations Board* v. *Jones & Laughlin Steel Corporation*, 301 US 1, although only over the dissenting opinions of the four conservative members of the bench. Activist opposition was weaker in *United States* v. *Carolene Products Company*, 304 US 144 (1938), where the constitutionality of the Filled Milk Act of 1923 prohibiting interstate trade in adulterated milk was upheld. The importance of the case lies in Justice Stone's "preferred freedoms" declaration in the fourth footnote. Following Cardozo's opinion in *Palko* v. *Connecticut*, 302 US 319 (1937), Stone distinguished between property rights and civil rights. Regulation of commerce would, he wrote, henceforth be presumed constitutional unless it plainly was not, but legislation which concerned freedoms protected by the Bill of Rights would not be so presumed:

> There may be narrower scope for operation of the presumption of constitutionality when legislation appears on its face to be within a specific prohibition of the constitution, such as those of the first ten amendments, which are deemed equally specific when held to be embraced within the Fourteenth. (*United States* v. *Carolene Products Company*, 304 US 152 (1938))

Congress's scope for commercial regulation (the interstate commerce clause notwithstanding) was thereby extended but differentiated from citizenship rights, which were accorded special protection. *Carolene* heralded the Court's confirmation of its presumption of the constitutionality of Federal laws addressing economic, financial and commercial policy, broadly construed. By 1941, all four conservative Justices who had reacted against the New Deal had retired. Following *West Coast Hotel* and *Carolene*, Roosevelt's attempt to legitimate national direction of American politics through Presidential leadership of Congress won the Court's unqualified approval.

For the doctrine of dual sovereignty, and the associated retention of certain commercial powers by the states, the implications were plain:

1. In *United States* v. *Darby Lumber Company*, 312 US 100 (1941), the Court unanimously upheld Congress's right to prohibit the shipment in interstate commerce of goods produced by children, thereby overruling *Hammer* v. *Dagenhart*, 247 US 251 (1918).
2. In *Wickard* v. *Filburn*, 317 US 111 (1942), the Court upheld the Executive's power to set acreage quotas for wheat even where none was distributed in interstate commerce.
3. The Court's judgment in *American Power and Light* v. *SEC*, 329 US 90, 104 (1946) completed what *Wickard* had hastened: defining the "interstate commerce" power was a matter for Congress and not the Courts: "The power," the Court held, "is as broad as the economic needs of the nation". The case symbolized the realization of Federal supremacy over the States in commercial and economic policy.

The "interstate commerce" and "necessary and proper" clauses were used by the Court to sustain the constitutionality of the public accommodation sections in Title II of the Civil Rights Act of 1964 in *Heart of Atlanta Motel Inc.* v. *United States*, 379 US 241 (1964), and *Katzenbach* v. *McClung*, 379 US 294 (1964). The Court chose this route because it was thereby enabled to confront the question of racial discrimination in public facilities without confronting the question of whether the Fourteenth Amendment could be held to apply not only to State governments but also to private persons and businesses.) In *Heart of Atlanta Motel*, the Court held that:

> the action of the Congress in the adoption of the Act as applied here to a motel which concededly serves interstate travelers is within the power granted it by the Commerce Clause of the Constitution.

In *Katzenbach* it was held that Mr McClung was engaged in interstate commerce by virtue of his purchasing 46 per cent of the meat used in the kitchen of his restaurant from beyond the borders of the State of Alabama: he was accordingly engaged in interstate commerce. Implicitly rejecting the activism of the Hughes Court against New Deal legislation, the Warren Court here declared that:

> The absence of direct evidence connecting discriminatory restaurant service with the flow of interstate food, a factor on which the appellees place much reliance, is not, given the evidence as to the effect of such practices on other aspects of commerce, a crucial matter. The power of Congress in this field is broad and sweeping; where it keeps within its sphere and violates no express constitutional limitation, it has been the

rule of this court, going back almost to the founding days of the Republic, not to interfere. The Civil Rights Act of 1964, as here applied, we find to be plainly appropriate in the resolution of what the Congress found to be a national commercial problem of the first magnitude. We find it in no violation of any express limitations of the Constitution and we therefore declare it valid.

The reasoning was scarcely compelling. Commercial considerations were not a significant motivation in the passage of Civil Rights Act of 1964. President Johnson and a majority in Congress intended the Act to expunge racial segregation in the South, and thereby asserted the supremacy of Federal over States' rights. The import of the Court's judgment in *McClung* was clear: if the appellant could be compelled to integrate his restaurant in Birmingham on the grounds of interstate commerce, so could all owners of public facilities. A century after the Fourteenth Amendment, Federal power over the States in civil rights was at last unambiguously enforced.

Whereas the interstate commerce and "necessary and proper" clauses were previously constraints upon Congress, the Court after 1937 viewed them as licences. In this regard, the constitutional law of interstate commerce's development was effectively complete with the judgment in favour of the Federal regulatory authority in *American Power and Light* v. *SEC* in 1946. The Court's reasoning there constrained Warren and his colleagues to decide *McClung* as they did, once the interstate commerce power was selected as the ground for determining the case. Since 1937, there has been only one significant departure from the principle that the interstate commerce and necessary and proper clauses were for Congress to define, and the view that dual sovereignty had no force: in 1976, Rehnquist wrote the opinion for a split Court in *National League of Cities* v. *Usery*, 426 US 833. Rehnquist declared amendments to the Fair Labor Standards Act extending regulation of earnings and hours to employees of State and city governments unconstitutional. The Court's slender majority sought to distinguish between constitutional Congressional regulation of private corporations, and unconstitutional regulation of the States, and implicitly resurrected the Tenth Amendment. The opinion held that the legislation injured the sovereignty of every State government and the constitutional right of State governments to act independently in matters of their "integral operations" and "traditional functions". Congress had, in the Court's view:

sought to wield its power in a fashion that would impair the States' ability to function effectively in a Federal system . . . We hold that insofar as the challenged amendments operate to directly displace the States' freedom to structure integral options in areas of traditional governmental functions, they are not within the authority granted Congress [by the commerce clause].

The Court's protection in *Usery* of governmental functions integral to the operations of State and local government survived for just eight years. By a majority of 5 to 4, the Court in *Garcia* v. *San Antonio Metropolitan Transit Authority*, 469 US 528 (1984), overturned *Usery*, finding that restraints on Congress's use of its powers under interstate commerce were political rather than judicial.

The facts of this now famous case were as straightforward as those in *Usery*. The San Antonio Metropolitan Transit Authority (SAMTA) sought a declaratory judgment in Federal District Court that, contrary to the finding of the Wage and Hour Administration of the Department of Labor, the decision of the Court in *Usery* exempted its bus operations from the minimum wage and overtime provisions of the Fair Labor Standards Act (FLSA). Applying the principle in *Usery*, the District Court found for SAMTA, holding that the operation of city buses was a traditional governmental function and therefore exempt from Federal interstate commercial regulation. Blackmun wrote the majority opinion, declaring that the fact of State sovereignty under the Tenth Amendment provides no clear guide as the boundary between Federal and State power:

> the Framers chose to rely on a Federal system in which special restraints on Federal power over the States inhered principally in the workings of the National Government itself, rather than in discrete limitations on the objects of Federal authority. State sovereign interests, then, are more properly protected by procedural safeguards inherent in the structure of the Federal system than by judicially created limitations on Federal power.

Powell dissented, powerfully:

> The fact that Congress generally does not transgress constitutional limitations on its power to reach State activities does not make judicial review any less necessary to rectify the cases in which it does so. The States' role in our system of government is a matter of constitutional law, not of legislative grace.

Powell's position is attractive, but provides no principle by which a division of functions might be found. None the less, *Usery* is (so far) the exception in Federal constitutional law since 1937, not *Garcia*: the latter is fully in accord with the preferred freedoms doctrine of Justices Cardozo and Stone in *Palko* and *Carolene*, and of the right of Congress to define the nature and limits of interstate commerce. Such abstention is unsatisfactory constitutional law, but it has dominated the Court's thinking in modern times. For that reason, the importance of *Garcia* is frequently exaggerated (though the costs to State and local government of complying with the judgment were estimated at between $2 and $4 billion): Blackmun's reasoning there was implicit in all but one of the Court's judgments on interstate commerce after *West Coast Hotel*. There remains the tension between, on the one hand, the Court's claiming the power to strike down violations of the Commerce Clause, and on the other the Court usually declining to strike down any provisions. It is unclear even that the Court's 5 to 4 decision in *United States v. Lopez*, 115 S. Ct 1624 (1995), by which it struck down as an unconstitutional exercise of the commerce power Congress's prohibition of the carrying of firearms within schools (an action which is in any case a felony under the laws of most states), has the broad implications that some contemporary commentators argued. Although the judgment was the first since *Carter v. Carter Coal Co.* in 1936 in which the Court had held Congress to have exceeded the limits of the interstate commerce power, Justice Thomas was the only member of the Court explicitly to urge the adoption of a much more restrictive understanding of the commerce clause's application.

Federalism, Civil Rights, and Criminal Procedure

The long struggles in the Federal Courts for the establishment of civil rights notionally guaranteed by the Fifteenth Amendment were examined in Chapter 4. All the cases discussed there had importance for the subject of this chapter – the balance between Federal and State power: *Smith* v. *Allwright* (1944); *Baker* v. *Carr* (1962); *Reynolds* v. *Sims* (1964); *Wesberry* v. *Sanders* (1964); and *South Carolina* v. *Katzenbach* (1965), together ended dualist Federalism in civil and voting rights, made State governments more representative, disposed of "States' rights" arguments in defence of segregation, and federalized them in law and practice.

Similarly in rights of the accused, the Warren Court presided over a significant extension of Federal standards to the States. In *Mapp* v. *Ohio*, 367 US 643 (1961), and *Ker* v. *California*, 374 US 63 (1962), the Court established a position towards which it had moved for some time – that the Fourteenth Amendment incorporated procedural rights of accused people. These two cases had the highly significant consequence that procedures under which State police and authorities searched private property and seized evidence as part of a criminal investigation must conform to Federal constitutional standards. Evidence presented in State criminal cases which did not was thereafter ruled inadmissible (although later cases under Burger and Rehnquist weakened the rule).

In *Malloy* v. *Hogan, Sheriff*, 378 US 1 (1964) and *Griffin* v. *California*, 381 US 957 (1965), the Court reversed its long-standing position that the Fifth Amendment right against self-incrimination applied only to Federal, and not State, authorities: the Fifth Amendment was incorporated into the Fourteenth. Similar incorporation occurred regarding the rights of accused people to a defence counsel "in all criminal prosecutions", as specified in the Sixth Amendment. *Gideon* v. *Wainwright*, 372 US 335 (1963) overturned *Betts* v. *Brady*, 316 US 455 (1942) by extending the guarantee of legal representation to indigent people charged with serious crimes under State law. The Fourteenth Amendment's reach was extended still further in 1972 under Burger, when in *Argersinger* v. *Hamlin*, 407 US 25, the Court held that accused individuals were entitled to a defence counsel in all cases where imprisonment might follow conviction. *Miranda* v. *Arizona*, 483 US 436 (1966) set rigorous Federal procedural standards for the admission of evidence through confession in State criminal trials, thereby guaranteeing compliance with the Fifth Amendment's protection against self-incrimination. In the words of Warren, writing for the Court, a suspect:

> must be warned prior to any questioning that he has the right to remain silent, that anything he says can be used against him in a court of law, that he has the right to the presence of an attorney, and that if he cannot afford an attorney one will be appointed for him prior to any questioning if he so desires. After such warnings have been given, and such opportunity afforded him the individual may knowingly and intelligently waive these rights and agree to answer questions or make a statement. But unless and until such warnings and waiver are demonstrated by the prosecution at trial, no evidence obtained as a result of interrogation can be used against him.

In personal morality and privacy, too, the ability of State governments to prohibit contraceptives and abortion were, respectively, struck down and restricted by the Court in *Griswold* v. *Connecticut*, 381 US 479 (1965) and *Roe* v. *Wade*, 410 US 113 (1973). The latter overturned State laws restricting abortion in the first three months of pregnancy, while *Webster* v. *Reproductive Health Services* 492 US 490 (1989) limited *Roe*'s scope by upholding five provisions of a Missouri Statute regulating the circumstances under which late abortions should be performed, and banning the use of public employees and facilities to perform abortions not necessary to save the mother's life; the Court thereby granted greater scope to the State legislatures to determine abortion policy. In these cases, the Court wrestled with difficult and contentious cases of personal freedom but the cases also concerned Federal–State relations. Whereas the (heavily Catholic) State of Connecticut had prohibited the use of contraceptives, other States had not; in *Griswold*, the Court struck down all State restrictions in favour of a right to privacy which it thought implicit in the Ninth Amendment. Both in *Roe* and *Webster*, the Court again confronted questions of privacy and individual rights, but also of whether the Federal Courts or state Legislatures should judge them, and of the permissible boundaries of such judgments.

Federalism: Structure and Process of Intergovernmental Fiscal and Policy Relations

Constitutional law supplies only the framework within which relations between the three levels of government in the United States are conducted.

The substance comprises their interaction in the formation, legitimation, implementation, and evaluation of public policy. Federal, State, and local politics meet in Congress with the legitimation of policy despite the formal exclusion of State and local governments from the Federal legislative process. Yet the House of Representatives is composed of politicians elected from single-member Districts, whose electoral fortunes depend heavily upon their sensitivity to local opinion in order to deter otherwise plausible opponents. Combined with a Congressional Committee system which divides legislative labour by function corresponding with District, State, or regional interests, local influence upon Federal legislation is assured, as white southern thwarting of civil rights initiatives until the 1960s shows vividly. However, three layers of government provide opportunities to reformists as well as to conservatives. Denied redress by State government, the civil rights movement turned to parts of the Federal government. Northern congressmen and senators provided one audience, but alone they were insufficiently strong. Black people accordingly turned to the Supreme Court (southern State courts and Federal courts in the southern States were barriers, not openings), and later to the Federal executive.

Mixing of the three levels is as evident in policy implementation as in formation. Most programmes authorized and appropriated by the Federal government are not implemented by them directly, but by State and local governments. The latter are also required to meet much of the cost of Federal programmes which they administer from State and local taxpayers: Medicaid, the Federal programme that pays some of the poor's hospital costs, is an example. As power in Washington is less separated than shared by separated institutions, so the formulation and implementation of most policy is less separated into discrete Federal and State functions than shared by them. Most policy areas involve all three layers of government in their formation and implementation. Even foreign and defence policy, constitutionally the preserve of the Federal government (and mainly of the President) is influenced by regional, State, and local considerations, as the discussion in Chapter 13 shows.

Intergovernmental Fiscal Relations

Measured by their revenue bases, their capacities and will in the making of public policy, the relative importance of the three levels has changed during the twentieth century. In 1933, the Federal government spent the least of all three levels of government. By 1978, it spent nearly twice as much as the two lower levels combined (some 64.4 per cent of all government spending), and more than 500 Federal programmes providing grants to State and local governments had been established. By 1993, the Federal share had fallen slightly, to 61.0 per cent. As the major changes by the Supreme Court between 1937 and 1946 weakened the standing of the States in constitutional law, so growing fiscal dependency further reduced the extent to which the States could plausibly claim to be sovereign. Financing public services delivered locally from a mixture of Federal, State, and local taxes nullified the doctrine of dual sovereignty, and established that of interactive Federalism, combining shifting elements of co-operation and conflict.

The potential for the expansion of the Federal government's revenue base can be dated precisely to 3 February 1913, when the Sixteenth Amendment to the constitution was ratified. Federal grant-in-aid programmes had begun with President Lincoln's signature of the Morrill Act in 1862, providing for Federal support of agricultural colleges on public land. Others, many directed to agricultural support in various forms, followed. However, only with the Sixteenth Amendment could significant new initiatives by the Federal government through grant-in-aid programmes be undertaken. Programmes for agricultural extension started in 1914, for highway construction (which included a dollar-for-dollar match between Federal and State funds) through the Federal Road Aid Act in 1916, for vocational education via the Smith-Hughes Act in 1917, and for public health in 1918.

Having gained new financial leverage, Congress began to set conditions for the disbursement of grants. Amendments in 1921 to the 1916 Federal Road Aid Act required periodic Federal assessments of State highways departments' capacity to implement the programme to standards set by the US Department of Agriculture, designated as the programme co-ordinator and dispenser of the grants. The move stirred resentment among the States, which grew when similar provisions followed in other programmes. The question went to the US Supreme Court, which determined in *Massachusetts v. Mellon*, 262 US 447 (1923), that since the grants were merely an inducement and not foisted upon the States, no violation of States' sovereignty occurred. States had to choose between accepting grants under Federal conditions and having no Federal support at all. Most chose to accept.

The setting of conditions mattered less in the early 1920s, when grant programmes were small, than in the period between 1933 and 1980, when they became very large. For example, Federal support to States for highway construction grew sharply with the Interstate Highway Act of 1957, but Congress and Federal agencies attached clear conditions to the grants. In the 1960s, Federal grants to support education programmes of State and local governments was made contingent upon the compliance of States with Federal requirements: the 1964 Civil Rights Act empowered the Commissioner of Education to withdraw Federal aid to segregated schools. Most of the growth in Federal grants between the Federal Road Aid Act Amendments in 1921 and the zenith of Federal aid to the States in the late 1970s was in such "categorical" form – grants made for particular purposes under specified conditions.

The Sixteenth Amendment presaged a shift from local governments' dominance of revenue-raising. Prior to its ratification, local governments accounted for 59 per cent of aggregate government expenditure, and the States for 6 per cent. By 1936, four years into Roosevelt's presidency, these figures had altered, to 36 per cent and 14 per cent respectively, and by 1970, a year into Richard Nixon's Presidency, to 23 per cent and 13 per cent. (In wartime, of course, the balance shifted sharply and temporarily against sub-Federal governments, because the Federal government has responsibility for all national expenditure on national defence. In 1944, Federal agencies accounted for 90 per cent of all government spending.)

The central difficulty in domestic policy is, as Walter Heller, a former Chairman of the Council of Economic Advisers, once expressed it, that "prosperity gives the national government the affluence and the local government the effluents". Problems occur locally, be they homeless and drug-dependent youth of northern cities; unemployed former coal-miners of Appalachia; farmers in remote mid-western towns bankrupted by low grain prices; or the problems of public transport in urban and rural areas. Local and State governments have a more rigid fiscal base than the Federal government, and different taxes have different buoyancies. Income taxes provide most of the Federal government's revenue; sales taxes are the main source for the States, and property taxes are the mainstay of local governments, especially for local school districts. Apart from the direct and indirect effects of the Sixteenth Amendment, taxes on income are, especially in times of inflation, buoyant: as taxable income rises, so does total revenue. If the tax system is progressive, a rise in taxable income will produce a disproportionately large rise in taxation. By contrast, a rise in general income levels does not produce a proportionate increase in sales taxation. Thus the greater the extent to which a government relies upon income taxes, the greater the revenue increase it can obtain without the (politically unwelcome) step of raising tax rates. By contrast, property tax rates have to be increased if revenue from property taxes is to increase faster than the rate of economic growth.

Dillon's Rule has significance for attempts by States' to broaden local governments' revenue bases, and so to revitalise relations between them and the States. Twenty-nine States authorize local sales taxes; thirteen permit income levies for certain local governments; thirty-one allow local tax increment financing; and twenty-six facilitate local governments access to bond markets. This revitalization has occurred as prospects for growth of Federal assistance to States and localities have dimmed. From Roosevelt's Presidency to Carter's, State and local government programmes were increasingly financed by Federal authorities. In March 1933, Federal grants to state and local governments accounted for only 1.5 per cent of State and local expenditure; in Carter's second year, they accounted for 26.2 per cent.

Federal grants made direct to local governments (circumventing State governments) accounted for 2.5 per cent of local revenue in 1955, and 17.5 per cent in 1978, by which time direct aid accounted for a-quarter of all Federal grants. Since 1979, such fiscal dependence has broadly stabilised (as Table 9.5 on p. 313 shows).

Enhancement of Federal fiscal resources notwithstanding, most public services were, at the end of Herbert Hoover's Presidency in 1933, delivered and financed by State and local governments; Federal grants-in-aid were of only marginal importance. Hoover left the Presidency and Roosevelt entered it in circumstances of deep national economic crisis which had inflicted fiscal damage upon governments at all levels. Revenue fell as GNP halved in three years. State governments, responding in part to the requirements of most State Constitutions that their budgets be balanced, coped by reducing capital investment and aid to local governments. While the dependence of cities and other local governments upon property taxes afforded them some protection from heavy falls in revenues from taxes on income, rural domination of State Legislatures caused States to be less generous in their grants to cities than to rural counties (see Table 9.1).

Elected to office by a new coalition dominated by working-class voters, Roosevelt had compelling political reasons for confronting, and if possible alleviating, the cities' plight. Federal authorities accordingly began to expand direct financial aid to cities rather to than disburse it through State capitals. The sums were small, but the principle was established, and grants rose rapidly (see Tables 9.2 and 9.3). They grew again with the Housing Act of 1948 and the Interstate Highways Act of 1956 (see Exhibit 9.3 on p. 306), before accelerating during the Great Society of Lyndon Johnson's Presidency. Direct Federal aid to cities, besides meeting substantive needs, also enhanced cities' political standing: Dillon's Rule notwithstanding, after 1933 many cities were better able to assert autonomy from their States.

As the New Deal and the Second World War required expansion of the Presidency and Federal bureaucracy, so it effected an expansion of Federal regulation. Many responsibilities that were previously the preserve of the States were now assumed by the Federal authorities. A sample of New Deal legislation indicates the extraordinary sweep of the revolution in regulation, which transformed relations between Federal and State governments (see Exhibit 9.2).

These New Deal programmes established new Federal activities and new Federal regulations; many supplanted or supplemented State regulations. Federal programmes did not, however, eliminate State regulation. Many States set stricter standards for commercial activities, welfare policy, and civil rights than did the Federal government: the governments of California, Michigan, New York, and Pennsylvania all adopted "little New Deals". Other States set less strict standards, exploiting the scope which much New Deal legislation gave for State discretion within Federal parameters. For

TABLE 9.1

Revenues and Expenditure of Federal, State and Local Governments, 1927–44, $millions

	Federal tax revenues	State and local tax revenues	Federal expenditure	State and local expenditure
1927	3,364	6,087	3,533	7,810
1932	1,813	6,164	4,266	8,403
1934	2,942	5,912	5,941	7,842
1936	3,882	6,701	9,165	8,501
1938	5,344	7,605	8,499	9,988
1940	4,878	7,810	10,061	11,240
1942	12,265	8,528	35,549	10,914
1944	48,663	8,774	100,520	10,499

Sources: *United States Historical Statistics*, Series Y 569; Series Y 605; Series Y 657; Series Y 671.

TABLE 9.2

Local Government Revenue, by Source Before and During the New Deal, $millions

	Total revenue from Federal, State and local sources	Fiscal transfers from Federal sources	Transfers from States	Total from local sources
1927	6,333	9	596	5,728
1932	6,192	10	801	5,381
1934	6,363	83	1,318	4,962
1936	6,793	229	1,417	5,147
1938	7,329	167	1,516	5,646
1940	7,724	278	1,654	5,792

Sources: *United States Historical Statistics*, Series Y 796; Series Y 798; Series Y 799; Series Y 800.

TABLE 9.3

State Government Revenue, by Source, Before and During the New Deal, $millions

	Total revenue from all sources	Fiscal transfers from Federal government	State sources	Local governments
1927	2,152	107	1,994	51
1932	2,541	222	2,274	45
1934	3,421	933	2,452	36
1936	4,023	719	3,265	39
1938	5,293	633	4,612	48
1940	5,737	667	5,012	58

Sources: *United States Historical Statistics*, Series Y 710; Series Y 712; Series Y 714; Series Y 713.

EXHIBIT 9.2

A Sample of New Deal Legislation Bearing Upon Federal–State Relations

- The **National Labor Relations Act (1935)** enhanced labour unions' rights to organize and bargain collectively, established the National Labor Relations Board, and banned certain unfair practices by employers. The measure was initiated by Senator Robert Wagner and was at first opposed by the President, only to win his support after the extent of Congressional backing became apparent. Three years later, the Fair Labor Standards Act set a minimum wage of twenty-five cents per hour, and a maximum working week for some workers of forty-four hours.

- Following a report by his Cabinet Committee on Economic Security, Roosevelt proposed to Congress in 1935 that a system of social insurance be established. The **Social Security Act (1935)** that resulted instituted old age pensions financed by compulsory contributions from employees and employers (except for agricultural and domestic workers) under the Old Age, Survivors, and Disability Insurance system (OASDI). It also established rudimentary systems of welfare for the elderly poor, a similarly-organized and parsimonious welfare system for the care of dependent mothers and children (Aid to Families with Dependent Children), for the disabled and the blind, and a skeletal Federal–State system of unemployment insurance.

- Agriculture largely fell under Federal control with the **Agricultural Adjustment Act (AAA) (1933)** and the **Soil Conservation and Domestic Allotment Act (1936)** which largely replaced it. Production was regulated, and payments were made to farmers by means of a tax on the processing of food. The **Agricultural Marketing Act (1937)** made provision for product marketing agreements. The **Agricultural Adjustment Act (1938)** established average allotments and production quotas which, with crop loans and parity payments to farmers, effectively set minimum prices for some products.

- The **Glass–Steagall Act (1933)** separated commercial and investment banking, increased Federal Reserve Board powers over national banks, and created the Federal Deposit Insurance Corporation to insure bank deposits. The 1935 Banking Act reorganized the Federal Reserve Board, formed the Federal Open Market Committee to fix short-term interest rates, and enabled the Board to set reserve requirements.

- Scattered and varied state regulation of radio and telephone companies fell under Federal control with the Federal Communications Commission's establishment by the **Communications Act (1934)**.

- The Federal Power Commission, created under Hoover's Presidency in 1930 as a conservation agency, acquired new powers over generating companies by the **Federal Power Act (1935)**, and over interstate natural gas by the **Natural Gas**

---

example, the Social Security Act (1935) gave discretionary powers to States regarding the Aid to Families with Dependent Children (AFDC) programme in setting criteria for eligibility and levels of benefit; but it conspicuously omitted to define a single national standard for either eligibility or benefits. (In the final decade before AFDC's abolition under the *Personal Responsibility and Work Opportunity Reconciliation Act of 1996*, payments still varied

Act (1938). Also in power generation, but with a much broader remit, the Tennessee Valley Authority (TVA) undertook major public works in the construction of hydro-electric plants, flood control, the promotion of conservation, the control of water-borne diseases, and the stimulation of economic activity (which the generation of electricity did so much to promote) in general. Old southern perceptions of the Federal government, owing more to folk-memories of Reconstruction than to the possibilities of economic development, began to be modified as TVA's benefits accrued to the region. The Authority not only fostered economic growth in a poor region, but began to soften racial politics.

- The **Merchant Marine Act (1936)** replaced the Shipping Board with the Federal Maritime Commission (FMC) and authorized it to set prices, approve or disapprove of routes, and supervise shipping practices.

- The **Motor Carrier Act (1935)** brought interstate bus companies under the control of the Interstate Commerce Commission with the power to set fares. Three years later, the **Civil Aeronautics Act** established the Civil Aeronautics Authority (later the Civil Aeronautics Board) to regulate fares, license routes, and control mergers and acquisitions.

- Consumer rights were advanced by two Acts in 1938: the **Food, Drug, and Cosmetic Act** granted to the *Food and Drug Administration (FDA)* the power to test and license drugs and to test the safety of cosmetics, and to the Department of Agriculture the authority to set food quality standards. The Wheeler–Lea Act gave the Free Trade Commission, an old Progressive agency, the power to prohibit unfair and deceptive business acts or practices.

- Roosevelt's foundation in May 1935 of the *Rural Electrification Administration (REA)* altered more rural Americans' lives than any of his other acts. The programme begun (and, by the 1960s, virtually completed) by the REA to supply electricity to the 90 per cent of rural dwellers who in March 1933 lacked it, was an extraordinary symbolic and substantive achievement of Federal government in the New Deal. By 1940, the proportion of rural Americans having an electricity supply had increased from 10 per cent to 40 per cent. Electricity, often supplied by co-operatives when private companies would not do so, transformed the quality of rural life, improved agricultural productivity, and gave New Deal Democrats in Congress a significant platform on which to run for re-election. The REA was especially welcome to Roosevelt's southern supporters, to whom it provided a solid argument against defenders of States' rights.

widely: the average monthly payment per family in 1993 varied from $748 per month in Alaska to $120 per month in Mississippi.) Had Roosevelt bowed to liberal pressures for more radical redistribution, conservative opposition in Congress would have been greater (and possibly successful).

Opposition to Federal welfare programmes was heavy but especially intense from southern conservatives, since they feared the social and political consequences of black workers achieving some financial independence from white employers. Determined to preserve his electoral coalition of northern industrial states and segregated southern rural ones, Roosevelt's programmes offered little direct help to black people in the south: the 1935 Social Security Act's exclusion of agricultural workers and domestic workers was designed to bar black people. White southern businessmen and farmers benefited from AAA programmes, but black sharecroppers and tenant farmers did not. Far from undermining segregation, the New Deal largely accommodated it. The price for southern electoral support in Presidential elections and (less reliably) political support from southern Committee Chairmen in legislative battles, was Roosevelt's acquiescence in Jim Crow: the President proposed no civil rights legislation. However, black Americans not in agricultural or domestic employment benefited from the provisions of the 1935 Social Security Act, and black people were appointed to positions in the administration (although they were usually segregated from white workers). The latter was a remarkable departure from past Democratic practices, especially those of President Woodrow Wilson. Washington, in which most of those black Federal bureaucrats worked, nevertheless remained completely segregated.

While the leaders of most New Deal agencies conformed to southern segregationist practices, Federal bureaucrats' own autonomy in setting the rules for the implementation of policy were occasionally exploited to advantage. The clearest instance was in the National Youth Administration (NYA). By establishing direct links between the Federal government and southern black and Hispanic people, by its resistance to racial wage differentials, and by employing black administrators, the NYA did more than other New Deal agencies to alleviate poverty among young black people in the south. Between 1932 and 1938, most black voters responded to changed circumstances by shifting their allegiance from the party of Lincoln to that of Franklin Roosevelt.

The discretion deliberately granted to State governments by Congress in drafting New Deal legislation created wide disparities in the quality of services supplied which the intervening sixty years have not removed. New programmes and changes in constitutional interpretation altered Federalism from dual to co-operative, but the simple categories do not capture the complexity: Federalism changed rapidly during Roosevelt's Administration in commercial policy, less rapidly in welfare policy, and was virtually static in civil rights. If dual sovereignty was past, state autonomy was vigorously defended, and in certain respects remained intact. In welfare policy, state autonomy was sufficient (as the Alaska and Mississippi AFDC payments show) to modify Federal policy decisively according to States' fiscal capacities and political choices. In civil rights, they enabled many northern states to enact civil rights laws, and southern ones to sustain segregation.

Some New Deal legislation explicitly supported existing state commercial regulations. The Connally Hot Oil Act prohibited interstate trade in oil produced in violation of such controls upon production as States imposed, and the Miller–Tydings Act (1937) exempted States having resale price maintenance from Federal anti-trust legislation. Other New Deal programmes, by providing employment and public works programmes to ease unemployment, established links not only between three levels of government, but also between society and Federal agencies. Penetration of the Federal government by groups had always characterized American politics; the systematic peacetime penetration of society by the Federal government was a contribution of the New Deal. Federal agencies increasingly presented themselves, and were increasingly regarded, as both legitimate and needed participants in promoting State and local welfare.

All was grist to Roosevelt's electoral mill: throughout, the New Deal's alteration of relationships between Federal, State, and local governments was heavily informed by the President's political calculations. The New Deal coalition of 1932 had to be consolidated and (if possible) expanded; to that end, Federal programmes were formulated and implemented. The principle included relief programmes: the Public Works Administration (PWA), established by Roosevelt in 1933, helped to construct by 1939 two-thirds of all new Courts and school buildings in the United States, more than a third of its hospitals, and many hundreds of public works projects, large and small. Electrification of the railway linking New York and Washington was financed by the PWA, as were the building of the Triborough Bridge and Lincoln Tunnel in New York, 30th Street Station in Philadelphia, and many ships for the US Navy. The New Deal's physical legacy symbolises its transformation of Federal–State relations, introducing new Federal life to every State, Congressional District, and County.

The Great Society

The development of intergovernmental fiscal relations proceeded apace after Roosevelt's death (see Exhibit 9.3).

Lyndon Johnson's politics were shaped by Franklin Roosevelt's. In his speech at the University of Michigan on 22 May 1964, Johnson committed his Administration to a major programme of Federal domestic policy initiatives which, in the phrase supplied by his speechwriter, Richard Goodwin, he termed the "Great Society". Partly because he realised the political benefits of doing so, Johnson declared the "Great Society" to be a natural extension of the New Deal that he had supported enthusiastically when a young Congressman in central Texas.

The Great Society marked the second dramatic forward movement of the regulatory and grant-making roles of the Federal government, not only in

---

EXHIBIT 9.3

Federal Grants under Presidents Truman, Eisenhower, and Kennedy

- Federal grants-in-aid more than trebled during Truman's eight years in the White House, from $844 million to $2,329 million (although the statistics for his Presidency are distorted by the fiscal effects of demobilisation, the Cold War, and the Korean War). The number of Federal grant programmes, including the important **Housing Act (1949)**, more than doubled, to seventy-one.

- Eisenhower's Presidency was lethargic only by comparison with the frenetic pace of the New Deal and Great Society. As Table 9.4 shows, real Federal intergovernmental aid more than doubled between Eisenhower's election in 1952 and Kennedy's in 1960 sixty-one grant programmes were added under Eisenhower, including the large interstate highway programme in 1956, and the environmental grants programmes for sewage treatment and the control of water pollution in the same year.

- Kennedy also used the Federal grant-in-aid as a primary instrument of policy implementation, notably in his regional development programme for Appalachia which informed Johnson's own anti-poverty programme.

TABLE 9.4

Federal Intergovernmental Grant-in-Aid (GIA) to State and Local Governments by Function from before the New Deal to the close of the Great Society, 1930–70, $millions

Year	Total GIA	Public assistance	Health	Education	Misc, welfare	Highways
1930	100	–	> 0.5	22	1	76
1932	214	–	–	24	2	186
1934	1,803	–	–	22	2	222
1936	1,015	28	4	37	37	224
1938	790	216	15	48	86	247
1940	967	271	22	51	187	165
1942	926	375	29	151	139	158
1944	983	405	60	136	99	144
1946	844	439	71	58	133	75
1948	1,581	718	55	120	335	318
1950	2,212	1,123	123	82	402	429
1952	2,329	1,178	187	156	333	420
1954	2,958	1,438	140	248	519	538
1956	3,441	1,455	133	276	751	740
1958	4,794	1,795	176	308	816	1,519
1960	6,838	2,059	214	441	896	2,942
1962	7,703	2,432	263	491	1,348	2,783
1964	9,774	2,944	322	579	1,507	3,644
1966	12,519	3,528	365	1,595	2,147	3,975
1968	18,173	5,319	823	2,781	3,588	4,197
1970	23,585	7,445	1,043	3,017	5,041	4,392

Source: *United States Historical Statistics*, Series Y 638/51.

education, welfare, social security, urban housing and transport policy, and the alleviation of poverty, but also in civil rights. The Federal role lay primarily in initiation, legislation, and evaluation (or oversight); implementation lay mainly with State and local governments. Most Federal programmes required the involvement of State and local governments for their implementation; the possibility that the Federal government might itself implement the programmes it partly funded was never seriously considered by the administration. Under Johnson's leadership, more than 200 new Federal programmes of grants to States, cities, counties, school districts, local communities and charities were authorized. Most were "categorical grants", authorized by Congress for particular purposes under defined conditions, rather than as block grants for State and local governments to use as they wished. Categorical grants suited Congress and executive agencies because they reinforced links between lower-level governments and Federal authorities. The mirrored division of labour in the fragmented Federal bureaucracy and Legislature increased both the opportunity and the incentive to make grants both categorical and conditional.

Within this new, complex system of Federal grants, cities were especially prominent recipients, both directly and indirectly; the extension of Federal grants to governments below the States and to non-governmental groups was a distinctive feature of the Great Society. None the less, at its close in 1968, States still received 80 per cent of all Federal grants. States themselves also became more important sources of aid to local governments during the Great Society period (as they had during the New Deal), but Federal aid grew more rapidly still: by 1971, Federal aid was the largest single channel of intergovernmental grants. Moreover, approximately a fifth of state aid to local governments originated from the US Congress, with the States acting as sluices (see Table 9.4).

The Great Society comprised six major Federal programmes. One, the Model Cities Program, is discussed briefly in the following chapter; the remaining five are considered here:

The War on Poverty

The War on Poverty, launched by the Economic Opportunity Act (EOA) (1964), was designed to eliminate poverty and free Americans from welfare support. Responsibility for the Act's administration was placed in the Office of Economic Opportunity (OEO), a statutory agency within the EOP in order to by pass established departmental fiefdoms in the Federal bureaucracy; implementation avoided State bureaucracies wherever possible, not least because southern ones would have striven to perpetuate discrimination in the programme's implementation. Like the Appalachian Regional Commission inaugurated under President Kennedy, and the 1966 Model Cities programme, EOA was a "target grant" programme. Whereas most Federal programmes are functionally specific, these three had several specified purposes but were directed to defined areas or to specified demographic groups. The Act called for the "maximum feasible participation of the residents of the areas and the members of groups served": the OEO contracted with non-governmental community groups to develop anti-poverty programmes.

Although Johnson's anti-poverty programme enjoyed considerable success, its deliberate avoidance of established bureaucracies in the States and cities and its invitation to local communities and individuals to "participate" angered Democratic politicians whose support the President needed elsewhere.

The Elementary and Secondary Education Act (1965)

Education has figured prominently in Federal policy and politics since the Northwest Ordinance of 1787 required every township in the Northwest Territories to provide free public education. The 1917 Smith–Hughes Act's authorization of Federal support for State and local governments' vocational education programmes was supplemented by the Lanham Act in 1940. It authorized Federal subsidies to "Federally-Impacted Areas": school districts whose property tax-bases were reduced by the presence of large numbers of tax-exempt Federal buildings. In his 1952 platform for the Presidency, Eisenhower declared himself to be opposed to further Federal aid to education. However, he regarded the Soviet Sputnik programme as sufficiently alarming to propose the National Defense Education Act of 1958 to support modern language and science education. Widespread resistance to Federal control of local schools began to be outweighed by fears for national security in the Cold War. President Johnson's Elementary and Secondary Education Act (ESEA) (1965) extended the principle of Federal support.

Protestant objections to financing Catholic schools (nominally on the grounds that such support violated the First Amendment's separation of Church and State), and Catholic resistance to Federal support for non-Catholic schools only, were overcome by the Act's support for school children rather than for Schools themselves. ESEA was presented as compensation for the poverty of States, schools, and individual children; it was not intended to be an undiscriminating programme of Federal assistance. Federal grants were calculated according to the formula of 50 per cent of a State's expenditure per school child multiplied by the number of children in the State from families below the Federal poverty line. The formula was made more redistributive in 1967 by permitting States to receive Federal grants, either on the basis of 50 per cent of that which it spent per pupil, or 50 per cent of the average amount per pupil across the United States. In practice, State and local governments' implementation of ESEA thwarted the Act's compensatory intent: most school districts benefited, irrespective of their pupils' impoverishment.

Civil Rights Legislation, and the Twenty-third Amendment Abolishing the Poll Tax

In conjunction with Supreme Court judgments regarding electoral redistricting, the Civil Rights Act of 1964, the Voting Rights Act of 1965, and ratification of the twenty third Amendment, eliminated southern States' capacity to abridge the civil and voting rights of black Americans. (It also made all State governments more responsive to black people dependent upon public services, and so led to higher tax-bases and an increase in the number and scope of State government education and welfare programmes.) The 1964 Civil Rights Act and the 1965 Voting Rights Act were discussed in Chapter 3. The 1968 Civil Rights Act made racial discrimination in most housing markets unlawful, thereby further restricting the ability of State and local governments to protect or sanction instances of discrimination by private individuals.

Amendments in 1965 to the 1935 Social Security Act

These provided for a payroll tax paid as part of Social Security to an insurance fund (Medicare) to pay for hospital care for the elderly and disabled. The scheme is wholly Federal, its conditions are uniform, benefits are earned and therefore a matter of entitlement and not of annual Congressional appropriation. The "Part A" Medicare Trust Fund receives salary deductions and premiums, and pays hospital costs for the elderly and disabled for up to sixty days. The "Part B" Medicare premium pays an insured person's doctors' fees. A scheme to provide a rudimentary system of medical care for the indigent poor (Medicaid) was established by the same legislation. Medicare was the only significant departure among Great Society programmes from the principle of Federal grants-in-aid, being legitimized instead by enriching the politically secure insurance provisions of the 1935 Social Security Act.

Of all the amendments initiated by President Johnson in 1965, Medicaid causes the greatest difficulties for fiscal relations between levels of government. It is means-tested, financed by Federal matching funds to State and local governments for welfare recipients and for others who, while not dependent upon welfare, cannot pay their medical costs. As a redistributive welfare programme, Medicaid is administered by the States. To qualify for Federal matching funds, a State government that establishes a Medicaid programme (all States except Arizona do so) must include within its scope all in receipt of welfare, and additional categories specified in the Federal law: the blind, the disabled, and the elderly. States enjoy additional discretion in implementation through their power to determine eligibility rules and benefit levels. Since 1993, the federal agency that administers Medicaid, the Health Care Financing Administration, has permitted states to experiment with a variety of managed care systems in attempts to restrain the programme's rampant cost inflation.

The Job Corps Program

The Job Corps Program was authorized by the Economic Opportunity Act of 1964 (EOA, the main legislative vehicle for the Johnson Administration's anti-poverty programme) and designed to provide remedial education and training programmes for adolescents to enable them to enter the labour market. As such, the programme marked a Federal foray into a field of policy in which the United States was becoming increasingly deficient by comparison with its major international competitors.

Nixon, Reagan and the New Federalisms

President Nixon wisely recognised the importance, and shrewdly discerned the political benefits, of (in his words) a "New Federalism" involving the replacement of categorical Federal funding with a mixture of block grants and the disbursement of funds unrestricted by use. Its general purpose was to devolve decision-making about programmes funded in part by Federal grants to State governments and to Federal bureaucrats employed outside Washington. The political motivation was to weaken Democratic power-bases in Congressional Committees and Federal agencies in Washington. The primary vehicle which Nixon used was General Revenue Sharing (GRS). Implemented in 1972, it comprised a substantial additional source of Federal funds which State and local governments could use as they chose, and not as Congress specified.

GRS was abolished during Ronald Reagan's Presidency, ironically as part of an attempt to reduce Federal power by decreasing Federal spending. Reagan declared his intention in his inaugural address of attacking not only Federal grants to lower-level governments but (implicitly) of the Federal bureaucracy and the Federal Courts by restoring the place of the Tenth Amendment to the place it had occupied in *Schechter* (see pp. 289–90):

> It is my intention to curb the size and influence of the Federal establishment and to demand recognition of the distinction between the powers granted to the Federal government and those reserved to the states or to the people.

The President emphasized his determination to reduce the number and value of Federal grants to States, and in 1982 dubbed a programme for reducing Federal expenditure on redistributive policy "New Federalism". It comprised a devolution in responsibility for the funding of AFDC and Food stamps from the Federal government to the States, one of Reagan's perennial objects. The President expected local control of welfare to result in lower levels of benefit, thereby increasing the possibility of tax reductions. Seeking to lessen the fiscal burdens upon the States resulting from transfer in order to win their support, he offered to assume full Federal funding for Medicaid, to establish a trust fund from Federal excise taxes to compensate states further, and by 1987 to have reduced Federal excise taxes. If achieved, his proposal would have enabled States to compensate by imposing additional excise taxes themselves.

Reagan's New Federalism proposals foundered upon the illogical division of responsibility for welfare programmes from medical aid programmes to the poor. Moreover, the enthusiasm of many Governors for Federal assumption of Medicaid costs was diminished by their assuming responsibility for AFDC and Food Stamps. The Food Stamps programme had reduced disparities in entitlements between welfare recipients among the States; the cost of taking it over would encumber poor States. By the same token, State governments with relatively generous Medicaid benefits and broad entitlements were reluctant to acquiesce in Federal standards which cut benefits and narrowed entitlements. For political reasons, such States would probably be constrained to supplement low Federal benefits with their own programmes.

There were few attractions in the swap proposals for many States, and none for local governments. Their fiscal support from Federal agencies would under Reagan's plan have been redirected via the states. As State budgets moved into deficit in the early 1980s, radical shifts in Federal–State financing of major programmes added to the proposals' fiscal risk. Negotiations between the National Governors' Association (NGA) and the White House on a revised package failed largely because Governors sought firmer assurances of a Federal floor beneath State income maintenance levels than the administration, beset by ideological pressure from some officials to any Federal welfare standards, economic recession, and growing fiscal crisis, felt able to give.

Reductions in Federal Grants

New Federalism's failure must not obscure President Reagan's transformation of intergovernmental relations by reductions in Federal grants. What Reagan failed to accomplish quickly by New Federalism, reductions in Federal grants and State taxpayer resistance achieved more slowly. Resistant to the reduction of categorical grants though Members of Congress and Senators are, Reagan persuaded Congress to cut Federal grants between 1980 and 1985 extensively and deeply: their value fell by almost a quarter in real terms during these years. The greatest reduction occurred in 1981, when the Omnibus Reconciliation Act eliminated sixty programmes and consolidated a further seventy-seven into nine new block grants, giving States greater discretion in how they should be spent. The Administration also succeeded in persuading Congress to tighten eligibility rules for AFDC and Medicaid – a Hamiltonian twist in a purportedly Madisonian plot.

Reductions in Federal aid under the 1981 Omnibus Reconciliation Act, and later cuts in controllable expenditure under Bush and Clinton's Presidencies, still left many Federal grant-in-aid programmes intact. However, the small amount of new finance that Congress made available was directed mainly to reformulated programmes. For example, the Education Consolidation and Improvement Act (ECIA) authorized Federal expenditure on compensatory education for pupils from poor families, and especially for those in poor communities. At the time of writing the Act accounts for about 80 per cent of all Federal education grants to lower-level governments, but is no more than a modified authorization of funds previously disbursed under ESEA. The parts of ESEA that remained were consolidated by the 1981 Act into one of nine block grants to State and local governments.

The changes have had two distinctive and significant consequences. First, payments to individuals in 1994 accounted for more than 50 per cent of the total value of Federal grants-in-aid. Since the late 1970s, there has been a decisive shift of federal policy-making from, in John Kincaid's phrase, "places to persons" (Kincaid, 1994). Between 1980 and 1994, Federal aid to State and local governments for payments to individuals increased as a percentage of GDP from 1.2 to 1.9 per cent, and as a percentage of federal outlays from 5.5 to 9.0 per cent. In constant (1992) dollars, the absolute amount has increased from $56.7 billion to $124.6 billion, with a commensurate shift from capital to current consumption (Office of Management and Budget, 1998). The largest single component among such payments to individuals is in respect of Medicaid, which grew from $2.7 billion in 1970 to $95 billion in 1996 (more than a-third of all Federal Grants to States). The restrictions placed in the 1980s and 1990s on those discretionary Federal grants-in-aid not directed to individuals resulted in approximately 90 per cent of all Federal domestic expenditure growth in the early 1990s being accounted for by increases for Medicaid, food stamps, child nutrition, and foster care.

Second, Federal aid to cities has fallen: the ending of GRS and of Urban Direct Action Grants (UDAG) has reduced Federal support. Forced by the overall budget ceiling to choose between programmes, the House Appropriations Subcommittee on HUD-Independent Agencies decided in September 1988 to allocate UDAG's appropriation to saving NASA's space station programme. Furthermore, the replacement of many categorical grants by block grants increased the scope for states to divert funds from cities with falling populations (and hence ebbing political influence over both State Legislatures and the US Congress) but further concentrated policy problems.

As the following chapter on the politics of cities and suburbs shows, reductions in Federal support for cities was a deliberate political act: neither the President nor his Congressional supporters depended upon urban support. Reagan refused to meet bipartisan delegations of American city mayors after 1981, and disdained groups such as the National League of Cities which represented their interests.

The data show that President Reagan effected a sharp change in intergovernmental fiscal (and hence political) relations. Federal aid to the States declined as a proportion of Federal outlays during Reagan's Presidency from 16.5 per cent to 10.8 per cent, and of State–local expenditure from 25.2 per cent to 21 per cent (see Table 9.5). Congress has attempted to ease local government's fiscal problems by directing most of the increase in Federal categorical grants since 1980 to local governments rather than through the States. However, increases in these grants have been small in absolute terms, and tiny in comparison with any of the previous five decades. Moreover, the categorical proportion of Federal aid was larger in 1986 (the midpoint of Reagan's second term) than it had been in Carter's last year (81.4 per cent as opposed to 79.3 per cent), and grew still further with the elimination of GRS in 1986.

TABLE 9.5

Federal Grants in Aid, 1970–95

Year	Current dollars							Constant (1987) dollars	
	Total grants ($bn)	Average annual percentage change	Grants to individuals		Grants as percentage of			Total grants ($bn)	Average annual percentage change
			Total ($bn)	Percentage of total grants	State–local government outlays	Federal outlays	GDP		
1970	24.1	17.8	8.7	36.3	19.0	12.3	2.4	73.6	11.3
1975	49.8	2.8	16.8	33.7	22.6	15.0	3.3	105.4	0.6
1980	91.5	1.8	32.7	35.7	25.8	15.5	3.5	127.6	−0.2
1985	105.9	1.6	49.4	46.6	20.9	11.2	2.7	113.0	0.8
1988	115.4	2.1	62.4	54.1	17.7	10.8	2.4	110.8	0.7
1989	122.0	5.6	67.4	55.2	17.3	10.7	2.4	112.2	1.3
1990	135.4	10.5	77.1	57.0	19.4	10.8	2.5	119.5	6.3
1991	154.6	13.3	90.7	58.7	20.5	11.7	2.7	130.9	9.1
1992	178.1	14.3	110.0	61.8	21.5	12.9	3.0	146.8	11.5
1993	193.7	8.4	121.5	62.7	21.9	13.7	3.1	155.5	5.8
1994	210.6	8.4	131.1	63.3	23.0	14.4	3.2	165.9	6.5
1995 (est.)	228.0	8.0	140.4	63.9	N/A	14.8	3.2	174.7	5.2

Source: Advisory Commission on Intergovernmental Relations, Washington, DC.

Remedies for Shrinkage of Federal Support

Sudden changes in patterns of Federal grants-in-aid to State and local governments prompted them in the 1980s and early 1990s to seek a remedy by increasing their own revenue. Many State and local governments also reduced services as part of a politically uncomfortable struggle to satisfy both taxpayers and those dependent upon public support. States and cities were doubly squeezed by requirements imposed upon them by Congress and Federal agencies to assume increasing proportions of Federal programme costs. (Medicaid poses particularly severe problems of this kind.) As a result, in the 1980s and early 1990s, many State governments experienced severe financial strain: State legislatures and bureaucrats tightened eligibility requirements and reduced benefit levels, both for their own programmes and for those (of which Medicaid is a key example) partly funded from Federal sources. Most States raised taxes after the 1981 Omnibus Reconciliation Act which, while not fully compensating for reductions in Federal support, have in several cases (including Connecticut and New Jersey) prompted fierce resistance by taxpayers and so caused political difficulties for State governments.

Shrinkage of Federal support has had painful consequences for local governments, especially for many cities. Between 1980 and 1992, State aid to local governments increased from $90 billion to $198 billion, more than a quarter of all State government expenditure. Three-fifths of State aid to local governments was directed to education: The next largest category, public welfare, accounted for approximately 15 per cent. Variation in the pattern of aid by State to local government is enormous. Nevertheless, in general, the increases fully compensated local governments neither for the direct Federal grants that they had lost, nor for the rapid changes in employment patterns in the private sector.

Dillon's Rule poses difficulties for local governments because compliance with State regulations carries inescapable costs for the local governments whose programmes are regulated. In an attempt to ease their fiscal circumstances, local governments have therefore lobbied States not only for additional funds in compensation for lost Federal grants but also for relaxation of regulatory burdens upon them. Some States responded: in the cause of promoting economic development, the government of Texas cut the costs to its cities and counties of its planning requirements. In most States, however, the bulk of counties' budgets is determined by programmes written in Washington and in State capitals; the scope for discretionary spending at the local level is consequently small.

In California, a taxpayers' revolt resulted in the passage of Proposition 13 in 1978 which cut property taxes by 57 per cent, and in Proposition 4 in 1979, by which public spending by the State, county and local governments was controlled by a restrictive formula. Californian counties were especially badly affected by the heavy reductions in property tax revenue: unlike cities, they have no sales tax, and unlike the State, no income tax. Accordingly, most Californian Counties have reduced, and some have eliminated entirely, services such as libraries in order to maintain spending on programmes (such as prisons) which they are bound under Federal or State law to provide. Counties across the United States are therefore increasingly squeezed between mandatory programmes of the Federal and State governments that they must implement, and severe constraints upon their capacity to raise revenue. The 1986 Tax Reform Act even limited local governments' freedom to raise capital finance through tax-exempt bonds, while ending tax concessions on depreciation and investment tax-credits. Many local governments accordingly began to charge user fees for public services.

Despite taxpayers' resistance to higher taxes, prosperous States were able in the mid-1980s to provide substantial assistance to local governments. In FY 1986, Massachusetts spent 10 per cent of its annual Budget on financial support to governments within the State; ten other States (some of them poorer, some of them more conservative, some of them both) spent less than 1 per cent. Dillon's Rule also enables States to determine the degree of taxing freedom that local governments enjoy. In response to the loss of $182.5 million in GRS funds from the Federal government, Illinois permitted its 101 counties to increase their sales taxes. Revenue produced by the increases was three times larger than the GRS funds that had been lost. Although politicians usually regard the raising of taxes as unattractive, local governments have been forced to rely more heavily upon their own tax-payers to finance local programmes. Local governments' adjustment to such new circumstances has varied: for middle-class white suburbs, the change has been uncomfortable but not insuperably difficult. For declining cities such as Detroit and Newark, the change has been disastrous because, as explained further in the following chapter, the local tax-base is too weak to support increases in tax-rates.

In intergovernmental relations as in much else, Mr Clinton's Presidency has been one of policy and political flux. He initiated some progressive reforms, and (especially after the Republicans' recovery of Congressional majorities after the 1994 mid-term Congressional elections) acquiesced in extremely conservative ones. In welfare reform, he did both: having made the subject a plank in his campaign for the Presidency, he finally conceded leadership on the matter to conservative Republicans in the 104th Congress. The Personal Responsibility and Work Opportunity Reconciliation Act, which he signed into law in the summer of 1996, ended the AFDC programme (ADC before 1939) established by Roosevelt's Social Security Act of 1935 which had been designed to relieve poverty among children. At the programme's outset in 1935, all recipients were children. Most recipients were children even after the inclusion of mothers in the programme from 1939; in 1992, the AFDC caseload was 9.2 million children (of whom half were under the age of six, and a quarter under the age of three), and 4.4 million adults. Most of the latter were mothers but only 7.6 per cent were teenagers. Senator Moynihan, a moderate Democratic US Senator from New York, observed that the legislation had as its premise the notion that "the behavior of certain adults can be changed by making the lives of their children as wretched as possible. This is a fearsome assumption".

The 1996 Act is important not only as a legislative event, but also as a continuation of a process of retreat from earlier practices: welfare support has become increasingly tied to work requirements for recipients, especially since the Family Support Act of 1988 required that all states run "welfare-to-work" programmes typically comprising short-term training on seeking and retaining employment, and assistance in finding a post. States have also availed themselves of waivers from Federal programme requirements to experiment with different AFDC provisions or to increase work incentives. The 1996 Act considerably extends these arrangements by further limits to cash support and increasing the incentive to find and keep a job. By deciding to sign the Act, Clinton achieved his immediate object of preventing Senator Dole, the Republican Presidential nominee, from exploiting the subject of welfare reform to his advantage. Quite apart from the beneficial electoral effects for Mr Clinton of neutralising the question, the substance of the Act (the first example of the transformation of a major individual entitlement programme into a block grant to the States) contained the following chief provisions:

- State entitlements to matching federal funds are ended by the new law: under Temporary Aid to Needy Families (TANF), States receive a fixed (nominal) amount of money equal to the payments received in the early 1990s for AFDC and related welfare-to-work programmes.
- Any parent who has received 24 months of assistance in programmes funded through TANF must be working or in a work programme to be eligible for receipt of further funding.
- By 1997, 25 per cent of all families in the State in receipt of TANF support were required to be working at least 20 hours per week; by the year 2002, 50 per cent of all such families must be working at least 30 hours per week.
- States face mandatory time limits on support: no family may receive funding from TANF if an adult in that family has already received five years of assistance during his or her lifetime. Some scope exists for States to tighten or loosen these limits.
- The Act limits able-bodied 18–50 year olds to three months of food stamp benefits every three years unless they work at least 20 hours a week.
- States are permitted to deny Medicaid to adults who are deleted from the welfare lists because of their failure to meet work requirements, and to

decide for themselves whether to deny Medicaid coverage to legal immigrants.
- Illegal immigrants are prohibited from receiving low-income child nutrition programmes.

By the year 2002, the Act is projected to save $54.1 billion, of which $23.3 billion will be saved by cutting food stamp benefits by 13 per cent. The Supplemental Income programme, providing income to the poor elderly, blind, and disabled, is to be cut by 12 per cent. The poorest households with incomes below half of the Federal poverty level ($6,250 for a family of three) will lose an average of $540 a year in food stamp benefits. In the House, Republican support for the measure was nearly complete: the only two Republicans to vote against it were Cuban-Americans from Florida, who objected to provisions denying assistance to legal immigrants.

There is little reason to think that the Act has overcome the conflict (first identified by Henry Aaron in *Why is Welfare so Hard to Reform?* (1973)) between the goals of support for those who cannot work; provision of incentives for those able to work; and the need to keep programme costs and caseloads low. As Rebecca Blank has argued (1997), there is even less reason to think that States, which, as the Great Depression of the early 1930s showed, are much less well fitted to act counter-cyclically than is the Federal government, will be able to meet the needs of welfare recipients since, irrespective of differences in programme design between States, welfare is a powerfully counter-cyclical programme.

Yet by ending AFDC and creating the cash-limited TANF block grant to the States, Congress effectively delegated complete discretion over welfare programmes' design to state governments with limited fiscal capacity and political will. States may, effectively, determine which groups are entitled to apply for welfare support, the amount that they may receive, and the length of time for which they may receive it. Not unusually for conservative measures that ostensibly devolve decision-making powers, however, the 1996 Act also imposes conditions (or "mandates") upon the States, as indicated in the above list of provisions. For a measure designed to liberate individuals from the yoke of welfare dependence through devolutionary principles, the Act is remarkably coercive and centralist.

Conclusion

America's vastness has always affected the character and structure of its politics and government. Despite having a political culture that is in many respects inchoate and diverse, and (broadly) a decentralized political system, the United States is a stable and modern political order. Amidst the centrifugal forces of Federalism, ethnicity, class, and religion, there are powerful centripetal forces that enable the system to cohere. The most important of them is the legitimacy conferred upon America by the deliberate nature of its creation, and the simultaneous rejection of European political systems. The Federal Constitution dispersed and fragmented government; as the Civil War showed, although the Union of States was permanent, it was not centralized. The implication of developments since 1937 is that there are few limitations in constitutional law upon the centralization of power in the Federal government. But although constitutional law now acts more as licence to the Federal government than as a fetter upon it, fiscal incapacity constrains the forces in Washington, which, between the New Deal and Richard Nixon's Presidency, altered the balance of power between Washington and State capitals. The Federal government's extensive regulatory power notwithstanding, more power over policy initiative (and, in the case of welfare, discretion over implementation) now lie beyond the nation's capital than they did between Franklin Roosevelt's first year in office and Jimmy Carter's last.

10

The Politics of Cities and Suburbs

The Subject

The subject of this chapter is the nature of politics and policy in America's Metropolitan Areas, and the cities and suburbs that comprise them. The theme is that, with the exception of their solid electoral support for Democratic Presidential and Congressional candidates, the condition of America's cities is strikingly varied. Consistent with this theme, a threefold categorization into *declining*; *diverse*; and *dynamic* cities is developed and applied. Although suburbs reveal some differences of condition, development, and prospect, the factors that unite them are more powerful than those that divide them. More recent phenomena than cities, the causes of suburbs' growth are strikingly similar, and their social and political significance comparable. This chapter will show that the politics of racial segregation, for so long a rural southern question, has in the twentieth century also become an urban and suburban one: suburban development has taken the form it has at the speed it has in part because urban areas, especially those in the north and east, have attracted huge inward black migration. In their political attachments, suburbs remain areas of Republican strength, Clinton's qualified successes in his Presidential campaigns notwithstanding.

The Structure of City Government

Governments of cities in the United States take one of three general forms:

(i)   The *mayor–council* system, comprising a mayor elected in a city-wide poll, and a council elected on the basis of wards represented by councillors throughout the city. The mayor is a chief executive, and the council legislates. The balance of power between the executive and the legislature varies considerably according to the provisions of city charters. In its strongest form, the mayor and council plan emerged out of the disorder and corruption of the late nineteenth century. It typically provides for a single-chamber council with legislative and financial powers, but no direct control over administrative officers. An elected mayor appoints all departmental heads, and has the power to dismiss them; in these decisively important respects, the mayor is a chief executive. Where the mayor–council plan was in the late nineteenth or twentieth centuries supplemented by local, ethnically homogeneous, bases of party politics organized by a large number of highly-organized officials in precincts and wards (such as in Chicago), party control of contracts and patronage often followed.

While strong forms of the mayor–council plan are much commoner than weaker ones, the latter variants do exist, normally providing for a mayor (who may be little more than a figurehead) sharing power with the council and other elected officials. Approximately half of America's 7,000 cities with a population of 2,500 people or more (including Chicago and New York) use the mayor–council plan in one form or another.

(ii) The *Commission* system is one in which elected commissioners have specified functional responsibilities for a city's government. In the wake of the Civil War, it was common for southern state governments to intervene in the business of cities when the latter found themselves in financial difficulty by way of establishing boards of commissioners to administer the city. Such practices were broad antecedents, but the proximate cause of the major change in city governance represented by the Commission system's introduction was a natural disaster: on 8 September 1900, a tidal wave killed thousands and destroyed much property at Galveston, Texas. The incapacity of Galveston's existing system of government to cope with the disaster undermined local confidence to such a degree that the Government of Texas appointed a commission of five local businessmen to run the city during the emergency. The temporary commission itself appointed a committee to draft a new constitution (charter) for the city. Such was the sense of urgency that the new charter became law within six months. Modelled loosely upon a private corporation, it established a board of five commissioners, all of whom were (after further revisions to the charter) popularly elected. One of the five was designated as mayor, with general supervisory powers; each of the other four had executive and legislative responsibility for a part of the city's administration.

The change created improved transparency, legitimacy, and effectiveness. Faced with Galveston's success, Houston and a number of other Texas cities duly followed suit. Politicians elsewhere also sat up and took notice: in Iowa, the city of Des Moines established a variant upon the Galveston arrangement by adding to it key elements of the Progressives' anti-corruption and transparency proposals, including non-partisan nominations and elections (by which the party label was prohibited for local elections); the establishment of civil service rules in the local bureaucracy (to prevent patronage becoming the base for party-suffocating democracy); and the introduction of the initiative, referendum, and recall (by which voters held politicians to account). In the short run, the system proved to be appealing: by 1914, more than 300 cities had instituted commission systems of government. In the longer run, however, the lack of a single executive diminished its appeal. Of 7,000 cities in America, barely 150 still use the system; Galveston itself abandoned it in 1960, adopting instead the council–manager plan.

(iii) Under the *Council–Manager* plan, sometimes known as the "Staunton Plan" after the city in Virginia where it was first employed shortly before the First World War, the mayor and council appoint a general manager to exercise operational control of a city's executive departments. The arrangement, which owes much to quaint but earnest Progressive nostrums about the desirability of separating politics from administration, is now used in nearly 3,000 cities, but is especially popular in western and south-western states: Dallas, Phoenix, and San Diego all employ it. Approximately 125 counties use a form of the system for their own government under the *County–Manager* plan.

Three categories commonly used in discussion of the subject ("Metropolitan Area"; "Central City"; and "Suburb") are now defined and considered.

Types of Metropolitan Areas

Standard definitions of Metropolitan Areas were first published by the Bureau of the Budget (as it then was) in 1949, using the term "Standard Metropolitan Area"; the nomenclature was altered in 1959 to "Standard Metropolitan Statistical Area", and again in 1983 to "Metropolitan Statistical Area"; the criteria for defining such areas have also been altered (in 1958, 1971, 1975, 1980, and 1990). Eighty per cent of Americans live in Metropolitan Areas, although such areas account for only 10 per cent of the land area of the United States.

In the United States there are eighteen Consolidated Metropolitan Statistical Areas (CMSAs) (all of which, and all of the subdivisions of which, are – outside New England – based on county boundaries). CMSAs are vast urban and suburban conurbations, of which the following (with 1994 populations in parentheses) are examples: Dallas – Fort Worth, Texas (3.36 million); New York – Northern New Jersey – Long Island (19.8 million); and San Francisco – Oakland – San Jose, California (6.5 million). Their component areas are designated Primary Metropolitan Statistical Areas (PMSAs), and are typically single or adjoining cities. The following (again with 1994 populations in parentheses) are examples of PMSAs: Forth Worth – Arlington, Texas (1.4 million); Newark, New Jersey (1.6 million); and San Francisco, California (1.6 million).

Metropolitan Areas outside CMSAs are termed Metropolitan Statistical Areas which, according to the 1990 criteria, are defined by containing within their borders (i) one city with 50,000 or more inhabitants; and (ii) a total metropolitan population of 100,000 or more inhabitants. Examples include Albuquerque, New Mexico (with a 1994 population of 875,000); Nashville, Tennessee, (1.07 million); and Savannah, Georgia (276,000).

The proportions of land area and population accounted for by Metropolitan Areas have grown considerably since 1960. A comparison of decennial US Census data from 1960 with those from 1990 shows the following:

- In 1960, 63.0 per cent of the population lived in Metropolitan Areas; in 1990, 74.3 per cent did so.
- In 1960, Metropolitan Areas accounted for less than 9 per cent of the total land area of the United States; in 1993, they accounted for 19.0 per cent.

In 1993, there were 268 Metropolitan Areas in the United States, covering more than 673,000 square miles, and containing more than 203 million people. In 1990, the majority of Americans lived in one of the thirty-nine Metropolitan Areas (MSAs) of one million or more inhabitants. Crucially, however, within the MSAs, average city populations grew between 1970 and 1990 by only 2 per cent while suburban population of the 39 MSAs rose by 55 per cent. (Hughes and Sternberg, 1993, pp. 5–7). The fastest-growing MSAs lay in the south and west. Atlanta, a good example of such an MSA, is both a central city of 500,000 inhabitants and an MSA, comprising twelve counties and 100 suburbs, with two million inhabitants.

Central Cities

In the case of both an MSA and a CMSA, the largest city within it (such as Atlanta in the previous example) is designated a "central city". The Bureau of the Census defines a "central city" by its employment and commuting characteristics, classifying it as such if it meets one or more of three criteria:

(i)   Cities with populations of at least 250,000 or at least 100,000 inhabitants working within their limits.
(ii) Cities with populations of at least 25,000, employment/residence ratios of at least 0.75, and out-commuting of less than 60 per cent of resident employed workers.
(iii) Cities with populations of betweeen 15,000 and 25,000 that are at least a third as large as the largest central city, and that meet the employment/ residence ratios and out-commuting standards for cities with populations of at least 25,000 (Bureau of the Census, 1991).

Suburbs

Suburbs are areas of low-density population within MSAs beyond the borders of central cities. The creation of residential suburbs was stimulated by an antipathy to urban corruption and violence, and, as black migration from the rural south to northern cities gathered pace from 1920 onwards, from white citizens' fear of black people. Pressure for new housing from returning soldiers after both world wars drew the Federal government into providing loans to construction companies to build suburban housing, and making loans to veterans to buy them. In this setting, Abraham Levitt and Sons was a major innovator on the east coast after the Second World War, drawing upon his experience gained through building workers' houses for the Federal government during the war. The firm designed extensive new suburban housing developments outside New York and Philadelphia, employing techniques of mass industrial production for common structural components, thereby sharply reducing building costs.

The suburban house and garden (in American terminology, "yard") became acceptable analogues for the rural farm, especially since the dominant style of construction was of a colonial style common in country areas and commoner in the national culture. At the time of its construction, the company's development at Hempstead, New York, was unprecedentedly large. Supported by federally guaranteed mortgages through the Federal Housing Authority (for civilians) and the Veterans' Administration (for demobilized soldiers), it eventually comprised more than 17,400 houses and 82,000 residents. Owners' stewardship of the new properties was subject to the company's continuing scrutiny, even to the extent of the species of trees planted in gardens being a matter of company decision. Marketed as the epitome of individual choice, Levitt's houses were in fact the barely-differentiated products of a mass market for white, car-dependent, consumers (Jackson, 1985, pp. 236–7).

Intellectual Importance of Cities and Suburbs

Cities and suburbs (Metropolitan Areas) are the densest markets for business and political activity: city halls are meeting places, literal and metaphorical, for business's unelected owners and the people's elected representatives. Politicians have a duty (which they occasionally discharge) to pursue the public interest; and business expresses a claim (which has a veneer of plausibility) to be similarly motivated. But each side also has driving sectional interests: ambitious politicians seek votes and power for themselves as individuals, while businessmen seek higher profits and lower taxes. As Chapter 3 showed, the white male franchise preceded, rather than followed, America's industrial revolution; that fact has resulted in the tensions between the economic power of business and the political power of elected governments usually lying at the surface of America's metropolitan politics.

The faithfulness or otherwise of metropolitan government in the United States to core American democratic values has a wider significance for the plausibility of those values. Cities are highly concentrated examples of American democracy at work. Where that democracy has become corroded by the public interest's marginalization, cities have degenerated into squalid examples of a pathological condition in American politics. Such pathologies have, however, also offered opportunities to reformers seeking to use failed city governments as laboratories for the improvement of public life. Accordingly, opposition to the abuse of city governments' patronage and contracting powers provided the platform for urban reform movements in the United States during the Progressive period, as civil service reform had become an earlier cause at Federal level (see Chapter 8).

During the period of entrenched corruption of city government, the subject of attack by the Progressives' reforms in the thirty years before the First World War, public interest was in some cities subverted in corrupt financial relations between politicians and businessmen. Progressivism disinfected cities. Its proponents reformed city government:

- Through the introduction of primary elections.
- In some cities by introducing city managers (non-partisan administrators) to replace the elected mayor.
- In some states by introducing non-partisan local elections.
- In many cities by replacing most patronage appointments by nonpartisan civil servants recruited by merit, so reproducing locally what Congress had legislated for the Federal government under the Pendleton Act of 1883 (see Chapter 8).

Progressivism could not, however, solve the problem posed for representative government by the juxtaposition of concentrated economic and political interests in America's metropolitan areas, since the problem is partly beyond democratic solution: irrespective of their political views, elected politicians have no option when formulating their cities' fiscal policies but to take the needs of business fully into account. That imperative is particularly apparent when a city's economy is dominated by one or a few economic interests with powerful common concerns: examples include the influence of investment banks in New York City; the insurance industry in Hartford; steel companies in Pittsburgh until the 1970s; the gaming industry in Las Vegas; and real estate agents and property developers everywhere. Under such circumstances, city politicians' autonomy from corporate interests is limited, and the risk to the public interest correspondingly high.

Arising from the volatile interaction of politicians, voters, and businessmen, and from the structural influences of race and class, three important theoretical questions arise from study of the politics of metropolitan areas:

- The first is the central problem in political science, tidily encapsulated in the title of Robert Dahl's (1961) seminal study *Who Governs?* To expand the question is to enquire where power is located, how it is distributed in different kinds of political system, and the implications of answers for the principle usually celebrated as the supreme characteristic of democracy: equality of representation expressed in the equal worth of one vote with others.
- The second problem is that of how and why the autonomy that cities have from interest groups varies. In so far as their autonomy is qualified, are cities to be understood as responsive not to the preferences of individual citizens but to those of disproportionately influential groups such as investment bankers or property developers? If they are, what are the implications for the accountability of elected politicians in cities? If they are not, is the autonomy of city governments so marked that governments' accountability to citizens is damagingly qualified?
- The third problem is that of locating the public interest. Is it merely the result of the interaction of groups and parties? Or is it something quite distinct and separate, to be protected from the exercise of private pressure over public policy?

Who Governs?

In *Who Governs?*, Robert Dahl (1961) brought pluralist theory to its highest empirical and theoretical pitch. Sharing the dominant view in American political science that the central questions of the distribution of power in American society and the adequacy of American democracy could most usefully be observed in cities, he examined decision-making about public policy in New Haven, Connecticut (conveniently, the town in which his University is sited). Dahl's study provides a powerful rebuttal of Floyd Hunter's (1953) study, *Community Power Structure*, in which he examined political power in Atlanta, Georgia. Employing a curious (and flawed) methodology, Hunter asked prominent citizens whom they regarded as the most powerful local people. Forty emerged from the exercise as enjoying economic power so great that, beside them, the mass of Atlanta's citizenry had virtually none. In so far as Hunter's research is well-founded, the implications for pluralist accounts of group power are grave; and the implications for democratic accountability more generally are yet more severe. However, Hunter's study shows only that those whom he chose to interview regarded certain other individuals as being powerful; it does not constitute a sound test of the distribution of power.

By his support for pluralist interpretations against Hunter's elitist model, Dahl rejected structuralist understanding of city government; his understanding of political power leaves ample scope for political activity as a variable that shapes outcomes. There is nothing determinist in his account.

The familiar criticism that his interpretation of American metropolitan democracy is naïvely optimistic is groundless. He does *not*, for example, claim:

(i)   That New Haven's plural distribution of political power is typical of all cities: he did not find there the "semi-dictatorship occasionally found in other American communities" (not least in the south, and in machine-based cities of the North, such as Chicago).

(ii) That New Haven is an ideal-type democracy: "Like every other political system, of course, the political system of New Haven falls far short of the usual conceptions of an ideal democracy; by almost any standard, it is obviously full of defects" (Dahl, 1961, p. 311).

(iii) That participation in a city's politics is the same among those with high incomes as among those with low incomes, or that support for the rules, procedures, and essential characteristics of the democratic system is uniform. On the contrary, Dahl argues that participation in politics and support for the regime are greater among those with high incomes than among those with low; among those of high status than those of low; among those with considerable education than those with little; and among white-collar employees than blue-collar ones. But he develops these claims by arguing, not entirely convincingly, that low *rates* of participation among the worse-off is more than offset by their greater number.

Using New Haven as his single case-study, Dahl explicitly rejects de Tocqueville's argument that political culture ("the whole moral and intellectual state of a people") explains why democracy is sustained in the United States. (De Tocqueville, 1969). The power of the democratic myth, Dahl argues, has led to a confusion between the high rates of political participation that some democratic theorists think desirable in a democracy, and those much lower ones that, in fact, obtain. De Tocqueville's observation that the rate of political activity in democratic regimes is higher than the rate of uncoerced political activity in authoritarian ones has led to the conceit that politics is, for most people in democratic societies, central to their lives. Those "who are deeply concerned with political affairs . . . sometimes find it difficult to believe that most other people are not" (Dahl, 1961, p. 280). In fact, Dahl found that in New Haven, governance was only a fragment of social life.

Dahl's detailed research led him to conclude that American cities were transformed between the early nineteenth century and the mid-twentieth century from "a system in which resources of influence were highly concentrated to a system in which they are highly dispersed", contingent upon particular local circumstances. Inequalities that remain are not, he holds, cumulative; they therefore threaten neither democratic values nor democracy's health.

While not sharing Dahl's pluralist assumptions, Clarence Stone accepts Dahl's stress upon the importance of political action and calculation. In his *Regime Politics* (Stone, 1989), a compelling study of policy and politics in Atlanta, he explains the post-war development of the city's politics in terms of the need to bridge the gap between the State and the market, between the politics of representation as expressed through the ballot box, and the city's need to stimulate private investment. He holds that what he terms Atlanta's "urban regime" is founded upon successive accommodations between mainly white business elites and the city's black middle class; the black lower class is, he finds, effectively excluded from political power. Without seeking to generalize from his case, he argues that, in Atlanta, strong governance can be brought about only with the active collaboration of business (Stone, 1989, p. 234).

Neo-elitist, Marxist, and Public Choice theorists reject the primacy of politics and political calculation, holding instead that market considerations dominate, but differ on the question of whether cities can be analysed as self-contained units or are merely epiphonomena of larger political and economic forces. Among neo-elite theorists, E. E Schattschneider and Matthew Crenson stand out for the clarity of their analyses. In his book *The Semi-Sovereign People*, Schattschneider (1960) memorably observed that "the flaw in the pluralist heaven is that the heavenly chorus sings with a strong upper-class accent", and that the system of pressure upon government "mobilized bias" in favour of private, organized elites and against the public, unorganized lower class. (Dahl had acknowledged this possibility explicitly, but rejected the claim that such social structures were static.) The thrust of his analysis was that there was a disjunction between the proclamations that the formal rules and processes of American politics provided for plurality, and the awkward evidence suggesting that the processes of policy-making (not least those in Metropolitan Areas) were not. Working-class, female, black, and poor were, when Schattschneider published his study, little represented in positions of corporate or governing power; they are little better represented at the time of writing, in 1997.

Crenson, in *The Unpolitics of Air Pollution* (1971), a study of the declining cities of Gary, Indiana, and East Chicago, argued that local business elites had the capacity and the incentive to control the agenda by excluding from public consideration those matters which they did not wish to have raised. As P. Bachrach and M. S. Baratz had noted in the early 1960s (Bachrach and Baratz, 1962; 1963), the pluralists' method, that of analysing observable behaviour, left the power to control the political agenda out of consideration.

Racial Disadvantage and Rebellion

Dahl and his fellow pluralists failed to predict, or explain convincingly the violent revolts of black urban Americans against the system of city government in particular, and of politics in general. The period of greatest unrest in northern and western cities lay between the riot in the Watts district of Los Angeles in the summer of 1965, and the extensive rioting in Detroit and Washington in 1967/8. The timing was remarkable: the Watts riot occurred a year after passage of the Civil Rights Act of 1964, and days after President Johnson signed the Voting Rights Act of 1965 into law. Fuelled by the passage of the income tax cut in early 1964, the economy had begun to grow above its long-term trend rate, with the result that rates of black unemployment fell sharply. At a time of profound change in their condition before the law and of some improvement in economic prospects, and during the Presidency of a man who did more than any other President in the twentieth century to liberate black Americans from their oppression, black Americans rebelled. By marching peacefully in the teeth of southern white violence, southern blacks had in the early 1960s altered northern white perceptions of their plight, so strengthening prospects for passage of the key civil and voting rights legislation of 1964 and 1965. In rebelling violently against a system of politics which continued to exclude and marginalize them, northern blacks forced a decisive further change in the national agenda. Notwithstanding the shattering impact which their rebellion had upon the Democratic Party's national coalition and hence upon Vice-President Hubert Humphrey's chances of election to the Presidency in 1968, black educational, economic, social and political advance rapidly became an issue of immeasurably greater national salience than it had been at any other point since Reconstruction.

The pathologies of racially-divided American cities remain. The Los Angeles riots of April–May 1992 served as a vivid, if momentary, reminder to white suburban Americans of the embedded problems of central cities. As explained later in this chapter, the nature of labour markets in American cities at the end of the twentieth century is that white citizens are vastly more likely than black ones to be employed in highly-paid, private-sector, professional, managerial, advanced manufacturing, research, consultancy, corporate services, and white-collar occupations generally; and that black workers are much more likely to be employed in poorly-paid service and public sector posts, in restaurants, cafes, and unskilled manufacturing jobs. Rewards to unskilled and semi-skilled labour are declining rapidly, while rewards to cognitive workers are rising; and public support for the disadvantaged is falling sharply. Poorly-educated black urban poor are therefore triply exposed to the harsh distribution effects of markets. Beyond lawful economic activity lie the rewards and risks of markets in drugs. In those markets, black people are more likely than any other racial group to fall victim to violence, and to be imprisoned.

Violent black urban revolt in the 1960s and early 1990s revealed a deep racial inequality resistant to solution by the democratic procedures and norms that had assisted in the dissolution of other racial and ethnic divisions in America's cities, and in the gradual inclusion of successive waves of immigrants. Black citizens' explosion of rage at their continuing exclusion not only from power in government but also from social and economic advance through government altered their relationships with their fellow citizens of other races; within political science, it exposed a major flaw in the pluralists' account of the distribution of power in America's cities.

Public Interest and Private Interests

Marxists such as I. Katznelson in his remarkable book *City Trenches* (1981), about the restructuring of Washington Heights in north Manhattan, New York City, hold that the needs of capital are by the very nature of liberal democracy's operation in a capitalist society served (directly or indirectly) by the State, the fact of governments' popular election notwithstanding. Katznelson holds that attempting to study cities in isolation is misguided. There is general agreement among Marxist analysts of metropolitan politics that the nature of capitalist economies requires the liberal democratic state to act in the (as some of them suppose, homogeneous) interests of capital. In holding that "structure is all", Marxist writers have improbable intellectual allies among proponents of currently fashionable public choice theory, the product of utility-maximizing individualistic assumptions about human behaviour deriving from micro-economics. Paul Peterson, a stimulating exponent of public choice theories of metropolitan development in his *City Limits* (1981), shares the Marxists' dismissal of the explanatory value of political action, but contends, unlike all Marxists, that the pressures for and shared interest in economic development override all others. He explains the weakening of redistributive policies during the 1980s, and their effective eclipse between 1981 and 1996 by the supreme need that all cities and other local governments have for policies that "maintain or enhance the economic position, social prestige, or political power of the city, taken as a whole" (Peterson, 1981, p. 20). A probable, but not a logical, consequence, Peterson argues, is that the need to attract capital causes the needs of the poor and disadvantaged to be excluded. Competition between cities, he holds, "drives distribution off the metropolitan political agenda and puts the promotion of economic development in top position". (Peterson, 1981, p. 34). Many Federal, State, and local welfare programmes have been heavily cut since the early 1980s, while economic development has indeed been promoted vigorously by cities competing with each other for business investment. Yet the link that Peterson makes between the two phenomena is less secure than might be supposed.

In practice, the link can be better explained by the calculations of politicians about either their electoral coalitions, or their conceptions of the public interest, as it can by a structural account that marginalizes political activity. Neither Marxism nor public choice theory has anything to say about political activity, or about how the imperatives to which local states are supposedly subject are translated into policy through political action and conflict. An understanding of politics which holds that political activity is purely epiphenomenal upon the overriding need of local States to attract and retain capital is one that cannot explain change within a city over time, or differences between cities at any one point in time: its explanatory value is, accordingly, slight. Although the different examples of New York and Detroit lend some support to a structuralist interpretation of metropolitan politics, and, by implication, of liberal democratic politics generally, a full explanation demands the inclusion of an account of how politicians calculate and manoeuvre to build and retain coalitions of electors and of interests (see for example, Mollenkopf, 1983). Neither is foreordained; and neither is epiphenomenal.

Declining, Diverse, and Dynamic Cities: Different Fiscal Fates

Most cities in the north and mid-west, such as Pittsburgh, Cleveland, and Chicago, were established as a result of industrialization; some, such as Boston, New York, and Philadelphia, were founded before industrialization but grew rapidly as manufacturing output and employment rose during the industrial revolution. Even with the hindsight of a century and more, the rapidity of change effected by manufacturing's growth is startling: the proportion of the population living in central cities between 1850 and 1920 rose from less than 20 per cent to more than 50 per cent; and the national population rose four times, to 106 million. Industrial production at the end of the period was a thousand times greater than at its beginning (Mollenkopf, 1983, p. 12). The industrial city was defined by a concentration of labour and manufacturing capital, and white ethnic groups living in discrete housing areas.

Table 10.1 shows those counties with the highest population growth rate, and those with the greatest rate of population decline in the thirteen years between 1980 and 1992 (though the trends have been apparent throughout the post-war period). The fifteen fastest growing counties are mostly suburbs; all are in the south, south-west, and west. The fifteen counties suffering the greatest population falls are all cities in the north-east and mid-west. In most cases, these counties are coextensive with central cities. Most of the expanding counties are co-extensive with suburbs surrounding cities. The names of the central cities, almost all of which are *declining* cities within the meaning of the typology listed below, are given in parentheses; where appropriate, the names of the nearest cities to the growing suburbs are also indicated.

American cities are not homogeneous entities. There are three distinct types. The first, *declining* group, comprises cities whose economies are deteriorating absolutely. The group includes cities such as East St Louis, Gary, and Buffalo, whose origins lie in nineteenth-century manufacturing

TABLE 10.1

Highest Population Rates of Growth and Decline by County, 1980–92

Highest population growth rate, 1980–92		Largest population decline, 1980–92	
County	Percentage rate	County	Number
Flagier, FL (Suburbs of Jacksonville; Orlando; and Daytona Beach)	207.7	Wayne, MI (Detroit)	−241,664
Douglas, CO (Suburb of Denver)	191.4	Philadelphia, PA (Philadelphia)	−135,638
Camden, GA	181.7	Allegheny, PA (Pittsburgh)	−115,799
Matanuska−Susitna, AK (Anchorage suburbs)	152.2	Cook, IL (Chicago)	−114,287
Hernando, FL (Tampa suburbs)	146.5	Cuyahoga, OH (Akron)	−87,191
Osceola, FL (Orlando suburbs)	141.9	Essex, NJ (Newark)	−77,884
Fayette, GA (Atlanta suburbs)	140.0	St Louis, MO (St Louis)	−69,068
Gwinnett, GA (Atlanta suburbs)	134.9	Orleans, LA (New Orleans)	−68,332
Dawson, GA (Gainesville suburbs)	116.5	Baltimore, MD (Baltimore)	−60,645
Elko, NV	116.3	District of Columbia (Washington, DC)	−53,211
Nye, NV	115.6	Erie, NY (Buffalo)	−43,183
Washington, UT	112.3	Lake, IN (Gary; and East Chicago)	−41,099
Denton, TX (Dallas suburbs)	105.9	Mahoning, OH (Youngstown)	−23,880
Charlotte, FL (Cape Coral suburbs)	104.0	St Louis, MN (Duluth)	−23,727
Collin, TX (Dallas suburbs)	101.2	Kanawha, WV (Charleston)	−23,645

Source: Bureau of the Census.

and which enjoy little infusion of human or financial capital. Large parts of cities such as these are now empty and derelict, many of their taxpaying companies and people having left. The critical mass of population (and hence of politicians) committed to policies of economic growth and investment is absent. Few, if any, fast-growing companies remain in such cities; those citizens who do so are disproportionately poor, ill-educated, and are either dependent upon public benefits or exist on the fringes of low-skilled, low-pay, and low-benefit jobs in fragile labour markets.

The second, *dynamic* group, comprises those cities such as Austin, Dallas, Phoenix, Raleigh, and San Diego, which continue to grow and whose governments are committed to their doing so. The population of Phoenix, for example, grew by 58 per cent between 1970 and 1990. Located mainly in the south, south-west, and west, such cities are twentieth-century creations of Federal and State governments rather than nineteenth-century creations of an unfettered market. They typically have the following characteristics: a much higher proportion of educated white citizens among their populations than cities of the first and third types; large research universities heavily dependent upon Federal and State subventions, subsidies, and corporate contracts; a significantly lower proportion of people outside or on the fringes of the labour market; and lower densities of unionization. Such cities have depended for their creation and growth not upon basic manufacturing industries such as steel, textiles, or heavy engineering, but upon direct Federal fiscal subsidies for the capital cost of providing water resources and electricity. Indirect Federal and State subsidies support service industries and education, while the Federal government, through its purchase of weapons systems for the US armed services in the Second World War and the Cold War which followed, provided a huge boost to such new urban and suburban economies.

The third, *diverse* group, is more complex than the first two. It comprises cities that, having their origins either in industrial or pre-industrial America, have shown their ability to adapt to economic change (especially with respect to their loss of manufacturing employment) primarily through the breadth of their economic and cognitive activity. Boston/Cambridge and New York are good examples: both, critically, contain several world-class universities which attract faculty from throughout the world, and export graduates of high quality, not only to regional economies but also throughout the United States and abroad. Partly because of its outstanding universities, Boston in particular has attracted research, development, and advanced manufacturing companies on a large scale to replace old industries. New York's strength lies in the vigour of its internal economic diversity: it has retained some of its old clothing industry while expanding its international primacy in entertainment, corporate services, and finance. The example of New York's developmental path, and the constraints under which its city government works, are examined in greater detail later in this chapter.

Markets' Measurement of Cities' Health

Capital markets show how private markets price the varying fiscal health of cities in these three categories. Like other local governments in the United States, cities raise money by issuing bonds, some of them of short-term maturity, but most of longterm. Their sale finances capital investment in (for example) roads, school building, airport construction and improvement, public transport, water purification and waste treatment, and housing; during the 1980s, municipal bonds were increasingly issued to finance school building and repair, but decreasingly to finance public housing. In 1992, local governments (cities and counties) in the United States had outstanding debts of $18.4 billion in short-term bonds, and $409.1 billion in long-term bonds. The price of such debt in municipal bond market varies considerably, depending upon the creditworthiness of the city or local government concerned. Where, as in the cases (for example) of Minneapolis or Omaha, market analysts judge that a city's creditworthiness is high, the price of its bonds on the market will be high and the interest rate payable on the bonds low. Where, as in the cases of Washington DC, or St Louis, such analysts think a city's creditworthiness much weaker, the price of its bonds on the market will be low, and the interest rate payable on the bonds high. For city treasurers and taxpayers, the former condition brings pleasure, but the latter pain. Just as credit ratings agencies such as Moody's regularly publish alphabetic ratings for companies' creditworthiness, so they also issue such ratings for cities, thereby providing market participants with a simple indication of cities' fiscal health.

States also finance capital investment by selling bonds, but they are typically higher-quality financial instruments than those sold by cities; most therefore command higher prices. That is itself a telling sign of the concentration of financial strain in cities rather than in suburbs and rural areas. Table 10.2 shows the great variation in revenue, taxation, and indebtedness of the largest American cities. As the data in the table imply, for every dollar which the government of New York City received in taxes in 1996 it paid nearly twenty cents in debt servicing. The city's total outstanding debt in late

TABLE 10.2

City Governments – Ten Largest Cities' Revenue and Debt, 1992

Cities ranked by population, 1990	Revenue								Debt outstanding
	Total	General revenue						Utility and liquor store	
		Total	Intergovernmental		Taxes				
			From state and local government	From Federal government	Total	Property	Sales		
New York	44,888	36,782	13,330	1,150	17,141	7,899	3,432	1,993	34,984
Los Angeles	6,993	3,889	385	137	1,933	774	578	2,141	8,003
Chicago	4,514	3,298	565	256	1,592	596	855	228	6,012
Houston	1,802	1,417	23	41	779	400	359	235	3,962
Philadelphia	3,471	2,818	717	157	1,483	440	73	587	3,835
San Diego	1,427	1,174	142	92	383	156	194	125	1,646
Detroit	2,043	1,567	576	130	551	215	44	169	1,685
Dallas	1,371	1,083	16	42	505	295	201	122	3,586
Phoenix	1,152	988	230	82	334	117	197	103	2,310
San Antonio	1,427	555	96	22	224	124	94	839	4,239

Source: US Bureau of the Census.

1996 was $30 billion, only a little less than its annual budget of $33 billion. Capital underinvestment in roads, bridges, and school buildings in the 1970s and 1980s has produced in New York an accumulation of infrastructural projects requiring significant investment. The city cannot afford to borrow more because its debt burden is high; on the other hand, it cannot afford not to borrow more, because its infrastructural needs are so great. The city's bond ratings are low, but the high interest rates it is therefore obliged to pay result in its debt being attractive to investors.

Table 10.3 shows that, despite the reductions in the flow of Federal funds to State and local governments in the 1980s, total intergovernmental revenue from the Federal and State governments to some cities remains a large proportion of general revenue:

- A *dynamic* city (such as Houston) with a buoyant tax base may have only a trivial dependence upon intergovernmental fiscal aid: $39 per person per annum as compared to $478 per person per annum from taxes.
- A *declining* city (such as Detroit) may in fact draw more money per capita from intergovernmental fiscal aid than it is able to do from its weak tax base: Detroit, indeed, takes $686 per person per annum in intergovernmental revenue, but only $536 per person per annum from taxes.
- A *diverse* city's dependence upon intergovernmental fiscal aid typically and predictably lies between cities in the first two groups: although New York continues to draw more from taxes ($2,341 per person per annum) than it does from intergovernmental revenue, its dependence upon the latter is high ($1,977 per person per annum).

TABLE 10.3

Largest Cities' Finances: 1992

Cities ranked by 1990 population	General revenue		Intergovernmental revenue		Taxes		General spending		Outstanding debt	
	Total ($m)	Per capita ($)	($m)	Per capita ($)	($m)	Per capita ($)	($m)	Per capita ($)	($m)	Per capita ($)
New York	36,782	5,023	14,480	1,977	17,141	2,341	34,331	4,688	34,984	4,778
Los Angeles	3,889	1,116	522	150	1,933	554	3,534	1,014	8,003	2,296
Chicago	3,298	1,185	822	295	1,592	572	3,281	1,179	6,012	2,160
Houston	1,417	869	64	39	779	478	1,452	890	3,962	2,430
Philadelphia	2,818	1,777	874	551	1,483	935	2,823	1,780	3,835	2,418
San Diego	1,174	1,057	233	210	383	345	1,084	976	1,646	1,482
Detroit	1,567	1,524	706	686	551	536	1,577	1,534	1,685	1,640
Dallas	1,083	1,076	58	58	505	502	1,373	1,363	3,586	3,562
Phoenix	988	1,005	312	317	334	339	924	940	2,310	2,349

Source: Bureau of the Census.

Three Faces of Metropolitan Politics: Suburbanization; Race and Ethnicity; and Poverty

Suburbanisation

The metropolitan population of the United States first exceeded rural population in the first term of Franklin Roosevelt's Presidency; suburban population first exceeded central city population in 1970; and by the 1992 election, suburban voters comprised a majority of the US voting-age population (and a significantly larger proportion of those who actually voted).

The development of Metropolitan Areas in the second half of the twentieth century has been characterized by three major developments:

1. The dramatic weakening of cities' traditional employment bases in manufacturing. Most employment growth in new manufacturing activities (such as software engineering, pharmaceuticals, telecommunications, and aerospace) has occurred in suburbs, sometimes under the stimulus of Federal government procurement policies (particularly in defence).
2. The displacement of white ethnic groups in cities by more recent internal migrants from the rural south (African-Americans) and immigrants from abroad (Hispanic-Americans and Asian-Americans).
3. The dispersal of white populations from high-density central cities to low-density suburbs. Lost employment in city manufacturing has partly been replaced by employment in State and local government, service industries (such as entertainment, universities and research institutes, and health-care), and corporate services (such as law, accountancy, and management consultancy), and finance.

Of the many instances of white America's dependence upon Federal spending for the maintenance of its employment and quality of life, Federal and State subsidies to white Americans' evacuation of cities from 1940 onwards has been one of the most consequential – socially, economically, and politically. Despite their commonly being regarded as expressions of private-sector economic decisions, the development of suburbs has depended heavily upon public subsidy. Indeed, as Kenneth Jackson persuasively argued in his important book *Crabgrass Frontier*, the creation of suburbs has been a deliberate and sustained Federal policy, albeit one not acknowledged as such (Jackson, 1985, p. 293). As was explained in Chapter 9, President Eisenhower's successful proposal to Congress that it authorize and appropriate funds for a interstate highway system comprised a major Federal initiative, especially for a fiscally conservative Republican President, and was a significant stimulus to suburban development. State and local governments have throughout the twentieth century also funded (with Federal assistance) large roadbuilding programmes at public expense. Most of the State and local schemes were designed to link cities (until the 1960s, overwhelmingly the most important sites of employment) and suburbs (until the same decade, primarily residential areas). New public roads linking suburbs with cities not only liberated those (in the main, white) citizens with the cars to drive on them, but were provided free at the point of use. By the same token, such roads served as effective barriers to those (often black and Hispanic) citizens without cars, or the funds to pay for fuel. Fast highways increased the ease with which white citizens might leave cities, either to live, as was previously the case, or both to live and work, as has come to be typical. The highway programmes of Federal, State, and local governments did much to undermine the Federal government's nascent city infrastructure investment programme in the 1949 Housing and Urban Renewal Act. Earlier, at the New Deal's beginning, Congress's establishment in June 1933 of the Home Owners Loan Corporation (HOLC) at Roosevelt's behest led to Federal bureaucrats putting in place an elaborate system of rating rules which measured communities' property values according to considerations of racial and ethnic homogeneity and quality. As D. S. King has shown, the Federal Housing Authority (FHA), also established during the New Deal but under racially conservative Congressional oversight until well after the passage of the 1968 Civil Rights Act with its "open housing" clause, assiduously advanced segregated housing (King, D. S., 1995(b)). It granted mortgage insurance to private builders who (as the FHA knew and certain of its Congressional defenders intended) systematically discriminated against non-white Americans in the sale of housing: of nine million new houses built between the FHA's establishment and 1950, more than 99 per cent were not for sale to non-whites (King, 1995(b), p. 194).

Having been created as residential areas from which white residents commuted to work in cities, suburbs have in the second half of the twentieth century become the most rapidly growing sites of economic activity and employment in the United States. During the second half of the twentieth century, suburbia has increasingly accommodated the cars and their users. As late as 1946, there were only eight shopping centres in the entire United States; in 1994, there were more than 40,000. Almost all such malls are suburban, not central city, phenomena and all are located close to highways so that they may be supplied by trucks and accessed by private cars. Malls have in turn been supplemented by drive-in fast-food outlets; drive-in banks; and, in an especially crass twist of history, drive-in churches. Without the combination of private road transport, Federally-subsidized road construction, and Federally-subsidized mortgages, CMSAs could neither have been established nor sustained.

When manufacturing was concentrated in cities, investment in public transport was high. As manufacturing's concentration there has declined, so too has investment in public transport. Only sudden and substantial oil price increases in 1973/4 and 1979/80 caused political attention to focus fleetingly again upon collective solutions to a collective problem. In practice, the impetus behind the development of public transport has foundered upon two rocks:

1 Developing collective transport for voters who undertake various commuting journeys among many low-density suburbs is more complicated and expensive than developing collective transport solutions for workers within cities, or between a few suburban centres and a core city. The provision of public transport and the sharing of cars to work are easier where population and workplace densities are high: of the five counties in the United States where the use of public transport or the sharing of cars for commuting are highest, four are in New York City where between half and two-thirds of workers travel by bus, train, subway, or in carpools, while the fifth (technically not a county at all) is Washington DC, which has an excellent subway and bus system. Public transport can serve concentrated city populations adequately; it cannot equally serve dispersed suburban populations in which individuals do not make well-established radial journeys into a city from a suburb, but rather differentiated journeys within and between suburbs. The failure of collective transport provision thereby illustrates the nature and a consequence of suburbanization. As John Kain (1992) has argued, city dwellers (disproportionately black and Hispanic) suffer from "spatial mismatch": hampered by poverty and insurance market failures, a high proportion of black and Hispanic Americans lack the means to live in the suburbs, have no private transport to enable them to reach the suburban labour market, and are confined to the city by a mass transport system that does not cater to their needs.

2. While public opinion polls show significant support for public transport, there is little indication that most voters (especially most suburban voters) are willing to pay increased taxes or to support new bond issues to finance the capital investment required or the running costs entailed. The transport consequences of suburbanization carry significant environmental costs, but the electoral risk for politicians who seek to restrict the use of cars is high: dispersed, low-density housing suburbs typically defeat collective public transport solutions, and depend upon individual car transport.

The rapid growth of white-collar professional jobs in suburbs has been accelerated not only by the provision of road and other transport links but also by advanced communications technologies, lower tax rates in the suburbs (because of a smaller welfare-dependent population), and tax breaks to mortgagees. Through its demand during the Second World War and afterwards for products from new industries, such as aerospace and electronics, the Federal government was an important actor in hastening suburban employment growth. The development of nuclear, chemical, and biological means of warfare, and electronic means of intelligence gathering, powerfully stimulated links between the Department of Defense, the intelligence agencies (see Chapter 13), research institutes and universities, and defence contractors and subcontractors. Almost all research and development work in support of such activity has occurred in the suburbs.

In the 1960s, most Americans commuted between home and work. They still do. In the 1990s, however, the median commuting journey is not between a low-density suburb and a high-density city, but between a home in one low-density suburb to a place of work in another, similar, suburb. The point's significance is that cities and the problems that press upon them can be understood only in the context of their wider relationship to the suburbs surrounding them, and hence of the networks of political and fiscal relationships that tie the fates of cities to the suburbs and to the rural townships beyond, to the governments of the fifty States, and to the Federal government.

Political and fiscal relations between States and cities have been deeply affected by suburbanization and the weakening tax base of the *declining* group of central cities. Although by Dillon's Rule cities are, formally, constitutionally subject to State governments, some enjoy substantial autonomy from them. They do so for two opposite reasons: either because city interests dominate the State Legislature, or because dominant rural and suburban interests in the State Legislature prefer to leave cities to address their burdensome problems in their expensive ways, permitting them to levy heavy property taxes on city residents. In times of fiscal buoyancy, of economic growth in cities, and of stable tax-paying populations, such autonomy was welcome to cities. As tax-payers have moved to the suburbs, and cities' manufacturing and commercial cores have crumbled, many cities have found themselves trapped between declining tax bases and remaining populations disproportionately dependent upon public welfare. The importance of large cities to government has been further reduced as city party machines have disappeared, and the Presidential nominating process has been thrown open to Primary and caucus voters.

More than two-thirds of jobs created in Metropolitan Statistical Areas since 1976 have been in suburbs. In manufacturing, the sector best placed to create highly-paid jobs for the unskilled and semi-skilled, the imbalance in the distribution of jobs is even more sharply marked, with many suburbs creating jobs three times more rapidly than they are attracting residents (Hughes and Sternberg 1993, p. 32).

Older suburbs have recently faced employment problems of a similar kind to those with which central cities have long been familiar. Many skilled technical and managerial jobs have been lost in older suburbs during the 1990s as large manufacturing and service corporations such as AT&T and IBM have cut costs heavily in order to adjust to the competitive threat presented by new, less rigid, and more adaptably profitable competitors operating in dynamic product markets. The fusion in the 1990s of computing and telecommunications technologies, coupled with intensifying global competition and restless waves of institutional investors seeking more profitable uses for their capital, has reduced employment stability in computing, electronics, and services. That stability underpinned the development of suburbia between 1945 and 1985 as it had the development of employment in steel manufacture, textiles, and engineering in America's cities in the first half of the twentieth century. White suburban voters' uncertainties about their future income streams in the face of the mobility of international capital have induced new apprehensions about employment security, intensified dissatisfactions with government and distrust of politicians, and prompted a hankering for the recovery of stability of expectations and life chances which, in the absence of concerted and co-ordinated action by national governments, may prove forlorn.

Race and Ethnicity

America is the product of immigrants and immigration. Native Americans are themselves descendants of Asian immigrants who came to what is now the United States via Alaska. European immigrants settled in America following Columbus's discovery of the land in 1492. Some Protestant sects came to pre-industrial America to escape religious persecution; in the fifty years after 1810, British, German, and Irish Catholic immigrants comprised the bulk of the total influx. In the latter twenty years of the century, the western European flow was augmented by Scandinavian immigration. The west European inflow was later supplanted by Italian, Austro-Hungarian, Polish, and Russian immigration between 1890 and 1910 when, on average, a million immigrants entered the United States annually. Until the passage in 1924 of the Immigration Act, the United States had a general "right of entry" approach to immigration; between 1924 and 1965, immigration was restricted by racial quota, and only with President Johnson's Immigration Act of 1965 were racial quotas relaxed. Where 75 per cent of immigrants before the 1965 Act were European, 75 per cent since 1965 have been non-European, primarily from Latin America and Asia. Until their post-war decline, American cities attracted almost all of this immigrant labour, as they were contemporaneously drawing heavy migrant labour from the south.

Cities have long had the prime role in assimilating immigrants into labour markets, into society, and into politics. As the discussion in Chapter 2 about urban party machines showed, immigrants were absorbed into (often ethnically-differentiated) urban society by political parties hungry for new party activists willing to supply labour in return for jobs and assistance. The vast capacities of cities' manufacturing and commercial businesses to absorb unskilled and semi-skilled labour maintained the attractions of cities to immigrants from western and southern Europe in the nineteenth century, and of black migrants from the rural southern states between the 1920s and 1960s. Despite the decline of their manufacturing bases, cities continue to act as magnets to foreign workers: service industries' demands for cheap labour absorb the largest part of Asian and (especially) Latin American immigrants. Nevertheless, among recent Latin American and (especially) Asian immigrants is a significant proportion of technically skilled and educationally advanced people: the statistical evidence indicates that the proportion is in fact higher among immigrants between 1980 and 1996 than in the population as a whole. The number of immigrants in the 1990s remains high, and their concentration in some ports of entry is correspondingly great: foreign-born nationals account for more than a third of the population in some Texas counties and in Queens, New York; the proportion of foreign-born people in Miami, Florida, is nearly a half.

Internal flows of migrant labour have been scarcely less dramatic, and their consequences comparably great: during the 1940s, the black population of Chicago grew by 77 per cent, from 278,000 to 492,000. In the 1950s, it grew by another 65 per cent, to 813,000, giving a typical black migration to Chicago of 2,000 or more people a week. By 1960, Chicago had more than half a million more black residents than it had had in 1940 (*The Promised Land*, p. 70). The arrival of black migrants has prompted the flight of many white citizens: the movement of black workers in the first half of the twentieth century from rural southern states to northern inner cities has been matched by the movement of white populations (in much larger numbers) in the second half of the century from cities to suburbs. The Supreme Court's schools desegregation judgment in *Brown* was directed primarily at the South, but its impact upon the north has, though delayed, been momentous. Between 1970 and 1993, the part of Chicago's population that was white fell from 64.6 per cent to 36.3 per cent; the part of New York's from 75.2 per cent to 38.4 per cent; the part of Boston's from 81.7 per cent to 58.0 per cent; and of Dallas's from 75.8 per cent to 49.8 per cent (Davis, 1993, p. 15). As white people have fled central cities for the suburbs, so the political influence of cities' representatives upon State governments and upon the Federal government has waned, and that of suburban representatives has grown. Not only do most American voters live in suburbs, but their racial, class, and educational characteristics are such that their voting participation is higher than the national average. Suburban influence upon national politics is therefore disproportionately great: suburban voters' agendas have effectively become the national agenda, and hence those of Presidential candidates. While other political developments help to explain diminished Federal support for cities since the early 1980s, the weaker influence of cities (many of them under black American control) upon State and Federal governments (all of them under white American control) has been elemental.

Although the number of (mainly professional, middle-class) black people living in suburbs has grown rapidly since the 1960s, almost all live in racially-homogeneous areas, just as those more numerous black citizens living in cities do. There are few significant racially-mixed suburbs in the United States, and scarcely more areas of racially-mixed housing, either. Although Americans work in integrated offices and factories, they live in segregated housing areas. Black Americans have experienced some improvement in life chances: they now have more than a token representation in the upper reaches of the major professions, in business, and in government (especially in the Armed Forces, but also in upper-level Federal, State, and local employment). They have achieved social mobility and career success (dreamt of, but not expected, by civil rights leaders in the early 1960s) through dramatically improved educational attainments, as Table 10.4 shows. The proportion of black Americans with four years or more of college-level education is more than four times greater than in 1960, and larger than for any of the three major Hispanic subgroups, an improvement proportionately better than that of white citizens. Black educational attainment nevertheless remains much worse than that of white people: only 12.9 per cent of black students complete four years or more of college-level education, compared to 22.9 per cent of white students.

An alternative interpretation of the data in Table 10.4 is that most Americans are poorly prepared to compete in fluid labour markets in which the gap between the rewards to cognitive workers and those to unskilled and

TABLE 10.4

Educational Attainment by Race and Ethnicity, 1960–94

Year	Total	White	Black	Hispanic			
				Total	Mexican	Puerto Rican	Cuban
Completed four or more years of High School							
1960	41.1	43.2	20.1	NA	NA	NA	NA
1970	52.3	54.5	31.4	32.1	24.2	23.4	43.9
1980	66.5	68.8	51.2	44.0	37.6	40.1	55.3
1990	77.6	79.1	79.1	50.8	44.1	55.5	63.5
1994	80.9	82.0	82.0	53.3	46.7	59.4	64.1
Completed four or more years of college							
1960	7.7	8.1	3.1	NA	NA	NA	NA
1970	10.7	11.3	4.4	4.5	2.5	2.2	11.1
1980	16.2	17.1	8.4	7.6	4.9	5.6	16.2
1990	21.3	22.0	11.3	9.2	5.4	9.7	20.2
1994	22.2	22.9	12.9	9.1	6.3	9.7	16.2

Source: US Bureau of the Census.

semi-skilled workers is growing. From approximately 1973, the real earnings per hour of unskilled workers have fallen steadily. Even in 1964, the Welfare Commissioner of New York conceded that "Maybe we are going to have to accept that many able-bodied people are never going to be engaged in economically productive employment" (Banfield, 1974, p. 100). In the late 1990s, job prospects are much poorer for uneducated able-bodied individuals – especially for black and Hispanic uneducated able-bodied people – than they were even in 1964. It is doubtful that such permanent exclusion from employment for many black and Hispanic Americans is consistent with the maintenance of public order, and it is certain that it is not consistent with American values of opportunity and inclusion.

Poverty

The needs of those city dwellers on the fringes of volatile labour markets and beyond them, coupled with the physical infrastructural needs of cities themselves, have met with less sympathetic ears in Congress since Mr Reagan's Presidency than they did under the five Democratic administrations between 1932 to 1980. Greater inequality (measured by the fiscal resources available to city and suburban local governments, and by income between city and suburban residents) has resulted. Such inequality has increased further as a result of competition between the governments of cities and suburbs to attract capital and human resources of high quality, but to deter those individuals and groups (partly through creative use of zoning laws) likely to be dependent upon, rather than contributing to, a local government's tax-base.

Cities were established for business purposes; where they have flourished, they have done so because business itself has flourished. As S. B. Warner argued in 1968, "The tradition of privatism has always meant that the cities of the United States depended for their wages, employment, and general prosperity upon the aggregate success and failures of thousands of individual enterprises, not upon community action" (Warner, 1968, p. 4). With economic importance came political and cultural importance or, as in the case of New York, economic primacy and cultural centrality. The counterpart of Warner's observation is, as he acknowledged, that what the private market could not do well, or neglected, American cities have been unable to overcome (ibid., p. x). Until the mid-1970s, it was possible to argue, as Banfield did, that while there existed much poverty and racial discrimination in American cities, "there is less of both than ever before" (Banfield, 1974, p. 2). Yet at the twentieth century's end, the plight of the urban poor remains much as it was at the beginning: American central cities contain many who have no significant access to health care; who have exceedingly poor educational facilities (and lower educational attainments than the average in some Third World countries); who lack the training and education to participate in the job market; who are daily exposed to criminal activity and violence; and who live in shattered social structures and squalid housing. All of the poorest and most deprived urban areas in the United States that share these characteristics are inhabited by racial and ethnic minorities. The segregated concentration of the black and Hispanic poor in such areas is growing rather than diminishing (Hughes and Sternberg, 1993, p. 22).

The connections between social deprivation and urban crime appear to lack political salience for most suburban Americans. In the mid-1960s, a progressive reforming liberalism survived even the challenges of urban rioting, as the report of the Kerner Commission (1967), shows: "Warring on poverty, inadequate housing and unemployment, is warring on crime. A civil right law is a law against crime. Money for schools is money against crime. Medical, psychiatric, and family-counselling services are services against crime. More broadly and most importantly every effort to improve life in America's 'inner cities' is an effort against crime" (Kerner Commission, 1967, p. 6).

A consequence of the effective abandonment of declining central cities by Federal and State governments has been a rapid expansion of the number of adults on probation, in prison, or on parole. The number increased from 1.84 million in 1980 (the last full year of Jimmy Carter's Presidency), to 3.71 million in 1988 (the last year of his successor, Ronald Reagan's), and to 4.76 million in 1992 (the last full year of George Bush's Presidency). Of the 4.76 million imprisoned in 1992, 1.78 million were black Americans (Bureau of the Census, *Statistical Abstract of the United States, 1996*, Table 354). Not only are many more Americans imprisoned now than at the end of Carter's Presidency, the use of capital punishment has increased, too: excluding those appealing against their convictions, 688 people (270 of them black, Hispanic, or of other non-caucasian race) were under sentence of death in 1980; by 1993, 2,716 persons (1,150 of them black, Hispanic, or of other non-caucasian race) were under sentence of death (Bureau of the Census, *Statistical Abstract of the United States, 1996*, Table 354).

John Kennedy's and Lyndon Johnson's Presidencies marked the peak of optimism about the good that government might do for cities, as the Model Cities programme illustrates. Members of Congress rejected Johnson's proposal that the policy be targeted on a few cities, and spread the programme more thinly to distribute the benefits among Congressional Districts (and hence among themselves). The programme's effectiveness was thereby reduced, but a much larger constituency for its reauthorization and reappropriation was created: aggregate Federal grants-in-aid to cities grew rapidly up to 1980. The weakening of the progressive impulse in both major political parties as the Democrats' fissures widened in the late 1960s and 1970s, and the Republican Party's ingestion of southern conservatism under Richard Nixon's leadership, at first marginalized and then extinguished the Party's north-eastern and north-western reforming liberal wings.

Mr Carter's defeat was highly significant. At Reagan's behest, the Federal government abandoned most urban aid programmes during the 1980s: the Community Development Block Grant, and the Urban Development Block Grant were abolished, while the Comprehensive Employment and Training Act of 1973 was replaced by the poorly-funded Jobs Training and Partnership Act of 1982. At Reagan's request, Federally-assisted public housing provision was virtually ended. A consequence of Mr Reagan's Presidency was the spawning of a lively academic debate about the respects in which, and the extent to which, the sharp change in fiscal policy effected in 1981 affected the nature of Federal welfare policy. In urban policy, however, the data show that the legislative cuts effected in that year significantly reduced some Federal programmes and eliminated others altogether. Unable both by reason of his own anxieties and by Congressional opposition to restrain the growth in Federal entitlement programmes from which Republican voters benefited as much as Democratic ones, but forced by the rapid growth in defence spending which he sponsored to make cuts elsewhere, Reagan cut especially deeply into those programmes upon which poor, urban, Democratic voters depended. In the House, his political support came primarily from suburban and rural Republicans, with some support from rural southern conservative Democrats. Reagan opposed Federal aid to cities and local governments, and successfully pressed for the abolition of President Nixon's General Revenue Sharing in 1986, and Carter's Urban Development Action Grants (which had supplied nearly $5 million for some 3,300 projects in declining cities (Kincaid, p. 208). Under President Clinton, health-care reform that would have provided some medical cover to those in low-paying jobs without medical insurance failed. Contrary voices were without significant political effect: the Milton S. Eisenhower Foundation's report entitled *Investing in Children and Youth, Reconstructing Our Cities* (1983) proposed major new expenditure upon programmes targeted at inner-city youth, including job training; education, welfare, and health care reform; and drug prevention. There has been no Federal response, and there is little likelihood of there being one.

Politicians, Businessmen, and Economic Growth:
The Example of New York City

The health of Metropolitan Areas depends upon private investment decisions. The autonomy of civil society is a necessary, if insufficient, condition for democracy's health; accordingly, democratic governments ought not to attempt to dictate to civil associations. In the case of relations between business corporations and city governments however, the relative weakness of the latter poses significant political difficulties, because businessmen always have the option of going elsewhere. Knowing that businessmen can leave concentrates municipal minds. For example, the then mayor of New

York, Ed Koch, worked strenuously between 1985 and 1987 to persuade the National Broadcasting Company (NBC) not to leave New York for an alternative (and cheaper) corporate headquarters in New Jersey. Koch eventually secured a deal by which NBC renewed its lease on its New York headquarters and invested in improved facilities there, with the assistance of inducements providing for tax incentives worth more than $97 million over thirty years. Each of Mayor Koch's successors in New York City Hall has concluded significant package deals with other major corporations to induce them to remain; mayors of other cities have also been compelled to strike bargains (some even larger than Koch's with NBC) with corporations that exploit to the full their freedom to move operations between competing cities and counties.

City mayors are correspondingly obliged to calculate carefully the consequence for their tax-paying population of increasing city taxes in order to finance public programmes designed to assist the needy. Like corporations, tax-payers (especially those with highly-marketable skills and high incomes) are free to leave cities whose tax rates they deem intolerably high, or whose pathologies of urban life (such as the visibility of the destitute and homeless) they come to find unacceptable: this openness of city borders, contrasting vividly with national States' immigration controls at international borders, limits the freedom of city goverments to act. Cities lack the coercive powers of the national State, a weakness with profound implications: the controls over regulation of money, trading of goods and services across international borders, the establishment of a defence policy, and movement of capital and people, all of which the Constitution grants to the Federal government, are denied to all sub-Federal governments.

In the cases both of corporations and individuals, the freedom to move from one city or State to another has been used intensively. Some cities (such as New York) have responded in the 1980s and 1990s by restraining public expenditure growth in order to cut taxes on citizens and businesses whose presence is required for future prosperity. Others (such as Detroit and Newark) have sought to compensate for reduced flows of Federal and State fiscal support by increasing public expenditure but at the cost of hastening the flight to the suburbs of citizens and corporations. In both cases, city politicians have to take account not only of the probable responses of individual and corporate tax-payers to changes in local tax rates but, crucially, of the responses of members of their electoral coalitions to changes in public policies. Yet the task of courting business does not fit naturally or easily with the democratic purpose of winning elections. In New York, as in other cities whose governments have strained to retain those tax-payers and job creators they have and to attract new ones, Mayors Ed Koch (1981–9), David Dinkins (1989–93), and Rudolph Giuliani (1993–) have all been obliged to create policies for their city's economic development consistent with their maintenance of majority electoral coalitions. Koch (a Jewish

Democrat who became steadily more conservative during his term of office), Dinkins (a black liberal Democrat), and Giuliani (a moderately conservative Republican whose relations with the State party were conflictual) had different coalitions. Yet all three found difficulty in maintaining their *electoral* coalitions while pursuing New York City's economic development by maintaining *governing* coalitions of support including, critically, the investment banks to which the city sold its debt; all three were nevertheless constrained to pursue both.

Politicians have sometimes resolved the conflicting demands of their electoral coalitions and economic development by financing public policy programmes (including redistributive ones) through creating debt. In the 1970s, New York Mayor John Lindsay, an example of that now nearly extinct breed of liberal Republicans, resolved the tensions between meeting the demands of his electorate and financing them by increasing the size and frequency of bond issues. In explaining why Lindsay made that choice, Martin Shefter has also shown that it had ineluctable consequences: a fiscal crisis resulted, in which the city was obliged to pay increasingly high interest rates on debt that bankers and brokers were otherwise unwilling to buy (Shefter, 1992). A plausible short-term expedient, Lindsay's was a policy with disastrous medium-term implications: destroying New York's credit worthiness with the markets drove the city into the arms of a Federal government in 1975 which, under President Gerald Ford, had the strongest political motive for stigmatizing New York as an exemplar of urban fiscal irresponsibility for which Democrats could be blamed (especially after Lindsay's change of party affiliation). Ford exacted heavy cuts in redistributive expenditure as the price for Federal assistance. New York's debt servicing costs fell from nearly a third of its tax revenue in the mid-to-late 1970s to approximately a tenth by 1990. Belated infrastructural improvements that had been postponed in order to reduce expenditure, coupled with a stagnant local tax base, have since 1990 combined to increase the debt burden once more.

There is no easy solution to the matrix of difficulties under which New York, like other large cities, labours and which its debt problem represents: it needs to borrow in order to finance capital improvements to schools, roads and bridges, without which businesses and individual taxpayers may opt to leave the city. However, it cannot afford to increase its debt burden significantly because, first, its total outstanding debt ($30 billion in mid-1996) is high, and close to the limit imposed by the State constitution; second, because new debt is expensive (the market gives it a high-risk rating, so forcing it to be sold at an interest premium); and third, because the city's tax rates are already so high that to raise them would provoke political resistance from Mayor Giuliani's core constituents. Establishing capital spending as the priority is politically sensible for a conservative Republican such as Giuliani, since the dependent poor form no part of his electoral coalition. Accordingly, he has sought at every turn to cut current redistributive spending, even at the price of further reducing the City's meagre provision for the homeless, few of whom vote at all and none of whom vote for him (*New York Times*, 27 August 1996, p. B3).

Conclusion

New York surmounted the fiscal crisis of the 1970s following the application of Presidential leverage; its government confronts the gathering difficulties of the late 1990s by cutting its redistributive activity and taking fuller account of the demands of highly mobile business, and of tax-paying voters for lower tax rates. The constraints upon the government of New York City, as of other cities, are several and tight: decisions about levels and types of taxation, borrowing, and expenditure are important in their own right, politically consequential, and morally weighty (though often unrecognised as such). Political choices at all levels of government are, by their very nature, difficult, but those made by politicians and officials in cities are especially so because they lack the range of choices and sanctions available to the US Federal government. The examples of Detroit and other *declining* eastern and mid-western cities illustrate the rapidity with which the decay of manufacturing and the flight of tax-paying populations to safer, whiter, suburbs can enfeeble a city's commercial health. Yet as New York and many other *diverse* examples suggest, cities are not condemned to secular decay and degradation: resilient and creative city politicians can and do attract new capital while enriching the employment prospects and cultural life of the cities' inhabitants. New York's commercial life is, if arguably less dynamic than before the 1960s, still exceptionally vigorous. Its international importance in finance and the entertainment industry, for example, is undimmed. Detroit's government, on the other hand, failed to take sufficiently full account of business demands, as a result of which capital and (mostly white) tax-paying voters left for the suburbs and much of the city's commercial centre was abandoned to the destitute, dependent upon a shrinking tax-base and the whims of a Federal and a State government increasingly deaf to the demands of urban voters.

11

Domestic Economic Policy

The Economic Policy Process

Gloomy assessments of its condition, prospects, and relative decline notwithstanding, the American economy remains the largest and most efficient in the world. Since the oil price shocks of 1973 and 1979, the United States has achieved higher rates of output growth than many other industrial countries, but smaller improvements in productivity. Having averaged about 2.4 per cent between 1890 and 1973, the annual rate of growth in productivity (defined as output per hour of all persons working in the non-agricultural business sector) fell to 0.7 per cent between 1973 and 1990. Output growth in that period was mainly a function of increased inputs, especially of hours worked and increased participation by women in the labour force. New waves of immigrants entered labour markets, too. During the 1980s, the United States created more jobs than any of its major competitors; the corollary was that real wages stagnated. Between 1990 and 1995, however, productivity grew at about 2 per cent per annum, and then rose sharply to 3.5 per cent between June 1994 and June 1995, before reverting to the long-term trend rate. Measuring productivity is more difficult than it was because of the continued relative decline of American manufacturing and the growth in services (manufacturing now accounts for only 18 per cent of US GDP compared to more than 30 per cent in the 1950s, whereas services now account for 55 per cent of GDP). It appears that services are experiencing significant productivity gains, but the extent of such gains is more of a guess than a calculation. Through increasing by more than a half between 1991 and 1995, investment spending is a proximate explanation, but that surge is itself not easily accounted for.

US productivity nevertheless remains the highest in the world. However, the conventional wisdom, heavily propagated by Mr Clinton's administration both before and after his re-election victory in 1996, that US output growth was especially rapid during his first term, is false: between the first quarter of 1992 and the second quarter of 1996, the US economy expanded at an annual rate of growth of 1.8 per cent – only a little more than the European Union (EU), and less than Japan (but much more than Britain). According to the OECD's (1997) *Economic Outlook* at the beginning of 1997, the annual growth rates from the latest cyclical peak to 1998 gives an annual growth rates of 1.9 per cent in the US, compared to 2.7 per cent per annum over the 1979–89 cycle.

The well-being of all other economies continues to depend on the health of the US economy. The proportion of US GDP exported has, throughout the twentieth century, been lower than that in the country's major competitors. Although the proportion has grown since 1945, it still stands at only 11 per cent. The US dollar is the largest internationally-traded currency: huge quantities of the currency are held overseas by foreign governments and companies, most commodities are dollar-denominated, and so is the United States government's own debt. No other country enjoys the immense advantage of borrowing abroad in its own currency to fund its own debt.

Decisions that Federal, State, and local governments make about taxing and spending affect the economy's condition in the aggregate and its regional and local components. Decisions of individuals and corporations also affect the economy, but the Federal government's taxing and spending decisions exert the greatest single influence, because its budget is greater than all State and local budgets combined (accounting for more than 20 per cent of GDP) and because, unlike the Constitutions of many States, the US Constitution does not prohibit the Federal government from running a fiscal deficit.

Economic policy processes in all democracies are conflictual. In America, however, conflict is intensified by the fragmentation of politics, and a cultural antipathy to big government. More especially, the weakness of Executive authority renders policy-making exceptionally fraught: the formation, legitimation, implementation and evaluation of American economic policy require agreements between politicians in autonomous and competitive institutions. Since the objectives, perspectives, electoral bases of support, ideological preferences, and institutional interests of the politicians and officials who participate in the process diverge more frequently and in more directions than they converge, achieving such co-operation is difficult. Public powers over Federal economic policy are shared between the single elected member of the Executive Branch, that Branch's many unelected officials, the 535 elected members of the United States Congress, and the independent quasi-public Federal Reserve System. Public officials contribute to economic policy-making in the knowledge that most economic decision-making power remains in private and corporate hands.

Notwithstanding his constitutional restrictions, the President remains the single most important participant in the economic policy process. No other politician or official in government, and no individual in the private sector, rivals the Presidency's institutional capacity for economic policy leadership. The President has the power, and indeed the obligation, to identify economic policy objectives and to set the agenda for action: lacking authority, he must seek to persuade those whose support he needs but is unable to require. He acts, therefore, with or against Congressional politicians who themselves have (and use) powers of initiation, formalization, legitimation, implementation, and evaluation. The President's prospects of securing assent for his policy preferences are, therefore, institutionally hampered – and designedly so. This unpromising circumstance may be either mitigated or exacerbated by exogenous factors at best only partially within the President's influence. Among these are the partisan and ideological balances within Congress; the identity and policy preferences of appointees to Executive Branch agencies and regulatory authorities (especially the Federal Reserve System); public opinion; the proximity of elections; and the international political, military, and economic contexts within which policy is formulated and advanced.

In contrast to the President's leadership of the armed forces in peace and war, he has no power of command in economic policy. Authority rests, ultimately and constitutionally at least, with Congress and not with the President. Presidential leadership in economic policy is problematic, not only because of intellectual uncertainties about the effectiveness of different policy instruments and their relationship to each other, but also because of high political risks for the many people and institutions involved in its formulation. Of this difficulty's several dimensions, the reconciliation of fiscal and monetary policy is the most forbidding. Presidents must try to make fiscal and monetary policy economically and politically congruent because of the broad macroeconomic duties assumed by all Presidents since March 1933, and imposed upon them by the Employment Act of 1946 (see p. 352). Nevertheless, the separation of powers, and the Federal Reserve Board's substantial autonomy, usually cause the President to be a supplicant rather than an executive.

A President's part in economic policy derives from Article II of the Constitution. He exercises further powers and responsibilities through the delegation of powers to him from Congress by the Federal Reserve Act (1913), the Budget and Accounting Act (1921), the Employment Act (1946), and the Budget and Impoundment Control Act (1974), together with their subsequent amendments. Throughout the twentieth century, but particularly since 1932, the political fate of United States Presidents has in large part been dependent upon the achievement of steady output growth, low inflation and high employment, which Presidents and scholars alike understand normally to be prerequisites for electoral victory. Inauspicious as their prospects for success are, Presidents must attempt to influence macroeconomic outcomes, not least because their re-election prospects hang upon them, as Presidents Carter and Bush discovered in 1980 and 1992 respectively.

The first section of this chapter comprises an examination of the institutional participants in the economic policy process. There is no examination in the chapter of the roles played by interest groups because Chapter 7 includes a discussion of the business and labour lobbies' influence upon economic policy. Important though it is to the health of the American economy, trade policy is considered not here, but in Chapter 12 as part of the discussion of foreign policy.

The second section examines the fiscal policy process; and the third section gives an assessment of the effectiveness of recent Budget reforms and policy, and of the calibration of fiscal and monetary policy.

Participants in Economy Policy-making

The Executive Branch

The Executive's interests in economic policy are divided institutionally between Presidential and departmental components. To this extent, the Federal government's making of economic policy reflects the general difficulty of Presidents in attempting to formulate and implement policy across an administration over which they have constitutional and statutory jurisdiction, but incomplete authority. Within the departmental component, agencies and departments have vested interests in the Federal Budget, not least because it affects their activities. Although not simply (or primarily) budget-maximisers, senior bureaucrats have a prudential continuing political commitment to their agencies' fiscal health. Annual appropriations for many Federal programmes ensure that senior bureaucrats must have regard to Congressional opinion about them.

The Federal government is the largest single participant in the American economy: decisions made by Executive officials, and laws and regulations written by Congress, have consequences for the level and character of economic activity. All governments in the United States affect the economy by implementing public policies and issuing regulations. Tightening Federal or State regulations governing (for example) the discharge of carcinogens into the air, may be desirable public policy but, like all regulation, it imposes costs upon the polluter, its employees, and consumers, while benefiting those affected by pollution. Regulation of markets has none the less always been preferred to nationalization as an instrument of public policy in the United States.

Governments also intervene in the economy by raising revenue, and by expenditure, both on their own and in support of other governments' programmes. Vast public procurement programmes inescapably cause governments (indirectly) to affect economic activity: in the 1995 fiscal year, the Federal government spent more than $202 billion on private sector goods and services. Many individuals, companies, and localities depend for their survival upon Federal orders. This pattern is especially marked in the case of defence equipment which, in law and in practice, is subject to detailed Federal control: defence procurement programmes powerfully affect patterns of investment, and research and development, in private industry and commerce.

In most years since 1945, the Federal government has run a fiscal deficit on a budget larger than that of all State and local governments combined. By 1994, the Federal government had accumulated gross debts of $4.6 trillion; it needs regularly to raise more. The US Treasury, which exercises authority delegated by Congress for the government's debt management, covers the shortfall between expenditure and revenue by selling US Treasury securities. With a range of maturities of between two and thirty years, demand from dealers in Treasury securities markets sets the price of the debt. Decisions regarding the financing of the Federal government's debt have the potential to affect the economy's condition significantly. Unlike bonds issued by many private corporations and some American cities, Treasury bonds are entirely secure. They are so because they are backed, in the official phrase, "by the full faith and credit" of the United States government.

The Council of Economic Advisers

Reflecting the twin imperatives of economic crisis and international conflict which spawned its birth and growth, the Executive Office of the President (EOP) has the management of economic and national security policy as its two major activities. In addition to several advisers within the White House Office itself, the Employment Act (1946) established the Council of Economic Advisers (CEA) in the EOP in order to promote policies designed to secure full employment, an institutional expression of Keynesianism. The CEA is a staff, not a line, agency and has one client, the President of the United States. Its three members are appointed by the President, subject to the advice and confirmation of the Senate.

The 1946 Act established the objectives of seeking "maximum employment, production, and purchasing power". It requires the President, at the start of each session of Congress, to present an *Economic Report of the President*, which comprises an analysis of economic trends and conditions, presents a programme for implementing the President's policy objectives, and makes recommendations for necessary legislation. Since the economic crises following the oil price increases of 1973 and 1979, and the rise of monetarist influence, the CEA has set less store by the objective of full employment set by the 1946 Act, but its members continue to advise the President on macroeconomic policy. Members of the CEA since 1946 have in their different ways attempted to provide such means for intelligent and informed Presidential decision-making.

Walter Heller, Chairman of the CEA under Kennedy and Johnson, identified five functions the Council enjoyed under these Presidents, and which have been retained by later Presidents:

1. *Provision of information to the President.* Under Kennedy and Johnson, this included (a) keeping the President informed of "economic events, trends, and prospects" as the 1946 Employment Act required; (b) responding to Presidential requests for information, advice, and interpretation of data and events; (c) briefing the President on economic policy for press conferences or for private meetings with journalists. All three functions continue.

2. *Speech-writing*. This includes preparing drafts of Presidential speeches, and commenting on drafts prepared by others. CEA Chairmen have always had the subsidiary, public, task of representing the President's policies to business corporations and associations, to labour unions, and to the press. The preparation of the *Economic Report of the President* falls under this heading. The *Report* offers the President the opportunity to win Congressional, interest group, and public support for his policies.

3. *Briefing of the President*. The CEA briefs the President for his meetings on economic policy with Cabinet members, interest-group representatives, members of Congress, and foreign heads of government. The CEA also seeks to persuade the President of the merits of certain policy choices. During Kennedy's Administration, the broadly Keynesian Council persuaded the President of the utility of fiscal fine- tuning in promoting faster economic growth. In 1969 and 1970, President Nixon's CEA, influenced more by Milton Friedman's theory of the natural rate of unemployment than by Keynesian theories of demand management, argued that the defeat of inflation should be the administration's first priority, even at the price of accepting a higher "natural rate of unemployment". Paul McCracken and his colleagues on Nixon's CEA were less successful in persuading the President of this object's political desirability than Heller and his colleagues had been with regard to fiscal policy in 1963, and failed completely to prevent the President's startlingly pragmatic imposition of wage and price controls in 1971.

4. *Responsibility for the legislative programme*. The CEA had special responsibility for the President's legislative programme under Johnson. Although new and expensive legislative initiatives have been rarer since the mid-1980s, the CEA continues to review, with a team of senior White House staff, proposals for the following year's legislative programme, and to assign special responsibility to the economic staff of the Council for the analysis of programmes with particular significance for the economy.

5. *Special activities*. In Chairman Heller's formulation, this simply referred to President Kennedy's use of the CEA "to represent him in interagency discussions on particular policy problems". Such a role, apparently nebulous, in fact reveals the intimacy of the Council's relations with the President, and the Council's determination to assert itself at the centre of his administration. The influence of the Council in later years has typically been a function of the political skill of its Chairpersons.

The Office of Management and Budget (OMB)

The Executive's budgetary policy is co-ordinated in the Office of Management and Budget (OMB), whose history was discussed briefly in Chapter 4. Established by the Budget and Accounting Act (1921) in the Treasury, the

Bureau of the Budget was moved to the EOP by the 1939 Reorganization Act. The change resulted from Roosevelt's wish to have more immediate staff assistance, the 1937 Brownlow Commission's agreement with his view, and Congress's accession to both. The Bureau provided the Presidency with an office to examine the Budget proposals from each of the Executive Departments and form them into a coherent overall package reflecting the President's priorities for submission to Congress in an annual Budget message. The Bureau was renamed the Office of Management and Budget in 1970, reflecting President Nixon's desire to centralize management of the Executive Branch in the EOP, and thereby to politicize it. Prior to the 1974 Budget Reform Act, the message related to the Budget for the fiscal year beginning on the first day of July following; since 1974, the fiscal year has begun on 1 October and ended on 30 September. The OMB's role in the formation of the Federal Budget is examined in greater detail below.

The Executive Departments

Chapter 8 showed that the Federal bureaucracy has two distinctive features:

1. Unlike government bureaucracies in France or the United Kingdom, the Federal bureaucracy's loyalties are divided. Its members attend not just to Presidential preferences but also to Congressional ones. Only White House staff are exempt from Congress's scrutiny, and even they are dependent upon Congress for their salaries. Congress remains the first branch of government.
2. The American Federal bureaucracy is highly fragmented. Executive agencies within departments are semi-autonomous. Having loyalties both to the Chief Executive and to Congress (which authorizes their existence and activities, and has the power of the purse over them), departments have ample political space. Presidential policies are not easily co-ordinated across departments. The President depends upon the semi-autonomous Department of the Treasury for developing and implementing fiscal policy, and upon the OMB within the EOP for formulation of a budget prior to its submission to Congress. The President's political writ runs for a shorter distance than his constitutional position as Chief Executive implies, and sub-governmental networks are the primary influences upon policy.

The Treasury

The Secretary of the Treasury is the main financial officer of the US government and economic adviser to the President, in which role he has overall responsibility for macroeconomic policy. He is also responsible for international financial policy, and for the management of the government's debt, by which he determines the quantities and maturities of debt to be raised through quarterly refinancing.

The Treasury Department is organised in a similar way to other Federal departments: the Secretary and a few officials have responsibilities covering the entire activities of the department. Immediately below the Secretary are two Under-Secretaries: one has responsibility for International Affairs, and the other for Finance. However, most of the Department's work is led by political appointees at Assistant Secretary level in specialist agencies and sections including Economic Policy; Fiscal Policy; Domestic Finance; International Economic Policy; and International Monetary Affairs. In all cases, the Assistant Secretaries are supported by political appointees and civil servants engaged in economic analysis and forecasting, and in preparing policy advice to the Under-Secretaries and thence to the Secretary and the President.

The Department of Commerce

The Secretary of Commerce is the President's main adviser on business and commercial policy. The department traditionally has close links to business groups and itself often represents business interests to other Federal agencies. In addition to the Department's semi-autonomous agencies (including the Bureau of the Census, the Patent and Trademark Office, and the National Oceanic and Atmospheric Administration) most of its agencies are concerned with economic development within the United States, with the promotion of exports, and with representing American business interests in international trade. The Economic Affairs division collects data on economic activity, particularly on consumer spending and capital formation, levels of inventories, and prospects for output and employment. Some of the Department's work overlaps with that of the Treasury, the Department of Labor, and the Council of Economic Advisers, The Department consequently has to compete with others to exert influence upon the President's policy.

The Federal Reserve Board and Federal Reserve Banks

Membership, Independence and Constraints of Operation

By the 1913 Federal Reserve Act, and the Banking Acts of 1933 and 1935, Congress chose to vest exclusive responsibility for monetary policy in the Federal Reserve Board, the central bank of the United States. As a regulatory body, the Federal Reserve Board's members are appointed by the President, with the advice and consent of the Senate. Therefore neither the President, nor the Secretary of the Treasury, nor Congress directly controls monetary policy. The Board guards jealously its managerial and operating independence: its budget is not subject to review by the President or the OMB. Great as its formal powers are, however, the Board's capacity to use them is constrained by its sensitivity to political pressure and the prospect of such pressure. The mere possibility that it might be applied is usually sufficient to affect its decisions: discounting for the future is the stock-in-trade of unelected officials as it is of politicians, and of financial market-makers. In political practice, therefore, the Board is constrained, although the tightness of the constraints vary with circumstances. Arthur Okun, President Johnson's last Chairman of the CEA, rightly concluded that the Board enjoys independence within, but not from, the administration.

Attempts by Congress to constrain Board policy decisions have similarly been unsuccessful. A Congressional resolution in 1974 requiring the Board to inform Congress biannually of its money supply targets has been met with the provision of several broad target ranges, leaving the Board considerable freedom. Even when such targets have been missed, Congressional oversight has been weak and without effect. The Humphrey–Hawkins Full Employment Act (1978), Congressional Keynesianism's last gasp, required the Board to state whether its monetary targets were consistent with the President's macroeconomic policy, but this requirement has similarly been circumvented by the use of wide monetary target ranges in order to preserve its discretion, and by its unwillingness to accept responsibility for economic policy outcomes (which luxury Presidents are denied).

The Board itself comprises seven full-time members appointed by the President, subject to Senate confirmation, each for a fourteen-year term. This period is longer than any President may serve, and longer than most members of either the House or Senate in fact do. Formal independence from the Executive is thereby assured. Furthermore, no American President may remove a Board member. Presidents of the twelve district banks in major cities together comprise the Federal Reserve system serve on the Federal Open Market Committee (FOMC), membership of which is divided into voting and non-voting members. Five District Presidents (the President of the Federal Reserve Bank of New York is always one) have voting powers on the FOMC, together with all seven members of the full Board. The Board's domination of the twelve Reserve Banks is enhanced by two factors:

(i)   It appoints Presidents of Reserve Banks; and
(ii)   The United States' capital market is national – a familiar fact, but one with clear political implications for the Board's internal operations.

It is in this setting that the Board has special responsibility for the containment of inflation through regulation of the money supply. No significant means of monetary control are held by any other agency or institution. Three hundred and fifty highly specialized economic research staff work for the Board. Many do so for a large part of their careers, attracted in part by salaries fixed not on civil service scales but set by market forces: the most senior staff earn considerably more than the Chairman or Governors. The staff is as large as it is because of what H. Stein (1988, p. 341) regards as the Board's operating premise "that it must be continuously informed about everything that goes on in the economy", and be able to supply analyses to the Board which enable it to adjust policy in the light of it. In practice, this means that there are on the staff specialists in every sector of the economy, from machine tools to futures markets in agricultural commodities.

Elected politicians in Congress and the White House retain some influence over monetary policy. The President's power to nominate the Chairman and Governors enables him to shape the Board's composition, while the Senate's power of confirmation permits it to examine his choices. Even fourteen-year terms do not exempt Board members from political pressures. Under the Federal Reserve Act (1913) the Federal Reserve Board is Congress's creation, but not its creature: Congress may alter its structure, rules, and remit. The Board has indeed periodically been the subject of pressure from populist members of Congress, anxious to bring the central bank under closer political control. In practice, there is little overt interference, partly because the Board's members understand that their technical judgements about policy are made in the context of intensely competitive democratic politics. As with the Supreme Court, so with the Reserve Board: its formal autonomy increases rather than diminishes its sager members' awareness of the contingent character of its legitimacy and power.

There are, however, two good arguments to be made in support of holding the Board more accountable to elected politicians; the first has to do with the principle of accountability in a democratic society, and the second derives from the composition of the Board's personnel. With regard to the first, it is not *prima facie* justifiable that a political system characterised above all else by the use of elections as a legitimating device for the holding of public office should leave the determination of monetary policy in the hands of individuals formally accountable to no one. The argument is the stronger for the Board's being wholly unrepresentative of America: most Governors have been male, white, and either academics (in January 1993, no fewer than five had PhDs in Economics) or bankers. Those feared to be radical, or whose views depart from the acceptable middle ground of monetary thinking, are rarely considered for membership of the Board, regardless of their ability. Not only does the Board draw upon a narrow range of activities, it tends to select its membership, and especially its Regional Presidents, from among its own. Necessary though experience is, it is not clear that the narrow backgrounds of most Board and District Bank members and of the Board's staff are entirely advantageous. Populists and liberals have regarded the self-perpetuating character of the System's narrow personnel selection as evidence of its threat both to democratic accountability and to the interests of individual borrowers.

The Board hovers uncertainly on the fringes of government, exploiting its centrality to macroeconomic policy and its autonomy to arrive at a unique constitutional arrangement. In practice, its equivocal status has worked to its institutional advantage, and (usually) to the benefit of monetary policy itself. Congressional politicians who have shaped the Board's constitution by Statute prize the arrangement's utility. By granting the Board autonomy from electoral politics, wise politicians implicitly acknowledge the temptations open to them were the control of monetary policy to be theirs as completely as is that of fiscal policy. Manipulating interest rates for electoral advantage of Congressional majorities would be too enticing to resist, but the consequences would be damagingly destabilizing. (On the one occasion in the post-war period when the Board acceded to ferocious Presidential pressure, that of President Nixon's harassment of Chairman Burns in 1971–2, the lagged effects on inflation were disastrous.) By delegating responsibility to the FOMC, Congress implicitly accepts that monetary judgements should be made as dispassionately as possible and comparatively free from immediate political pressures, which since the early 1970s have warped Congress's own formation of fiscal policy.

Congress

Congress is the first branch primarily because it creates most of government and finances all of it. Congress, and Congress alone, has the power of the purse, determining what public money the Federal government raises and spends. Whatever taxes are raised by the Federal government are raised by Congress. Whatever funds are spent on government programmes are appropriated by Congress or, increasingly, through entitlements included in authorizing bills which Congress writes. By authorizing programmes, Congress permits them to exist. By appropriating funds for programmes, Congress provides finance for the authorized programmes up to and including the maximum specified in the authorizing legislation. Except for entitlement programmes, no programme can be financed without appropriations being voted.

Entitlement programmes include Social Security, Medicaid, Medicare, and many Veterans' Administration programmes. Expenditure upon them occurs not through Appropriations Bills, but because the authorizing legislation identifies certain groups of citizens as being entitled to receive money or services. In such cases, the authorizing legislation entails expenditure, and the Appropriations Committees lack jurisdiction. Entitlement programmes therefore further enhance the power of tax-writing Committees in both Chambers. Since Social Security and Medicare are financed through the revenue-raising process, both fall within the jurisdiction of the House Ways and Means, and Senate Finance, Committees – thereby affording them control of both taxation for the programmes and the programmes themselves.

Congressional Budget Committees

In 1974, Congress altered significantly the means by which it raised and spent public money. The 1974 Budget and Impoundment Control Act (BICA) established Budget Committees in both Chambers so that the budget might be examined in its entirety. Prior to the Act's passage, the spending and taxing parts of the Budget were not examined as a whole by a single Committee. To set recent budgetary procedures in context, a brief review of the pre-reform system of budget formation is appropriate, particularly because the new Budget Committees did not supplant the old revenue-raising and Appropriations Committees, but supplemented them.

House Ways and Means Committee

The Constitution places the power of taxation with Congress, and grants the House of Representatives primacy in the process. Article I, Section 7, states that: "All bills for raising revenue shall originate in the House of Representatives; but the Senate may propose or concur with amendments as on other bills". The Senate has, therefore, to wait until the House has voted on a Tax Bill before it may act. Once the House has done so, the Senate's freedom of action is complete, thereby enabling the Senate to play a major role if the opportunity exists. Prior to the 1974 Budget reforms, the Ways and Means Committee enjoyed sole jurisdiction over Revenue Bills within the House (and hence, because of the origination clause, initiating power over such Bills).

The Ways and Means Committee was established in 1802, with responsibility for both taxation and appropriations, but its appropriating powers were reduced in the succeeding sixty-three years and extinguished with the founding of the House Appropriations Committee in 1865. Until the Subcommittee Bill of Rights in 1973, Ways and Means enjoyed special influence within the House because it had no Subcommittees. Furthermore, legislation which it reported was sent to the Floor by the Rules Committee under a "closed" rule which permitted no amendment to be tabled. The House was therefore obliged to accept or reject the Bill as a whole, thereby enhancing the Committee's influence over the Bill's fate. Moreover, under the rules of the House, the Committee's business was "privileged", which meant that the Speaker could place it on the Calendar ahead of other business.

Although the seniority rule gave all Chairmen between Speaker Cannon's overthrow in 1910 and the Committee reforms pushed through the Democratic caucus by the large class of Democratic freshmen in January 1975 considerable autonomy, it gave Chairmen of the Ways and Means Committee special influence. The confluence of favourable procedural rules gave Wilbur Mills, Chairman of the Committee from 1957 to 1974, as decisive an influence over fiscal policy as any single elected politician has ever enjoyed in the United States. Until the combination of his personal downfall and internal Congressional reforms, no tax legislation moved into law without his personal *imprimatur*. He knew the United States Tax Code well, appreciated its provisions' significance for different groups and individuals, and was a clinically accurate judge of colleagues' sentiment in Committee and on the House Floor. Mills was, in an era of powerful Chairmen, the most powerful Chairman of the most powerful Committee in Congress.

Senate Finance Committee

The House Ways and Means Committee's counterpart in the Senate is the Finance Committee. Its right to conduct hearings on taxation policy and legislation only after the House has acted has diminished only slightly its influence over fiscal policy. Congress's bicameral structure invariably causes a Bill to be treated differently by the two Chambers; like other legislation, a Tax Bill drafted in two forms is sent to a Conference Committee. Members drawn from Senate Finance, and House Ways and Means determine the Bill's final text, which must then proceed to the Floor of both chambers for a final vote, generally under procedural rules precluding amendment.

Tax-writing Conference Committees

Politics does not stop at the Conference Committee door. Chairmen of the Senate Finance, and House Ways and Means Committees have never been averse to employing Conference Committees as fora in which to secure objectives they have been unable to attain in earlier Congressional deliberations.

Appropriations Committees

Article I, Section 9, of the Constitution decrees that the Federal government spend only those monies properly appropriated:

> No Money shall be drawn from the Treasury, but in Consequence of Appropriations made by Law; and a regular Statement and Account of the Receipts and Expenditures of all public Money shall be published from time to time.

Appropriations Committees may not appropriate funds until the Legislating (Authorizing) Committees have authorized spending levels for a programme. In the twenty-five years prior to the 1974 Budget and Impoundment Control Act, most Legislating Committees authorized programmes annually, thereby reducing the time available to Appropriations Committees subsequently to act, and challenging the political primacy of Appropriations Committees. A frequent consequence of the resulting pressures upon the Congressional timetable has been that Appropriations Bills were often not enacted into law by the beginning of the new fiscal year. The 1974 reforms have not disposed of the problem: new Budget procedures have made punctual completion of appropriating even more difficult. Consequently, when Appropriations Bills lie unenacted by a new fiscal year, Congress must pass a "continuing resolution" for a limited period (sometimes for as short a period as a day or two, occasionally for much longer), by which spending continues at the level for the previous year until a new Appropriations Bill establishes new spending levels. Without appropriations, all but the most essential government activities stop: departments and agencies close, Federal employees are sent home, and fiscal transfers to State and local governments cease. During the rancorous budget negotiations of 1990, Congress passed five continuing resolutions, as successive deadlines for the completion of the appropriations process passed without agreement having been reached.

The full Appropriations Committees are large in order that the thirteen Subcommittees in each chamber should have sufficient members to hold hearings on draft legislation, and thereby to oversee the expenditure of funds appropriated earlier. Since Appropriations Committees in both Chambers regained their power over appropriations in the years following the First World War, appropriating has been undertaken less by full Committees than by Subcommittees. Jurisdictions of the Senate and House Appropriation Committees are identical, and those of their Subcommittees are nearly so. Procedures for appropriations legislation derive from dividing Appropriations Bills between departments and agencies. Thus the work of the House Appropriations Committee is divided between its thirteen Subcommittees, each of which corresponds to an Executive Department or group of agencies, the EOP, the Judiciary, and the Legislature. All are financed by appropriations, providing heavy burdens for the Subcommittees.

Prior to Congressional reform in the early 1970s, the House Committee was composed mainly of senior Congressmen, usually from safe seats and virtually immune to defeat in Primaries or general elections. Their conservatism was expressed in their marginal reduction of Budget requests made by the President. By concentrating the power to appropriate in one Appropriations Committee in each Chamber, the House and the Senate indicated their determination to control spending which, in the peacetime years between the early 1920s and the mid-1960s, they did with remarkable effectiveness.

General Accounting Office

In addition to creating the Bureau of the Budget, the Budget and Accounting Act of 1921 also established the General Accounting Office (GAO), led by the Comptroller General. The Dockery Act of 1894 had established a Comptroller within the Treasury; the 1921 Act altered the Comptroller's status from an Executive official removable by the President to one who, though appointed by the President, could be removed from office only by joint resolution of both houses of Congress. As the creation of the Bureau of the Budget (BOB) reflected the President's growing managerial responsibilities, and its move to the Executive Office EOP in 1939 reflected Congress's recognition of the need for more satisfactory coordination of the Federal government's expenditure, so the GAO's establishment confirmed Congress's intention to oversee the Executive's expenditure of monies which it had appropriated.

Congress will not cede powers without retaining oversight, either directly through Committee hearings, or indirectly through the creation of an agency, owing its primary responsibility and political allegiance to Congress rather than to the Executive. A legislative agency, the GAO is Congress's main investigating arm. Although the bulk of its work is auditing, Congress has also given it the wider remit of examining the Federal government's efficiency and effectiveness. Most of its reports are available publicly.

Congressional Budget Office

Created by the Budget and Impoundment Control Act of 1974 (BICA), the Congressional Budget Office (CBO) is a non-partisan agency of the Legislative Branch, providing objective and impartial analysis of the budget, current and alternative fiscal policies, and the economy generally. Its professional standards are high. Unlike those made by the highly politicized OMB in the EOP, its forecasts of budget deficits are dispassionate; in the past that has often made them a more reliable guide to the likely size of the fiscal deficit. Between 1993 and 1996, however, CBO projections of the budget deficit were little better than OMB's, and both were consistently pessimistic. Tiny errors in forecasts matter, not least because the budget deficits which they project determine the size both of expenditure cuts required and tax cuts that can be afforded. Forecasting errors can therefore have disproportionately large consequences for politicians engaged in bargaining over cuts in programmes required to effect budget cuts.

Objects and Processes of Economic Policy-Making

Policy Objectives and Policy Instruments

In common with the governments of most advanced democracies, the United States government has pursued four economic policy objectives in the post-war period. Conveniently, they are codified in the 1946 Employment Act:

1. Maintenance of high employment.
2. Promotion of economic growth.
3. Maintenance of price stability.
4. Maintenance of a favourable balance of payments.

In pursuit of these purposes, the Federal government nominally has fiscal (taxation and public spending policies), monetary, and trade policy at its disposal. Its objectives have not differed materially from those of other western States. The two primary differences in policy between the United States, and Japan and most western European States, have lain first, in the policy instruments employed, and second, in institutional design. The Federal government has not adopted an industrial policy of the kind that Germany, France, and Japan have had (although many of the fifty States have implemented industrial policies of their own).

The institutional setting within which policy is made in the United States is exceptional. No other central government functions within a comparably tight constitutional straitjacket, still less one tailored in the late eighteenth century. Fragmenting structures fragments process. This is quintessentially so in the case of economic policy, where taxing and spending powers are divided between Congress and the Presidency, and between the Federal government and the States. Article I of the Constitution gives the House precedence over the Senate in the origination of Revenue Bills, requires that all money drawn from the Treasury be in the form of appropriations made by law, and requires that national accounts be published. The presentment clause of Article I introduces the Executive to the fiscal feast by providing that all Bills shall be presented to the President for his signature or veto. On Article I and the Sixteenth Amendment providing for a Federal income tax hang all the constitutional laws enabling and constraining the Federal government in the making of fiscal policy.

Economic Policy Choices

In macroeconomic policy, Presidential relations with Congress are primarily fiscal in nature; and those with the Federal Reserve System, entirely monetary. All economic policy choices are none the less, tightly interrelated. At its simplest, the two consequences of interrelatedness are, first, that a President's decision regarding problem *A* will have consequences for problems *B*, *C*, and *D*, and the range of choice with respect to those problems; second, policy problems have no coherent structural analogues and so fail to fit into tidy organizational channels. The problem of governance for the President is thereby compounded. Macroeconomic policy has throughout the post-war period exemplified both consequences, as Presidents and their advisers have long appreciated.

With a single client, the CEA's advice is untainted by parochial agency perspectives, and so has eased the problem for Presidents' economic leadership of the divisions between the Presidential and Departmental segments of the Executive. None the less, the CEA has not been a panacea for the Executive's maladies. Recent Presidents have established other co-ordinating units, such as Ford's "Economic Policy Board", Bush's "Economic Policy

Council" (EPC), and Clinton's "National Economic Council" to imprint the President's strategic and tactical priorities more fully upon departments. Under President Bush, the EPC was a co-ordinating and advisory body whose meetings were usually chaired by the Secretary of the Treasury. Consisting of the Chairman of the CEA; the United States Trade Representative; the Secretaries of Agriculture, Commerce, Labor, State, and Treasury; and the Director of OMB, the EPC advised President Bush on domestic and international economic policy. The latter was especially important in considering US trade policy in the Uruguay Round of the GATT negotiations: the different interests represented by the several departments which comprise the EPC had no other forum in which policy questions could be considered. The EPC's location in the EOP assisted Bush in formulating policy commanding the support of his Cabinet colleagues in the departments whose interests are most directly at stake in GATT.

The Federal Budget Process Prior to 1974

Roosevelt and his successors used the Budget to set their political priorities between programmes by submitting annual fiscal recommendations to Congress. No other single delegation of power from Congress has done more than this to enable Presidents to set the national agenda. Whether that opportunity is seized and fiscal leadership given (as Roosevelt and Eisenhower did throughout their Presidencies, and Reagan did briefly in 1981) or squandered (as Carter did in 1980, and Reagan did after 1981) depends upon Presidential judgement and skill, and not formal statutory authority.

Prior to the implementation of BICA in the 1976 Fiscal Year (FY76), budgeting was a closed and mainly private process in which no examination was made of the national budget as a whole. Decisions about spending and taxing were made by different politicians in different committees, but budgetary fragmentation did not result in fiscal indiscipline: the seniority rule, the recruitment to Revenue and Appropriations Committees in both Chambers only of those whom Congressional leaders trusted to act responsibly and to defer to the established norms of the Committees, made for tight political control of fiscal policy by Congress. Within the Executive Branch, budgets were drafted incrementally: in submitting their requests to BOB/OMB, agencies typically (and rationally) added a small percentage to their appropriations for the previous fiscal year. The BOB ensured that the many budget requests it examined did not breach the President's overall budget targets.

Congressional Appropriations Subcommittees invariably reduced the budget requests for individual agencies. Departments, agencies, the BOB, and the President expected them to do so – hence the inflated requests made by departments and agencies to the BOB, and by the President to Congress. Congress none the less acceded to incremental budgeting: the economy's steady growth made it affordable and politically attractive by dispensing with the need to set priorities between different categories of spending. Although deficits were usually incurred, the Federal deficit declined as a percentage of GNP. Total Federal debt therefore also grew absolutely, but shrank as a percentage of GNP. Peacetime Budget requests of twentieth-century Presidents were until the late 1960s designed not to result in substantial deficits. Subsequent restraining action of the Appropriations Committees reduced any deficit still further. Congressional tax-writing Committees confirmed this culture of fiscal conservatism by generally resisting attempts to cut income taxes. Even in 1965, the first year of President Lyndon Johnson's "Great Society", when spending on social, welfare and educational policies was rising quickly, the budget deficit was only $1.4 billion – about half the size of the deficit in the peacetime year of 1955 during the fiscally conservative administration of President Eisenhower – and a trivial 0.2 per cent of GNP.

Expenditure on the Vietnam War disrupted stable incremental budgeting. Costing $27 billion per annum by 1967 (a third of total defence appropriations), the war accounted for almost all of the Federal deficit in that year, and burst the institutional banks of financial restraint. Rapidly rising expenditure on the Vietnam War therefore destabilized Government finances, led to the unsettling of the dollar, and to the inflation that engulfed the American economy in the 1970s. Struggles over how to finance the war unhinged not only the Revenue Committees but also the Appropriations Committees of both Chambers, and damaged relations between them.

In theory, Appropriations Committees retained complete authority to appropriate funds within the limits set by the authorizing or Legislative Committee. In practice, controls exercised by Appropriations Committees diminished significantly from the 1960s onwards, for three reasons:

1. The very act of *authorizing* a programme vests it in practice with a claim upon *appropriations*. The capacity of the Appropriations Committees to resist authorizing legislation either by declining to appropriate, or by appropriating at levels significantly below those authorized, is limited. Powerful as both Committees were, their members were bound to take account of political pressures from elsewhere in Congress. This pressure intensified with the practice of Authorizing Committees in the years after 1945 not to make permanent authorizations (thereby effectively ceding funding decisions to Appropriations Committees), but temporary ones for a year or two (thereby keeping Appropriations Committees on a shorter political leash).

2. An increasing proportion of Congressional spending has by-passed the Appropriations Committees in the post-war years. A large proportion of Johnson's "Great Society" programmes were funded by long-term contract authority not subject to annual review by Appropriations

Committees. The decreasing proportion of the budget that is in fact controllable under current law by the Appropriations Committees is examined below.

3. The House Appropriations Committee's closed meetings, its culture of fiscal conservatism, its hierarchical structure, and the protection of its legislation on the Floor of the House, were all altered by the wave of Congressional reforms of the early 1970s. The dispersal of authority within the House had special significance for "Control" Committees such as Ways and Means and Appropriations, whose authority and standing had depended heavily upon them. The decision of the House Democratic caucus in 1974 to make appointment to Chairs of Appropriations Subcommittees subject to full party caucus votes in Congress significantly weakened their autonomy. Furthermore, the powers of Appropriations and tax-writing committees were modified by the 1974 budget reforms.

The Budget and Impoundment Control Act (1974)

The Budget and Impoundment Control Act of 1974, the single most important reform of economic policy-making since the 1946 Employment Act, arose out of the growing fiscal disorder between 1968 and 1973 and the wider institutional conflict between Congress and the Executive during the Nixon Presidency. Vast expenditure on the Vietnam War in the late 1960s, coupled with growing domestic spending, the circumvention of established appropriations control procedures, and the political divisiveness of raising income taxes and cutting domestic spending in 1968, had placed budget-making under severe strain by the time Nixon became President (see Tables 11.1 and 11.2). Facing opposition majorities in both the House and the Senate, Nixon attempted to govern without Congress, a strategy which the Constitution ensured would eventually fail but which did so only at a damagingly high cost.

Where Congress appropriated funds to programmes of which Nixon disapproved, he impounded them. Prevented from vetoing parts of Appropriations Bills (the "line-item" veto which the Governors of forty-three States possess, and which in April 1996 Congress granted to Presidents in the weak form of an enhanced rescission power), Presidents Truman, Eisenhower, and Kennedy had all impounded funds which Congress had added to their defence budgets for particular projects. Nixon's use of impoundment was on a different scale and of a different kind: appropriations above the amounts he requested were commonly reduced to his preferred levels or abolished altogether. Bellicosity marked all President Nixon's dealings with Congress, but unashamedly so with respect to budgetary politics. He declined to recognise what was plain in Constitutional Law and in Statute: the White House's budgetary recommendations had no

TABLE 11.1

Outlays by Budget Enforcement Act Categories, 1962–98 (in billions of US dollars)

Fiscal year	Defense	Programmatic spending	Domestic discretionary spending	Net interest	Total
1962	52.6	33.1	14.0	6.9	106.8
1963	53.7	34.1	16.3	7.7	111.3
1964	55.0	36.9	19.5	8.2	118.5
1965	51.0	37.8	22.1	8.6	118.2
1966	59.0	41.6	26.1	9.4	134.5
1967	72.0	48.0	29.1	10.3	157.5
1968	82.2	57.1	30.9	11.1	178.1
1969	82.7	61.7	30.5	12.7	183.6
1970	81.9	69.7	34.3	14.4	195.6
1971	79.0	83.0	39.7	14.8	210.2
1972	79.3	96.3	44.5	15.5	230.7
1973	77.1	111.5	48.3	17.3	245.7
1974	80.7	126.6	51.1	21.4	269.4
1975	87.6	164.9	62.0	23.2	332.3
1976	89.9	184.2	77.9	26.7	371.8
1977	97.5	197.4	91.3	29.9	409.2
1978	104.6	220.6	105.3	35.4	458.7
1979	116.8	239.2	113.8	42.6	503.5
1980	134.6	282.3	128.7	52.5	590.9
1981	158.0	329.8	136.1	68.7	678.2
1982	185.9	361.0	127.0	85.0	745.7
1983	209.9	399.4	129.7	89.8	808.3
1984	228.0	393.5	134.9	111.1	851.8
1985	253.1	434.0	145.2	129.5	946.3
1986	273.8	449.1	146.8	136.0	990.3
1987	282.5	463.8	146.3	138.7	1,003.8
1988	290.9	493.0	157.7	151.8	1,064.1
1989	304.0	530.0	168.1	169.3	1,143.7
1990	300.1	605.2	181.2	184.2	1,243.2
1991	319.7	635.9	193.9	194.5	1,324.4
1992	302.6	687.1	212.7	199.4	1,381.7
1993	292.4	707.0	226.9	198.8	1,403.4
1994	282.3	752.7	240.8	203.0	1,451.7
1995	273.6	782.4	252.0	232.2	1,515.7
1996	266.0	822.5	250.1	241.1	1,560.3
1997	268.0	880.1	262.5	247.4	1,631.0
1998	260.1	945.7	268.0	249.9	1,687.5

Source: Office of Management and Budget. *The Budget for the Fiscal Year 1998. Historical Tables*, Table 8.1

TABLE 11.2

Revenues, Outlays, Deficit, and Debt Held by the Public, $billions:
Deficit as Percentage of GNP, 1962–94

Fiscal	Total revenues	Total outlays	Deficit (−) or surplus (current $billions)	Deficit (−) or surplus (as percentage of GDP)	Gross Federal debt
1962	99.7	106.8	−7.1	−1.3	302,928
1963	106.6	111.3	−4.8	−0.8	310,324
1964	112.6	118.5	−5.9	−0.9	316,059
1965	116.8	118.2	−1.4	−0.2	322,318
1966	130.8	134.5	−3.7	−0.5	328,498
1967	148.8	157.5	−8.6	−1.1	340,445
1968	153.0	178.1	−25.2	−2.9	368,685
1969	186.9	183.6	3.2	0.3	365,769
1970	192.8	195.6	−2.8	−0.3	380,921
1971	187.1	210.2	−23.0	−2.1	408,176
1972	207.3	230.7	−23.4	−2.0	435,936
1973	230.8	245.7	−14.9	−1.1	466,291
1974	263.2	269.4	−6.1	−0.4	483,893
1975	279.1	332.3	−53.2	−3.4	541,925
1976	298.1	371.8	−73.7	−4.3	628,970
1977	355.6	409.2	−53.6	−2.7	706,398
1978	399.6	458.7	−59.2	−2.7	776,602
1979	463.3	503.5	−40.2	−1.6	829,470
1980	517.1	590.9	−73.8	−2.7	909,050
1981	599.3	678.2	−78.9	−2.6	994,845
1982	617.8	745.7	−127.9	−4.0	1,137,345
1983	600.6	808.3	−207.8	−6.1	1,371,710
1984	666.5	851.8	−185.3	−4.9	1,564,657
1985	734.1	946.3	−212.3	−5.2	1,817,521
1986	769.1	990.3	−221.2	−5.1	2,210,629
1987	854.1	1,003.8	−149.7	−3.3	2,346,125
1988	909.3	1,064.5	−155.1	−3.1	2,601,307
1989	991.2	1,143.7	−152.5	−2.8	2,868,039
1990	1,032.0	1,253.2	−221.2	−3.9	3,206,564
1991	1,055.0	1,324.4	−269.4	−4.6	3,598,498
1992	1,091.3	1,381.7	−290.4	−4.7	4,002,136
1993	1,154.4	1,409.4	−255.0	−3.9	4,351,416
1994	1,258.6	1,461.7	−203.1	−3.0	4,643,705

Source: Congressional Budget Office, *The Economic and Budget Outlook: Fiscal Years 1990–1994,* drawn from Tables F-1 and F-2, pp. 130–1; Office of Management and Budget, *The Budget for the Fiscal Year 1998,* Historical Tables, Table 1.3.

privileged standing, and Presidents were obliged to implement public laws, regardless of whether they approved of them. Laws appropriating funds to government programmes were in this respect no different from other public laws; Congress's authority to mandate spending was constitutionally incontestable.

Nixon none the less resisted, forcing Congress to sue Cabinet Secretaries to ensure that appropriations should be spent as required by law. As impoundments of defence appropriations undertaken by Truman, Eisenhower, and Kennedy suggest, Congress has in any case declined to eliminate all Presidential spending discretion for fear of being seen to abridge the President's role as Commander-in-Chief. Recognizing the desirability of granting Presidents some discretion over the spending of appropriated funds, the 1974 Act legitimised two forms of impoundment – rescissions and deferrals – under specified conditions. The Act required that for appropriated funds to be rescinded (cancelled altogether) according to Presidential wishes, the House and Senate would have to pass a Bill or a Joint Resolution of Congress within forty-five days of continuous Congressional session following the President's action. The Act set a less demanding condition for the sustaining of a Presidential decision to defer the spending of lawfully-appropriated funds: in this case, either the House or the Senate had to veto the proposed deferral for it to be halted.

INS v. *Chadha,* 462 US 919 (1983), which declared vetoes of executive actions by one house of Congress unconstitutional, removed the constitutional basis for deferrals under the 1974 Act. In *City of New Haven* v. *United States,* 809 F.2d 900 (DC Cir 1987), plaintiffs from Congress and several city governments brought suit in Federal District Court, challenging President Reagan's deferral in his 1987 Budget of funds appropriated for urban aid programs, arguing that had the constitutionality of a one-house veto been in doubt when the 1974 Act was passed, the contingent powers of deferral would not have been granted to the President. The plaintiffs won their case in District Court and the judgment was sustained unanimously by the Circuit Court in January 1987. Congress subsequently incorporated the Appeal Court ruling in its revisions to the Gramm–Rudman–Hollings Act of 1985 (as explained below). That Act prohibits deferrals on the grounds of policy disagreement, permitting them under three conditions only: for contingencies, emergencies, and as permitted by particular laws. Deferrals are regarded as being approved unless specifically disapproved by either House of Congress (an indication of the extent to which Congress ignored the provisions of *INS* v. *Chadha*). Congress's codification of procedures governing deferral and rescission has made impossible any future emulation of Nixon's defiance, but, especially in the wake of the enhanced rescission powers passed into law in 1996, permits greater Presidential discretion than was allowed before 1974.

The 1974 Budget Act addressed three problems:

1. Presidential *abuse of impoundment*.
2. The growing difficulty Congress faced in formulating a *coherent fiscal policy* in the wake of the oil price shock of October 1973 (especially with respect to the increasing difficulty Congress had in passing Appropriations Bills before the beginning of the fiscal year to which they referred).
3. Widespread dissatisfaction with what appeared an *uncontrolled growth* in Federal expenditure.

The first problem concerned the balance of power between Congress and the Presidency, the second the inadequacy of Congress's own procedures for formulating policy, and the third the Federal government's capacity to determine priorities and enable members of Congress and Senators to make difficult budgetary choices. To these ends, the Act established new House and Senate Budget Committees, and a Congressional Budget Office providing a centre of economic expertise (thereby enabling Congress to subject budget analyses and estimates from OMB to its own critical analysis). A new budget calendar was set, the beginning of the fiscal year moved from July to October, and a clear timetable for budget decisions was established. The new Budget Committees did not supplant the existing Appropriations and Tax-writing Committees, but supplemented them: the resulting timetable has therefore to accommodate separate but contingent decisions by the Budget, Appropriations, and Tax Committees. This muddled and unsatisfactory compromise occurred because of the unwillingness of members of the established (and prestigious) Appropriations, Senate Finance, and House Ways and Means committees to risk losing influence in a comprehensively reformed fiscal policy committee structure.

The Act stipulates that in March of every fiscal year, House and Senate Budget Committees examine reports from other committees on the budgets for programmes falling within their jurisdictions. The Budget Committees then prepare a first resolution which, since revisions to the procedure in 1981, has set a ceiling on spending and a floor on revenue on the first day of the next fiscal year, unless Congress decides to adopt a second resolution. It was this first budget resolution, coupled with the binding reconciliation procedures originally included in the second resolution set for passage by September, which Reagan exploited in 1981 to secure heavy cuts in previously-authorized spending over a three-year period.

Neither the Appropriations Committees nor the Tax-writing Committees in the two Chambers enjoy in the last years of the century the positions of privilege they once did, despite rules being set for the two Budget Committees which have limited their effectiveness. The Appropriations Committees operate under tight fiscal constraints: the Gramm–Rudman–Hollings Act I and II, coupled with the Omnibus Budget Reconciliation Act (OBRA) of

1990, and the Budget Act of 1997 have jointly greatly reduced the freedom of action appropriators previously enjoyed. While that part of the Federal budget that is controllable under current law by Appropriations Committees is small, it is upon these programmes that most budgetary restraint was focused until Congress belatedly (in the mid-1990s) turned to the problem presented by the growth of entitlements.

Appropriations Subcommittee Chairpersons have adjusted to Budget Committee ceilings by exploiting such freedom of manoeuvre as they continue to retain. Nominally, their freedom is considerable, since the Committee exercises control over the salaries of all Federal employees (including themselves, but excluding the President and Federal Judges, whose incomes are Constitutionally protected), defence, education, housing, transport, and over Federal programmes, scientific research institutes, and grants-in-aid to State and local governments. In practice, new spending may now be undertaken only where cuts are made in other programmes; the room for manoeuvre is consequently small, and their power reduced commensurately. Special additions to appropriations in order to appease or please colleagues must be matched by reductions elsewhere.

Renewed Budget Reform (1985): The Gramm–Rudman–Hollings Act (I)

Budget reform in 1985 was prompted by the unprecedented growth in peacetime of the fiscal deficit. Introduced in the Senate in September of 1985, the Balanced Budget and Emergency Deficit Control Act was signed into law by President Reagan within three months. The operation's haste reflected widespread anxiety about the apparent inability of President and Congress to control expenditure. Named Gramm–Rudman–Hollings (GRH) after its principal sponsors, the Act required Congress to pass one budget resolution instead of two, and made reconciliation of overall targets for expenditure with taxation obligatory rather than optional. Reconciliation had never been used on the second resolution as the 1974 Act specified but, because of timetabling pressures after the passage of all the authorization, appropriations, and taxation legislation, solely on the first. As S. Collender has noted, GRH also obliged Congress to include reconciliation instructions in budget resolutions (Collender, 1990):

> Every budget resolution must "to the extent necessary to effectuate the provisions and requirements of such resolution" specify the amount by which new budget authority, budget authority provided in previous years, new entitlement authority, credit authority, and revenues must be changed.

Furthermore, each budget resolution had under GRH also to direct individual Committees in the House and the Senate to recommend changes in laws falling within their jurisdictions to achieve the spending changes required. Committees are therefore instructed by the resolution to enforce assumed reductions or increases in taxation and spending. Apportioning the changes is a matter for the Committees. Progressively declining deficit ceilings were written into law, and sequestration procedures were instituted for cuts in spending to be made automatically if deficit ceilings ("maximum deficit amounts") were breached. Statutory obligation automatically applied enabled politicians to avoid making unpalatable choices. In the event, however, the deficit in Fiscal Year (FY) 1986, the first year of GRH's operation, exceeded the ceiling by $50 billion, so making attempts to comply with the Act even harder. Reflecting political hostility and distrust between the Democratic House majority and the Republican administration, GRH made detailed provision for sequestration procedures. Anxious to prevent OMB controlling sequestration, and aware of the constitutional difficulty that would flow from placing responsibility with CBO (since it was a wholly Congressional agency), GRH allocated responsibility to the GAO whose head, the Comptroller-General, is appointed by the President but (uniquely) subject to removal by Congress.

Challenges to and Later Revision of the 1985 Act (GRH II)

Immediately after the passage of GRH, Democratic Congressman Mike Synar brought suit in Federal District Court challenging the law's constitutionality. The Court held that Congress had acted unconstitutionally by vesting executive power in an officer subject to removal by Congress. The Supreme Court subsequently upheld the District Court's judgment, in *Charles A. Bowsher* v. *Mike Synar et al.*, 478 US 714 (1986). The White House, alarmed more by the prospect of defence cuts than the deficit's growth, submitted an *amicus curiae* brief supporting Synar's suit. Since the point and purpose of Congress seeking a means for implementing sequesters was that it would be automatic and that Congress would have no immediate, direct control over it, the loss of the automatic provision vitiated GRH.

When, in the summer of 1987, the government approached the limits of its borrowing authority, Senator Gramm used the bill providing for an extension of the borrowing limit to pass a new version of GRH. President Reagan's displeasure at the prospect of defence cuts being imposed by a revised sequester process was exceeded only by his determination to veto any legislation providing for a tax increase. The President and many of his Republican allies, who had so frequently criticised Congress for fiscal irresponsibility had, however, painted themselves into a corner. Reluctantly, the President signed the Balanced Budget and Emergency Deficit Reaffirmation Act (GRH II) into law in the autumn of 1987. It set FY 1993 for the final disappearance of the Federal deficit, either through Congress's own budget cuts, or by automatic sequesters administered by OMB.

Although the constitutionality of the new procedure was not in doubt, GRH II's fiscal provisions were implausible. Crucially, the law did not stipulate that the actual deficit had to meet the target, merely that the projected deficit do so. That flaw enabled Congressional politicians to manipulate economic assumptions in order to comply technically with the law while failing to contain either the general growth in federal spending or, under the sting of interest groups defending the huge social security, Medicare, and veterans' programmes, the growth in mandatory programmes uncontrollable under appropriations law.

It remains one of the striking characteristics of the Federal budget process that Presidents and Congresses declare their support for a "balanced budget" (usually without specifying what they mean by it) without proposing one (as any President could) or writing one (as any Congress could). Declaring support for fiscal virtue requires less political courage than practising it.

Omnibus Budget Reconciliation Act (OBRA) of 1990

The failure of GRH II stimulated further corrective action in 1990, in the form of the Budget Enforcement Act (formally, Title XII of the Omnibus Budget Reconciliation Act (OBRA) of 1990) which provided for a clear distinction between discretionary and mandatory spending. As James Thurber has argued (Thurber, 1996), the BEA, passed in implicit recognition of GRH II's failure to effect reductions in the actual deficit, was constructed in an attempt to force politicians to make zero-sum choices between different expenditures and different taxing options. The attempt to set binding deficit reduction targets was abandoned; however, budget procedures were centralized, so enhancing the Congressional Leadership's power. The BEA's main provisions were:

- Congress's freedom to propose extra spending was further restricted, with the qualification that increases in the size of the fiscal deficit in the event of war or recession were permitted. Appropriations bills had to comply with spending caps for defence, foreign aid, and discretionary domestic spending, adjusted for inflation, for FYs 1991–3. Appropriations that broke the caps were not to be brought to the Floor of either Chamber.
- Automatic spending cuts under GRH were replaced by three "sequesters", taking effect fifteen days after Congress adjournments. The first offset only those discretionary appropriations exceeding statutory limits; the second offset increases in entitlement payments designated as "non-exempt" in law (a small proportion of total entitlements); the third took effect only if the first two had not eliminated the excess deficit, but covered all non-exempt spending.
- Authorizing Bills increasing entitlements, and Taxation Bills reducing revenue, were not to be considered for action on the Floor of either

Chamber unless offset by cuts in other entitlements or increases in other revenues.

- Social Security receipts and expenditures were no longer included in Budget calculations. The trust fund into which social security payments were made was in substantial surplus because the number of people in employment will grow to the century's end. Its removal from the calculation reduced the political difficulty caused to Senators and Representatives by pressure to reduce entitlement spending, but increased the likelihood of larger deficits.

The BEA also enhanced OMB's influence over legislative proposals from executive agencies by requiring it to determine the fiscal consequences of every proposal for entitlement payments. Since the law limited discretionary spending and required that entitlement increases be offset by revenue increases or entitlement cuts elsewhere, the power of the Congressional Budget Committees over the Budget was reduced, and confined to determining expenditure priorities within each of three discretionary spending categories. Automatic procedures therefore largely displaced decision-making by politicians, indicating that Congressional procedures for aggregating interests have been significantly weakened since the mid-1960s.

The BEA was effectively extended until FY 1998 by President Clinton's five-year deficit reduction plan embodied in the Omnibus Budget Reconciliation Act of 1993. The means for the accumulated deficit reduction of $500 billion over the five FYs 1994–8 were further restraints upon discretionary programmes, and a range of tax increases (which Republicans exploited to the President's disadvantage in public opinion polls, and to the advantage of Mr Gingrich and his conservative Republican colleagues in their successful battle to gain a House majority in 1994). Although the BEA's rules helped to contain discretionary spending, a major restraining influence was that the end of the Cold War permitted large cumulative cuts to be made in defence appropriations. President Clinton's preference for cutting the fiscal deficit rather than alleviating poverty among the poorest Americans indicated his abandonment of his Democratic Presidential predecessors' broadly liberal commitments since the Social Security Act of 1935. That preference was confirmed by his decision shortly before the Presidential election of 1996 to sign legislation which abolished the main Federal welfare programme, Aid to Families with Dependent Children. Strikingly, Clinton evinced no enthusiasm for cutting the major programmatic entitlement programmes of Medicare and Social Security, each of which was heavily protected by the votes and interest representation of many millions of middle-class recipients.

The New Republican Majority

The politics of budget-making were altered by the Republicans' gaining of a majority in the Congressional mid-term elections of 1994. One of the main planks in the Republicans' "Contract with America" was a proposal to amend the Constitution to require a balanced budget. Under the leadership of Newt Gingrich at the height of his powers as Speaker in January 1995, the House passed the proposal by 300 to 132, but the measure just failed to win passage in the Senate. Later attempts to revive the proposal also met with defeat.

As the Republicans had successfully exploited the Democrats' support for Clinton's tax rises in the 1993 budget negotiations, so Clinton successfully attacked the Republicans in 1996 for having twice forced the closure of federal agencies in the winter of 1995/6 as part of their campaign to secure a budget deal satisfactory to them. Whereas it had previously normally been the case that continuing resolutions were passed to enable the federal government to continue in operation, Gingrich and his allies in the Republican House leadership, their calculations distorted by inflated ambition, decided in 1995 to force the issue. As Senator Dole had rightly warned, the Speaker's tactic was a disastrous political error: Gingrich's sway over Republican House colleagues fell sharply as the full extent of public displeasure became apparent. Mr Clinton, accomplished at the politics of adjusting his own political position to that of the median voter, prospered through successfully stigmatizing Gingrich and his allies as extremists while actually embracing fiscal austerity.

The 1997 Balanced Budget Agreement

Clinton's drift to fiscal conservatism moved a stage further in the summer of 1997 with his support for a Fiscal 1998 budget resolution heavily promoted by the Republican majority (see Table 11.3). The House Concurrent Resolution 84 provided for a balanced budget by 2002 to be achieved by net reductions in the deficit of more than $204 billion. Significant spending reductions were effected in mandatory programmes, sharpening the burden of deficit reduction on the poor, who had already suffered heavy reductions with the cuts in the food stamps programme and the abolition of AFDC in 1996: cuts of $115 billion over five years were effected in Medicare (serving 37 million elderly and disabled Americans); and of $16 billion in Medicaid (serving some 42 million poor children, women, and impoverished disabled and elderly). Tax changes included reductions in capital gains and estate taxes, and tax credits for children.

Monetary Policy

Powers and Actions of the Federal Reserve Board

As earlier discussion showed, the President lacks even nominal direct control over monetary policy. The power to set the discount rate is the Federal Reserve Board's alone, giving it special responsibility for the achievement of

TABLE 11.3

The 1997 Budget Agreement : Spending Outlays by Functional Category

Fiscal Year	1997	1998	1999	2000	2001	2002
Science, space and technology	17.0	16.9	16.5	16.0	15.9	15.7
Energy	1.9	2.2	2.4	2.3	2.0	1.9
Natural resources	22.4	22.4	22.7	23.0	22.7	22.3
Agriculture	9.9	11.0	11.3	10.7	9.5	9.1
Commerce, housing credit	−9.6	1.8	3.3	8.6	11.6	12.8
Transportation	39.5	40.9	41.3	41.4	41.3	41.2
Community development	12.1	10.4	10.9	11.0	11.4	8.4
Education, social services	50.5	56.1	59.3	60.7	61.9	62.3
Health	127.4	137.8	144.9	153.9	163.1	171.7
Medicare	191.3	201.8	211.5	225.5	238.8	250.8
Income security	237.8	247.8	258.1	268.2	277.3	285.2
Social security	366.4	384.1	402.8	422.8	443.9	466.8
Veterans	39.4	41.3	41.9	42.2	42.5	42.7
Courts, police, prisons	20.7	22.6	24.5	25.2	25.9	24.9
Defence	266.6	266.0	265.8	268.4	270.1	272.6
International affairs	14.5	14.6	14.6	15.0	14.8	14.8
General government	13.9	14.0	14.4	14.7	14.1	13.1
Net interest	247.6	248.6	252	247.7	241.7	236.9
Offsetting receipts	−47.4	−48.8	−44.4	−46.0	−50.0	−64.1
Total Spending	**1,622.1**	**1,692.2**	**1,753.9**	**1,811.1**	**1,858.5**	**1,889.1**
Revenues	**1,544.9**	**1,601.8**	**1,644.2**	**1,728.1**	**1,805.1**	**1,890.4**
Deficit (−) or surplus	**−67.2**	**−90.4**	**−89.7**	**−83.0**	**53.3**	**1.3**

Source: House Budget Committee.

economic stability (and especially for the containment of inflation) by manipulating short-term interest rates. Institutional control of United States economic policy is, therefore, bicephalous. Moreover, the contrast between the formation of monetary and of fiscal policy is sharp. Monetary policy is developed in a small, cohesive, unit whose members are more respectful of technical analysis than of electoral pressures, and whose institutional circumstances facilitate the making of technical judgements and exempt them from electoral reprisal. By contrast, fiscal policy has since the early 1970s been developed and implemented publicly in conditions of extreme electoral sensitivity in open hearings and mark-up sessions of Congressional Committees and Subcommittees.

The quasi-autonomous Federal Reserve provides an appropriate means whereby both President and Congress may influence indirectly the formation of monetary policy while exempting themselves from blame for its consequences. Congress thereby acknowledges its limited capacity to form policy quickly and coherently. Equally, successive Presidents have acknowledged that Congresses will withhold from them greater influence over monetary policy than that granted by the Federal Reserve Act of 1913. Congress is a full constitutional participant in economic policy-making. Its bicameral, fragmented, condition prevents it from exercising leadership in circumstances where speed of response and technically-informed anticipation are at a premium. The Board may accommodate fiscal policy, or move against it. In the long term, its ability to counteract the decisions of elected politicians is slight; in the short term, it may act autonomously, as it did in the latter part of Carter's Presidency. The Board works through three policy instruments, each exercised (in ways that doubtless cause President Andrew Jackson to turn in his grave) through the Federal Reserve's trading office in New York:

1. It may buy Treasury bonds from private brokers or sell them in "open-market operations". Purchases from brokers increase banks' reserves (directly so if bonds are bought from banks themselves; indirectly if through brokers who then deposit the proceeds from the sale). Increased reserves leach through to increased Treasury bond purchases, which raise their price, decrease interest rates on bonds in the Treasury market, increase the money supply, and so stimulate private spending. Selling Treasury bonds reverses this sequence of events. In practice, the Board is constantly engaged in the markets, pushing prices and rates of government securities in their perfectly inversely varying directions.
2. It may encourage or discourage bank borrowing by lowering or raising the "discount rate" – the rate of interest which it charges on short-term (fifteen days or less) loans to banks or other depository institutions.
3. It may alter the reserve requirement ratio which it imposes upon banks.

Of the many difficulties to which regulation of interest rates by these three means gives rise, the consequential problem of reconciling fiscal and monetary policy is perhaps the greatest. Difficult enough intellectually, the structure and culture of United States government render it yet harder. The Employment Act of 1946 was not directed to the Federal Reserve Board or its role, although in Congressional hearings in 1952, the Board graciously indicated that it was willing to accept the objectives of the Act "provided it is explicitly within the framework of a stable price level". In fiscal policy, by contrast, no such arrangement exists. If monetary policy is made by unelected experts in private, then fiscal policy is formed by elected amateurs in public. Significantly, too, professional staff on Congressional Committees and Subcommittees, and those who work for individual Members of Congress and Senators, are less insulated by professional cultures and norms than are the members of the Federal Reserve.

Processes of Economic Policy-Making: An Assessment

Three explanations can be advanced for the fiscal crisis in which the United States became enmired after 1981:

1. The *new processes* were themselves to blame.
2. The deficit results from the *policy choices* made by the Reagan Administration and accepted by Congress in 1981.
3. Institutional reform made the *formation* and *legitimation* of fiscal policy more difficult.

In support of item 1 above three arguments have been advanced: first, that privacy and closure were prerequisites for institutional disaggregation to be overcome and aggregate budgetary outcomes to be consistent internally and with Presidential preferences; second, that the openness of policy processes has encouraged greater interest group influence over policy, and increased the difficulty which members of Congress have in resisting them; and finally, that the Budget process ought to be regarded as part of the wave of Congressional reforms in the mid-1970s which have made Congress a more responsive representative institution, but one that is less capable of aggregating interests.

In support of item 2, it has been contended, first, that the correlation between institutional reform and fiscal chaos is spurious and that, as Hogan (1985) argued, changed political and economic conditions have disrupted old orders. Second, it is argued that the source of the structural deficit lies in the Reagan Administration's failure to reduce entitlement spending in 1981, and its increase in defence spending by 42 per cent in real terms between FY 1981 and FY 1988. Third, the revenue base was driven down. Congress's passage of the Economic Recovery Tax Act in 1981 reduced Federal revenues by $749 billion between FY 1982 and FY 1986. A correction in 1982 of approximately $100 billion altered the speed, but not the downward direction, of the Federal government's revenue base. Fourth, Reagan's budgetary exercises were predicated upon optimistic economic assumptions. Some within the Reagan Administration knew perfectly well that the result would be large and growing deficits, but anticipated that Congress would respond by cutting domestic spending still further. To a limited extent, it did so: starting in 1982, Congress reduced spending and increased taxes in 1983, 1984, 1985, and 1987, but expenditure was not cut to the level required to hold the deficit steady. The explanation for the failure is that most of the budget was, and is, either uncontrollable under existing authorization law (Social Security and Medicare are clear examples); uncontrollable if the United States were not to breach international obligations (interest payments on the national debt); or ran counter to the President's wishes (defence spending was to increase in real terms by historically large amounts in peacetime). The remainder accounted for only a small proportion of Federal expenditure.

In support of item 3 is an integrated institutional approach predicated on the assumption that institutions matter and that they shape policy outcomes. Institutional structures and rules do not determine such outcomes, but condition them. Thus, the failure of the 1974 Act and subsequent reforms to establish an entirely new committee structure for fiscal policy, and the provision in the House for rotation of the Chair is explained by the threat to existing bases of power, promotion to which had governed Congressional politicians' career planning and calculations. The Budget Committees were thereby weakened, and their capacity to make enforceable collective choices for Congress as a whole diminished. They are able to overcome this weakness only on exceptional occasions. Reagan's exploitation in 1981 of the reconciliation provisions of the first Budget Resolution under the procedures amended in 1980 is the best example of the interaction of procedure and political opportunity.

For many, the inadequacy of Budget processes since 1974 is revealed by the rarity with which the making of fiscal policy overcomes particularistic interests, ironically illustrated by the later incapacity of Congress to make good the fiscal damage done by choices made in 1981. Current institutional structures in Congress offer weak incentives to elected politicians for the overcoming of electoral and interest group pressures. Presidents Reagan and Bush renounced fiscal policy as an instrument of macroeconomic stability, with the consequence that disproportionate emphasis during their administrations was placed on monetary policy (over which they exercise at best marginal influence). Congressional direction of fiscal policy has, since 1981, largely been devoted to addressing the aggregate consequences of the sharp upward thrust given to the fiscal deficit by President Reagan's spending and taxing policies in that year. By the end of 1986, Reagan had accumulated a larger aggregate fiscal deficit than all his thirty-nine predecessors combined: the national debt nearly trebled during the eight years in which he occupied the White House. Institutional reform did not make fiscal deficits of unprecedented size and proportion in peacetime inevitable, but did reduce the obstacles to their creation. Had such proposals come before the four revenue and Appropriations Committees of the House and the Senate in the period before the reforms to Committee rules and the Budget process of the early to mid-1970s (themselves products of the poisonous distrust that had arisen between the White House and Congress), it is unlikely they would have made legislative progress. In 1981, they made a rapid, though ill-considered, passage into law.

Differences between the institutional circumstances governing the formation of fiscal and monetary policy have had damaging political consequences since 1981 because of the ideological crusade on behalf of income tax rate cuts, huge increases in defence spending financed by borrowing on international capital markets, and deficient policy processes. When ideological fervour informs the formation of public financial policy, as it did in the early 1980s, modified institutional barriers were too weak to resist, while the incentives for elected politicians to remedy the error were for too long insufficient.

Conclusion

The worst of the fiscal stress is well past: as a proportion of GNP, the fiscal deficit peaked in 1983 at 6.3 per cent, and fell thereafter until recession caused it to rise in 1990. With the ending of growth in the defence budget in real terms from 1985 onwards, and the onset of absolute reductions from 1990 as the collapse of the Soviet Union became apparent, the budget deficit shrank as a proportion of GNP to less than 2.0 per cent by 1996. That reduction was achieved only with the aid of a vigorous and prolonged period of economic expansion (and so of growth in Federal revenues). Current institutional processes provide inadequate solutions to major fiscal crises because they provide powerful incentives for elected politicians to support favoured programmes and to reject the deficit that results. Institutions whose rules reward irresponsibility risk failure.

Making fiscal policy has, since the growth of Federal budget deficits in the early 1970s and the contemporaneous internal reforms of Congress, never been less than disordered, and on occasion incapacitated. Fiscal policy in Washington is formed in an institutional setting and through political processes which now exaggerate rather than mitigate the weakness of the central State, the disaggregation of the Congressional policy-making process, and its permeability to external influence. Important institutional controls, a neutral and expert BOB in the Executive Branch, powerful and semi-autonomous Taxation and Appropriations Committees in Congress which have shared interests in fiscal order, have been undermined by internal reform and the entrepreneurial independence of legislators whose incentives to reach rational aggregate outcomes are insufficient for the public interest to be achieved. In this unpromising setting, the incoherence of the President's 1981 fiscal package and the diminishing share of the Federal Budget that is effectively controllable, have together produced historically high fiscal deficits, a reduced revenue base, and a quadrupled national debt. During most of the 1980s, it also produced a large external deficit (which is linked to the fiscal deficit because of the low savings ratio in the United States), and a residually chaotic policy in respect of the external value of the dollar.

Government's general purpose is to effect collective action which cannot be undertaken by private individuals, associations, or corporations. This task is necessarily difficult in the United States because of the fragmentation that characterises its political institutions. Reforms of the budget processes at both ends of Pennsylvania Avenue and changes in Congress's committee structure, culture, and rules perversely made the task of effecting collective action in pursuit of collective economic policy purposes even harder. In conjunction with muddled and incoherent policy choices, the results were for too long deeply damaging.

12

Foreign and Defence Policy

Foreign Policy, Defence Policy, and the National Interest

The United States is the world's sole superpower. Its economy is the largest in the world and its armed forces the most potent. No other State has the capacity and will to project force around the globe or in the air above it. Nor does any other State commit such vast financial, technical, and human resources to gathering intelligence about the military, political, diplomatic and commercial capacities and intentions of other States, whether friendly or hostile. The formation of United States foreign policy, the means of its implementation, and the ends to which policy is directed, are of critical significance to the international political system. They also affect scholarly understanding of American government itself, since competitive struggles within and between institutions of government occur over foreign and defence policy as much as over domestic policy: this chapter examines these processes. Policy content is considered only in so far as it illuminates structure and process.

Too much can be made of the majority opinion in *United States* v. *Curtiss-Wright Export Corporation*, 299 US 304 (1936), which is usually, but erroneously, identified as the definitive judgment on the broad and implied powers of the President in foreign affairs (in contrast to his limited and specified powers in domestic ones). Justice Sutherland's judgment set only distant boundaries to Presidential power, but the President's powers are in practice more vigorously contested than the Juctice's breathless account might suggest. While greater than in domestic policy, and while Presidents have from the first exercised powers which they claim to be implied by Article II of the Constitution (see Appendix 1), their realizable extent is shaped by the exigencies of politics, Congressional support, and public opinion. Without the latter two, implied powers amount to little over the long term; with them, they can occasionally be as great as Sutherland wrongly suggested they always are.

While defence policy should *serve* and not drive foreign policy, the relationship is rarely this straightforward. Defence might be expected to be a realm in which the articulation of a "national interest" by the agencies of the Federal government is least subject to amendment by parochial interests. It does so incompletely, because different bureaucratic, economic, and political pressures on structural, logistical, and foreign economic policy-making constrain the President and affect the long-run direction and content of policy. Foreign policy is only one determinant of defence policy: it is also shaped by the modes and costs of acquiring weapons systems, the political momentum of established defence relationships, bureaucratic power, and Congressional support for existing deployments.

As Appendix 3 indicates, the framers of the Constitution were as disinclined to grant the President free rein in the formation of foreign and defence policy as in domestic policy. None the less, from granting the power to negotiate treaties, and the bestowal of the power of Commander-in-Chief of the United States' armed forces to the President by Article II, Sections 2, Presidents since George Washington have claimed substantial implied powers over the making of foreign and defence policy.

The Presidential prerogative over waging war under Article II, Section 2 has been expansively defined by most twentieth-century Presidents to include the initiation of hostilities. Formal declarations of war by Congress are rare; the deployment of US armed forces in battle is not. The United States engaged in military conflict without a Congressional declaration of war in Korea between 1950 and 1953; in Lebanon in 1958 and 1985; in Vietnam between 1961 and 1975; in the Dominican Republic in 1965; in Cambodia in 1970; in Grenada in 1985; and in Panama in 1989. In 1991, the President sought and received Congressional approval for a military attack to liberate Kuwait from occupying Iraqi forces. In addition, covert operations occur throughout the world under the auspices of the CIA. These have led either through direct action or sponsorship to the overthrow of existing governments and the establishment of new ones, usually in the Third World.

Institutional Participants

The President

The distinguished constitutional scholar, Edward Corwin, once famously observed that the Constitution "is an invitation to struggle for the privilege of directing American foreign policy". The struggle is conducted almost entirely between the two elected branches: while significant cases have come before the Supreme Court, Executive–Legislative struggle since the Nixon Presidency has not tempted Federal courts to pass judgment on the allocation of powers. The President is the single most important participant in foreign and in defence policy, and the Constitution grants him special powers in respect of them. The Article II clause conferring the authority of

Commander-in-Chief upon the President vests him with a singular power: in war (though not in peace) the President lacks competitors as well as peers. US soldiers follow Presidential commands. Addressing immediate external threats to national security requires organizational clarity and political singularity: they meet in the President. However, conflict about the war power's nature and extent was not disposed of by the constitutional text; nor has it been settled by the subsequent disputes about it.

Whereas in war the power of Commander-in-Chief owes little to persuasion and almost everything to authority, his power over foreign and defence policy in peace is shared with Congress, and with the civilian and military bureaucracies. Even in peace, however, the President has both an obligation and an opportunity to lead: US foreign policy is not merely what Presidents declare it to be, but is nearly so. Since the abandonment of isolationism as a guiding principle of US foreign policy, most Presidents have accepted the force of the first and the utility of the second, though not to Congressional or public acclaim.

Congress's influence on foreign and defence policy is usually exerted in one of two forms, and a President would be unwise to ignore either:

- In the *setting of bounds* to what is *politically acceptable*. Development of United States policy towards the Middle East between 1989 and 1992 was thus conducted by President Bush and Secretary of State Baker virtually autonomously from day to day and week to week. However, it was not undertaken independently of Congress, external interest groups, public opinion, or foreign states. Although the President's role as Chief Diplomat is formally ensured by Article II, prudent Presidents secure the domestic foundations of their negotiating position before committing their political capital abroad.

- In *modifying* particular Presidential proposals. Congress has often sought to modify Presidential policy, both during its development and after its pronouncement. Informal meetings and conversations between the Congressional leadership, members of relevant Congressional committees, and the President and his advisers shape policy during formulation. Formal hearings before Congressional committees at which administration witnesses are examined, and after which they give their assessments of Congressional sentiment to agency heads and the White House, offer further opportunities for influence. Finally, the ratification of Treaties allows the Senate to judge Presidential policy after its establishment. As the Senate's refusal to ratify the Versailles Treaty in 1919 and SALT II in 1979 showed, this power can have momentous consequences: President Carter's withdrawal of the SALT II Treaty in the teeth of Senate opposition to it was important in itself, as well as for its reflecting new anxieties within Congress about the erosion of America's military power in the wake of the Soviet invasion of Afghanistan.

Setting the Foreign Policy Agenda

The President's capacity and opportunity to set the foreign policy agenda derive from his legitimacy, a function of his status as the only nationally elected official. While defining options in policy formation requires the involvement of other parts of the Executive Branch, the pronouncement of foreign policy is primarily the Presidents' responsibility. Yet Congress's willingness to grant the President virtually unfettered discretion in determining United States foreign policy is a product of the Cold War rather than of peace. The change from the American-led alliance against Nazi Germany to the American-led alliance against Soviet Communism was institutionally nearly seamless: Franklin Roosevelt and Harry Truman as Commanders-in-Chief during the Second World War gave way to Harry Truman as Commander-in-Chief during the Cold War.

Truman, who laid the legal, organisational, doctrinal, and political foundations of America's vast military power in the Cold War, none the less depended upon Congress. His need for authorizations and appropriations constrained him, as did his need for bipartisan Congressional support for his policy of containing the Soviet Union and for rebuilding western Europe. Truman's achievement of Republican support for his active, internationalist, assumption of Western leadership against Soviet expansionism was neither inevitable nor straightforward. In using the Presidency to seek public, Congressional, and especially Republican, support, Truman sought approval for a decisive change in American attitudes and policy. The United States had hitherto resisted entanglement in foreign alliances because its leaders perceived high risk in such embroilment, especially with a corrupt European politics fundamentally at odds with American values.

Washington's warning against foreign alliances in his Farewell Address of September 1796 became established as a principle of American foreign policy. The United States, he urged, should eschew "habitual hatred or an habitual fondness towards any nation", and "steer clear of permanent alliances with any part of the foreign world". With the abrogation of the French alliance, isolationism survived even the tuggings at the American heart of the 1848 revolutions. Prior to 1861, the United States took part in no international conference, and few American politicians claimed that American interests were much affected by European events. As late as Franklin Roosevelt's first term, when the rationale for isolationism had weakened, isolationist Republicans continued to attribute American entry into the First World War to Wilson's determination to protect the arms trade and to save bankers from ruin. Such views were fuelled by persistent distrust of Britain and France, sympathy for Germany, and populist antipathy to finance. For some, these sentiments concealed anti-Semitism. Entry into the Second World War occurred only after the deployment of isolationist arguments similar to those of a century before. The US declaration of war on Japan came on 8 December 1941 after Japanese naval aircraft had sunk the US Pacific Fleet at Pearl Harbor the previous day. Germany and Italy declared war on the United States four days later.

The technological advances that made delivery by air of nuclear weapons possible rendered American boundaries permeable to threats from an ideologically hostile and expansionist enemy in a bipolar international system. Truman adeptly exploited the development, using the Presidency to symbolize national purpose in new international involvements designed to protect American interests. Departing from the tradition embraced by all his predecessors of eschewing permanent alliances, Truman sought the advice and won the support of key Congressional leaders for the doctrine which bore his name, and by which the United States began its post-war immersion in the defence of western Europe and other allies. He acted similarly in winning the support of Arthur Vandenberg, Republican Chairman of the Senate Foreign Relations Committee, for the Marshall Plan of aid to western Europe.

Throughout the Eisenhower and Kennedy Administrations, and for the first three years of the Johnson Administration, an anti-communist ideological purpose united Presidents and Congresses. Such agreement failed to settle the question of determining the boundary between the Constitutional allocation of the power Congress to declare war and the power of the President to wage it. This latent problem apart (which in any event resists tidy resolution), such disagreement as there was over policy owed more to politicians' attempts to trump others' anti-Communist sentiments with fiercer ones of their own than to a questioning either of the premises of foreign policy or of the constitutionality of Presidential leadership. There was little divergence of strategic view: of the ten Treaties submitted to the Senate between 1953 and 1961, none were defeated, and eight were approved with seven or fewer votes against. Moreover, Eisenhower took careful note of the political harm that President Truman's failure to consult extensively with Congress over the sending of US forces to Korea had caused in 1950. Accordingly, when considering US options in responding to an attack by Communist China on Formosa (now Taiwan) in 1955, Eisenhower sought and secured a Joint Congressional resolution of approval, underpinning the legitimacy of any actions which he might take later.

In these circumstances, Presidential leadership in foreign policy faced little serious constitutional challenge, notwithstanding attempts by the isolationist Republican Senator Bricker to restrict the President's powers to negotiate treaties and executive agreements. Presidents Truman, Eisenhower, Kennedy, and Johnson set US policy in the Cold War with a freedom comparable to that of Presidents Wilson and Roosevelt during the two world wars. However, Presidents Johnson's and Nixon's frequently deceitful policy in Vietnam eventually disrupted the pattern of Congressional deference to Presidential leadership, epitomized in the Gulf of Tonkin Resolution of

1964 and in Congressional support for financing the war. Vietnam's human and financial costs were appallingly severe, and its political consequences for the Democratic Party and the New Deal coalition bitterly divisive. The trust that Congress was willing to repose in Presidents pursuing the bi-partisan policy of opposition to what had since 1948 been regarded as an expansion of territorial control sponsored by the Soviet Union was thereby eroded.

Presidential leadership in foreign policy has not vanished: the advantages of executive singularity ensure that it cannot. None the less, Congress is less willing now than it was between 1941 and 1967 to acquiesce in the President's agenda, especially in light of the dominant pattern since 1968 of split party control between the White House and Capitol Hill, which has so frequently turned questions of relations between the Presidency and Congress into partisan ones.

The National Security Council and National Security Staff

The National Security Council (NSC) was established by the National Security Act of 1947, and placed in the EOP by Truman's Reorganization Plan No. 4 (1949). The Council is chaired by the President and has three other members: the Vice-President, the Secretary of State and the Secretary of Defense. The Director of Central Intelligence (the CIA head), and the Chairman of the Joint Chiefs of Staff are, in accordance with the National Security Act, respectively intelligence and military advisers to the Council. There is a substantial National Security Staff, the NSC's secretariat, led by the Assistant to the President for National Security Affairs (National Security Adviser or NSA), a position created within the White House at President Eisenhower's direction and replicated by each of his successors.

Within the statutory shell provided by the National Security Act and its amendments, operating procedures of national security advice within the White House are determined by Presidents themselves. Their practices have varied. In one respect, however, there has been broad similarity between administrations: the post of National Security Adviser has become one of the most important in government. It has been used by (among others) McGeorge Bundy under President Kennedy, Walt Rostow under President Johnson, Henry Kissinger under President Nixon, Zbigniew Brzezinski under President Carter, and Colin Powell under President Bush, to shape national security policy. Nixon, distrustful of Federal bureaucracies in general and of the State Department in particular, readily acquiesced in the systematic exclusion of Secretary of State William Rogers from most significant foreign and defence policy decisions by his NSA, Henry Kissinger, simultaneously forming major new policy initiatives bilaterally and exclusively with him. All Secretaries of State and Defense are handicapped by the advantage enjoyed by NSAs of close proximity to the Oval Office, and of daily scheduled private meetings with the President. Even President Carter, who entered office bent upon ending the marginalization of the State Department, eventually fell under the influence of Zbigniew Brzezinski to the disadvantage of both his Secretaries of State.

President Reagan's detachment from foreign policy decision-making left room in the Iran-*Contra* affair of 1986–8 for two of his NSAs, Robert McFarlane and John Poindexter, to conduct an illegal foreign policy operation in defiance of Congress, separately from both the Departments of State and Defense. The breaking of the law besmirched Reagan's Presidency, a consequence of which the President seemed only faintly aware. Furthermore, as the *Report of the President's Special Review Board* on the scandal showed, the blurring of the boundary between advising the President (which is the NSA's proper role) and executing policy (which is not) harmed US interests and damaged the integrity of foreign policy-making. The debacle also illustrated anew that although clear decision-making procedures are important, they are easily subverted by staff and Presidents.

The importance of the NSC, as distinct from the NSA and the national security staff, has varied. Eisenhower, whose preference for formal modes of decision-making was clearest in security matters, established a highly-structured system consisting of the NSC itself, a planning board, and an operations co-ordinating board at the centre of foreign policy decision-making. Kennedy, his Democratic successor, found such formalism ineffective, and adopted *ad hoc* task forces in an attempt to ensure that policy problems were identified precisely and the options clearly distilled. Working in the guise of an executive committee of the NSC, the group of thirteen that clarified the President's options during the Cuban Missile Crisis of 1962 succeeded in removing Soviet missiles from Cuba without publicly humiliating Nikita Khrushchev, the First Secretary of the Soviet Communist Party. Kennedy made informality work; Johnson, his successor, could not. Confining decision-making to trusted advisers rather than opening channels to those whose analyses would infirm and challenge his own views, Johnson thereby impaired decision-making on Vietnam, his besetting foreign policy predicament.

Eisenhower, more skilled in bureaucratic politics than his critics allowed, understood what Johnson, Nixon, Carter, and Reagan did not: established procedures in which the NSA brokers, communicates, advises the President, and co-ordinates policy development with the Departments of State, Defense, and other agencies benefit both Presidents and the Presidency. The temptations to seek control over policy formation and the esteem of officials within and outside the administration, which together have fuelled the aspirations and careers of many NSAs, may damage the needs of the President. There are recurrent problems of co-ordination within the Executive Branch: tensions result from the Executive Branch's fragmentation, the gulf between the EOP and the Departments, and the struggle for control over both the processes of policy-making and the content of policy itself.

Resolution of both requires the full engagement, understanding and resolve of a resourceful President but few meet this standard.

Office of the United States Trade Representative (USTR)

The USTR was created by Executive Order in 1963, and placed in the EOP by the Trade Act of 1974. The Office is directed by the USTR, a member of the President's Cabinet with the rank of Ambassador. She or he is assisted by three Deputy USTRs, each of whom also holds the rank of Ambassador; two are based in Washington and one in Geneva, home of the World Trade Organisation (WTO). Following the success enjoyed by President Carter's Trade Representative, Robert Strauss, in leading American negotiators during the Tokyo Round, the President published a Reorganization Plan in 1979 which strengthened USTR's standing within the administration. Implemented by Executive Order in January 1980, it conferred the responsibility of setting and administering overall trade policy upon the Office, and designated the USTR the chief US representative for the following:

- All matters touching upon *GATT*.
- Discussions concerning *trade* and *commodity policy* held within the ambit of the Organisation for Economic Co-operation and Development (OECD).
- All other *bilateral* and *multilateral negotiations* concerning trade policy, direct investment incentives and disincentives to trade, incentives and barriers to cross-border investment.

The major trade Act of 1988, the Omnibus Trade and Competitiveness Act, codified the authority granted by the 1980 Executive Order and added the important duty of implementing enforcement actions under Section 301 of the 1974 Trade Act designed to eliminate barriers to American exports in foreign markets by designating particular practices as "unfair". (The politics of identifying countries which USTR deem to be in violation of Section 301 were important for what they revealed about the Executive's understanding of broader US foreign policy interests and in the development of the US's bargaining position during the Uruguay Round negotiations begun in 1986: countries the United States could afford to offend (such as India) were named; and those it could not (such as Japan) escaped.) The formation and implementation of US trade policy have greater importance in the early 1990s than formerly, since economic hazards to American security have largely displaced military threats in the wake of the implosion of the Soviet Union.

The nature of trade policy naturally attracts the attention of many government agencies and interest groups. Companies which trade abroad; labour unions dependent upon the jobs such trade generates or threatens;

cities; Congressional districts; States; and regions with economic interests at stake bring pressure to bear on the administration and Congress to protect domestic markets from foreign competition, or to open foreign markets to American competition. During the 1970s and 1980s, for example, many States instituted economic sanctions of their own against the South African regime; and some were slower to remove them than the Federal government wished. The involvement of Departments such as Agriculture and Commerce ensures that sectional pressures from affected groups are brought to bear. In the Uruguay Trade Round, for example, efficient American exporters of beef, grain, and oilseeds sought to open foreign markets that were wholly or partly closed to them. These interests were so powerful that they dominated the American negotiating position and overwhelmed the smaller, less efficient, producers of commodities such as sugar, peanuts, and tobacco which could not withstand freer international trade. The role of promoting agricultural exports is reflected in the Department's organisation, where an Under-Secretary leads the Foreign Agricultural Service (FAS), an agency that administers export assistance and foreign food assistance programmes and is represented abroad in more than sixty US embassies by agricultural scientists and economists.

The Department of Commerce

The 1988 Act delegates to the US and Foreign Commercial Service (an agency within the Department of Commerce) responsibility for commercial representation and jurisdiction over trade policy in US embassies and consulates abroad. The Commerce Department is thereby effectively charged with, and the State Department excluded from, the implementation of trade policy determined by the USTR. The Bureau of Export Administration within the Department has responsibility under the 1987 Export Administration Act for promoting American exports of non-agricultural goods, and supervising countervailing duty and anti-dumping Statutes. In implementing the latter, the department is lobbied by domestic industries affected by foreign imports whose prices are artificially low because of subsidies provided to foreign producers, and of goods being sold in the US market at prices below those in their domestic market, respectively. Three Assistant Secretaries have responsibilities for other aspects of trade policy.

The Department of Commerce is deliberately designed by Congress to be receptive to complaints by American companies (the department's traditional clients) and politicians about allegedly unfair trading practices. Its structure and programmes encourage such receptivity through triangular political relationships between the private sector, executive agencies, and Congressional Subcommittees. The deliberate placing of the USTR Office within the EOP offers some prospect to American negotiators of their being able to negotiate trade agreements without being subverted by the activities of kaleidoscopic domestic interest groups. Given the intensity with which protectionist pressures are applied in Congressional politics, it is striking that Presidents have retained such autonomy in making trade policy. It is doubtful that this pattern will continue so happily as the salience of trade politics grows: resistance to delegating "fast-track" negotiating authority to Presidents has grown rapidly, especially among Congressional Democrats.

The Treasury Department

The Treasury participates in foreign policy through its responsibility for the management of the world's largest trading currency, the US dollar. The department's other international responsibilities include the US external balance, tariff policy, and the management of the public debt. Its international role has become more demanding with the end of United States economic hegemony and the growth of its interdependence with the international economy. The fact of American economic hegemony in 1945 is widely known, but its extent too little appreciated. In 1945, the United States accounted for 50 per cent or more of total world GNP, exported more than twice as much as it imported, and effectively determined (by reason of the dollar's dominance) other countries' monetary policies. To that extent, Bretton Woods was a political fig-leaf, and an earnest symbol of self-restraint. West European dependence upon American policy was symbolised by the Marshall Plan in 1947, but had been an established fact two years before. American hegemony lasted for barely twenty-five years, but American dominance continues.

The end of the United States's hegemony was expressed in the collapse of the Bretton Woods order in 1971, vividly symbolised by the United States's running a trade deficit for the first time in its modern industrial history, and by ending the right of governments to convert surplus dollars into gold. The increasingly multinational character of production, the rapid growth in capital movements across national boundaries, the ending of dollar–gold convertibility, the weakening US balance of payments, and the vigorous economic recoveries from war in Western Europe and Japan, undermined American capacity to determine international monetary policy. That development was underlined by the rising proportion of the United States's GNP absorbed by international trade, with its accompanying exposure of the American economy to developments and pressures beyond its control.

A decade later, foreign pressures increased: as the fiscal deficit grew in the early to mid-1980s and the savings ratio remained obstinately low, Treasury debt was bought in larger quantities by foreign customers. The US external deficit also grew rapidly, adding to weaknesses which pushed the Treasury more deeply into foreign policy. The relative decline of the US economy in the 1980s was put into fuller perspective at the end of the decade by the sudden collapse of the Soviet and East European economies, whose consequent vulnerability and dependence upon new sources of multilateral finance from the International Monetary Fund (IMF) dominated by the United States lent further weight to the Treasury's voice. As the United States dominates the IMF, it also dominates the World Bank and the Inter-American Development Bank; as important sources of development finance internationally, so they were significant sources of Treasury influence on American foreign policy.

The Justice Department

Four bureaux of the Justice Department are involved in foreign policy: the FBI; the US National Central Bureau (USNCB); the Immigration and Naturalisation Service (INS), and the Drug Enforcement Administration (DEA). (The first of these is not considered below, but in the next section, dealing with the intelligence community.)

- USNCB represents the United States in INTERPOL and has assumed greater importance in recent years as international police co-operation has grown with intensified efforts to defeat terrorism. The Agency co-ordinates the work of Federal intelligence and law enforcement agencies, police services at Federal, State, city and local levels of government in the United States and between the United States and police services abroad.
- Since its creation in 1891, INS has had responsibility for administering laws governing entry to the United States, and for issuing regulations of its own. The United States continues to absorb large numbers of immigrants. In particular, increased flows of illegal immigrants across the Rio Grande has caused domestic political problems in southern California, New Mexico, and Texas, and difficulties in relations between the United States and Mexico. The agency's role has assumed greater significance as Congressional and public interest in the problem has grown.
- The DEA was created in 1973 by President Nixon's Reorganization Plan No. 2, which amalgamated four agencies into one. It is charged with the tasks of investigating drug-trafficking between States within the US and between the US and foreign countries; and with breaking drug manufacturing and distribution networks. In addition to field offices throughout the United States, the DEA is represented in fifty foreign countries.

The Intelligence Community

The intelligence "community", in the misleadingly comforting euphemism, is large and extensive. As might be expected in light of the discussion in Chapter 8, it is also riven with interagency conflict and competition. The size of the annual appropriations by Congress to the several agencies comprising the community are officially declared to total $26 billion. The Director of Central Intelligence (DCI) has nominal command of all intelligence gathering, assessment, and operations but is more usually reduced to co-ordinating the different efforts of disparate agencies, the existence of some of which (the so-called "black" agencies) is officially denied. The publicly-acknowledged agencies include the Central Intelligence Agency (CIA), whose Director is always also the DCI.

The CIA

The CIA was established by the National Security Act of 1947 as the NSC's intelligence advisory service and the co-ordinating agency for the Federal government's entire intelligence work. Such an advisory and co-ordinating role has been hampered by the characteristic dispersion of functions among a number of agencies. In practice, other parts of the intelligence community have resisted attempts by the DCI and some Presidents to centralize political authority and budgetary control, with the result that other intelligence agencies have operated independently of both the CIA and DCI. Not only has the CIA's co-ordinating role often been foiled by other agencies, but the Agency's twin roles of intelligence operative and policy advocate have impaired its analytical objectivity. Even conservative Presidents with a harshly realistic understanding of international politics have privately expressed dissatisfaction with the CIA's work. For example, Richard Nixon regarded the CIA with a contempt similar in kind and intensity to that which he expressed about most Federal government agencies: he complained to his senior aide, Bob Haldeman, in the summer of 1971 that "The CIA tells me nothing I don't read three days earlier in the *New York Times*. The CIA isn't worth a damn" before defining intelligence as "how to spend $5 billion and learn nothing" (Haldeman, 1994).

Its covert activities have caused the CIA to be regarded with suspicion – especially by liberals and democrats. In 1973, the CIA organised the overthrow of Salvador Allende's elected government in Chile and its replacement by General Pinochet's bloody military dictatorship. The CIA was simultaneously engaged in co-ordinated, illegal, domestic operations with the FBI against Nixon's political opponents. Abuse of its power angered Congressional liberals and prompted President Carter to restrain the Agency by attempting to enforce the 1947 Act. However, under his successor, the DCI's authority over other intelligence agencies was again reduced, and budgets for covert work increased. Establishment by the House and Senate of Select Committees on Intelligence to oversee the CIA has necessarily had only limited success. Intelligence operations require secrecy; democratic procedures require disclosure and accountability.

In 1975, Congress attempted, by the Hughes–Ryan Amendment to the 1974 Foreign Assistance Act, to hold the CIA accountable by expanding the number of Oversight Committees and requiring reports to be made to them about covert actions. The Senate created a new Select Committee on Intelligence in 1976, and the House followed suit a year later. After the failure of the Iranian hostage rescue, Congress's determination to check the CIA weakened, and Hughes–Ryan was replaced by the less restrictive Intelligence Oversight Act of 1980. It required the CIA to report to the Select Committees only, and permitted the President to launch covert operations without prior notification if he judged that vital interests were at stake. As the mining of Nicaraguan harbours, the covert war against the *Contras*, and the Iran-*Contra* episode revealed, President Reagan showed scant regard either for the spirit of the Act, or for Congressional prerogatives. Congress's enthusiasm for restraining the CIA cooled in the 1980s, partly because providing additional information to Select Committees deflected criticism: consulting them was not only required by statute, but often politically advantageous. Tensions none the less persist.

Other Intelligence Agencies

Agencies that operate under the Secretary of Defense's authority but remain within the intelligence community include the National Security Agency which, with the world's most extensive and advanced electronic signal gathering system, intercepts and decodes communications of both allied and enemy states; the Central Imagery Office, which has charge of intelligence gathered by satellite; and the Defense Intelligence Agency, which provides the Secretary and the Joint Chiefs of Staff (JCS) with analyses drawn from the intelligence gathering still undertaken (to the detriment of the Defense Department's efficiency) by the four individual services. The Secretary of State depends heavily upon the Bureau of Intelligence and Research, headed by an Assistant Secretary of State, for the intelligence input into his or her decisions. The Bureau is, in turn dependent for raw material on reports from US embassies and stations abroad and the information that other agencies choose to supply.

Three other Departments also have substantial intelligence functions: Justice, Treasury, and Energy. Within the Justice Department, the FBI's role is counter-espionage. This broad remit has in the past been subject to abuse by some Presidents and FBI Directors in order to harass domestic opponents: Martin Luther King, for example, was subjected to intensive surveillance throughout his entire political career as part of a campaign by J. Edgar Hoover to label him as having Communist sympathies. During the Nixon Administration, the Justice Department illegally wiretapped many domestic organizations under cover of the President's duty to protect national security, in violation (as the Supreme Court later determined) of the Fourth Amendment.

The Treasury's overt intelligence operations are conducted through its employees overseas, who gather information on the economic policies and prospects of foreign states. Its covert intelligence work takes place through two specialized agencies within the Department: the Bureau of Alcohol, Tobacco, and Firearms; and the Secret Service. The former monitors smuggling and illegal trading in the three specified goods, while the latter not only protects the President and VIPs but also gathers intelligence on threats to them that it seeks to forestall, and leads the Federal government's anti-counterfeiting work. The Department of Energy's intelligence work is largely confined to ensuring compliance by foreign states with the Nuclear Non-Proliferation Treaty, and with gathering intelligence on the testing by foreign states of nuclear weapons. The first has assumed much greater importance since the exposure by the International Atomic Energy Agency of the Iraqi nuclear weapons programme, and the new opportunity detected by the United States to access and end North Korea's nuclear weapons programme.

The Department of State

Older even than Treasury or Judiciary, the State Department was established by an Act of Congress on 27 July 1789 as the Department of Foreign Affairs, and renamed the Department of State in September of the same year. In 1995 it was staffed by 24,600 employees, 10,000 of whom are foreign nationals working in embassies or consulates abroad (see Exhibit 12.1). The department's Congressional appropriation in 1996 was $5.5 billion, the second-smallest Congressional appropriation to a Cabinet-level executive department. Its American employees are divided roughly equally between postings abroad and in Washington. 4,200 are employed as Foreign Service Officers (FSO), the corps of professional diplomats who represent the United States government abroad in 164 Embassies; in twelve missions; one US interests section; sixty-six consulates general; fourteen consulates; three branch offices; and forty-five consular agencies.

The majority of Federal civilian employees in foreign postings are drawn from other agencies: approximately 85 per cent work for the Agency for International Development (AID); the Arms Control and Disarmament Agency, (ACDA); the US Information Agency (USIA); the Central Intelligence Agency (CIA); and domestic departments and agencies with international responsibilities such as the Departments of Agriculture, Commerce, and Treasury. Such bureaucratic splintering exacerbates the difficulties of co-ordinating foreign policy and the State Department's prospects of leading it, despite the Foreign Service traditionally regarding other agencies disdainfully as being parasitic upon the central purposes of diplomacy.

US Ambassadors are drawn both from the ranks of career FSOs and from the pool of political appointees, both those to whom the President has

---

EXHIBIT 12.1

The Department of State

Seven principal officials based in Washington comprise the top layer of the State Department: the Secretary of State himself, the Deputy Secretary, and five Under-Secretaries. Below these seven are nineteen Assistant Secretaries in charge of the Department's *bureaux*, its key operating units in Washington (see below). Within each bureau are directors of individual offices, civil servants and foreign service officers (FSOs).

As in other departments, the Secretary of State is always a political appointee, as are most of his or her six colleagues at principal level. (The only exception is that the Under-Secretary for Political Affairs is always a career official, well-placed to bring experience and continuity to the Department.) His or her four Under Secretary Colleagues (for Global Affairs; for Economic and Agricultural Affairs; for International Security Affairs; and for Management) are invariably political appointees.

In Washington, the State Department is organised into *bureaux*, units similar in origin and function to agencies in other departments. Each is headed by an Assistant Secretary. Conforming to the pattern throughout the Federal bureaucracy, every bureau except one has a parent Subcommittee in Congress. The exception is the Department's Congressional Relations office, which co-ordinates appearances by Administration officials in Congressional hearings, especially the Senate Foreign Relations Committee, and the House Foreign Affairs Committees. Seven bureaux have functional remits, and five geographic areas: Africa; East Asia and the Pacific; Europe and Canada; Inter-American Affairs; Near East and South Asia. Assistant Secretaries in the latter five have charge over the development of US policy towards the countries and regions within each, and chair interdepartmental groups in the National Security Council (NSC) system which prepare papers for the Council and implement Council decisions.

---

obligations for their contributions to his election campaign, and those with abilities and attributes of potential benefit to the President and the country. Ambassadorships in London and Paris are coveted by, and usually awarded to, close supporters. Most Ambassadors to African and Latin-American countries are career diplomats, since the postings have little attraction and much danger. Not unnaturally, the use of Ambassadorships as rewards to political friends causes all manner of tensions in the State Department between appointees and career diplomats.

Together with the Deputy Assistant Secretaries and Office Directors assigned to cover individual countries within each Bureau, State Department officials receive from embassies abroad reports of conversations and meetings, and information from the other intelligence-gathering agencies. In the light of their accumulated understanding, they interpret the material and, with other departments and agencies, develop policy options for the Secretary of State, the NSC and the President towards countries and groups of countries in the region. The involvement of other departments and agencies in foreign policy denies regional bureaux a monopoly of control over information, analysis, and policy formation within the Executive Branch; Executive Branch fragmentation obliges each bureau to co-ordinate constantly with others.

Many State Department officials have relevant academic expertise before joining the State Department (linguistic ability, and advanced academic training in a social science are prized advantages) but all, to a greater or lesser degree, acquire it in the course of their careers. But expertise is not always welcomed by new political administrations or political appointees, especially where policy issues are ideologically charged. Nor has analytical detachment always been highly prized: upon his appointment as President Nixon's National Security Adviser, Henry Kissinger's distrust of State Department professionals and obsessive concern for his own political influence and status led him to circumvent not only regional bureaux in the Department but also, in secret preparations for a *rapprochement* with China in 1972, to exclude the State Department from the process altogether. If the President deems a policy question sufficiently important, State Department expertise is (ironically) often nullified, since the important questions are decided by the President in consultation with senior staff and the Secretary of State rather than at bureau level in the Department. This pattern has applied to all questions touching upon US relations, both with major allies and adversaries in the post-war period, thereby reducing the influence of the otherwise prestigious Bureau for European Affairs (which had responsibility for covering both NATO and Warsaw Pact members).

The politicization of the State Department, as of other Federal agencies, is necessary and inevitable if the President is to have any prospect of enforcing his policy priorities. Fear of jeopardizing their careers under a President from a different party is usually a sufficient reason for officials to avoid adopting a radical or polar position in a controversial matter. Aggregation of these individual tendencies lends some substance to the claim that the State Department is characterized by a culture of cautious incrementalism which can be overcome only by energetic leadership of appointees loyal to the President and the Secretary of State. Innovative Secretaries of State are therefore inclined to form policy in small groups loyal to them rather than to clients. Having attempted to formulate policy without the aid of the State Department when merely the President's National Security Adviser, Kissinger continued to view the Department with suspision once he became Secretary of State in his own right. Not all Secretaries have distrusted the department (Cyrus Vance and Warren Christopher both worked with it rather than against it), but many have. Three years into the post, President Bush's Secretary of State, James Baker, continued to work with trusted staff within his office on the Department's seventh floor, even when he attempted to broker an immensely complicated Middle East peace. Political loyalty in

Washington is generally more highly prized by department secretaries than is detached expertise. Such a disposition none the less carries the price of uneven attention to potential crises, and of discontinuity between administrations, and exacerbates the fragmentation of the policy-making community rather than overcomes it.

The Department of Defense

The Department of Defense was established in 1949 by Congressional amendments to the National Security Act of 1947. It comprises the Office of the Secretary of Defense, the military departments and military services within those departments; the Chairman of the Joint Chiefs of Staff and the Joint Staff; the unified and individual commands; the Defense Agencies, and the Department's field stations. The Secretary of Defense's authority over this most complex of all departments was increased by the Defense Reorganization Acts of 1958 and 1986 (see p. 398). Unlike the Secretary of State, the Secretary of Defense directs an agency with a huge budget whose disposition is of vital importance to defence contractors, subcontractors and suppliers, and thus to employees of contractors, and to their representatives in Congress. Acquisition of weapons systems presents one of the purest examples of distributive policy-making by Congress, comprising business worth tens of billions of dollars annually to corporations, and consequently generating intense group pressures on the Department and the Congress's Armed Services Committees, who make procurement decisions. Additionally, the Secretary of Defense is subject to political pressures from Members of Congress proposing the expansion of defence facilities in their Districts or, as is now more often the case, attempting to resist their closure.

Since the Secretary of Defense is designated in law as the "principal defense policy adviser to the President", and is responsible "for the formulation of general defense policy and policy related to all matters of direct and primary concern to DOD", he requires a large civilian management team within the Pentagon. Attempting to implement administration policy in so vast a bureaucracy accustomed to incremental budgeting and decision-making, and standard operational procedures is exceptionally difficult. Accountability of civil servants and military officers in the Department to the Secretary, the President, and to Congress is often weak. Public alarm at a rash of procurement scandals within the Department helped Senator Goldwater during the mid-1980s to build a coalition for improved management structures and procedures in the Pentagon, with the object of reinforcing accountability. Within the "Office of the Secretary of Defense" (itself a large management structure) there are several senior assistants to the Secretary and the Deputy Secretary. Despite its nominal unification, each armed service maintains its own structure within the Department and, like agencies in other departments, has substantial operating autonomy.

The Joint Chiefs of Staff (JCS)

The JCS organization comprises the Chairman; the Vice-Chairman; the Chief of Staff, United States Army; the Chief of Naval Operations; the Chief of Staff, United States Air Force (USF); and the Commandant of the Marine Corps (the Marines are, in principle, a command within the Department of the Navy, but regard themselves as a separate armed service). By their statutory authority, the Joint Chiefs represent military opinion to the President and the Secretary of Defense.

Although, in law, the armed forces have always been under complete civilian control, their lack of authority in policy matters has not prevented them from exercising influence, often to the advantage of individual branches of the armed forces. None of the four armed services has ever supported a unified Defence Department, because it would threaten its own interests. The combination of cultural and structural differentiation has proved to be an obstacle to Presidents, Secretaries of Defense, and Chairmen of Congress's Armed Services Committees, who have periodically attempted to develop a more rational and efficient organization. The capacity of individual services to advance their own interests at the expense of those of the nation and the taxpayer has often been apparent. Competition is injected into the organization by its representational character: as the JCS represent the four services, so the military members of the Joint Staff (the JCS secretariat) of approximately 400 are drawn equally from the four services. The JCS possesses formidable bureaucratic capacity to resist Presidential initiatives, as its successful opposition to President Carter's attempt to end production of the B1 Bomber vividly showed.

Many members of the JCS regarded the organization less as a co-ordinating mechanism than as a forum for pressing their sectional claims and interests. As the JCS was unable to overcome the US Armed Forces' fragmentation, so relations between the Army, Air Force, Navy and Marines within the Pentagon and in theatres of operation were often poor, leading to inept organization and inadequate co-ordination in both peace and war.

Goldwater–Nichols Act (1986)

In an attempt to reduce the damaging competitive rivalry and strife between the four armed services, the Defense Reorganization Act of 1986 (the Goldwater–Nichols Act) enhanced the role of the JCS and weakened individual service departments' influence within the Defense Department. The Act also increased the authority of the Chairman of the JCS, in two respects:

1. By designating him/her as the *principal military adviser* to the President, NSC and Secretary of Defense. However, it grants him neither

membership of the NSC nor direct command over US forces; the JCS Chairman is entitled merely to transmit orders from the President to Commanders-in-Chief (CINCs), but not to give them himself.

2. Colleagues and staff within the JCS organization are now under the Chairman's authority, and serve at his direction, so increasing their incentive to supply disinterested analyses. General Colin Powell, appointed Chairman by President Bush, put the powers granted him by the 1986 Act to effective use during the Gulf War of 1991 while leaving field command to a Commander-in-Chief (General Schwarzkopf), as the Act required.

The Goldwater–Nichols Act has given the Chairman greater opportunity to influence the President's defence and national security thinking, and it requires him to advise the Secretary of Defense on priorities between different requests of colleagues in the four major commands. The Chairman is also required to assist the President and the Secretary of Defense by providing for:

- *strategic direction* of the Armed Forces;
- their *budgeting*;
- *comparison* of US *military capabilities* with those of other States;
- preparation of *contingency plans*, and the *logistic* and *mobility plans* for them to be fulfilled.

The Legislative Branch

Congress's influence over foreign and defence policy varies with the type of policy. In crisis management, it is minimal. In war, it is insignificant in the short term when there is a premium upon supporting forces in the field. Even in the medium-to-long term, it is slight while the President's direction of war meets with success and enjoys public support. When these two conditions are not met, Congressional opinion can reflect the (often divided) sentiments of wider public opinion. Both Presidents Truman and Johnson eventually encountered such medium-to-long-term political difficulties with Congress and public opinion as their conduct of Asian wars faltered.

In strategic foreign policy, Congress exercises more influence. Here the Executive enjoys less autonomy and depends upon Congressional authorizations and appropriations for foreign and military aid, upon Congress's willingness to support Presidential trade policy, and upon the Senate's willingness to ratify Treaties. In structural defence policy-making, the Executive enjoys little autonomy and is heavily dependent upon the Military Installations and Construction Subcommittees of the House and Senate Appropriations Committees, and of the (authorizing) House and Senate Armed Services Committees. Congress has the opportunity to involve itself in these second and third types of foreign and defence policy, not only through authorization and appropriations but also in Committee hearings called to examine problems and controversies. Increases in Subcommittees' autonomy from full committees and the huge increases in Congressional staff resources in the 1970s complicated the patterns of Executive–Congressional interaction in both strategic and structural policy. The lengthy list of Congressional Committees and Subcommittees with jurisdiction over parts of foreign and defence policy hints at the complexities of the policy process that results.

Interest Groups

Foreign states with which the United States maintains diplomatic relations have direct representation to the Executive in Washington, and the opportunity to represent their varied interests to Congressional, media, group, and public opinion. Foreign countries may be regarded as groups seeking to influence US policies to their advantage. Allies such as Britain, Canada, Germany, and Italy enjoy such close, collusive, ties with the United States that diplomatic activity between them is constant, wide-ranging, and generally co-operative. Differences of policy are rarely serious, and since 1945 none (including Suez in 1956) have threatened diplomatic rupture: relations are conducted primarily at official level between Embassy officials and Executive departments. Disagreements remain, but they are mostly confined to trade, where in any case EU States are formally represented in trade negotiations by the European Commission, and not individually.

Other foreign States have different relations with the United States. Even Israel, the single largest recipient of both US Foreign Aid and Military Aid, had a less stable and amicable relationship under President Bush and Secretary of State Baker. The Israeli Embassy accordingly pursues a broader range of contacts and employs different techniques in pressing for increased aid, and in opposing US sales of military equipment to Israel's adversaries. Israel bolsters its political strength with the administration by cultivating friendly relations with the Pentagon, with Members of Congress and Senators, and through the maintenance of close contacts with pro-Israel PACs, by steering funds to Congressional supporters and away from opponents. Israeli causes are in any case strengthened enormously by the large and influential activities and writings of Jewish academics, journalists, and business people. These have been insufficient to prevent the United States from adopting a Middle East policy at variance with Israel's own, but they have, so far, limited the divergence between the two States and have been sufficient to preserve the American guarantee of the sanctity of Israel's borders and security.

Most foreign governments have a more difficult task in influencing American policy. Declared enemies during the Cold War such as the Soviet

Union and the Warsaw Treaty Organisation (WTO) clients had no prospect of modifying American policy while Communist regimes remained in power. Nor, in the short term, could the United States weaken Communist control over territories east of the River Elbe. In the longer term, however, diplomacy offered the possibility that American interests might be advanced: the encouragement of *détente* challenged rather than accommodated members of the WTO, as the fitful progress of negotiations on arms control with the Soviet Union, and on the Conference on Security and Co-operation in Europe (CSCE) illustrated. By encouraging the stirrings of civil society in Eastern Europe and restraining internal oppression by Communist governments, CSCE served the foreign policy interests of the United States.

As the processes of trade negotiations and the institutions of the EU show, the United States must increasingly pursue diplomacy with non-State actors. The new importance of the United Nations following the end of the bipolar international order and the Soviet Union's collapse was first seen to American advantage in the Gulf War, waged under the cover of UN authorization. During the 1960s and 1970s, the United States Mission to the United Nations was often engaged in hostile exchanges with other member States; diplomacy has been publicly calmer since the end of the Cold War. The UN is increasingly both a forum and an instrument of US policy, as it was during the Korean War. As the utility of interstate relations diminishes with the increased salience of issues (such as environmental pollution, human rights and economic development) susceptible to solution only through international organizations, the importance of their representation in Washington may grow, and that of individual States (or at least advanced European ones) decline.

Foreign States and transnational actors exist alongside domestic groups whose agendas either extend to international affairs or which are founded primarily upon them. They include ethnic and national pressure groups; economic groups; human rights organisations; intellectual and research organizations on the fringes of government itself; state and legal governments; the electronic and print media; and public opinion:

- Among *ethnic and national groups* are: the Congressional Black Caucus, which has taken a close interest in, and at the margins exercised influence over, US policy towards South Africa; the National Association for Arab Americans; and the ten major pro-Israel PACs which help to fund supporters' election campaigns.
- *Economic groups*: these include the defence contractors (whose roles are examined on p. 413) in structural defence policy-making, companies which stand to gain or lose from particular trade agreements to which the United States is a party, and labour unions with interests in trade or in the prohibition of imports made by workers employed in oppressive circumstances.

- *Human rights groups*: these include Asia Watch, an organization specialising in the perpetually demanding tasks of gathering intelligence on the abuse of human rights in Asian countries, and in the difficult task of persuading Congress and the Executive to lobby for their remedy; and a host of liberal and Church-based organizations with similar purposes.
- *Intellectual and research organizations*: often of an ideological persuasion, these include the Council for Foreign Relations, an influential group representing elite business, financial, and intellectual interests and perspectives on US foreign policy; the Centre for International Economics, a successful research institute conducting research on international trade; the Brookings Institution, a moderately liberal think-tank; the Centre for Strategic and International Studies, a predominantly conservative research institute once attached to Georgetown University; and the American Enterprise Institute, a conservative, pro-business organization linked to many Republican politicians and to some conservative Democrats. Different administrations are susceptible in different degrees to the research produced by members of these think-tanks. Presidents also draw upon their own personnel when staffing their administrations, and Members of Congress and Senators when staffing their offices. By the same token, think-tanks draw upon those who leave the Executive and Legislative Branches.
- *State and local governments*: most of these seek to attract capital from abroad. To that end, most States and large cities maintain representative offices in foreign countries. Through the National Governors' Association, the National League of Cities, and other representative organizations, lower-level governments attempt to influence policy deliberations within both the Executive and Congress on questions affecting State and local commercial and political interests.
- *Electronic and print media groups*: coverage by television network news of foreign affairs is usually slight and superficial, and often banal: even avid readers of the best American daily newspapers have difficulty in following political developments in major countries such as Germany, Japan, Brazil, and Italy. This parochialism helps to ensure that few know much of foreign affairs, except those who watch Public (non-commercial) Television and read the foreign press (see Exhibit 3.1 on p. 81). Commercial television and the domestic press none the less influence the political agenda, are subject to influence by government press officers, and occasionally to control by them, as during the invasion of Grenada, when journalists were prevented from reporting it. However, they are also able to shape public thinking and undermine government propaganda: the coverage accorded the Tet offensive in 1968 exposed as hollow the administration's claim that the war was being won, hastened President Johnson's withdrawal from the race for the Democratic nomination, and caused US policy in Vietnam to be reassessed.

Processes of Foreign and Defence Policy-Making

Crisis Policy

Crisis policy proceeds according to the broad outline of contingency plans (preparation for the launching of attacks by the Soviet-led WTO on the Central European front preoccupied Pentagon and NATO planners for the entire Cold War). Never the less, however imaginative the planning work or accurate the intelligence assessments, the unexpected usually happens, and invariably has unforeseen consequences: for example, Japan's attack upon Pearl Harbor in December 1941 not only precipitated the entry of the United States into the Second World War, but also transformed the nature of the domestic debate about continuing isolation from the politics of great power rivalry. And consequences of a different kind flowed from the Gulf of Tonkin crisis in 1964: it galvanized Congress to give the President leave (by margins of 415 to 0 in the House and 98 to 2 in the Senate) to respond to aggression as he thought fit. It thereby granted him *carte blanche* in a war which eventually cost the lives of 56,000 Americans, and more than a million Vietnamese, and helped to disable the Democratic Party in Presidential elections for a generation.

The President's Powers in Crises

The Constitution unequivocally grants the power to Congress to declare war (see Appendix 1). Yet delegates to the Philadelphia Convention acknowledged that the Legislature was too unwieldy and sluggish an institution to respond to sudden attacks. Only six wars (including that in the Gulf) have ever been declared by Congress. That the President's powers as Commander-in-Chief, the maker of war, include the power to order military responses to attack is universally acknowledged. Even Jefferson, the most assiduous critic of Executive power, accepted this understanding and acted upon it as President in ordering a response to the British attack upon the USS *Chesapeake* in 1807. Had Soviet armoured forces launched the massive thrust through the Fulda Gap in northern Germany after 1949 for which contingency NATO planners prepared, Congress might well have had no time in which to declare war: the President would certainly have waged it.

Such ideal-type cases are straightforward and prompt no serious constitutional controversy. Presidents not only may but *must* defend the country against sudden attack: they may not decline to respond if the price of delay is defeat. The Constitution provides for government in emergency as well as in normality; the rights it defends are vitiated if the Republic it constitutes is destroyed by war. President Lincoln thus acted by suspending *habeas corpus* and imposing a blockade upon the rebellious southern States in April 1861, when Congress was in recess. He merely sought (and secured) retrospective Congressional approval. Even under Franklin Roosevelt and Harry Truman, the Commander-in-Chief clause was abused during time of war: in *Korematsu* v. *United States*, 323 US 214 (1944), the Supreme Court upheld the internment of 100,000 people of Japanese descent that Roosevelt had ordered. However, President Truman received shorter shrift from the Court in *Youngstown Sheet and Tube Co.* v. *Sawyer*, 323 US 579 (1952) for his attempt to seize private property under his Commander-in-Chief powers in what he claimed to be the national interest (see p. 102).

Where individual and property rights are not involved, the Supreme Court has avoided controversies about the war power, regarding them as political questions for resolution between the Executive and the Legislature. The Gulf of Tonkin resolution, for example, provoked no intervention by the Court. From its passage in August 1964 until the end of his Presidency, Johnson regularly secured Congressional appropriations for the expanding war, including the vast bombing campaign in February 1965 and the deployment of ground troops in July of the same year. Johnson regarded securing his political base in Congress for the war as his first priority. In doing so, the President attempted to pursue a middle course between conservative and liberal critics whose ranks swelled from the middle of 1967 onwards, when prospects of winning seemed as remote as those of withdrawal. A President's political need of Congressional support for his foreign and defence policy effectively obliges him to consult with Congress, whatever view individual Presidents may take of their implied powers under the Commander-in-Chief clause. That which the Constitution does not require of the President, politics of coalition-building may.

Consultation with Congress neither saved Johnson's Presidency nor won the war that split his party, for his policy in Vietnam depended partly on deceit and deception, not least of himself. As the prospect (and conception) of victory receded, doubts about the means, purpose, morality, and constitutionality of the huge effort grew. Partisan and ideological circumstances changed with Richard Nixon's election in 1968: facing Democratic majorities in Congress, Nixon chose to conduct the war alone, taking account of Congressional advice only when it suited his domestic purposes. Disregarding State Department advice and concentrating policy formulation and implementation in the White House restricted Congress's capacity to oversee the conduct of the war. Such reasoning informed the tight control of the invasion of Cambodia in April 1970, which Nixon justified as an exercise to protect the lives of Americans in Vietnam. Under its Chairman William Fulbright, the Senate Foreign Relations Committee had, as early as 1965, considered whether Presidential war powers were being unconstitutionally extended. He exposed as bogus Johnson's claim that the US invasion of the Dominican Republic in April of that year was for the purpose of protecting American lives rather than that of intervening to prevent a change of government inimical to American interests. That led him to consider whether Congress had also been misled in the information about the supposed North

Vietnamese attack upon the USS *Maddox* in the Gulf of Tonkin in the summer of 1964, which had enabled Johnson to seek Congressional approval for expanded war measures.

From 1965 onwards, therefore, debate about the propriety and conduct of the war in South-East Asia became entangled with the constitutional problem of the scope offered by the Commander-in-Chief clause. Johnson claimed that the Gulf of Tonkin resolution was an affirmation of broad Presidential powers; Madisonian critics such as Senators Fulbright and McGovern disagreed. Two factors complicated the problem. The first was that the administration misled Congress about the circumstances under which the USS *Maddox* was attacked. Had it been known that the ship was in North Vietnamese and not international waters, the justification in international law for the administration's action would have collapsed. The emergency was, as Fulbright himself later argued, contrived. The second was that, as Johnson claimed throughout his term in office, and as Nixon asserted when the Gulf of Tonkin resolution was finally repealed in 1970 amidst bitter Congressional dispute about the war's expansion into Cambodia, the President had no need of the resolution. Both claimed that the Commander-in-Chief clause gave him sufficient authority to act virtually as he chose; the Gulf of Tonkin resolution was a political cover that was finally removed.

This was no confined or arcane constitutional question: its origins, course, and resolution resonated through American society and politics. It broke two Presidents, damaged the Presidency, and eventually induced vigorous reassertions of Congressional prerogatives. The dispute's importance was plain: if the President could commit American troops to war without Congressional authorization in circumstances other than those of response to sudden attack, an important constraint upon Presidential power was nullified. Moreover, if the Executive's purpose in supplying information to Congress was to deceive rather than to inform, the bonds of trust upon which bipartisanship in foreign policy had been built, were shattered. The claim that the Constitution afforded Presidents powers in foreign and defence policy without let or hindrance offered a Caesarist corruption rather than a Hamiltonian interpretation of Articles I and II with sinister implications for a democratic Republic.

Congress's response began with Fulbright's Senate investigations. Having co-sponsored the Gulf of Tonkin resolution in 1964, he spent his last years in public life resisting Johnson and Nixon's claims that Presidential war powers were inherently flexible, a euphemism for their being determined by the President. His own "Sense of the Senate" resolution, the so-called National Commitments Resolution (1969), declared that grants of power from Congress to the Executive in foreign policy would henceforth be limited in extent and duration, unlike the Gulf of Tonkin Resolution which was general and open-ended. The National Commitments Resolution was not law, but marked the beginning of the reassertion of Congressional powers. It preceded the invasion of Cambodia and the revelation of the full extent of American military involvement in adjoining countries.

Undeclared Presidential war in Cambodia prompted Senators Cooper and Church to attempt to define conditions under which a President could act unilaterally abroad. Although the measure eventually passed the Senate in compromise form, it failed in the House, which was less inclined to challenge the assertion of Presidential foreign policy prerogatives. The Chairman of the National Security Policy Subcommittee of the House Foreign Affairs Committee attempted in both the 91st and the 92nd Congresses to pass a resolution, but as Church–Cooper was too restrictive for the House, so his own versions were insufficiently so for the Senate.

Following President Nixon's order for the bombing of Hanoi and Haiphong during Christmas 1972, resistance to attempts by Congressional liberals to limit Presidential war-making powers weakened. The end of the bombing, followed by the withdrawal of US combat forces in March 1973, did not terminate American engagement: President Nixon ordered a secret bombing campaign of Cambodia. When, as was inevitable, the new air war became known, Congress denied appropriations. Although Nixon vetoed the Bill, he eventually agreed to end all US combat operations in South-East Asia. Nixon's bombing of Cambodia weakened those who sought an accommodation with the President. The War Powers Resolution (1973), passed under Senator Javits's leadership over the President's veto, required the President to report to the Speaker and the President *pro tempore* of the Senate within forty-eight hours of the initiation of hostilities, on their circumstances, nature, extent and likely duration. The resolution required the President to consult with Congress "in every possible instance" before introducing armed forces into hostilities or circumstances where hostilities were clearly imminent. It further gave Congress the authority to end hostilities within sixty days, and required the President to withdraw US forces within sixty days with another thirty days being allowed for the withdrawal operation if the President declared it necessary. The timetable could be suspended by Congress declaring war or granting specific support for the President's action.

Every President since 1973 has regarded the War Powers Resolution as unconstitutional. Neither in the *Mayaguez* incident of 1975, where President Ford ordered the use of military force without prior consultation with Congress, nor in the rescue of US citizens from Saigon in 1975, did he consult with Congress. Nor did President Carter do so prior to attempting a rescue of American hostages in Teheran in 1980. Although the Supreme Court has declined to adjudicate upon it, the Resolution's constitutionality is doubtful, and not merely because it might be regarded as infringing a President's power as Commander-in-Chief. The Resolution in fact grants to the President and Congress powers that the Constitution does not: the waging of undeclared war for up to ninety days, and Congressional restrictions upon the President's command of deployed forces. Nuclear exchanges may occur in the two days between initiating hostilities and reporting to Congress. Less dramatically, such a period may make it politically impossible for Congress to question their deployment for fear of being regarded as treacherous. The War Powers Resolution has not diminished the President's capacity to set the agenda: as Commander-in-Chief, he can initiate and implement policy. It leaves wide scope for Presidential discretion regarding the form and timing of consultation and a choice as to whom he consults. The Resolution's silences permit Presidents latitude sufficient for them to act without significant hindrance.

The Resolution has, in practice, thus had less effect than Javits hoped for, whatever its constitutionality. However, Congress is no longer the pliant creature it was in August 1964. The intense debate in Congress over the wisdom of granting President Bush a free hand in the Gulf in 1991 showed that while the bilious distrust marking relations between Johnson, Nixon, and Congress had faded, reluctance to cede war powers remained. Both because of the disastrous conduct of the war in South-East Asia between 1964 and 1973, and because of Congress's own powerful sources of bureaucratic and analytical expertise in its specialist professional staff, no sweeping grant of authority to the President similar to that in the Gulf of Tonkin Resolution is likely to be made in the future.

Strategic Policy

In contrast to crisis policy and the war power, Congress exercises continuous influence upon strategic policy. Its decisions about the recipients, amounts, and conditions of foreign and military aid; trade policy; ratification of Treaties; confirmation hearings of senior Administration officials; its oversight of Executive Branch decision-making; hearings on human rights violations; its controls over arms exports; its authorizing weapons purchases and appropriating funds to pay for them, are all instances of Congress's broad powers over strategic policy. In the politically contentious development of American policy towards the newly unified China–Hong Kong in 1997, for example, Congressional pressures were strong and conflictual. House Majority Leader Richard Gephardt's policy of opposition to Chinese tyranny, for example, was carefully calculated to boost his Presidential election prospects in the year 2000 by appealing to conservative anti-Communists who feared Chinese imperial ambitions; to liberals who abhorred Chinese denial of human, civil, and political rights; and to labour unions whose members feared the loss of jobs to Chinese competition. Other Congressional pressures on President Clinton reflected commercial interests in opening up trade and investment opportunities in the newly unified China–Hong Kong. Clinton's strategic judgement that the China question ought to dominate the attention of American foreign policy-makers for the remainder of his second term and thereafter necessarily had to contend with such pressures, as well as with discontent from liberal supporters, who remembered vividly the President's earlier (now abandoned) insistence upon Chinese compliance with minimum standards of human rights observance.

The Defense Department's "Quadrennial Defence Review", notionally established to examine the major strategic purposes and modalities of US defence policy, also shows Congress's influence. Indeed, Congress itself required that the department undertake the periodic reviews, retaining for itself, consistent with the argument in the section below on structural policy, the right to determine the mix of modalities (especially base-closures) necessary to enable the United States to meet its self-imposed standard of having the capacity to fight two major regional wars simultaneously.

The Constitution's designation of the President as Chief Diplomat is subject to three qualifications:

- Appointments of Ambassadors and of appointees to non-civil service posts in the Executive Branch (save the President's immediate staff) are subject to *Senate confirmation.*
- The President's Treaty-making power is subject to the *advice* and *consent* of two-thirds of the Senate.
- Congress retains full *authorizing* and *appropriating* powers over foreign and defence policy.

Treaties and Executive Agreements

Presidents have generally secured consent more easily when they have sought advice prior to and during the negotiation of Treaties: Senators respond with warmth to courting, but with heat to neglect. Inadequate consultation risks misjudgement of negotiating positions with foreign states, and so defeat in the Senate. President Carter's negotiation of SALT II divided the Democratic party in the Senate; President Reagan's proposed sale of AWACS aircraft to Saudi Arabia in 1982 did much the same to his party through his attempt to avoid a legislative veto by the House and the Senate. The law of anticipated consequences obliges Presidents to take account of opinion in the Senate Foreign Relations Committee and of the full Senate (in the case of Treaties), and the reactions in both Chambers (in the case of authorizing and appropriating legislation) before seeking support on Capitol Hill. Drafting of policy proposals only after full consultation reflects political sagacity, not weakness. The need for Senate ratification, coupled with the wisdom of securing bi-partisan support, informed Presidents Truman and Eisenhower's approach to strategic policy formulation. Such an approach does not ensure foreign policy success, but does offer some prospect of domestic tranquillity.

Presidential failure to secure Senate ratification of Treaties can alter the entire course of US foreign policy, as the Senate's rejection of the Treaty of

Versailles in 1920 showed. The Senate's action flowed partly from partisanship (symbolised in Wilson's unwise exclusion of senior Republicans from the American delegation to Versailles), his unwillingness to consult fully with the Senate prior to establishing his own negotiating position, and his unyielding opposition to compromise with key Senators who sought an amendment of the Treaty's Tenth Article in order to preserve Congress's prerogative to declare war and commit US forces. President Carter's Panama Canal Treaty of 1979 would have been defeated had the Senate leadership not visited Panama to secure amendments necessary for ratification. Carter lacked both the confidence and the foresight to consult influential Senators during the Treaty's negotiation, which would have obviated the need for remedial action later.

The North Atlantic Treaty (1949) illustrates the utility for Presidents of close political collaboration with the Senate. Consultation between the Senate Foreign Relations Committee and the State Department was close throughout the drafting of the Treaty. Moreover, the ground was prepared by a Senate Resolution calling for a collective security organization linking the United States and western Europe; this Resolution was drafted by State Department officials and senior Senators including Arthur Vandenberg and Thomas Connally. Bridging the separation of the Executive and Legislature in the cause of "advice and consent" has both force and value, as even Alexander Hamilton acknowledged in *Federalist* No. 75. The constitutional law regarding the termination of Treaties is less clear than their ratification, although potentially of comparable moment. The Court's majority holding in *Goldwater* v. *Carter*, 444 US 996 (1979) that the question is political, and thus beyond the Court's jurisdiction, does not close the matter; it is likely to return for adjudication when Congress next challenges a President's termination of a Treaty.

Recent Presidents have sometimes viewed the prospect of securing the ratification of Treaties as insufficiently certain or excessively cumbersome, and so have resorted to concluding Executive Agreements. The destroyer-bases swap arrangement with Britain in 1940 (more than a year before the United States was brought into the war) is the most celebrated example. Roosevelt took the step because he (justifiably) feared that the Senate would reject a Treaty taking the United States a step further from neutrality. From the President's constitutional authority to recognise foreign governments, he must have an implied power to conclude agreements with foreign states. (He may also be given authority to negotiate agreements by delegated authority – foreign trade legislation protects individual members of Congress from taking responsibility for agreements which serve national, but not local, interests.) Executive Agreements risk involving the President and Congress in disputes over their respective powers, but conflict has usually occurred when agreements are concluded secretly, or touch the heart of the nation's foreign policy commitments. In the first case, the Senate cannot act if secrecy is maintained; in the second, Congress may protect Senate prerogatives by refusing to appropriate funds for the Agreement's implementation, or by so amending authorizing legislation that the Agreement is vitiated.

Foreign and Military Aid

Congress's power of the purse over US foreign and defence policy is clearly evident with regard to foreign and military aid. The President requests aid budgets, but Congress retains complete autonomy in law-making: it determines the identity of beneficiaries, the budget's size and the allocation of funds. Foreign aid attracts attention disproportionate to its cost. Unpopular with constituents, many of whom erroneously suppose it to be a large proportion of Federal expenditure, and even more of whom think it wasteful, the foreign aid budget is the object of intensive lobbying by foreign governments to whom the aid is important, but also (for example) from human rights organisations such as Amnesty International and Asia Watch (see p. 402), whose officials regularly testify against US military aid being granted to regimes that flout human rights. Members of the House and the Senate also choose to give Committee and Subcommittee hearings on foreign aid publicity, because the annual legislative rounds of authorization and appropriation enable them to question officials on US policies towards States and regions.

The cyclical appropriations process not only guarantees Congress influence over administration policy but also enables distributive politics to be played (see Tables 12.1 and 12.2). As with structural defence policy, military aid gives Senators and Congressmen opportunities to direct Federal spending towards businesses in their State or District. Foreign aid gives them the opportunity to appeal to fiscally conservative voters by attempting to cut the President's foreign aid budget request, or alternatively (for example) to appeal to Jewish voters by supporting increased aid to Israel. Since the redistribution of power within Congress in the early 1970s (see Chapter 5), the foreign aid budget has become more politicized and subject to detailed control. This development has been most apparent with human rights and international drug trafficking. Congress requires the State Department to report annually on human rights abuses in foreign countries, which may be taken into account when determining aid. The department's report became embroiled in controversy during Mr Reagan's Administration when, for reasons of *realpolitik*, he sought increased financial support for regimes in central America which had deplorably bad human rights records. The Anti-Drug Abuse Act (1986) required the Executive to certify whether foreign countries were or were not co-operating with American efforts to end international trafficking in drugs: President Reagan reported that General Noriega was co-operating even as it became evident that the Panamanian leader was personally profiting from a huge drug-smuggling operation

TABLE 12.1

**US Foreign Aid: Commitments for Economic Assistance,
by Region and Selected Countries, 1985–93, $millions**

Region and country	1985	1990	1991	1992	1993
Europe	284	160	606	514	469
Near East	3,270	2,199	2,754	2,205	2,124
of which:					
Egypt	1,065	901	783	893	748
Israel	1,950	1,195	1,850	1,200	1,200
Asia	781	873	749	511	375
of which:					
Pakistan	250	276	96	–	6
Philippines	183	314	328	201	83
Sub-Saharan Africa	839	621	865	891	783
Latin America	1,506	1,486	1,075	855	780
of which:					
Costa Rica	196	78	42	24	9
El Salvador	376	200	180	234	172
Guatemala	76	86	60	34	33
Nicaragua	–	220	215	43	128
Panama	74	396	40	15	6
Non-regional	1,453	1,607	1,598	1,693	2,018
Total	**8,132**	**6,964**	**7,668**	**6,819**	**7,059**

Source: *United States Statistical Abstract, 1996*, table 1297.

TABLE 12.2

US Foreign Military Aid by Region and Selected Countries, 1985–93 $million

Region and country	1985	1990	1991	1992	1993
Europe	1,736	939	1,007	960	863
of which:					
Portugal	128	87	101	102	91
Spain	403	2	2	1	–
Middle East	2,833	3,236	3,182	3,158	3,158
of which:					
Egypt	1,177	1,296	1,302	1,302	1,302
Israel	1,400	1,792	1,800	1,800	1,800
East Asia	416	383	233	32	22
of which:					
Indonesia	34	2	27	2	–
Philippines	42	143	203	28	18
South Korea	232	1	1	1	-
Africa	279	39	38	17	24
Latin America	269	234	237	124	74
of which:					
El Salvador	136	181	67	23	11
Honduras	67	21	34	6	3
Non-regional	58	63	61	56	1
Total	**5,801**	**4,894**	**4,760**	**4,348**	**4,143**

Source: *United States Statistical Abstract, 1996*, table 1296.

conducted with American knowledge. Violation of Congressional trust during the Vietnam War and Iran-*Contra* continue to exercise a chilling effect upon the conduct of foreign policy. Congress will not grant greater administrative discretion to the Executive as long as its members, or a majority of them, distrust it. The problem worsened in the 1980s as the split partisan control of the two elective branches appeared to have become the dominant pattern.

Trade Policy

Trade policy presents fewer but significant opportunities to Congress, which has deliberately chosen to place primary responsibility for negotiating in GATT with the USTR, a part of the EOP whose officials are responsible to the President. To delegate responsibility (for example) to an agency of the Department of Commerce would expose trade negotiators to greater and more numerous pressures from Congress and private interests alike. By affording the USTR autonomy from narrow interests, and granting the President "fast-track" negotiating authority, Congress implicitly recognizes the United States's overriding interest in maintaining a liberal trading regime.

Sectional interests none the less abound. In the Uruguay Round, they included agricultural and service industries seeking unfettered access to foreign markets; agricultural interests opposed to lifting barriers against competitive imports; textile manufacturers seeking continued protection from high tariffs; supporters of programmes benefiting US producers under "Buy American" programmes, and opponents of the GATT panel ruling which held that the administration's ban on the importing of tuna caught in nets not certified as friendly to dolphins violated GATT rules. Such an *ad hoc* alliance has only one interest in common: opposition to the aggregation of interests in one Treaty.

Structural Policy

Structural policy includes the procurement of weapons and weapons systems; the construction, expansion, reduction, and closure of defence bases and facilities; and the hiring, deploying and organising of military personnel. An excellent example of distributive policy, it consists in the Federal government purchasing goods and services from private businesses with public funds. Except for the lively market in guns sold to American citizens to defend themselves against other American citizens, the Federal government is a monopsonist in the domestic market for weapons. The sale by US defence contractors of weapons and weapons systems to foreign governments is tightly regulated in statute, and overseen by Congress.

Structural policy ties the Executive, Congress, and groups together unusually tightly. Defence contractors depend for their profits, and their employees for their jobs, upon decisions made by the President, the Pentagon, and (most of all) by Congress. They decide which weapons systems are to be bought, in what quantities, under what conditions, from whom, and over what period. Structural defence policy therefore matters for the domestic economy as a whole, for local economies dependent upon defence contractors, and so for American politics in general. Decisions about structural policy are politically informed. To that extent, the location and status of military bases, the number, type, and mix of weapons systems do not necessarily address the United States' actual defence needs.

The power of the purse and single-member Districts ensure that structural policy is a product of politicians' calculations about the significance of their decisions for their careers. Local politics obstructs policy-making in the national interest: developing a rational policy for United States' military bases has been bedevilled by Congress's fragmentation. Between the 1930s and early 1970s, southern domination of key committees caused a large proportion of expenditure on weapons and bases to be directed to the South, known by sceptical northerners in the United States Army as the region where Federal highways connect Federal bases. Only with the slight reduction in real defence spending from 1986 onwards, and the sharper reductions following the Soviet Union's disintegration, did Congress establish a procedure for overcoming this costly collective action problem. Base closures are now proposed to Congress by the Secretary of Defense and voted on in a single package. It is effectively a closed bureaucratic rule which, like the closed rule under which the House Ways and Means Committee once operated in Congress, has the advantage of enforcing hard choices by overcoming particularism.

The new procedure has not diminished politicians' proclivity to judge the country's defence equipment needs by their own political interests. Defence contractors duly exploit this weakness by distributing subcontracts widely, so that as many Senators and Congressmen as possible have vested interests in defending weapons projects from elimination. Production runs are expensively extended, and research and development programmes continued, to protect Congressional politicians from opponents' attacks. Policy is consequently often driven by the weapons acquired instead of weapons being bought to serve a particular policy.

At nearly $245 billion, Congress's appropriation to the Department of Defense for the 1997 fiscal year was nearly a hundred times greater than that to the State Department (see Table 12.3, which breaks this figure down by

TABLE 12.3

Defence Appropriations, Fiscal Year 1997
(measured in thousands of dollars of New Budget Authority)

Category	Clinton's request	House Bill	Senate Bill	Final Bill
Military personnel	69,782,830	70,115,160	69,802,587	70,016,500
Operations and maintenance	78,462,166	80,555,383	78,956,595	79,163,222
Procurement	38,137,109	45,513,657	44,124,082	43,815,484
Research and development	34,745,672	37,511,031	37,434,464	37,441,121
Miscellaneous	13,147,417	13,165,317	14,285,137	13,400,567
Other agencies	303,239	355,955	294,039	340,664
Total (including adjustments)	234,678,433	245,216,503	244,896,904	244,277,558

Source: Senate Appropriations Committee.

category). The figures conceal the politics behind their establishment, but every weapons system on the list has its constituency of supporters in Congress who find merit in it because part of the system is manufactured in their District. For example, Congressman Hochbrueckner, the liberal Democratic Representative from Long Island, New York, strove in 1989 to maintain production of the Grumman F14-D against the Defense Department (no less) which sought to end it; Grumman's main base is on Long Island. Buddy Darden, the Democratic Member of Congress for Georgia's 7th District, spent much of 1986 and 1987 attempting to persuade both the Air Force and his colleagues in Congress of the superiority of Lockheed's C-5 transport over McDonnell-Douglas's C-17. Lockheed's main facility is in his District; McDonnell-Douglas's is not. Although Hochbrueckner and Darden sit on the House Armed Services Committee, they failed to save their favoured projects. However, since such decisions are usually choices between competing systems, others gained.

Each of the armed services has a vested interest in its own overseas bases, often in countries with weak and undemocratic regimes, where the service has its own network of contacts with the armed services of the host government and may pursue its own bureaucratic interest in the guise of its own foreign and defence policy. Without representatives in Congress, these bases may become particularly vulnerable at a time of budgetary constraints and defence cuts.

Conclusion

In foreign and defence policy, the model of a fragmented and separated political system is less straightforwardly applicable to American government. First, the constitutional authority of the Federal government relative to the fifty States is much greater than in domestic policy. Second, with the exceptions of foreign aid and structural defence policy-making, the President's prerogatives are more numerous and substantial than in domestic or economic policy. The Executive's autonomy from Congressional and interest group pressures is consequently more extensive.

The President lacks competition in forming and executing foreign policy only during the management of crises and wars, and then only in the short term. It is quite different in other areas of foreign and defence policy formation. In the construction of defence bases; in the procurement of weapons systems and other supplies; in foreign aid policy; in strategic policy towards regions and countries; in the development of trade policy and the export of sensitive items of high-technology equipment; in immigration policy; and in questions of human rights and their abuse in foreign countries, Congress, intellectuals, journalists, interest groups, and public opinion play different, and often important, roles. Even where the autonomy of the Executive Branch is greatest, it is constrained. Even where government appears to be unified, symbolized in the lonely responsibilities of the President as Commander-in-Chief of the world's sole remaining military superpower, the politics of competition and fragmentation remain latent and are readily activated.

13

Conclusion

The bicentenary of the Republic's founding coupled with the deep Federal fiscal crisis induced close examination of the capacity of the government established by the Constitution to address social and economic policy disorders. Notwithstanding the deficit's virtual disappearrance, there remain serious and widely-shared apprehensions about the suitability of the Constitutional design, and the extent to which policy problems have social, historical, and political roots. Five particular criticisms are illustrative, though not exhaustive, of this central problem.

The gravest problem facing the United States at the end of the twentieth century is the persisting relative deprivation of black Americans. Among other minorities, only Native-Americans suffer greater disadvantage; for them, America's promise of assimilation has failed – as their separation on reservations attests. Shamefully, their misery is little noticed by most Americans, and (no less shamefully) by most of us who write about American society and politics. For black Americans, however, there has until recently remained the possibility that the promise of assimilation would solve their predicament. Shedding the stigma of inferiority under southern state governments' racist laws through the Federal government's belated intervention between 1954 and 1965 was a hugely important step towards such solution. As Nathan Glazer has argued (Glazer, 1997), those legal and political achievements, for which many Americans had long struggled, refuelled liberal optimism about the integration of black and white in schools, employment, and housing: that which had been accomplished in respect of all other racial groups (save for the forgotten native-Americans) could, it was anticipated, now be achieved for black Americans. Since the mid-1960s, many black Americans have known educational opportunity and success, and the occupational advance and financial security which often results. Yet, significant though their advances have been, their greater number remain enmired in multiple and crippling disadvantage from birth: the generational transmission of prejudice and racism resists simple legal remedy. Fissures in American society which separated black Americans from whites before the Civil Rights Act of 1964 separate them still: while many black Americans now work in integrated offices, few attend integrated schools, and almost none live in integrated neighbourhoods. Segregation *de jure* was ended in

1964; its persistence *de facto* grievously damages black American lives and mocks the confident assertion that all are created equal.

Congress's own collective decision-making is widely thought to be corrupted by the private financing of campaigns and the uncompetitive character of most Congressional districts. Aided by sophisticated campaign consultants, politicians appear better adapted to satisfying group and individual demands than to identifying a public interest, and expressing it through legislation and action. Popular distrust of politicians and deep cynicism about their ethical standards and motives have increased. Congress's procedures, norms, rules, composition, capacities, and roles have altered greatly and repeatedly over two hundred years. As Chapter 5 showed, Congress's institutional evolution has continued under electoral, endogenous, and exogenous political pressures throughout the period of modern United States' government from Franklin Roosevelt's Presidency onwards. Partly as a result of the greater transparency of its procedures and behaviour of its members, the details of Congress's intimate webs of political and financial relations with interest groups are plainer in the final decade of the twentieth century than they were during the final decade of the nineteenth. Never the less, the fact of corruption in those relations characterizes Congressional politics in the 1890s better than it does in the 1990s. While distrust of Congress spilled over in the 1992 and 1994 Congressional elections into intense disapproval of individual Members of Congress (causing the premature retirement of many who anticipated defeat), similar sentiments have been a recurrent feature of American politics, fuelled by an abiding suspicion of government and politicians. Public opinion poll data lend some support to the claim that popular distrust of government (especially of Federal government) has become both deeper and more extensive since the poison of Vietnam and Watergate entered politics. American government remains infected with, and deeply affected by, that poison. Yet the Waco siege and the Oklahoma bombing, though novel in the form of the anti-government sentiments they expressed and to which they gave rise, are not at all novel in the fundamental antipathy to government on which they draw as the discussion in Chapter 1 showed. The ambiguities of the Constitution, in which revolutionary values coexist with principles of stable government, leave open spaces for Jacksonian sentiments to express themselves, and often to do so with violence.

The utility of parties to government is widely thought to have fallen as party organization has weakened. It is ironic that the much-vaunted decline of party in the United States should since the 1960s have been held responsible (partly by some, but apparently wholly by others) for the difficulty of effecting collective choice. In the last decade of the nineteenth century and for the first two decades of the twentieth, party was regarded (with good reason) as destructive to the public interest and intrinsically corruptive by reason of its control of government patronage and contracts.

City parties throughout the north-eastern States, and Courthouse parties in much of the South, bore rich testimony to this view. As parties gradually fell under public control (symbolised in the extension of the direct Primary), their capacity for independent action founded upon a powerful organization withered – although the extent of the withering varied with the tightness of the public control assumed by State governments. During the twentieth century, therefore, parties have lost control, but not necessarily influence, over nominating procedures. Yet at both State and Federal levels, parties are inescapably hampered in their capacity to address the problem of effecting collective choice in a fragmented system by themselves being products of that system. Accordingly, they are divided between elected branches and levels of government; in a system of separated powers, parties can accomplish only occasionally, and with difficulty, that which they normally perform almost automatically in a semi-fused, unitary, state such as Britain.

The weak central State is hamstrung by powerful social interests which protect expensive claims on the public purse, notably entitlement programmes in which the great majority of voters (especially middle-class ones) have powerful stakes. The division of government in the United States at Federal and State level renders not only the notion of the State problematic, but also its structure weak and its boundaries both uncertain and permeable to societal influences. These are not recent developments, but intended consequences of constitutional structure. The Federal government's growth in the twentieth century has mitigated such weakness by creating a large peacetime national security apparatus, but has merely confirmed and reproduced it elsewhere in the creation of large Federal, State, and local bureaucracies which themselves reflect the fragmentation of the constitutional design. The result is a complex system of governments interacting with each other in the formation, legitimation, implementation, and evaluation of public policy, accountable to different electorates at different times, limited by Federal and State systems of judicial review, and everywhere lobbied and penetrated by interest groups pressing their claims upon politicians, their members of staff, bureaucrats, and Judges. The extensiveness and intensiveness with which governments across the United States are penetrated by interest groups have grown rapidly in the post-war period, as the number, diversity, resources, professional competence, and litigiousness of interest groups have increased. Groups with vested interests in government policies now advance and defend their claims with assiduous creativity. That such advancing of particular interests need not necessarily serve a collective interest was understood as well by Madison in 1787 as it was by Olson in 1965. The difficulties that both individualism and interest group liberalism pose for government, necessarily great in democracies, are accentuated in the United States because of the potent mixing of individualism as a supreme political value with a structure of government which accommodates it at the price of aggregating interests only with difficulty.

The quality of Presidents is commonly regarded as both damagingly low, and to have declined. In fact, no secular decline in the integrity, intellectual power, political dexterity, or leadership capacity of Presidents is apparent. The short-run deficiency in the third and fourth of these between 1974 and 1981 revealed no underlying trend (as Ronald Reagan showed between 1981 and 1989); nor did a similar short-run weakness of intellectual command between 1981 and 1989 (as Bill Clinton quickly showed in early 1993). The integrity that was absent in Richard Nixon's conduct of the Presidency was present in that of both of his successors (Gerald Ford, and Jimmy Carter). With the spectacular exception of Lincoln, a comparison of the cast of Presidents in the second half of the nineteenth century compares poorly, not well, with that of the second half of the twentieth. The system of national nominating Conventions, whose effective replacement after 1968 by Primaries and caucuses was held by many scholars to be responsible for the production of unsuitable and undistinguished candidates, had itself not reliably supplied candidates of high quality. It is doubtful whether any system of Primaries and caucuses in the 1920s could have nominated candidates less distinguished, more barren of ideas or devoid of purpose, than the nominating Conventions that produced Warren Harding and Calvin Coolidge.

At different points since the late 1960s, these five claims (and variations upon them) have been well ventilated in major newspapers, especially *The Washington Post* and *The New York Times,* in public (especially elite) opinion, and among many students of government. While the fundamental problem of effecting collective choice remains severe in the United States, the degree of difficulty which it presents has not markedly increased in the Republic's two hundred years. Politics remains the activity by which decisions are collectively made, enforced, modified, and rejected. The success which political systems enjoy in these respects offers a means by which their efficiency may be judged. For democracies, the standard of judgement is more severe, since they must engage in such collective action while fully respecting the dignity and autonomy of civil society, and of individual rights, while holding themselves accountable to the electorate, and operating consensually but under law. The fundamental problem presented by politics in the United States, especially in the Federal government, is that collective decisions are exceptionally difficult to make in a multiply-fragmented system that inhibits articulation of the public interest, penetrated by a vigorous, diverse, and rapidly-developing civil society. The high premia placed upon democratic accountability and individual rights accordingly make the governing of the United States uncommonly demanding.

The composition, content, and ordering of the agenda of public policy in the United States are competitively determined and subject to change. While the items high on the Federal agenda in Mr Clinton's second term appear to be forbiddingly complex and resistant to collective public remedy, there are no good grounds for judging current problems of public policy as being more severe than the combination of deep economic depression and world war with which Franklin Roosevelt was faced, or the threatened sundering of the United States that Abraham Lincoln successfully overcame, or the creation and establishment of the Republic to which Washington, Adams, Jefferson, Madison, and Jackson in their several ways devoted themselves. As the citing of these examples suggests, the Presidency is not only the centrepiece of the United States Constitution and of its politics, but provides the starting point for understanding the Republic's capacity to endure. It does so because the Presidency is a symbol of the country's ability to reconstitute itself, the means whereby old problems may be examined afresh, new objectives identified, and old values invoked anew. The Constitution grants little authority to Presidents but, as this book has shown, manifold opportunities to his competitors and nominal allies to deflect, demur, and delay. Yet the Constitution offers the possibility of renewal by giving a new President not only heavy responsibilities but also the fresh opportunity to lead this most diverse of nations and complex of governments. The cyclical prospects of change and possibilities of progress are not the least of the Constitution's complex legacies.

Appendix 1

The Constitution of the United States

We the People of the United States, in order to form a more perfect union, establish Justice, insure domestic tranquillity, provide for the common defence, promote the general Welfare, and secure the Blessings of Liberty to ourselves and our Posterity, do ordain and establish this Constitution for the United States of America.

Article I

Section 1.   All legislative Powers herein granted shall be vested in a Congress of the United States, which shall consist of a Senate and a House of Representatives.

Section 2.   The House of Representatives shall be composed of Members chosen every second Year by the People of the several States, and the Electors in each State shall have the Qualifications requisite for the Electors of the most numerous Branch of the State Legislature.

No Person shall be a Representative who shall not have attained to the Age of twenty-five years, and been seven Years a Citizen of the United States, and who shall not, when elected, be an Inhabitant of that State in which he shall be chosen.

Representatives and direct Taxes shall be apportioned among the several States which may be included within this Union, according to their respective Numbers, which shall be determined by adding to the whole Number of free Persons, including those bound to Service for a Term of Years, and excluding Indians not taxed, three fifths of all other Persons. The actual Enumeration shall be made within three Years after the first Meeting of the Congress of the United States, and within every subsequent Term of ten Years, in such Manner as they shall by Law direct. The Number of Representatives shall not exceed one for every thirty Thousand, but each State shall have at Least one Representative; and until such enumeration shall be made, the State of New Hampshire shall be entitled to chuse three, Massachusetts eight, Rhode-Island and Providence Plantations one, Connecticut five, New-York six, New Jersey four, Pennsylvania eight, Delaware one, Maryland six, Virginia ten, North Carolina five, South Carolina five, and Georgia three.

When vacancies happen in the Representation from any State, the Executive authority thereof shall issue Writs of Election to fill such Vacancies.

House of Representatives shall chuse their Speaker and other Officers; and shall have the sole Power of Impeachment.

Section 3.   The Senate of the United States shall be composed of two Senators from each State, chosen by the Legislature thereof, for six Years; and each Senator shall have one Vote.

Immediately after they shall be assembled in consequence of the first Election, they shall be divided as equally as may be into three Classes. The Seats of the Senators of the first Class shall be vacated at the Expiration of the second Year, of the second Class at the Expiration of the fourth Year, and of the third Class at the Expiration of the sixth Year, so that one-third may be chosen every second Year; and if Vacancies happen by Resignation, or otherwise, during the Recess of the Legislature of any State, the Executive thereof may make temporary Appointments until the next Meeting of the Legislature, which shall then fill such Vacancies.

No Person shall be a Senator who shall not have attained to the Age of thirty Years, and been nine Years a Citizen of the United States, and who shall not, when elected, be an Inhabitant of that State for which he shall be chosen.

The Vice President of the United States shall be President of the Senate, but shall have no Vote, unless they be equally divided.

The Senate shall chuse their other Officers, and also a President pro tempore, in the Absence of the Vice President, or when he shall exercise the Office of President of the United States.

The Senate shall have the sole Power to try all Impeachments. When sitting for that Purpose, they shall be on Oath or Affirmation. When the President of the United States is tried, the Chief Justice shall preside: And no Person shall be convicted without the Concurrence of two thirds of the Members present.

Judgement in Cases of Impeachment shall not extend further than to removal from Office, and disqualification to hold and enjoy any Office of honor, Trust or Profit under the United States: but the Party convicted shall never the less be liable and subject to Indictment, Trial, Judgement and Punishment, according to Law.

Section 4.   The Times, Places and Manner of holding Elections for Senators and Representatives, shall be prescribed in each State by the Legislature thereof, but the Congress may at any time by Law make or alter such Regulations, except as to the Places of chusing Senators.

The Congress shall assemble at least once in every Year, and such Meeting shall be on the first Monday in December, unless they shall by Law appoint a different Day.

Section 5.   Each House shall be the Judge of the Elections, Returns and Qualifications of its own Members, and a Majority of each shall constitute a Quorum to do Business; but a small Number may adjourn from day to day, and may be authorized to compel the Attendance of absent Members, in such Manner, and under such Penalties, as each House may provide.

Each House may determine the Rules of its Proceedings, punish its Members for disorderly Behavior, and, with the Concurrence of two thirds, expel a Member.

Each House shall keep a Journal of its Proceedings, and from time to time publish the same, excepting such Parts as may in their judgement require Secrecy; and the Yeas and Nays of the Members of either House on any question shall, at the Desire of either House of one fifth of those present, be entered on the Journal. Neither House, during the Session of Congress, shall, without the Consent of the other, adjourn for more than three days, nor to any other Place than that in which the two Houses shall be sitting.

Section 6.   The Senators and Representatives shall receive a Compensation for their Services, to be ascertained by Law, and paid out of the Treasury of the United States. They shall in all Cases, except Treason, Felony and Breach of the Peace, be privileged from Arrest during their Attendance at the Session of their respective Houses, and in going to and returning from the same; and for any Speech or Debate in either House, they shall not be questioned in any other Place.

No Senator or Representative shall, during the Time for which he was elected, be appointed to any Civil Office under the Authority of the United States, which shall have been created, or the Emoluments whereof shall have been encreased during such time; and no Person holding any Office under the United States, shall be a Member of either House during his Continuance in Office.

Section 7.   All Bills for raising Revenue shall originate in the House of Representatives; but the Senate may propose or concur with Amendments as on other Bills.

Every Bill which shall have passed the House of Representatives and the Senate, shall, before it becomes a Law, be presented to the President of the United States; If he approve he shall sign it, but if not he shall return it, with his Objections to that House in which it shall have originated, who shall enter the Objections at large on their Journal, and proceed to reconsider it. If after such Reconsideration two thirds of that House shall agree to pass the Bill, it shall be sent, together with the Objections, to the other House, by which it shall likewise be reconsidered, and if approved by two thirds of that House, it shall become a Law. But in all such Cases the Votes of both Houses shall be determined by Yeas and Nays, and the Names of The Persons voting for and against the Bill shall be entered on the Journal of each House respectively. If any Bill shall not be returned by the President within ten Days (Sundays excepted) after it shall have been presented to him, the Same shall be a Law, in like Manner as if he had signed it, unless the Congress by their Adjournment prevent its Return, in which Case it shall not be a Law.

Every Order, Resolution, or Vote to which the Concurrence of the Senate and House of Representatives may be necessary (except on a question of Adjournment) shall be presented to the President of the United States; and before the Same shall take effect, shall be approved by him or being disapproved by him, shall be repassed by two thirds of the Senate and House of Representatives, according to the Rules and Limitations prescribed in the Case of a Bill.

Section 8.   The Congress shall have Power To lay and collect Taxes, Duties, Imposts and Excises, to pay the debts and provide for the common Defence and general Welfare of the United States; but all Duties, Imposts and Excises shall be uniform throughout the United States;

To borrow Money on the credit of the United States;

To regulate Commerce with foreign Nations, and among the several States, and with the Indian Tribes;

To establish an uniform Rule of Naturalization, and uniform Laws on the subject of Bankruptcies throughout the United States;

To coin Money, regulate the Value thereof, and of foreign Coin, and fix the Standard of Weights and Measures;

To provide for the Punishment of counterfeiting the Securities and current Coin of the United States;

To establish Post Offices and post Roads;

To promote the Progress of Science and useful Arts, by securing for limited Times to Authors and Inventors the exclusive Right to their respective Writings and Discoveries;

To constitute Tribunals inferior to the supreme Court;

To define and punish Piracies and Felonies committed on the high Seas, and Offences against the Law of Nations;

To declare War, grant letters of Marque and Reprisal, and make Rules concerning Captures on Land and Water;

To raise and support Armies, but no Appropriation of Money to that Use shall be for a longer Term than two Years;

To provide and maintain a Navy;

To make Rules for the Government and Regulation of the land and naval Forces; To provide for calling forth the Militia to execute the Laws of the Union, suppress Insurrections and repel Invasions;

To provide for organizing, arming, and disciplining the Militia, and for governing such Part of them as may be employed in the Service of the United States, reserving to the States respectively, the Appointment of the Officers, and the Authority of training the Militia according to the discipline prescribed by Congress;

To exercise exclusive Legislation in all Cases whatsoever, over such District (not exceeding ten Miles square) as may, by Cession of particular States, and the Acceptance of Congress, become the Seat of the Government of the United States, and to exercise like Authority over all Places purchased by the Consent of the Legislature of The State in which the Same shall be, for the Erection of Forts, Magazines, Arsenals, dock-Yards, and other needful Buildings; – And

To make all Laws which shall be necessary and proper for carrying into Execution the foregoing Powers, and all other Powers vested by this Constitution in the Government of the United States, or in any Department or Officer thereof.

Section 9.   The Migration or Importation of such Persons as any of the States now existing shall think proper to admit, shall not be prohibited by the Congress prior to the Year one thousand eight hundred and eight, but a Tax or duty may be imposed on such Importation, not exceeding ten dollars for each Person.

The Privilege of the Writ of Habeas Corpus shall not be suspended, unless when in Cases of Rebellion or Invasion the public Safety may require it.

No Bill of Attainder or ex post facto Law shall be passed.

No Capitation, or other direct, tax shall be laid, unless in Proportion to the Census or Enumeration herein before directed to be taken.

No Tax or Duty shall be laid on Articles exported from any State.

No Preference shall be given by any Regulation of Commerce or Revenue to the Ports of one State over those of another; nor shall Vessels bound to, or from, one State, be obliged to enter, clear, or pay Duties in another.

No Money shall be drawn from the Treasury, but in Consequence of Appropriations made by Law; and a regular Statement and Account of the Receipts and Expenditures of all public Money shall be published from time to time.

No Title of Nobility shall be granted by the United States: And no Person holding any Office of Profit or Trust under them, shall, without the Consent of the Congress, accept of any present, Emolument, Office, or Title, of any kind whatever, from any King, Prince, or foreign State.

Section 10.   No State shall enter into any Treaty, Alliance, or Confederation; grant Letters of Marque and Reprisal; coin Money; emit Bills of Credit; make any Thing but gold and silver Coin a Tender in Payment of Debts; pass any Bill of Attainder, ex post facto Law, or Law impairing the Obligation of Contracts, or grant any Title of Nobility.

No State shall, without the Consent of the Congress, lay any Imposts or Duties on Imports or Exports, except what may be absolutely necessary for executing its inspection Laws: and the net Produce of all Duties and Imposts, laid by any State on Imports or Exports, shall be for the Use of the Treasury of the United States; and all such laws shall be subject to the Revision and Control of the Congress.

No State shall, without the Consent of Congress, lay any Duty of Tonnage, keep Troops, or Ships of War in time of Peace, enter into any Agreement or Compact with another State, or with a foreign Power, or engage in War, unless actually invaded, or in such imminent Danger as will not admit of delay.

Article II

Section 1.   The Executive Power shall be vested in a President of the United States of America. He shall hold his Office during the Term of four Years, and, together with the Vice President, chosen for the same Term, be elected, as follows.

Each State shall appoint, in such Manner as the legislature thereof may direct, a Number of Electors, equal to the whole Number of Senators and Representatives to which the State may be entitled in the Congress: but no Senator or Representative, or Person holding and Office of Trust or Profit under the United States, shall be appointed an Elector.

The electors shall meet in their respective States, and vote by ballot for two Persons, of whom one at least shall not be an Inhabitant of the same State with themselves. And they shall make a List of all the Persons voted for, and of the Number of Votes for each; which List they shall sign and certify, and transmit sealed to the Seat of the Government of the United States, directed to the President of the Senate. The President of the Senate shall, in the Presence of the Senate and House of Representatives, open all the Certificates, and the Votes shall then be counted. The Person having the greatest Number of Votes shall be the President, if such Number be a Majority of the whole Number of Electors appointed; and if there be more than one who have such Majority, and have an equal number of votes, then the House of Representatives shall immediately chuse by Ballot one of them for President; and if no Person have a Majority, then from the five highest on the List the said House shall in like Manner chuse the President. But in chusing the President, the Votes shall be taken by States, the Representation from each State having one Vote; A quorum for this Purpose shall consist of a Member or Members from two thirds of the States, and a Majority of all the States shall be necessary to a Choice. In every Case, after the Choice of the President, the Person having the greatest Number of Votes of the Electors shall be the Vice President. But if there should remain two or more who have equal Votes, the Senate shall chuse from them by Ballot the Vice President.

The Congress may determine the Time of chusing the electors, and the Day on which they shall give their Votes; which Day shall be the same throughout the United States.

No Person except a natural born Citizen, or a Citizen of the United States, at the time of the Adoption of this Constitution, shall be eligible to the Office of President; neither shall any Person be eligible to that Office who shall not have attained to the Age of thirty five Years, and been fourteen Years a Resident within the United States.

In Case of the Removal of the President from Office, or of his Death, Resignation or Inability to discharge the Powers and duties of the said Office, the same shall devolve on the Vice President, and the Congress may by Law provide for the Case of Removal, Death, Resignation or Inability, both of the President and Vice President, declaring what Officer shall then act as President, and such Officer shall act accordingly, until the Disability be removed, or a President shall be elected. The President shall, at stated Times, receive for his Services, a Compensation, which shall neither be encreased nor diminished during the Period for which he shall have been elected, and he shall not receive within that Period any other Emolument from the United States, or any of them.

Before he enter on the Execution of his Office, he shall take the following Oath or Affirmation: - "I do solemnly swear (or affirm) that I will faithfully execute the Office of President of the United States, and will to the best of my Ability, preserve, protect and defend the Constitution of the United States".

Section 2.   The President shall be Commander in Chief of the Army and Navy of the United States, and of the Militia of the several States, when called into the actual Service of the United States; he may require the Opinion, in writing, of the principal Officer in each of the executive Departments, upon any Subject relating to the Duties of their respective Offices, and he shall have Power to grant Reprieves and Pardons for Offences against the United States, except in Cases of Impeachment.

He shall have Power, by and with the Advice and Consent of the Senate, to make Treaties, provided two thirds of the Senators present concur and he shall nominate, and by and with the Advice and Consent of the Senate, shall appoint Ambassadors, other public Ministers and Consuls, Judges of the Supreme Court, and all other Officers of the United States, whose Appointments are not herein otherwise provided for, and which shall be established by Law; but the Congress may by Law vest the Appointment of such inferior Officers, as they think proper, in the President alone, in the Courts of Law, or in the Heads of Departments.

The President shall have Power to fill up all Vacancies that may happen during the Recess of the Senate, by granting Commissions which shall expire at the End of their next Session.

Section 3.   He shall from time to time give to the Congress Information of the State of the Union, and recommend to their Consideration such Measures as he shall judge necessary and expedient; he may, on extraordinary Occasions, convene both Houses, or either of them, and, in case of Disagreement between them, with Respect to the Time of Adjournment, he may adjourn them to such Times as he shall think proper; he shall receive Ambassadors and other Public Ministers; he shall take Care that the Laws be faithfully executed, and shall Commission all the Officers of the United States.

Section 4.   The President, Vice President and all civil Officers of the United States, shall be removed from Office on Impeachment for, and Conviction of, Treason, Bribery, or other high Crimes and Misdemeanors.

Article III

Section 1.   The judicial Power of the United States, shall be vested in one Supreme Court, and in such inferior Courts as the Congress may from time to time ordain and establish. The Judges, both of the supreme and inferior Courts, shall hold their Offices during good Behaviour, and shall, at stated Times, receive for their Services, a Compensation, which shall not be diminished during their Continuance in Office.

Section 2.   The judicial Power shall extend to all Cases, in Law and Equity, arising under this Constitution, the Laws of the United States, and Treaties made, or which shall be made, under their Authority; – to all Cases affecting Ambassadors, other public Ministers and Consuls; – to all Cases of admiralty and maritime Jurisdiction; – to Controversies to which the United States shall be a Party; – to Controversies between two or more States; between a State and Citizens of another State; – between Citizens of different States,– between Citizens of the same State claiming Lands under Grants of different States, and between a state, or the citizens thereof, and foreign States, Citizens or Subjects.

In all Cases affecting Ambassadors, other public Ministers and Consuls, and those in which a State shall be party, the supreme Court shall have original jurisdiction. In all other Cases before mentioned, the supreme Court shall have appellate Jurisdiction, both as to Law and Fact, with such Exceptions, and under such Regulations, as the Congress shall make.

The Trial of all Crimes, except in Cases of Impeachment, shall be by Jury; and such Trial shall be held in the State where the said Crimes shall have been committed; but when not committed within any State, the Trial shall be at such Place or Places as the Congress may by Law have directed.

Section 3.   Treason against the United States, shall consist only in levying War against them, or in adhering to their Enemies, giving them Aid and comfort. No Person shall be convicted of Treason unless on the Testimony of two Witnesses to the same overt Act, or on Confession in open Court.

The Congress shall have Power to declare the Punishment of Treason, but no Attainder of Treason shall work Corruption of blood, or Forfeiture except during the Life of the Person attainted.

Article IV

Section 1.   Full Faith and Credit shall be given in each State to the public Acts, Records, and judicial Proceedings of every other State. And the Congress may by general Laws prescribe the Manner in which such Acts, Records and Proceedings shall be proved, and the Effect thereof.

Section 2.   The Citizens of each State shall be entitled to all Privileges and Immunities of each Citizens in the several States.

A person charged in any State with Treason, Felony, or other Crime, who shall flee from Justice, and be found in another State, shall on Demand of the executive Authority of the State from which he fled, be delivered up, to be removed to the State having Jurisdiction of the Crime.

No Person held to Service or Labour in one State, under the Laws thereof, escaping into another, shall, in Consequence of any Law or regulation therein, be discharged from such Service or Labour but shall be delivered up on Claim of the Party to whom such Service or Labour may be due.

Section 3.   New States may be admitted by the Congress into this Union; but no new State shall be formed or erected within the Jurisdiction of any other State; nor any State be formed by the Junction of two or more States, or Parts of States, without the consent of the Legislatures of the States concerned as well as of the Congress.

The Congress shall have Power to dispose of and make all needful Rules and Regulations respecting the Territory or other Property belonging to the United

States; and nothing in this Constitution shall be so construed as to Prejudice any Claims of the United States, or of any particular State.

Section 4. The United States shall guarantee to every State in this Union a Republican Form of Government, and shall protect each of them against Invasion; and on Application of the Legislature, or of the Executive (when the Legislature cannot be convened) against domestic Violence.

Article V

The Congress, whenever two thirds of both houses shall deem it necessary, shall propose Amendments to this Constitution, or, on the Application of the Legislatures of two thirds of the several States, shall call a Convention for proposing Amendments, which, in either Case, shall be valid to all Intents and Purposes, as Part of this Constitution, when ratified by the Legislatures of three fourths of the several States, or by Conventions in three fourths thereof, as the one or the other Mode of Ratification may be proposed by the Congress; Provided that no Amendment which may be made prior to the Year One thousand eight hundred and eight shall in any Manner affect the first and fourth Clauses in the Ninth Section of the first Article; and that no State, without its Consent, shall be deprived of its equal Suffrage in the Senate.

Article VI

All Debts contracted and Engagements entered into, before the Adoption of this Constitution, shall be as valid against the United States under this Constitution, as under the Confederation.

This Constitution, and the Laws of the United States which shall be made in Pursuance thereof; and all Treaties made, or which shall be made, under the Authority of the United States, shall be the supreme Law of the Land; and the Judges in every State shall be bound thereby, any Thing in the Constitution or Laws of any State to the Contrary notwithstanding.

The Senators and Representatives before mentioned, and the Members of the several State Legislatures, and all executive and Judicial Officers, both of the United States and of the several States, shall be bound by Oath or Affirmation, to support this Constitution; but no religious Test shall ever be required as a Qualification to any office or public Trust under the United States.

Article VII

The Ratification of the Conventions of the nine States, shall be sufficient for the Establishment of this Constitution between the States so ratifying the Same.

DONE in Convention by the Unanimous Consent of the States present the Seventeenth Day of September in the Year of our Lord one thousand seven hundred and Eighty seven and of the Independence of the United States of America the Twelfth. IN WITNESS whereof We have hereunto subscribed our Names.

George Washington

Presid^t and Deputy from Virginia

Appendix 2

Amendments to the Constitution of the United States

(The first ten amendments were proposed on 25 September 1789 and declared ratified on 15 December 1791.)

First

Congress shall make no law respecting an establishment of religion, or prohibiting the free exercise thereof; or abridging the freedom of speech, or of the press; or the right of the people peaceably to assemble, and to petition the government for a redress of grievances.

Second

A well regulated Militia, being necessary to the security of a free State, the right of the people to keep and bear Arms, shall not be infringed.

Third

No Soldier shall, in time of peace, be quartered in any house, without the consent of the Owner, or in time of war, but in a manner to be prescribed by law.

Fourth

The right of the people to be secure in their persons, houses, papers and effects, against unreasonable searches and seizure, shall not be violated, and no Warrants shall issue, but upon probable cause, supported by Oath or affirmation, and particularly describing the place to be searched, and the persons or things to be seized.

Fifth

No person shall be held to answer for a capital, or otherwise infamous crime, unless on a presentment or indictment of a Grand Jury, except in cases arising in the land or naval forces, or in the Militia, when in actual service in time of War or public danger; nor shall any person be subject for the same offence to be twice put in jeopardy of life or limb; nor shall be compelled in any Criminal Case to be a witness against himself, nor be deprived of life, liberty, or property, without due process of law; nor shall private property be taken for public use, without just compensation.

Sixth

In all criminal prosecutions, the accused shall enjoy the right to a speedy and public trial, by an impartial jury of the State and district wherein the crime shall have been committed, which district shall have been previously ascertained by law, and to be informed of the nature and cause of the accusation; to be confronted with the witnesses against him; to have compulsory process for obtaining Witnesses in his favor, and to have the Assistance of Counsel for his defence.

Seventh

In suits at common law, where the value in controversy shall exceed twenty dollars, the right of trial by jury shall be preserved, and no fact tried by a Jury shall be otherwise re-examined in any Court of the United States, than according to the rules of common law.

Eighth

Excessive bail shall not be required, nor excessive fines imposed, nor cruel and unusual punishments inflicted.

Ninth

The enumeration in the Constitution, of certain rights, shall not be construed to deny or disparage others retained by the people.

Tenth

The powers not delegated to the United States by the Constitution, nor prohibited by it to the States, are reserved to the States respectively, or to the people.

Eleventh

(Proposed 4 March 1794; declared ratified 8 January 1798.)

The Judicial power of the United States shall not be construed to extend to any suit in law or equity, commenced or prosecuted against one of the United States by Citizens of another State, or by Citizens or Subjects of any Foreign State.

Twelfth

(Proposed 9 December 1803; declared ratified 25 September 1804.)

The electors shall meet in their respective states, and vote by ballot for President and Vice-President, one of whom, at least, shall not be an inhabitant of the same state with themselves; they shall name in their ballots the person voted for as President, and in distinct ballots the person voted for as Vice-President, and they shall make distinct lists of all persons voted for as President, and of all persons voted for as Vice-President, and of the number of votes for each, which lists they shall sign and certify, and transmit sealed to the seat of the Government of the United States, directed to the President of the Senate; – The President of the Senate shall, in the presence of the Senate and the House of Representatives, open all the certificates and the votes shall then be counted; – The person having the greatest number of votes for President shall be the President, if such number be a majority of the whole number of Electors appointed; and if no person have such majority, then from the persons having the highest numbers not exceeding three on the list of those voted as President, the House of Representatives shall choose immediately, by ballot, the President. But in choosing the President, the votes shall be taken by states, the representation from each state having one vote; a quorum for this purpose shall consist of a member or members from two-thirds of the states, and a majority of all the states shall be necessary to a choice. And if the House of Representatives shall not choose a President whenever the right of choice shall devolve upon them, before the fourth day of March next following, then the Vice-President shall act as President, as in the case of the death or other constitutional disability of the President. The person having the greatest number of votes as Vice-President, shall be the Vice-President, if such number be a majority of the whole number of Electors appointed, and if no person have a majority, then from the two highest numbers on the list, the Senate shall choose the Vice-President; a quorum for the purpose shall consist of two-thirds of the whole number of Senators, and a majority of the whole number shall be necessary to a choice. But no person constitutionally ineligible to the office of President shall be eligible to that of Vice-President of the United States.

Thirteenth

(Proposed 31 January 1865; declared ratified 18 December 1865.)

Section 1. Neither slavery nor involuntary servitude, except as a punishment for crime whereof the party shall have been duly convicted, shall exist within the United States, or any place subject to their jurisdiction.

Section 2. Congress shall have power to enforce this article by appropriate legislation.

Fourteenth

(Proposed 13 June 1866; declared ratified 28 July 1868)

Section 1. All persons born or naturalized in the United States, and subject to the jurisdiction thereof, are citizens of the United States and of the State wherein they reside. No State shall make or enforce any law which shall abridge the privileges or immunities of citizens of the United States; nor shall any State deprive any person of life, liberty, or property, without due process of law; nor deny to any person within its jurisdiction the equal protection of the laws.

Section 2. Representatives shall be apportioned among the several States according to their respective numbers, counting the whole number of persons in each State, excluding Indians not taxed. But when the right to vote at any election for the choice of electors for President and Vice-President of the United States, Representatives in Congress, the Executive and Judicial officers of a State, or the members of the Legislature thereof, is denied to any of the male inhabitants of such State, being twenty-one years of age, and citizens of the United States, or in any way abridged, except for participation in rebellion, or other crime, the basis of representation therein shall be reduced in the proportion which the number of such male citizens shall bear the whole number of twenty-one years of age in such State.

Section 3. No person shall be a Senator or Representative in Congress, or elector of President and Vice President, or hold any office, civil, or military, under the United States, or under any State, who, having previously taken an oath, as a member of Congress, or as an officer of the United States, or as a member of any State legislature, or as an executive or Judicial officer of any State, to support the

Constitution of the United States, shall have engaged in insurrection or rebellion against the same, or given aid or comfort to the enemies thereof. But Congress may by a vote of two-thirds of each House, remove such disability.

Section 4.   The validity of the public debt of the United States, authorized by law, including debts incurred for payment of pensions and bounties for services in suppressing insurrection or rebellion, shall not be questioned. But neither the United States nor any State shall assume or pay any debt or obligation incurred in aid of insurrection or rebellion against the United States, or any claim for the loss or emancipation of any slave; but all such debts, obligations and claims shall be held illegal and void.

Section 5.   The Congress shall have power to enforce, by appropriate legislation, the provisions of this article.

Fifteenth

(Proposed 26 February 1869; declared ratified 30 March 1870.)

Section 1.   The right of citizens of the United States to vote shall not be denied or abridged by the United States or by any State on account of race, color, or previous condition of servitude.

Section 2.   The Congress shall have power to enforce this article by appropriate legislation.

Sixteenth

(Proposed 12 July 1909; declared ratified 25 February 1913.)

The Congress shall have power to lay and collect taxes on incomes, from whatever source derived, without apportionment among the several States, and without regard to any census or enumeration.

Seventeenth

(Proposed 13 May 1912; declared ratified 31 May 1913.)

The Senate of the United States shall be composed of two Senators from each State, elected by the people thereof, for six years; and each Senator shall have one vote. The electors in each State shall have the qualifications requisite for electors of the most numerous branch of the State legislature.

When vacancies happen in the representation of any State in the Senate, the executive authority of such State shall issue writs of election to fill such vacancies: PROVIDED, That the legislature of any State may empower the executive thereof to make temporary appointments until the people fill the vacancies by election as the legislature may direct.

This amendment shall not be so construed as to affect the election or term of any Senator chosen before it becomes valid as part of the Constitution.

Eighteenth

(Proposed 18 December 1917; declared ratified 29 January 1919.)

After one year from the ratification of this article, the manufacture, sale, or transportation of intoxicating liquors within, the importation thereof into, or the exportation thereof from the United States and all territory subject to the jurisdiction thereof for beverage purposes is hereby prohibited.

The Congress and the several States shall have concurrent power to enforce this article by appropriate legislation.

This article shall be inoperative unless it shall have been ratified as an amendment to the Constitution by the legislatures of the several States, as provided in the Constitution, within seven years from the date of the submission hereof to the States by the Congress.

Nineteenth

(Proposed 4 June 1919; declared ratified 26 August 1920.)

The right of citizens of the United States to vote shall not be denied or abridged by the United States or by any States on account of sex.

The Congress shall have power, by appropriate legislation, to enforce the provisions of this article.

Twentieth

Proposed 2 March 1932; declared ratified 6 February 1933.)

Section 1.   The terms of the President and Vice-President shall end at noon on the twentieth day of January, and the terms of Senators and Representatives at noon on the third day of January, of the years in which such terms would have ended if this article had not been ratified; and the terms of their successors shall then begin.

Section 2.   The Congress shall assemble at least once in every year, and such meeting shall begin at noon of the third day of January, unless they shall by law appoint a different day.

Section 3.   If, at any time fixed for the beginning of the term of the President, the President-elect shall have died, the Vice-President-elect shall act as President until a President shall have qualified; and the Congress may by law provide for the case wherein neither a President-elect nor a Vice-President-elect shall have qualified, declaring who shall then act as President, or the manner in which one who is to act shall be selected, and such person shall act accordingly until a President or Vice-President shall have qualified.

Section 4.   The Congress may by law provide for the case of the death of any of the persons from whom the House of Representatives may choose a President whenever the right of choice shall have devolved upon them, and for the case of the death of any of the persons from whom the Senate may choose a Vice-President whenever the right of choice shall have devolved upon them.

Section 5.   Sections 1 and 2 shall take effect on the 15th day of October following the ratification of this article.

Section 6.   This article shall be inoperative unless it shall have been ratified as an amendment to the Constitution by the legislatures of three-fourths of the several States within seven years from the date of its submission.

Twenty-First

(Proposed 20 February 1933; declared ratified 5 December 1933.)

Section 1.   The eighteenth article of amendment to the Constitution of the United States is hereby repealed.

Section 2.   The transportation or importation into any State, Territory, or possession of the United States for delivery or use therein of intoxicating liquors, in violation of the laws thereof, is hereby prohibited.

Section 3.   This article shall be inoperative unless it shall have been ratified as an amendment to the Constitution by convention in the several States, as provided in the Constitution, within seven years from the date of the submission hereof to the States by the Congress.

Twenty-Second

(Proposed 21 March 1947; declared ratified 3 March 1951.)

Section 1.   No person shall be elected to the office of the President more than twice, and no person who has held the office of President, or acted as President, for more than two years of a term to which some other person was elected President shall be elected to the office of the President more than once. But this Article shall not apply to any person holding the office of President when this Article was proposed by the Congress, and shall not prevent any person who may be holding the office of President, or acting as President, during the term within which this Article become operative from holding the office of President or acting as President during the remainder of such term.

Twenty-Third

(Proposed 17 June 1960; declared ratified 3 April 1961.)

Section 1.   The District constituting the seat of Government of the United States shall appoint in such manner as the Congress may direct:

A number of electors of President and Vice President equal to the whole number of Senators and Representatives in Congress to which the District would be entitled if it were a State, but in no event more than the least populous State; they shall be in addition to those appointed by the States, but they shall be considered, for the purposes of election of President and Vice President, to be electors appointed by a State; and they shall meet in the District and perform such duties as provided by the twelfth article of amendment.

Section 2.   The Congress shall have power to enforce this article by appropriate legislation.

Twenty-Fourth

(Proposed 27 August 1962; declared ratified 4 February 1964.)

Section 1.   The right of citizens of the United States to vote in any primary or other election for President or Vice President, for electors for President or Vice President, or for Senator or Representative in Congress, shall not be denied or abridged by the United States or any state by reason of failure to pay any poll tax or other tax.

Section 2.   The Congress shall have power to enforce this article by appropriate legislation.

Twenty-Fifth

(Proposed 6 July 1965; declared ratified 23 February 1967.)

Section 1. In the case of the removal of the President from office or of his death or resignation, the Vice President shall become President.

Section 2. Whenever there is a vacancy in the office of the Vice President, the President shall nominate a Vice President who shall take office upon confirmation by a majority vote of both Houses of Congress.

Section 3. Whenever the President transmits to the President pro tempore of the Senate and the Speaker of the House of Representatives his written declaration that he is unable to discharge the powers and duties of his office, and until he transmits to them a written declaration to the contrary, such powers and duties shall be discharged by the Vice President as Acting President.

Section 4. Whenever the Vice President and a majority of either the principal officers of the executive department of such other body as Congress may by law provide, transmit to the President pro tempore of the Senate and the Speaker of the House of Representatives their written declaration that the President is unable to discharge the powers and duties of his office; the Vice President shall immediately assume the powers and duties of the office as Acting President.

Thereafter, when the President transmits to the President pro tempore of the Senate and the Speaker of the House of Representatives his written declaration that no inability exists, he shall resume the powers and duties of his office unless the Vice President and a majority of either the principal officers of the executive department or of such other body as Congress may by law provide, transmit within four days to the President pro tempore of the Senate and the Speaker of the House of Representatives their written declaration that the President is unable to discharge the powers and duties of his office. Thereupon Congress shall decide the issue, assembling within forty-eight hours for that purpose if not in session. If the Congress, within twenty-one days after Congress is required to assemble, determines by two-thirds vote of both Houses that the President is unable to discharge the powers and duties of his office, the Vice President shall continue to discharge the same as Acting President; otherwise, the President shall resume the powers and duties of his office.

Twenty-Sixth

(Proposed 23 March 1971; declared ratified 30 June 1971.)

Section 1. The right of citizens of the United States, who are 18 years of age or older, to vote shall not be denied or abridged by the United States or any state on account of age.

Section 2. The Congress shall have the power to enforce this article by appropriate legislation.

Twenty-Seventh

(Proposed 1789; declared ratified 7 May 1992.)

No law varying the compensation for the services of the Senators and Representatives shall take effect, until an election of Representatives shall have intervened.

Appendix 3

Constitutional Allocation of Powers over Foreign and Defence Policy

Powers Granted to Congress

Under Article I, Section 8:

"The Congress shall have power:

"To lay and collect taxes, duties, imposts and excises, to pay the debts and provide for the common defense and general welfare of the United States; but all duties, imposts and excises shall be uniform throughout the United States;

"To define and punish piracies and felonies committed on the high Seas, and Offenses against the Law of Nations;

"To declare War, grant letters of marque and reprisal, and make rules concerning captures on land and water;

"To raise and support armies, but no appropriation of money to that use shall be for a longer term than two years;

"To provide and maintain a Navy;

"To make rules for the government and regulation of the land and naval forces;

"To provide for calling forth the militia to execute the laws of the Union, suppress insurrections and repel invasions;

"To provide for organizing, arming, and disciplining the militia, and for governing such part of them as may be employed in the service of the United States, reserving to the States respectively, the appointment of the officer, and the authority of training the militia according to the discipline prescribed by Congress;

"To exercise exclusive legislation . . . over all places purchased by the consent of the legislature of the state in which the same shall be, for the erection of forts, magazines, arsenals, dock-yards, and other needful buildings."

Powers Granted to the President

Under Article II, Section 2:

"The President shall be the Commander-in-Chief of the Army and Navy of the United States, and of the militia of the several states, when called into the actual service of the United States.

"He shall have power, by and with the advice and consent of the Senate, to make treaties, provided two-thirds of the Senators present concur; and he shall nominate, and by and with the Advice and Consent of the Senate, shall appoint Ambassadors.

"He shall receive Ambassadors . . . and shall commission all the officers of the United States".

Further Reading

Journals and Newspapers

The output of research on United States government and politics in scholarly journals is vast. It is essential to keep up with articles in the following major journals:

American Political Science Review
British Journal of Political Science
Comparative Politics
Journal of Politics
PS
Political Science Quarterly
Political Studies.

Detailed coverage of current events is available in two (expensive) specialist weekly publications: *Congressional Quarterly Week Report*, and *National Journal*. The formerly liberal *New Republic*, and the persistently conservative *National Review*, provide varying weekly perspectives on current events, while *The Almanac of American Government*, published biennially, is an excellent guide to the politics of every US Senator and Congressman. *The New York Review of Books* is a good and pleasurable source of political debate. *The New York Times*, and *The Washington Post* remain America's two best newspapers, but are nearly impossible to obtain in Europe; some of their reports and editorials are reprinted in *The International Herald Tribune*, obtainable throughout Europe. Both *The New York Times* and *The Washington Post* are, however, now conveniently obtainable on the Internet and on CD-ROM. *The Wall Street Journal*, a daily financial newspaper, is now published outside the United States as well as within it; its coverage of economic news is first class.

The quality of European analysis of American politics varies: all of the British so-called "quality" newspapers report daily on American politics, but often unimaginatively. *The Financial Times* is the clearest exception to this rule: its coverage of United States' economic questions is usually excellent. The *Economist*'s coverage is occasionally useful.

1 Introduction

French constitutions were once regarded merely as "periodical literature"; the *Constitution of the United States of America*, endless subject of disputatious interpretation, could never be so stigmatized. It is central to United States government and politics; reading it and thinking about it in the context of American history is essential if United States government and politics are to be understood. For the same reason, *The Federalist Papers*, early and sophisticated propaganda in defence of the proposed Constitution, remain essential reading; Isaac Kramnick's "Introduction" to the Pelican edition is splendid. Louis Hartz's classic liberal exposition of American political values, *The Liberal Tradition in America*, together with Charles Beard's *An Economic Interpretation of the Constitution,* which advances a radical, if unpersuasive, interpretation of the motives and interests of the Constitution's founders, are

438

important and stimulating arguments. Among the plethora of scholarly work on the Constitution's operation, Maurice Vile's *Constitutionalism and the Separation of Powers* has lasted well and fully repays reading. Louis Fisher's more recent *Constitutional Dialogues* is a subtle and perceptive interpretation of the most important and complex constitutional relationships in United States government: those between Congress and the Executive. Seymour Martin Lipset's *The First New Nation* and his *Continental Divide* offer informed, comparative, and historically rich interpretations of the Republic's founding, development, and distinctiveness. Byron Shafer addresses himself to some of the many facets of the problem of American exceptionalism in his excellent edited collection of essays *Is America Different?* Robert Singh's *The Farrakhan Phenomenon* is a splendid critical analysis with much of importance to say about the immediate subject and the wider questions of extremism in America. James Gibson's *Warrior Dreams* sets right-wing militia groups in their appropriate, historical and cultural contexts, whilst Richard Hofstadter's *The Paranoid Style in American Politics* is a magisterial treatment.

2 Political Parties

Leon Epstein's *Political Parties in the American Mold* is a fine interpretation of the distinctiveness of political parties in the United States. Nelson Polsby's *Consequences of Party Reform* examines what its title declares; Byron Shafer's *Quiet Revolution* is a much more detailed, scholarly, account of party reform. On party organization, A. J. Reichley's *The Life of the Parties* is an authoritative plea for party revival, while Alan Ware's *The Breakdown of Democratic Party Organization* is a sophisticated argument about the decomposition of the organizational base of parties. Sundquist's *Dynamics of the Party System* is a fine study of alignment and realignment of political parties, while Key's superb *Southern Politics*, and Bass and De Vries's *The Transformation of Southern Politics* explore the tortured history of the great regional exception to most rules about party politics in the United States. Katznelson's *City Trenches* advances a compelling argument about the weakness of class as a basis for party politics in the United States. Stanley Greenberg's revised edition of *Middle Class Dreams* is a stimulating account of a suppposed middle-class rebellion against the Federal government and the two major political parties.

3 Elections and the Politics of Participation

Three problems of major interest receive extensive attention in the literature: (i) for whom Americans vote; (ii) why voting participation is comparatively low; and (iii) why Presidential elections have recently so often had different partisan outcomes to Congressional ones.

With regard to (i), Polsby and Wildavsky's *Presidential Elections* is the best introductory text. Burnham's *Critical Elections and the Mainsprings of American Politics* remains a classic study. Nie, *et al.*'s *The Changing American Voter*, and Smith's *The Unchanging American Voter* address the same problem with different data. P. M. Williams's "Party Realignment in Britain and the US", in the *British Journal of Political Science*, vol. 15, no. 1 (1985) sets the American debate about realignment in a comparative context. *Primary Colors* is an entertaining novel about the entirely fictional campaign of an unprincipled southern Governor running for President in the early 1990s. Shafer and Claggett's *The two Majorities* is an important and illuminating account of, in the authors' words, "the grand substantive framework for political conflict".

With regard to (ii), Piven and Cloward's *Why Americans Don't Vote* has provoked much controversy and debate, as Bennett's article "The Uses and Abuses of

Registration per cent Turnout Data" in *PS* (June 1990), and the ensuing exchanges in the same journal show. E. C. Ladd's *Where Have all the Voters Gone?* is a useful study, as is W. D. Burnham's essay "The Turnout Problem" in A. J. Reichley's edited collection *Elections American Style*.

With regard to (iii), Beck *et al.*'s article "Patterns and Sources of Ticket-Splitting on Subpresidential Voting", *American Political Science Review*, vol. 86 no. 3 (1992), together with Jacobson's excellent study *The Electoral Origins of Divided Government* and Shafer's stimulating article "The Election of 1988 and the Structure of American Politics", *Electoral Studies*, vol. 8 no. 1 (1989) provide a good interpretation of the nature and dimensions of one of the most fascinating problems in American politics.

Gerald Pomper's *The Election of 1996* contains useful articles on a number of aspects of the 1996 election, including an especially good piece by Anthony Corrado on campaign finance.

4   The Presidency and the Politics of Leadership

Still the defining study more than thirty years after it was first written, Neustadt's *Presidential Power* is a subtle and brilliant scholarly proof of the proposition that the Presidency and Congress are locked in complex relationships of mutual political dependence. Unfortunately, Neustadt's work is more often cited than it is read. Bob Haldeman's *The Haldeman Diaries*, available in fullest form on CD-ROM and in shortened form in hard copy, are superb; they comprise the finest single source of published evidence on the Nixon Presidency, and are rich with insights into the institution of the Presidency itself. Another excellent source, available only in hard copy, is Joseph Califano's *The Triumph and Tragedy of Lyndon Johnson*.

Louis Fisher also sets the Presidency in the appropriate context of relations with the other two branches in the third, revised, edition of his *Constitutional Conflicts between Congress and the President*, and in the second edition of his *The Politics of Shared Power*. James Sterling Young's *The Washington Community 1800–1828* (1966), a study of the dilemmas of leadership in Jeffersonian America but with much to tell us about modern American politics, has (with Neustadt's *Presidential Power*) a good claim to be one of the dozen finest books ever written on United States politics. Rockman's *The Leadership Question* (1984) is a stimulating study, exceptionally well-grounded in the comparative literature on political leadership, as is Macgregor Burns's *Leadership* (1978). Relations between Presidency and Congress are scrutinized in Peterson's *Legislating Together*, and in Jones's study of President Carter, *The Trusteeship Presidency*. Leuchtenburg's *In the Shadow of FDR* explains well the consequences of Franklin Roosevelt's restructuring of government, policy, and politics in the United States. Studies of individual modern Presidents and Presidencies abound. Among the best are Leuchtenburg's *Franklin D. Roosevelt and the New Deal*, Greenstein's ambitious (though not entirely persuasive) interpretation of Eisenhower's leadership, *The Hidden-Hand Presidency*, and Lou Cannon's excellent book, *President Reagan*.

5   Congress and the Politics of the Legislative Competition

Attracted by the prospect of quantification through the statistical analysis of Congressional voting patterns, American political scientists have written more widely on Congress than on either the Presidency or the Supreme Court. Jones's large textbook, *The United States Congress*, is a splendid introduction. Another distinguished student of Congress, Richard Fenno, has written extensively on the subject; his *Congressmen in Committees* (1973) and *Home Style* (1979) have been the most influential. The first analyses Members of Congress at work on Capitol Hill, while the second examines them at work in their Districts. The influence of electoral considerations on Congressional behaviour is the subject of Mayhew's classic study *Congress: The Electoral Connection*, and of Fiorina's scarcely less well-known *Congress: Keystone of the Washington Establishment*. Fowler and McClure's enjoyable and informative *Political Ambition* examines the problem of the factors that determine who runs for Congress. Sinclair's *The Transformation of the US Senate* is one of the best recent studies of the smaller Chamber. Fenno has written a series of studies of individual Senators: his excellent *The Making of a Senator* is a case study of the Senate career of Danforth Quayle; *Learning to Legislate*, is a study of Arlen Specter; *The Emergence of a Senate Leader*, examines Senator Pete Domenici's role in budgetary politics; while *The Presidential Odyssey of John Glenn* considers that Senator's failed Presidential bid. Questions of political process are considered by Dodd and Schott in their highly intelligent, if dated, *Congress and the Administrative State* and by Smith in his *Call to Order: Floor Politics in the House and Senate*. Hall's article "Participation and Purpose in Committee Decision Making", *American Political Science Review*, vol. 81, no. 1 (1987) is seminal; his book *Participation in Congress* is an impressively fine (and useful) piece of social science research. Hibbing and Theiss-Morse's *Congress as Public Enemy* offers a careful account and analysis of the American public's opinion of the Federal legislature. Two very useful edited collections of essays are Cox and Kernell's *The Politics of Divided Government* (1991), and Davidson's *The Postreform Congress* (1992). Robert Singh's *The Congressional Black Caucus* is a finely-crafted and stimulating research monograph on an important, if little-studied, organization.

6 The Supreme Court and the Politics of Adjudication

Congressional Quarterly Weekly Report is a great help in keeping up to date with judgments when they are handed down in a rush during the summer, and the November issue of the *Harvard Law Review* contains a useful account of the preceding term's judgements. The many American law school journals also contain articles in which the Court's judgments are examined. However, there is no substitute for reading the full decisions in the original: all good law libraries contain a full run of printed Supreme Court judgments and on-line facilities to appropriate databases. Now, too, anyone with an Internet connection can quickly find the full texts of Supreme Court judgments for easy downloading or printing. Hall's *The Oxford Companion to the Supreme Court, of the United States* is a magnificent and enjoyable compendium with concise explanatory entries on Court rules, procedures, cases, controversies, points of law, and Justices.

With respect to the large secondary literature, Richard Hodder-Williams's The *Politics of the US Supreme Court* and David O'Brien's *Storm Center* are excellent introductions to the subject. Hodder-Williams's article, "Six Notions of 'Political' and the United States Supreme Court", in *British Journal of Political Science*, vol. 22 no. 1 (1992) provides a helpful analysis of a problematic concept. Schwartz's *Super Chief: Earl Warren and his Supreme Court* is an admirable study of one of the greatest Chief Justices in the Court's history, while Blasi, in his edited collection entitled *The Burger Court*, and Schwartz in *The Ascent of Pragmatism* advance our understanding of the Court under Earl Warren's less remarkable successor. Michael Perry's *The Constitution in the Courts* is a skilful and subtle interpretation of the problems of original intent. Witt's *A Different Justice: Reagan and the Supreme Court* is a useful examination of that frequently conflictual relationship, while in *The Judicial Process*, Abraham gives an indispensable comparative treatment of courts in Britain, France, and the United States.

7   Interest Groups

Truman's *The Governmental Process* (1951) and Latham's *The Group Basis of Politics* (1952) are classic pluralist statements; Dahl's *Who Governs?* (1961) is social scientific research of the highest quality, and still essential reading. Schattschneider's *The Semi-Sovereign People* (1960) is a less sanguine account of the distribution of political power. Dahl and Lindblom's *Politics, Economics, and Welfare* (1953) still has the capacity to surprise. Cater's *Power in Washington* is an early but excellent interpretation of the power of subgovernments in Washington; Heclo's later article, "Issue Networks and the Executive Establishment", in King (ed.), *The New American Political System* (1978) is a clever interpretation of a more fluid system than that which Cater analysed. Building on the theoretical foundations established in his seminal book *The Logic of Collective Action* (1965), Olson considered the relationship between interest group activity and economic decline in *The Decline of Nations* (1982). Walker's article, "The Origins and Maintenance of Interest Groups in America", *American Political Science Review*, vol. 77 no. 2 (1983) addresses himself to the same theoretical problem with which Olson was concerned in 1965. Lindblom's *Politics and Markets* (1977) marked a change of view by one of the most distinguished scholars of interest groups, confirmed in his later Presidential address to the American Political Science Association, reprinted as "Another State of Mind", *American Political Science Review*, vol. 76 no. 1 (1982). Gaventa's *Power and Powerlessness* is an excellent application of Lukes's theory developed in *Power* (1974) to a coal-mining community in Appalachia. Wilson's *Unions in American Politics* is a good introduction to labour unions in the United States. Among recent articles, Peterson's "The Presidency and Organized Interests", *American Political Science Review*, vol. 86 no. 4 (1992), and Quinn and Shapiro's "Business Political Power: the Case of Taxation", *American Political Science Review*, vol. 85 no. 3 (1991) are excellent.

8   Bureaucracy: The Fourth Branch of Government

Crenson and Rourke's essay "By Way of Conclusion: American Bureaucracy since World War II", in Galambos's edited collection *The New American State*, provides a brief introduction to the subject. Fuller accounts may be found in Rourke's own *Bureaucracy, Politics, and Public Policy* (3rd edn) and "Bureaucracy in the American Constitutional Order", *Political Science Quarterly*, vol. 102, no. 2 (1987), in Johnson and Libecap's *The Federal Civil Service System and the Problem of Bureaucracy*, and in Woll's *American Bureaucracy*. Seidman and Gilmour's *Politics, Position, and Power* (4th edn) is a politically sensitive interpretation of the fourth branch. Dodd and Schott's *Congress and the Administrative State* is admirable, though now rather dated. The delegation of Congressional powers to agencies is further examined in McCubbins and Page's essay "A Theory of Congressional Delegation", in McCubbins and Sullivan's edited collection, *Congress: Structure and Policy*; the other half of that problem, Congressional oversight of agencies' operation through the appropriations and authorization processes, is well treated in Aberbach's *Keeping a Watchful Eye* (1990). Distributive politics has received considerable attention: Arnold's *Congress and the Bureaucracy: A Theory of Influence* is excellent, while Rich's "Distributive Politics and the Allocation of Federal Grants", *American Political Science Review*, vol. 83 no. 1 (1989), and Hird's "The Political Economy of Pork: Project Selection at the US Army Corp of Engineers", *American Political Science Review*, vol. 85, no. 2 (1991) are excellent pieces of research. Moe considers the persistent problem for Presidents of how they might exercise influence over bureaucrats only nominally subordinate to them in his essay "The Politicized Presidency", in Chubb and Peterson's *New Directions in American Politics*; Wood and Waterman's article on the same subject "The Dynamics of Political Control of the Bureaucracy", *American Political Science Review*, vol. 85, no. 3 (1991) repays reading.

9 Federalism and Intergovernmental Policy-Making

Good introductions are to be found in Dye's *American Federalism*; Elazar's *American Federalism: A View from the States*; Reagan and Sanzone's *The New Federalism*; Riker's *Federalism: Origin, Operation, and Significance*; Walker's *Toward a Functioning Federalism*; and Wright's *Understanding Intergovernmental Relations*. O'Toole's edited collection entitled *American Intergovernmental Relations* is a useful introductory reader. Sam Beer's splendid book, *To Make a Nation*, is fine scholarship founded on his long immersion in the subject. Chubb explores the difficulty of altering the balance of power between the Federal and State governments in his essay "Federalism and the Bias for Centralization", in Chubb and Peterson's *New Directions in American Politics*. Mackay considers the development of policy embracing the Federal and State governments in his *Domestic Policy and Ideology*, and Kettl asks hard questions about difficult problems of regulatory growth in *The Regulation of American Federalism*, using a detailed case study of a programme administered by the Department of Housing and Urban Development. Nathan *et al.*, in *Reagan and the States*, and King in "The Changing Federal Balance", in Peele *et al.*, (eds), *Developments in American Politics*, examine developments in federalism under President Reagan. The general subject of politics below the Federal level is nowhere better introduced than by Burns, *et al.* in their excellent *State and Local Politics*. Governorships provide the subject of Larry Sabato's valuable *Goodbye to Good-time Charlie*, and Governors' relations with State Assemblies the subject of Alan Rosenthal's *Governors and Legislatures: Contending Powers*. The processes of election to, and the structures and processes of politics within State Assemblies themselves, are considered in Rosenthal's *Legislative Life*.

10 The Politics of Cities and Suburbs

The web-site run by the Bureau of the Census, a Federal agency within the Department of Commerce, contains excellent sources of data on demographic change. The Bureau also publishes periodically the *State and Metropolitan Area Data Book*, a rich source of statistics on sub-Federal government.

Lineberry and Fowler's paper "Reformism and Public Policies in American Cities", *American Political Science Review* (1967), remains a useful account of the variants of mayoral systems.

Federal sponsorship of suburban growth is compellingly examined by Jackson in *Crabgrass Frontier*, while the failure of mass transport to accommodate new spatial circumstances is the subject of Kain's excellent paper "The Spatial Mismatch Hypothesis: Three Decades Later", *Housing Policy Debate*, vol. 3, no. 2 (1992).

The location and distribution of power are explained in different ways by, among others, Hughes and Sternberg in *The New Metropolitan Reality*; Dahl in *Who Governs?*; Hunter in *Community Power Structure*; Stone in *Regime Politics*; Schattschneider in *The Semi-Sovereign People*; and Crenson, in his stimulating book *The Unpolitics of Air Pollution*. Katznelson's fine *City Trenches* is a stimulating attempt to develop a Marxist account of urban politics, while Paul Peterson's *City Limits* is a structuralist argument of a different, public choice, sort. Mollenkopf's *The Contested City*, and *Phoenix from the Ashes*, are outstandingly fine analyses which accord to political activity its appropriately full place.

Lemann's *The Promised Land* explores the hopeful migration of southern black citizens to northern cities and the evaporation of their hopes in northern ghettoes.

While Banfield's *The Unheavenly City Revisited* held out in 1974 the prospect of qualified optimism about the future of cities, Leon Dash's fine and closely-focused study of the appallingly severe deprivation suffered by the poorest urban black Americans, *Rosa Lee*, holds out little.

11   Domestic Economic Policy

The web-sites run by the Office of Management and Budget, and the Congressional Budget Office, contain a wealth of statistical detail in Presidential budget proposals and Congressional budget legislation.

Congressional Quarterly Weekly Report and *National Journal* provide detailed accounts of the authorization and budgetary processes. Collender produces an annual *Guide to the Federal Budget* which is an essential reference. The best account of the reform of budgetary law in the 1970s is in Sundquist's *The Decline and Resurgence of Congress*. Hogan provides an assessment of the effectiveness of those reforms in his article "Ten Years After: the US Congressional Budget and Impoundment Control Act of 1974", in *Public Administration*, vol. 63, no. 2 (1985). Other sources on the politics and procedures of the budget are Savage's *Balanced Budgets and American Politics* and Stein's *Presidential Economics*. Mr Reagan's bout of tax-cutting and aggregate budget increases are addressed by Stockman in his badly-written but revealing account, *The Triumph of Politics*, by Penner in his edited collection, *The Great Fiscal Experiment*; and by Friedman in *Day of Reckoning*. The history of the budgetary process is the subject of Stewart's *Budget Reform Politics*, Fisher's *Presidential Spending Power*, and of Schick's *Congress and Money*. Monetary policy is examined in Mayer's edited book, *The Political Economy of American Monetary Policy*, and by Woolley in *Monetary Politics*. Greider's *Secrets of the Temple* is a sensational but entertaining account of Federal Reserve perfidy during the 1980s. Berman's *The Office of Management and Budget and the Presidency, 1921–1979* provides a good account of the development of that key institution within the Executive Office of the President. Brownlee's edited collection *Funding the Modern American State, 1941–1995* contains much important scholarship on the history of taxation and public finance.

12   Foreign and Defence Policy

The literature in this field is vast, but as with economic policy, so Sundquist's *The Decline and Resurgence of Congress* provides the single best account of the struggle between the two elective branches over policy in the 1960s and 1970s. *Congressional Quarterly Weekly Report* and *National Journal*'s detailed reports provide a useful running account of the bargaining between Presidency, Congress, and interest groups over the formation of foreign and defence policy. Kegley and Wittkopf's *American Foreign Policy* is a good introductory textbook, and John Gaddis's *Strategies of Containment* a superb account of relationship between the United States and the Soviet Union during the Cold War. Rubin's *Secrets of State* is a study of the State Department's role in the formation of United States' foreign policy, and Christopher Shoemaker's *The NSC Staff* an examination of the National Security Council's secretariat. The intelligence community provides the subject for Johnson in *America's Secret Power: The CIA in a Democratic Society*, and Bamford's *The Puzzle Palace*. The Vietnam War has spawned a minor publishing industry of its own, but Halberstam's *The Best and the Brightest* retains its capacity to shock, while Gelb and Betts's *The Irony of Vietnam*, the three volumes of Gibbons' *The US Government and the Vietnam War*, and Berman's *Planning a Tragedy* repay careful reading. The list of memoirs by former participants is very large. Among the best are Kennan's

Memoirs, Nitze's *From Hiroshima to Glasnost*, and Monteagle Stearns's *Talking to Strangers*. Kissinger's two volumes, *White House Years* and *Years of Upheaval*, should be read in conjunction with Shawcross's *Sideshow* and Seymour Hersh's *The Price of Power*. Strobe Talbott's *Endgame* and *Deadly Gambits* are splendidly revealing accounts of nuclear arms negotiations between the United States and the Soviet Union. More general arguments about the processes of foreign and defence policy-making processes are Destler, *et al.*'s *Our Own Worst Enemy*, and George's *Presidential Decisionmaking in Foreign Policy*. International economic policy is the subject of Bergsten's "The World Economy after the Cold War", *Foreign Affairs*, vol. 69, no. 2 (1990), Spero's *The Politics of International Economic Relations*, and Macchiarola's edited collection of essays *International Trade: The Changing Role of the United States*.

Bibliography

Aberbach, J. (1990) *Keeping a Watchful Eye* (Washington, DC: Brookings Institution).

Abraham, H. J. (1982) *Freedom and the Court*, 4th edn (New York: Oxford University Press).

Abraham, H. J. (1986) *The Judicial Process*, 5th edn (New York: Oxford University Press).

Abrams, C. (1955) *Forbidden Neighbors*, New York pp. 229–35.

Abramson, P. R. and Aldrich, J. H. (1982) "The Decline of Electoral Participation in America", *American Political Science Review*, vol. 76 no 3.

Anonymous (1996) *Primary Colors* (London: Vintage Books).

Ambrose, S. E. (1985) *Rise to Globalism*, 4th edn (Harmondsworth: Penguin).

Arnold, R. D. (1979) *Congress and the Bureaucracy: A Theory of Influence* (New Haven, Conn: Yale University Press).

Bachrach, P. and Baratz, M. S. (1962), "Two Faces of Power", *American Political Science Review*, LVI, 4.

Bachrach, P. and Baratz, M. S. (1963), "Decisions and Nondecisions: An Analytical Framework, *American Political Science Review*, LVII, 3.

Bamford, J. (1983) *The Puzzle Palace* (New York: Penguin).

Banfield, E. C. (1974) *The Unheavenly City Revisited* (Boston: Little, Brown).

Bass, J. and De Vries, W. (1976) *The Transformation of Southern Politics* (New York: Basic Books).

Bauer, R., Pool, I. and Dexter, L. A. (1963) *American Business and Public Policy* (New York: Atherton).

Beard, C. (1913) *An Economic Interpretation of the Constitution* (New York: Macmillan).

Beck, P. A., Baum, L., Clausen, A. and Smith, C. E. (1992) "Patterns and Sources of Ticket-Splitting on Subpresidential Voting", *American Political Science Review*, vol. 86 no. 3.

Beer, S. (1993) *To Make a Nation* (Cambridge, Mass.: Belknap Press).

Bellesiles, M. A. (1996) "The Origins of Gun Culture in the United States, 1760–1865, *The Journal of American History* (September), p. 425.

Bennett, S. E. (1990) "The Uses and Abuses of Registration and Turnout Data", *PS* (June).

Bergsten, C. F. (1990) "The World Economy after the Cold War", *Foreign Affairs*, vol. 69, p. 2.

Berman, L. (1979) *The Office of Management and Budget and the Presidency, 1921–1979* (Princeton, NJ: Princeton University Press).

Berman, L. (1982) *Planning a Tragedy* (New York: W.W. Norton).

Bernstein, M. H. (1955) *Regulating Business by Independent Commission* (Princeton, NJ: Princeton University Press).

Bickel, A. (1955) "The Original Understanding And the Segregation Decision", *Harvard Law Review*, vol. 69, no. 1.

Binder, S. A. and Smith, S. S. (1997) *Politics or Principles? Filibustering in the United States Senate* (Washington, DC: Brookings Institution).

Blank, R. M. (1997) "The 1996 Welfare Reform", *Journal of Economic Perspectives*, vol. 11, no. 1.

Blasi, V. (ed.) (1977) *The Burger Court* (New Haven, Conn.: Yale University Press).

Bureau of the Census (1975) *Historical Statistics of the United States* (Washington: DC, United States Government Printing Office).

Bureau of the Census (1991) *State and Metropolitan Area Data Book, 1991* (Washington DC: US Government Printing Office).

Bureau of the Census, *Statistical Absract of the United States, 1996* (Washington, DC: USGPO).

Burnham, W. D. (1970) *Critical Elections and the Mainsprings of American Politics* (New York: W.W. Norton).

Burnham, W. D. (1987) "The Turnout Problem", in A. J. Reichley (ed.), *Elections American Style* (Washington, DC: Brookings Institute).

Burns, J. M., Peltason, J. and Cronin, T. (1984) *State and Local Politics*, 4th edn (Englewood Cliffs, NJ: Prentice-Hall).

Burns, J. M. (1978) *Leadership* (New York, Harper & Row).

Campbell, A., Converse, P. Miller, W. and Stokes, D. (1960) *The American Voter* (New York: John Wiley).

Cannon, L. (1991) *President Reagan* (New York: Touchstone).

Cater, D. (1965) *Power in Washington* (London: Collins).

Chubb, J. E. (1985) "Federalism and the Bias for Centralization", in J. E. Chubb and P. E. Peterson, *New Directions in American Politics* (Washington, DC: Brookings Institution).

Chubb, J. E. and Peterson, P. E. (1985) *New Directions in American Politics* (Washington, DC: Brookings Institution).

Collender, S. (1990) *Guide to the Federal Budget* (Washington, DC: Urban Institute Press).

Conlan, T. (1988) *New Federalism* (Washington, DC: Brookings Institution).

Constitution of the United States of America, The.

Corrado, A. (1997) "Financing in the 1996 Elections", in W. D. Burnham, *The Election of 1996* (Chatham: Chatham House).

Corwin, E. (1957) *The President Office and Powers* (New York: New York University Press).

Cox, G. W. and Kernell, S. (1991) *The Politics of Divided Government* (Boulder, Col.: Westview Press).

Crenson, M. and Rourke, F. E. (1987) "By Way of Conclusion: American Bureaucracy since World War II", in L. Galambos (ed.), *The New American State* (Baltimore, MD: Johns Hopkins University Press).

Crenson, M. (1971) *The Unpolitics of Air Pollution* Baltimore, MD: Johns Hopkins University Press).

Dahl, R. (1961) *Who Governs?* (New Haven, Conn.: Yale University Press).

Dahl, R. and Lindblom, C. (1953) *Politics, Economics, and Welfare* (University of Chicago Press).

Dash, L. (1996) *Rosa Lee* (New York: Basic Books).

Davidson, R. H. (1992) "The Senate: If Everyone Leads, Who Follows?", in L. C. Dodd and B. I. Oppenheimer (eds), *Congress Reconsidered*, 4th edn (Washington, DC: CQ Press).

Davidson, R. (ed.) (1992) *The Postreform Congress* (New York: St Martin's Press).

Davidson, R. H. and Oleszek, W. J. (1981) *Congress and its Members* (Washington, DC: CQ Press), ch. 9.

Davis, M. (1993) "Who killed LA?", *New Left Review*, vol. 197.

de Tocqueville, A., *Democracy in America,* Anchor Books, 1969, p. 287.

Destler, I. M., Gelb, L. H. and Lake, A. (1984) *Our Own Worst Enemy*, New York, Simon & Schuster.

Dodd, C. and Oppenheimer, B. I. (1997) *Congress Reconsidered*, 6th edn (Washington, DC: CQ Press).

Dodd, L. C. and Schott, R. L. (1979) *Congress and the Administrative State* (New York: John Wiley).

Douglas, W. O. (1970) *Points of Rebellion* (New York, Random House).

Duverger, M. (1954) *Political Parties* (London, Methuen).

Dye, T. R. (1990) *American Federalism* (Lexington, Mass.: Lexington Books).

Elazar, D. (1972) *American Federalism: A View from the States* (New York: Crowell).

Eldersveld, S. J. (1982) *Political Parties in American Society* (New York: Basic Books).

Epstein, L. (1986) *Political Parties in the American Mold* (Madison, Wis.: University of Wisconsin Press).

Fairclough, A. (1995), *Race and Democracy* (Athens, GA: University of Georgia Press).

Feigert, F. B. (1984) "On the 'Decline' in Congressional Party Voting", Paper presented at the annual meeting of the Southern Political Science Association, Savannah, Georgia.

Fenno, R. (1973) *Congressmen in Committees* (Boston, Mass.: Little, Brown).

Fenno, R. (1979) *Home Style* (Boston, Mass.: Little, Brown).

Fenno, R. (1989) *The Making of a Senator* (Washington, DC; CQ Press).

Fiorina, M. (1974) *Congress: Keystone of the Washington Establishment* New Haven, Conn.: Yale University Press).

Fisher, L. (1975) *Presidential Spending Power* Princeton, NJ: Princeton University Press).

Fisher, L. (1987) *The Politics of Shared Power*, 2nd edn (Washington, DC: CQ Press).

Fisher, L. (1988) *Constitutional Dialogues* (Princeton, NJ Princeton University Press).

Fisher, L. (1991) *Constitutional Conflicts between Congress and the President*, 3rd edn (Lawrence, Kan.: University Press of Kansas).

Fowler, L. L. and McClure, R. D. (1990) *Political Ambition* (New Haven, Conn.: Yale University Press).

Freeman, B. I. (1965) *The Political Process* (New York: Random House).

Friedman, B. (1988) *Day of Reckoning* (New York: Random House).

Gaddis, J. (1982) *Strategies of Containment* (New York: Oxford University Press).

Gaventa, J. (1980) *Power and Powerlessness* (Oxford: Clarendon Press).

Gelb, L. and Betts, R. K. (1979) *The Irony of Vietnam* (Washington, DC: Brookings Institution).

George, A. (1980) *Presidential Decisionmaking in Foreign Policy* (Boulder, Col.: Westview Press).

Gibbons, W. C. (1989) *The US Government and the Vietnam War: Part II, 1961–1964* Princeton, NJ: Princeton University Press). 1986.

Gibson, J. (1994) *Warrior Dreams* (New York: Hill & Wang).

Glazer, N. (1997) *We are all Multiculturalists Now* (Cambridge MA: Harrard).

Gray, V. and Jacob, H. (1996) *Politics in the American States*, 6th edn (Washington, DC: CQ Press).

Greenberg, S. (1996) *Middle Class Dreams* (New Haven, Conn.: Yale University Press).

Greenstein, F. (1982) *The Hidden-Hand Presidency* (New York: Basic Books).

Greenstein, F. (1990) *Leadership in the Modern Presidency* (Cambridge, Mass.: Harvard University Press).

Greider, W. (1987) *Secrets of the Temple* (New York: Simon & Schuster).

Gunther, J. (1947) *Inside US* (London: Hamish Hamilton).

Gurr, T. R. and King, D. S. (1987) *The State and the City* (Chicago University Press).

Halberstam, D. (1992) *The Best and the Brightest* (New York: Random House).

Haldeman, R. (1994) *The Haldeman Diaries* (Santa Monica, Calif.: Sony Corp).

Hall, K. (1992) *The Oxford Companion to the Supreme Court of the United States* (New York: Oxford University Press).

Hall, R. (1987) "Participation and Purpose in Committee Decision Making", *American Political Science Review*, vol. 81 no. 1.

Hall, R. (1996) *Participation in Congress* (New Haven, Conn.: Yale University Press).

Hall, R. and Wayman, F. (1990) "Buying Time: Moneyed Interests and the Mobilization of Bias in Congressional Committees", *American Political Science Review*, vol. 84 no. 3.

Hamilton, A., Madison, J. and Jay, J. (1987) *The Federalist Papers*, intr. Isaac Kramnick (Harmondsworth, Penguin).

Hanson, R. C. (1996) "Integovernmental Relations", in V. Gray and H. Jacob (eds), *Politics in the American States*, 6th edn (Washington, DC: CQ Press).

Hartz, L. (1955) *The Liberal Tradition in America* (New York: Harcourt, Brace, Jovanovich).

Heclo, H. (1978) "Issue Networks and the Executive Establishment", in A. King (ed.), *The New American Political System* (Washington, DC: American Enterprise Institute).

Hersh, S. (1983) *The Price of Power* (New York: Summit Books).

Hird, J. A. (1991) "The Political Economy of Pork: Project Selection at the US Army Corp of Engineers", *American Political Science Review*, vol. 85, no. 2.

Hodder-Williams, R. (1980) *The Politics of the US Supreme Court* (London: Allen & Unwin).

Hodder-Williams, R. (1992) "Six Notions of 'Political' and the United States Supreme Court", *British Journal of Political Science*, vol. 22 no. 1.

Hofstadter, R. (1948) *The American Political Tradition* (New York: Knopf).

Hofstadter, R. (1966) *The Paranoid Style in American Politics* (London: Jonathan Cape).

Hogan, J. (1985) "Ten Years After: the US Congressional Budget and Impoundment Control Act of 1974", *Public Administration*, vol. 63 no. 2.

Hughes, M. A. and Sternberg, J. E. (1993) *The New Metropolitan Reality* (Washington, DC: Urban Institute).

Hunter, F. (1953) *Community Power Structure* (Chapel Hill, University of North Carolina Press).

Jackson, K. T. (1985) *Crabgrass Frontier* (New York: Oxford University Press).

Jacobson, G. C. (1990) *The Electoral Origins of Divided Government* (Boulder: Westview Press).

Johnson, L. (1989) *America's Secret Power: The CIA in a Democratic Society* (New York: Oxford University Press).

Johnson, R. N. and Libecap, G. D. (1994) *The Federal Civil Service System and the Problem of Bureaucracy* (University of Chicago Press).

Jones, C. O. (1988) *The Trusteeship Presidency* (Baton Rouge, La.: Louisiana State University Press).

Kain, J. (1992) "The Spatal Mismatch Hypothesis: Three Decades Later", *Housing Policy Debate*, vol. 3, no. 2.

Katznelson, I. (1981) *City Trenches* (Chicago University Press).

Kegley, C. W. and Wittkopf, E. R. (1991) *American Foreign Policy*, 4th edn (New York: St Martin's Press).

Kennan, G. (1967) *Memoirs* (Boston: Little, Brown).

Kerner Commission (1967) *The Challenge of Crime in a Free Society* (Washington, DC: USGPO).

Kettl, D. F. (1987) *The Regulation of American Federalism* (Baltimore, MD: Johns Hopkins University Press).

Key, V. O. (1949) *Southern Politics* (New York: Knopf).
Key, V. O. (1955) "A Theory of Critical Elections", *Journal of Politics*, vol. 17 no. 1.
Kincaid, J. (1994) "Governing the American States" in G. Peele *et al.* (eds.), *Developments in American Politics 2* (Basingstoke: Macmillan), p. 209.
King, D. S. (1992) "The Changing Federal Balance", in G. Peele, C. J. Bailey and B. Cain (eds), *Developments in American Politics* (London: Macmillan).
King, D. S. (1995(a)) *Actively Seeking Work?* (Chicago University Press).
King, D. S. (1995(b)) *Separate and Unequal* (Oxford: Clarendon Press).
Kissinger, H. (1979) *White House Years* (London: Weidenfeld & Nicolson/Michael Joseph).
Kissinger, H. (1982) *Years of Upheaval* (London: Weidenfeld & Nicolson/Michael Joseph).
Kluger, R. (1975) *Simple Justice*, vols I and II (New York: Knopf).
Krasner, S. (1978) *Defending the National Interest* Princeton (Princeton, NJ: University Press).
Ladd, E. C. (1977) *Where Have all the Voters Gone?* (New York: W.W Norton).
Lamis, A. P. (1984) *The Two-Party South* (New York: Oxford University Press).
Latham, E. (1952) *The Group Basis of Politics* (Ithaca, NY: Cornell University Press).
Leman, N. (1991) *The Promised Land* (New York: Knopf).
Leuchtenburg, W. (1963) *Franklin D Roosevelt and the New Deal* (New York: Harper & Row).
Leuchtenburg, W. (1989) *In the Shadow of FDR*, rev. edn (Ithaca, NY: Cornell University Press).
Lindblom, C. (1977) *Politics and Markets* (New York, Basic Books).
Lindblom, C. (1982) "Another State of Mind", *American Political Science Review*, vol. 76 no. 1.
Lipset, S. M. (1963) *The First New Nation* (London: Heinemann).
Lipset, S. M. (1990) *Continental Divide* (London: Routledge).
Lowi, T. (1979) *The End of Liberalism*, 2nd edn (New York: Norton).
Lowi, T. (1985) *The Personal President* Ithaca, NY: Cornell University Press).
Lukes, S. (1974) *Power* (London: Macmillan).
Macchiarola, F. J. (ed.) (1990) *International Trade: The Changing Role of the United States* (New York: Academy of Political Science).
Mackay, D. (1989) *Domestic Policy and Ideology* (Cambridge University Press).
Mayer, T. (ed.) (1990) *The Political Economy of American Monetary Policy* (Cambridge University Press).
Mayhew, D. (1974) *Congress: The Electoral Connection* (New Haven, Conn.: Yale University Press).
McCloskey, R. G. (1960) *The American Supreme Court* (University of Chicago Press).
McCubbins, M. D. and Page, T. (1987) "A Theory of Congressional Delegation", in M. D. McCubbins and T. Sullivan, *Congress: Structure and Policy* (Cambridge University Press).
McCubbins, M. and Schwartz, M. (1984) "Congressional Oversight Overlooked", *American Journal of Political Science*, vol. 2, no. 1 February.
McPherson, H. C. (1972) *A Political Education* (Boston, Mass.: Little, Brown).
McPherson, J. M. (1988) *Battle Cry of Freedom* (New York: Oxford University Press).
Miller, M. (1974) *Plain Speaking* (London: Coronet).
Milton, S. Eisenhower Foundation (1993) *Investing in Children and Youth, Reconstructing our Cities*, Washington, DC.
Moe, T. (1987) "The Politicized Presidency", in J. E. Chubb, R. P. Nathan and F. C. Doolittle (eds), *Reagan and the States* (Princeton, NJ: Princeton University Press).
Mollenkopf, J. H. (1993) *The Contested City* (Princeton, NJ: Princeton University Press).

Mollenkopf, J. H. (1994) *Phoenix in the Ashes,* new edn (Princeton, NJ: Princeton University Press).

Morris, C. R. (1996) *The AARP* (New York: Times Books)

Nader, R. (1965) *Unsafe at Any Speed* (New York: Grossman).

Neustadt, R. E. (1990) *Presidential Power and the Modern Presidents* (New York: Free Press).

Nie, N. H., Verba, S. and Petrocik, J. R. (1979) *The Changing American Voter* (Cambridge, Mass.: Harvard University Press).

Nitze, P. (1989) *From Hiroshima to Glasnost* (London: Weidenfeld).

O'Brien, R. (1990) *Storm Center*, 2nd edn (New York: W.W. Norton).

Oleszek, W. J. (1996) *Congressional Procedures and the Policy Process*, 4th edn (Washington, DC: CQ Press).

Olson, M. (1965) *The Logic of Collective Action* (Cambridge, Mass.: Harvard University Press).

Olson, M. (1982) *The Decline of Nations* (New Haven, Conn.: Yale University Press).

Organization for Economic Co-operation and Development (1997) *Economic Outlook* (Paris: OECD)

O'Toole, L. J. (ed.) (1985) *American Intergovernmental Relations* (Washington, DC: CQ Press).

Peirce, N. and Hagstrom, J. (1983) *The Book of America* (New York: W.W. Norton).

Penner, R. (ed.) (1991) *The Great Fiscal Experiment* (Washington, DC: Urban Institute Press).

Perry, M. (1994) *The Constitution in the Courts* (New York: Oxford University Press).

Peterson, M. (1990) *Legislating Together* (Cambridge, MA.: Harvard University Press).

Peterson, P. (1981) *City Limits* (Chicago University Press).

Peterson, P. (1991) *New Directions in American Politics* (Cambridge, Mass.: Harvard University Press).

Peterson, P. E. (1992) "The Presidency and Organized Interests", *American Political Science Review*, vol. 86, no. 4.

Piven, F. F. and Cloward, L. R. A. (1989) *Why Americans Don't Vote* (New York: Pantheon).

Polsby, N. (1969) "Goodbye to the Inner Club", *Washington Monthly*, August.

Polsby, N. (1983) *Consequences of Party Reform* (New York: Oxford University Press).

Polsby, N. and Wildavsky, A. (1988) *Presidential Elections* (New York: Free Press).

Pomper, G. *et al.* (eds) (1996) *The Election of 1996* (Chatham: Chatham House).

Pool, I. and Dexter, L. A. (1963) *American Business and Public Policy* (New York: Atherton).

Price, D. (1989) "The House of Representatives: A Report from the Field", in L. C. Dodd and B. I. Oppenheimer (eds), *Congress Reconsidered*, 4th edn (Washington, DC: CQ Press).

Quinn, D. P. and Shapiro, R. Y. (1991) "Business Political Power: The Case of Taxation", *American Political Science Review*, vol. 85 no. 3.

Reagan, M. D. and Sanzone, J. G. (1981) *The New Federalism*, 2nd edn (New York: Oxford University Press).

Reichley, A. J. (ed.) (1987) *Elections American Style* (Washington, DC: Brookings).

Reichley, A. J. (1992) *The Life of the Parties* (New York: Free Press).

Rich, M. J. (1989) "Distributive Politics and the Allocation of Federal Grants", *American Political Science Review*, vol. 83 no. 1.

Riker, W. (1964) *Federalism: Origin, Operation, and Significance* (Boston: Little, Brown).

Rivlin, A. (1992) *Reviving the American Dream* (Washington, DC: Brookings Institute).

Rockman, B. (1984) *The Leadership Question* (New York: Praeger).

Rosenstone, S. J., Behr, R. L. and Lazarus, E. H. (1984) *Third Parties in America* (Princeton, NJ: Princeton University Press).

Rosenthal, A. (1981) *Legislative Life* (New York: Harper & Row).

Rosenthal, A. (1990) *Governors and Legislatures: Contending Powers* (Washington, DC: CQ Press).

Rourke, F. E. (1987) "Bureaucracy in the American Constitutional Order", *Political Science Quarterly*, vol. 102 no. 2.

Rourke, F. E. (1984) *Bureaucracy, Politics, and Public Policy*, 3rd edn (Boston: Little, Brown).

Rubin, B. (1985) *Secrets of State* (New York: Oxford University Press).

Sabato, L. (1983) *Goodbye to Good-time Charlie* (Washington, DC: CQ Press).

Savage, J. D. (1988) *Balanced Budgets and American Politics* (Ithaca, NY: Cornell University Press).

Schattschneider, E. E. (1942) *Party Government* (London: Holt, Rinehart & Winston).

Schattschneider, E. E. (1960) *The Semi-Sovereign People* (New York: Holt, Rinehart & Winston).

Schick, A. (1980) *Congress and Money* (Washington, DC: Urban Institute Press).

Schwartz, B. (1983) *Super Chief: Earl Warren and his Supreme Court* (New York: New York University Press).

Schwartz, B. (1985) *The Unpublished Opinions of the Warren Court* (New York: Oxford University Press).

Schwartz, B. (1990) *The Ascent of Pragmatism* (Reading, Maas.: Addison-Wesley).

Seidman, H. and Gilmour, R. (1986) *Politics, Position, and Power*, 4th edn (New York: Oxford University Press).

Shafer, B. (1983) *Quiet Revolution* (New York: Russell Sage).

Shafer, B. E. (1988) *Bifurcated Politics* (Cambridge, Mass.: Harvard University Press).

Shafer, B. E. (1989) "The Election of 1988 and the Structure of American Politics: Thoughts on Interpreting an Electoral Order" *Electoral Studies*, vol. 8 no. 1.

Shafer, B. E. (ed.) (1991) *Is America Different?* (Oxford: Clarendon Press).

Shafer, B. E and Claggett, W. J. M. (1995) *The Two Majorities* (Baltimore: Johns Hopkins University Press).

Shawcross, W. (1986) *Sideshow*, 2nd edn (London: The Hogarth Press).

Shefter, M. (1992) *Political Crisis, Fiscal Crisis* (New York, NY: Columbia University Press).

Shoemaker, C. (1991) *The NSC Staff* (Boulder: Westview Press).

Sinclair, B. (1989) *The Transformation of the US Senate* (Baltimore, Md: Johns Hopkins Press).

Singh, R. (1997) *The Farrakhan Phenomenon* (Washington, DC: Georgetown University Press).

Singh, R. (1998) *The Congressional Black Caucus,* (Thousand Oaks, CA: Sage).

Sklar, M. J. (1988) *The Corporate Reconstruction of American Capitalism, 1890–1916* (Cambridge University Press).

Skowronek, S. (1982) *Building a New American State* (Cambridge University Press).

Smith, E. (1989) *The Unchanging American Voter* (Berkeley, Calif.: University of California Press).

Smith, S. S. (1989) *Call to Order: Floor Politics in the House and Senate* (Washington, DC: Brookings Institution).

Sorauf, F. (1976) *Party Politics in America*, 3rd edn (Boston: Little, Brown).

Spero, J. E. (1990) *The Politics of International Economic Relations*, 5th edn (New York: St. Martin's Press).

Stein, H. (1988) *Presidential Economics* (Washington, DC: American Enterprise Institute).

Stein, H. (1989) *The Fiscal Revolution in America* (Chicago University Press).

Stewart, C. (1989) *Budget Reform Politics* (Cambridge University Press).

Stockman, D. (1986) *The Triumph of Politics* (London: The Bodley Head).

Stone, C. (1989) *Regime Politics* (Lawrence: University of Kansas Press).

Stubbing, R. A. with Mendel, R. A. (1986) *The Defense Game* (New York: Harper & Row).

Sundquist, J. (1973) *Dynamics of the Party System* (Washington, DC: Brookings Institute).

Sundquist, J. L. (1981) *The Decline and Resurgence of Congress* (Washington, DC: Brookings Institute).

Talbott, S. (1979) *Endgame* (New York: Harper & Row).

Talbott, S. (1985) *Deadly Gambits* (London: Picador).

Thurber, J. (1996) *Rivals for Power* (Washington, DC: CQ Press).

Truman, D. (1951) *The Governmental Process* (New York: Knopf).

United States Office of Management and Budget (1997) *Budget of the United States Government, Fiscal Year 1998, Historical Tables* (Washington, DC: United States Government Printing Office).

Vile, M. (1967) *Constitutionalism and the Separation of Powers* (Oxford University Press).

Walker, D. B. (1981) *Toward a Functioning Federalism* (Cambridge: Winthrop Publishers).

Walker, J. (1983) "The Origins and Maintenance of Interest Groups in America", *American Political Science Review*, vol. 77 no. 2.

Ware, A. (1985) *The Breakdown of Democratic Party Organization, 1940–1980* (Oxford: Clarendon Press).

Warner, S. B. (1968) *The Private City* (Philadelphia, Pa: University of Pennsylvania Press).

Warren, E. (1977) *The Memoirs of Chief Justice Earl Warren* (New York: Doubleday).

Wayne, S. (1978) *The Legislative Presidency* (New York: Harper & Row).

Wildavsky, A. (1974) *The Politics of the Budgetary Process* (Boston: Little, Brown).

Williams, P. M. (1979) "Party Realignment in Britain and the US", *British Journal of Political Science*, vol. 15, no. 1

Wilson, G. (1979) *Unions in American Politics* (London: Macmillan).

Witt, E. (1986) *A Different Justice: Reagan and the Supreme Court* (Washington, DC: CQ Press).

Woll, P. (1977) *American Bureaucracy*, 2nd edn (New York: W.W Norton).

Wolman, H. (1996) "Theories of Local Democracy in the United States", in D. King and G. Stoker (eds), *Rethinking Local Democracy* (London: Macmillan).

Wolpe, B. C. and Levine, B. J. (1996) *Lobbying Congress*, 2nd edn (Washington, DC: Congressional Quarterly).

Wood, R. (1970) "When Government Works", *Public Interest*, vol. 18, Winter.

Wood, R. and Waterman, L. (1991) "The Dynamics of Political Control of the Bureaucracy", *American Political Science Review*, vol. 85, no. 3.

Woolley, J. (1984) *Monetary Politics* (Cambridge University Press).

Wright, D. (1983) *Understanding Intergovernmental Relations* (Pacific Grove, CA: Pacific Grove).

Wright, J. R. (1990) "Contributions, Lobbying, and Committee Voting in the U.S. House of Representatives", *American Political Science Review*, vol. 84 no. 2.

Young, J. S. (1966) *The Washington Community 1800–1828* (New York: Columbia University Press).

Index

Note: Page numbers in **bold** type refer to illustrative figures or tables.